STRATEGIC INITIATIVES IN EVANGELICAL THEOLOGY

THE
ANALOGY
OF FAITH

THE QUEST FOR
GOD'S SPEAKABILITY

ARCHIE J. SPENCER

IVP Academic

An imprint of InterVarsity Press
Downers Grove, Illinois

InterVarsity Press
P.O. Box 1400, Downers Grove, IL 60515-1426
ivpress.com
email@ivpress.com

InterVarsity Press® is the book-publishing division of InterVarsity Christian Fellowship/USA®, a movement of students and faculty active on campus at hundreds of universities, colleges and schools of nursing in the United States of America, and a member movement of the International Fellowship of Evangelical Students. For information about local and regional activities, visit intervarsity.org.

All Scripture quotations, unless otherwise indicated, are taken from the New American Standard Bible®, copyright 1960, 1962, 1963, 1968, 1971, 1972, 1973, 1975, 1977, 1995 by The Lockman Foundation. Used by permission.

Cover design: Cindy Kiple
Interior design: Beth McGill
Images: Yellow Christ by Paul Gauguin at Albright Knox Art Gallery, Buffalo, New York, USA / Bridgeman Images

ISBN 978-0-8308-4068-7 (print)
ISBN 978-0-8308-9709-4 (digital)

Printed in the United States of America ∞

Library of Congress Cataloging-in-Publication Data

Spencer, Archie J., 1959-
  The analogy of faith : the quest for God's speakability / Archie J. Spencer.
    pages cm. -- (Strategic initiatives in evangelical theology)
  Includes bibliographical references and index.
  ISBN 978-0-8308-4068-7 (pbk. : alk. paper)
  1. Analysis (Philosophy) 2. Analogy (Religion) 3. Knowledge, Theory of (Religion) 4. God (Christianity) 5. Jesus Christ--Person and offices. I. Title.
  B808.5.S676 2015
  231'.042--dc23

                                                                    2015022988

P 23 22 21 20 19 18 17 16 15 14 13 12 11 10 9 8 7 6 5 4 3 2 1

Y 34 33 32 31 30 29 28 27 26 25 24 23 22 21 20 19 18 17 16 15

To all my teachers past and present,

and especially to my first one in theology,

Dr. R. A. N. Kydd, whose love for the discipline

remains an indelible memory in my life.

CONTENTS

◆

ACKNOWLEDGMENTS

◆

Every scholarly work has various forms of support, and this book is no exception. I have had excellent encouragement on many levels. On one level, though, it has been a lonely project. Normally one has the opportunity to test one's ideas with fellow scholars and like-minded individuals who take the time to read and correct your manuscript on the way. This has not been possible in the present case for various reasons, so I must take full responsibility for all remaining errors, lapses in argument and general misunderstandings. At the end of the day, in respect to analogy at least, most of us are still students and precious few, experts. To be sure I have had many enlightening conversations with interested parties and colleagues, for which I am grateful. To these individuals I say simply, thank you for all your help. I would also like to thank IVP, Gary Deddo and David Congdon for the opportunity and guidance toward the publication of this book.

This book has its roots in concerns that go all the way back to my time as a doctoral student at the University of Toronto, and thus it represents many years of thought on the matter. Because the issue of analogy was tied so closely to my decision to study theology, I had to come to some satisfactory understanding of it before I could continue in a more dogmatically descriptive modality. The problem of analogy is hardly settled herein. Many will take issue with my description of the problem and its proposed solution. But, thankfully, the problem of analogy has largely been settled for me personally, and I am looking forward to moving on.

Further motivation on the matter has come from a decade-long ecumenical encounter with the Catholic fraternity, Communion and Liberation (founded by Monsignor Luigi Giussani, †2004), who have cheered me on despite the fact that I come to conclusions that may be seen as ecumenical closure on some levels by some scholars. I do want to represent an ecumenical spirit in this endeavor, so I am thankful to my many friends in CL who have taught me the true meaning of ecumenism. There are too many to mention by name so, again, simply but sincerely, thanks, CL!

Doing theology well is impossible without a context for teaching and scholarship, and I have been fortunate to be able to pursue my studies in such a place. One needs sabbaticals, libraries, TAs and students to teach. So I must also say a big thanks to all my students, friends and colleagues at Associated Canadian Theological Schools, Northwest Baptist Seminary, Trinity Western University, Vancouver School of Theology Library, St. Marks College Library and Regent College Library for allowing me to pursue this project in various ways. I must especially mention here my TAs, Erika McAuley, Bethany Scratch and Randene Larlee, for all their help with manuscript editing and administrative assistance.

I also owe a big debt of gratitude to my family, who stood by me even when this project required long absences from them. I look forward to having more time with Matthew, Janisa, Mike and my grandchildren, Julia and Mason, in the near future. The final word of thanks must go to my wife, Shelley. Neither of us had any idea I would be doing this kind of work when we met almost thirty-five years ago, but she has stuck with me through thick and thin. She is my constant companion and friend, as well as my editor, data entry/formatting expert and the ultimate motivator. For her my gratitude knows no bounds! The work is also offered finally as an express desire to know God, to love God and to share God, and so to render him the service of thanks, as befits the true mode of our being.

Lent 2015
Archie J. Spencer

ABBREVIATIONS

CD	Karl Barth. *Church Dogmatics*. Edited and translated by G. W. Bromiley and T. F. Torrance. Vols. I-IV. Edinburgh: T & T Clark, 1973, 2007.
GGW	Eberhard Jüngel. *Gott als Geheimnis der Welt: Zur Begründung der Theologie des Gekreuzigten im Streit zwichen Theismus und Atheismus.* Tübingen: Mohr Siebeck, 1977.
GMW	Eberhard Jüngel. *God as the Mystery of the World: On the Foundations of the Theology of the Crucified One in the Dispute Between Theism and Atheism.* Translated by D. Guder. Grand Rapids: Eerdmans, 1983.
IJST	*International Journal of Systematic Theology*
KD	Karl Barth. *Die Kirchliche Dogmatik, Band I-IV.* Zürich: Evangelischer Verlag-Zolliokon A.G., 1932–1967.
LCL	Loeb Classical Library. Cambridge, MA: Harvard University Press, 1912–.
ModT	*Modern Theology*
NovT	*Novum Testamentum*
NTS	*New Testament Studies*
NV	*Nova et Vetera*
PL	Patrologia latina. Edited by J.-P. Migne. 217 vols. Paris: 1844–1864.
SCG	Thomas Aquinas. *Summa Contra Gentiles*
SJT	*Scottish Journal of Theology*
ST	Thomas Aquinas. *Summa Theologiae*
TDNT	*Theological Dictionary of the New Testament.* Edited by Gerhard Kittel and Gerhard Friedrich. 10 vols. Grand Rapids: Eerdmans, 1976.
TEGP	Werner Jaeger. *Theology of the Early Greek Philosophers: The Gifford Lectures, 1936.* Oxford: Oxford University Press, 1947, revised 1952.
TLG	Thesaurus Linguae Graecae
ZNW	*Zeitschrift für die neutestamentliche Wissenschaft und die Kunde der älteren Kirche*

INTRODUCTION

All that I know is that I know nothing.

SOCRATES

For what do we know if we do not know what is in our mind,
since all we know, we cannot know except with our own mind.

SAINT AUGUSTINE

◆

Christian theological discourse has always had to contend with the attempt, on the part of some, to confine its claims to the knowledge of transcendence to that which we are actually capable of intuiting within the realm of finite experience. To a good degree, this was the state of religious knowledge of the classical, philosophical world that Christianity was born into, at least on the side of what Augustine described as "rational religion." Therefore, to establish its authority, linguistic capacity and necessity, Christian theology has always had to make claims to transcendent revelation beyond experience, and to prioritize such claims in respect to knowledge gained by experience. In order to limit this claim to transcendent revelation, Christians, in various ways, have pointed to either one or two books, namely, the book of Scripture and/or the book of nature. With respect to the book of Scripture we have claimed, with this book's own self-claim, that God has totally revealed himself in the event of his Word, the λόγος, Jesus Christ, to which the book of Scriptures bears exclusive witness. Classically, we have prioritized this book and generally submitted the knowledge gained from the book of nature to it, in hopes that over time we would see their concordance. With the assumption of such concordance as an inevitable outcome for divine knowledge, Christian theology has often felt free to ground its sentences in either one or the other, or more often both, of these "books." We were and are able, we claim, to make the book of Scripture talk to and confirm the book of nature, and vice versa, on the basis of the assumption that an inherent transcendent relation exists between Creator and creature that enables our sentences to speak responsibly, truthfully and certainly of the nature of this relationship. Furthermore, we are able to do so in ways that are hopeful for the creature's continued existence in the future, given the fact that immediate experience did not, and still does not, always seem to confirm such hope.

The problem with such knowledge of the divine was that our language often failed to do justice to these claims in respect to "knowledge." That is, language was, is and always will be creaturely in that it is built on and limited to our experience of the world. Therefore we had to conceive (as according to some claims, the mind was inevitably created to do) of a form of linguistic predication that respected transcendence on one side and the reality of God's speaking and existing in space and time on the other. The overall solution to this ontological difference was embodied, more often than not, in the concept of analogy. In very real terms, analogy came to represent the possibility, or depending on one's point of view, the impossibility, for such linguistic discourse. Thus at various points in its history Christian theology returns to such a principle in the hopes of clarifying, reaffirming and/or reconfiguring the ontological, epistemological, logical and transcendent ground for such a conception. But lest we Christians think we have been wise in our own eyes with the discovery of this middle ground, we should know that it was already a part of classical Greek heritage long before its appropriation by Christianity. Analogy represented, for both worlds, the possibility of theology, that is, speaking about divinity using creaturely language. In the long run this book is an analysis of this possibility from a Protestant point of view with precisely the same hopes for the possibility of theology.

Given the prominence of the crisis of linguistic discourse about the divine in the modern to late modern period, this book intends to place itself among the many other efforts, negative and positive, that have been carried out on this question in recent times. It does so in full recognition that yet another book on the issue of analogy seems unwarranted. However, given the history of this problem for Christian theology there is always a need, it seems, to push the boundaries of what we know about it and to be reminded of the foundational conceptualities that inform it in the first place. Because so much is at stake with analogy, there will always be a need to clarify, reformulate and reappropriate it in respect to revelation. As Augustine asks, if we do not know what the mind knows, then what do we know? The answer of Socrates and the later skeptical school of Carnades, "all we know is that we know nothing," is not adequate for Christian theology. Thus theology must push to the boundaries of how it knows what it knows. Or, for that matter, what it knows about how it knows. The possibility of theology is motive enough, especially in Protestant theology today, to undertake a revised study of analogy in the interest of its faith. At a time when Protestant theology is at its own "crossroads," as Gerhard Sauter puts it, we must now face again, as Protestants, the crucial task of theology in the twenty-first century, if for no other reason than that this is the crying need of the church today. "Theology can fulfill its task only if it is really rooted in the life and work of the church, that is, if it is faithful to what God has entrusted it to proclaim and to consent to—unconditionally and under all circumstances."[1] If Protestant theology is to do this, it must revisit the ground of its own existence and possibility.

In this work we will approach the state of affairs just described in terms of two debated starting points that have consistently been appealed to as answers to the problem of the speakability and knowledge of God. These terms are oftern referred to in the Latin expression as *analogia entis* and *analogia fidei*, the analogy of being and of faith, respectively. We will briefly define these from the outset so as to avoid any confusion. We should remember, though, that these principles will receive considerable development and expansion throughout this book and so these definitions are provisional at this point.

The more debated of these concepts is that of the *analogia entis*. A straight

---

[1]Gerhard Sauter, *Protestant Theology at the Crossroads* (Grand Rapids: Eerdmans, 2007), p. xix.

definition hardly seems possible since it has become such a hotly debated issue. Multiple definitions and nuances are often appealed to. The "analogy of being" as a phrase received programmatic coinage in the period of Thomistic scholasticism just after the death of Thomas Aquinas himself. Its ultimate formulation as a concept occurs in the famous work by Thomas de Vio, Cardinal Cajetan, titled *The Analogy of Names* (*De Nominum Analogia*). The coinage *analogia entis* is usually attributed to the sixteenth-century Catholic theologian Francisco Suárez. The analogy of being is based on the assumption that a likeness or analogy exists between the infinite being of God and the finite being of his creation. This likeness, or similarity-resemblance, lies at the basis of all arguments for the existence of God and serves as the power and capacity of language to speak of God in terms of his being and perfections. It is a mode of signification that depends on an a posteriori identification of attributes of being in the creature that must be assumed to exist in God in a more perfect and a priori way. Such qualities accrue to the creature by virtue of the act of creation upon which God imprints these qualities. It has since been developed in more complex modes of expression, but this is the essence of its function according to medieval scholasticism. In its development within that period it comes to be seen as a critical component of a larger metaphysical scheme; indeed it is often synonymous with the essence of metaphysics as a science of being in the service of theology. More must be said and will, of course, but this should suffice to guide the reader in the early going.

The concept of the *analogia fidei* was not originally thought of as a competing principle with analogy of being for grounding theological speech, but it eventually became so in the interest of avoiding certain metaphysical principles that were seen to be contrary to the biblical mode of revelation, even a supplanting of it. Initially the term was simply shorthand for the gospel, but it came to mean, in contradistinction to the analogy of being, the *use* of the gospel, in its clarity and simplicity, as a limit and corrective to all theological science. Where the Scriptures were a clear and unambiguous expression of the revelation of God in Jesus Christ of Nazareth, there a test for the accuracy and faithfulness of theological sentences and words could be had. In the mid-twentieth century, and indeed before that in the Reformation, it came to be associated with a relationship between Creator and creature that is solely dependent on the event of the incarnation, as Word, as witnessed to in Scripture, for linguistic expression of the content of revelation. As we shall see, it will receive considerable expansion as a christological principle wherein God and humanity are expressed in a relation of correspondence, to which all theological statement must become obedient, in terms of the limits of the speakability and knowability of God. This brief definition of *analogia fidei* will take on more significance in the second half of this work, the clarity of which certainly constitutes one of the critical aims herein.

In 1994 John Webster published a set of articles written by various scholars on the theology of Eberhard Jüngel, titled *The Possibilities of Theology*.[2] In the introduction to the book Webster explains the profound effect that the work of Jüngel had on his own discovery of theology, and its contemporary reemergence as a viable discipline.[3] This book came out during a period of hiatus when it appeared that Protestantism in the English-speaking world was perched on the precipice of deciding to abandon Christian theological self-description altogether. In a unique and powerful way Jüngel seemed capable of straddling the worlds of postmodern hermeneutics, bibilical studies, philosophy and dogmatics, while through this synthesis enabling responsible speech about God to emerge in the conflicting denials and affirmations of the possibility of "God-talk" taking place in all these disciplines.[4] Aside from Webster himself, it appeared to me that no such complementary English theology, or English-speaking theologian, in the Protestant tradition seemed capable of navigating these fields simultaneously as did Jüngel. Furthermore, what Jüngel brought to the discussion was a penetrating grasp of the theology of the one continental theologian whose works promised to be able to make a difference for Protestant theology, namely, Karl Barth.[5] In the nearly two decades since the publication of Webster's book, one can say, with a good degree of certainty, that Christian theological self-description in the Protestant faith now seems far from dead in its mainline expressions in North America, if not in its sectarian expressions.

---

[2] John Webster, ed., *The Possibilities of Theology: Studies in the Theology of Eberhard Jüngel in His Sixtieth Year* (Edinburgh: T & T Clark, 1994).
[3] Ibid., p. 6.
[4] Ibid., p. 2.
[5] Ibid.

Though it is true that the discipline of Christian theology, or Christian dogmatics, has as many detractors as it ever had, it is also true that since the works of scholars such as Barth and Jüngel have been made more readily available, the disciplines of systematic, historical and philosophical theology have been very much on the rebound. But despite this renaissance in Protestant theology, on the scholarly level at least, the question of "the possibility of theology" for the church and the academy remains submerged beneath layers of suspicion and neglect.

In a very real sense theology (Catholic, Protestant, Orthodox or otherwise) will always remain under the threat of denial simply by virtue of what it desires to comprehend and that this is ultimately deemed "incomprehensible." Even the apostle Paul could not fully fathom the "mystery" of the gospel in terms of any dimensions, height, breadth, depth and/or length.[6] Jüngel and Barth were keenly aware of both the possibilities and limits of theology as discourse. Webster notes with astuteness that, of all the concerns that Jüngel brings forward in his critical works in dogmatics, hermeneutics, philosophy and bibilical studies, it is the function of language and its capacity to speak meaningfully of God that is paramount.[7] In its essence the so-called postmodern turn, as epitomized in the works of Jacques Derrida at least, is precisely about this issue. In both Barth's works and, following his influence, in Jüngel's, it is the question of analogy that crystallizes this concern for the possibility of responsible speech that corresponds to God.[8] This question, as to the precise nature of the relation or correspon-

---

[6]The Pauline epistles are full of affirmations of the transcendent dimensions of revelation and our inability to fully grasp the "incomprehensible" gospel, meaning, of course, the revelation of God in Jesus Christ (Eph 1:15-23; 3:17-19; Rom 16:25-27; 1 Tim 1:17). Paul was well aware of the interplay between the mystery of revelation and the revelation of mystery that language was now called on to express.

[7]John Webster, *Eberhard Jüngel: An Introduction to His Theology* (Cambridge: Cambridge University Press, 1986), p. 40.

[8]*CD* I/1, p. 76. Barth writes, "Church proclamation has to be accompanied and confronted by Church theology, especially dogmatics. In distinction from all scattered answers to irrelevant questions, theology, and especially dogmatics, is the concentrated care and concern of the Church for its own most proper responsibility. In making its proclamation the raw material of dogmatics, it does the one thing it really needs apart from proclamation itself and the prayer that it may be right, the one and only thing it can do as the Church in relation to the obvious center of its life. For how should not this be the one thing needful when it is not just a matter of right answers to the divine call as with its other functions (and this is certainly to be taken seriously too), but also of the correct representation of the divine call itself, and therefore of the service of God in the supreme sense of the term? And how should not serious reflection on the background

dence between God and the world on which theological language rests, remains a central issue. As such, the question of analogy is synonymous with the question of the basis, possibility and limitations of theology. Ingredient in this issue is the key decision about the relative freedom of God and humanity, their ontological perspecuity, grace, salvation, works, ethics and the adequacy of human language in refering to God. In the late modern period what we say about analogy, how we define it, defend it and use it, is determinative of key aspects of theology. In short, it is synonymous with the problem of theology.

THE PROBLEM: ESTABLISHING A BASIS FOR THINKING AND SPEAKING ABOUT GOD ANALOGICALLY

The history of the term *theology* is bound up with the interplay between ontology, epistemology and rationality. The word, after all, belonged to the Greeks and not to Christianity in the first instance. Yet the term has come to mean quite different things to all religious and philosophical traditions, both historically and in our own time. If the term has a unifying concept, it centers on the problem of how "God" may be thought and spoken of in creaturely conceptualities. This fundamental problem, in turn, is centered on the question of how words may be used legitimately within such a context. As noted above, the shared answer among various religious traditions has often gone under the rubric "analogy," which is itself by no means uniformly defined and/or understood. God may be thought and consequently spoken of, it is often affirmed, by means of analogy, in such a way that what we know and discover about ourselves, and creation, in some inadequate way reflects or resembles the Creator. This implies that the question of analogy is attended by, or has ingredient within it, ontological questions and presuppositions often referred to in part of the Christian tradition as the "analogy of being" (*analogia entis*).

The history of the discussion about the (in-)adequacy and yet the inevitability of analogy can be said to be further bound up with the question of

---

of biblical exegesis and with reference to the practice of preaching be the only thing that has to be done, and can in fact be done, about this one thing (always apart from prayer)?" Jüngel echoes these concerns in his book *God's Being Is in Becoming: The Trinitarian Being of God in the Theology of Karl Barth*, trans. John Webster (Grand Rapids: Eerdmans, 2001), pp. 17-27.

epistemology. How is it that we know what we know about ourselves, let alone God? With regard to God, analogy raises the questions: How do we know? What do we know? And to what extent can we ever know the divine, from within creation itself? In recent ecumenical and contextual theology, the problem of analogy, expressed under this disputed phrase, "analogy of being," has once again been forced back on the theological agenda in Protestantism and Catholicism. This has been especially demonstrated in the now-famous Regensburg address delivered by Pope Benedict XVI in September 2006.[9] This address amounts to a renewed call for rational thought about the divine-human relation precisely on the grounds of the analogical possibilities of speech. While the phrase "analogy of being" seems to be getting much of the press in response to this call, not all that is said about it corresponds to what was the actual state of affairs concerning the historical development of the phrase within these faith traditions. This problem not only obscures what may actually be attained in the interest of theology along the lines of analogy, but it is also misrepresentative of the best efforts at analogical method within these traditions.

What is needed in the current theological context is a more careful treatment of analogy that clarifies the issue in terms of a christological point of reference. Not only this, but such treatment would also prescribe an understanding of analogy that clarifies what is at stake metaphysically,

---

[9]In the controversial address Pope Benedict XVI writes: "In all honesty, one must observe that in the late middle ages we find trends in theology, which would sunder this synthesis between the Greek spirit and the Christian spirit. In contrast with the so-called intellectualism of Augustine and Thomas, there arose with Duns Scotus a voluntarism, which, in its later developments, led to the claim that we can only know God's *voluntas ordinata*. . . . God's transcendence and otherness are so exalted that our reason, our sense of the true and good, are no longer an authentic mirror of God, whose deepest possibilities remain eternally unattainable and hidden behind his actual decisions. As opposed to this, the faith of the Church has always insisted that between God and us, between his eternal Creator Spirit and our created reason there exists a real analogy, in which—as the Fourth Lateran Council in 1215 stated—unlikeness remains infinitely greater than likeness, yet not to the point of abolishing analogy and its language. God does not become more divine when we push him away from us in a sheer, impenetrable voluntarism; rather, the truly divine God is the God who has revealed himself as logos and, as logos, has acted and continues to act lovingly on our behalf. Certainly, love, as Saint Paul says, 'transcends' knowledge and is thereby capable of perceiving more than thought alone (cf. Eph 3:19); nonetheless it continues to be love of the God who is Logos. Consequently, Christian worship is, again to quote Paul—λογικη λατρεία, worship in harmony with the eternal Word and with our reason (cf. Rom 12:1)." See "Faith, Reason and the University: Memories and Reflections," *Libreria Editrice Vaticana* (2006): 10.

epistemologically and theologically. This would further enable analogical speech along the lines of the Protestant commitment to the analogy of faith. Thus, while the substance of the first part of this book is partly a corrective to recent misappropriations of analogical method, it is also, for the most part, positive in its outcome in that it will issue in a viable theological procedure that draws on all of the traditions, but from the point of view of Protestant theology. In particular, the two Protestant theologians already mentioned, Barth and Jüngel, who have set the tone for the debate, will be called on to aid us in this christological filling-out of analogy. Barth's doctrine of revelation leads him to posit an *analogia fidei* that is christologically defined, as a means whereby thought and speech about God may proceed in a way that is faithful to the divine revelation as witnessed to in Holy Scripture. Jüngel's theological method was the first and is still one of the best Protestant attempts at a further definition of such a method, with his proposal for an "analogy of advent." This method was christological in substance.

Building on their approaches to the problem, both of which flow out of a deep historical sense for analogy, this book proposes to delineate more directly the connection between revelation and analogy by giving more content to the christological orientation of Barth as it relates to the "linguistic turn" in Jüngel. This will include connecting the doctrine of "revelation as event" in the Gospel of John more concretely to the concept of theology as second-order witness to the event. It will also include a theological evaluation of the more philosophical proposal of Jüngel's "analogy of advent" in order to invest more of the interest of revelation as event into the linguistic turn. Along the way we will root this revised analogical method in a more historically grounded concept of analogy than do some current offerings along this line. What this means for theology is that a procedure will emerge that allows for thinking and speaking about God in ways that demonstrate both the adequacy of language to convey the knowledge of God and yet the incapacity of language to be "freighted" with the being of God. Such an approach respects the ontological difference between God and creation but makes the relational similarity (based on christologically oriented revelation) the acid test of our knowledge of God and humanity.

A BRIEF OUTLINE

With this central intention in mind, we shall proceed as follows. Chapter one will be given over to describing in a very intentional and focused way the emergence of the problem of predication about the divine that inevitably led to the use of analogy. Recent reappropriations of the Catholic doctrine of the *analogia entis* as an important linguistic tool for theology, in ecumenical dialogue, have raised the question as to how this concept had been previously employed and to what degree in its application it has tended to smuggle into Christian theology a totalizing metaphysical epistemology that is possibly alien to the Word of God. This chapter will clarify and justify the concerns of Protestant theology in its rejection of this totalizing metaphysic by locating the problematic nature of the *analogia entis* within the classical invocation and determination of the concept of analogy. This task will be undertaken in order to demonstrate that indeed certain elements of the Platonic, Aristotelian and Neoplatonic cosmogonies and theogonies traded on a clear metaphysics of being that at times put God and humanity within the same species of being, thus tending toward an undue deification of humanity and/or anthropocentrizing of God in theological predication. At the heart of this tendency was the Platonic concept of cause-effect-resemblance (CER). This principle became the latent power of all subsequent philosophical and theological systems that traded on this cosmological principle, in its theological sentences.

Having established the classical concept of analogy, the rest of chapter one will offer a summary of the historical process by which the concept of analogy, understood on the basis of the classical development of CER, entered into Christian theological discourse. The key here will be an analysis of Augustine's epistemology, his linguistic model for divine predication and its basis in his doctrine of the Trinity, especially as it relates to his theology of illumination, creation, the soul as *imago Dei* and "vestiges of the Trinity" in creation. All of these Augustinian principles trade on the Neoplatonic concept of CER, in various ways. In the process of this investigation into the original sources of Augustine, it will become very clear that it was Augustine, not Aquinas, who first formally instituted analogical ways of theological speech. Since the problem of *vestigium trinitatis* is a highly refined species of analogical predication, it is not surprising that, for Protestant theology at least, it proved to be a questionable way to do theology. The fact is that Augustine, through Anselm, Pseudo-Dionysius and Boethius, bequeathed to Aquinas an analogical method that had CER at its core, and this remained a determinative principle in Aquinas's understanding of analogy due to his use of causal argumentation.

Having traced out the process whereby analogy comes into Christian usage, it will then be the task of chapter two to demonstrate precisely how Aquinas contributed a somewhat confused method of analogy that left the Catholic tradition open to multiple interpretations of the Thomistic concept, especially in its relationship to metaphysics. The net result was that the church often opted for a philosophical ontology that left revelation and Christian theology open to synergistic tendencies. This synergistic ontology can be attributed to many factors, but few are as important, or little understood, as the influence of a Proclan (i.e., relating to Proclus) and Pseudo-Dionysian Neoplatonism mediated through the structure of Aquinas's *Summa Theologiae, Prima Pars*. Here we will employ not only the *ST* but also the *Summa Contra Gentiles* (*SCG*) and other works to demonstrate that if Aquinas cannot be finally pinned down on this, then at the very least he is open to the kinds of ontological-epistemological misinterpretations that did take place and indeed were sanctioned for long periods of time as the accepted Thomistic doctrine of analogy. Naturally, this will lead us to our discussion of developments after Aquinas wherein the *analogia entis* takes shape as a concept with a metaphysical ontology in view, namely, in distinction from the univocal position of Duns Scotus, and in the exposition of Cardinal Cajetan's interpretation of Aquinas's theory of analogy.

This book will take a position in the history of the debate about analogy that will assume a modality of how theology in the Middle Ages was actually done, not how it ought to have been done had it been true to a "Catholic doctrine of the *analogia entis*." This phrase, "Catholic doctrine of the *analogia entis*," is the basic description of the concept as exposited by Erich Przywara, Hans Urs von Balthasar and their followers in the twentieth and twenty-first centuries. In this book, however, we will have to conclude that such a static and normative interpretation of the *analogia entis* cannot be identified either in actuality or as the spirit of what was intended. We must also assume that the concept of the *analogia entis* was more often than not either undefined, or, if it was defined, it was so as a "metaphysics" on the basis of which existed a theological-philosophical epistemology. When late medieval theology divided theological language into univocal forms of predication on the one hand, in the philosophical analysis of Duns Scotus, and analogical predication as a middle way between univocity and equivocity, on the other, in the foundational interpretation of Cardinal Cajetan's *The Analogy of Names*, it set in place a mode of theological speaking that became the single most influential method from Aquinas to Suárez. This was a formative period for Catholic theology that saw the rise of Molinism on the one hand and Jesuitism on the other, both of which traded heavily on the Dominican master Cajetan's interpretation of Aquinas. It is, therefore, no surprise that the Catholic Church has since had to contend with the inner tensions of Dominican theology. On the one hand, Dominicans want a less synergistic reading of Aquinas, and on the other, Jesuits want a more synergistic reading. This state of affairs in Catholic theology has persisted and was a major reason why Barth and other Protestants were not able to see in Catholic theology a use of analogy that did not somehow involve itself in a totalizing, synergistic metaphysics incipient in what they understood as the "analogy of being."

Two late medieval theologians, among others, attempted to correct this Jesuistic-Molinist misinterpretation by reviewing and "correcting" Cajetan's view of Aquinas's doctrine of analogy, namely, Fransisco Suárez and the Dominican Sylvester of Ferrara. However, as Hampus Lyttkens and George Klubertanz's analysis of the history of analogy clearly points out, neither work actually corrected Cajetan in the direction of a flat contradiction. Rather, they refined Cajetan's view along the lines of the analogy of "intrinsic attribution," which turns out to be a subspecies of the analogy of proportionality, the single method of analogy that Cajetan attributes to Aquinas. This is especially the case with Suárez. Thus the modern attempts to appeal to Suárez over Cajetan, in the works of Battista Mondin, Erich Przywara, von Balthasar and their current followers, do not solve the problem they have with Cajetan's reduction of Aquinas to a single view of analogy. In fact, they are already predisposed to the metaphysics of being ingredient in the traditional view precisely because they come at it from the Jesuistic-Molinist point of view. In the final analysis the appeal to a "Catholic view of the analogy of being" is just as committed to a synergistic metaphysics of being as Cajetan's. Furthermore, such a view is inevitable from the point of view of Aquinas's confused use of analogy, despite their call for a form of analogy that is similar in expression to the Protestant concept of the analogy of faith. It will be finally suggested, though not fully defended herein, that this is largely due to the failure of Catholic theology, in its synergistic mode, to rest theological predication squarely on a christological basis.

The lion's share of this study, chapters three to five, will be devoted to an exposition of the concept of the analogy of faith as the most viable option for theological predication, one that is best expressed in a combined approach based on the work of Barth and Jüngel, especially through their invocation of "correspondence," which turns out to be the key idea in any conception of analogy. At its core, then, our proposal is ecumenical, because it is essentially christological. In this respect, at least, it shares the concerns of von Balthasar with respect to an *analogia fidei*, even if it disagrees with his assessment of Barth on this issue.

The previous analysis of the development of the concept of the analogy of being, in chapters one and two, will put us in the best possible position in chapter three to understand what was at the heart of Barth's categorical rejection of this method as "the invention of the Antichrist," and how, therefore, his proposal for an "analogy of faith" was substantial, not just a slogan placed over against the Catholic view. Those who criticize Barth's view as dismissive, reductionistic or self-contradictory have often fallen victim to twin dangers in reading Barth. The first is a general lack of close reading of Barth himself, a fact we must note but cannot demonstrate in its fullness. The second is in reading Barth ahistorically in terms of his own development. Here the excellent work of Bruce McCormack's *Karl Barth's Critically Realistic Dialectical Theology* will aid us in establishing the place that Reformed thought had in Barth's development at this crucial juncture. Within a genetic-historical understanding of Barth's rejection of the analogy of being that follows the Reformed-Scholastic criticism and rejection of it, one can see the emergence of a christological tone in Barth's theology that intensifies in his later work and becomes the central concept in his invocation of analogy in the *CD*. Even in the early 1920s Barth was already trying to find a place for analogical predication on a christological basis, though dialectic remains a central impulse throughout his works. At the end of the day we cannot see in Barth's rejection of the analogy of being a contradiction to his later invocation of the analogy of faith. The dialectical feature in Barth's theology is precisely the testing of all analogical predication by the christological criteria as the single root of God's self-revelation. Barth's rejection of the analogy of being must be seen not just in the places where he takes the matter up directly but in the whole fabric of his concern for the singularity of revelation in all doctrinal expression.

Several locations within the *CD* can help us see this in Barth: his treatment and rejection of the possibility of any concept of a *vestigium trinitatis* in creation and the related natural theological appeal to an *analogia causalitatis*, as well as his formal treatments of the themes of *analogia relationis* and election. We will use these sections in Barth's *CD*, understood within the total context of his development of dogmatics, to underscore his concerns with Catholic theology. However, these are by no means exhaustive of what Barth means in his rejection of the analogy of being in favor of the analogy of faith. Rather, they are clear expressions of his central concern with the method, and they remain normative for him throughout. In the final analysis, these sections of the *CD* express his concern for responsible speech about God that corresponds to the substantial christological event of God's own self-giving. Thus theology can only point us to an analogy of faith. But the analogy of faith is no empty concept in Barth's theology. In the final section of this chapter we will trace this out in terms of Barth's own christological definition of analogy. The goal is to uncover the *analogia fidei* that provides such a powerful mode of expression in which theological predication can find its full bearing. Nevertheless, it remains a concept that is not fully fleshed out in Barth's theological corpus. It is worked out to the degree that his *CD* is one grand attempt at a christologically grounded *analogia fidei*, but Barth's critics are often inattentive to this feature of his work.

One of the most astute Barth scholars in this respect is Jüngel. He is one of a very few Protestant scholars who have attempted to spell out Barth's appeal to the analogy of faith in terms of a consistent theory of how analogy ought to be employed. He calls this the "analogy of advent." His proposal, which combines a statement regarding the ambiguous function of language, together with a specifically social-linguistic understanding, offers a means for the christological delineation of the analogy of faith. Unpacking this in christological terms will be our final task. When taken together with Barth's treatment of analogy, the concept of correspondence, based on the biblical witness to God's self-revelation in Jesus Christ, becomes a fruitful mode of theological predication.

The design of this book leads us quite naturally to chapter four and the single most innovative approach to analogical method in Protestant theology to date. Jüngel is no doubt partly responsible for putting the issue of analogy back on the agenda of theology in both Catholic and Protestant circles today. What few realize, however, is that his was more than an attempt to correct both traditions. His whole intent in *God as the Mystery of the World* is to give back to theology its proper task of speaking and thinking responsibly about God but with special reference to the "Word of the Gospel" as the possibility of anthropomorphic speech, precisely because God reveals himself as human. For Jüngel, God is thinkable, speakable and knowable as correspondence, which is a linguistic event known from Scripture as Jesus Christ of Nazareth. If analogy were to be exclusively grounded therein, responsible speech about God becomes possible as the expression of God's self-revelation in the God-Man, that is, in the inclusion of humanity in and with God's self-revelation. Within a fully orbed Christology, a specifically Protestant and yet ecumenical concept of theological method can emerge. Historical event, parabolic and metaphorical performance as "a being led by the hand" (*manuductio*), together with participated existence makes theology not only legitimate and possible, but also necessary. Participation, performance and parable: these are the three christological keys to theological speech. Taken together they form the core of what is meant by the *analogia fidei*. Working this out takes us into our last chapter.

Thus the final chapter will begin to do what Jüngel did not do with any depth. Jüngel's approach, and almost all other approaches to analogy, has often fallen prey to the failure to clearly and sufficiently ground analogy christologically. Jüngel attempts to do this but limits what he means by Christology to the concept of parable as speech act. While he points to the incarnation, he does not exposit it from the point of view of the correspondence of faith. If anyone can be said to have taken this necessary christological connection in analogy more seriously, it is Barth. In chapter five we shall return to Barth's concept of correspondence as exposited in his doctrine of Jesus Christ as electing and elected God and man in order to demonstrate anew why the nature of theological language has to exist in the nexus of an unresolved dialectic. Barth's doctrine of Jesus Christ as electing God and elected man is the *locus classicus* for defining this correspondence. When Christ the God-Man is the consistent point of reference for Christian theology, two features of language emerge. First, it must be recognized, with the church fathers among others, that language cannot bear the weight of human being, let alone divine being. So there will always be an aspect of inexpressibility in the theological task that remains core to its self-expression.

But, and here is where so much criticism of theology falls short, we may conclude that language is adequate to give us the concept of God especially when it has constant and primary reference to the God of the Bible, Jesus Christ. He is the one true analogy. All three approaches to analogy, participation, performance and parable, require of the inquirer a personal investment that cannot be gainsaid where theology wishes to speak of divine revelation. Theology therefore participates in advent. Theology is itself reflective of an "analogy of advent." In this analogy of advent creation and cross become the locus of the formal presence of God as performance, not as necessity, nor as negation, but as a "freely added plus," a more-than-necessary God. As Jüngel puts it so well, "God's advent into human language constitutes a language gain (*Sprachgewinn*)."[10] Theology as such not only points to this coming of God in the incarnation in metaphorical and parabolic ways but also itself participates in this coming-to-be. Human speech about God is fully responsible and possible when it corresponds to the full range of the incarnation as the participation, performance and parable of God in creation, in the person of his Son, Jesus Christ, in real-historical terms. These are, so to speak, the three "acts" of theology, contained in Scripture, that correspond to the event of revelation. Barth's Chalcedonian Christology confirms the broad outlines of what theology, as *analogia fidei,* should look like. It is a form of theological predication that has the potential to transcend all of the internal boundaries within so-called orthodox Christianity.

---

[10]*GMW*, pp. 290-93; *GGW*, pp. 395-97.

Finally, I shall argue that this analysis of analogy in the history of theology requires us to privilege the *analogy of faith*. Analogy and speech are inseparable acts that embody a necessary performance from the perspective of a participation in God that is inimical to Christian theology. But it is a participation limited to and caused by God's direct correspondence to us in his Word. As such, this book may be offered as a christological foundation for revelation, which gives us the unique features of the Christian God of the Bible, Father, Son and Holy Spirit. In this sense, rather than a method, it is already theology as prolegomena. The content itself yields the method. The words *science* and *method* are modern ciphers for entry into the task of theology in and with God's self-revelation. It is faith seeking understanding, one *intellegere*, one *fides*, one God and Father of us all.

1

THE CLASSICAL CHRISTIAN ROOTS
OF THE PROBLEM OF ANALOGY

◆

THE PRIMITIVE AND PLATONIC ORIGINS
OF "THEOLOGY" AND ANALOGY

At what point in the history of Western thought did the problem of speaking
about God, in a way that counted as the knowledge of God, arise? The
general answer is that it arose among the Greeks, especially among their
philosophers. Greek philosophy marks its origins from the time of the Io-
nians, especially Thales, Anaximander and Anaximenes. Aristotle referred
to this group of philosophers as "the physicists."[1] It was here, in the school
of Miletus, that the classical cosmogonic, theogonic, psychogonic myths and
physical (natural) philosophy first met, then diverged. The Hesiodic interpretation of Greek mythology in the form of poetry marks the beginning of
a shift from the mere rational organization of mythological story to the
more radical form of rationality that no longer derives its impetus from the
myths themselves but from human experience and its given reality, expressed in the phrase τὰ ὄντα ("existing things"). In making this move, the
Ionian philosophers shifted from a standpoint that Aristotle understood to
be a theological-mythological view (terms he sometimes uses synony-

---

[1]Aristotle, *Metaphysics* A, p. 983b, line 6. See especially Γ, 1005a, lines 31-33, where he refers to
them as ἀλλὰ τῶν φυσικῶν (literally, "some naturalists" who study τῆς ὅλης φύσεως σκοπεῖν καὶ
περὶ τοῦ ὄντος, "the whole of nature and concerning existing things"). All citations of classical
literature in this book will follow the citation numbering of the TLG. Translations are taken
primarily from the TLG or the LCL. See also S. Kirk and J. E. Raven, eds., *The Presocratic Philosophers* (Cambridge: Cambridge University Press, 1957, 1983).

mously) to a physico-ontological, and thus "scientific," worldview.[2] However, as most classics scholars would point out, the reduction, elimination and/or allegorical reinterpretation of mythology does not equal a nontheological view of the cosmos for these "physicists."[3] Thales understands that to call "Oceanus" the genesis of everything is to call him the source of all physical, spiritual and ethereal phenomena, the ὄντα.[4] The one statement of Thales that we do have preserved, within his physical philosophy, is his statement πάντα πλήρη θεῶν, or "everything is full of the divine."[5] While this may be a competing view, other than physics and/or mythology, it is no less theological in the Greek sense of the term. In fact it may represent a synthesis of the other, opposing conceptions of cosmology. The same can be said of the other Ionian philosophers, though in different words.[6]

But why is this Milesian starting point notable for our project here? Almost three centuries later, Plato recites Thales's dictum "everything is full of the divine" in such a way that it indicates he viewed the Presocratics as holding to a theological view of the world, and that indeed this dictum summarized well the beginning and end of all philosophy and theology.[7] Plato seems to think, contrary to what Aristotle would later say, that this indicates

---

[2]Aristotle, *Metaphysics* A, 980a-b.

[3]John Burnet notes that even Xenophanes, the founder of the so-called Eleatic school, was predisposed to explaining the world in light of the principle of divinity. Even if it was a rather pantheistic god, it was still a god who differed from the world in respect to organs of sense, since "he sees all over, thinks all over and hears all over." See John Burnet, *Greek Philosophy: Thales to Plato* (London: MacMillan, 1961). See also F. M. Cornford, *From Religion to Philosophy: A Study in the Origins of Western Speculation* (Princeton, NJ: Princeton University Press, 1912, rev. 1991), pp. 124-59.

[4]Cf. Aristotle's account of Thales in his *Metaphysica* (*Metaphysics*) and the physical philosophers in greater detail in his *De anima* (*On the Soul*) I.2, 405a, lines 1-19; 411a, line 7.

[5]Aristotle and Plato attribute this basic statement to Thales. Cf. Plato, *Laws* 10, 899b; *De anima*, 411a, line 7 (καὶ Θαλῆς ᾠήθη πάντα πλήρη θεῶν εἶναι). On this point see *TEGP*, pp. 11-37; Burnet, *Greek Philosophy*, pp. 34-36.

[6]See *TEGP*, p. 198. Jaeger comments, "In reality it matters very little whether Thales coined the term or not: the spirit of the early Greek philosophy of nature finds its expression in these words."

[7]Plato, *Laws*, 899b. Plato says the following with respect to this pantheistic statement of Thales: "Concerning all the stars and the moon, and concerning the years and months and all seasons, what other account shall we give than this very same,—namely, that, inasmuch as it has been shown that they are all caused by one or more souls, which are good also with all goodness, we shall declare these souls to be gods, whether it be that they order the whole heaven by residing in bodies, as living creatures, or whatever the mode and method? Is there any man that agrees with this view who will stand hearing it denied that 'all things are full of gods'?" (TLG). See also Aristotle, *De anima* I.5, 411a, lines 1-2; *TEGP*, pp. 22-23; Ingolf U. Dalferth, *Theology and Philosophy* (Eugene, OR: Wipf and Stock, 1988).

a theological interest on the part of the physicists rather than the fostering of an agnostic or atheistic attitude in contrast to mythology, which Aristotle often disparaged.[8] Eventually, one of Plato's students, Philip of Opus, came to understand the statement of Thales to be the best possible place to begin the study of *being*.

Admittedly it is not possible to reconstruct Thales's full philosophy as expressed in the short sayings we have available to us. Neither is it possible to develop a complete argument from Plato or Aristotle that this particular concept of an intuition of the divine from the observation of nature forms the bedrock of their approach to the knowledge of God; but it is most certainly possible to illustrate that this statement represents Plato's and the overall Milesian attitude, especially as it relates to natural theology, the study of being and the problem of human speech about the divine in general. That is to say, both Thales and Plato understood experience (physics, nature) of the phenomena (τὰ ὄντα) as a source of our knowledge about God. The knowledge of the divine is embedded in the cosmos itself and requires only reflective reasoning to bring it out. Here, for the first time in Middle Eastern culture, philosophy emerges as the critical pointer to theology. In fact, with Thales's dictum, philosophy arrives at its own self-assured position, on whose foundations the mythological view of the world lies, but now limited and confined to the reasonable explication of experience.[9] Through the Milesian physical philosophers the connection between nature and the divine is made in ways that are critical to Plato's later, mature philosophy of religion and his use of analogy as a tool for speaking about the divine.[10] This

---

[8]Plato, *Laws*, 967a. Says Plato: "For they imagine that those who study these objects in astronomy and the other necessary allied arts become atheists through observing, as they suppose, that all things come into being by necessary forces and not by the mental energy of the will aiming at the fulfillment of good" (TLG). Here Plato clearly sees something hidden in nature that nature points us to, vis-à-vis the divine, rather than turning us away from it.

[9]See *TEGP*, p. 23. Jaeger notes rather cryptically, "To many of us today it seems hardly possible to look back any further than this primary philosophical experience of significant being; and yet we can see that man's repose in being is not taken as a matter of course. Philosophy is rather the supreme stage of a new self-assurance on man's part, under whose foundations lie vanquished a wild army of darksome forces" (the darksome forces being mythology, or more simply unknowing, which gives rise to mythology).

[10]*TEGP*, pp. 25-26. Jaeger writes in conclusion, "The development of the idea of kosmos means both a new way of looking upon the organization of the state as derived from eternal laws of Being, and a re-creation of religion in terms of the idea of God and the divine government of the world as revealed in nature. That this is not peculiar to Anaximander but remains intrinsi-

influence is most certainly passed down through the centuries in both philosophy and theology and remains a fundamental way of posing the problem
of how we may speak of the divine from our observation of nature such that
our way of speaking constitutes knowledge of God.

Plato's conception of analogy. Plato was the originator of a theory of CER
that introduced order, design and divine participation into the universe of
sensible things, and in such a way that those "sensibles" reflect the eternal,
indelible pattern of the divine artificer. This was a theory he developed in
light of Milesian attempts at explaining the divine-creaturely connection
they intuited as basic to nature. This much at least can be said on the basis
of the *Timaeus* and its subsequent reception. Space does not permit its full
elaboration here.

From the time of Plato's adoption of the Milesian attitude (that everything
is full of the divine), theories of opposition, dialectic, analogy, difference,
similitude and logic abounded in early Greek cosmogony, theogony and psy-
chogony, and their explicating disciplines, theology and philosophy. Aristotle
himself invokes this reliance on a range of styles of argumentation in his
Physics and *Metaphysics*, and of course he is often criticized for embedding
his own philosophical doctrines in his interpretation of these principles of
logic and argumentation, not the least of which is his concept of analogy.[11]
This is so much the case that in respect to analogy one often loses sight of
what Plato taught regarding it and how he employed it. Plato's understanding
and employment of analogy emerges from this common appeal to opposites
found in Presocratic and Socratic traditions. In Plato, furthermore, this
appeal to analogy emerges in his understanding of the general antithesis he

---

cally bound up with the new philosophical approach, is clear from the way it recurs in Anaximenes" (*TEGP*, p. 36).

[11]Aristotle, *Physics*, 188a, lines 15-37; *Metaphysics*, 1004b, lines 29-31; 1075a, line 28; 1087a, lines
29-31. In a context in which he is speaking of analogy Aristotle states: "With regard to this kind
of substance, then, let the foregoing account suffice. All thinkers make the first principles
contraries [πάντες δὲ ποιοῦσι τὰς ἀρχὰς ἐναντίας], as in the realm of natural objects, so too in
respect of the unchangeable substances. Now if nothing can be prior to the first principle of all
things, that first principle cannot be first principle if it is an attribute of something else. This
would be as absurd as to say that 'white' is the first principle, not qua anything else but qua
white, and yet that it is predicable of a subject, and is white because it is an attribute of something else; because the latter will be prior to it. Moreover, all things are generated from contraries as from a substrate [ἀλλὰ μὴν γίγνεται πάντα ἐξ ἐπαντίων ὡς ὑποκειμένου τινός], and
therefore contraries must most certainly have a substrate" (TLG).

posits between being and the world of becoming in the earliest cosmogonies, such as Hesiod's *Theogony*. Plato's theory of the relation between these two principles is subtle and was developed over time. The axis in appealing to one from the point of view of the other is, however, always the same, that is, by means of analogical arguments. There is an absolute difference between what, in the *Phaedo*, is "divine, immortal, and intelligible, uniform, indissoluble and even constant and true to itself," on the one hand, and what is "mortal, manifold, human, unintelligible, dissoluble and never constantly true to itself" on the other. At the heart of analogy, in Plato's use of the device, sits a principle of *absolute dissimilarity* in arguing from becoming and being and vice versa. In this respect Plato is different from his predecessors, and perhaps even Aristotle, in terms of what analogy could achieve for talk about the transcendent realm. Analogy, for Plato, functions in as a principle of linguistic reference between two quite different realms, but as a similarity that is discriminating and not, as it sometimes is for the Presocratics, as a principle of logic between members of a single world of reality.[12] In Plato, then, analogy stands as a sort of reasoning from experience. Analogy, reason and experience are closely connected in the *Timaeus*. As Lyttkens puts it, "In the *Timaeus*, Plato begins an account of the origin and structure of the world by some theoretical remarks on knowledge." That is,

> he proceeds from the fact that the nature of our concepts depend upon the objects they represent. We differentiate between the world and its prototype, and it is likewise necessary to differentiate between concepts referring to prototypes and to images. While the former are fixed and unchangeable, the latter—emanating from an image—are only imaginary, and analogous to the former. Being bares the same relation to becoming as truth does to belief.[13]

---

[12]On this aspect of Plato's thought see especially G. E. R. Lloyd, *Polarity and Analogy: Two Types of Argument in Early Greek Thought* (Cambridge: Cambridge University Press, 1966), pp. 23-24; Cornford, *From Religion to Philosophy*, p. 259. See also Hampus Lyttkens, *The Analogy Between God and the World: An Investigation of Its Background and Interpretation of Its Use by Thomas of Aquino* (Uppsala: Almquist and Wiksell, 1952). His remains one of the most substantial treatments of analogy as it emerges in the classical period, and I gratefully acknowledge partial dependence on it for what follows in this section.

[13]Lyttkens, *Analogy Between God and the World*, pp. 24-25. He cites Plato's *Timaeus*, section 29c, "The concepts built on the image are said to be, 'ἀνὰ λόγον τε ἐκείνων ὄντας· ὅτιπερ πρὸς γένεσιν οὐσία, τοῦτο πρὸς πίστιν ἀλήθεια,' ('analogous thereto and possess likelihood; for as Being is to Becoming, so is Truth to Belief')" (TLG).

In his very thorough treatment of *Plato's Earlier Dialectic*, Richard Robinson points out that while a "method of analogy" in Plato's dialogues is
discussed very little, it is much used. Indeed, it is often employed in the
so-called middle dialogues where Plato regularly uses an analogy in order
to help the reader "see the truth" of his propositions. However, as G. E. R.
Lloyd points out, "This is true not merely of the middle dialogues but of the
whole Platonic corpus."[14] When Plato's uses of analogy are brought into comparison with his scattered formal statements on analogy, also understood as
"paradigm" and/or "illustrative example," it will be seen that he refers often
to the *deceptiveness of resemblances*.[15] It is no exaggeration to say that the
middle and late dialogues of Plato rely more heavily on analogy to help us
understand truth than any other form of argumentation. *Cratlyus, Parmenides, Theatetus, Meno* and *Phaedo* all testify to this, but perhaps none
more than *Gorgias* and the *Republic*.[16] Furthermore, "a very large number of
Platonic analogies, perhaps more than half, contain the joint notions of
techne-episteme, which is in English the tetrad knowledge-science-art-
technique."[17] For Plato, this is a key element in lending linguistics its capacity
to express the otherwise inexpressible. What is critical in his use of analogy
is the never-mentioned, but always assumed, presence of the universal, the
whole, as the basis of all analogy. This is the principle we are calling "cause-
effect-resemblance," or CER. Plato's key analogy, found in *Cratylus, Laws*
and the *Republic* is "idea:knowledge::sensibles:opinion." This is a "major cord
in Plato's theoretical philosophy."[18] That is, idea is the primary cause of a distinction, but a distinction in relation, between knowledge and opinion. The
universal principle of idea is the one concept against which all analogates are
to be seen, and yet not seen, in the sense that the analogy is only meant to point
to it, not describe it as an "epagoge."[19] The claim is to be able to see one thing
by virtue of an insight from another relation. "It is an intuition of a 'universal'

---

[14]Lloyd, *Polarity and Analogy*, p. 389.

[15]Richard Robinson, *Plato's Earlier Dialectic* (Ithaca, NY: Cornell University Press, 1941), pp. 214-
15.

[16]Ibid., pp. 217-18. Robinson explains that analogy is, for Plato, the best way to infer a universal
or ideal without sacrificing the opacity of reality or the transcendent character of that ideal world
on which the analogy trades.

[17]Ibid.

[18]Ibid., p. 218.

[19]Ibid., p. 217.

but a particular kind of intuition . . . a sort of seeing and not seeing. One case cannot give us insight into another unless it gives us insight into the universal covering both"; and yet analogy refuses to mention the universal directly.[20]

Thus in Plato analogy very easily moves from being a form of intuitive knowledge of the universal to an illustrative and explanatory example of it, with the resulting tendency to identify the analogy with the thing itself, rather than merely interpreting it.[21] Where the intention is to suppress the universal as not identical, the result is often that the universal becomes linked, by illustrative means, to an analogy as a "case or species" of the universal. That the universal idea is supposed to be subversively present in opinion is a given, but the danger is toward an identity or similarity without dissimilarity. Plato steadfastly resists this tendency. There are not two universals, or more than one idea and opinion, but only one universal that informs both cases, which means there really is only one case, the universal. In this sense it is really univocal. When the analogy falls into illustration it sets up an image (εἰκών), which makes that which is otherwise impossible to see "vivid and persuasive." A pure analogy should not do this in reality; it must allow for ambiguity and dissimilarity in all cases.

This at least accords with Plato's discussions of analogy and imagery in the *Republic*, the *Statesman* and the *Timaeus*. It is interesting that Plato spends considerable time discussing other methods of discourse and argumentation hypothetically in his dialogues, but uses them very little, while at the same time he spends little time discussing analogy hypothetically, but employs it often. Both Robinson and Lyttkens note that it is significant that the word ἀναλογία occurs only once in the dialogues *Republic*, *Statesman* and *Epinomis* and a mere three times in the *Timaeus*. In each case Plato is referencing the mathematic concepts of proportionality. In the *Republic* it is about the divided line (section 534a), in the *Statesman* it is a jocular reference to geometry (section 257b), and in the *Timaeus* it refers to *the proportionality inherent in the demiurgic construction of the physical universe*

---

[20]Ibid. This ambiguity in the use of analogy, in its very principle, is ever present.

[21]Plato, *Cratylus*, sections 387-90. For Plato, naming is almost essentially equivalent to the entity so named. He writes: "Then in naming also, if we are to be consistent with our previous conclusions, we cannot follow our own will, but the way and the instrument which the nature of things prescribes must be employed, must they not? And if we pursue this course we shall be successful in our naming, but otherwise we shall fail" (*Cratylus*, section 387d).

(sections 32b, 37a, 56c). The word itself is seemingly confined to these mathematical references in terms of any theoretical meaning of analogy. Does this not mean a concept of analogy is theoretically operative in Plato's philosophy? Though he does not use the word *analogy* to describe the intuition of reality, he means something close to that, especially in terms of his understanding of geometry. Plato saw geometry as a basic summation of the universe, a belief he received from Pythagoras and summed up in the statement: "Look for the proportions in reality, for they are there and you will find them."[22] In Plato's mind geometry is the language and creative power of the gods, who embedded proportionality in both the structure of reality and its knowability, within the physical world.[23] As such analogy is expressive of unity, or as "the finest of bonds . . . which makes itself and the things it binds, as much one as possible, and this is most finely achieved by proportion."[24] Again the Pythagorean axiom comes to the fore in the *Philebus*, where Plato says, "We ought always to assume and search for one form concerning everything on each occasion, for we shall find it there."[25]

Furthermore, while it is true that we have no clear discussion of the word *analogy* in Plato, he does discuss two words that have essentially the same meaning and use, namely *paradigm* and *image* (παράδειγμα, εἰκών). If, with Robinson, we agree that his discussions of these concepts "offer something approaching discussions of analogy," then we can certainly learn more about the role of analogy in Plato's thought than if we restrict ourselves to his actual use of the term ἀναλογία.[26] Space does not permit a full analysis of

---

[22]Plato, *Gorgias*, section 508a. The concept bares striking similarity to Thales's dictum "everything is full of the divine." Plato encourages the search for this "one idea" as though it were the essence of wisdom: "Now you, as it seems to me, do not give proper attention to this, for all your cleverness, but have failed to observe the great power of geometrical equality amongst both gods and men: you hold that self-advantage is what one ought to practice, because you neglect geometry" (TLG).

[23]Plato, *Timaeus*, sections 31a-32a.

[24]Ibid.

[25]Plato, *Philebus*, section 16d, which reads: "We must always assume that there is in every case one idea of everything and must look for it—for we shall find that it is there [οὖν ἡμᾶς τούτων οὕτω διακεκοσμημένων ἀεὶ μίαν ἰδέαν περὶ παντὸς ἑκάστοτε θεμένους ζητεῖν εὑρήσειν γὰρ ἐνοῦσαν], and if we get a grasp of this, we must look next for two, if there be two, and if not, for three or some other number; and again we must treat each of those units in the same way, until we can see not only that the original unit is one and many and infinite, but just how many it is. And we must not apply the idea of infinite to plurality until we have a view of its whole number."

[26]Robinson, *Plato's Earlier Dialectic*, pp. 222-23.

the two cases we may address in Plato where these discussions of paradigm and image take place (specifically the *Republic*, 368a-c, 434d-435a, and the *Statesman*, 277a-279e), so we shall rely here on the conclusions drawn from Robinson, a recognized authority on this matter in Plato.[27]

The first and most critical conclusion Robinson comes to in Plato's discussion of paradigm and image, as substitutes for the concept of analogy, is that neither form of comparison leads one to logical conclusions. They only suggest, for Plato, the possibility of hypothesis. In the analogy big letter:small letter::city:man, we recognize justice in the man when we see it in the city, just as looking at big letters from the same distance helps us see the small letters. We can say that our previous knowledge of x, although opaque, "is enough to guide us reasonably well" in the choice of analogates, and our choice of these guides us back to a clearer knowledge of x, but x is the beginning and end of each. It is a way of suggesting a hypothesis but not a logical deduction of one x from other analogates.

In light of this first conclusion, two further and related conclusions remain for Plato, which he puts forth as cautions in the use of analogy. The analogates can only be based on some *resemblance*, and, subsequently, conclusions based on resemblance are risky. Yet, despite this risk, Plato uses analogies throughout and very often draws quite significant conclusions from them, not the least of which is the analogy already mentioned, idea: knowledge::sensibles:opinion. In fact, the analogy big letter:small letter::city:man is a key point in his political philosophy vis-à-vis justice. In short, we must agree with Robinson when he writes, "There is no harmonization of these conflicting judgments, such as an attempt to state when analogy is good and when it is bad; and the prevailing opinion, which runs against analogy, seems to condemn Plato's own predilection for analogies in his dialogues."[28] So Plato disparages the use of analogy as a method of logic, yet uses analogies all the time to suggest and put forward his own hypotheses. Robinson offers two possible explanations for this paradoxical view of analogy in Plato, and these explanations accord well with Plato's suspicion of analogy as a form of argument that is dangerous because resemblance is not identity.

---

[27]Ibid., pp. 232-33.
[28]Ibid., p. 230.

One of these is the assertion in the *Phaedrus* that a wise man would write philosophy down only as a form of play, or as a reminder to those who know. It follows that the dialogues are either amusements or memoranda; and it would be possible to justify their use of images on that ground, or Plato might have adapted to this purpose the distinction, common enough in the dialogues, between teaching and discovering.[29]

That is, analogy may be good as a teaching tool but not good as a means of inductive reasoning or discovery of knowledge. It could serve as *manuductio*, but not as a form of epistemic justification. Analogies are needed to conduct us onto the right way of knowledge from sensible appearances, wherein the idea is imperfectly imitated, and where recollection may lead us, via analogy, from the visible to the invisible. Such a use of analogy has been recognized from Aristotle to Aquinas, with some considerable refinement in each, and among others, but it is Platonic in its essence.

Summary. What can be ascertained as the primary principle driving the initial use of analogical speech as applied to the suprasensible? One could say that, up to and including Plato's works, analogy is an appeal to an innate resemblance between that which presents itself to the senses as knowable, via rational reflection on CER, and that to which it points, which ordinarily is considered to be "suprasensible" on any other basis, be it the transcendent "idea(s)," the "ideas in the divine mind," or as we shall soon see, the Neoplatonic "one" and the Aristotelian "unmoved mover." It seems that there is an essential element to all predication about the relation between the sensible and supersensible. It is a CER that sits at the heart of Platonic ontology. While this ontology will come under serious criticism in Aristotle's *Metaphysics*, in the long run both his theory of analogy and the net result of his *Metaphysics* in that respect remain essentially Platonic, if only in a Neoplatonic form. It is to this part of the puzzle that we must now look in our attempt to demonstrate the essentially classical and Platonic-ontological roots of the subsequent medieval appropriation of analogy, and therefore, in the following pages of this study, to a necessarily Christian and christological caveat that is needed in order to employ analogy in theology.

---

[29]Ibid., pp. 233-34.

ARISTOTLE ON METAPHYSICS OF BEING, PSYCHOLOGY AND ANALOGY

With this basic Platonic understanding of analogy in mind, we move now from the sketch of developments within the Platonic corpus to a preliminary description of Aristotle's approach to speaking about divine realities. Here we come fully into the employment of more "scientific" views of epistemology, ontology, analogy and logic. In history the treatment of Plato and Aristotle has often been suggestive of an absolute difference between them, and this was particularly the case in the crucial epoch of Christian history between A.D. 900 and 1275, a period that has had no small implications for subsequent theological method. Make no mistake that what we have to say here about Aristotle's relationship to Platonic thought will have considerable implications for the traditional view within Thomism regarding Aquinas's appropriation of analogy in his *ST* and the *SCG*.

At this juncture we want to demonstrate three features of Aristotle's formation of his concept of analogy (he also uses the word *metaphor* but clearly means something like Plato's concept of analogy as *proportional comparison*). We want to demonstrate, first, his indebtedness to Plato's understanding of CER as the fundamental basis of his concept of analogy. Second, we want to exposit and exploit his fourfold theory of causality in light of this principle. Third, we want to briefly clarify the ontological implications of this CER for further developments toward the analogy of being. Our conclusion here will suggest that Aristotle's theory of analogy involves very similar ontological/metaphysical commitments to Plato's cosmology, and to theology in Aristotle's fully developed *Metaphysics*.[30] Having established the pervasive use of a CER in the development of Greek thought as a whole, we will be in a position to see, in the following sections of this chapter, how it was transmitted into Christian theology via Neoplatonism—by Augustine, in particular, but he was by no means the only one. This will put us in an optimal position to uncover some of the basic impulses in-

---

[30]Perhaps one of the most challenging, if also most idiosyncratic, interpretations of Aristotle's *Metaphysics* as it relates to analogy and the science of "being qua being" is Ralph McInerny's multiple studies on these and related issues, the most important of which include: *The Logic of Analogy: An Interpretation of St. Thomas* (The Hague: Martinus Nijhoff, 1971); *Aquinas and Analogy* (Washington, D.C.: Catholic University of America Press, 1996); *Preambula Fidei: Thomism and the God of the Philosophers* (Washington, D.C.: Catholic University of America Press, 2006).

forming Aquinas's appropriation of analogy, especially in the *SCG* and the *ST* but also in some of his smaller works. It will be discovered that, in his understanding of analogy, Aquinas is working with the very same concept of CER and that he received this from his Neoplatonic sources, especially Proclus, through Pseudo-Dionysius, as much as he received it from Aristotle's formal theory. This fact, as we have said, has important implications for the ontological orientation of the analogy of being and for the later Protestant critique of the concept. It is a fact that is largely ignored or misunderstood among some current theologians who want to use the concept of the analogy of being as a new touchstone for a revised metaphysical theology, which they see as essentially Catholic but which appears to be more classical than Catholic.

    Cause-effect-resemblance in Aristotle. In what sense can it be said that Aristotle shares with Plato a principle we are calling CER, especially in light of Aristotle's apparent rejection of the Platonic doctrine of idea, on the basis of which Plato's conception of CER exists? At first glance the task of answering this question seems impossible, but keeping in mind the apparent inconsistency in Aristotle's argument mentioned above, indeed a very good case can be made for such shared ground. Plato works his cosmology out on the basis of the concept of preexistent forms, or ideas, which serve as the substantial reality of all apparent things. Furthermore, we can discern the form through an analysis of CER. Indeed, Aristotle's *Metaphysics* begins precisely at this point in terms of describing what the nature of knowledge is for the knowing person. He suggests, "All men by nature desire to know."[31] This desire is innate, nonpragmatic and theoretical in orientation. Furthermore, it ascends by degrees from sensate knowledge, leading to memory and finally to the knowledge of "universals." The stress is decidedly on the universal, rather than the sensate form of knowledge. Aristotle writes, "We do not consider the senses to be wisdom. . . . They do not tell us the reason for anything."[32] Sensate knowledge can be affected by circumstances, whereas universal knowledge remains unaffected by anything past, present or future. The reason for this is that universal knowledge is substantially curtailed by its form (εἶδος). Aristotle illustrates this point as follows: "To

---

[31]Aristotle, *Metaphysics* A, 980a, line 1.
[32]Ibid.

have a judgment that when Callias was suffering from this or that disease, this or that benefitted him, and similarly with Socrates and various other individuals, is a matter of experience; but to judge that it benefits all persons of a certain type, considered as a class, who suffer from this or that disease . . . is a matter of art."[33] He says this in order to point out the fact that while "experience is knowledge of particulars, art proceeds on the basis of a universal εἶδος or 'form.'" Now unless Aristotle intends something wholly new by his use of the word *form* (a point we do not have access to because he never states this), we must assume he is using the word *form* in its Platonic sense. The word also occurs in his *Logic* and the *Physics*, where he offers a more technical definition of it, but its etymology and use at this critical juncture in the *Metaphysics* is unmistakably Platonic. The term has a central place in Platonic thought, where its fundamental meaning is its connection with the phenomena, which, despite their entry point within the flux of nature, appear always to point to something beyond themselves.[34] As Plato develops this doctrine it becomes attached to the theory that all phenomena "somehow participate in the forms," the changeless principles of universal knowledge. Crucially, Aristotle places his point of departure within this Platonic conception of form.[35] That is, Aristotle seems to make the same distinction between particulars and universals, and precisely that the knowledge of one, particulars, leads to or contains within it the other. What is even more telling is that the universal is superior to the particular. The reason is that while the sensate knowledge that informs the art of medicine may be good for Callias, it may not be good for or helpful to the human species in general. But it has a universal principle of the good of all that underlies it. That is, it points us to a universal.

At this point in his *Metaphysics*, Aristotle accuses Plato of teaching a theory of forms that confuses matter with substance as essencce.[36] Aristotle relates this more confused view to the Presocratic tendency to make air, earth, water and fire, "either individually, or in some combi-

---

[33]Ibid.
[34]Joseph Owens, *The Doctrine of Being in Aristotelian Metaphysics: A Study in the Greek Background of Medieval Thought* (Toronto: Pontifical Institute for Medieval Studies, 1951), p. 81. I gratefully acknowledge dependence on Owens's magisterial study in what follows in this section.
[35]Ibid., p. 13.
[36]Ibid.

nation, the reality of which all other existent things are but variations of this, or these, basic elements."[37] He posits instead that the true nature of physics is its εἶδος. Matter can contain essence as form only because it possesses the potential to receive form. Matter does not have its own nature as such.[38]

While Aristotle criticizes Plato for failing to offer an explanation of final causality in his cosmology, Aristotle seems to end up back at the same place, that is, the need to intuit reality as something ingredient in particular sensibles but not identical with it, yet being the formal cause of its existence.[39] These causes are needed in order to understand (following his hierarchy of the forms of knowledge) the material, the form in things, their native force (arguing back to a prime mover), and the purpose for which they exist. Crucially he adds that their efficient cause must bear some resemblance in form to the effect "because all four causes ultimately coincide with the formal cause, (that is with the idea)."[40] As we shall see shortly, this understanding of the four causes underwrites the whole of the Aristotelian system of knowledge and its ontology. At this juncture the question must be and indeed has been asked. Joseph Owens puts it best: "Does this reasoning mean that knowledge according to form is precisely knowledge of the cause? Do the notions 'cause,' 'form' and 'universal' ultimately coalesce? Does 'cause' mean 'form'?"[41] For this study it is not really necessary that Aristotle answer with a categorical yes or no. The fact is we cannot ultimately judge, because Aristotle's *Metaphysics, Categories* and/ or *Physics* are simply unclear on this matter. It may well be that we can say yes, based on Aristotle's doctrine of the soul, where "mathmaticals" take on the aura of motive force, as in Plato's *Timaeus*. But even here we cannot decide in the absolute affirmative. What the question does indicate for our study, when taken together with Aristotle's need to return to Plato's theory of idea(s) to make his "formal cause" argument work, is that there is no Aristotelian concept of analogy apart from a similar CER that we see in

---

[37]Aristotle, *Metaphysics* E, 1014b, lines 26-35.
[38]Ibid., 1014b, line 35, through 1015a, line 5.
[39]Aristotle, *Physics*, 198a, lines 14-20.
[40]Ibid.
[41]Owens, *Doctrine of Being*, pp. 95-96.

Plato's invocation of the quasi-religious orientation of the universe.[42]

In his discussion of causality and metaphysics, Aristotle intimately connects cause with εἶδος, or "form." In the final analysis, knowledge of the cause implies knowledge of the universal, a fact that many modern classics scholars have made clear. It is a central factor leading to the reassessment of Aristotle's ultimate dependence on a Platonic form of argument from causality.[43] Owens suggests that this apparent identification of form and cause will have significance for Aristotelian philosophy, though he does not pursue this. It can be argued that one immediate implication is that insofar as the notion of causality is central to Aristotelian *Metaphysics* of "being qua being," his *Metaphysics* is itself a species of Platonic ontology, even Neoplatonic, especially in respect to its epistemological grounding of the knowledge of universal causes, expressible as knowledge through proportional analogy.[44] One would agree with Owens that a "prudent reserve" should be exercised here, but the fact that the question has been raised already puts Aristotelian independence from the Platonic doctrine of ideas in doubt. If that is so at the very opening of his *Metaphysics*, it is only confirmed and lent credibility when we give further consideration to Aristotle's formal doctrine of the four causes. As per Owens, one cannot appeal to etymology in order to exonerate Aristotle here. Owens states the problem delicately, given his Catholic heritage, and the implications of his study for the received "orthodox" interpretation of Aristotle via Aquinas. "The problem can only be noted and kept in mind for subsequent examination. But its importance can readily be suspected. If Entity . . . is the cause of Being, the Aristotelian notion of cause may play a decisive role in the investigation of this subject."[45]

In sum, in the Aristotelian demarcation of wisdom as a special knowledge of the universal, inherent in form and derived through an analysis of cause through effect, wherein the effect resembles the cause, he has made the principle of cause something much different from the mere sensible intuition of things, motion and existence. Analogy appears to have an ontological as well as an epistemological weight, as the following analysis of his doctrine of the

---

[42]Ibid.
[43]Ibid., p. 88.
[44]Ibid.
[45]Ibid.

fourfold cause seems to further indicate. Indeed it becomes almost impossible to sever causality and its implications for analogy from Aristotle's doctrine of being qua being and its underlying Platonic cosmology.

Aristotle's four causes as his epistemological basis of wisdom. To begin with, in coming to an understanding of the employment of CER we must keep in mind that, for Aristotle, wisdom is the knowledge of the form (or universal) in the sensible, not mere sensible intuition itself. However, at the epicenter of Aristotle's *Metaphysics* sits the very famous argument from causality, which allows him to establish the basis on which the existence of a prime mover may be known. This argument from causality involves an approach to the concept of "cause" (αἴτια) in Aristotle that cannot be entirely separated from Plato's understanding of motion and causality, especially as it emerges in Plato's cosmology. This is the clear result of any close investigation of this argument from the four causes, which he carries out precisely in an attempt to overthrow the Platonic view. We have already seen that for Aristotle the purest and best form of knowledge, which he calls wisdom, is the knowledge of original, prime causes of the sensible. This he calls knowledge of the universals, or forms. Form and cause inhere in such a way that knowledge of one is knowledge of the other. The words are almost synonymous. For both Plato and Aristotle the central fact about all observable phenomena in the physical universe is the principle of motion. "Cause," however it is to be understood, is the key to the explanation of the motion of manifoldness. Locomotion is recognized from the beginning as a form of the prime motion of the universe. While this is suggested in Plato's *Laws*, it is in Aristotle a central principle of his explanation of the physical universe. Indeed, locomotion is one of four species of motion that correspond to the four types of causes.[46] Therein, the unifying feature of this argument is its appeal to cause, whatever the agency, coagency or intermediating agency. Any knowledge that comes forth as wisdom must account for these four causes, but especially as they point to a prime cause, or a prime mover, that is "unmoved." Aristotle repeats the argument from the *Physics*, noted above, here in the *Metaphysics*, but this time in direct connection with "first philosophy" (metaphysics) as opposed to a general physical explanation for

---

[46] Aristotle, *Physics* I, 184b, lines 10-25.

things. He writes that there are only two ways in which the science of meta-physics can be divine:

> A science is divine if it is peculiarly the possession of God, or if it is concerned with divine matters. And this science alone fulfills both of these conditions for (a) all believe that God is one of the causes and a kind of principle, and (b) God is the sole or chief possessor of this sort of knowledge. Accordingly, although all other sciences are more necessary than this, none are more ex-cellent. The acquisition of this knowledge, however, must in a sense result in something which is the reverse of the outlook with which we first approached the inquiry. All begin, as we have said, by wondering that things should be as they are . . . because it seems wonderful to everyone who has not yet perceived the cause that a thing should be measurable by the smallest unit. Thus we have stated what is the nature of the science which we are seeking and what is the object which our search and our whole investigation must attain. It is clear that we must obtain knowledge of the primary causes, because it is when we think that we understand its primary cause that we claim to know each par-ticular thing. Now there are four recognized kinds of causes [τα δ' αἴτια]. Of these we hold that one is the essence or essential (οὐσια) nature of the thing since the "reason why" of a thing is ultimately reducible to its formula, and the ultimate "reason why" is a cause and principle: Another is the matter or substrate; the third is the source of motion; and the fourth is the cause which is opposite (at the other end) to this, namely the purpose or good; for this is the end of every generative or motive process.[47]

This passage comes as a conclusion after Aristotle has worked through the Presocratic, Socratic, Pythagorean and Platonic attempts at identifying properly the cause of the generation and manifoldness of the universe. Ar-istotle concludes that Plato did not take proper account of all the causes and that he confuses the formal and material cause, leading to a falsification and admixture between form and matter.[48] This is the problem Aristotle sets out to fix with his identification of the four causes and how they may point to an essential form in matter, without confusion. From Aristotle's perspective, the essential missing ingredient in Plato's cosmology is an understanding of prime matter that must be assumed as a separate entity, which has the po-

---

[47] Aristotle, *Metaphysics* A, 983a-b.
[48] Plato, *Timaeus*, 35a.

tential to receive form but does not actually do so until it is joined to form.[49]

What does Aristotle means by "cause" (αἴτια), here, in his reference to primary and fourfold causality? Keep in mind that *the key concept is cause and its proximity to the Platonic concept of form.* This being the case, our conclusion must be that, while Aristotle's employment of causal argumentation may be an improvement on the Platonic conception of how form and matter come together, it nevertheless enfolds the Platonic conception of cause within his "new" system of theoretical knowledge or wisdom.[50] How do we know this to be the case? To begin with, this is a fact that has been recognized by scholars such as Edward B. Caird, Philip Merlan, Leo Elders, Harold Cherniss, Werner Jaeger and a host of others. As such, they have concluded, the Aristotle we know today is not the independent Aristotle of the Middle Ages. If indeed this is the case, then this conclusion has enormous implications for our understanding of Aquinas's appropriation of analogy in his primary *Summae*, and thus any present attempt to establish theology on the basis of a revised analogy of being.

Furthermore, here, in Aristotle's *Metaphysics*, we are at a place where he refers to "one cause" as the "entity" and the "what-is-being" (for the question of why is ultimately reduced to the logos, and the primary "why" is the cause and principle).[51] In this connection he also refers to the earlier works of the Presocratics up to and including Plato on causality as "investigation of being," by which he means the ultimate nature of things. He sees the four causes as empirically perceptible in the observation of the universe, as either part of that universe, material and efficient causes, or as above these as generative or consummative causes. It would appear that these are equivocal principles or analogous to such. Thus they need no justification beyond pointing them out. As far as Aristotle can see, these are apparent to all empirical observation. But this assumption does little to explain the proximity of cause to form and what that proximity might mean for the knowledge (wisdom) he seeks. Aristotle seems unaware that "cause" functions as more than a mere physical principle in his or, for that matter, Plato's philosophy.

---

[49]See, for instance, Harold Cherniss, *Aristotle's Criticism of Plato and the Academy* (New York: Russel and Russel, 1944), pp. 199-200.

[50]Compare Aristotle's understanding of formal cause as stated above with Plato's understanding of CER in *Timaeus*, sections 35a-38d.

[51]Aristotle, *Metaphysics* A, 983a, line 26; *Physics*, 194b, lines 23-25.

The movement from cause to the identification of form in matter, leading to knowledge of the universals, is so sleight of hand that it hardly throws any light on his virtual equation of cause-form-universal. Cause is real as it presents itself to the senses, but form and universal are abstractions. Wisdom is the ability to cognize the cause as resembling form, which constitutes the knowledge of the universals.[52] "If form and universal, as studied by wisdom (though they also constitute wisdom), continue to show identification with cause," in the sense determined by the *Metaphysics*, "they must mean real elements of things. They will have to be conceived on the model of physical principles. Accordingly, if wisdom treats the most universal it will be dealing with something highly real, and not with an abstraction."[53] There seems to be absolute coherence here between cause, as empirically observed, and the reality of universals known through cause as "form." Again, it appears that Plato's "form," "idea" or "universal" has been collapsed into "cause." If this is the case, then not only does Aristotle share Plato's view of analogy, which assumes similarity and likeness between cause and effect as a witness to the form embedded in the universe, but he has lifted it to the status of an ontology of being that is universal.

It is no accident that in the Middle Ages the employment of the analogy of being always struggled to avoid this univocity, sometimes unsuccessfully. If the science of the highest causes (formal and teleological cause) is ultimately the science of the most real, then the formula "being qua being," which Aristotle says is the subject matter of the study of these causes, means a unity of beings, which is a Neoplatonic principle par excellence.[54] It may well be that many Thomists and Aristotelians will take issue with this interpretation, but this, at any rate, seems to be the implication of Aristotle's introduction to his *Metaphysics*. Whatever may be said against this interpretation of causality in Aristotle, it must be seen against this "basis of inquiry" on which Aristotle himself begins. His goal in the *Physics* and in book A of the *Metaphysics* is to establish causality on a more firm footing. He is not here concerned with the equation of cause-form-universal; nevertheless, the

---

[52]The proximity of Plato's "ideas" to Aristotle's "universals" is clearly visible here.

[53]Owens, *Doctrine of Being*, p. 90.

[54]We should note that, for Plotinian Neoplatonism, being is a unity, but it points beyond itself to the One.

assumption of their equation has no small implications for his doctrine of being qua being. Wisdom is the knowledge of the εἶδος, which is the unchanging principle in all particulars. Thus we may conclude with Owens that "if wisdom is the study of ultimate causes, and the ultimate in the order of cause is solely the form, then wisdom will be primarily a study of form."[55] Thus the expression of this wisdom may be named by analogy as a CER.

Again, the point here is not whether one approaches this knowledge through the senses, via CER, or whether such a pattern is in the mind, which recalls this CER. The point is, cause may be known through the effect, *but the meaning of the relationship is form in the cause.* This form is expressible by means of analogy. Analogy, therefore, can point us to wisdom, which is the knowledge of the universal cause of all. This means that the notion of cause, insofar as it points us to the intelligible form in a thing, *accrues to things as their fundamental being.* The form is the element in a particular, which is its unchangeable being, in contrast to composite matter without form. Form is what a thing is. "They are what it is. But what a thing necessarily and unchangeably and definitely 'is,' is its form. The *genera*, the matter or the composite may be the 'what-is' of the thing. But only its form can be its 'What-is-Being.'"[56] In short, analogical predication about the form in things trades on an ontological reality inherent in the analogy. As such, analogy is a substitute for metaphysics. So, when Heidegger critiqued the analogy of being in his work *Aristotle's Metaphysics Θ 1-3,* he rejects Aristotle's metaphysics, and all subsequent metaphysics of being, precisely because he thinks it impossible that language may be freighted with the being of the divine in terms of the form in things.

> In each of its inflections the word "being" bears an essentially different relation to *being itself* (*Being qua Being*), from that of all other nouns and verbs of the language, to the essence that is expressed in them. From this it may be inferred that the foregoing considerations regarding the word "being" are of greater importance than other remarks about the word and linguistic usage in connection with things of any sort what so ever. But even though we have here a very special and fundamental connection between word, meaning, and being, in which so to speak the thing is missing, we must not suppose that it

---

[55]Owens, *Doctrine of Being,* p. 92.
[56]Ibid., p. 94.

will be possible to sift out the essence of being itself from a characterization of the word meaning.[57]

Whether or not Heidegger is overstating his case against metaphysics, the problem he identifies is there in Aristotle, and it is a problem that very much stalked medieval appropriations of analogy, after Aristotle.

Aristotle's understanding and use of analogy. The place of Aristotle in the Western metaphysical tradition was assured by his students, who collected and collated most of his works, including the *Metaphysics*. In the Middle Ages his philosophy was considerably forwarded by Aquinas, Maimonides, Ibn Rushd (Averroes) and Ibn Sina (Avicenna), all of whom not only rediscovered his work but also applied it to their various religious epistemologies. Very few scholars questioned the independence of Aristotelian causal argumentation until the nineteenth and twentieth centuries. Heidegger, in a careful approach to classical philosophy, first raised questions about the problematic ontology that sat at the heart of both Platonic and Aristotelian *Metaphysics*. The problem begins with Parmenides of Elea.[58] To Heidegger's way of thinking, both Plato and Aristotle were concerned ultimately with the Parmenidean problem of oneness of being, something Plotinus was more honest about than most, in the Platonic and Aristotelian schools. Heidegger saw this as having considerable implications, not just for Aristotle's doctrine of being qua being and the "unmoved mover," but also for the epistemological basis on which Aristotle allows for the possibility of speech about the divine, especially the analogical aspect of that epistemology, grounded as it was in a concept of CER. He comments on the Aristotelian concept of analogy, as it is later formed into analogy of being, as follows: "The analogy of being—this designation is not a solution to the being question, indeed not even an actual posing of the question, but the title for the most stringent *aporia*, the impasse in which ancient philosophy,

---

[57]Martin Heidegger, *Aristotle's Metaphysics Θ 1-3* (Indianapolis: Indiana University Press, 1995), pp. 34-35; see also his *An Introduction to Metaphysics* (New York: Doubleday, 1961), pp. 74-75. He refers to *analogia* as "the most stringent *aporia*" handed down to theology by Plotinus, in his sixth Ennead and repeated in the Middle Ages, leading eventually to Meister Eckhart's pronouncement that God "is not at all," because analogy fails to establish the possibility of a referent to being in any substantial way (*Aristotle's Metaphysics*, p. 38). We may therefore infer from the above quotation that Heidegger saw language as already predisposed to an impossibility to say anything meaningful about being.

[58]Aristotle, *Metaphysics*, 1026a, lines 13-19.

and along with it all subsequent philosophy for today is enmeshed."[59] Heidegger's criticism of the analogy of being, especially as it is related to the medieval appropriation of Aristotle and his penchant for the description of being as ἕν, after Plotinus, indicates clearly that analogy in its Latin form is equally indebted to a henology.

When Aristotle turns to analogy as a mode of speech about the divine, he demonstrates clearly that he is dependent on the Platonic conception of CER.[60] He takes up the concept of analogy in a number of places, including a crucial discussion of analogy in relation to metaphor. He sees analogy as a species of metaphor, which he calls the "analogy of the name." Metaphor occurs when there is a transference of a name from one entity to another, different reality, or entity. In his *Poetica* he delineates these analogies under four types. "Metaphor consists in giving the thing a name that belongs to something else; the transference being either from genus to species, or from species to genus or from species to species, or on grounds of analogy."[61] Now it is the analogical use that Aristotle finds interesting in terms of its significance for how language may function.

> Analogy is for Aristotle a means of expressing the relation of species to genus
> where genus stands for the unity of being, but a unity which cannot be said
> synonymously. Being, according to Aristotle, cannot be reduced to genus because it is neither a homonym nor a synonym. Yet "Being," like the "*One*" that
> goes together with it, is what is for the most part said of the whole.[62]

For Aristotle, "being" is the ultimate conception under which all difference and sameness may be considered. As such it is not itself a category. Analogy expresses the difference and the sameness of this relation in language. It is his mode for expressing "a particular kind" of meaning in language, which expresses "a oneness of meaning without being a genus for this unified meaning."[63] That is, words may be brought into an analogical relation in such a way that they necessarily cosignify "one common sense." For instance, *healthy* can be said of a condition, an item (herbs) or an activity (walking),

---

[59]Heidegger, *Aristotle's Metaphysics*, p. 38.
[60]See especially Aristotle's *Poetica* 21, 1457b; *Metaphysics* Δ, 1016b; *Nicomachian Ethics* 1131a, line 30, through 1131b, line 10.
[61]Aristotle, *Poetica* 21.
[62]Heidegger, *Aristotle's Metaphysics*, p. 31.
[63]Ibid.

but it can take on a different meaning depending on the analogy. But the concept of health is carried forward in each instance.

Heidegger is absolutely right to suggest that in Aristotle this is not a function of logic, because in analogy ordinary logic breaks down. This is precisely why analogy can be used to relate similar yet quite different conceptions. "Language itself can in no way be understood logically—a fact that we are only now gradually realizing."[64] This is the critical ingredient that sits at the heart of Aristotle's descriptions of analogy in the *Poetica* as follows:

> Metaphor consists in giving the thing a name that belongs to something else ... there are four terms so related that the second (B) is to the first (A), as the fourth (D) to the third (C); for one may then metaphorically put D in lieu of B, and B in lieu of D. Now and then, too, they qualify the metaphor by adding on to it that to which the word it supplants is relative. It may be that some of the terms thus related have no special name of their own, but for all that they will be metaphorically described in just the same way.[65]

Here Aristotle clearly assumes the classical understanding of analogy as mathematical proportionality as expressed in the formula a:b::c:d. Such comparisons allow for a naming by analogy, even though they are individually, essentially differentiated, to the point of a total dissimilarity. What makes them capable of being used in an analogy is their capacity to be compared on the basis of a shared "relation." For example, in the analogy "old age is to life as evening is to day," neither of the four elements have any similarities. But when they are brought together in this analogical fashion, the one thing they have in common is the relation between the words *old age* and *evening*. Both express the idea of the relationship between time, life and passing away. The analogy is immediately understood not because of what is said or written but because of the association of the relation of lateness to time as it relates to existence. Analogy presupposes that this transferability in language is basically understood by all rational beings and that it can be expressed linguistically. Certainly this seems to be a rational conclusion to draw from the very exercise we have just engaged in, by analogy. However, the question we are asking concerns the use of analogy

---

[64]Heidegger, *Aristotle's Metaphysics*, p. 32. While this may not be true of all language, it is certainly true of certain types.

[65]Aristotle, *Poetica* 21-22.

when speaking about the supersensible realities, specifically God. Therein lies the problem that sits at the heart of all analogical predication, Platonic, Aristotelian, Thomistic or otherwise. To speak of God *per analogiam*, in the manner suggested here by Aristotle, means that a level of knowledge must be assumed to already exist between God, God's relation to God's self and all existents that are assumed to exist apart from him yet, when brought into comparison, are known in terms of the common relation between them, including the divine. That is to say, Aristotle assumes a relationship of dependence between existent things and God as the cause of their existence, with cause being the common relation, despite the absolute dissimilarity.

For Aristotle analogy is a different matter altogether than mere univocity and equivocity. In analogy the same word may have different meanings but can be related, by analogy, to *one other thing* in terms of similarity. This one thing may serve as the hermeneutically first thing in relation to which other things can be named. These words, which may serve as hermeneutical first things, are, according to Aristotle, *paronyma*, or words derived through comparison.[66]

> There are many senses in which a thing may be said to "be," but all that "is" is related to one central point, one definite kind of thing, and is not said to be by a mere ambiguity. The statement, "everything is healthy" is related to health, one thing in the sense that it preserves health, another in the sense that it produces it, another in the sense that it is a symptom of health, another because it is capable of it . . . so too there are many senses in which a thing is said to be but all refer to one starting point.[67]

As we can observe, there are many things that can be called healthy, but all must be related in some particular way to the proto-concept of health as the final ground of all meaning for its differentiated usage. Analogy is needed in all the sciences because of the fact of this interrelatedness on which all else that goes by the name "health" ontologically depends. In analogy all the names are related to an ontologically prior concept. This is expressed in Aristotle's *Metaphysics* as follows: "It is clear then that it is the work of one science also to study the things that are, *qua* being. . . . But everywhere

---

[66]Aristotle, *Metaphysics* Γ, 1003a, lines 25-37.
[67]Ibid.

science deals chiefly with that which is primary, and on which other things depend, and in virtue of which they get their names."[68] Clearly Aristotle recognizes an ontological relation that sits at the heart of all analogical meaning, a meaning in which different entities have differing relationships to a common entity, after the pattern of CER. The question is, how is this form of analogical speech related to that which, as we have seen, Aristotle designates specifically as "analogy," namely, mathematical proportionality? What, according to Aristotle, is the common principle on which all analogical usage in any branch of knowledge is used?

It would appear to be the concept of *relation*. In his recent exposition of Aristotle's doctrine of analogy, R. E. White notes that while direct comparisons, in Aristotle's understanding, yield little advance in knowledge because the comparisons are obvious,

> by contrast, [for Aristotle,] the indirect, analogical, comparisons are seen as philosophically interesting comparisons and can appropriately be drawn between things that have no obvious properties in common. The analogical comparisons are always governed by the formula A is to B as C is to D, or more explicitly, "$R(A, B) = R(C, D)$," and a relation "R" where the way in which "$C + D + R$" will be specified depends upon the discipline being studied.[69]

In all these, and here White is correct, "perhaps the only theme to unite them is the idea that analogy enables us to make comparisons between phenomena too 'remote' to be compared directly."[70] Unfortunately, Aristotle only employs analogy as a consistent form of epistemology in his biological works. We are left to infer, as do many who come after him, what the implications are for metaphysics and theology. Some indirect references are made, but no consistent employment of analogy emerges in the later two "sciences."

Needless to say, much has been made of what we think Aristotle meant by analogy in theology and metaphysics. In short, all agree that the concept of relation is central to Aristotle's variations on the use of analogy and that this principle governs both the metaphysical and epistemological implications of his use of analogy. To be sure, Aristotle's understanding of analogy

---

[68]Ibid., 1003b, lines 15-22.
[69]R. M. White, *Talking About God: The Concept of Analogy and the Problem of Religious Language* (London: Ashgate, 2010), pp. 48-49.
[70]Ibid.

is qualitatively and quantitatively an advance on Plato's. But it is no less concerned with comparison based on a similarity to be located in dissimilar objects. This matter will arise again in a critical way in chapter four.

While it is certainly true that Aristotle understands dependence in causal relations in a way that differs from Plato, vis-à-vis the theory of ideas, the operative principle in the form of analogy (attribution) seems to trade on the same principle of CER that we observed in Plato, especially his cosmogony, and as we have seen, in Aristotle's doctrine of causality. This dependence of relation is the universal reason for employing analogy in this fashion. Here we must, with Jüngel, draw a significant conclusion that is often overlooked when considering Aristotle's use of analogy (and subsequently Aquinas's):

> To describe the lingual-logical relationship of different things which are "referred to something one and common," on which everything else depends and after which it is named [Aristotle] uses the term *anagogē*. Under the influence of Neoplatonic commentaries on Aristotle, [in the Middle Ages] the aspect of dependence was translated from the logical and hermeneutical context to the ontological during the period of scholasticism, so that the hermeneutical dependence of any *analogatum* on this analysis flowed over into the ontological dependence of being. The hermeneutical first thing appears as the ontological origin which under certain circumstances can also be thought of as the ontic causer.[71]

As we shall see, this claim can be demonstrated to be an accurate rendition of what happened to analogy.

Summary. Aristotle demonstrates a deep dependence on Plato more than a total difference, though they obviously do not share the same approach to philosophy. Aristotle's approach to metaphysics as science constitutes a monumental moment for Western thought. But it is clear he could not have achieved it without Plato. Aristotle was discovered amid the attempt to bring his teaching together with Plato's in order to unite all branches of knowledge. This task emerged out of the Platonic school more than it did the peripatetic schools of thought. It began with the Middle Platonists but was carried out under what would later be known as Neoplatonism. Thus Neoplatonism is

---

[71]*GMW*, p. 272.

really the driving force in appropriating Aristotle's ideas. We have now demonstrated that indeed CER forms the fundamental basis of Aristotle's theory with respect to speaking about God. We have also seen that this is the force of his argument in his employment of the concept of causality. Clearly his theory moves the principle of CER forward toward a conception of the analogy of being, though he does not use this phrase. Thus his theory of analogy involves very similar ontological/metaphysical commitments to those that have been observed in the development of Platonic and indeed Presocratic thought. His concept of analogy, especially as it relates to causality and the divine ideas, remains Platonic and prepares the way for a Neoplatonic conception of analogy.

CAUSE-EFFECT-RESEMBLANCE AND ANALOGY: THE NEOPLATONIC CONNECTION

All along the line thus far we have made oblique references to a school of thought that will come to have enormous consequences for Christian theology, namely Neoplatonism. The question as to the appropriateness of Neoplatonic philosophy in Christian theological discourse is, of course, a critical discussion in our time and cannot be our main focus here. But what we shall have to say about its influence on theological method, especially in the medieval period, will scarcely be missed by the attentive reader.[72] The predominant modality of speech about God that emerges out of the Neoplatonizing of Christian theology becomes known as *via negativa* ("way of negation") or apophatic theology. The method has its roots in Platonic cosmology and is developed to some degree in the Middle Platonists, Plutarch, Apuleius, Alcinous (Albinus), Basilides and Minarius. It is mimicked somewhat in Philo of Alexandria and the Christian Platonists of the East, especially Clement, Origen and Gregory of Nyssa. The method of discourse is systematized in Plotinus and perfected in his subsequent disciples Porphyry, Iamblichus and especially Proclus's *Elements of Theology*. In Christian

---

[72]Recently certain schools of thought have sought to revive Neoplatonic metaphysics in the interest of Christian theology. The leading school of thought is, by far, the group of scholars known as radical orthodoxy. This has not been undertaken without severe criticism, however, especially from classics scholars working within this field of scholarship. See, for instance, Wayne J. Hankey and Douglas Hedley, eds., *Deconstructing Radical Orthodoxy: Postmodern Theology, Rhetoric and Truth* (Burlington, VT: Ashgate, 2005).

theology, it is either highly influential or even formalized in Augustine, Boethius, Anselm and Pseudo-Dionysius, the latter being its most ardent adherent. The connection between Proclus and Pseudo-Dionysius is a critical factor for this development, especially in respect to Aquinas, as we shall see in chapter two. The Plotinian approach to speech about and knowledge of the divine will have decisive consequences for the Augustinian and Thomistic employment of analogy.[73]

Neoplatonism, in its pure Plotinan expression, holds to six principles, which are also common, it is claimed, to the Platonic tradition.

1. Reality is immaterial rather than material.

2. Thus the visible and sensible is unreal but has reference to a higher level of being in which the image they reflect is more real.

3. Knowledge, therefore, is to be sought through intuition, not primarily through sense perception.

4. The vehicle by which the real may be related to the unreal is the soul, which is immortal by virtue of its reality as an emanation from the One.

5. Thus the highest good that can be known is the real.

6. This knowledge is identical to the beautiful, the good, the true, and as such is the One.

---

[73]There are many places one could go to to understand the essence of Neoplatonism and its roots in Middle Platonism. The following have been helpful in the analysis here: A. H. Armstrong, ed., *The Cambridge History of Later Greek and Early Medieval Philosophy* (London: Cambridge University Press, 1967; Armstrong is perhaps the most recognized scholar of Neoplatonic thought in the history of the discipline); Deirdre Carabine, *The Unknown God: Negative Theology in the Platonic Tradition, Plato to Eriugena* (Louvain: Peeters, 1995); John Dillon, *The Middle Platonists, 80 B.C. to A.D. 220*, rev. ed. (Ithaca, NY: Cornell University Press, 1996); Stephen Gersh, *Middle Platonism and Neoplatonism: The Latin Tradition*, 2 vols. (Notre Dame, IN: Notre Dame Press, 1986); Stephen Gersh and Maarten J. F. M. Hoenen, eds., *The Platonic Tradition in the Middle Ages: A Doxographic Approach* (New York: Walter de Gruyter, 2002); Lenn E. Goodman, ed., *Neoplatonism and Jewish Thought* (Albany: State University of New York Press, 1992); John Gregory, *The Neoplatonists: A Reader*, 2nd ed. (New York: Routledge, 1999); Parviz Morewedge, ed., *Neoplatonism and Islamic Thought* (Albany: State University of New York Press, 1992); Dominic J. O'Meara, ed., *Neoplatonism and Christian Thought* (Albany: State University of New York Press, 1981); Basil Tatakis, *Byzantine Philosophy*, trans. Nicholas J. Moutafakis (Indianapolis: Hackett, 2003); R. T. Wallis, *Neoplatonism*, 2nd ed. (London: Duckworth, 1995). For extensive research, issues and the classical approach to Neoplatonic research, see the journal *Dionysius* (Halifax: Dalhousie University Press), published since 1977 and established by the Neoplatonism scholar A. H. Armstrong.

Of these primary features of Neoplatonic thought, points 2 and 4 stand in close proximity to the two principles that underlie the Neoplatonic conception of analogy. These principles also underlie Plotinus's doctrine of the One and lead him to adopt a Platonic conception of the divine idea as the identity between the ideas and the divine mind. These ideas are latent in the creation and lead to a knowledge, however opaque, of the divine mind through contemplation. But of course at the end of all contemplation we come to the realization that the One ultimately "dwells in unapproachable light." These principles were most evident not in any theory of analogy per se but in the analogical mode of exegesis that dominated the Neoplatonic system of "commentary" and their mode of reflection and contemplation. Scholastic commentary as exegesis of texts was a system of knowledge and education that would come to have enormous significance in the Middle Ages.

Neoplatonic exegesis and analogical rules. Tracing out the features of this form of exegesis will illustrate well how analogy actually functioned in formative Neoplatonism. This cannot be discovered in any set of principles or rules laid down by Plotinus or others. However, it can be demonstrated to be the core method for speech about the divine in two respects. First, there is the Neoplatonic penchant for allegorical exegesis, and second, there is the Proclan approximation of the "rules" by which such exegesis and analogy exists in Neoplatonic discourse. We will employ the basic findings of John Dillion's article "Image, Symbol and Analogy: Three Basic Concepts of Neoplatonic 'Allegorical Exegesis'" to help us see these exegetical principles in action. In this article Dillon attempts to, in his words, "sort out, through an examination of some individual contexts, the possible difference of meaning between two basic terms of Neo-Platonic allegory, *eikon* and *symbolon*, and in this connection the use of the term *analogia/ analogon*."[74] He is concerned to lay bare the "rules" that govern Neoplatonic exegesis. "By what system does one recognize in a given text an image or symbol of metaphysical reality? How can one learn to recognize the correct 'analogia'?"; here he is suggesting that *analogia* is the aim of the allegorical inter-

---

[74]John Dillon, "Image, Symbol, and Analogy: Three Basic Concepts of Neoplatonic 'Allegorical Exegesis,'" in *The Significance of Neoplatonism*, ed. R. Baine Harris (Albany: State University of New York Press, 1976), pp. 247-48.

pretation of the icon (εἰκών) or symbol (σύμβολον).[75] While he recognizes
that there is no clearly defined set of rules for discerning analogy as a
method in Neoplatonic literature, he affirms that they are there in the exegetical practice nevertheless. Indeed there cannot be any one set of rules
for allegorical exegesis, since the hermeneutic is a free and open-ended
practice often dependent on the master who practices it. One cannot learn
these rules except insofar as one is "sitting at the feet of one's master."[76]
Indeed, the most one can deduce from the practice of arriving at a correct
analogy through observation of symbols and icons is the fact that they
depend on a relational "similarity."

Interestingly, Dillon relies on Proclus's *Commentary on Plato's Timaeus*
to demonstrate this somewhat vague principle of allegorical exegesis.[77] On
the basis of this text, and in connection with the Pythagorean theory that
influences Proclus, a three-level system of exegesis is set out that analogically
mirrors the three hypostases of Neoplatonism, namely, being, life, and intellect or mind. The first two stages, reflective of the Pythagorean education
of novices, are to point out the εἰκών and then to interpret the σύμβολον in
the text. The *Republic*, for instance, is an εἰκών of the creation of the universe,
while the story of Atlantis, contained therein, is "symbolic" since, as Proclus
puts it, "myths in general tend to reveal the principles of reality (τὰ
παράδειγματα) through symbols." So while they point to the πράγματα,
which is the substance of reality, they do so only on the basis of a one-to-one
correspondence, based on the observable features of the σύμβολον and
εἰκών. As such we can compare image and archetype through σύμβολον and
εἰκών. As with Plato, for instance, this method of exegesis posits a one-
to-one relation between the Good and the sun, in that both are sources of
visibility, "and even of existence, to the entities subordinate to them [life],
the world of sensible objects and the world of intelligible objects."[78] These
three modalities reflect the three roles for deriving exegetical meaning of
a text. Εἰκών is a reflection or resemblance, a "mirror image" or a "direct
representation" of an original, its paradigm. A symbol relates one thing to

---

[75]Ibid.
[76]Ibid.
[77]Ibid.; Proclus, *Commentary on Plato's Timaeus*, TLG I.29, 31-32.
[78]Dillon, "Image, Symbol and Analogy," p. 250.

its paradigm through a process of "standing in place of" in a way that "fits together" a corresponding reality in "a higher realm." Dillon uses the illustration of a statue of Winston Churchill (icon) as opposed to a cigar (symbol). Both can point to a reality in different ways.[79] But already the problem of the incapability of something physical referring to something suprasensible arises.

Plato's analogy between the sun and the Good also anticipates that difficulty. The sun may be a symbol of the Good because its means of referral does not assume a one-to-one similarity. Indeed some resemblances can be inferred—source of visibility, existence, subordinated relationship and so on—but such analogies fail to represent an icon from the paradigm that inspires the analogy. What, if anything, makes one an icon and the other a symbol? Proclus provides an answer to this question in his *Commentary on the Republic*, wherein he distinguishes εἰκών and σύμβολον as they relate to Plato's employment of myth. In his mind the principle of transcendent order in the ideas must have some reflection or somehow be represented in the seemingly disordered and scandalous behavior of the gods in the Homeric myths. But such representation can only be indirect because "these symbols have obviously no resemblance . . . to the essential natures of the gods. But myths must surely, if they are not to fall short utterly of representing the truth, have some resemblance to the nature of things . . . the contemplation of which they are attempting to conceal by means of the screens of appearance."[80] If symbol is a form of concealment in speaking about "essential natures of the gods," so also, in Plato, is the tendency to use iconic myths to "conceal his transcendent intentions about the gods," yet these "images" do in some way represent "the realities of the secret theories hidden within them."[81] Now, as Dillon makes abundantly clear, there is no consistent ordering of references to mythological σύμβολον or εἰκών in Proclus that would indicate a prioritizing of the capacity of one over the other to represent these divine realities. Rather, both concepts in Proclus become allegorical means whereby he—and therefore we—may begin to speak "analogically" of the divine. It would seem to be the case that myths, as σύμβολον

---

[79]Ibid., p. 251.
[80]Ibid.
[81]Ibid.

and εἰκών, but especially the latter, can represent the divine in different ways, and that they also "provide no problems to those who are willing to follow out the ἀναλόγια."[82]

Here Proclus combines the concept of symbolic and iconic representation under the term *analogy*. In the vast majority of Neoplatonic writers after Plotinus, *analogy* has its root meaning in the Platonic conception of proportionality, and Proclus is no exception. In fact, a careful observation of his *Commentary on Plato's Timaeus* I, 33, lines 4-7, would lead one to conclude that proportionality is at the core of what he means by analogy, even if it avoids any kind of formulation like a:b::c:d. According to Dillon, for Proclus, analogy, in the context of allegorical exegesis proper, "signifies the correspondence between the surface meaning of the text and the metaphysical truths of which it is an expression. This must have been seen as a sort of fixed mathematical relation."[83] Such analogies had to be the means whereby the symbols and icons could be labeled, so as to name what divine realities they might point to. As one studied and learned through allegorical practice, these analogies become easier to identify.[84]

In his *Commentary on Plato's Parmenides*, Proclus privileges analogy over icon and symbol as the primary means whereby we may disclose the divine representation we often find on the surface of the text. These analogies not only exist on the surface, but they also extend to the author, the subject matter and the overall mode of discourse in the text. In the text of the *Parmenides* of Plato, for instance, Proclus sees Parmenides, the philosopher, as an analogy of the "un-participated divine νοῦς," while Zeno is "analogous to that νοῦς which is participated in by the divine soul."[85] Socrates is the representation of νοῦς as one "capable of receiving the divine forms." But Proclus sees analogy as being able to contain multiple levels of meaning taken together. Parmenides, Zeno and Socrates are an ἀναλόγια "according to which they represent respectively the three moments of Being, life and mind within the hypostasis of νοῦς."[86] While it is clear that no set of rules for allegorical interpretation seems forthcoming in Neoplatonic literature,

---

[82]Ibid., p. 255.
[83]Ibid.; Proclus, *Commentary on Plato's Timaeus* I, 1.5-1.7.
[84]Dillon, "Image, Symbol and Analogy," p. 256.
[85]Ibid.; Proclus, *Commentary on Plato's Parmenides*, TLG.
[86]Dillon, "Image, Symbol and Analogy," p. 257.

one can affirm with confidence that analogy "is the principle upon which allegorical exegesis is based."[87] In fact, this is consistent with Plato's own use of allegory and analogy as discussed above. Variations on interpretation and the representation of divine realities can in no way be confined to rules that regulate their appearance, interpretation and understanding. Such a set of rules would defy the view one sees, since the One eminates throughout the universe as mind. This lack of determination as to the rules for employing analogy will later make it virtually impossible to establish a "method of analogy" in Aquinas's writings. This was in fact what motivated Cardinal Cajetan to attempt such a narrative in his *The Analogy of Names*.[88]

Summary. So much for an initial description of the classical roots and the theoretical development of the concept of analogy. It is firmly rooted in the Platonic cosmological principle of CER. We must emphasize here that we have only surveyed the development. Many questions must go unanswered. More will be said about the Neoplatonic-Proclan influence on the medieval appropriation of Neoplatonic analogy in chapter two, where the brief analysis here will be shown to be critical to later employment of analogy in Aquinas. Our single goal in this opening exploration of the problematic relationship between the capacity of language to speak of the divine and divine transcendence has been to show that analogy was the most natural recourse of the classical world and that such analogical speech depended on a principle of CER. The degree to which, or not, Christian theology may or is even bound to follow this inclination will be left until the latter three chapters. Our goal in the first two chapters of this book is to demonstrate, as much as possible, the actual uses to which analogy was put in order to uncover its metaphysical orientation. Plato's employment of analogy and his conception of cosmology live from the central principle of CER. The Aristotelian attempt to formalize the relationship between language and "first science" is ultimately dependent on this essential Platonic (or at least Middle-Neoplatonic) cosmology.[89] It

---

[87]Ibid.

[88]On this see especially G. P. Klubertanz, S.J., *St. Thomas Aquinas on Analogy: A Textual Analysis and Systematic Synthesis* (Chicago: Loyola University Press, 1960), pp. 121-23.

[89]Proclus, in his very influential attempt to establish the possibility, shape and scope of "theology" in contradistinction to Christianity, in *The Elements of Theology*, will inadvertently be one of the leading voices influencing Aquinas in respect to analogy, via Pseudo-Dionysius's *Divine Names*.

is confirmed in the general philosophical and exegetical orientation of Neoplatonism, which becomes its main vehicle of transference into Christian practice. However, it remains unclear to us exactly how analogy fully comes into Christian theology itself in a manner and mode that reflects these classical roots. Again, this is a crucial question if we want to speak clearly about the possibility of speaking, thinking and knowing divine realities. In very many respects the questions of epistemology, ontology, faith, reason and theology are decided in respect to how one answers this question. The unfortunate fact about analogy is that the history of the development of analogical method is fraught with misunderstanding, complexity and misrepresentation. Going forward, we will continue to use the principle of CER as a cipher to help us understand the continuing force analogical speech comes to exert in theology. The question of the nature of the analogy of faith, with which the final three chapters of this book are concerned to exposit, can only be properly comprehended against the backdrop of this discussion. With that in mind, we are now ready to answer the next crucial question, whither the use of analogy in Christian theology?

THE AUGUSTINIAN APPROPRIATION OF
CAUSE-EFFECT-RESEMBLANCE

Augustine's attitude toward the classical philosophers has been well summed up in his famous dictum, "We are to take from them in order to devote it to the purpose of preaching the Gospel."[90] In keeping with the sentiment ex-

---

It is ironic, therefore, that Christian theology will receive its mode of analogy in part from a man who wished to establish it on quite another basis. Indeed, one could say that the problem of analogy is anticipated, summarized and formalized in his opening proposition, πᾶν πλῆθος μετέχει πηι τοῦ ἑνός, "every manifold in some way participates Unity." Proclus, *The Elements of Theology*, trans. E. R. Dodds (Oxford: Clarendon Press, 1963, 2004), p. 3.

[90]Augustine, *De doctrina christiana* (PL vol. 34). See also R. P. H. Green, trans., *Augustine: On Christian Teaching* [*De doctrina christiana*], Oxford World's Classics (New York: Oxford University Press, 1997); *On Christian Belief*, ed. Boniface Ramsey, trans. Edmund Hill, Ray Kearney, Michael Campbell, Bruce Harbert and Michael Fiedrowicz (New York: New City Press, 2005). It contains *True Religion, The Advantage of Believing, Faith and the Creed, Faith in the Unseen, Demonic Divination, Faith and Works* and *Enchiridion*. We will draw on two sources for our interaction with Augustine's text. The first is PL, edited and published by J.-P. Migne between 1844 and 1855, which contains the majority of Augustine's writings in the original Latin and can be found at pld.chadwyck.com. We will also have recourse to *S. Aurelii Augustini Opera Omnia, editio Latina*, much of which is from the PL, with the addition of a few texts missing in Migne.

pressed there, in the mature Augustine, we shall not be attempting to prove in this section that Augustine was a thoroughgoing Platonist/Neoplatonist. Indeed, we need not go so far in order to establish the fact that a Platonic way of speaking about God (based on CER) does enter Christian discourse, in a methodological way, through Augustine. In its most reified form this "way" is through analogy, most expressly put forth by Augustine in the principle of *vestigium trinitatis*. This we must say with little doubt.[91] Though there is considerable discussion about precisely how Augustine came to be exposed to particularly Neoplatonic doctrine, there can also be no question that he was both exposed and heavily influenced, especially where theological method, cosmology, psychology, epistemology and metaphysics are concerned. As Gerald Bonner notes, "The discovery of Neoplatonism was unquestionably a major event in the history of Augustine's development."[92] In

---

It can be found at augustinus.it/latino/index.htm. For English translations, we will rely on the new series by J. E. Rotelle and B. Ramsey, eds., *The Works of Saint Augustine: A Translation for the 21st Century* (New York: New City Press, 1990); William Harmless, ed., *Augustine in His Own Words* (Washington, D.C.: Catholic University of America Press, 2010); Gerald Bonner, *St. Augustine: Life and Controversies*, 3rd ed. (New York: Morehouse, 2002); Serge Lancel, *Saint Augustine* (London: SCM Press, 2002); Peter Brown, *Augustine of Hippo: A Biography*, rev. ed. (Berkeley: University of California Press, 2000); Allan Fitzgerald, ed., *Augustine Through the Ages: An Encyclopedia* (Grand Rapids: Eerdmans, 1999); Henry Chadwick, *Augustine of Hippo: A Life* (New York: Oxford University Press, 2009); Chadwick, *Augustine: A Very Short Introduction* (New York: Oxford University Press, 2001); Carol Harrison, "Augustine," in *The Early Christian World*, ed. Philip Esler (New York: Routledge, 2001), 2:1205-23. The following were also very helpful: Lewis Ayres, *Augustine and the Trinity* (Cambridge: Cambridge University Press, 2010); Luigi Gioia, *The Theological Epistemology of Augustine's De Trinitate* (Oxford: Oxford University Press, 2008); James J. O'Donnell, *Augustine: A New Biography* (New York: HarperCollins, 2005); Pierre-Marie Hombert, *Nouvelles recherches de chronologie augustinienne*, Collections des Études Augustiniennes, Série antiquité 163 (Paris: Institut d'Études Augustiniennes, 2000); Goulven Madec, *Introduction aux 'Revisions' et à la lecture des oeuvres de saint Augustin*, Collection des Études Augustiniennes, Séries Antiquité 150 (Paris: Institut d'Études Augustiniennes, 1996). The following studies in particular have deeply influenced my reading of Augustine herein: the biography by Peter Brown, cited above; Robert J. O'Connell's *St. Augustine's Early Theory of Man* (Cambridge, MA: Harvard University Press, 1968) and his magisterial treatment of Augustine, titled *The Origins of the Soul in St. Augustine's Later Works* (New York: Fordham University Press, 1987). See also John Rist, *Augustine: Ancient Thought Baptized* (Cambridge: Cambridge University Press, 1994); Mary T. Clark, *Augustine*, Outstanding Christian Thinkers Series (Edinburgh: T & T Clark, 2005); György Heidl, *Origen's Influence on the Young Augustine: A Chapter of the History of Origenism* (Notre Dame, IN: Notre Dame University Press, 2003). See also the excellent work *Augustine Through the Ages: An Encyclopedia*, ed. A. D. Fitzgerald (Grand Rapids: Eerdmans, 1999). Many other works will be noted in passing along the way.

[91]Gioia, *Theological Epistemology of Augustine's De Trinitate*, pp. 22-23; Ayres, *Augustine and the Trinity*, pp. 280, 288-89.

[92]See R. Dodaro and G. Lawless, *Augustine and His Critics, Essays in Honour of Gerald Bonner* (London: Routledge, 2000), p. 4.

order to effectively connect Augustine and his successors to the classical understanding of analogy, which he indirectly baptized as the standard mode of speech about the divine, we will have to first understand his connection to the Neoplatonic elements ingredient in his epistemology. Therefore we shall first investigate his cosmologically driven epistemology, in order to clarify how Augustine both differs from and has affinity with the Platonic and Neoplatonic tradition. Only then are we in a position to understand why the mature Augustine opts for an epistemology ultimately dependent on an ontological theory of analogies of the Trinity (*vestigia trinitatis*) in his most significant and influential theological work, *De Trinitate*.[93] The analogical approach to the knowledge of the triune God is, for Augustine, the only *ratio* that can make the doctrine of the Trinity intelligible to us in our speech about God. Though other theologians before Augustine traded on similar analogies (for instance Gregory of Nyssa), his becomes expressive of a standard mode of speech about God thereafter.[94] A brief glance at Boethius's philosophical theology and Anselm's ontological proof clearly demonstrates the dominance of this Augustinian method, though we cannot take the time to establish this herein. It was also in this vein that Peter the Lombard wrote his *Sentences* and Bonaventura his *Summa*.[95] These figures constitute the primary influences on mid-to-late medieval theology, especially the thirteenth century.

Augustine's cosmologically driven epistemology: Illuminated intellect. We begin with Augustine's epistemology simply because it contains within

---

[93]Augustine, *The Trinity*, trans. Edmund Hill (New York: New City Press, 1991).

[94]On vestiges of the Trinity in Gregory of Nyssa, see David Bentley Hart's article, "The Mirror of the Infinite: Gregory of Nyssa on the Vestigia Trinitatis," *ModT* 18, no. 4 (2002): 541-61.

[95]Peter the Lombard, for instance, begins his whole treatise on a very strong epistemological note with an invocation of Augustine's *De Trinitate*, stating: "The things, therefore, which one is to enjoy, are the Father and the Son and the Holy Spirit. However the same Trinity is a certain most high Thing and common (property) to all enjoying It, if however It ought to be called a thing and not the Cause of all things, if however even a cause. For it is not easy to find a name, which convenes with so great an excellence, which the one God is better said (to be) except 'this Trinity.' Moreover the things, which one is to use, are the world and the created things in it. Whence (St.) Augustine in the same (book), 'This world is to be used—not enjoyed—so that *the invisible things of God, understood through those things which have been made, may be perceived* [*conspiciantur*], that is, as from temporal things there are only eternal ones, which one is to enjoy, which are eternal and incommutable; but all others one is to use, so that one arrives at the thorough fruition of these.' Whence (St.) Augustine in the tenth book *On the Trinity*: 'We enjoy things cognized, in which very things the delighted will takes rest for its own sake; but we use those things which we refer to the other, which one is to enjoy'" (*The Sentences of Peter the Lombard*, trans. G. Silano [Toronto: Pontifical Institute of Mediaeval Studies, 2007], p. 7 [PL vol. 192]).

it, as an enduring and relatively stable aspect of his theology, all the necessary assumptions that go into his analogical method. By *epistemology*, in the context of Augustine's philosophy, we do not mean merely the "justification of belief," an oft-repeated shorthand definition more germane to modern thought. Knowing truth with certainty was not relegated to a static system of thought in either Augustine or the late patristic-classical era in which he lived. Rather, one spoke of knowledge as a way, a journey or a road, traveled on by means of various human faculties, including intellect (mind), *ratio* (reason) and illumination, all contained within the soul and understood as its "higher faculties." The principles of knowledge and understanding were the products of the proper function of these faculties. Very early on in his life Augustine developed certain principles with regard to the way of knowledge from which he would never stray very far, even in his mature theology. Again, it has been well documented that it was his encounter with the *libri Platonici* that led to some of these fundamental epistemological developments.[96] Prior to this his position on the possibility of the certainty of knowledge was deeply influenced by the skepticism of Manichaeism. No clearer starting point can be adduced than when Augustine writes: "But then, after reading certain books of the Platonists which taught me to seek for a truth which was incorporeal, I came to see your invisible things, understood by those things which are made."[97] Herein is the kernel of his philosophical and theological epistemology. Precisely how one understood the "invisible things" from the "things that are made" involved Augustine in a system of knowledge at once rooted in a generally accepted cosmology. We know the invisible by observation of the visible, recognizing in the visible the imprint of the invisible.

One of the earliest places where this is worked out with more clarity and precision is in his early work *Contra Academicos*. Though his doctrine of illumination receives refinement and precision as a theological instrument of the mind in his mature work, it retains the largely Platonic meaning in which it was worked out in this earlier work.[98] Emerging as he was from

---

[96] Augustine, *Confessions* 7.20-26.

[97] Ibid., 7.9.13.

[98] Compare, for instance, Augustine's *Contra Academicos* I-II (PL vol. 32) with his *De Trinitate* XIV-XVI (PL vol. 42); Hill, trans., *The Trinity*. For the English translation of *Contra Academicos* see Johannes Quasten, ed., *Contra Academicos*, trans. John J. Omera, Ancient Christian Writings

the spirit of a heavily skeptical school, he felt it needful, "for the sake of our life, our morals, our souls," to offer a counterargument to skepticism. He also wanted to make it clear that while philosophical reason can be a starting point for certainty about truth, it finally needed an illumination that transcended mere philosophical reason. To get at this he divides knowledge into two categories, "sense knowledge" and "intellectual knowledge." Augustine understands that, without the capacity for reflective reason, our senses may well lead us astray. For instance, the refraction of light through water would lead us to believe that whatever we put into water might appear to us to be broken; however, rational intuition, repeating the laws of refraction, tells us that this is an illusion.[99] Later on he will explain that our senses are actually driven by an innate capacity to intuit an object as to its relationship to our "affections."[100] Our senses enable us to become aware of an object, but it can only become an aspect of knowledge when it corresponds to the mind through the imaginative and intellective function of the soul. Knowledge of the object presented to the senses "is contained in the mind as memory."[101]

The soul, according to Augustine, is active in every moment of sensory input. The object presents itself to the senses, but the sensation is entirely an internal matter enabled by the soul through memory.[102] An image of every object we encounter through the senses already exists in the mind. The object, the senses, the image and memory constructed in the encounter are all essential elements to knowledge, but only the soul is the active agent in knowing. Our "perception" of all sensibles is, as he writes elsewhere, "an action upon the body not hidden from the soul."[103] Objects external to the knower are necessary but not sufficient means for knowledge. At times one can look right at an object but not see it because of some other preoccupation of the mind. It takes the engagement of the intellectual aspect of the soul to "really see" an object.[104] What the eye sees is more than a function of

---

12 (Westminster, MD: The Newman Press, 1950).

[99] Augustine, *Contra Academicos* II.9.22 (*Ancient Christian Writings* 12:76).

[100] Augustine, *Epistolae* 122.2 (PL vol. 33).

[101] Augustine, *Contra Academicos* IV.13 (*Ancient Christian Writings* 12:133).

[102] Ibid., III.13 (*Ancient Christian Writings* 12:135).

[103] Augustine, *De quantitate animae* 24.46 (PL vol. 32).

[104] Ibid., 27.53.

the physical faculty of sight. Much later he will say that it requires the "mind's eye" to really see.[105] Memory, therefore, is more than a capacity to recollect past images presented to the mind. "It is actively involved in mediating between what we perceive through the senses and what we understand in the mind."[106] The senses are entirely reliable when combined with the understanding of the mind, which is able to account for the principles of mediation between perception and understanding. This latter aspect is the basis of all intellection. We pass from sensory knowledge to intellective knowledge when we think about and formulate thoughts and propositions with respect to sensory data.

The "skeptics," toward whom Augustine partly aims his *Contra Academicos*, would only allow that these thoughts and propositions may, or only probably, point to knowledge. However, there could be no certainty, so judgment must be suspended. Augustine noted that the skeptics, those in the tradition of Carnades, Seneca or the Pyrrhonian school, treated this "probable knowledge" as near-truth, to which he retorted: "If someone who had never seen your father said, on seeing your brother that he was like your father, you would consider him a madman or fool."[107] So, he says, are the academics when they say that "in daily life they follow what is truth-like although they do not know what the truth is."[108] So Augustine concludes,

> Therefore the question between us is whether the arguments [of the academicians] make it plausible that nothing can be perceived and that one should not assent to anything. Now if you prevail, I'll gladly yield. Yet if I can demonstrate that it's much more plausible that the wise man be able to attain to the truth and that assent need not always be withheld, then you'll have no reason, I think, for refusing to come over to my view. . . . It is enough for me that it is no longer plausible that the wise man knows nothing.[109]

Augustine produces such propositions, accepted as basic axioms within skepticism itself (for instance, the law of noncontradiction), as a fundamental truth, demonstrable through reason. So, likewise, are mathematical

---

[105] Augustine, *De Trinitate* XI.3.6.
[106] Ibid., 8.14.
[107] Augustine, *Contra Academicos* II.7.16 (PL vol. 32).
[108] Ibid., II.7.19.
[109] Ibid., II.13.30:34-43; III.14.30:20-21; III.14.31:45-49.

propositions. There is a sense in which, though we may doubt all things, including our own existence, "we cannot doubt the fact that we doubt."[110] In his mature theology he will add that our own human self-awareness is sufficient to establish the truth of our own existence. "Hence you know that you exist; you know you live; you know you understand."[111] This initial intuition regarding the relationship between sensory knowledge and intellectual knowledge is a concern for Augustine throughout his life, and he fills in the gaps in his subsequent works. In the final analysis skeptics must be hoisted on their own petard, namely the "truth" that we can know nothing for certain.

The key that unlocks the nature of the relationship between that which the senses perceive and that which the mind understands Augustine calls *divine illumination*. He begins to work this doctrine out in his subsequent "more directly Christian" works like *De magistro* (*The Teacher*) and *De libero arbitrio* (*On Free Choice*). These works deal directly with the relationship between objectivity and intellectual knowledge in reference to transcendent truth. In *The Teacher*, Augustine is concerned to show how intellectual knowledge is possible by means of a rarefied theory that conflates his received Platonism with his Christian faith. In this work he will refer to this new epistemology as *illuminatio*, we think, for the first time. According to Augustine the human mind can change, but truth is static. Therefore truth can only arise in the mind when aided by the presence of an "illuminating" light, which shines within the mind. This theory appears to be a heightened expression of the Platonic theory of recollection through anamnesis, which literally means "unforgetfulness." The following is his earliest known explanation of it: "But when things are spoken of which we perceive through the mind, that is through intellect and reason, we are talking about things which, being present, we see in that inner light by which he himself who is called the inner man is illuminated, and in which he delights."[112] That is, as he would later explain, knowledge of the truth for us is innate insofar as the Creator has endowed the mind with a natural capacity to know truth because we are created in his image. The Creator is in and with his creation

---

[110]Augustine, *De vera religione* 73 (PL vol. 34); *De civitate Dei* XI.26 (PL vol. 41).
[111]Augustine, *De Trinitate* X.10.14 (PL vol. 42); *De beata vita* II.7 (PL vol. 32).
[112]Augustine, *De Trinitate* X.10.14; *De magistro*.

through the rational capacity of the human mind. This is his λόγος, or Word, or Wisdom, indeed Christ himself, in us as our teacher, who leads us into all truth. "For illumination is participation in the Word, namely in that life that is the light of humanity."[113] This inner light in Augustine's mature theology is referred to almost exclusively in christological terms. But its original intuition is Platonic, as much as one would like to think it is purely biblical, especially in its connection with recollection and anamnesis. A brief comparison with Plato confirms this.

Plato considered all learning to be a mere process of awakening to what the mind already knows. Education is "recovering," through recollection, "the knowledge of oneself, that is in oneself."[114] Plato demonstrates this process at length in the *Meno*, the conclusion of which states that all learning is internal to the learner.[115] Here Augustine largely agrees with the Platonic understanding of mimesis—that is, innate reason, which is capable of grasping the educational process as that related to any external cause or process. Peter King offers a very succinct summary of the Platonic roots of Augustine's theory of illumination in his introduction to his new translation of *De magistro*, as follows:

> Consider the following example. You recite to yourself the steps of a mathematical proof while attempting to understand it. You are merely parroting the proof. Yet in thinking it through you suddenly have a flash of insight and see how the proof works—you comprehend it, and thereby recognize its truth. We commonly describe this difference with a visual metaphor—the "flash of insight"— . . . "enlightenment" and so on. Augustine calls it "illumination." . . . The power that reveals the truth to us, Augustine maintains, is Christ as the teacher operating within us. The very understanding we have testifies to God's presence in the world, since mind is illuminated with knowledge by the inner teacher.[116]

How is it that Augustine is able to identify Christ as the inner teacher? And how is this to be seen as an improvement on the Platonic concept of learning? Augustine is not clear on this, and the answer to both these questions must

---

[113] Augustine, *De Trinitate* IV.4; *De civitate Dei* I.10.2.
[114] Plato, *Meno* 85d 4; 6-7.
[115] See Plato, *Meno* 98a, 3-5; see also P. King, ed. and trans., *Augustine: Against the Academicians and The Teacher* (Indianapolis: Hackett Press, 1995), p. 7.
[116] King, "Introduction," in *Augustine: Against the Academicians*, p. 8.

still be, to some degree, located in his appropriation of Platonism. In his later refinement of the theory of illumination, Augustine finds it necessary to ground the claim of Christ as internal teacher in a more generally philosophical conception of the "divine origin" of all truth. That is, he qualifies the subjectivity of the truth we may come to know by placing it within an ascending scheme of ever-increasing objectivity, a scheme that directly reflects the Neoplatonic hierarchy of knowing.

In his subsequent work *De libero arbitrio* (*On Free Choice*), he notes that, though mutable, human knowledge is qualified by its subjective orientation; its objective reality emerges in the process of existence, life and knowing (the Neoplatonic *esse, vivere* and *intelligere*).[117] As such, given the fact that intelligence is reflective of divine transcendence, the source of objective truth must be equally transcendent. So coming to truth through an experience of illumination is actually an encounter with the divine. "This truth, above the human mind, and illuminating man's natural acts of judging and apprehending essences, is an immutable wisdom identifiable with God."[118] As such, wisdom is the missing step in the Neoplatonic triple way of knowing—that is, the missing "fourth step." Thus wisdom becomes the aim of knowing the truth, as *veritas*. It is identified with its absolute objectivity.[119] "Because truth is superior to the human mind, characterized as it is by immutability and eternity, it is not subject to the mind; it is not 'constructable' by it. Wisdom is the highest truth and is the 'self-same' (*ipsum*)."[120]

Keeping in mind that both Plato and Plotinus do not have this fourth level, it would appear that Augustine has indeed lifted the process of learning, christologically, to a hitherto unforeseen moment. But this judgment, though promising, is premature. Augustine's position, despite its christological framing, is actually quite consonant with the Middle Platonic process of knowing, wherein the λόγος functions in much the same way in the hierarchy of intellection.[121] Origen of Alexandria was very influenced by these

---

[117]Augustine, *De libero arbitrio* III.21.60 (PL vol. 32).
[118]Clark, *Augustine*, pp. 118-20; Rist, *Augustine: Ancient Thought Baptized*, pp. 76-77.
[119]Augustine, *De Trinitate* IV.4; *De civitate Dei* X.2.
[120]Ibid.
[121]For an excellent exposition of these fourfold Middle Platonic systems see Robert Berchman, *From Philo to Origen: Middle Platonism in Transition* (Chicago: Scholars Press, 1984); Heidl, *Origen's Influence*, pp. 58-59.

Middle Platonic theories, and there is little doubt that Augustine was acquainted with his thinking. At the heart of his theory of illuminations sits,
by Augustine's time, the well-known, Platonically inspired theory of "the
divine ideas," as we briefly mentioned above. Augustine will later teach that
the prototypes, or forms-ideas, of all realities are "primordial forms in the
mind of God in accord with which he creates."[122] A number of recent studies
have established this appropriation of the "divine ideas" in Augustine. In his
comprehensive study on the subject of the divine ideas, Vivian Boland comments on Augustine as follows: "For Augustine the ideas are the eternal
rationis rerum according to which all things have been created. They are
contained in the Word, who is the wisdom or art of the Father."[123] Augustine
shows no awareness of Plotinus's philosophical criticisms of the "demiurgic"
understanding of the ideas, although for theological reasons he shares the
conviction that "the ideas are the divine mind—that is, what is in the Word
is the Word."[124] It could also be that, in Augustine, there is a possible tendency to identify the Plotinian νοῦς with the Johannine λόγος, though the
evidence for this is as of yet inconclusive.[125] At any rate it seems clear that
Augustine has adopted some form of the Platonic conception of the "divine
ideas," and this does inform his theory of illumination. There are radical
differences that I think absolve Augustine from a completely Neoplatonic
worldview. But the influence is nevertheless strong and deep.

Elsewhere Augustine again takes up the question of the divine ideas, in
terms of how it informs this theory of illumination. It emerges in question
forty-six of his *Eighty-Three Different Questions*. In this discussion he asserts
that the divine ideas give truth its ontological "form" as truth. He also says
that this world of the intelligible, as the substance of the divine mind, is "to
be identified with the Word of God" and was the agency through whom
"God the Father, Son and Holy Spirit created all that exists, or ever will exist."[126]
The ideas are, as such, eternal and with God, since God cannot add or take
away anything from his being. In *De civitate Dei* (*The City of God*), Au-

---

[122]See also Vivian Boland, *Ideas in God According to Saint Thomas Aquinas*, Studies in the History
　　of Christian Thought 69 (Leiden: Brill, 1996), pp. 85-86; Clark, *Augustine*, p. 19.
[123]Boland, *Ideas in God*, p. 85.
[124]Ibid., pp. 85-86.
[125]See Paul Henry, "Augustine and Plotinus," *Journal of Theological Studies* 38, no. 2 (1937): 20-21.
[126]Augustine, *De Trinitate* IV.3.

gustine affirms:

> And if God, as Plato continually maintains [he means Plotinus], embraced in
> his eternal intelligence the ideas both of the universe and of all the animals,
> how then, should he not with his own hand make them all? Could he be
> unwilling to be the constructor of works, the idea and plan of which called
> for his ineffable and ineffably to be praised intelligence?

Furthermore, "God, as Plato constantly reminds us, held in his eternal understanding the forms, not only of the entire universe, but also of all animate
beings. Forms are in the Son of God, in the Word."[127] So at the very least we
may agree with Mary Clark when she affirms, "These divine ideas are the
standards [for Augustine] by which judgments concerning temporal realities
are made, and the mind has access to them by illumination."[128]

By now the connection between Augustine's epistemology, most essentially stated in his theory of illumination, and his understanding of analogy
are coming into focus. This focus will grow in intensity as we look into his
theory of the soul as *imago Dei*, particularly its noetic aspect, and his understanding of it as a *vestigium trinitatis*. That a Platonic cosmology (either
from Plato, Middle Platonism and/or Neoplatonism, or some combination
thereof) informs his understanding of how we can know the truth, and how
we may speak about it, now seems unquestionable. John Rist, in his *Augustine: Ancient Thought Baptized*, summarizes this influence, in respect to
speech about God, in Augustine as follows. In Augustine's epistemology:

> We conclude that the contents of our memories are of two sorts: images of
> particular objects, experiences and events in time and historical sequence—
> these are our immediate concern in considering questions of skepticism; and
> "things themselves" recognized by the mind, namely the objects of mathe-
> matics, logic and above all metaphysics, that is the Platonic forms which in-
> variably by "nature" or in accordance with our learning, by acquisition, con-
> stitute the finitude of the mind. Such "ideas," as Augustine had learned from
> Plotinus, are both in the mind of God and somehow also present to what
> Plotinus calls our human "upper soul."[129]

---

[127] Augustine, *De civitate Dei* XVI.26-28.
[128] Clark, *Augustine*, p. 19.
[129] Rist, *Augustine: Ancient Thought Baptized*, pp. 76-77.

These images and ideas will eventually form the basis of Augustine's mature theology of the soul, its noetic aspect, its creation in the image of God and therefore its analogical (and so ontological) capacity to intuit the triunity of God.

In sum, it should be abundantly clear by now that Augustine's theory of illumination is critical to his epistemology and ontology. The principle has been variously interpreted. In the *ST* of Aquinas we understand it as an aspect of what Aristotle called the "agent, or active intellect," in which Aquinas affirms that the agent intellect illuminates the sensory image received by the passive intellect (the location of the sensory faculty), with the active intellect thereby abstracting the universal form of the real contained in the image.[130] This, he thinks, is what Augustine was referring to in designating the active intellect and the "light of the mind." Aquinas agrees that this is divine in origin, but so innate as to yield itself to be known even by the secular philosopher. It could also be that his theory of illumination is best represented in the Ockhamist theory that divine illumination is merely a matter of discovering through reason the already-existing impression of the divine forms on the mind.[131] As the human mind develops into a greater awareness, it relies on these impressed forms to judge matters of perception and experience. This is a very influential view and also finds a following, before William of Ockham, in Anselm, Boethius, Peter the Lombard, Bonaventure and so on. In order to do final justice to this expansion of Augustine's theory of illumination, one would need to offer a synthesis of all his critical passages on the soul and his doctrine of the image of God, which is a task beyond our scope here. But such a synthesis has been done, and if Robert J. O'Connell and Ronald Nash are right, this synthesis leads to the view that the forms are, for Augustine, "in the mind" and "are the *a priori* virtual conditions for knowledge."[132] They are a priori because they cannot be derived from experience. They are natural because they are in the mind even when they are not objects of thought.[133] And, finally, the forms are preconditions of *scientia* because knowledge becomes possible only when

---

[130]*ST* I, q. 84.
[131]William of Ockham, *Dialogus*, trans. John Scott (London: The British Academy, 1999), 1.4, pp. 25-28.
[132]Ibid., p. 440.
[133]Ibid.

these universals are applied to the images from sensation.[134] It would seem
then that the human mind is patterned after the structure of the divine ideas.
While it is true that, for Augustine, this "inner light" needs the external
prodding of an "outer light," it still constitutes a reflection of Platonic anthropology in its essence. It is, and always remains for Augustine, the essential and natural epistemological point of contact. A further elaboration
of his doctrine of the soul, in respect to mind as a *vestigium trinitatis* and
therefore the veritable *imago Dei*, will bear this out.

As with his doctrine of illumination, we see in Augustine's understanding
of the soul as mind a decidedly Neoplatonic bent. It is clear that he adopts
certain aspects of the classical Platonist doctrine of the soul in terms of its
immateriality and existence apart from the body. He also clearly espouses a
similarity between human mind and divine mind that is rooted in the
concept of the "divine idea." His own view fits well with the Neoplatonic
synthesis of Platonic and Aristotelian thought. His understanding of mind
as an image of the Trinity is most certainly an advance on the quasi-
trinitarian understandings of Porphyry, Plotinus and other Neoplatonists.
The mind is that aspect of created order which most closely resembles divinity. Therefore, to know it is to know the divine in the most intimate terms
possible for a finite mind.[135] We can also certainly agree that Augustine's
doctrine of the mind, though somewhat indebted to Plato and Plotinus,
nevertheless moves beyond them both. "Memory for Augustine is more
than Platonic reminiscence, though certainly it is a relation to the forgotten
or innate principles and to the origins of the mind's knowing and loving."[136]
Augustine appears to close off the Plotinian option for an inaccessible *one*
beyond mind, preferring a more Middle Platonist allowance for a unity of
knowledge of the self and God.[137] But he shares completely the Neoplatonic
concept of incorporeality of mind. "The fundamental difference between
Augustine and Plotinus is that Augustine is able to carry his self-reflectivity

---

[134]Ibid.

[135]See Augustine, *De quantitate animae liber unus* 34.77 (PL vol. 32); *De diversis quaestionibus
LXXXIII liber unus* 51.2 (PL vol. 40); *De Genesi ad literam imperfectus liber* 16.60; *De civitate Dei*
11.26.

[136]Hankey, "Mind," in Fitzgerald, ed., *Augustine Through the Ages*, pp. 566-67.

[137]Augustine, *De vera religione liber unus* 3972 (PL vol. 34); *Confessions* VII.1.1-2; *De Trinitate*
XIV.12.

all the way through."[138] This was a principle made possible by Augustine's affirmation of Christ as the incarnate Word, revealed both to the senses and to the mind. That is, mind is what makes us capable of union with God. "Ultimately, this is owed to the Trinitarian form [analogously understood] of both the divine and human mind."[139] A brief look at Augustine's theology of creation, especially in respect to his understanding of the biblical concept of *imago Dei*, confirms this fundamentally Neoplatonic conception of the human soul. When we finally lay out Augustine's doctrine of analogy, it will be clear that, in respect to theological method, vis-à-vis speech about God, a Platonic cosmology of CER is its essential form.

Imago Dei *as vestige of the Trinity.* Augustine's thinking about the human mind as a vestige of the Trinity is not confined to his formal treatment of the theme in his *De Trinitate*. For example, Augustine's insistence on the simultaneous creation of body and soul, form and matter in *De Genesi ad litteram* has important implications for his doctrine of the *imago Dei* and its similarity to the Holy Trinity. Augustine offers his views partly in an attempt to overcome the apparently disparate descriptions of the creation of man and woman in Genesis 1–2. It is largely in line with interpretations that had been advanced by the likes of Origen and other fathers of the church. Augustine reads the first two chapters of Genesis as two separate stages in the creation of one humanity, male and female, in the image and likeness of God, respectively.[140] Both the body and soul were joined in one simple creative act on one day, but the soul was "fully formed on the first day 'in its own proper being' and hidden until breathed into the body."[141] In Augustine's works the problem of the soul's relation to the body is by no means explained in direct terms. In fact, from its early description in *De immortalitate animae* to the later *De Genesi ad litteram*, there does not seem to be any clear resolution of this problem in Augustine.[142] Here Plotinus's influence seems to persist. In some sense the soul must preexist apart from the body. It would appear that the embodiment of the soul is to be seen as representing God's bringing creation to its perfection. Whether this represents the pre-

---

[138]Hankey, "Mind," p. 567.

[139]Augustine, *De vera religione* 39.72; *Confessions* VII.1.1-2; *De Trinitate* XIV.12.

[140]Henri Crouzel, *Origen* (New York: Harper & Row, 1989), pp. 4-5.

[141]Augustine, *De Genesi ad litteram* VII.24.35; see Heidl, *Origen's Influence*, p. 379.

[142]Augustine, *De immortalitate animae* I.5; compare Plotinus, *Enneades* IV.7.

existence of individual souls, or, along with Plato and Plotinus, a world soul, is unclear. As we have suggested, Augustine seems hesitant to draw a firm line between a purely "biblical description" and a Platonized form of that biblical description.[143] There is a sense in which Augustine sees embodiment in terms of its incorruptible state, "as the Platonists do." He writes, "Plato you see, says that the gods are both mortal by the connection of the body and soul, and yet are rendered immortal by the will and decree of their maker.... Plato ... affirms that it was granted by the Supreme, as a boon to the gods He had made, that they should not die, that is, should not be separated from the bodies with which he had made them."[144]

The ambivalence in these early and later texts is not overcome in the doctrine of the soul as image in the *De Genesi ad litteram*. He ends his meditations on Genesis 1–2 with "conclusions" that are quite tentative in respect to how soul and body are to be combined, and in what respect the combination is reflective of the image of God. "In fact, the conclusions are 'far from being conclusive,' at all."[145] O'Connell's suggestion in this regard is striking. "The soul may have been made out of some sort of spiritual matter; or it may be the result of a *defluxio*, a flowing downward of a spiritual creature (one possible form that 'spiritual matter' might take) enjoying a life of happiness; or it may have been made, not of any matter at all, but out of nothing."[146] Only corporeal elements and an "irrational soul" have been definitely excluded as conceivable "matter" for the soul's original creation, and no light whatever has been shed on what the soul's creation out of nothing "might positively entail."[147] At the end of the day, Augustine is faced with coming to terms with the incipient dualism that marked theories of the soul's origins in his own time. How to do justice to the absolute incorporeality of God, the creation of the human soul in his image and its existence in body remains a point of ambivalence in his theology. The problem, simply put, is how to adopt aspects of Plato's, Plotinus's and Origen's insight respecting the incorporeality of the soul, which Augustine clearly wants to

---

[143] Augustine, *De civitate Dei* XIII.16-17.

[144] Ibid., XIII.16.

[145] Robert J. O'Connell, *The Origin of the Soul in St. Augustine's Later Works* (New York: Fordham University Press, 1987), pp. 216-17.

[146] Ibid.

[147] Ibid.

affirm, without falling into the dualist error.[148] At the end of the day Augustine cannot be said to have fallen into that error. However, he remains unclear and hesitant. It is only in respect to his answer to the question of the connection between image of God and the divine that his inclinations become clear, especially as they are worked out in terms of a doctrine of the *vestigium trinitatis*.[149]

In his *Soliloquies*, Augustine prayerfully seeks to understand himself as soul in relation to the divine. Since one obviously cannot begin such a divine and human self-understanding with the divine perspective, one must start with oneself. Self-understanding is, in the words of Rist, "the 'core' of Augustine's thought."[150] In this particular work, in the process of trying to understand soul apart from its embodiment, Augustine ends in a position quite apart from the view of the body-soul relationship put forward in the *De Genesi ad litteram*. In this subsequent attempt at the understanding of God from the rational aspect of the soul, Augustine affirms the likeness of the soul to God in its unity and multiplicity, that is, its oneness and threeness. This is a position that he says we not only find in the scriptural understanding of the image of God in Genesis and Romans but that is a natural aspect of our knowledge of God apart from Scripture and the essence of the principle of illumination, or "faith that seeks understanding."[151]

There are two overarching reasons why Augustine feels compelled to seek the knowledge of God and the soul in their connection. One reason is, as Rist suggests, Platonic.[152] Augustine was impressed with the Platonic "emphasis on the superiority of the soul over the body" and was himself convinced that something about this rang true, especially in its "emphasis on the God-likeness of the soul."[153] The other reason was theological; if embodiment of the soul was a negative development, according to Plato, why does the Christian faith "celebrate the corporeality of soul" as good in its essence?[154] Of these two motives one would think that the theological mo-

---

148Ibid., p. 219.
149Rist, *Augustine: Ancient Thought Baptized*, pp. 92-147.
150Ibid., p. 92.
151Ibid.
152Ibid.
153Ibid.
154Ibid.

tivation, informed as it was by a biblical view of *creatio ex nihilo*, would dominate, but this is not always the case, especially in Augustine's doctrine of the *imago Dei* as a vestige of the Trinity. One could also say the same about his doctrine of original sin wherein the concupiscence of the body is blamed as the location of innate, universal propensity to sin.[155]

> Above all, Augustine claimed to have learned from the Platonic books that God is immaterial, and when he considered man's creation in that image and likeness of God (Gen. 1:26), he naturally held that we are an image of what is immaterial. Hence, he maintained, as late as the time of the *De Trinitate* (completed after 420), where the most detailed treatment of the topic can be found, that what is an image of God must itself be immaterial.[156]

To be sure, Augustine sees this as a shared doctrine between the Platonists and Christianity. But this is the Platonic principle he uses to interpret Genesis 1:26 and not vice versa. The problem posed with the adoption of the Platonic principle of incorporeality is how the corporeal soul is to be seen as an image of the triune God.

The problem is expressed at length in Augustine's *De Trinitate* as follows:

> We shall have tarried long enough among those things that God has made, in order that by them He himself may be known that made them. "For the invisible things of Him from the creation of the world are clearly seen, being understood by the things that are made." . . . I have quoted these words . . . for this reason, that no one of the faithful may think me vainly and emptily to have sought first in the creature, step by step through certain trinities, each of their own appropriate kind, until I come at last to the mind of man, traces of that highest Trinity, which we seek when we seek God.[157]

Laying aside all concerns about the right ordering of the soul's relation to the body in Augustine's thought, though its grounding in Scripture is critical, one has to recognize immediately the classical roots of Augustine's identification of the highest in creation with the highest God, as mind. This is surely no accident. Neither is it completely a gift to Augustine from the Bible. It is, to say the least, a principle framed in synthesis between Scripture

---

[155] Augustine, *Contra Iulianum haeresis Pelagianae defensorem libri sex*, I.6.25 (PL vol. 44).
[156] Rist, *Augustine: Ancient Thought Baptized*, p. 94.
[157] Augustine, *De Trinitate* XV.2.

and the Platonic tradition, with the weight on the Platonic side being no small matter of "baptism." "From the time of his conversion, Augustine wished to maintain both that it is man's soul which is created in the image of God, and that man himself is some kind of composite of two substances, soul and body."[158]

Two of the most authoritative commentators, Rist and O'Connell, agree that in this aspect of Augustine's thought some sort of dualist account of humanity is essential to Augustine, though Augustine fails to answer precisely why.[159] For lack of a better explanation, we may posit that one of the primary reasons has to do with how we know and therefore how we express God. That is, it goes back to Augustine's epistemology. In Augustine, analogy, based as it was on a similarity between the triunity of human being as soul and the triunity of God, is the central means for expressing God from a creaturely point of view. Such a view entails no mere similarity or likeness, however, but rather is based on the classical understanding of the mind as an ontological and epistemological modality of the CER embedded in creation itself.

> For Augustine, then, soul and body are separate substances. Unlike soul, body requires a place and makes contact with other bodily objects, which also requires a place. Soul, though present in our bodies, need not be so, and can "live" among non-bodily objects. The forms and the truths available to the soul are in no way tied to their spatial instantiations; but neither, of course, are the soul's judgments necessarily in line with the impressed ideas, which it possesses. . . . It is the soul, not the body which "remembers," "understands" and "loves."[160]

In this respect we may agree with O'Connell when he suggests that the *De Trinitate* is as much an investigation into the origin, nature and construction of the human soul as it is an investigation into the doctrine of the Trinity.[161] Indeed Augustine's initial affirmation that the knowledge of God begins with an exploration of the self seems to support this.[162]

---

[158]Rist, *Augustine: Ancient Thought Baptized*, pp. 94-95.
[159]Ibid.; O'Connell, *Origin of the Soul*, pp. 246-47.
[160]Augustine, *De Trinitate* VIII.3, 4; XV.22.42.
[161]O'Connell, *Origin of the Soul*, pp. 247-48.
[162]Augustine, *De Trinitate* IX.4.1f.

Augustine begins his theory of the image of God in the *De Trinitate*, book VIII, with the same starting point as the *De Genesi ad litteram*, that is, that Genesis 1:26 refers to the image as located in the soul, making the human a substantially different entity than nonhuman creatures. "This rules out from the very start any notion that man, *qua* incarnate—the soul *qua* embodied in the 'animal' body of the *De Genesi ad litteram*—is to be regarded as the seat of God's image."[163] But where, in the soul itself, is this image contained? Is it to be sought in "sense perceptions" or "phantasms"? Is it the will, or action? No, it would appear that this must be discovered through an exercise of the mind. When one does this, one discovers that the image is a vestige of the Trinity in the mind, but only vaguely perceivable as such. In fact a complete metaphysics of the human must always be penultimate. It is a historical fact that Augustine changed his view of the soul, its relation to the body and its origin at several key junctures in his career, including his conversion to Christianity, where he begins to favor a literal interpretation of embodied soul, in his debate with Pelagius. In that debate he wants to distance himself from a strict interpretation of corporeal soul. Both O'Connell and Rist note that, at the end of the process, in the *De Trinitate* books XIII-XV, he denies the possibility of a complete metaphysics of the human because, like our knowledge of God, it can only be partial and incomplete. Conversely, we cannot deny, as Pierre Hadot does, that his understanding of image as triune image is a metaphysics of being of sorts.[164] Hadot had suggested that Augustine's understanding of a psychological image, as analogy of the Trinity, is less imbued with ontological features than either Plotinus or Victorinus, as some assert, because Neoplatonists saw this image as an image of the ontological structure of divine being itself.[165]

But the starting point in humanity is ontological nevertheless. It is merely "a different kind of ontological image or even a different way of expressing an ontological image."[166] As such we contain, within our soul, an image of the whole Trinity. "Augustine's minimal meaning is that our means are constituted by three activities, only formally distinct, which he prefers to

---

[163]Ibid.; O'Connell, *Origin of the Soul*, p. 248.
[164]Rist, *Augustine: Ancient Thought Baptized*, p. 145.
[165]Pierre Hadot, "L'image de la Trinite," *Studia Patristica* 6 (1962): 404-5.
[166]Rist, *Augustine: Ancient Thought Baptized*, p. 145.

identify as 'self-mentoring,' 'self-understanding' and 'self-willing.'"[167] These three distinctions he further reduces to mind, love and knowledge, which are imperfectly reflected in the soul but are perfect in God, as of one substance. "Similar reasoning suggests to us, if indeed we can anyway understand the matter, that these things (i.e. love and knowledge) exists in the soul [mind] and that, being as it were involved in it, they are so evolved from it as to be perceived and reckoned up substantially, or, so to say, essentially."[168] Within the human, at least imperfectly, these three are substantially united. "Wherefore love and knowledge are not contained in the mind as in a subject, but these also exist substantially, as the mind itself does; because even if they are mutually predicated relatively, yet they exist each severally in their own substance."[169] The difference between one's knowledge of oneself and God's self-knowledge is precisely the *limit* of the analogy. God knows himself perfectly, whereas we know our self imperfectly (though we can become more "Godlike" as we progress in self-knowledge).

In his *De Trinitate* XIV.11, Augustine affirms that we are still capable of achieving near-divine status despite the fall. We have an innate *capax Dei* in certain regions of the soul.[170] The principle of knowledge Augustine seems to arrive at is that the "substantial" difference between our self as "self-knowers" and God as self-knower is the imperfection of our self-knowledge and the perfection of God's. The structure of the analogy pertains to an ontological relation in mind as in some sense a shared essence, perfect in God but imperfect in humanity. If this is not an ontology based on analogy, it is very akin to it. "The root of our knowledge is neither knowledge of intelligibles, nor of sensible objects, but of ourselves (ultimately in God)—though of ourselves *qua* intentional agents."[171] It is clear that Augustine sees the soul as more akin to the spiritual nature of the divine and therefore as, substantially and really, like, or similar to, the three persons of the Trinity.[172] In this effort to find in the soul an image of the Trinity, Augustine emphasizes "the consubstantiality of the mental acts," "ruling out" any distinction between

---

[167]Ibid., p. 147.
[168]Augustine, *De Trinitate* IX.4, 6.
[169]Ibid.
[170]On *capax Dei*, see Augustine, *De Trinitate* XIV.8–11.
[171]Rist, *Augustine: Ancient Thought Baptized*, p. 146.
[172]Augustine, *De Trinitate* IX.2.2–5.8; X.11.17–12.19; XIV.8.11–12.

the soul and its faculties, "except insofar as there is a 'function in relation' between them."[173] Mind, love and knowledge were equal to the single sub-stance of the soul. It was its essence. However, the soul does not recognize itself as an image of the Trinity until, in self-contemplation, it "remembers God as Trinity." To know our self substantially as self-loving is to know God as, in himself, self-loving and as expressed as self-loving in his participation with creation through his Word of Wisdom. "This Wisdom is an actualized participation of God in and with the Word of God, and vice versa, that rep-resents the Father's self knowledge and self love."[174]

Furthermore, the soul cannot be an exact image because we lack any el-ement within the soul that resembles the simplicity and absolute oneness of the divine essence.[175] There is therefore the possibility of the knowledge of God as Trinity within the human soul, but we could not, on the basis of that analogy, know him as absolutely simple. When Augustine speaks of God as "absolutely one" and of a "simple substance," he means that God is "one essential being." To support this view of God he cites Exodus 3:14 as biblical justification. But by "I Am Who I Am," he understands God's being as one essence in three persons, not in the strictly monotheistic terms often attributed to this passage in the Hebrew understanding. The three are intrinsic as relations to the one substance or being of God.[176] Essence, in Augustine's parlance, means being-ness, be-ing. "Doubtless, He [God] is substance, if this is a better word, essence (*essentia*) or what the Greeks call οὐσία. For as wisdom (*sapentia*) is from what it is to be wise, and as knowledge is what it is to know, so *essence* derives from what it is to be (*esse*)."[177] As such, God alone is "truly *esse*," for he alone is im-mutable and eternal. God does not exist as we do. He is "being itself" (*ipsum esse*), but we exist between being and nonbeing. So, unlike Plotinus (as it re-lates to his understanding of the One but not mind), the good, or the One, is not beyond being, but the very essence of being.[178] The attribute of immuta-bility, rather than becoming the definition of God in his essence, singles out the absolute simplicity of his essence. "Because God is, and supremely is, He

---

[173]Ibid., IX.4.7; X.11.18.
[174]Ibid.
[175]Augustine, *De Trinitate* XV.5.7, 7.11, 9.16.
[176]Ibid., V.2.3; VII.4.7.
[177]Clark, *Augustine*, p. 40.
[178]Augustine, *De civitate Dei* XII.2.

is immutable."[179] Other words and compound phrases are added to emphasize the absolute simplicity of the divine essence, such as "truly being," "properly being" and/or "primarily being." These phrases try to attest to the fact that in God the divine ideas are immutable, from all eternity, and are the meaning of what it is for God to self-subsist.[180]

Clearly this interpretation of Exodus 3:14 is considerably indebted to a Platonic understanding of *esse* and anticipates in no small measure the definition of God as *ipsum esse subsistens* in Aquinas's *ST*. Herein it serves as the basis for Augustine's reasoning that our creation in the image of God is to be analogically understood in terms of the triune Being. "There is in Augustine's thought-world the basis for reasoning analogically from finite existent to the supreme existent ('I am who I am'), from good things to the Supreme Good (doctrine of creation), and from beautiful realities to that 'Beauty— ever ancient ever new.'" Yet, "he himself reasoned from the experience of intellectual knowledge to the existence of transcendent truth, perfect Being and creative soul, through love of all beings."[181] This all traded on the assumption and conviction that God is everywhere present as the pattern within creation. Reading back from the effect, we may distinguish the cause. Not only does theological knowledge need this, but theological speech is impossible without such an analogy.

In sum, Augustine's whole theological development, including his "conversion" from Manichaeism, to Neoplatonism, then to Christianity, and the subsequent development of his theology, his mode of epistemological discourse, has to assume the Platonic understanding of CER as basic. We see this in his discovery of the "Platonic books," his adaptation of Platonic cosmology and anthropology to the Christian doctrine of *creatio ex nihilo*, and his ambivalence toward a doctrine of the soul from his early to later theology. The last half of the *De Trinitate* is a testimony to his need for analogy as CER, to make sense of it all in linguistic terms. His anticipation of the modality of analogy, which we can now briefly sketch, would be eventually built into a standard mode of discourse in subsequent Latin theology, especially in the works of Peter the Lombard and Bonaventure.

---

[179] Ibid., XII.25.
[180] Augustine, *De Trinitate* VII.4.9; *De doctrina christiana* XII.2.
[181] Augustine, *De Trinitate* VII.4.9; Clark, *Augustine*, p. 41.

Augustine's anticipation of analogy. Herein lies the crux of the matter as
far as analogical speech in Augustine is concerned. The knowledge of God
is always indirect, mere likeness (*similarity*) even though mediated by a
perfect *likeness* (image), namely the divine Wisdom, the Word, yet mitigated
and controlled by *dissimilarity*. This is the question that has dogged discourse about divinity from the beginning. In understanding God from his
creation, by analogy, how far can we know God's essential being? Can creation really teach us both to know and speak about God, analogically? Are
its limitations its own self-negation as knowledge? Is this knowing, speaking
and thinking perpetually an unknowing, unspeaking, unthinking, in short
a denial, even here in Augustine? Deidre Carabine thinks that precisely here,
in Augustine's use of analogy, the seeds of a negative theology can be clearly
seen.[182] To be sure, Augustine affirms with Paul in Romans 1:18-20 that a
knowledge of God can be ascertained by the natural (unenlightened) mind
from the observation of creation. However, Augustine reduces creation here
to an internal principle of mind.[183] "By making use also of that which God
has made, insofar as we could, we have warned those, who demand reason
concerning such things, that they should behold the invisible things of Him
through those that were made (Rom. 1:20), especially through that rational
or intellectual creature which was made in the image of God."[184] Then again,
at the end of the same passage in the *De Trinitate*, Augustine cautions, "But
lest anyone should so compare this image . . . as to think it similar to this
same Trinity in every respect, I have warned him . . . that he should rather
behold this likeness, of whatever sort it may be, the great unlikeness that
there also is."[185] Again, Augustine's Platonic hesitation of mind makes it difficult to know whether it is what the image says positively, or what it fails to
say, that constitutes the knowledge of God as Trinity. There is a sense in
which already *Deus absconditus* is more an aspect of the knowledge of God
as "knowledge" (as opposed to "unknowing") in Augustine.

Given the preponderance of available *vestigia* in creation and the rational
soul, one would assume this knowledge of God is essentially positive. But

---

[182]Carabine, *Unknown God*, pp. 272-73.
[183]See especially Augustine, *In Evangelium Ioannis tractatus* 23.10 (PL vol. 35); *De Trinitate* XV.39.
[184]Augustine, *De Trinitate* XV.39.
[185]Ibid.; see also Augustine, *De vera religione* XXIX.52.

here, Augustine falls silent. He does not distinguish between positive and negative knowledge of God. The paradigm can therefore be read as either inviting *kataphatic* release or instituting *apophatic* reserve. It would appear that silence on this is a preference for the apophatic. Augustine shares one important principle with classical and Christian writers of his time, namely, that God was "ineffable." That is, God, by his very nature as God, is "past finding out," in the sense that only God knows God, absolutely as God. Indeed this is what distinguishes him from his creation.[186] God cannot be expressed in language any more than he can be comprehended in and/or by our mind. Our own lack of self-knowledge is an indirect, apophatic indication of the perfect self-knowing of God. God surpasses all knowing, thinking and speaking so that we must hold to a *doctrina ignorantia* in respect to our knowledge of God.[187] Augustine's interest here is that the analogy permits correct rather than incorrect speech about God. But he sees the knowledge of God as *Deus absconditus* to be the essence of what it is to know God.[188] Again Carabine's conclusion would seem to fit. "While it is true that Augustine does not develop an explicit and systematic method of affirmation and negation, as Pseudo Dionysius will do, that does not mean that the principles of negative theology can be simply relegated to the background of his thought."[189] Indeed where theological language is concerned it seems very much front and center. In this respect he is very close to Plotinus. Nevertheless, "it remains true that Augustine was first and last a man who accepted, lived and preached the reality of the Christian message, and for him, that message was expressed in the dialectical truth of revelation itself: God is most hidden and yet most revealed."[190]

Summary. Given what we have observed so far, it would appear that Lyttkens's conclusions on Augustine's contributions to analogical method are considerably overstated. Lyttkens writes,

> Even if Augustine actually teaches that there is a likeness of creation to God, he nevertheless does not use analogy as a logical aid in explaining that our

---

[186]See Augustine, *Enarrationes in Psalmos* 85, 12; *Epistula* 130, 14.27.

[187]See Augustine, *Epistula* 130, 15.28.

[188]Augustine, *Epistula* 120, 3.13; *De Trinitate* VIII.2.3; see Lyttkens, *Analogy Between God and the World*, p. 115.

[189]Augustine, *De Trinitate* VIII.2.3; Carabine, *Unknown God*, p. 276.

[190]Carabine, *Unknown God*, p. 277.

names of God, though inadequate are nevertheless justified. He is cognizant of analogy in the form of proportionality. He has also studied and is acquainted with Aristotle's theory of the categories, but makes no use of analogy as a category. Nor does he use analogy as an aid in teaching a direct likeness between the Trinities of God and the Soul.[191]

It is true that neither his doctrine of the soul nor his doctrines of *creatio ex nihilo*, the *imago Dei*, illumination or *vestigium trinitatis* yield a method as such. But the development of these doctrines in Augustine raises considerable difficulties for speech about God, which later doctrines of analogy were supposed to effectively address but never fully succeeded. Anselm and Boethius are classic examples of the attempt to address this problem, both of whom inherit the modality of doing so directly from Augustine.

By way of summary, what can we affirm about the problem of analogy and its entry into Christian theological modes of discourse thus far? We have been able to establish that the classical concept of analogy arose as a modality of speech about the divine because of its basis in a cosmological conception of CER. Having traced its development in classical thought, we have shown that this basic cosmology entered into a Christian theological discourse in a determinative way in Augustine, especially through his epistemology, cosmology, anthropology and, preeminently, in his doctrine of the creation, summarized in the human soul as an *imago Dei* that is as a *vestigium trinitatis*. It has also become clear that the Augustinian solution to the problem of the ineffability of God, as an object of our love, remained a problem for theology in subsequent tradition. It should be clear by now that the possibility of speech about God was wholly framed, determined and answered with the considerable aid of Platonic/Aristotelian/Neoplatonic thought. As we shall see in the next chapter, it was precisely this classical framing of the problem that led Aquinas to analogy as a middle way. The degree to which analogy solves this problem, and thus transcends the Platonic problem altogether, is precisely the point about which no clarity in Aquinas can be had. It will be sufficient for us to demonstrate merely this point in order to show how Aquinas is sometimes read in the Catholic tradition along univocal lines wherein God's being and ours are species of the

---

[191]Lyttkens, *Analogy Between God and the World*, p. 121.

same genus. To be sure, this is a perversion of what Aquinas must have intended by resorting to analogy. In fact he did so to avoid it. But it is a fact that it does happen, and Aquinas's works inadvertently give aid and comfort to this interpretation in a number of places. What the problem ultimately witnesses to is the necessarily Neoplatonic point of CER from which Aquinas is forced to start, and this determines much in Aquinas's doctrine of analogy, to which we must now turn.

2

THOMAS AQUINAS AND THE MEDIEVAL APPROPRIATION OF ANALOGY

◆

No treatment of analogy, medieval or modern, Protestant, Orthodox or Catholic, can bypass the significance of Aquinas's understanding and formulation of the concept contained in various places of the *Corpus Thomisticum*. This current study would not only be remiss to leave it out of the account, but it would also be considerably hampered in its attempt to positively put forth an understanding of the *analogia fidei* as an alternative to the *analogia entis* and indeed to distinguish them as qualitatively different modes of signification. It would be equally problematic to avoid taking into account the development of the theme in the works on analogy subsequent to Aquinas, especially in the seminal treatment by Thomas de Vio, Cardinal Cajetan, and his formal definition of the Thomistic doctrine of analogy in *The Analogy of Names* (*De Nominum Analogia*). So much of the discussion in our time depends on how we view these developments, especially in their respective metaphysical contexts. In order to establish the claim that the *analogia entis* is considerably enmeshed in a metaphysics of being that may hamper or disqualify it as a mode of theological signification, the case must be made against current interpretations of the history of Thomistic thought about analogy that try to exonerate Aquinas's view by casting a negative light on Cajetan's view. There is too much at stake in the argument to avoid this complex set of concerns at this point.

Therefore in this chapter we will focus mainly on Aquinas but also draw attention to these post-Thomistic developments in terms of expositing the actual state of affairs that existed once a firm Thomistic conception appears in its authoritative form. This does not necessarily happen with Aquinas himself, but it does so in later Thomistic development.

We will will take a position in the history of the debate about analogy that will focus on how analogy in the later Middle Ages was variously understood. We will not make assumptions about how it "ought to have been understood" had it been true to the "Catholic doctrine of the *analogia entis*," as some have argued today.[1] We will have to establish that such a static and normative interpretation of the *analogia entis* cannot be fully identified as essentially the same as Aquinas's view. In fact, the concept of the *analogia entis* was, more often than not, either undefined, or defined as a metaphysics on the basis of which a theological-philosophical epistemology was attempted and largely established. This was a basis for theology that ultimately gave philosophy, rather than revelation, the pivotal role in theological epistemology. In the minds of some Protestants, it obviated theology as such. In that era such a mode for theology required a reversal of the order of relation, at least, if not the outright denial of the role of philosophical reason by some, especially Luther. Our main goal in this chapter is to demonstrate how Aquinas contributed a confused method of analogy that left the Catholic tradition open to multiple interpretations of the Thomistic principle, both in terms of philosophical and theological interpretations.[2] The net result was that the church

---

[1] See especially Erich Przywara, *Analogia entis* (München: Johannes Verlag, 1932, 1962); *Schriften I, Fruhe religose; Schriften II, Religionsphilosophische; Schriften III, Analogia entis, Metaphysik: Ur-St'ruktur und All-Rhythmus* (Einsiedeln: Johannes Verlag, 1962). For Hans Urs von Balthasar on analogy, see "Analogie und Dialektik: Zur Klärung der theologischen Prinzipienlehre Karl Barths," *Divus Thomas* 22 (1944): 171-216; "Analogie und Natur: Zur Klärung der theologischen Prinzipienlehre Karl Barths," *Theologisch Zeitschrift* 23 (1945): 3-56; *Convergences: To the Sources of Christian Mystery,* trans. E. A. Nelson (San Francisco: Ignatius, 1983); "Creation and Trinity," *Communio* 15 (1988): 285-93; *Explorations in Theology,* 5 vols. (San Francisco: Ignatius, 1988–1991); *The Word Made Flesh,* trans. A. V. Littledale and A. Dru, 2 vols. (New York: Ignatius, 1964-1965); *Glory of the Lord: A Theological Aesthetics [Herrlichkeit: Eine theologische Asthetik I-III],* ed. and trans. J. Fessio and J. Riches, 7 vols. (San Francisco: Ignatius, 1982-1991; vol. 1, *Seeing the Form [Herrlichkeit I: Schau der Gestalt],* 1961, 1967, trans. E. Leiva-Merikakis, 1982, 1989; vol. 2, *Studies in Theological Style: Clerical Styles [Herrlichkeit II; Fdcher der Stile],* 1962, 1969; trans. A. Louth et al., 1984); *Theo-drama: Theological Dramatic Theory [Theodramatik I—IV],* 5 vols. (San Francisco: Ignatius, 1988); *Theologik,* 3 vols. (Einsiedeln: Johannes Verlag, 1985-1987); *The Theology of Karl Barth [Karl Barth Darstellung und Deutung seiner Theologie],* trans. E. T. Oakes (San Francisco: Ignatius, 1962).

[2] See especially *ST* II, qq. 109-14, "Treatise on Grace"; M. J. Scheeben, *Nature and Grace,* trans. C. Vollert (London: Herder, 1954), pp. 5-6.

often opted for a philosophical ontology and/or epistemology that left revelation and Christian theology open to synergistic tendencies.

This tendency can be attributed to many factors but few are as important,
or little recognized, as the influence of a Proclan/Pseudo-Dionysian, Neoplatonic ontology (or better, henology) mediated through the structure of
the first part of Aquinas's *ST*.[3] The conceptions of analogy that emerge in
Aquinas can be shown as deeply influenced by this Neoplatonic cosmology.
To establish Aquinas's mature attitude toward analogy we will employ primarily, but not exclusively, the two great *Summae* of Aquinas, the *SCG* and
the *ST*. Recent scholarship on Aquinas, especially as it relates to the
structure of his *Prima Pars* and his employment of the concepts of causality,
divine idea and participation, make this position plausible.[4] As such, these

---

[3]The primary Latin texts of Thomas Aquinas employed in this work are provided by the Fun-
dación Tomás de Aquino, 2001–2013, www.corpusthomisticum.org. We will also have recourse
to the Leonine edition of the *Corpus Thomisticum, Editio aureo numismate donata Summo Pontiiice
Leone XIII* (Romae: Ex Typographia Forzani Et S., 1979). The primary English translations of
Aquinas's two *Summas* employed here are: *The Summa Contra Gentiles*, Dominican Fathers Edition of the Leonine Text (London: Burns and Oates, 1924); and *The Summa Theologica*, Dominican Fathers Edition of the Leonine Text (London: Burns and Oates, 1924). Various other
English translations will be noted where and when employed. We will note the use of any other
Latin editions as needed.

[4]On the Platonic and Neoplatonic influences on Aquinas, see the following, though the literature
is much broader than can be represented here: Thomas Aquinas, *Commentary on the Book of
Causes* [*Super Librum de causis expositio*], trans. Vincent A. Guagliardo, Charles R. Hess and
Richard C. Taylor, Thomas Aquinas in Translation 1 (Washington, D.C.: Catholic University of
America Press, 1996); Louis Bertrand Geiger, "La Participation dans la philosophie de S.
Thomas d'Aquin," 2nd ed., in *Bibliothèque thomiste* 23 (Paris: Vrin, 1995); Wayne John Hankey,
God in Himself: Aquinas' Doctrine of God as Expounded in the Summa Theologiae, Oxford Theo-
logical Monographs/Oxford Scholarly Classics (Oxford: Oxford University Press, 1987); Robert
John Henle, *Saint Thomas and Platonism: A Study of the Plato and Platonici Texts in the Writings
of Saint Thomas* (The Hague: Martinus Nijhoff, 1956); Mark D. Jordan, *The Alleged Aristotelian-
ism of Thomas Aquinas*, Étienne Gilson Series 15 (Toronto: Pontifical Institute of Mediaeval
Studies, 1992); Jean-Marc Narbonne, *Hénologie, ontologie et Ereignis (Plotin-Proclus-Heidegger)*
(Paris: Les Belles Lettres, 2001); Rudi A. te Velde, *Participation and Substantiality in Thomas
Aquinas*, Studien und Texte zur Geistesgeschichte des Mittelalters xlvi (Leiden: Brill, 2009). See
also te Velde's *Aquinas on God* (London: Ashgate, 2008). On the Aristotelian influences on
Aquinas, the following works were consulted (again, the list is far from exhaustive): Georges C.
Anawati, O.P., "Saint Thomas d'Aquin et la Mitaphysique d'Avicenne," in É. Gilson, ed., *St
Thomas Aquinas, 1274-1974*, 2 vols., Commemorative Studies (Toronto: Pontifical Institute for
Mediaeval Studies Press, 1974), 2:449-66; Brady Ignatius, O.F.M., "John Pecham and the Back-
ground of Aquinas's De Aeternitate Mundi," in Gilson, ed., *St Thomas Aquinas*, 2:141-79; M. D.
Chenu, O.P., "Creation et Histoire," in Gilson, ed., *St Thomas Aquinas*, 2:391-401; É. Gilson, *The
Christian Philosophy of St. Thomas Aquinas* (New York: Random House, 1956); P. Osmund
Lewry, O.P., "Two Continuators of Aquinas: Robertus de Vulgarbia and Thomas Sutton on the
'Peri hermeneias' of Aristotle," *Mediaeval Studies* 43 (1981): 58-130; Lakebrink Bernhard,

crucial elements in his thought also make it very reasonable to see him as extending Augustine's epistemology and natural theology along Neoplatonist lines, though not without a strong Aristotelian bent. As already stated, this is important in that at the very least he contributed indirectly to an ontological approach to theology that Protestant theology had to reject because it appears to place God and humanity within one genus of nature. In fact, Aquinas is more to be implicated than is often admitted by his Catholic interpreters, who want to see him purely as a biblical theologian.[5] If it can be demonstrated, as we will do here, that Aquinas cannot be pinned down on analogy in any final way, then at the very least he is open to the kinds of ontological-epistemological misinterpretations that did take place and indeed were sanctioned for long periods of time as the accepted Thomistic doctrine of analogy, understood as *analogia nominum* but later as *analogia entis*.

This close analysis of analogy in the *Summae* of Aquinas (with some reference to other works as well) will lead us naturally in the second section of this chapter to our discussion of developments after Aquinas wherein the *analogia entis* takes shape as a concept with a metaphysical ontology in view, namely, in contradistinction to the univocal position of Duns Scotus, and in line with Cajetan's interpretation of Aquinas's theory of analogy in *The Analogy of Names*.[6] We will confirm our findings with respect to the meta-

"Analektik und Dialektik: Zur Methode des Thomistischen und Hegelschen Denkens," in Gilson, ed., *St Thomas Aquinas*, 2:459-88; A. Llano Cifuentes, "The Different Meanings of 'Being' According to Aristotle and Aquinas," *Acta Philosophica* 10 (2001): 29-44; J. Chua Soo Meng, "Reginald Garrigou-Lagrange OP on Aristotle, Thomas Aquinas, and the Doctrine of Limitation of Act by Potency," *The Modern Schoolman* 78, no. 1 (2000): 71-87; J. Talanga, "On the Immortality of the Mind in Aristotle and Thomas Aquinas," *Filozofska Istraživanja* 13, no. 1 (1992): 31-43.

[5]For a recent example of this reluctance, see Thomas Joseph White, O.P., "How Barth Got Aquinas Wrong: A Reply to Archie J. Spencer on Causality and Christocentrism," *NV* 7, no. 1 (2009): 241-70, and his essay, "'Through Him All Things Were Made' (John 1:3): The Analogy of the Word Incarnate According to St. Thomas Aquinas and Its Ontological Presuppositions," in Thomas Joseph White, O.P., *The Analogy of Being: Invention of the Antichrist or the Wisdom of God?* (Grand Rapids: Eerdmans, 2011), pp. 246-79. See also my "Causality and the *Analogia entis*: Karl Barth's Rejection of Analogy of Being Reconsidered," *NV* 6, no. 2 (2008): 329-76.

[6]The key point of discussion has been, and likely will remain, Cardinal Cajetan's monumental influence on Aquinas interpretation especially as it relates to his *De Nominum Analogia*, ed. P. N. Zammit and P. H. Hering (Rome: Angelicum, 1951). For the best English translation see Edward A. Bushinski's edition, with introduction, Cardinal Cajetan, *The Analogy of Names and The Concept of Being* (Pittsburgh, PA: Duquesne University Press, 1953).

physical nature of the *analogia entis* by means of a brief analysis of the problems that present themselves with respect to this approach, especially in reference to univocity.

AQUINAS'S CONCEPTION OF ANALOGY IN HIS MAJOR WORKS

The question of naming God intelligibly in the **Summa Theologiae, Prima Pars.** Aquinas, like one of his predecessors and oft-quoted authorities, Pseudo-Dionysius, begins his system of theology by questioning the adequacy of his received authority, in this case *The Sentences* of Peter the Lombard, though he does not mention them directly. Aquinas argues that a whole new approach to *doctrinam sacram* is in order so as to provide what is really needful but presumably missing from previous efforts, and to avoid "useless questions, articles and arguments" that arise because the study follows a predetermined order rather than "the order of the subject matter itself."[7] In short, what the discipline of theology itself demands is an ordering of the subjects in a way that is completely different from that of Peter Lombard.[8] Peter Lombard begins with the received Augustinian description of the soul's quest for the beautiful, the truthful and the good. The *ST* begins by announcing the subject matter of the sacred science as *De Deo*, a starting point Aquinas receives from his opening authoritative sources, Aristotle and Pseudo-Dionysius.[9]

In the first forty-five questions of the *Prima Pars*, Aquinas moves, in a comparably Neoplatonic fashion, from the Aristotelian conception of the unity of separate substances, through to the conceptual divisions of the operations and on to the real relations in opposition, back to the unity of separate substances.[10] Though Aquinas uses Aristotle's description of theology as *Metaphysics*, or first science, this now allows him to "imitate Proclus and

---

[7] *Secundum ordinem disciplinae* (*ST* I, q. 1, art. 6-7).

[8] Peter the Lombard's approach in *The Sentences* does not question his received authority at all (Peter the Lombard, *The Sentences, Book I: The Mystery of the Trinity*, trans. Giulio Silano [Toronto: Pontifical Institute of Mediaeval Studies, 2007], pp. 5-6).

[9] Hankey, *God in Himself*, p. 23.

[10] Here Aquinas follows Proclus's *Elements of Theology*. Compare, for instance, Aquinas's ordering of the treatment of the *esse*, *De Deo*, with Proclus's treatment of the "One" in his first three propositions of his *Elements of Theology* (*ST* I, qq. 2-26, *De Deo*; *Elements of Theology*, A. Pro 1-3). This pattern of dealing with the science of theology is also observable, according to Aquinas, in the *Celestial Hierarchy* of Pseudo-Dionysius, as per *ST* I, q. 75, pr.

embrace the whole of causal reality within theology's exitus-reditus framework."[11] How so? "Whereas, by Thomas's account, only the material belonging to *res* [in the *res signa*] in Lombard's scheme could be given such a structure, in his own *Summa* the whole course of theology falls within it."[12] As Aquinas affirms, "But in sacred doctrine all things are treated under the aspect of God, either because they are God Himself, or because they refer to God as their beginning and end. . . . The subject matter of the principles and of the whole science is contained virtually in the principles."[13] Here Aristotle and a Neoplatonic form of logic are brought together as a formal basis for a science, in this case theology. As Wayne Hankey suggests, "The Aristotelian and Proclan theologies seem to fit neatly together so as to constitute Thomas' unification of theology as science of the first principles and as *Summa* or systematic treatment of reality as a whole. Each contributed what the other lacked. Aristotle had not shown how what is other than the first emerged from it and is related to it."[14] Both Aristotle and Proclus, one from the point of view of God as the highest thought of a philosophical science, the other from the point of view of God as the absolute source, end their respective "theology" with the unknowability of God in his essence.[15]

What is the significance of this starting point and methodological shift in the *ST*? Simply put, it demands a reading of the *ST* that accounts for all sources on both sides of these theological methods.[16] It will not do to elevate one over the other as authoritative. "These considerations must make impossible the view that Thomas' thinking becomes less Dionysian after the *Commentary on the Sentences*.[17] Only after this commentary can the full implications for a theology of a gradual *exitus* and a complete *reditus* of reality, from and to God, be developed in form and content."[18] Ultimately, says Hankey, "The whole argument [of the *ST*] is assimilated to the logic of *exitus et reditus* and it is to the traditions which transmit this logic to Thomas

---

[11]Hankey, *God in Himself*, p. 26; see also endnote 1, p. 162.
[12]Ibid., p. 27.
[13]*ST* I, q. 1, art. 7, res.
[14]Hankey, *God in Himself*, p. 27.
[15]Ibid., p. 28.
[16]Ibid.
[17]Ibid., p. 29 n. 42.
[18]Ibid.

that we must be alert."[19] Hankey goes on to apply this understanding of Aquinas to the whole of the *Prima Pars*, with some very significant conclusions as a result. But for our concerns here, vis-à-vis analogy, what he discovers regarding the function of the arguments for the existence of God and the possibility of naming God, in questions 12 and 13, is critical to a revised understanding of Aquinas's appeal to analogy. At any rate Hankey's reading of Aquinas should give us cause for great caution in appointing a "Catholic doctrine of the *analogia entis*" and its serviceability toward a new "metaphysical theology."

There are many aspects of Aquinas's thought that are affected by this revised understanding of his procedure in the *ST, Prima Pars*. Of particular interest to this study are the questions concerning the naming of God and his attributes. For instance, in the opening movements of Aquinas's *ST*, we certainly may affirm that the mediation of revelation in creation, vis-à-vis language, envisions such language as essential to creation itself. As creation yields knowledge of God via CER, language can only carry this relation analogically. Analogy, on this account, cannot be just a principle of logic, as such. It is ingredient in the way of the relation between God and the world.[20] This attitude is confirmed in Aquinas in his understanding of naming and the intelligibility of language as knowledge, either as positive predication or negative attribution.

Surprisingly, as we saw with Augustine, the accent in the *Prima Pars* seems to be more weighted on the side of *via negationis*. Question three of *ST* begins with negations that leave only one possible positive predicate under the conditions of the merely self-evident revelation of *De Deo*, that of oneness, or simplicity. Here we are in the realm of God's singular, exclusive, divine substance. In the consideration of his operations, subsequent to this question, certain positive predicates will obtain, but always with the understanding that they are considered under this unity; "since God is absolute form, or rather absolute being, He can in no way be composite."[21] Obviously the substantial simplicity of God is the ground of

---

[19]Ibid.

[20]See Étienne Gilson, *The Christian Philosophy of St Thomas Aquinas*, trans. L. K. Shook (New York: Random House, 1956), p. 358.

[21]*ST* I, q. 3, art. 7, res. See *ST*, Dominican Fathers ed., p. 40.

all assertions regarding his operations. Interestingly, this accords well with the Proclan-Dionysian logic with which Aquinas begins. Compare, for example, the above statement from the *ST* with Proclus when he states the following in his *Elements of Theology*, proposition 8: "All that in any way participates in the Good is subordinate to the primal Good which is nothing else but Good."[22] While everything that has existence can be said to participate the Good, its goodness is derivative and imperfect. The One, however, is goodness itself. We can say of particular things that they are good, by participation and abstraction, but not that they are "the Good," as with the self-identical "One."

Pseudo-Dionysius repeats this understanding of "the Good" in his *De divinis nominibus* as follows:

> How else are we to understand the sacred Word of God when it declares that the Deity, speaking of itself, had this to say: "Why do you ask me about what is Good? No one is Good but God above." . . . I have discussed all this elsewhere and I have shown how in scripture all the names appropriate to God are praised regarding the whole, entire, full and complete divinity rather than any part of it, and that they all refer indivisibly, absolutely, unreservedly, and totally to God in His entirety. Indeed, as I pointed out in my *Theological Representations* anyone denying that such terminology refers to God in all that He is may be said to have blasphemed. He is profanely daring to sunder absolute unity.[23]

Earlier in book one, section three, of the *Divine Names* he again invokes Proclus's *Elements* directly as having taught him about divine simplicity and the unity of divine causation, which is the basis of the passage just cited.[24] The expression he uses there is directly out of Proclus, "A *henad* unifying every *henead*."[25] Such citations between Aquinas's *ST, Prima Pars*, Proclus and Pseudo-Dionysius can be illustrated in many other places. Here we are merely noting that the modality of naming God according to his operations must follow the same logic that determines his understanding of the substantial and absolute simplicity of God. Pseudo-Dionysius follows a Proclan

---

[22]Proclus, *Elements of Theology*, trans. Dodd, p. 9.

[23]Pseudo-Dionysius, *The Complete Works*, ed. and trans. P. Rorem and C. Luibheid, Classics of Western Spirituality (New York: Paulist, 1987), pp. 58-59.

[24]Ibid., p. 50; Pseudo-Dionysius, *Divine Names* I.1.

[25]Ibid.; compare propositions 1-6 of *Elements of Theology* with *Divine Names*, TLG I, 588b.

logic, "which separates the simple from the complex and so substance from activities."[26] He does so for the same reasons, namely, to "make it intelligible why, in treating God, unity should be divided from the distinct persons and substance from the operations."[27]

Thus it was Pseudo-Dionysius who transmitted this logic to Aquinas. Throughout his *Divine Names*, Pseudo-Dionysius always draws the names of God back into the unity from which they proceed. In fact the *Divine Names* ends with the concept of simplicity, or oneness, as the quintessential descriptor of God, other than remaining silent. "But the transcendent unity defines the one itself and every number. For it is the source, and the cause, the number and the order of the one, of number, and of all being."[28] Precisely here is where we must root our understanding of Aristotle's place in Aquinas's *ST*. Again we cite Hankey's analysis:

> Understanding Thomas' own peculiar synthesis of the diverse theological logics which he inherited has enabled us to recognize why the nine questions which first name God were preceded by a proof for God's existence. Furthermore, we have some hold on why the proof starts with the moving sensibles. Discovering how Thomas' ordering of the five ways differs from the sequence of the four causes in Aristotle's various listings points us to the notion of motionless motion. This idea suggests a means of unity, being and essence and also of unifying knowledge and the knowledge of God. If motionless motion describes the logic of a circle by which God's name, "simple," is joined to his name, "one," after he is extended into infinity and seen to exist in all things . . . then we may well have found what unites God's being and his activities, and what enables affirmative predication of Him.[29]

But this is clearly the result of a combination of the Platonic system of knowledge, through mind, and the Aristotelian theory of sensory perception, which was the common heritage of Aquinas's immediate context.[30] A number of conclusions flow from this analysis that have important con-

---

[26]Proclus, *Elements of Theology*, p. 9.
[27]Ibid.
[28]Pseudo-Dionysius, *Divine Names* XIII.3, 980D, p. 129.
[29]Hankey, *God in Himself*, p. 58.
[30]This position completely contradicts Gilson's, put forth in his *Christian Philosophy of St Thomas*, pp. 362-63.

sequences for our current understanding of analogy and for Aquinas's understanding of it.

The *first* consequence is that Aquinas appears to be assimilating two forms of the knowledge of God, negative and positive, within two systems of knowledge, Platonic and Neoplatonic-Aristotelian, in order to provide for the possibility of positive knowledge of God expressible in language.[31] This fact has been confirmed, not only through Hankey's analysis of the *Prima Pars* but also by such scholars as M. D. Chenu and S. Gersh. In Pseudo-Dionysius the three ways of knowing God, in their order, are the *via negativa, via eminentia* and *via causalitatis*. In Aquinas these are affirmed but reversed, beginning with the way of causality (arguments for the existence of God), then negation (the simplicity of God) and emanation (the operations or works). "So Aristotle is restricted to conform to Dionysius and Dionysius is reordered to admit Aristotle."[32]

Second, the principle that mitigates the "positivity" of such a knowledge of God is the existence of God as the perfection of all predicates in unity, or, stated differently, his "absolute simplicity." In light of this principle the knowledge of God will only ever be "imperfect." That is to say, the principle that expresses the nature of the knowledge of God we can possess or express within the context of the sensible is only his "ineffability." In Aquinas, the "ineffability" or "incomprehensibility" of God constitutes the essence of his self-revelation as *De Deo*. "There is not in Thomas a complete and direct contradiction between the doctrine of God's being, on the one hand, and his teaching about the knowledge of it, and predications about God, on the other hand, but neither can there be a total consistency."[33]

But, *third*, the point is that ambiguity abounds in Aquinas's theology precisely because our predication cannot satisfy the full weight of divine

---

[31]For a full treatment of this approach to the knowledge of God in Aquinas, see the very important study by Gregory P. Rocca, *Speaking the Incomprehensible God: Thomas Aquinas on the Interplay of Positive and Negative Theology* (Washington, D.C.: Catholic University of America Press, 2004). In the long run, despite the claim of Rocca and others that there is balance in these epistemological polarities, the principle of the incomprehensibility of God, expressed as *De Deo*, or "God in Himself," stands as the principle that conditions positive knowledge on the side of the negative in Thomas.

[32]Hankey, *God in Himself*, p. 72.

[33]Ibid., p. 94.

being. This is where analogy not only does a service, but very often also a disservice in theology.[34] Such a disservice has sometimes accompanied the history of the interpretation of Aquinas. In his final chapter on the philosophical and theological implications of this understanding of Aquinas's indebtedness to Proclan Neoplatonism, Hankey summarizes the situation with respect to analogy in Aquinas. It is a conclusion with which our discussion of Aquinas's understanding of analogy must begin, because it represents well the ambivalence that sits at the heart of Aquinas's theological enterprise where predication about the divine is concerned. Hankey writes:

> Thomism misunderstood Thomas partly because it did not appreciate the difference between the existentialism it assumed and the Neoplatonized Aristotle Thomas found philosophically authoritative. . . . History provides the evidence for that unity of the two theologies, scriptural and philosophical, in which Aquinas believed and which is essential to his theological practice. They are both aspects of one thinking which is both human and divine or, alternatively, they are two forms of revelation.[35]

Precisely this aspect of Thomistic thought was, from time to time, embodied in theories of analogy built on his understanding. Heidegger criticized it for embodying a forgetfulness of being as onto-theology. Barth criticized it for positing two sources of revelation premised on one unitive conception of being. More will be said about the later criticism below. Here we are saying Aquinas's epistemological-analogical-metaphysical methodology embodied an ambiguity that often led theology in multiple and sometimes errant directions, but also sometimes in the right direction. Such was and is the actual status of Aquinas's understanding of analogy, which we are now in a position to demonstrate.

Analogy in the early texts and the **Summa Contra Gentiles**. We must preface our treatment of analogy in Aquinas's *Summae* with a brief summary of what has been discovered thus far in respect to analogy and its various interpretations in the tradition up to Aquinas. These are the key ideas that Aquinas must have been familiar with. *First*, there is the fact that the word

---

[34]See *GMW*, pp. 272-73.
[35]Hankey, *God in Himself*, p. 141.

analogy originates in a Greek context, and that this is critical to the Latin adaptation of it in theological method.[36] From its mathematical origins in

---

[36]On the concept of analogy in Aquinas, see especially Hampus Lyttkens, *The Analogy Between God and the World: An Investigation of Its Background and Interpretation of Its Use by Thomas of Aquino* (Uppsala: Almquist and Wiksell, 1952), pp. 110-11, and Battista Mondin, *The Principle of Analogy in Protestant and Catholic Theology* (The Hague: Martinus Nijhoff, 1963), p. 1. The literature on analogy, especially as it relates to Aquinas, is vast, to say the least. We can only note here the most standard works that are important to our own investigation: James F. Anderson, *The Bond of Being: An Essay on Analogy and Existence* (St. Louis: B. Herder, 1949); Anderson, *The Cause of Being: The Philosophy of Creation in St. Thomas* (New York: B. Herder, 1952); G. C. Berkouwer, *The Providence of God*, trans. Lewis B. Smedes (Grand Rapids: Eerdmans, 1952); John R. Betz, *After Enlightenment: The Post-Secular Vision of J. G. Hamann* (Oxford: Blackwell, 2009); Betz, "Beyond the Sublime: The Aesthetics of the Analogy of Being," *ModT* 21 (July 2005): 367-411 and *ModT* 22 (January 2006): 1-50; Erich Przywara, *Analogia entis: Metaphysics, Original Structure and Rhythm of All*, ed. and trans. David Bentley Hart (Grand Rapids: Eerdmans, 2014); B. Beumer, "*Gratia supponit naturam*. Zur Geschichte eines theologischen Prinzips," *Gregorianum* 20 (1930): 381-406, 535-52; Martin Bieler, "Karl Barths Auseinandersetzung mit der analogia entis und der Anfang der Theologie," *Catholica* 40 (1986): 241-45; Maurice Blondel, *L'action* (Paris: Presses Universitaires de France, 1995, repr. of 1983 ed.); Henri Bouillard, *Karl Barth, Genese et evolution de la theologie dialectique*, 3 vols. (Paris: Aubier, 1957); Bouillard, *The Knowledge of God*, trans. Samuel D. Femiano (New York: Herder & Herder, 1968); Stephen L. Brock, *Action and Conduct: Thomas Aquinas and the Theory of Action* (Edinburgh: T & T Clark, 1998); James J. Buckley, ed., *Knowing the Triune God: The Work of the Spirit in the Practices of the Church* (Grand Rapids: Eerdmans, 2001); David Burrell, *Faith and Freedom: An Interfaith Perspective* (Malden, MA: Blackwell, 2004); Burrell, *Knowing the Unknowable God: Ibn-Sina, Maimonides, Aquinas* (Notre Dame, IN: University of Notre Dame Press, 1986); Burrell, *Aquinas: God and Action* (Notre Dame, IN: University of Notre Dame Press, 1979); Burrell, *Analogy and Philosophical Language* (New Haven, CT: Yale University Press, 1973); W. Norris Clarke, *Explorations in Metaphysics: Being—God—Person* (Notre Dame, IN: University of Notre Dame Press, 1994); Clarke, *The One and the Many: A Contemporary Thomistic Metaphysics* (Notre Dame, IN: University of Notre Dame Press, 2001); Jean F. Courtine, *Inventio analogiae. Metaphysique et ontotheologie* (Paris: J. Vrin, 2005); Cardinal Cajetan Thomas De Vio, *The Analogy of Names and the Concept of Being* (Pittsburgh, PA: Duquesne University Press, 1953); Gilles Emery, *Trinity in Aquinas* (Ypsilanti, MI: Sapientia Press of Ave Maria College, 2003); F. E. England, *Kant's Conception of God: A Critical Exposition of Its Metaphysical Development Together with a Translation of the Nova Dilucidatio* (London: Unwin Brothers, 1928); Étienne Gilson, *Being and Some Philosophers* (Toronto: Pontifical Institute of Mediaeval Studies, 1952); Gilson, *The Christian Philosophy of St Thomas Aquinas*, translated by L. K. Shook (New York: Random House, 1955); Colin E. Gunton, *Act and Being: Towards a Theology of the Divine Attributes* (Grand Rapids: Eerdmans, 2003); Gunton, *Becoming and Being: The Doctrine of God in Charles Hartshorne and Karl Barth* (Oxford: Oxford University Press, 1978); Gunton, *Intellect and Action: Elucidations on Christian Theology and the Life of Faith* (Edinburgh: T & T Clark, 2000); W. J. Hankey, *God in Himself: Aquinas' Doctrine of God as Expounded in the Summa Theologiae* (Oxford: Oxford University Press, 1987); Martin Heidegger, *Being and Time*, trans. John Macquarrie and Edward Robinson (New York: Harper & Row, 1962); Heidegger, *Hegel's Phenomenology of Spirit*, trans. Parvas Emad and Kenneth Maly (Bloomington: Indiana University Press, 1988); Heidegger, *The Phenomenology of Religious Life*, trans. Matthias Fritsch and Jennifer Anna Gosetti-Ferencei (Bloomington: Indiana University Press, 2004); Heidegger, *What Is Called Thinking*, trans. J. Glenn Gray (New York: Harper & Row, 1968); Keith Johnson, "*Analogia entis*: A Reconsideration of the Debate Between Karl Barth and Roman Catholicism, 1914-1964" (PhD diss., Princeton Theological

the likes of Archytas and Euclid to its use in ethics and metaphysics in Aristotle, the classical understanding of the word is ultimately determined by the use Plato makes of it in his emphasis on proportion and/or proportionality. We may cite, for example, the analogies of "similar relations," or "forms of knowledge" (knowledge:opinion::thinking:imagination) that are especially understood as kinds of beings in relation to knowledge (being: becoming::knowledge:opinion).[37] There is, for Plato, a proportional relationship between elements within creation, knowledge and language that are inherent not to only our way of knowing but also our way of being.[38] This function of language is rooted in his cosmological conception of CER.

Second, Aristotle built a formal theory of analogy on this CER that re-

---

Seminary, 2008); Eberhard Jüngel, *God's Being Is in Becoming: The Trinitarian Being of God in the Theology of Karl Barth, a Paraphrase*, trans. John Webster (Grand Rapids: Eerdmans, 2001); Jüngel, *God as the Mystery of the World* (Grand Rapids: Eerdmans, 1983); Immanuel Kant, *The Critique of Judgment*, trans. J. H. Bernard (Amherst, NY: Prometheus Books, 2000); Kant, *Critique of Pure Reason*, trans. Lewis White Beck (New York: The Liberal Arts Press, 1956); George P. Klubertanz, *Introduction to The Philosophy of Being* (New York: Meredith, 1963); Klubertanz, *St. Thomas Aquinas on Analogy: A Textual Analysis and Systematic Synthesis* (Chicago: Loyola University Press, 1960); Norman Kretzman, ed., *The Cambridge History of Later Medieval Philosophy: From the Rediscovery of Aristotle to the Disintegration of Scholasticism, 1100-1600* (Cambridge: Cambridge University Press, 1988); Bernard J. Lonergan, *Verbum: Word and Idea in Aquinas*, ed. David B. Burrell (London: Darton, Longman & Todd, 1968); S. D. Long, *Speaking of God: Theology, Language and Truth* (Grand Rapids: Eerdmans, 2009); Long, *Saving Karl Barth: Hans Urs von Balthasar's Preoccupation* (Philadelphia: Fortress, 2014); Andrew Louth, *St John Damascene* (New York: Oxford University Press, 2002); Ralph McInerny, *Aquinas and Analogy* (Washington, D.C.: The Catholic University of America Press, 1996); McInerny, *The Logic of Analogy* (The Hague: Martin Nijhoff, 1971); McInerny, *Rhyme and Reason: St. Thomas and Modes of Discourse* (Milwaukee: Marquette University Press, 1981); John Milbank, *Truth in Aquinas* (New York: Routledge, 2001); Milbank, *The Word Made Strange: Theology, Language, Culture* (Malden, MA: Blackwell, 1997); John S. Morreall, *Analogy and Talking About God: A Critique of the Thomistic Approach* (Washington, D.C.: University Press of America, 1979); Thomas Franklin O'Meara, *Thomas Aquinas Theologian* (Notre Dame, IN: University of Notre Dame Press, 1997); Joseph Owens, *The Doctrine of Being in the Aristotelian Metaphysics: A Study in the Greek Background of Mediaeval Thought* (Toronto: Pontifical Institute of Mediaeval Studies, 1951); Humphrey Palmer, *Analogy: A Study of Qualification and Argument in Theology* (London: Macmillan, 1973); Wolfhart Pannenberg, *Metaphysics and the Idea of God*, trans. Philip Clayton (Grand Rapids: Eerdmans, 1990); Gerald B. Phelan, *Saint Thomas and Analogy* (Milwaukee: Marquette University Press, 1941); Eugene F. Rogers, *Thomas Aquinas and Karl Barth: Sacred Doctrine and the Natural Knowledge of God* (Notre Dame, IN: University of Notre Dame Press, 1995); Philip A. Rolnick, *Analogical Possibilities: How Words Refer to God* (Atlanta: Scholars Press, 1993); Richard Swinburne, *Revelation: From Metaphor to Analogy* (New York: Oxford University Press, 1992); Carl G. Vaught, *Metaphor, Analogy, and the Place of Places: Where Religion and Philosophy Meet* (Waco, TX: Baylor University Press, 2004); Andrew N. Woznicki, *Being and Order: The Metaphysics of Thomas Aquinas in Historical Perspective* (New York: Peter Lang, 1990).

[37] See Plato's *Republic*, as cited in Robinson, *Plato's Earlier Dialectic*, pp. 222-23.

[38] See Lyttkens, *Analogy Between God and the World*, pp. 15-28; Mondin, *Principle of Analogy*, p. 2.

tained this essential epistemological-ontological orientation, though we may certainly not yet call it the "analogy of being." Neither may we call Aristotle the father of analogy per se; rather, he is its first formal theorist. Aristotle's improvement on the Platonic conception is to be found in its scientific-logical use.[39] But it is interesting to note, as we have seen, that at the most critical point of his discussion of a formal theory of analogy, he does not actually use the word *analogy*.[40] He proceeds to describe how terms may be used univocally and equivocally as two opposite extremes but does not name the middle mode as analogy. Rather, he calls such terms words "which do not differ by way of univocality." Analogy is applied to such middle terms only in the Middle Ages, though what is most often meant by it is a relation of proportion or proportionality, in some sense.[41] At times Aristotle uses the word *metaphor* as a substitute for analogy, or will refer to a logical argument as "reasoning by analogy," but this is only in the rare cases where he understands analogy as a subtype of metaphor.[42] However, in the majority of his uses of the words *analogy* and *metaphor* he means some relation in proportion.[43]

Third, in terms of its Greek etymology and use, it is introduced more formally into theological discourse by writers like Augustine, Boethius, Anselm, Pseudo-Dionysius and Proclus, where it carries forward the meaning of a CER between various aspects of creation and being, in similarity and dissimilarity with the divine. Forms of predication in language trade, either negatively or positively, on this perceived resemblance between creation and Creator. This principle of CER was formalized in the two principles: first, that "everything which by its existence bestows a character on others, itself primitively possesses that character, which it communicates to the recipient."[44] The second, related principle is that analogy constitutes a principle of ontological unity in which we may observe the relation of various levels, or degrees, of reality in a descending or ascending order.[45]

---

[39]See Aristotle, *Organon Topica*, TLG 106a-108a.
[40]Mondin, *Principle of Analogy*, p. 2.
[41]Ibid.; Aristotle, *Analytica Priora*, TLG 68b-69a.
[42]Aristotle, *Organon Topica* 124a, 15f; TLG 136b-137a.
[43]Mondin, *Principle of Analogy*, p. 2; see also *Principle of Analogy*, p. 3; Lyttkens, *Analogy Between God and the World*, p. 58.
[44]Proclus, *Elements of Theology* 18, 21.
[45]Proclus, *Commentary on Plato's Parmenides* 851, 8-9.

According to these principles our knowledge of reality is one of degrees, proportionate to the level both above and/or below our level of existence. Spiritual beings exist on a plain above and thus proportinately possess a greater knowledge, while our knowledge supersedes all levels below us.[46] It is critical that we understand this basic, unbroken use of analogy in Greek literature, and that it is precisely transferred into its Latin meaning.

Fourth and finally, while it is true that the Latin use of the word broadens the meaning of the term somewhat, the original conception of proportional relation through CER is never lost. The word *analogy* was used of various sacred images. It was often coupled with the word *fidei* as an indication of how one should proceed in reading and interpreting the gospel. *Analogia fidei* thus constituted a reference to the interplay between Scripture, doctrine and the intratextual tradition, that is, interpreting one part of Scripture that might be obscured by reference to a simpler and clearer text. But with Augustine, Anselm, Boethius, Bonaventure and others, the word most often has cosmological attachments like participation, similarity, similitude and metaphor, all retaining the basic Platonic-Aristotelian meaning of the word.[47]

These are the facts that are already ingredient in the concept of analogy that Aquinas takes up, adjusts and employs in various locations in his corpus. Indeed, it is Aquinas who broadens out certain meanings that have special significance for theological speech, along with the already-received meaning of similarity/dissimilarity (in reference to logical, physical, epistemological and metaphysical categories). By *analogy* Aquinas variously means either proportion, proportionality, resemblance, proportional distribution, degree of being, metaphor, simile, and/or other forms of predication. Furthermore, though *analogy* is the key term, in its place he will sometimes employ words like *proportionis*, *communitas* or *similitude*. Very often the meaning of proportion and similitude is to be understood within the context of the doctrine of the *imago Dei*, a precedent started in Augustine's *De Trinitate* and subsequently adopted by Aquinas.[48] However, the real expansion of the Latin meaning takes place after Aquinas, but is often based on what he says

---

[46]Pseudo-Dionysius, *Divine Names* I.1, 588a; *Ecclesiastical Hierarchy* I.2.372d.

[47]See Augustine, *De Trinitate* VIII-XV; Bonaventure, *Commentaria in Sententiis P. Lombardi* I, d, 3a; 1, q. 1-3.

[48]Augustine, *De Trinitate* XIII-XV.

and how he uses it. The most extreme expansion of the term is to be seen in Scotus, who insists that, rather than analogy being a middle way, it was another way of saying univocity. The very concept, in his mind, assumes a one-to-one comparison between God's being and existence and human being and existence. In fact, according to Scotus, no knowledge of God is possible without such univocity.[49] It is the differentiation between analogy as a middle way and analogy as univocity that remains the essence of the debate since Aquinas. The ultimate question is not, what is the Catholic doctrine of analogy? but, what is the proper interpretation of its use, especially in Aquinas? On this, agreement is hard to come by. This lack of consensus on the interpretation of the use to which Aquinas puts analogy is only too well demonstrated since Cajetan's famous attempt to reduce Aquinas's theory to a single form under the *Analogy of Names*. Successive attempts at "correcting" and "clarifying," even denying, Cajetan's approach have yielded only a greater degree of uncertainty, as the literature since testifies to.

In what follows here, only this lack of real corrective is really salient when considering the various criticisms of the so-called *analogia entis*. The real issue arises when contemporary scholars want to signify only one use of the *analogia entis* as truly "Thomistic" and therefore "truly Catholic," and so also the one most consistently used in the tradition. As we have said, this is an impossibility, as the following analysis of Aquinas will make clear. Perhaps the best summary we can offer on the state of scholarship on this question is the one offered by George Klubertanz when he suggests: "Textually Cajetan's followers have added very little to his work, although a number of special studies have been undertaken to prove that Cajetan's interpretation is faithful to the text of St. Thomas."[50] Here he is referring to Sylvester of Ferrara and Suárez. But even those who oppose Cajetan's interpretation nevertheless must "discuss Thomistic analogy in light of Cajetan's categories." Indeed Klubertanz himself is forced to admit that in all who oppose his approach to Aquinas, nevertheless "the preponderance of Cajetan's influence in the systematic elaboration of a theory of analogy is more readily appre-

---

[49]Duns Scotus, *Ordinatio*, bk. I, qq. 1-2, para. 27. See his complete works in *Opera Omnia*, 11 vols., Scotistic Commission (Vatican City: Typis Polyglottis Vaticanis, 1950).
[50]Klubertanz, *St. Thomas Aquinas on Analogy*, pp. 12-13.

ciated . . . and even when they disagree they use his frame of reference."[51]

Given this tendency to default to Cajetan's categories among post-Thomas interpreters, how may we best approach the interpretation of Aquinas's use of analogy in this respect? There is no question that, as for other post-Cajetan interpreters, his model will exert some influence here. Further factors influencing an interpretation have to do with the chronology of Aquinas's writings. What constitutes authoritative texts? Are all text to be taken into account, or is there a "key text" that should be used to interpret the rest? Both of these approaches to the texts of Aquinas have held sway among various Thomistic interpreters. Cajetan perfected the "key text" interpretation, while in our time Klubertanz has attempted to be comprehensive while keeping chronological and developmental factors in mind.[52] From either point of view we run into trouble.

It is not our task here to sort out a proper method at length but to indicate a *via media* between these two extremes. That is to say, while we agree with Klubertanz that the "key text" method "has resulted in essentially different syntheses, all of which are open to serious criticism," his approach, which includes a synthesis of all texts without assigning priority, has yielded a no less problematic description of Aquinas on analogy, and indeed ends up partially affirming Cajetan's approach while admitting to the near impossibility of a formal theory of analogy in Aquinas.[53] Furthermore, in terms of the emphasis Klubertanz places, he appears to overlook texts in the "mature" period of Aquinas's thought and their import for what is, after all, his greatest achievement and the pinnacle of his career, that is, the *ST*.[54] In his table of "chronological variations" as to where and when texts on analogy appear, and at what stage of Aquinas's development, again we agree with Klubertanz that it is "not simply a matter of chronological variation" in terminology that can explain the complexity of Aquinas's understanding.[55] At the same time we cannot dismiss the strong possibility of development of his thought on this, especially in his summative and programmatic works like the *SCG* and the *ST*. Indeed, along with a few other important and particularly clear texts,

[51]Ibid.
[52]Ibid., pp. 104-5.
[53]Ibid.
[54]Ibid., p. 19.
[55]Ibid., p. 22.

these texts shall be our primary focus in this present section.[56] However, the "key" is not any given text, but the function of analogy in these works and therefore what Aquinas thinks about analogy. So chronology, maturity of thought, and certain clear, programmatic texts, in the *Summae* and other selected works, will be our focus in expositing Aquinas.[57] Both of the *Summae* represent Aquinas's mature theological thought. There will also be some recourse to earlier and later texts in the *De veritate, De potentia* and the *Compendium Theologiae* that are very clear and are related to the Neo-platonic influences on his thought.

Cajetan adopted several comments by Aquinas in two of his early works in establishing his definition of analogy in Aquinas as *The Analogy of Names*; these were Aquinas's *Commentary on the Sentences I* and *De veritate*, which Cajetan sees as the key texts.[58] In both cases subsequent research has determined that these two earlier texts, though they add something to our understanding of Aquinas on analogy, cannot function as keys to interpret his whole "theory."[59] Cajetan used these early comments on analogy to limit what Aquinas might possibly mean by it and to establish his own "prefabricated" types of analogy. These texts and his subsequent classification have proven to be wholly unsatisfactory and continue to muddy the waters in our own time.

The beginning of what appears to be an orderly and theoretical treatment

---

[56]For an excellent collection and collation of the most important texts, see also Klubertanz's index of such in his *St. Thomas Aquinas on Analogy*, pp. 159-293, which includes a list of citations of every occurance of analogy in Aquinas.

[57]These texts are generally dated from 1261-1263; 1266-1268; 1269-1271.

[58]See Cajetan, *Analogy of Names*, pp. 12-18, in *III Libros Sententiarum* I.1.1.

[59]See especially Klubertanz, *St. Thomas Aquinas on Analogy*, pp. 14-15; Lyttkens, *Analogy Between God and the World*, pp. 310-11, 474-76. Lyttkens writes, "Summarizing the above, we find that St. Thomas only uses the analogy of proportionality as a logical aid in stating of God certain properties taken from creation, viz. in *De Ver.* 2.11. The analogy of proportionality must accordingly be said not to play that central part in St. Thomas, which is ascribed to him in Thomistic quarters." On p. 475 n. 6 he adds, "The passage in *De Pot. 7. 7* that is usually quoted does not mean likeness of proportion but stresses the difference between God's and creation's relation to *esse*. It is not clear, in *I Eth. Lect. 7*, that proportionality signifies more than the immanent *bonum*. *III Sent.* d. 1. 1. 1., refers to *analogia entis* between substance and accidents, not God and creation" (*Analogy Between God and the World*, pp. 475). While this conclusion has been generally accepted since, and followed by scholars, see also J. Hochschild, *The Semantics of Analogy: Rereading Cajetan's De Nominum Analogia* (Notre Dame, IN: University of Notre Dame Press, 2010). Hochschild tries to suggest that Cajetan does not intend his *De Nominum Analogia* to be a reinterpretation of Aquinas's view but rather is his own independent position.

of analogy, though it is also far from that, first occurs in book I, chapters 30-34 of the *SCG*, a recognized source of authority for what might be called the final theological principles in Aquinas's corpus. In the *SCG*, Aquinas indicates his purpose to be the declaration of "the truth, which the Catholic faith professes, while weeding out contrary errors."[60] In the many subsequent amendments to the *SCG*, Aquinas never undertakes to disavow this claim. He deals with the problem of analogy under the category of "divine names," asking, "What terms can be predicated of God?" Already in chapter 22 of book I he has set up a principle whereby we may both name and understand the relationship between God and the world, that is, the principle of participation. "Everything exists through having existence. Therefore nothing exists by its essence, but by participation of something, namely existence. Now that which exists by participation of something cannot be the first being, because that in which a thing participates in order to exist, is previous to that thing. But God is the first being, to which nothing is previous."[61] This principle will ultimately determine the nature of the *analogates* (that which is analogized) in relation to the *analogans*, the primary term to which the analogates are compared. As a necessary step in between, Aquinas posits that "in sequence to the above we may consider in what way it is possible to find in things a likeness to God, and in what way it is impossible."[62]

This principle, as a follow-up from the previous ontological conception of the "participation in being," will become the epistemological basis that makes analogy possible as a mode of speech about the divine. Aquinas explains the way likeness of being between the creature and Creator may or may not be affirmed, here following Pseudo-Dionysius.

> For effects that fall short of their causes do not agree with them in name and ratio, and yet there must needs be some likeness between them, because it is of the nature of action that a like agent should produce a like action, since everything acts according as it is in act; wherefore the *form* of the effect is found in its transcendent cause somewhat, but in another way and another ratio, for which reasons that cause is called equivocal. Yet for all the likeness (*similitude*) there is also a great unlikeness, so that, as heat is to the sun and

---

[60]*SCG*, bk. I, chap. 2.
[61]*SCG*, bk. I, chap. 22.
[62]*SCG*, bk. I, chap. 29.

dryness, both unlike and like in the sharing of heat, so God is both like and unlike those whom he creates. "God bestows all perfections on all things," and in consequence he is both like and unlike all.[63]

Appealing to Scripture, Aquinas locates this likeness preeminently in our creation after "the image and likeness" of God, but it is Pseudo-Dionysius who provides the framework for this doctrine of perfection in his *Divine Names*: "The same things are like and unlike to God; like according as they imitate Him, as far as they can, who is *not* perfectly imitable; unlike according as effects fall short of their causes."[64]

The likeness here is, for Aquinas, based on the possession of a "quality or form." However, such a quality or form is found in the creature imperfectly such that the participation in the likeness is "God's simply but not the creature's. And thus the creature has what is God's, and therefore is rightly said to be like God."[65] However, the reverse cannot be the case, since it cannot be affirmed that God has what belongs to the creature: "wherefore neither is it fitting to say that God is like his creature."[66] In book I, chapters 30-34, Aquinas builds his understanding of analogy on these doctrines of perfection and participation in terms of likeness and unlikeness, which at that point in the *SCG* is designed to protect the simplicity, aseity, freedom and eternity of God.

In order to do so Aquinas, in book I, chapter 29, lays the emphasis on the negative as follows: "Much less properly can it be said that God is assimilated to the creature. For assimilation denotes movement towards similarity, and consequently applies to one that receives its similarity from another. But the creature receives from God its similarity to Him and not vice versa. Therefore God is not assimilated to His creature, but rather, vice versa."[67] When in chapter 30 of book I Aquinas comes formally to his exposition of theological predication by analogy, it is precisely with this negative note that he begins,

---

[63]*SCG*, bk. I, chap. 29.
[64]Ibid. See also Pseudo-Dionysius, *Divine Names* ch. IX, 909b-c. On the Neoplatonic-Proclan background to this principle, see H. D. Saffrey, "Nouveaux liens objectifs entre le Pseudo-Denys et Proclus," *Revues scientifiques philosophiques et theologiques* 63 (1979): 3-16, 6-11, and his "New Objective Links Between the Pseudo-Dionysius and Proclus," in *Neoplatonism and Christian Thought*, ed. Dominic J. O'Meara, Studies in Neoplatonism: Ancient and Modern 3 (Albany: State University of New York Press, 1982), pp. 64-74.
[65]Pseudo-Dionysius, *Divine Names* ch. IX, 909b.
[66]*SCG*, bk. I, chap. 29.
[67]Ibid.

and it is clearly meant to mitigate the positive nature of theological predication: "What can and what cannot be said of God; also what is said of Him alone, and what is said of Him together with other beings?"[68] These are the questions that lie at the heart of the "theological naming" of God.

> For since every perfection of creatures is to be found in God, albeit in another, more eminent way, what ever terms denote perfection absolutely and without any defect whatever, are predicated of God and of other things. . . . But any term that denotes such like perfections together with a mode proper to creatures, cannot be said of God except by similitude and metaphor, whereby that which belongs to one thing is applied to another.

But some terms are nontransferable because "those which express . . . perfections together with the mode of supereminence in which they belong to God, are said of God alone, for instance . . . the first being and the like."[69] The whole structure of the *SCG* at this point indicates an anticipation of the structure of the *ST* and comes to the same position on divine predication.

In the *Prima Pars* of the *ST*, Aquinas begins the formal treatment of theology with the simplicity of God, followed by a discussion of the role of reason, vis-à-vis the arguments for the existence of God.[70] This is followed by an exposition on divine predication in questions 13 and 14 of the *ST*, with the supposition of analogy as a middle way between univocity and equivocity. So also the *SCG* proceeds in this way. "Seeing then that we intend by the way of reason to pursue those things about God which human reason is able to investigate, the first object that offers itself to our consideration consists in those things which pertain to *God in Himself*; the second will be the procession of creatures from Him; and the third the relation of creatures to Him as their end."[71] This is pretty much the same as the order of the knowledge of God established in the *Prima Pars*: the way of causality, emanation and negation, with resemblance as a process of return to the first cause, an *exitus-reditus*, if you will, and again reversing Pseudo-Dionysius to allow for Aristotle, but maintaining the Neoplatonic logic as essential substructure of the argument.

---

[68]*SCG*, bk. I, chap. 30.
[69]Ibid.
[70]Compare *SCG*, bk. I, chap. 30, to *ST* I, q. 1, art. 3, pr.
[71]*ST* I, q. 9.

Thus with the modifying doctrines of *perfection* and *participation* and the methodological procedure of the ways of *analogically* conceived *cause, emanation* and *negation*, Aquinas offers three modes of predication in the *SCG*. First, there are the names said of God alone, "that express a perfection along with a mode of super eminence," like highest Good, the first Being and so on. Such names may be used of creatures only in a metaphorical or analogical sense. There are also names that "express a perfection along with the mode that is proper to the creature," but these names can also only be said of God in terms of likeness, and therefore metaphorically or analogically.[72] Finally, there are names that designate perfection without imperfection. These "designate an absolute perfection without expressing the mode according to which it is found in a particular subject: These names are predicated of both God and other things: for example, goodness, wisdom, being and the like."[73] In each case it seems clear that it is the mode of signification that belongs to creatureliness that determines the mode of signification.

Aquinas is acutely aware of this problem. In all forms of theological predication it must be recognized, according to Aquinas, that the intellect begins with the knowledge it receives from our sensual circumstances, which cannot be transcended. In respect to theological predication, this results in an imperfection lying at the root of every mode of predication, an imperfection that does not "befit God," even though that which is signified in the name befits God in "some eminent way."[74] Aquinas offers the following example to illustrate his point:

> This is clear in the name of "goodness" and "good." For goodness has signification as something not subsisting, while good has signification as something created. And so with reference to the mode of signification no name is fittingly applied to God; this is done only with reference to that which the name has been imposed to signify. Such names, therefore, as Dionysius teaches, can be both affirmed and denied of God. They can be affirmed because of the meaning of the names; they can be denied because of the mode of signification.[75]

As we have already said in our discussion of the structure of the *Prima*

---

[72]*SCG*, bk. I, chap. 30.
[73]Ibid.
[74]Ibid.
[75]Ibid.

Pars, it would seem that here also the "sensible" is that with which we begin but represents the baseline in preparing the mind, with its memory, to ascend to the knowledge of God via divine predication through causality, negation and emanation. This confinement of predication to the sensible ought not to be understood as the absolute opposite of the divine simplicity, which in Aquinas is the object of theological knowledge. In order to refine the possibility of positive predication, in chapter 31 of book I he distinguishes between extrinsic and intrinsic attribution with respect to absolute perfections in God.[76] "And so too, the perfections of all things, which are becoming to other things in respect of various forms, must needs be ascribed to God in respect of His one virtue and this virtue is not distinct from His essence, since nothing can be accidental to Him, as we have proved."[77] That is to say, extrinsically we may denominate God as the cause of wisdom and intrinsically, "somewhat," by our participation in wisdom as similitude, we may denominate God as "wisdom itself." How may we do so if all we have to go on is our sensory perception? We may do so because "the like of this may be found in human cognitive powers and operative virtues. For the intellect by its one virtue knows all that the sensitive faculty apprehends by various powers, and many other things besides."[78] Aquinas does not explain the "various powers" and "many other things" but rests his case on a pre-existing cognitive power innate to sensual perception. Thus he starts from empirical sense perception in noting that predicates are only properly predicated of the creature first and that we must learn how they may be predicated of God as an attribute. Nowhere in the *SCG* does he attempt to fully explicate the presuppositions of this intrinsic-extrinsic attribution of predicates. Here his interest is in illustrating how from sensory perception the intellect may be able to rise to a higher knowledge. "Again the intellect, the higher it is, the more things it is able to know by means of one, while an inferior intellect can arrive at the knowledge of those things only by means of many."[79]

This leads Aquinas to a significant conclusion on the way to analogy, that

---

[76]Aquinas, *Scriptum super librum Sententiarum*, bk. I, XXI, q. 5; *De veritate*, q. 21, art. 4.
[77]*SCG*, bk. I, chap 31.
[78]Ibid.
[79]Ibid.; see also Hankey, *God in Himself*, p. 43.

is, "that nothing is predicated univocally" of God and other things. Aquinas never tires of reminding his readers of this where analogy is concerned. Neither names of shared perfection, between creature and Creator, nor names of supereminent perfections, exclusive to God himself, can be applied univocally. As we saw in *SCG* book I, chapter 29, "God is not a univocal cause." That is, in creation the imprint of the Creator on creation is not univocal in being and essence. Creation receives a form, but not one that is univocally identical to that of the agent; thus the name arising from the form imprinted cannot be univocal either. The CER is a similarity in dissimilarity as such, because "the forms of things whereof God is cause do not attain to the specifics of the divine virtue, since they receive severally and particularly that which is in God simply and universally."[80] Furthermore, whatever is predicated of several things univocally is "either genus, or species, or difference, or proper accident, and God is none of those things."[81] Aquinas's conclusion here in respect to univocal predication is important for our later study:

> What is predicated of some things according to priority and posteriority is certainly not predicated univocally. For the prior is included in the definition of the posterior, as substance is included in the definition of accident according as an accident is a being. If, then, being were said univocally of substance and accident, substance would have to be included in the definition of being insofar as being is predicated of substance. But this is clearly impossible. Now nothing is predicated of God and creatures as though they were in the same order, but, rather, according to priority and posteriority. For all things are predicated of God essentially. For God is called being as being entity itself. But in other beings predications are made by participation. . . . It is impossible, therefore, that anything be predicated univocally of God and other things.[82]

Precisely here is where univocal and analogical predication gets tricky. Aquinas's explanation of its impossibility may also be argued in favor of its possibility, depending on one's presuppositions and where one chooses to place the emphasis, vis-à-vis knowledge. Earlier in the *Commentary on the Sentences I* he denies that the predication of divine names is according to pri-

---

[80]*SCG*, bk. I, chap. 32.
[81]Ibid.
[82]Ibid.

ority and posteriority, but here he adopts it as necessary to all predication.[83] What does he mean by this seemingly contradictory assertion? The issue is somewhat critical because the phrase *per prius et posterius* is used throughout Aquinas's writings with respect to analogy. It is rooted in the CER argument for likeness-unlikness and occurs most often when he is treating the relationship between substance and accidents, a distinction he owes to Boethius as much as Aristotle. In his *De Principiis Naturae* he defines this in relation to his understanding of being.[84] As per Aristotle's "categories," being, says Aquinas, "may be predicated of substance, quantity, quality" and all other of Aristotle's categories. However, not all categories have being in the same way, or on the same level of intelligibility. "For all of these are called being because they are attributed to substance, their subject. Thus, being is predicated antecedently [*per prius*] of substance and consequently [*per posterius*] of the other categories."[85] There are variations on this phraseology, but what Aquinas means is that being may only be truly and intrinsically ascribed to substance first and accidents subsequently. That is, in any given analogy, being inheres in the one *analogans* as substance, then in the other *analogatum* as accident.[86]

What the distinction enables Aquinas to achieve is a capacity to distinguish what is imperfect in the predication of proper perfections to God and yet also to explain how the *analogatum* may possess the perfection as the *essential relation* between *analogans* and *analogatum*. As we shall see below,

---

[83]Aquinas, *Scriptum super librum Sententiarum*, Bk I, q. 2, art. 3.

[84]See Joseph Bobik, *Aquinas on Matter and Form and the Elements* (Notre Dame, IN: University of Notre Dame Press, 1998), pp. 63-79.

[85]Aquinas, *De Principiis Naturae*: "Being is predicated both of substance and of quantity, quality, and the other categories. However, it is not entirely the same intelligibility by which substance is being and quantity is being and the others are being. For all of these are called being because they are attributed to substance, their subject. Thus, being is predicated antecedently [*per prius*] of substance and consequendy [*per posterius*] of the other categories." See also his *De ente et essentia* cap. II.2; *ST* II, q. 61, art. 1, ad. 1; q. 120, art. 2. See Klubertanz, *St. Thomas Aquinas on Analogy*, pp. 65-66.

[86]Aquinas, *De ente et essentia* chap. II.2. See also his *Super librum de causis expositio*, proposition 22, where he writes: "For in all things that are below the first cause, we find some things existing perfectly, or complete, [while] other things [are] imperfect or diminished. The perfect seem to be those things that are self-subsistent in nature, which we signify through concrete terms, such as 'man,' 'sage,' and the like. But the imperfect are those things that are not self-subsistent, such as the forms 'humanity,' 'wisdom,' and the like, which we signify through abstract terms." Compare Proclus, *Elements of Theology*, proposition 115, which reads thus: "Every God is above being, above life and above intelligence" (per R. Taylor in *Commentary on the Book of Causes*).

this distinction plays a central role in the *ST* in respect to analogy. It is also critical to notice in the passage from book I, chapter 32, that this kind of predication involving substance and accident, wherein a name is predicated of one being substantially (and therefore essentially), and other beings (accidents) by participation, then the predicate exists in substantial being, really, and in accidental being, indirectly. This special mode of predication is of a "one to another," not of a "many to one," even if, as we have said, one's presuppositions may allow one to argue that way. This distinction between priority and posteriority is precisely what constitutes the ambiguous nature of all analogy so philosophically circumscribed. Aquinas is endeavoring to place God as the prior analogate but must use a philosophically conceived principle of relation purely based in the sensuous in order to try to ascend to the position of divinity as a principle of mind. But such a sensuous starting point appears to obviate any real knowledge of transcendence. Clearly Plotinus lurks in the background, via Boethius, perhaps also in the form of a Proclan-Dionysian appropriation of Aristotle. Thus Aquinas appears to equate being with substance, which will have consequences for how Aquinas will be perceived and received vis-à-vis theological speech about God.

Before proceeding to his final definition of analogy in book I, chapter 34, Aquinas dedicates a whole chapter to arguing against "equivocal predication." Of all the arguments put forward there, the one most important for our consideration is the argument *ad absurdum*. Aquinas writes, "If names are said of God and creatures in a purely equivocal way, we understand nothing of God through those names; for the meanings of those names are known to us solely to the extent that they are said of creatures. In vain, therefore, would it be said or proved of God that he is a being, good or the like."[87] That is to say, such equivocity can only yield anthropomorphism at best, and mere anthropology at worst. Confined as we are to the sensible, all claims to equivocity in predication must be reduced to that. However, if, as he notes at the beginning of *SCG*, book I, chapter 33, we must exclude equivocity by virtue of the fact that such predicates are predicated "without any order of reference to one another," then the opposite must be true, that is, that only names that are predicated of God by analogy of one to another are legitimate.

---

[87]*SCG*, bk. I, chap. 33.

These he calls names that follow "the order of cause to effect."[88]

Thus Aquinas comes to the third form of predication, which in the *ST* he will call the "middle way" or analogy. Those names predicated of God and other things must be said, not equivocally or univocally, but analogically, "that is according to an order of relation to some one thing."[89] There are two ways in which analogous predication may proceed in relation to "this one thing": that of the analogy of the many to the one and/or the analogy of one to another. Names that may be predicated of both God and the creature proceed by an analogy of one to another:

> Names said of God and creature are predicated . . . according to an order of reference [relation] to some one thing. This can take place in two ways. In one way, according as many things have reference to something one. Thus, with reference to one health we say that an animal is healthy as the subject of health, medicine is healthy as its cause, food as its preserver, urine as its sign. In another way, the analogy can obtain according as the order or reference of two things is not to something else but to one of them. Thus "being" is said of substance and accident according as an accident has reference to a substance, and not according as a substance and accident are referred to a third thing.[90]

According to this text, analogy, in theology, must proceed along the lines established in the second mode of the relation of one to another. Why? Aquinas explains in the same section that analogical naming as a relation of one to another, according to substance and accident, is based on the fact that there is a relationship of the name to knowledge, "since the name is a sign of intellectual conception."[91] That is to say, the act of naming already bespeaks a relation of priority insofar as that which comes first in reality is realized as knowledge.[92] "Wherefore being is said of substance previously to being said of accident, both in reality and according to the meaning of the word."[93] Here Aquinas wants to limit the theological scope and use of analogy and not permit an analogy of the many to the one or an analogy of two to a third. Wisdom, for instance, cannot be predicated of creatures and God as a *tertium*

---

[88]Ibid.
[89]*SCG*, bk. I, chap. 34.
[90]Ibid.
[91]Ibid.
[92]Ibid.
[93]Ibid.

quid, that is, in which they share this wisdom. This mode of analogy denies the supereminence of wisdom, reducing it to a shared nature of the same substance, however unequal.

This must certainly be true of terms that designate absolute perfections, such as *being*. Being is predicated of substance essentially. This is a principle in which God does not participate but is, essentially. His being and his essence are identical. "Wherefore being is said of substance previously to being said of accidents, both in reality and according to the meaning of the name."[94] At this point this does not constitute an analogy of proportion, proportionality or attribution, but simply an analogy of one to another. However, this form of analogy is still ultimately based on an intrinsic sharing of perfections between God and the creature, as Cajetan's analysis will make clear. In book I, chapter 30, of the *SCG* we have already seen that Aquinas denies the analogy of extrinsic attribution, that is, a form of analogy in which the *analogates* do not share, intrinsically, to the same degree at least, in the concept analogized. That is, they only share in their relation to *one common thing*. Here "intrinsic likeness" is implied by Aquinas when he says that "health" is actually prior in medicine but must be designated so on the basis of health of a human. The basis of this intrinsic likeness is the principle of CER. "Thus, the healing power in health-giving (medicines) is naturally prior to health in the animal, as cause is to effect; yet we *know* this power through its effect, we name it from that effect. Hence it is that health-giving is first in the order of reality, and yet health is predicated of animal first, according to the meaning of the term."[95] So, essentially, the truth in the thing and the truth as we know it intellectually are parallel to the relation between the health of the human and the health-giving power of medicine.

Thus the essence of the concept exists in the human even as it exists essentially in the things that cause it. The truth in the intellect is virtually the same as the health in the human. The analogical method put forward here then is a clear species of intrinsic analogy of attribution, even if it is not designated so. It is based entirely on a CER. More could be said about Aquinas's treatment of analogy in other, less specific contexts elsewhere in the *SCG*, but suffice it to say here that throughout this document the preferred

---

[94]Ibid.
[95]Ibid.

mode of analogy is that of one to another, which amounts to a form of analogy of intrinsic attribution. The standpoint from which Aquinas deals with analogy seems to be ontological-metaphysical, rather than epistemological and/or as a category of logic. This is so because he considers it from the perspective of a relationship between cause and effect, divine and human intellect, and divine and human being.

Can we find confirmation of this general attitude elsewhere in Aquinas's corpus? Certainly, but other statements and factors prohibit fixing the analogy of one to another as the final Thomistic form of analogy. However, we may certainly affirm that its metaphysical foundations occur everywhere in the Thomistic corpus, both early and late. In his *De potentia*, for instance, Aquinas tries to deal with some of the metaphysical implications of his understanding of analogy in book I, chapters 30-34, of the *SCG*. Clearly this earlier work was edited by Aquinas to accommodate these concerns.[96] Question 7 of the *De potentia* deals with the apparent contradiction between divine simplicity and a multitude of names, especially in light of the negative predicatory theory of Maimonides, who is one of Aquinas's primary interlocutors in this work. Here we will confine ourselves to what he says about analogy, especially as it confirms what we have found in Aquinas thus far. In the same work, Aquinas aims to demonstrate that the multiplicity of divine names is identical with the divine substance. In defense of this, Aquinas invokes the use of an analogy between God and the world, which he claims rests on two foundational metaphysical principles. The first is that creation and creatures are effects of God's divine agency; second, that this divine agency imprints on creation a CER. The central biblical doctrine he invokes as theological justification for these principles is creation in the image of God. As an image of the divine, the creature is created with an innate capacity to know the Creator. But, since image and likeness bespeak an indirect resemblance, this knowledge is only "imperfect." The term *imperfect* is not to be understood as "flawed," however, but understood in relation to the perfection that can only ever be predicated of God. That is, it points to an ontological difference. Thus all our knowledge, and the words we use to express it, can only ever be "imperfect," never univocal.[97] "Therefore, although these terms

---

[96]Aquinas, *De potentia*, q. 7, art. 7; *SCG*, bk. I, chap. 33.
[97]See Aquinas, *De potentia*, q. 7, art. 5.

which our intellect attributes to God from such conceptions *signify* the divine essence, they do not signify it perfectly as it is in itself, but as it is conceived by us. Accordingly we conclude that each of these terms signifies the divine essence, not comprehensively but imperfectly."[98] Thus, in contradiction to the negative theology of Maimonides and apophaticists, Aquinas affirms that names, however imperfect, do signify absolute perfections and may be properly predicated of the divine.

Yet in the very same breath he seems to concede the unknowability and unspeakability of God, stating: "Man reaches this highest point of his knowledge about God when he knows that he knows him not, inasmuch as he knows that which God is transcends whatever he conceives of Him."[99] Furthermore, says Aquinas, there is a clear ontological connection in CER that makes analogical naming possible. "An effect includes something whereby it is like its cause, and something whereby it differs therefrom: and this by reason of its matter or something of the kind."[100] Aquinas uses the example of the making of bricks to illustrate his point. Bricks must be hardened by fire, and in the process clay and fire share the property of heat. Also in the process, the bricks condense and harden, "due to the nature of the material."[101] In what way, then, may we accord likeness or resemblance between the brick and the fire? On the one hand, heat is ascribed to the fire "properly in a more immanent way since the brick is hot by being made hot, while the fire is hot by nature."[102] On the other hand, "if we ascribe to the fire that wherein the brick differs from the fire, it will be untrue and any term that signifies this condition of dissimilarity cannot be said of fire unless metaphorically."[103] It would be wrong, for instance, to ascribe density to fire on the basis of the density of the brick, or its materiality, and so on. Fire can be described as hard, however, metaphorically, "because of the violence of its action and the difficulty to quench it."[104] Aquinas now draws a very significant conclusion in respect to this study.

---

[98]Ibid.
[99]Ibid., q. 7, art. 5.
[100]Ibid.
[101]Ibid, q. 7, art. 5, ad. 8.
[102]Ibid.
[103]Ibid.
[104]Ibid.

Accordingly in creatures there are certain perfections whereby they are likened to God, and which as regards the thing signified do not denote any imperfection, such as being, life, understanding and so forth: and these are ascribed to God properly, in fact they are ascribed to him first and in a more eminent way than to creatures. And there are in creatures certain perfections wherein they differ from God, and which the creature owed to its being made from nothing, such as potentiality, privation, movement and the like.[105]

As we have already seen, such "perfections" cannot be ascribed to God and yet constitute the difference between God and creature. What is critical to note here is the fact that in the *ST* and elsewhere Aquinas invokes this passage as the ground of his description of analogy of "intrinsic attribution." In the context of his discussion of analogy in *De potentia*, the analogy of extrinsic attribution is clearly denied. God is good, or wise, not because he causes goodness or wisdom, but because he is goodness and wisdom, essentially. "Because He is wise, therefore does he cause wisdom?" Extrinsic attribution places the priority on the creaturely possession of the perfection, while intrinsic attribution places the priority on the divine essence as wisdom. Thus the multiplicity of divine names is a product of the incapacity of human intellect to comprehend the single essence of God. It must rely on a multiplicity of faculties innate to the human, through a CER, wherein God possesses these perfections eminently, and in a prior way.[106] Creatureliness reflects this essence indirectly as image.

To secure this analogy of intrinsic attribution, Aquinas must, in question 7, article 7 of the *De potentia*, deny both univocity and equivocity, again on the same basis as he does in *SCG*. Univocity is impossible because "God is not univocal cause," and equivocity is impossible because it would deny a relation of one to another. So it must be analogous predication on which theological language must trade. Furthermore, as in the *SCG*, there are two modes of analogy that may be employed. Though the terms of reference are different, Aquinas essentially respects what he has said in the *SCG*, book I, chapter 34. "The first is when one thing is predicated of two with respect to a third: thus being is predicated of quantity and quality with respect to sub-

---

[105]Ibid.
[106]Ibid.

stance. The other is when a thing is predicated of two by reason of a relationship between these two: thus being is predicated of substance and quantity."[107] The first is to be rejected because "the two things must be preceded by something to which each of them bears some relationship: thus substance has respect to quantity and quality."[108] This is impossible because it degrades the relation of the primary to the secondary. So the other is to be preferred because "in the second kind of predication this is not necessary, but one of the two must precede the other."[109]

Since God precedes the creature, the second kind of predication is applicable to him but not the other. Thus the analogy of many to the one, or, in the same way, the analogy of two to a third, is to be rejected. This argument is repeated in the *ST*. The reason for its rejection there is the same, as in all cases where Aquinas deals with it. For this kind of speech about God to be true "we should have to posit something prior to God."[110] That is to say, the analogy must be employed in such a way that God's *aseity*, freedom, simplicity, uniqueness and sovereignty are affirmed and safeguarded. Because of its proximity to univocity, any mode of analogy that suggests univocal proportion is rejected, it would seem, but as we shall see in the *ST*, with respect to proportion, this is not so clear. For reasons we shall state later, it would appear that the analogy of intrinsic attribution so clearly delineated here and in the *SCG* gets confused in the *ST*, in the commentaries of Aquinas on Pseudo-Dionysius's *De divinis nominibus* and in his commentary on Boethius's *De Trinitate*. It is in fact this confusion between analogy of intrinsic attribution and analogy of proportionality that drives the post-Thomistic discussion, even today.

As we can now see, earlier and later texts from Aquinas's corpus make a static view of analogy in Aquinas impossible. One of the reasons for this is indeed the mixture of logical, epistemological and metaphysical concerns that drive the method of analogy. For instance, how does one understand the principle of causal eminence that sits at the heart of Aquinas's description of analogy in his commentaries on Aristotle, Pseudo-Dionysius and

---

[107]Ibid., q. 7, art. 7.
[108]Ibid.
[109]Ibid.
[110]Ibid.; *ST* I, qq. 13-14.

Boethius?[111] Therein the language of priority and posteriority is supplemented by the language of causal eminence, especially in the analogy between Creator and creature. Qualities or perfections are described as being in God eminently and in the creature deficiently. The analogy then becomes one of proportion and/or proportionality, which he seems to reject elsewhere. Furthermore, in the *ST*, he uses other phrases like "analogy of proportion," "analogy of imitation" and "analogy of participation," all of which are rooted in some form of intrinsic analogy.[112]

The key in all these forms of analogy is the *causal relationship* on which they are based. Effects are direct products of causes, which are never in potential but always in actuality. All agents cause only insofar as they are in action, and all causes are in act only insofar as what they produce is their effect. Thus an examination of the effect yields some aspect of the cause and resembles the cause in that these effects receive it from the cause. Aquinas, as we have seen, divides these cause-effect-resemblances into univocal causes, equivocal causes and analogous causes.[113] Univocal causes have effects of the same species as the cause, while equivocal causes have effects of different species but the same genus. Analogous causes have effects that only resemble their causes, without being of the same species or genus. Transcendental perfections, such as goodness, wisdom and being, may be shared between analogous cause and effect, but the effects will differ in the specific formal perfections because all analogous causes ascribed to God possess these perfections "in a more eminent way."[114]

In his commentary on the *Liber de causis* Aquinas writes,

> Dionysius, however, corrects this position [i.e., Proclus with the Neoplatonists calling secondary causes "gods"] when they assert that the separate forms, which they call "Gods," exist in succession, so that one would be *per se*

---

[111]Causal immanence is the core of Aquinas's understanding of analogy. For a recent argument of this case see C. Davis and P. A. Riches, "Metanoia: A Theological Praxis of Revolution," in Creston Davis, John Milbank and Slavoj Žižek, eds., *Theology and the Political: The New Debate* (Durham, NC: Duke University Press, 2005), pp. 22-51.

[112]See Aquinas, *Super Boethium De Trinitate*, q. 2, art. 27, where he invokes causal eminence as a basis for an analogy of proportion.

[113]See Aquinas, *Super Boethium De Trinitate*, q. 2, art. 1, 8; *ST* I, q. 13; *Quaestiones disputatae De potentia Dei*, ed. Raymund Spiazzi (Taurini: Domus Editorialis Marietti, 1953), q. 7, art. 5.

[114]See Aquinas, *Expositio in Dionysium De divinis nominibus* cap. 18, lect. 1; *Liber de causis*, lect. 35.1.

goodness, another *per se* being, another *per se* life, and so on. . . . For it must be said that all of these are essentially the first cause of all things itself, from which things participate all such perfections. . . . How this can be he [Proclus] shows subsequently from the fact that, since God is being itself and the very essence of goodness, whatever belongs to the perfection of goodness and being belongs essentially to him as a whole, so that he is the essence of life, wisdom, power and the rest.[115]

Again this preserves the idea that a perfection exists in the primary cause in a "more eminent way." Aquinas nowhere defines precisely what he means by "a more eminent way," but we may ascertain from the *ST* that he means, following Augustine and Pseudo-Dionysius, that the eminence of perfection in God is its relation to divine simplicity. The identity of perfection with simplicity is its immanence, while the identity of a perfection's multiplicity is its presence imperfectly in an effect.[116] Elsewhere, in the commentaries on Boethius's *De Trinitate* and Pseudo-Dionysius's *De divinis nominibus,* analogy is a mode of discovery or a principle of logic, but principally the passage just cited points to our understanding of analogy as a similarity between God and the world. In each case it is CER in which a nonunivocal-nonequivocal form of analogy is used to describe the relation of the effect to its cause.[117] It remains the basic ontological control in his description of analogy in the *ST* and the *Compendium Theologiae*, to which we can now turn.

Analogy in the Summa Theologiae *and* Compendium Theologiae. Since the composition of Aquinas's great work, the *ST*, finished around 1272, not long before his death, it has been considered his most authoritative work by the Church. Thus what it had to say on matters of faith, philosophy and theological method should be accorded the utmost care and attention. However, in Thomistic scholarship such has not always been the case, especially in respect to what he has to say about analogy.[118] The *ST* is of course the final testimony to the fact that there is no unified theory of analogy in

---

[115]St. Thomas Aquinas, *Commentary on the Book of Causes*, trans. V. A. Guagliardo (Washington, D.C.: Catholic University of America Press, 1996), prop. 3, p. 22.

[116]See *ST* I, q. 17.

[117]Aquinas, *Super Boethium De Trinitate*, q. 4, art. 2; q. 6, art. 3; *Expositio in Dionysium De divinis nominibus*, cap. 2, lect. 3-4.

[118]The most standard and widely accepted for hundreds of years was that of Cajetan's, *Analogy of Names*.

Aquinas's works. "Rather he made do with a few vague remarks and that grammatical astuteness which [Burrell has] suggested as a replacement for intuition. Others, of course, organized those remarks of his into a theory, and that is what Aquinas has become famous for."[119] One could not have said it better than David Burrell here. In fact, he goes even further, issuing a rather severe indictment of those who see in Aquinas "a Catholic doctrine of the analogy of being": "The misunderstanding resulted in the usual way: The philosophical activity of the master became doctrine in the hands of his disciples. Constructing a theory turned analogy into a method and gave the discussion a particular turn: Does it work? The nearly unanimous conclusion has been that it does not."[120] We would do well to keep this in mind as we approach Aquinas's few comments on analogy in the *ST*. If there is no formal theory of analogy there, where one would have expected it, then we are not likely to find one elsewhere, even if we cobble together statements from all his works, as some have done.

The question of analogy in the *ST* comes up where one would expect it, in the section on the justification of the names of God in questions 13-14 of the *Prima Pars*. The very form of the question, "whether a name can be given to God?" already begs further questions. If the answer is no, why not? If the answer is yes, how so? The question is placed in the negative, not on the basis of some agnostic or atheistic interlocutor, but from within the apophatic tradition, namely Psuedo-Dionysius, who himself affirmed, according to Aquinas, that "it seems that no name can be given to God. For Dionysius says that, of Him there is neither name, nor can one be found of Him."[121] So also, it seems, that the Scriptures themselves prohibit the naming of God (Prov 30:4).[122] The context for the question is Aquinas's previous discussion with respect to the relationship between God and creation as a relationship of CER, in which he concludes that

> our natural knowledge of God begins from sense. Hence, our natural knowledge can only go so far in that it is led by sensible things. But our mind

---

[119]David Burrell, *Aquinas: God and Action* (Notre Dame, IN: University of Notre Dame Press, 1979), p. 55 n. 1.

[120]Ibid.

[121]*ST* I, q. 13, art. 1.

[122]*ST* I, q. 13, art. 1. The text asks a rhetorical question: "What is His [God's] name? Surely you know?" with the expected answer being that no one knows.

can go as far as to see the essence of God, because the sensible effects of God do not equal the power of God as their cause. Hence from the knowledge of sensible things the whole power of God cannot be known; nor therefore can his essence be seen. But, because they are his effects and depend upon their cause, we can be led from them so far as we know whether God exists, and to know of Him what must necessarily belong to Him, as the first cause of all things, exceeding all things caused by him.[123]

Here, in question 13, we have moved well beyond "whether God exists" and must now deal with "what must necessarily belong to him as the first cause." The problem is one of language, and precisely the creatureliness of language. All our language is configured through the senses and flows out of that experience. There are, as per Dionysius, no words or images that can do justice to God, who is above and beyond all experience and language. All we have to go on, apart from Scripture, is the knowledge that God exists as first cause, and since experience tells us we may know somewhat of a cause from its effects, this principle must be applicable to God, who is the cause of all things. Here Aquinas must separate out God's being, his existence in the unity of existence and essence, from his operations.

This treatment of the question of naming God follows the Neoplatonic pattern in terms of epistemology, of how we may know God. They, the operations, correspond to the differing levels of reality because they represent a division of substance. Thus a related question for Aquinas is "whether any names applied to God are predicated of Him substantially?"[124] The task of relating God's essence to his operations, as cause to effect, is not an easy one for Aquinas. To achieve it he relies in part on Aristotle's tentative division between primary and secondary act in the *De anima*. It would seem that our knowledge of the existence of God as first cause is already a predicate we make before we know the rules of predication, as though we are "thrown into the water" before we are given "swimming lessons."[125] Aquinas offers the following rationale as an answer to this perplexing problem: "It ought to be said that according to the philosopher, words are signs of concepts and concepts are likenesses of things. And so

---

[123]*ST* I, q. 13, res.
[124]*ST* I, q. 13, art. 2.
[125]The question is from Aristotle's *De anima* II.4; see Hankey, *God in Himself*, p. 81.

it is clear that words refer to things signified by means of an intellectual conception. And therefore, according as something is able to be known by an intellect, it is able to be named by us."[126]

Since, therefore, the intellect knows a cause from its effect, it can know by means of reason that there is not an infinite order of causes but, necessarily, some prime cause. Clearly, then, predication follows an ontological-epistemological route. Predication is dependent on knowledge, and knowledge on being. "The structure of God's being and the structure through which it is known ought then to be reflected in—indeed determinative of—what is said of him."[127] The logic of question 13 flows directly from his consideration of the simplicity of God as "God in Himself." The question begins as follows, "Because in the above we have considered God in Himself, it remains to consider how he is in our knowledge, that is how he is known from creatures."[128] So it is proper that he states in question 13, "Having considered what pertains to the knowledge of God, we ought to proceed to the treatment of the divine names; for everything is named by us as we know it."[129] Thus names belong to God as part of his perfection. The names signify God in that "they more properly belong to God than to creatures." We will recall the argument from the *SCG* that the names belong to God in a prior sense and to his effects *per posterius*.[130] These words are not mere synonyms, and neither are they to be applied univocally or equivocally. They are analogically applied to God first and then to creatures, through the order of knowing and naming it from the creature, "in the way a principle is related to an inferior cause." Thus, as far as what is signified through the name is concerned, "they are more primarily predicates of God than of creatures."[131] The order of relation, as we have seen in the *SCG*, is from God to the creature and not vice versa.

> Since therefore God is outside the whole order of creation, and all creatures are ordered to Him, and not conversely, it is manifest that creatures are really related to God Himself, whereas in God there is no real relation to creatures

---

[126]Ibid.
[127]Hankey, *God in Himself*, p. 82.
[128]*ST* I, q. 13, pr.
[129]*ST* I, q. 13.
[130]*ST* I, q. 13, art. 2.
[131]*ST* I, q. 13, art. 6.

but a relation only in idea, in as much as creatures are referred to Him. Thus, there is nothing to prevent these names which import relation to the creature from being predicated of God temporally, not by reason of any change in Him but by reason of the change of the creature.[132]

Thus in the words "God is wise" we do not simply mean that God is the cause of wisdom in creation. Rather we mean God essentially is wisdom. The name "wisdom" expresses God insofar as our intellect knows him to be such. He is this by virtue of an intrinsic relation, not a mere extrinsic relation. Thus the limitation is placed on the perfection from the side of creation. These perfections are in God immanently, from eternity, but we know them from his effects imperfectly.

This is also due to the fact that, as images of him, we are imperfect, in image and knowledge. In this respect both Pseudo-Dionysius and John Damscene are, as "Holy Doctors of the Church," correct. "Negative names applied to God or signifying His relation to creatures manifestly do not at all signify substance, but rather express the distance of the creature from Him, or His relation to something else, or rather, the relation of creatures to Himself."[133] In this case, these positive and negative predicates belong to God formally but are signified imperfectly. Aquinas distinguishes two principles for such predication. There must be a perfection signified and a mode of signification. "As regards what is signified by these names, they belong properly to God, and more properly than they belong to the creature, and are applied primarily to Him. But as regards the mode of signification, they do not properly and strictly apply to God; for their mode of signification applies to creatures."[134] The reason for these two modes of distinction is that "our knowledge of God is derived form the perfections which flow from Him to creatures, which perfections are in God in a more eminent way than in creatures. Now an intellect apprehends them as they are in creatures, and as it apprehends them it signifies them by names."[135]

Article 4 of question 13 offers the same arguments against synonymity of terms applied to God as in the *SCG* and *De potentia*, but in a condensed

---

[132]*ST* I, q. 13, art. 7.
[133]*ST* I, q. 13, art. 2.
[134]*ST* I, q. 13, art. 3.
[135]Ibid.

fashion. Aquinas's primary point appears to be that the perfections are not all reducible to a single meaning so that it would be redundant to say "God is good" or "God is wise" and so on.

> But even according to what was said above (article 2), that these names signify the divine substance, although in an imperfect manner, it is also clear from what has been said, that they have diverse meanings. For the idea signified by the name is the conception in the intellect of the thing signified by the name. But our intellect, since it knows God from creatures, in order to understand God, forms conceptions proportional to the perfections flowing from God to creatures, which perfections pre-exist in God unitedly and simply, whereas in creature they are received, divided and multiplied.[136]

So Aquinas, after a Neoplatonic fashion, concludes, "Therefore although the names applied to God signify one thing, still they signify that under many and different aspects, they are not synonymous."[137]

This leads Aquinas to the most crucial problem with respect to divine predication, expressed in article 5 of question 13. It has to do directly with the nature of theological language and its justification. It is, of course, the problem of univocity. Again, Aquinas strains to distinguish his position of analogical predication as a middle way between univocity and equivocity. We must keep in mind that for Aquinas, the epistemological grounds for the knowledge of God has previously been established on the basis of a CER already present to the intellect. This is the very same basis which not only Aristotle but especially the Neoplatonists have invoked for theology. Aquinas's argument here mirrors what we have already encountered in book I, chapter 31, of the SCG and in De potentia but with some significant alterations with respect to proportion. We may also say the same for his discussion of analogy in De veritate.[138] There is one important addition to his argument in the ST, against univocity, however, that receives scant attention elsewhere, and that is his rooting of predication in the absolute simplicity of God. Says Aquinas, "Univocal predication is impossible between God and creatures. The reason for this is that every effect which is not an adequate result of the power of the efficient cause, receives the similitude of the agent

---

[136]ST I, q. 13, art. 6.
[137]ST I, q. 13, art. 4.
[138]Aquinas, De veritate, q. 1, art. 4, ad. 4.

not in its full degree."[139] Thus far this adds nothing new to Aquinas's argument against univocity, but he continues with an important addition to his argument elsewhere, stating: "But in a measure that falls short, so that what is divided and multiplied in the effects resides in the agent simply, and in the same manner . . . all perfections pre-exist in God unitedly."[140]

Here again Aquinas runs up against the Neoplatonic problem of the one and the many. How, if not univocally, may we at least think of the multitude of perfections as witnessing to one simple divine essence? The solution does not really remove the potential for univocal predication. The following conclusion he gives makes this internal contradiction abundantly clear.

> Thus, when any term expressing perfection is applied to a creature, it signifies that perfection distinct in idea [in the mind of God] from other perfections; as for instance, by this term "wise" applied to a man, we signify some perfection distinct from a man's essence, and distinct from his power and existence and from all similar things; whereas when we apply it to God, we do not mean to signify anything distinct from His essence, or power, or existence. Thus, also this term wise applied to men in some degree circumscribes and comprehends the things signified; whereas this is not the case when applied to God.[141]

But of course this means that the term is incomprehensible; that is, the concept exceeds the capacity of the name to signify it. So it is said of a human one way and of God in a way that is supereminent to the same signification, thus it is not said univocally. The question as to whether Aquinas has sufficiently safeguarded himself here against a univocal understanding, or at the least against the idea that without a univocity of thought his theory of naming comes to naught, cannot be pursued at length. But we need merely note that Aquinas saw the problem, that is, that the mediation of the

---

[139]*ST* I, q. 13, art. 4. In *De veritate* Aquinas writes, "In those things which are related as cause and that which is caused, there does not obtain, properly speaking, a reciprocal likeness. We call the statue of Hercules similar to Hercules but not conversely" (*De veritate*, q. 4, art. 4, ad. 2). See also Aquinas's comments on causal proportion-proportionality in *Scriptum super Sententiis* III, distinction 1, q. 1, ad. 3; *De veritate*, q. 23, art. 7, ad. 9; *Super Boethium De Trinitate*, q. 1, art. 2, ad. 3; *ST* I, q. 13, art. 1, ad. 4; *Quaestiones quodlibetales*, quodlibet X, q. 8, art. 17, ad. 1; *Scriptum super Sententiis* IV, distinction 49, q. 2, art. 1, arg. 6, ad. 6. Aquinas never tires of pointing this out.

[140]*ST* I, q. 13, art. 4.

[141]*ST* I, q. 13, art. 5.

cause may be known, but not the mediator per se. For him the solution was
to be found in analogy, understood in a certain way. Scotus will say that this
way can work only under the conditions of univocity.

Here for the first time Aquinas links all the concepts that have predomi-
nated in other works. The idea of proportion leads to, but is understood in
relation to, an analogy of one to another, intrinsic versus extrinsic analogy,
and participation in perfection. These are all tied together in a basic understanding of CER. But the argument is nuanced, and embellished by new
terminology, such as "mode of the community of idea." Clearly the statement
is written in a much more methodological and programmatic format and
has the hint of a formal theory about it. Contrary to the way of univocity or
equivocity, Aquinas affirms that all names must be used of God "analogously," that is, "according to proportion."[142] There are two ways in which
names may be used analogously, apart and from divine predication, that is,
as rules of usage: "either according as many things are proportionate to one
[*multa habent proportionem ad unum*] . . . or according as one thing is proportionate to another [*unum habet proptorionem ad alterum*]."[143] In the first
case he illustrates it as follows: "thus for example 'healthy' is predicated of
medicine and urine in relation and in proportion to health of a body, of
which the former is the sign (urine) and the latter the cause (medicine)." In
the second case he uses the same example. That is, "'healthy' is said of medicine and animal, since medicine is the cause of health in the animal body."
Thus he concludes:

> And in this way some things are said of God and the creatures analogically
> and not in a purely equivocal nor a purely univocal sense. For we can name
> God only from creatures. Thus whatever is said of God and creatures, is said
> according to the relation of a creature to God as its principle and cause,
> wherein all perfections of things pre-exist excellently. Now this mode of the
> community of idea is a mean between pure equivocation and simple univo-
> cation. For in analogies the idea is not, as in univocals, one and the same, yet
> it is totally diverse as in equivocals; but a term which is thus used in a multiple
> sense signifies various proportions to some one thing.[144]

---

[142]Ibid.
[143]He bases this on Rom 1:18-21.
[144]ST I, q. 13, art. 5.

In comparison to what we have cited from Aquinas concerning analogy above, it is immediately clear that this is a much more densely packed definition. As per the *De potentia* and the *SCG*, the division of analogy appears to be the same, that of analogies of one to many and of one to another. But now the word *proportion* is inserted in each case. Again, the preferred mode that will serve the theological naming of God best is the analogy of one to another, or as Aquinas puts it here, "according as one thing is proportionate to another."[145] In the *De potentia* and the *SCG*, Aquinas uses two different illustrations for each case of analogy. In the case of many to one he uses the health, medicine, urine example; in the second he tends to use the example of the predication of *being*. In each case he illustrates the different modes of predication according to a CER. In this section he uses the health, medicine, urine example of both cases. In both analogies health is caused by medicine, with urine as the sign in the first case. Urine as sign is omitted in the second case but included in the concluding statement. What connects the cause, the effect and the sign (or relation) in each case? It is not that of urine, or medicine, but that of the effect "healthy." Health is the resulting analogous name that exists between the primary analogate, medicine, and the secondary analogate, urine. This is the causal relation or resemblance they have to one another.

What form of analogy is Aquinas wishing to make clear for theology? The point, it seems, is that "health" is intrinsic to both the primary and secondary analogates.[146] In this passage, extrinsic attribution is not brought into the equation. Aquinas has already established the basis for predication as rooted in the formal participation of God in his perfections, and the imperfect participation of the creation in those perfections, as the meaning but not the essence of perfections. Extrinsic attributions would leave the names of God empty, without content and, significantly, without a causal relation or resemblance between Creator and creature. But his primary concern remains the safeguarding of absolute, transcendent simplicity and freedom, so the mode of analogy thus fits that concern. This is always his concern when applying human language to describe God, however imperfectly. The question here, then, is not, which method best enables this naming?, but, which will avoid inappropriate naming? For Aquinas this is the analogy of

---

[145] Ibid.

[146] Aquinas, *Scriptum super Sententiis* IV, distinction 49, q. 2, art. 1, ad. 7.

one to another, *analogia unius ad alterum*, or better, *unum habet propo-tionum ad alterum*. This way of analogy is a way that moves from effect to cause and designates the relation from, or via, the effect to cause. This is in concert with what Aquinas teaches about knowing God from his effects. God cannot be designated from himself as cause, so the fundamental pre-supposition of a likeness of creation to God is the only basis on which our naming of God is possible. It will also mean that, for Aquinas, there is a limitation on the number of possible predicates that may be ascribed to God, precisely because we can only know God, *per se*, from his effect.[147]

What this means for Aquinas's understanding of analogy is that anal-ogous terms, which are predicated on the basis of causal relation of resem-blance, must ultimately be attributed to God intrinsically if they are to count as knowledge of God. In himself God is an equivocal cause, but from our point of view there remains only a relation of similarity in dissimilarity between cause and effect, allowing for the necessity of intrinsic analogous attribution.[148] Thus the same thing is meant with the example of being in the second case, as per *De potentia* and *SCG*, that is intended here. The reason he uses the same example in both cases here, in distinction from "being" in the *SCG* and *De potentia*, is that the example works better in terms of iden-tifying the difference between the two.

In sum, in the *ST* the analogous naming of God's perfections is based entirely on the relation of efficient causality between God and his creatures, just as in the example the predication of "healthy" is based on a relation of efficient cause between medicine and the body. In regard to "being," however, the example that has been here removed, the predication is based on "a re-lation of inherence of accident in substance" rather than a relation of effi-cient causality. What difference has this introduced into Aquinas's argument? In the case of an analogy of "one in proportion to another," God as cause is the primary analogate, whereas the predicate is secondary. In order to avoid any confusion between the primary and secondary analogate, vis-à-vis the sameness of being, Aquinas prefers the "health" example to "being." But the effect of the argument is the same. Aquinas continues to refer to analogy throughout the *ST*, but in every case Aquinas means *analogy* in terms of its

---

[147] Aquinas, *Super Isaiam*, cap 2, lect. 2; *De veritate*, q. 1, art. 7.
[148] *ST* I, q. 4, art. 3; I, q. 8, art. 5.

classical meaning of proportion, but not in every case as a mathematical sense of proportionality, though he means this in some cases.[149]

This critical alteration in Aquinas's description of analogy is confirmed in the last of his theological treaties, the *Compendium Theologiae*, where Aquinas once again summarizes his understanding of analogy with some expansion and revision of what he has said in his primary *Summae*. Therein he claims, once again, that names applied to God and other beings are predicated analogically, "that is according to their proportion to one thing." In comparing God with creatures, "as their first origin," we may attribute to God what we see as perfections in creatures. "This clearly brings out the truth that, as regards the assigning of the names, such names are primarily predicated of creatures, in as much as the intellect that assigns the names ascends from creatures to God."[150] That is, beginning with the sensible and intuiting perfections in the sensible, *names are a mode of ascent* wherein we come to knowledge of the supersensible. In theology, according to *via negativa* there comes a point in the ascent where names must be dropped altogether. "But as regards the things signified by the name, they are primarily predicated of God, from whom the perfections descend to other things."[151] Here again we see the pattern of *exitus-reditus*, which marks the structure of the *Prima Pars* of the *ST*, repeated in the *Compendium*. We may well cite Hankey's conclusion about question 13 in his *God in Himself*, as applicable here in the *Compendium*.

---

[149]See also 2. Cf. *ST* I, q. 8, art. 5; I, q. 16, art. 6; *SCG*, bk. I, cap. 34; Aquinas, *De potentia*, q. I, art. 1; *Sententia libri Metaphysicae*, bk. 4, lect. 1; bk. 7, lect. 4. In the last citation Aquinas is responding to the passage in Aristotle's *Metaphysics*, p. 1031a, lines, 1-14, about which Aquinas concludes: "For by reason of the fact that all the other categories get the notion of being from substance, the mode of being of substance, i.e., being a what, *is therefore participated in by all the other categories according to a certain proportional likeness*; for example, we say that, just as animal is the whatness of man, in a similar fashion color is the whatness of whiteness, and number the whatness of double; and in this way we say that quality has whatness, not whatness in an unqualified sense, but a whatness of this particular kind; just as some say, for example, in speaking of non-being from a logical point of view, that non-being is, not because non-being is in an unqualified sense, but because non-being is non-being. And in a similar way quality does not have whatness in an unqualified sense, but the whatness of quality." Aquinas seems to make the relation in the similitude stronger, not weaker, and intrinsic as opposed to extrinsic.

[150]Aquinas, *Compendium Theologiae*, pars Ia, caput 27. For a recent translation of the *Compendium*, see Thomas Aquinas, *Compendium of Theology*, trans. R. J. Regan (Oxford: Oxford University Press, 2009), p. 25.

[151]Aquinas, *Compendium Theologiae*, pars Ia, caput 43.

> There is a fundamental conformity between what is maintained about the being (or non-being), knowledge and predication of the first principle [or prime analogate] in the traditions upon which Aquinas draws. Yet, they say exactly opposed things. Further, although efforts have been made to resolve the difficulty by suggesting the contrary, Thomas believes there is coherence between ontology, knowing and naming. Clearly there is a unity on the subjective side. How we name God from creatures follows from how he is known through them and this is a result of their composed unity, in all three [ontology, knowing, or naming] there is division and unity.[152]

The problem, however, is that the subjective and objective in our knowledge of transcendence must be connected directly through God's essential being. Thus in the case of the *Summae* and the *Compendium*, at any rate, "incoherence occurs because our knowledge *in via* is not this direct essential knowledge. Yet Thomas' teaching about naming God is remarkably positive. Can this be justified without dissolving the unity of ontology, psychology and logic?"[153] Or, as Kant would eventually ask, on this basis, is *metaphysics* even possible? His answer is, of course, the problem that all Thomists still face today.[154]

Based on this analysis of Aquinas's treatment of analogy in the *Summae*, *De potentia*, the *Compendium Theologiae* and elsewhere, we may draw the following conclusions. *First and foremost*, we may say that, for the most part, in the *Summae* analogy has significant metaphysical implications in that the ontological basis of analogy is CER, whatever form of analogy Aquinas may seem to invoke. *Second*, the most common form of analogy, but not exclusively so, seems to be the intrinsic analogy of substantial relation expressed as the analogy of one to another (*unius ad alterum*), especially where names of absolute attributes are concerned. The aim in

---

[152]Hankey, *God in Himself*, pp. 94–95.

[153]Ibid.

[154]The problem with scholastic metaphysics, which Kant uncovered in his *Critique of Pure Reason*, has been well documented since. The following works are critical in this respect: I. Kant, *Critique of Practical Reason*, trans. L. W. Beck (Indianapolis: Bobbs-Merrill, 1956); Kant, *Critique of Pure Reason*, trans. N. Kemp Smith (New York: St. Martin's Press, 1929); Kant, *Prolegomena to Any Future Metaphysics*, trans. L. W. Beck (Indianapolis: Bobbs-Merrill, 1950); Kant, *Lectures on Philosophical Theology*, trans. Allen Wood and Gertrude M. Clark (Ithaca, NY: Cornell University Press, 1978); Kant, *The Cambridge Edition of the Works of Immanuel Kant: Lectures on Metaphysics*, ed. and trans. Kanrl Ameriks and Steve Naragan (Cambridge: Cambridge University Press, 1997).

such use, however, is to place a limit on theological epistemology via analogy in order to protect the simplicity and incomprehensibility of God. *Third*, and as a consequence, Aquinas rejects, on the surface at least, univocity, equivocity and the analogy of one to the many because they may subject God to being read as part of one genus being with creation, or to separate God from the world completely without relation. Still, for all, the absolute uniqueness and simplicity of God must be protected at all costs. Thus, *fourth*, it would seem that an analogy of proportionality is also rejected, though this is less clear, especially when he does seem to equate analogy of one to another with an analogy of one in proportion to another in terms of intrinsic attribution in the *ST* and the *Compendium Theologiae*. But there are also necessary considerations in respect to the creature that any account of analogy must allow for. So, *fifth*, the names predicated of God must be meaningful in terms of their predication, however imperfectly, of the creature. If there was a mere equivocity such that all naming is dissolved into the single essence of God, then either God is only knowable as the best possible wish of finite humanity for infinity, or the names are mere anthropomorphism that witnesses to nothing sure, by way of theological knowledge. This agnosticism also holds true for an analogy of extrinsic attribution, which denies the possibility of any real, essential similarity of being. Apparently, only the analogy of one to another along the lines of an intrinsic attribution allows for the real naming of real perfections of two distinct yet similar subjects, God and the human creature. But, and here is where confusion often enters the Thomistic model, the predication is according to priority and posteriority. A predicate belongs to God in a different, qualitative and original way than it belongs, imperfectly and derivatively, to the human. Though the meaning of a predicate as applied to God must be read from the effect, as its real and substantial meaning, the predicate signifies something real about the essence of God that nevertheless cannot be essentially in the effect. In this way, Aquinas attempts to do justice to both humanity and God as subjects in relation, but also, we think more importantly, in absolute distinction. There are other predicates than the supraessential, of course, and these also are participated between God and the creature and may be known, via priority and posteriority, by analogy.

These are the main features of Aquinas's doctrine of analogy, but, given
the diversity of his expressions and the myriad texts in which he says
other things, we cannot call this a "final theory of analogy" in Aquinas. It
is certainly not an "analogy of being" yet. But of course Cajetan would
change this perception of Aquinas in an important way with his *The
Analogy of Names*. But before we get to this, we need to discuss briefly the
philosophical, ontological, henological and epistemological under-
pinning of Aquinas's understanding of analogy thus far.[155]

The philosophical presuppositions in Aquinas's use of analogy. The very
first metaphysical-ontological category to consider is Aquinas's underlying
cosmology, which, through the principle of CER, is the basis not only of his
understanding of analogy but of being (*esse*) as well. Analogy serves Aquinas
in distinguishing theologically how we may transfer terms that designate
aspects of our knowledge of God from creation, that is, the works of God,
to God himself. As we have stated, for Aquinas it is axiomatic that creation
is the effect of a divine cause and therefore reflects this cause. While Aquinas
follows Aristotle in epistemological terms, that is, that knowledge comes via
sensory intuition of the universe as it presents itself, it is also merely a
starting place for the necessary movement to a higher form of intuition,
which is endemic to nature and mind itself. Space does not permit a full
exposition of Aquinas's understanding of form and matter, in potentiality
and actuality, but this Aristotelian explanation for existence of things, that
form comes to matter as actuality to potentiality, is at the base of Aquinas's
doctrine of creation out of nothing, *creatio ex nihilo*.[156] The relation of potentiality to actuality always pertains to how matter contains form and is
designed to explain how things come into existence with respect to constancy and change. How does motionless form relate to changing matter?
Matter is only ever potential, with the capacity to receive form. Form is ever
and always essential actuality. It is the power inherent in the possibility of

---

[155]The primary philosophical principles influencing Aquinas's development of analogy include
concepts such as act and potency, attribution, causality, effect, eminence, equivocity, essence,
likeness-unlikeness (similarity-dissimilarity), matter and form, metaphysics, participation,
perfection(s), predication, priority-posteriority (*prius et posterius*), potency, proportion, proportionality, substance, accident and univocity (Hankey, *God in Himself*, pp. 8-9).

[156]See Aquinas, *De Principiis Naturae* cap. 1-2; *SCG*, bk. II, cap. 39; *Quaestiones quodlibetales*,
quodlibet VII, q. 1, art. 3; see also Bobik, *Aquinas on Matter and Form*, pp. 183-99.

all existents.[157] Aquinas applies this distinction to all temporal existents.[158] All created things receive their being from God and are therefore, like matter and form, related as potentiality to actuality. God is himself *actus purus*, as such. All other actuality is secondary.

As we have already seen in our treatment of Aristotle above, Aquinas here adopts Aristotle's principle that gives matter actuality and being (*esse*). The form is the very *actus*, as the principle that emanates from the one, and gives *esse* to matter. As such, actuality—form—is perfect, whereas matter—potentiality—is imperfect. So then, the form is the likeness to God, which exists in all things. The point of the joining of form to matter, creating existents, is what Aquinas calls the *ordo*, or order of things.[159] There is in all creation, according to Aquinas, a double order in the process of creation. All existents are reciprocally ordered to one another, while all of them fulfill God's single purpose for creation. God's *ordo* is also his *decretum*, which is the primary and underlying order of all things, and therefore the governing principle of creation.[160]

The human intellect, as active agent intellect, is a principle he adopts from Aristotelian-Neoplatonic thought and always follows this foundational *ordo*, the ultimate purpose of which is God himself, the highest good.[161] Thus creation is essentially the expression of an order in which God goes out of himself, in a procession of degrees, and returns to himself by that same order. Therefore the *ordo* is equivalent to God's own *exitus-reditus*.[162] In the process of the return of all to God, there is a striving, among agent intellects, toward likeness through knowledge, again ordered by degrees of relative existence. Clearly the basis, even of his doctrine of *creatio ex nihilo*, is heavily indebted to the classical principle of CER, taught in primitive form in Plato's *Timaeus* but later perfected in Aristotle and Neoplatonism. The effect returns to the cause because it already possesses the similarity to the cause. The aspiration to likeness in created things for or toward their Creator is exactly parallel to

---

[157] Aquinas, *Sententia libri Metaphysicae*, bk. I, lect. 1.

[158] Aquinas, *Sententia libri Metaphysicae*, bk. I, lect. 15.3; *SCG*, bk. III, cap. 7.

[159] *SCG*, bk. I, cap. 42-43; bk. III, cap. 22-23; Aquinas, *Sententia libri Metaphysicae*, bk. I, lect. 12; *Expositio in Dionysium De divinis nominibus*, caput 4, lect. 6.

[160] *SCG*, bk. II, cap. 24. See Lyttkens, *Analogy Between God and the World*; see also *SCG*, bk. I, cap. 42.

[161] Aquinas, *Super Boethium De Trinitate*, pars. 1-2.

[162] So also Proclus, *Elements of Theology*, propositions 31, 33, 35; see also Plotinus, *Enneades* VI, 7, 2; *Expositio in Dionysium De divinis nominibus*, caput 4, lect. 3.

the classical doctrine of form to matter and its return. Augustine's *De Trinitate* is an example par excellence of the theological appropriation of this principle. The goal is henological, in the sense of absolute unity. All form-possessing existents are in relation toward unity.[163] This is the end toward which creation is ordered. God is, as such, the cause and end (*telos*) of creation. The task in existence is to know this order and to communicate it, downward and laterally, according to degree, and the only possible means for this is analogy. This is an analogy of effect to cause according to the *ordo* of creation.[164]

On the level of creation, then, and with respect to Aquinas's doctrine of *creatio ex nihilo*, we note that with creation *ex nihilo*, Aquinas sought, as did Augustine, to give an absolute beginning to creation in order to distinguish it from the Creator. This distinction was necessary for Aquinas because previous cosmologies, like those of Aristotle, Plato and the Neoplatonists, often failed to adequately distinguish God from creation, positing either an eternity of matter or a monistic system of thought. Obviously Aquinas, as did Augustine before him, felt the need to reinterpret the process of the coming-to-be of creation in order to safeguard not only the absolute difference of God from creation, but also the ontological perspicuity of creation itself. It remains a question of some debate as to the relative success of both Augustine and Aquinas in maintaining this distinction. But this is a question beyond the present scope of this study, though it does indirectly impinge on precisely how analogy has been historically understood. Two questions become important for Aquinas in this process: the existence and eternity of matter, and the origin and eternal existence of "divine ideas."

The question that most concerns us here is the latter, though the former question has no small implications for Aquinas's theology and understanding of analogy as well. In his exhaustive and excellent treatment of the history and development of "divine ideas," especially as the concept comes to Aquinas and is used by him, Vivian Boland contends that the notion of ideas in God, of all possible and real existents, "remains essential in [Aqui-

---

[163]*ST* I, q. 47, art. 3; II, q. 17, art. 4; Aquinas, *Expositio in Dionysium De divinis nominibus*, caput 4, lect. 1.
[164]Aquinas, *Super Boethium De Trinitate*, pars. I, 2-3; *SCG*, bk. I, cap. 33.

nas's] treatments of central theological themes." This underlines the necessary place the notion of divine ideas has for Aquinas. This is particularly so with respect to his theological epistemology in connection with the knowledge of God, and the certainty of speech about God. Part of the reason for its importance in Aquinas's corpus had to do with how one may speak of simplicity through a multiplicity of terms. "The question of simplicity and plurality thereby raised is not due simply to the limitations of human language in speaking of God. The divine essence [in Aquinas's thought] really is imitable in the myriad of ways in which God knows it to be imitable."[165] Therefore, Boland concludes, "for Aquinas it is necessary to speak of ideas in God in two senses, as a principle of knowledge and as exemplar cause."[166] Here, as we have seen with Plato and the Neoplatonists, "divine idea" and exemplar cause are connected through a CER, in that "because God's effects pre-exist [as divine ideas] in Him *secundum modum intelligibilim* (according to the mode of intelligence), the divine essence which is identical with the divine intelligence [mind] is *similitude omnium rerum* (a similarity in all things)."[167] In respect to analogy this exemplar causality is the ground of possibility to speak of God on the basis of his effects. This exemplar causality in connection with the divine idea is a philosophical principle implicit in Plato and explicit in Neoplatonism.

But to make exemplar causality work, one must assume that there is more than mere similitude between God's essence as cause and his effect as exemplar. Here there is a virtual identity between effect and cause when effect is understood to preexist in the mind of God. Thus, "his essence is the principle of everything that is made. For the Dionysian vision particularly the exemplars are the perfections of life, intelligence, being and goodness, divine attributes in which God, as the creative source and cause of all things, enables his creatures to participate."[168] So also then participation, a further philosophical principle from Platonism, becomes essential as a modality of naming, though, as Gregory Doolan recently pointed out,

---

[165]Vivian Boland, *Ideas in God According to Saint Thomas Aquinas*, Studies in the History of Christian Thought 69 (Leiden: Brill, 1996), p. 233.
[166]Ibid., p. 234; *ST* I, q. 15, art. 1.
[167]Boland, *Ideas in God*, p. 234.
[168]Ibid.

there are some differences between Aquinas and Plato on participation.[169] It is clear, according to Boland, however, that Plato remains Aquinas's most important source for his theory of exemplar causes and divine ideas, in that, as with Plato's cosmology, "God's bestowal of being and God's knowledge reach to the last and least of things and the divine ideas must, somehow, extend as far."[170] Boland affirms that this concept was received by Aquinas, through a combination of Neoplatonic-Dionysian sources and the Augustinian tradition.[171]

Summary. Both notions, exemplar causality and participation, are central to Aquinas's understanding of analogy, as particularly the work of Cornelio Fabro, Louis Bertrand Geiger, M. D. Chenu, Rudi te Veldi and others has demonstrated.[172] Clearly Aquinas draws these central ideas from Pseudo-Dionysius and the Proclan tradition adopted therein. Similarity, resemblance and likeness, as well as dissimilarity, unlikeness and difference, all are the stock and trade language of theological naming in Pseudo-Dionysius's *Divine Names*. Aquinas, through the concept of "divine ideas," as an aspect of the agent intellect, uses these notions to demonstrate positively how the many may speak of the one, while at the same time emphasizing its limitations. "Where Plato held for formal causality and univocal predication between idea and the thing, St. Thomas departs from the Platonist tradition by regarding efficient causality as fundamental, though still including final and exemplary causality properly understood, and by developing a theory of analogical predication."[173] These Neoplatonic conceptions, as Fabro points out, "[make] it possible to pass from finite to infinite being through analogical discourse, which has in participation, its beginning,

---

[169]Ibid., p. 19. See also Gregory T. Doolan, *Aquinas on the Divine Ideas and Exemplar Causes* (Washington, D.C.: The Catholic University of America Press, 2008), p. 195.

[170]Boland, *Ideas in God*, p. 134.

[171]See also Plato, *Parmenides* 130b-d.

[172]See Boland, *Ideas in God*, p. 259. See also Cornelio Fabro, *Participation et Causalite selon S. Thomas d'Aquin* (Paris: Louvain, 1961); Fabro, "The Intensive Hermeneutics of Thomistic Philosophy: The Notion of Participation," *Review of Metaphysics* 27 (1974): 449-91; Fabro, "Platonism, Neo-Platonism and Thomism: Convergencies and Divergencies," *Neo Scholastic* 44 (1970): 69-100; Fabro, "The Overcoming of the Neoplatonic Triad of Being, Life, and Intellect by Saint Thomas Aquinas," in Dominic J. O'Meara, ed., *Neoplatonism and Christian Thought* (London: Variorum Press, 1982), pp. 97-108, 250-55; L. B. Geiger, O.P., "Dissimilitude, Transcendence et Perfection du Principe Divin. Aperies et Solutions," *Dialogue* (1962): 17-35; John L. Farthing, "The Problem of Divine Exemplarity in St Thomas," *The Thomist* 49 (1985): 183-222.

[173]Boland, *Ideas in God*, p. 260.

middle and conclusion. Thus, the semantics of being are tied up with the tradition of analogy in a way that makes analogy an essential ingredient to a metaphysics of being."[174] This is a conclusion to which scholars such as Lyttkens, Klubertanz and others have also come to in respect to Aquinas's doctrine of analogy.

Much more could be said directly from Aquinas himself in this respect, but aspects of this discussion now move us on to the historical features of the interpretation of Aquinas's doctrine of analogy, where we will clearly see that sometimes more and less was made of this metaphysical attachment to analogy in Aquinas, sufficient to muddy the waters and cause considerable concern over the so-called Catholic doctrine of analogy. We are now in a position to see why Protestants, epitomized by Barth, could not adopt such a conception of analogy as a mode of theological speech, proposing instead an *analogy of faith*, christologically grounded. But before we get to this chapter, a basic summary of the problematic features of analogy as concieved along these lines will help to solidify the need for an alternative approach.

MEDIEVAL APPROPRIATIONS OF AQUINAS'S USE OF ANALOGY

We are now in a position to question any conception of a normative principle of Catholic theology called the analogy of being. To solidify the case against such an assumption, an analysis of the emergence of the very concept *analogia entis* is in order. It would seem that even in Aquinas the concept of the *analogia entis* was more often than not either undefined or defined as a philosophically inspired metaphysics of being on the basis of which existed a theological epistemology. Late medieval theology followed Aquinas in dividing theological language into univocal forms of predication on the one hand, in the philosophical analysis of Scotus, and analogical predication as a middle way between univocity and equivocity, on the other, in the foundational interpretation of Aquinas, historically interpreted to be represented in Cajetan's *The Analogy of Names*. This set in place a mode of theological speaking that became the single most influential method of analogy from Aquinas to

---

[174]Ibid.

Suarez, though by no means the only one.[175] The concept came to be known formally as the *analogia entis* therafter.

This was a formative period for Catholic theology that eventually saw the rise of Molinism on the one hand and Jesuitism on the other in late medieval theology, both of which traded heavily on the Dominican master Cajetan's interpretation of Aquinas.[176] It is therefore no surprise that the Catholic Church has since had to contend with the inner tensions of Dominican theology, which, on the one hand, wants a less synergistic reading of Aquinas, and, on the other hand, a Jesuistic-Molinist theology, which wants a more synergistic reading of their master.[177] This state of affairs in Catholic theology persisted in the early twentieth century and was a major reason why Barth and other Protestants were not able to see in Catholic theology a use of analogy that did not somehow involve itself in a totalizing, synergistic metaphysics incipient in what they understood as the "analogy of being."

Two late medieval theologians, Fransisco Suárez and another Dominican, Sylvester of Ferrara, among others, attempted to correct this Jesuistic-Molinist misinterpretation by reviewing and "correcting" Cajetan's view of Aquinas's doctrine of analogy. However, as Lyttkens and Klubertanz's analysis of the history of analogy clearly points out, neither work actually corrected Cajetan in the direction of a flat contradiction. Rather, both defined Cajetan's view along the lines of the analogy of "intrinsic attribution,"

---

[175]Hochschild offers a new "paradigm" for reading Cajetan's *The Analogy of Names*, in which he suggests that rather than trying to systematically describe Aquinas's thinking on analogy, Cajetan was more concerned about semantic issues that had arisen during his debate with certain Scotistic interpretations of Aquinas. He writes, "Most of the history of interpretations of Cajetan's *De Nominum Analogia* can be described . . . as representing a more-or-less coherent 'paradigm,' approaching *De Nominum Analogia* as if it were an interpretation or systematization of Aquinas, or a generically 'Thomistic' exposition of analogy. Recent historical scholarship, and reflection on the text of *De Nominum Analogia* itself, suggested the exhaustion of that paradigm, and pointed to the emergence of a new one, which approaches *De Nominum Analogia* as a text intending to answer the particular and focused questions recapitulated here" (*Semantics of Analogy*, p. 121).

[176]See Luis De Molina and Alfred J. Freddoso, trans., *On Divine Foreknowledge*, Cornell Classics in Philosophy (repr., Ithaca, NY: Cornell University Press, 2004); Thomas P. Flint, *Divine Providence: The Molinist Account: Cornell Studies in the Philosophy of Religion* (Ithaca, NY: Cornell University Press, 2006); Linda Trinkaus Zagzebski, *Dilemma of Freedom and Foreknowledge* (repr., Oxford: Oxford University Press: 1996).

[177]Barth's concerns with synergism in the Catholic tradition and Przywara's *analogia entis* are directly connected with the theology of Luis de Molina's work on divine providence, foreknowledge and freedom of the will. See *CD* II/1, pp. 576-77; *KD* II/1, p. 551.

which turns out to be a subspecies of the analogy of proportionality, the single method of analogy that Cajetan attributes to Aquinas.[178] This is especially the case with Suárez. Thus the modern attempts to appeal to Suárez over Cajetan, in the works of Mondin, Przywara, von Balthasar and their current followers, do not solve the problem they have with Cajetan's reduction of Aquinas to a single view of analogy. In fact they are already predisposed to the metaphysics of being ingredient in the traditional view precisely because they come at it from the Jesuistic-Molinist point of view.[179] In the final analysis the appeal to a "Catholic view of the analogy of being" is just as susceptible to a synergistic metaphysics of being as Cajetan's. Furthermore, such a view is almost inevitable from the point of view of Aquinas's confused use of analogy, despite its call for a form of analogy that is, in some places, similar in expression to the Protestant concept of the analogy of faith. It will be finally suggested, though not fully defended herein, that this is largely due to the failure of Catholic theology, in its synergistic mode, to rest theological predication squarely on a christological basis.

Scotus and the problem of univocity. In their heavily criticized book, *Truth in Aquinas,* John Milbank and Catherine Pickstock undertake a reinterpretation of Aquinas in respect to univocity that, in the words of one scholar, "offers a blatant misreading of Aquinas that ignores the ordinary canons of scholarly inquiry."[180] This was particularly so in respect to their understanding of the relationship between the theology of Aquinas and that of Scotus. It would appear that, for Pickstock and Milbank, the modern denial of theology was built on an onto-theological account of the univocity of being, first formulated by Scotus but anticipated in Aquinas and formalized in Suárez. The real culprit in this mix, however, was Scotus, whose theory of the univocity of being was the true harbinger of the metaphysical death of theology and was the ground that made it possible for modernity to proclaim this death. Kant was merely its instantiation.[181] Furthermore, it was a Cajetanian understanding of the analogy of being that

---

[178]See Klubertanz, *St. Thomas Aquinas on Analogy*, pp. 17-18.

[179]See especially Barth's comments on pp. 141-46 of *CD* I/2, where he links Przywara's understanding of analogy with a Marian theology that undergirds the Catholic synergistic doctrine of *cooperation*. See esp. p. 145.

[180]John Marenbon, "Aquinas, Radical Orthodoxy and the Importance of Truth," in Wayne J. Hankey and Douglas Hedley, eds., *Deconstructing Radical Orthodoxy: Postmodern Theology, Rhetoric and Truth* (Burlington, VT: Ashgate, 2005), p. 49.

[181]See John Milbank and Catherine Pickstock, *Truth in Aquinas* (London: Routledge, 2001), chap. 3.

made this unspeakability of God possible in modernity. Meanwhile, Pickstock
and Milbank provide us with a classic case of colonization of history in the interest of a "postmodern" deconstruction of the modernist grounds for the denial
of a metaphysically conceived theology. We will not respond directly to the
question of the role of Scotus in the history of philosophy herein.[182] Others have
taken this up in recent times and continue to do so.[183] Most are highly critical of
Pickstock and Milbank. However, the place of Scotus in respect of analogy is no
small matter, and it does seem he has a crucial role to play, especially in pro-
moting a misunderstanding of Aquinas on analogy and in encouraging a view
of analogy designed to avoid Scotus's theory of univocity, but precisely magni-
fying the problem associated with it by proposing the concept of the *analogy of
being*. Thus any understanding of the emergence and possible standardization
of this concept in the Middle Ages must account for his theory of univocity.

Scotus, in many ways, marks a transition in metaphysical thought from
Aquinas to Cajetan. In the 250 years that separate Aquinas from his follower,
Cajetan, some were attempting to resolve what had become an issue of confidence with respect to analogy and its ability to provide theology with a
basis for its own naming of God, at least in terms of Aquinas's understanding
of analogy. For many years after Cajetan, his solution to the problem, by
formulating the precise nature of Aquinas's theory of analogy, remained—
and in some ways still is—the standard interpretation of the analogy of
being. But it became so precisely because of a pressing need to resolve a
problem raised by Scotus and his theory of univocity.[184] Let us look briefly

---

[182]Marenbon, "Aquinas, Radical Orthodoxy," pp. 49-50. See also Richard Cross, "Duns Scotus and
Suarez at the Origins of Modernity," in Hankey and Hedley, eds., *Deconstructing Radical Orthodoxy*, pp. 65-78; Cross, *Duns Scotus: Great Medieval Thinkers* (New York: Oxford University
Press, 1999), pp. 35-37; Cross, "Where Angels Fear to Tread: Duns Scotus and Radical Orthodoxy," *Antonianum* 76 (2001): 7-41. This of course has already been identified as a problem that
sits at the heart of Thomistic metaphysics as well. See *GMW*, pp. 265-80.

[183]See especially Catherine Pickstock, "Duns Scotus: His Historical and Contemporary Significance," *ModT* 21, no. 4 (2005): 543-74.

[184]For works by Duns Scotus, see *Philosophical Writings: A Selection*, ed. and trans. Allan B. Wolter
(Indianapolis: Hackett, 1987). This edition contains *Quaestiones super libros Metaphysicorum
Aristotelis* and *Ordinatio*. See also Richard N. Bosley and Martin M. Tweedale, eds., *Basic Issues
in Medieval Philosophy: Selected Readings Presenting the Interactive Discourses Among the Major
Figures*, 2nd ed. (Orchard Park, NY: Broadview, 1997), which contains selections from *Ordinatio, Reportatio* and *Quaestiones super libros Metaphysicorum Aristotelis*; John Duns Scotus, *God
and Creatures: The Quodlibetal Questions*, trans. Felix Alluntis and Allan B. Wolter (Washington,
D.C.: The Catholic University of America Press, 1975); Scotus, "Commentary on the Sentences,"
in Eugene R. Fairwather, ed., *A Scholastic Miscellany: Anselm to Ockham* (Philadelphia: The

at this development in order to understand more clearly Cajetan's intentions in his *De Nominum Analogia*.

In the history of theology it was the dubious contribution of Scotus to modify the transcendentals (beauty, truth, goodness, cause and the One) so as not to imply transcendence that opens up a new modality of naming God. But the foundation of this modality, that is, comparison on the basis of CER, remained the same. As far as Scotus was concerned, to relegate these terms to the meaninglessness of transcendence was to rob language of its very power to signify something real and truthful. In Scotus's opinion, terms such as *being* were already obviated if the only content we could give such a term arose from the creaturely realm, but with the claim that, based

---

Westminster Press, 1956), pp. 428-36; Scotus, "The Oxford Commentary on the Four Books of the Sentences," in *Philosophy in the Middle Ages*, ed. Arthur Hyman and James J. Walsh (Indianapolis: Hackett, 1973), pp. 555-604; Allan B. Wolter, ed., *John Duns Scotus, A Treatise on God as First Principle*, 2nd and rev. ed. (Chicago: Franciscan Herald Press, 1983). Important secondary works include: Marilyn McCord Adams, "Final Causality and Explanation of Scotus's 'De Primo Principio,'" in Chūmaru Koyama, *Nature in Medieval Thought: Some Approaches East and West*, Studien und Texte zur Geistesgeschichte des Mittelalters 73 (Leiden: Brill, 2000), pp. 153-84; Egbert Peter Bos, "A Scotistic Discussion of 'Deus est' as a *propositio per se nota*. Edition with an Introduction," *Vivarium* 33 (1995): 197-234; Boulnois Olivier, "Puissance neutre et puissance obédientielle: de l'homme à Dieu selon Duns Scot et Cajétan," in Bruno Pinchard and Saverio Ricci, eds., *Rationalisme analogique et humanisme théologique: la culture de Thomas de Vio "Il Gaetano": actes du Colloque de Naples, 1-3 novembre 1990* (Napoli: Vivarium, 1993), pp. 31-69; Oliver, "Reading Duns Scotus: From History to Philosophy," *ModT* 21 (2005): 603-8; David B. Burrell, "John Duns Scotus: The Univocity of Analogous Terms," *The Monist* 49 (1965): 639-58; Richard Cross, *Duns Scotus on God* (Aldershot, UK: Ashgate, 2004); Cross, *The Metaphysics of the Incarnation: Thomas Aquinas to Duns Scotus* (Oxford: Clarendon Press, 2002); Cecil B. Currey, *Reason and Revelation: John Duns Scotus on Natural Theology* (Chicago: Franciscan Herald Press, 1977); André De Muralt, Valentín Fernández Polanco and Francisco León, *La estructura de la filosofía política moderna: sus orígenes medievales en Escoto, Ockham y Suárez* (Tres Cantos: Ediciones Istmo, 2002); Étienne Gilson, *Jean Duns Scot: Introduction à ses positions fondamentales*, Études de philosophie médiévale 42 (Paris: Vrin, 1952); Martin Heidegger, *Die Kategorien- und Bedeutungslehre des Duns Scotus* (Tübingen: J. C. B. Mohr, 1916); Joshua P. Hochschild, "Cajetan on Scotus on Univocity," *Proceedings of the Society for Medieval Logic and Metaphysics* 7 (2007): 32-42; Wolfhart Pannenberg, *Analogie und Offenbarung: Eine kritische Untersuchung zur Geschichte des Analogiebegriffs in der Lehre von der Gotteserkenntnis* (Göttingen: Vandenhoeck & Ruprecht, 2007; see esp. chap. 6: "Die kritische Auflösung der hochscholastischen Analogielehre und die These von der Univokation des Seins bei Duns Scotus," pp. 123-80); Catherine Pickstock, "Modernity and Scholasticism: A Critique of Recent Invocations of Univocity," *Antonianum* 78 (2003): 3-46; Michael Schulz, *Sein und Trinität: Systematische Erörterungen zur Religionsphilosophie G. W. F. Hegels im ontologiegeschichtlichen Rückblick auf J. Duns Scotus und I. Kant und die Hegel-Rezeption in der Seinsauslegung und Trinitätstheologie bei W. Pannenberg, E. Jüngel, K. Rahner und H. U. v. Balthasar*, Münchener theologische Studien 2, 53 (St. Ottilien: EOS-Verlag, 1997); Thomas Williams, ed., *The Cambridge Companion to Duns Scotus* (Cambridge: Cambridge University Press, 2003).

on the priority and posteriority of substance, it was knowledge of the divine at the same time. For Scotus, "being as being," or being itself, is the only true object of the human mind, and not just the study of the essence of things as they exist.[185] His *Treatise on God as First Principle* opens with precisely this affirmation.

> O Lord our God, true teacher that you are, when Moses your servant asked you for your name, that he might proclaim you to the children of Israel, you, knowing what the mortal mind could grasp of you, replied: "I am who I am," thus disclosing your blessed name. You are truly what it means to be, you are the whole of what it means to exist. Thus, if it be possible for me, I should like to know by way of demonstration. Help me then O Lord, as I investigate how much our natural reason can learn about the true being which you are if we begin with the being which you have predicated of yourself.[186]

Note well here that the being that is the object of study is not being in its creaturely modality but being revealed, or "the being God predicated of himself," that is, "God himself."

If this is the order of the knowledge of being, and therefore also the basis of naming, then "being" must be a univocal predicate since only it can encompass God and the creature, substance, and accident. Clearly the *ST* can be interpreted this way given its starting point as *De Deo*. The capacity of such transcendentals as being to apply across all categories cannot be accounted for merely on the basis of analogy, which only yields abstract, indirect and ambiguous knowledge. "For Scotus, therefore, it must be that such terms refer to something ingredient in every other notion."[187] That is, the application is univocal. Such is also the case with words like *good* and *cause*. "Now there are two properties of God which have reference to creatures, one is eminence in goodness, the other is causality."[188] But eminence (the idea that God is goodness itself) cannot be divided. Causality, however, appears to be diffused from primary to secondary causes. "According to some its divisions are: exemplar, efficient and final cause. Such [Aquinas?]

---

[185]See Scotus, *Treatise on God as First Principle* 1.2.
[186]Ibid.
[187]David Burrell, *Analogy and Philosophical Language* (New Haven, CT: Yale University Press, 1973), pp. 96-97.
[188]As cited in ibid., p. 97.

say that exemplar cause gives a thing its essential being. But I say here . . . that exemplar cause is not to be numbered alongside of efficient cause, for it is only as a concomitant factor of an efficient cause, that the exemplar in the mind of the artisan gives any being to a thing."[189] In short, cause, like goodness and being, is also a univocal concept. The reason is that an exemplar cause is essentially the same as a formal cause, "in view of its effects," and thus a principle of eminence, so more than mere cause. "For the more excellent being contains virtually the forms of other things and contains their unity."[190] That is, as we observed with Aristotle's tendency to collapse all other causes to formal cause, so also must a univocal predication of causal eminence be formal cause. As such, human intellect can, by means of univocals, have direct rather than merely indirect access to both the phenomena and the noumena. If there is a property that distinguishes God's being from ours, it is that we know these transcendentals in terms of finitude and embodiment, whereas God knows them as himself, infinitely. Infinity is thus the only attribute that escapes a univocal application and constitutes God's absolute perfection. For Scotus, the knowledge of God, via analogous transcendentals, is not enough to really know quid pro quo. Our concepts must be univocal to God and creation to be of any assistance. "Every univocal concept is sufficiently one that it would either be contradictory to affirm and deny it of the something, or else, if taken as a middle term of a syllogism, that the two other terms would be bound together by it without sophistical equivocation."[191]

This theory of univocity is often pushed to extremes in post-Scotist philosophy, and it is by no means a muted doctrine in Scotus himself. Burrell notes that he is pushed to a position "so notorious" because of a desire to contrast his view with that of Aquinas and his concept of analogy.[192] Scotus seems to have been motivated by Aquinas's "excessive agnosticism."[193] Yet it is a characterization of Aquinas's doctrine of analogy, that of Henry of Ghent and John of St. Thomas, more than it is Aquinas's conception of analogy. But

---

[189]Ibid.
[190]Ibid.
[191]Bernard Montagnes, *The Doctrine of the Analogy of Being*, trans. E. M. Macierowski (Milwaukee: Marquette University Press, 2004), p. 16.
[192]Burrell, *Analogy*, p. 175.
[193]Scotus, *Treatise on God as First Principle* 1.2

this is precisely the problem that Burrell fails to account for here. That is, the constant and regular "misrepresentation" of Aquinas on analogy in his heirs in the Catholic tradition. But this is no defense of Aquinas, since "misrepresentations" often become official interpretations, which is what happens with Cajetan's position. The fact remains that, regardless of whether it was Aquinas or Henry of Ghent, by Scotus's time there was a crisis of the speakability of God that drove Scotus to the "extreme" of univocity. It is very possible, as Burrell notes, that the view of analogy he is refuting is akin to the analogy of proportionality a:b::c:d, which of itself tends toward univocal predication, but in contradictory terms.[194] If this is so then, understandably, Scotus feels it necessary to launch a counterargument to analogy in the direction of univocity. But it was a problem he saw to be inimical to Aquinas, nevertheless. The unspoken fact is that, however Henry of Ghent may have misunderstood Aquinas, the assumption was that he was employing a Thomistic model of analogy. This is also the case with John of St. Thomas, as well as Cajetan; in fact, it will be a standard Catholic line that those who attack Thomistic doctrine are really attacking effigies of Aquinas, while Aquinas himself remains "safe and secure." Not much is ever said, for instance, about how these "effigies" of Aquinas tend to take on the status of official interpretation, which was certainly the case with Cajetan's reduction of Aquinas's "analogy of being" to intrinsic attribution or, effectively, the analogy of proportionality. That being the case, and the fact that Scotus himself had no small following in the Catholic Church, we may well ask what importance his view has for subsequent Catholic understanding of analogy. The answers to this question are diverse, but they include the possibility that there is always a drive toward either agnosticism or univocity in Catholic theology. Rarely does an analogy of being, understood as *unius ad alterum*, suffice of itself to satisfy the foundation of theological knowledge. This can be illustrated in the reasons Scotus himself gives for the rejection of analogy in favor of univocity.[195]

In Henry of Ghent, as in Aquinas, there is an assumption of the axiom of God's absolute simplicity, and this axiom means that "every multiplicity must be reduced to unity," and that this is also true for all "concepts" and

---

[194]Burrell, *Analogy*, p. 98.
[195]The author gratefully acknowledges his indebtedness to Montagnes and Burrell here.

names of God. Where two or more names of God introduce an apparent multiplicity—or worse, contradiction—then the claim to unify them under some general transcendental is "illusory" as far as Scotus is concerned.[196] If we are to speak of God and the creature under the one concept of being, then "being is said of everything under one formality." Under this univocal conception, being becomes "unqualifiedly most common" (*communisima simpliciter*), and this is the presupposition underlying all entities. If this is the case, then "ambiguity" with respect to the knowledge of it will not do. "On such an account, we dare not vacillate about our ability to be clear about being, for everything else hangs on it."[197] And there is the requirement of epistemology that "each faculty have its proper object: the intellect's is being."[198]

Such an approach to the science of being means we begin with a "clear and distinct idea of being," rather than a doubtful one.[199] "Now in our present condition, we can conceive being and apply it to God without being certain that the being is finite or infinite, created or uncreated."[200] That is, being, as applied to creature and Creator, is conceived as distinct. But if the concept of "being" is clear and distinct, "of itself it is neither one nor the other, but neutral as regards these modes." Its own proper content is univocal. "It encompasses everything that is, including uncreated being."[201] Thus it is able to have itself as the object of its own science.[202] It seems clear that Scotus saw in the "Thomistic" doctrine of analogy an incapacity to really express God or to name his perfections. To the degree that Aquinas himself expresses the ineffability of God, in the sense of his being "unnamable," this seems to be a legitimate concern of Scotus despite the "misrepresentation of his thought."[203]

But there is a further reason, according to Montanges, that Scotus rejects the "Thomistic" doctrine of analogy. "If to know God, we had to form a second concept (that of divine being) analogous to the first (that of created

---

[196]Montagnes, *Doctrine of the Analogy*, p. 117; Burrell, *Analogy*, p. 100.
[197]See Burrell, *Analogy*, pp. 100-101.
[198]Ibid.
[199]Ibid., p. 100.
[200]Ibid.
[201]Ibid.
[202]See Montages, *Doctrine of Analogy*, pp. 117-18; Scotus, *Ordinatio*, pars. 3.2-3.
[203]See *ST* I, q. 1, art. 13-15.

being), we would find ourselves in an impossible situation, since all our concepts originate from phantasms and the agent intellect."[204] If the concept "being" is not a phantasm, then we must not posit an absolute difference in being between Creator and creature, otherwise "being" comes to mean nothing. Being must somehow "be univocal within sensible representations." But this conception of being must be applied to God a priori and the creature a posteriori. However, this also requires a univocal concept of being. "Either we know God by means of just a necessarily univocal concept, or else, as Henry of Ghent claims, there must be two concepts in a relation of analogy, and God remains inaccessible."[205] Again, Scotus seems alert to a lacuna within Thomistic epistemology here that Aquinas allows for and Henry of Ghent exploits, in order to protect the simplicity of God. Burrell repeats the charge that such a conception of univocity "leads to a notion of being indistinguishable from 'the most common genus.'"[206]

Of course he is right, but would Scotus have taken this direction if "Thomistic" epistemology were not, in his mind at least, in danger of a differentiation beyond all simplicity, and so a net negative return for theological knowledge? Aquinas may not be directly charged with placing God and the human under one genus conception of being, but does his epistemology drive Scotus in this direction? One could argue that his emphasis on divine simplicity seems to require this. In our own time the charge is repeated, much to the protest of the Dominicans and other Thomists, and rightly so when explicitly applied to Aquinas himself. But do the *Summae* ultimately and inadvertently promote such an outcome in later medieval thought? Certainly here Scotus's reasons for rejecting analogy provide impetus in that direction. There are, of course, further reasons Scotus offers for rejecting analogy, but they essentially come to the same point, only now in relation to the "perfections" of God's "being." Just as "being" must be conceived univocally, so also must the other perfections.[207] From the point of

---

[204]Montagnes, *Doctrine of Analogy*, p. 117.

[205]Ibid.

[206]Burrell, *Analogy*, p. 101.

[207]As Scotus suggests, "Every metaphysical enquiry about God proceeds in the following manner: one considers the formal character [*raison*] of something; one eliminates the imperfection that this formal character would have in creatures; one posits this formal character separately by attributing to it the absolutely supreme perfection; and one attributes it to God in this form. ... Every enquiry about God therefore supposes that the intellect has the same univocal concept

view of pure logic Scotus was correct. This is why analogy in Aquinas and Cajetan can never be simply a matter of the logical function of language.

Cardinal Cajetan: The analogy of proper proportionality and metaphysics. This discussion of univocity in Scotus leads us quite naturally, in the history of medieval thought, to the anti-Scotist work of Cajetan. Ralph McInerny, in not just one but in all three of his major treatments of analogy and Thomistic thought, clearly singles Cajetan out as the most problematic and unfortunate interpreter of Thomas's conception of analogy.[208] On the one hand, he agrees with the most vehement attack on Cajetan in the modern period, in Étienne Gilson, in respect to analogy at least. On the other hand, against Gilson, he applauds as "entirely fitting" that his commentary on the *ST* "should be printed along with the work in the Leonine edition" of the same.[209] The story of this somewhat schizophrenic approach to Cajetan cannot be told in full here, but the history of this affirmation/dismissal of Cajetan, and his interpretation of Aquinas, has had no small impact on the attempts to reinterpret Aquinas's understanding of analogy in our own time. Indeed the internal weakness of the argument against Cajetan's interpretation of Aquinas on analogy seems to be that he is authoritative in all other respects of Aquinas's theology, especially his metaphysics, but is to be rejected, or heavily corrected, in this one crucial matter, except of course in respect to the terms in which he frames analogy.

The history of the treatment of Cajetan's *The Analogy of Names* reveals that it was considered almost impossible until the late twentieth century to dispense with Cajetan's basic understanding of Aquinas on analogy.[210] In the end, at least for Sylvester of Ferrara, Suárez and many others, Cajetan was considered to be right in most respects about Aquinas and analogy. It is debatable whether this was an agreement out of loyalty to the "grand master" of the Dominican Order and the most authoritative scholar of Thomistic metaphysics, or indeed there was considerable accord between Cajetan and Aquinas on all matters metaphysical, analogy included. A brief analysis of

---

there as it draws from creatures." Quoted in Montagnes, *Doctrine of Analogy*, p. 118 n. 22.

[208]McInerny, *Logic of Analogy; Aquinas and Analogy; Preambula Fidei*.

[209]McInerny, *Aquinas and Analogy*, pp. 3-4.

[210]Time does not permit a full exposition of the reception of Cajetan in modern times. Gilson's article on Cajetan is likely the place to begin: É. Gilson, "Cajetan et l'existence," *Tijdschrift voor Philosophie* (June 1953): 267-86.

The Analogy of Names, taken up in connection with Cajetan's own metaphysics of being contained in his commentary on Aquinas's *De ente et essentia*, shows him to be indeed a "grand master" of Thomism, and therefore
to be respected in all aspects of Aquinas's thought, analogy included. The
inclusion of his commentary on the *ST* with the Leonine edition of the same
confirms this, if nothing else.

Cajetan was barely in his grave before serious criticisms of his understanding of analogy began to emerge, starting with Sylvester of Ferrara, a
Thomist of the late sixteenth century. He was the first to recognize what
would come to be the standard critique of Cajetan's interpretation, that
is, that Cajetan bases his description on too small a range of texts from
Aquinas.[211] In recognition of the fact that Aquinas describes analogy in
multiple locations, Sylvester attempted to correct Cajetan's interpretation
by reference to the many texts in Aquinas that Cajetan left out, especially
the texts in the two *Summae*. Cajetan, in his estimation, failed to reconcile what appeared to be contradictory accounts of analogy in Thomas's
corpus. For instance, in the *ST*, Aquinas designates a primary *analogate*
to which all other *analogatum* are to be related. In *De veritate*, the key text
for Cajetan, however, there appears to be an "analogy of proportionality"
in which the various analogates express no such *direct* relation.[212] In
defense of Cajetan's failure to recognize this apparent contradiction, Sylvester reconciles the two texts by suggesting that "St. Thomas is here
merely rejecting the position that a name predicated absolutely of the
creature can lead directly to a knowledge of the Creator and be so predicated of Him; that St. Thomas does not intend to exclude a proportional
relationship between the analogates in such a way that one can be referred
to the other as to a first analogate."[213]

Sylvester finds similar explanations to help reconcile Cajetan and Aquinas
on many other "apparent contradictions," but in the end finds Cajetan to be
basically right in respect to the analogy of proportionality, just not careful

---

[211]Cajetan, *Analogy of Names*, pp. 10-12. The two texts from Aquinas are *Scriptum super librum
Sententiarum*, bk. I, distinction 19, q. 5, art. 2, ad. 1, and *De veritate*, q. 2, art. 11.

[212]See Lyttkens, *Analogy Between God and the World*, pp. 225-28; Klubertanz, *St. Thomas Aquinas
on Analogy*, pp. 10-11, for this analysis.

[213]Lyttkens, *Analogy Between God and the World*, pp. 225-28; Klubertanz, *St. Thomas Aquinas on
Analogy*, p. 11.

or thorough enough in his reading of Aquinas. In the final analysis, Sylvester is just as reductionistic as Cajetan. "Neither Sylvester nor his followers have justified the reductionism which characterizes his approach to St. Thomas' doctrine on analogy."[214] In the long run he understands the analogy of proportionality to be the one valid type of analogy in the two *Summae*, which appears to limit analogy to the analogy of one to another.[215]

The value of Sylvester's critique here is the fundamental recognition that Aquinas's thinking on analogy is by no means unified in any one theory. This will be used against Cajetan time and again, suggesting that his view of Aquinas is too restrictive and reductive and that the analogy of proportionality does not do justice to the principle of the analogy of one to another as an "intrinsic analogy" as described above in the two *Summae*. But such criticisms fall short of the actual unity of thought between Aquinas and Cajetan on matters metaphysical, as we shall now demonstrate.

Cajetan (1468–1534) was born in Gata, Italy, and became a Dominican novitiate at the age of sixteen. The order sent him to study philosophy and theology at Naples, Bologna and Pavia, where he first began to lecture on St. Thomas's thought. He was later appointed to the Chair of Thomistic Metaphysics at Padua, where he completed commentaries on Aquinas's *De ente et essentia*, the *SCG*, the *ST* and *The Sentences* of Aquinas. He was later appointed master general of the Dominican order and eventually made a cardinal by Pope Leo X in 1517.[216] Though he spent the last few decades of his

---

[214]Lyttkens, *Analogy Between God and the World*, pp. 225-28; Klubertanz, *St. Thomas Aquinas on Analogy*, p. 11. Klubertanz and Lyttkens come to similar conclusions here.

[215]Klubertanz, *St. Thomas Aquinas on Analogy*, pp. 11-12. Klubertanz notes, "Sylvester also attempts to reconcile St. Thomas' doctrine of an analogy *unius ad alterum* between creatures and their Creator (found both in the *Summa contra gentiles* and in the *Summa theologiae*) with his denial of an analogy of proportion in *De veritate*, q. 2, a. 11. Proportion must be merely one type of analogy *unius ad alterum*, which is a general designation that includes proportionality as well as proportion. Thus St. Thomas is rejecting only a direct proportion between God and creatures in *De veritate*, q. 2, a. 11, not all analogy of one to another, and affirming only one type of analogy of one to another (that is, proportionality) in the two *Summae*, not every type covered by this general term" (*St. Thomas Aquinas on Analogy*, p. 11).

[216]The complete works of Cajetan are as follows: Cajetan, *In De Ente et Essentia De Thomae Aquinatis Commentaria*, ed. M.-H. Laurent, O.P. (Turin, 1934); *In Summa Theologiae St. Thomae Aquinatis Commentaria*, Leonine ed. (Rome, 1882); *De Nominum Analogia, De Conceptu Entis*, ed. P. N. Zammit, O.P. (Rome: Angelicum, 1934); *In De Anima Aristotelis Commentaria*, ed. J. Coquelle, O.P. (Rome: Angelicum, 1938); *In Praedicamenta Aristotelis Commentaria*, ed. M.-H. Laurent, O.P. (Rome: Angelicum, 1939); *In Porphyrii Isagogen Commentaria*, ed. I. M. Marega, O.P. (Rome: Angelicum, 1934); *Opuscula Omnia* (Venice, 1956). The two English translations

career as vicar general of the church, and therefore out of the mainstream of academic life, his fame is entirely in respect to the latter. In his lifetime he was destined to counsel no fewer than four popes: Julius II, Leo X, Adrian VI and Clement VII. It is clear from all of this that we are dealing here with a "prince of the church," and no small figure in respect to authority. Mondin puts well the regard in which the church, for a long time, held his views on analogy. "Without any sign of hesitation or uncertainty, he systematically explains the whole Thomistic theory of analogy in such a way that neither he nor any subsequent philosophers for many years found reason to add anything to the fundamental principles and outlines laid down by him."[217]

Judging by the way he is commented on in today's scholarly circles, one would get the impression he was an obscurantist who muddied the waters of Thomistic metaphysics in a way that was counterproductive, misleading even. One certainly gets this impression from Gilson's critique of him.[218] Cajetan himself, however, was the consummate careful scholar, and it was scholarship that motivated his treatment of analogy in his *De Nominum Analogia* (*The Analogy of Names*).[219] He writes,

> motivated both by the obscurity of the subject itself and the deplorable scarcity of profound studies in our age, I intend to publish . . . a treatise on the analogy of names. An understanding of this doctrine is so necessary that without it one cannot study metaphysics, and ignorance of it gives rise to many errors in other sciences.[220]

From Cajetan's point of view, a collection of half-truths, misinterpretations and outright errors had led to a situation that threatened the very basis of the Thomistic synthesis, which, by his time, was the reigning philosophical and theological modality of the intellectual life of the Church, as well as the broader medieval culture.

---

of these works that we shall employ are his *The Analogy of Names* as noted above and his *Commentary on Being and Essence*, ed. and trans. L. H. Kendzierski and F. C. Wade (Milwaukee: Marquette University Press, 1964).

[217]Mondin, *Principle of Analogy*, p. 36.

[218]Other than those already noted above, see the list of Gilson's treatment of Cajetan in McInerny, *Preambula Fidei*, pp. 39-40.

[219]Cajetan, *Analogy of Names*, pp. 9-10. "For from the following discussions it will become clear that such theories have wandered over roads of ruin away from the truth which spontaneously manifested itself" (*Analogy of Names*, p. 9).

[220]Ibid.

As we have already mentioned, Cajetan builds his Thomistic doctrine of analogy on a few selective texts from the Thomistic corpus. One text is contained in an early work of Aquinas, his commentary on the *Sentences of Peter the Lombard*.[221] The other key text is from Aquinas's *On Truth* (*De veritate*), in which he deals with analogy in question 2. Of these two the most crucial text in terms of setting the problem is from the commentary on the *Sentences*, in which Aquinas divides analogy in terms of analogy "according to intention and not according to being, according to being and not according to intention, and according to intention and being."[222] For Cajetan, all forms of analogy spoken of in the Thomistic corpus fall under one of these categories, which he re-names analogy according to inequality, analogy of (*extrinsic*) attribution and analogy of proportionality.

His treatment of the first category, analogy of inequality, is brief and designed to show that in no way is it reasonable to suppose that Aquinas considers this approach valid. The analogy of inequality occurs when a word applied to two completely different entities means the same, but "the inequality of perfection" makes them incomparable—for example, *body* as applied to celestial and terrestrial beings. The "notion" of *body* remains the same, but "the notion of corporeity is not in inferior and superior bodies according to an equal grade of perfection."[223] This will always be the case with such words brought into comparison in this way, irrespective of genus and/or species. "For every genus can be called analogous in this way, as is clear from quantity and quality in the predicaments, and body, etc."[224] But this is not properly analogy. As analogy it is a "misuse" of terms. "For to speak of something according to priority and posteriority is broader than speaking analogically . . . as a matter of fact they are univocal, and therefore the rules of univocal terms must be observed with respect to them."[225] Such forms of analogy cannot serve theology, therefore.

The next form of analogy treated is that of extrinsic attribution (*secundum intentionem et non secundum esse*) and is illustrated with the classic Aristo-

---

[221] Aquinas, *Scriptum super librum Sententiarum*, bk. I, distinction 19, q. 5, art. 2, ad. 1.
[222] Ibid.
[223] Cajetan, *Analogy of Names*, pp. 11-12.
[224] Ibid.
[225] Ibid.

telian/Thomistic appeal to "health" as it applies to medicine, urine and animal. He defines it as follows.

> Analogous by attribution are those things which have a common name, and the notion signified by this name is the same with respect to the term but different as regards the relationships to this term. For example, the name healthy is common to medicine, urine and animal, but the notion of all insofar as healthy expresses different relationships to one term, namely healthy.[226]

Animal is a "subject" of health, while urine is a "sign" of health, and medicine its "cause." "In this example it is perfectly clear that the notion of health is not entirely the same nor entirely different, but to a certain extent the same and to a certain extent different."[227] Note here that this "one term" unifies a diversity of relationships, at least in terms of its extrinsic applicability to animal and urine. It is extrinsic to medicine as its cause.[228] "The example of health in *III Metaphysics* refers to the final cause, the example of medical, in the same text, pertains to efficient cause, the analogy of being (*analogia entis* likewise mentioned in the same text) pertains to material cause, and finally the analogy of good, given in *I Ethics* refers to exemplary cause."[229] Cajetan outlines four conditions inimical to this form of analogy. First, it is conditioned by "extrinsic denomination," so that only the primary analogate realizes the perfection formally, whereas the others have it by extrinsic denomination. That is, the animal, as the prime analogate, has health formally, while the other *analogatum*, medicine, and so on, "are called healthy not because of health inherent to them, but extrinsically after the health of the animal, insofar as they signify it, etc."[230] Thus, "secondary analogates are denominated from the numerically single perfection of the primary analogate on the basis of the various relations that obtain between them and the primary analogate."[231] The second condition follows from this in that "the one thing which is the term of the diverse relationships in

---

[226]Ibid., pp. 15-16.
[227]Ibid.
[228]Ibid. He relies here on Aristotle's *Metaphysics* III-IV, p. 1003a, line 32, through p. 1003b, line 15.
[229]Cajetan, *Analogy of Names*, p. 15. Here he refers to Aristotle's *Nicomachian Ethics* I.6, p. 1096b, line 26.
[230]Cajetan, *Analogy of Names*, p. 17.
[231]Klubertanz, *St. Thomas Aquinas on Analogy*, pp. 8-9.

analogous names of this type is one not merely in concept but numerically."[232] That is, the health intrinisic to the subject, animal, is one and the same as the health extrinsic to the urine and medicine. This is so universally, as concept, and particularly, as it relates to the one subject, animal. The multiplication of particulars does not mean a division of the perfection, health. "For what is common by extrinsic denomination does not multiply its denominator in the denominated in the same way as a universal term is multiplied in its univocates."[233] To hark back to the example of *body* in relation to terrestrial and celestial being, obviously *body* is qualitatively different in each case, though univocally denominated.

This leads to a further—often overlooked, but critical—third condition on the use of analogy of extrinsic attribution. It is essentially a metaphysical condition. "The primary analogate is put into the definition of the others with respect to the analogous name." Why so? Because the secondary and tertiary *analogatum* only have the name predicated of them by virtue of their relation to the primary analogate, "in which the perfection expressed by it is formally realized."[234] Urine and medicine only mean something in relation to health by virtue of the animal's intrinsic possession of the quality, health. This relation to the "one thing" dominates Aquinas's understanding of analogy in subsequent works and expresses the metaphysical unity of all perfections under the concept of simplicity. In all forms of analogical predication this unity must be protected from any division among *analogatum*. It is a condition that applies not only to intrinsic and extrinsic attribution, but also to proportional analogy, proportionate analogy and all their subtypes. This conditional use of extrinsic attribution is dominated by the problem of the one and the many all along the line. It leads to a final condition on the use of analogy of extrinsic attribution, one that deepens this metaphysical orientation in analogy. In such uses of analogy, "the diverse relationships [among the analogates] are implied in such an indeterminate and confused way that the primary relationship is signified distinctly or almost distinctly, but in the others in a confused manner and by way of re-

---

[232]Ibid.
[233]Cajetan, *Analogy of Names*, pp. 19-20.
[234]Ibid.

duction to the primary relationship."[235] Klubertanz explains this condition nicely: "the analogous concept involved (health) contains distinctly the perfection of the primary analogate."[236] Klubertanz infers correctly that this is something like an analogy of proportion, here considered not as a separate form of analogy, but as a form of the analogy of extrinsic attribution.[237]

Thus, according to Cajetan, we may conclude the following from this second form of analogy. The perfection analogized is common to all analogates "not merely as regards the external word."[238] Here there is a hint of a possible intrinsic analogy wherein the quality is "somehow" intrinsic to all *analogatum*. Certainly extrinsic denomination does not mean the analogates only possess a likeness of quality. The quality "somehow inheres" in all *analogatum*. Thus used, absolutely, the quality "stands for the primary analogate" so that "there is nothing prior to the primary analogate in which the whole perfection expressed by the analogous term is formally realized."[239] In his subsequent treatment of the Thomistic employment of the analogy of extrinsic attribution, Cajetan notes that there are no new additions to this or the other two categories of analogy in Aquinas, because "it embraces analogy according the *genera* of causes."[240] For, to the primary and other analogates, the analogous term is common in such a way that it "does not posit or signify anything prior to them and for this reason it is called analogy of one to another, everything different from the primary analogate being identified with the one."[241] The consequence of this identification of the analogy of attribution with the analogy of one to another will lead later scholars to posit this, and not proportionality, as Aquinas's preferred type, but with the added dimension of intrinsicality hinted at in Cajetan. It can also be referred to in Cajetan as the analogy of proportion. It is, finally, an incorrect form of analogy, but more acceptable than the first. The problem remains that such terms of use may be fraught with "'ambiguities,' as the Arabic scholars called them."[242]

[235]Ibid.

[236]Klubertanz, *St. Thomas Aquinas on Analogy*, pp. 8-10.

[237]Ibid. See also Lyttkens, *Analogy Between God and the World*, p. 239.

[238]Cajetan, *Analogy of Names*, p. 20.

[239]Ibid., p. 21.

[240]Ibid.

[241]Ibid.

[242]Ibid.

According to Cajetan, there is an extension of this use of analogy, into proportionality, which may more properly serve theological denomination. He now takes this up as a third species of analogical predication. The extension includes analogical attribution but specifically under the category of proportionality. What does this mean? This is the analogy Aquinas designates as "according to the intention and according to 'to be'" and, according to Cajetan, this is the preferred analogical method to be identified with that discussed in *Questiones disputate de veritate.*[243] This is analogy "in the proper sense."[244] "Analogous by proportionality are those things which have a common name, and the notion expressed by this name is proportionally the same."[245] Thus, in terms of similarity, there is proportionality between *analogatum*. Seeing may be proportionately applied to intellect and/or to the physical faculty of sight in ways that are similar yet qualitatively different. It is critical, however, to distinguish terms used in proportion and those implying proportionality. First, proportion is a quantitative difference, as in 2:4::3:6. In this analogy 4 and 2 are twice in proportion and therefore are similar as divisible numbers. Proportionality, however, speaks of a similitude in that proportions are compared, as in 2:4::3:6. But philosophers have transferred this mathematical analogy designated proportion "to express any relationship of conformity, commensuration, capacity, etc."[246] As a result they have "extended the use of the term propor-

---

[243] Aquinas, *De veritate*, q. 2, art. 11a.

[244] Cajetan, *Analogy of Names*, p. 24; P. Descoqs, *Institutiones Metaphysicae Generalis* (Paris, 1925), pp. 227-28, adds a number of texts in Aquinas to support this, but especially Aquinas, commentary on Aristotle's *Nicomachian Ethics*. See Aquinas, *Sententia libri Ethicorum*, bk. I, lect. 7, para. 5-14. "In another way, one name is predicated of many according to notions which are not entirely diverse but agree in some one point. Sometimes [they agree] in this that they refer to one principle. . . . Sometimes in this that they refer to one end. . . . Sometimes according to diverse times in this that they refer to one end. . . . Sometimes according to diverse proportions to one subject . . . or according to one proportion to diverse subjects. . . . Thus [the Philosopher] says that good is not predicated of many according to entirely diverse notions . . . but rather according to analogy, i.e. according to the same proportion, insofar as all good things depend upon one first principle of goodness or are ordered to one end. . . . Or also all things are called good according to analogy, i.e. according to the same proportion, as sight is a good of the body and the intellect of the soul. Hence he prefers this third mode because it is taken according to goodness inherent to things, whereas the first two modes are according to separate goodness, by which a thing is denominated [good] in a less proper sense." See also Aquinas, *De veritate*, q. 2, art. 11; *De potentia*, q. 7, art. 7; and *Sententia libri Metaphysicae*, bk. V, lect. 8.

[245] Cajetan, *Analogy of Names*, p. 25.

[246] Ibid. See Aquinas, *De veritate*, q. 23, art. 7, ad. 9.

tionality to every similitude of relationships. It is in this sense that we use the terms in the present study."[247] This, too, is a critical juncture in Cajetan's account, since many contemporary scholars do not read proportion in terms of mathematics but in terms of degrees in cause-effect-resemblances. As we can see, however, the mathematical background cannot be so easily expunged, especially given Aquinas's understanding of proportion in the *De veritate* and the passage from the commentary on *Ethics* just cited above.[248] What makes proportionality the proper modality of analogy for Cajetan is the fact that only in this way do all of the *analogatum* possess in an *intrinsic* way the analogous quality or perfection, albeit only in a similarity and not an absolute identity. It is perfectly represented in the prime analogate and imperfectly, yet proportionately, represented in the secondary *analogatum*. "The former clear concept is simply many concepts and only proportionately one; the latter or confused (*con-fused*) concept is simply one and proportionately many."[249]

The analogy of proportionality can occur in two ways, one metaphysical, another more proper. Metaphysical proportionality does not allow a property to be intrinsically applied to all *analogatum* in the analogy. Only this form of analogy "excels," because "it arises from the genus of the inherent formal causality," since it predicates intrinsic perfections inherent in all *analogatum*, and not just extrinsically. It also is the most faithful to the tradition of analogical speech in Greek philosophy, "from whom we have borrowed the term."[250] In Cajetan's mind analogy and proportionality are used synonymously in Greek philosophy, such as Aristotle, who defines these terms as "whatever things are related to one another as one thing to another."[251] This is also true of the Neoplatonic and Arabic appropriation of analogy.

Here is the crucial point that Cajetan wants to make, and the substantial reason why he attempted a clarification of the meaning and use of analogy in Aquinas.

---

[247]Cajetan, *Analogy of Names*, p. 23.
[248]See Aquinas, *De veritate*, q. 23, art. 7, ad. 9.
[249]Cajetan, *Analogy of Names*, pp. 25-26.
[250]Ibid., p. 28.
[251]Ibid.

> Speaking of the community of Good to those things which are said to be good [Aristotle] says: "They are not considered similar to what is equivocal by chance, but certainly 'being from one' or 'all tending to one' or rather what is one by analogy." Adding an example of analogy, he says, "Just as in the body there is sight, so in the soul there is intelligence." In these words he not only reveals to an attentive reader that the name analogy expresses what we have said about it, but by using the word rather, implies that this analogy must be proposed in metaphysical predications.[252]

The import of analogy then, for Cajetan, has more at stake than the ability to name God and his predicates. It is the heart of the possibility of metaphysics because it is the only mode of access to said metaphysics. "By means of the analogy of proportionality we know indeed the intrinsic entity, goodness, truth, etc. of things, which are not know from the preceeding analogy," or otherwise.[253] Metaphysics without such an analogy of proportionality is unreflective, unskilled metaphysics, at heart. This is what, in Cajetan's mind, Aquinas meant by prescribing an analogy of proportionality or "according to 'to be' *and* according to intention." The reason he prescribes this over other methods is essentially metaphysical. It is that "the analogates are not considered equal in the perfection expressed by the common name, nor in the 'to be' of this perfection, yet they agree proportionally both in the perfection expressed by that name and in its 'to be.'"[254]

As Klubertanz and Lyttktens, among others, note, Cajetan had many followers and defenders in the church's tradition, including John of St. Thomas, Maurilio Penido, Gerald Phelan and, to a degree, Klubertanz himself. Those who have disagreed have done so either entirely within the terms set by Cajetan himself (such as Sylvester and Suárez) or hold views outside the mainstream and therefore tend to be "idiosyncratic."[255] What is routinely missed by both the critics and the promoters of Cajetan's view of analogy is the underlying reason for his writing *The Analogy of Names* to begin with. He sees it as essential to a proper metaphysics. It is interesting to note how some contemporary scholars, wanting a new metaphysics without Cajetan,

---

[252]Ibid.
[253]Ibid., pp. 28-29.
[254]Ibid., p. 29.
[255]For example, McInerny, Przywara and von Balthasar.

have ignored the importance of his argument for metaphysics. If it is true that he has so severely misled us on Aquinas's view on analogy, would it not also naturally apply that he has misled us on Aquinas's metaphysics, since metaphysics requires analogy? A brief comparison here leads us to conclude that just as there is considerable accord between Cajetan and Aquinas on metaphysics, so also there must be considerable accord between their views of analogy, regardless of the criticisms of Cajetan's reductionism. If this is the case, then certainly a new appraisal of Cajetan's view of analogy is called for, just as it also calls for a reappraisal of Aquinas on analogy.[256] Precisely such is the case in respect to the metaphysical principle of causality as it relates to analogy and being in Aquinas and Cajetan.

Metaphysics of being in Cajetan and Aquinas. To grasp the roots of any conception of the "analogy of being" as it was commonly understood by the time of Cajetan and up to Suárez, it is necessary to have a clear conception of Aquinas's notion of the existence of being. The topic is a daunting one and can only be sketched in its broad strokes here, though its import for any conception of analogy will be immediately recognized. Cajetan understood Aquinas's metaphysics to be the basis of any employment of analogy, as can be demonstrated from his commentary on Aquinas's *De ente et essentia*.[257] In this commentary, citing Aquinas as his authority, Cajetan agrees with the Scotist position that being is "a single formal concept to represent substance and accidents, God and creatures." Indeed beings, which present a real, albeit simply analogical, likeness, can be represented by a unique concept expressing that which brings them together. "Now, created being is like substantial being, *in virtue of the relation* of causality, which in each instance ties the first term to the second (a relation of exemplarity for what is created, of emanation for the accident)."[258] It is upon this basis that Cajetan says Aquinas builds his metaphysics of being. As Montagne and others note, this position appears to be Scotistic and therefore univocal.[259] Yet it is historically understood as a position he builds from Aquinas in response to Scotism. Whether Cajetan falls into univocity of being here depends, of course, on

[256]Hochschild, *Semantics of Analogy*.
[257]For comprehensive treatment of Cajetan on this work, see Montagnes, *Doctrine of Analogy*, pp. 122-23.
[258]Montagnes, *Doctrine of Analogy*, p. 122.
[259]Ibid.

how one understands *esse* in Aquinas. Aquinas's general position may be briefly summarized as follows.

The two foundational ideas in Aquinas's conception of reality are those of participated being (existence) and absolute being (essence). The order of being as *ipsum esse subsistens* is absolute being followed by participated being.[260] He calls God *qui est* (he who is) in the sense of primary or foundational being. As self-subsisting being, God is the formal, efficient, final and exemplar cause of all existents.[261] This is a position known in the classical philosophical traditional as "existentialist."[262] That is to say, Aquinas defines the essence of things as their existence, and God as the essence of all existence, though we cannot know his essence except in the fact that he exists. Here Aquinas is the first to distinguish between essence and existence, although he does so by building on a tradition extending back to Plato through Aristotle, Augustine and Boethius. For Aquinas, as opposed to Aristotle, a substance (οὐσία, *substantia/essentia*) is composite. It is an essence that has received existence. In the conferral of existence on an essence, through substance, what was possible (as an idea in the mind of God) has become actualized. In the case of physical existence, this is actualized when a form receives matter (as opposed to Aristotle where matter receives form). Thus act and potency, existence and essence, form and matter, are correlatives of existence.[263] Being is that which is conferred,

---

[260] Aquinas, *De ente et essentia, prooemium: Quia vero ex compositis simplicium cognitionem accipere debemus et ex posterioribus in priora devenire, ut, a facilioribus incipientes, convenientior fiat disciplina, ideo ex significatione entis ad significationem essentiae procedendum est.* Translation: "Since we ought to acquire knowledge of simple things from composite ones and come to know the prior from the posterior, in instructing beginners we should begin with what is easier, and so we shall begin with the signification of being and proceed from there to the signification of essence."

[261] *ST* I, q. 1, art. 2-3.

[262] Aquinas, *De ente et essentia*, caput I. See also Owens, *Doctrine of Being*, p. 90.

[263] Aquinas, *De ente et essentia*, caput II. "In composite substances we find form and matter, as in man there are soul and body. We cannot say, however, that either of these is the essence of the thing. That matter alone is not the essence of the thing is clear, for it is through its essence that a thing is knowable and is placed in a species or genus. But matter is not a principle of cognition; nor is anything determined to a genus or species according to its matter but rather according to what something is in act. Nor is form alone the essence of a composite thing, however much certain people may try to assert this. From what has been said, it is clear that the essence is that which is signified by the definition of the thing. The definition of a natural substance, however, contains not only form but also matter; otherwise, the definitions of natural things and mathematical ones would not differ. Nor can it be said that matter is placed in the definition of a natural substance as something added to the essence or as some being beyond the essence of the thing, for that type of definition is more proper to accidents, which do not have a perfect

through actuality, on an essence, or better, substance.[264] This is in contradiction to Aristotle because he proposes a form-to-matter motion of existence in line with his view of the eternity of matter and the absence of any
concept of the beginning of creation.[265] Form and matter are collapsed in
Aristotle, when considered under the conditions of existence, change and
motion.[266] For Aquinas, nothing exists without needing to be explained in
terms of its possibility and actuality. Essence and existence are distinguished in a world of motion and change, with the terms *substance* and
accident. In God, essence and existence are one, undivided, because in God
de ente et essentia sunt indivisa.[267] To know what God is, existence itself, or
being itself, is not thereby to know his essence, which indeed we cannot
know.[268] This is in contrast with the univocal understanding of being in
Scotus, who defines God as "infinite being."[269]

According to Aquinas and Cajetan, creatures participate in existence by
virtue of their creation, and therefore theoretically exist in a way distinct
from the existence of God.[270] The difference is that their existence is by
participation and thus not self-subsistent existence. These two concepts,
being and participation in being, both arguably from the Platonic tradition,
are the core concepts of Aquinas's metaphysics of being. What gives human
being its existence is the fact that God, as pure being, is the cause of all other
realities. Human being is real because it is participated being. But, as with
the Neoplatonic tradition, being is the name given to the essential emanation of the one as *exitus* and *reditus*. It is unified by virtue of its participation in intellect. This is its reality.[271] In this sense creatureliness is not
coterminous with existence or being. Participated being refers to a principle
that transcends creation itself. Being in this sense is absolutely other than
its embodiment. It is, as such, not identical with being (*esse*). The same is

---

essence and which include in their definitions a subject beyond their own genus. Therefore, the
essence clearly comprises both matter and form."
[264]Ibid.
[265]Ibid.
[266]Ibid.
[267]Ibid., caput II.
[268]Ibid.; *ST* I, q. 13.
[269]Scotus, *God as First Principle* 4.1.
[270]Aquinas, *De ente et essentia*, caput III.
[271]Ibid.

true of all individual existences. Yet participation underscores a principle of similarity and likeness to all other *esse*, because their origin is the actuation of existence, and that in God who is pure actuality himself. Thus the human creature is proportionally similar to God and all other beings through this status of actuated being. The likeness between God and human creatures, then, is *omne agens agit simile sibi*.[272] If this is an accurate, albeit also all too brief, description of Aquinas's metaphysics of being, then certain consequences flow from it for analogy in general and for Cajetan's description of Aquinas's concept of analogy and his own Thomistic metaphysics.

First, contrary to Aristotle, Aquinas and Cajetan appear to ground reality not so much on the basis that an entity has form, but as it has existence or being (*esse*). It also appears that God is *ipsum esse subsistens*, that is, primary being or being itself. Thus, in his description of God, it is being (*esse*) that is the root of all forms of predication with respect to God. Causality (efficient, final and exemplar) is the modality by which we name, through effects. As effects we participate in cause to the degree that there is a CER.[273] This is not directly an emanationist understanding wherein being in God and in the creature are indistinguishable. The being of creatures is an imitation of the being of God, not an identity. As God is, in proportion to his essence, the creature is in proportion to theirs. God's essence is his own, ours an effect of his cause: Our being is finite, his infinite. Our being is caused by God, conserved by God, and yet created in the image of God in such a way that our existence points to his essence as existence. We imitate God as existents who actualize our own being. This is the substance of our participation in divine being, but without identity.

Second, if we hark back to what we said about analogy in Aquinas, certain aspects of his metaphysics of being now make his understanding of analogy clearer. It seems that indeed his metaphysics does not allow for any univocity or equivocity in naming the predicates of God, "being" the chief among them. Yet, the absolute difference between being and beings, and between finite beings, must somehow be overcome, since an absolute difference renders predication on the basis of comparison impossible. When we predicate being of an entity, we are saying it is similar in its dissimilarity and

---

[272]Aquinas, *De ente et essentia*, caput IV.
[273]Ibid.

dissimilar in its similarity. This is the way of analogy, but it trades on difference, primarily, and is therefore ultimately ambiguous. It was for this
reason that Scotus posited univocity—not because he wanted to be philosophically monist, but because analogy predicated on an absolute difference
was ultimately agnostic, vis-à-vis the names of God. If we posit that being
is predicated as a genus, then there is no real differentiation in being. Yet
difference makes the predicate "being" incomprehensible. Either way the
tendency is toward nonbeing. Thus Aquinas, and after him Cajetan, posits
analogy as a middle form of discourse that expresses the ambiguity of predicates, so that the incomprehensibility of the absolute simplicity of God may
be preserved. Metaphysical analogy is at one and the same time similarity
and dissimilarity. However, as we saw in Aquinas's analogy of one to another,
through CER, one may posit an *intrinsic* similarity of the absolutely different
as a basis for naming this absolutely different.[274] Let us now look briefly at
Cajetan's metaphysics to see whether indeed he follows his master into a
metaphysics of being, and thus a metaphysical analogy of being per se.

Indeed, Cajetan's metaphysics, if we are to take his commentary on Aquinas's *De ente et essentia* as a basis, essentially tries to establish three core
aspects of Aquinas's metaphysics. *First*, the principle of God as *ipsum esse
subsistens*, that is, God as existence itself. *Second*, that this self-existence is
the ground, unity and simplicity of all the perfections of God. *Finally*, Ca-

---

[274]For the above analysis see J. P. Reilly, *Cajetan's Notion of Existence* (The Hague: Moulten, 1971),
   p. 28. See also James F. Anderson, *An Introduction to the Metaphysics of St. Thomas Aquinas*
   (Chicago: Henry Regnery, 1953), pp. 36-37. See especially p. 39 and his *Reflections on the Analogy of Being* (The Hague: Martin Nijhof, 1967). Anderson's conclusions are critical to a proper
   reading of the difference between proportional and intrinsic comparisons between divine and
   human being, analogically. "What may be called 'the univocist position in ontology' results
   from the attempt to grasp being by means of a kind of abstract 'logical' conception. We mean
   that the partisans of this view have assumed that being must have a simple unity like that proper
   to *quidditative* concepts in some formal logic. Reference is made to the mentality of wishing to
   subsume all things under what the Cartesians called 'clear and distinct ideas.' The trouble is that
   no transcendental-existential object can be attained in this manner; it can be seen only metaphysically thanks to what has been called the judgment of existence. Of course 'being' is the
   chief of such objects; not an essence, it is really common to all that is or truly can be. . . . It is
   a fact, moreover, that Francisco Suarez, an influential sixteenth century Scholastic, similarly
   considered that 'being' must have a 'simple unity' like that proper to formally logical concepts.
   It may be said that this view (still so influential) leads logically to the destruction of all ontological analogy; that in the measure that analogy of attribution ('intrinsic attribution' in Suare-
   zianism) is stressed and proportionality denied, analogy will tend to resolve itself into univocity" (*Reflections on the Analogy*, pp. 62-63).

jetan, following Aquinas, demonstrates that as *esse subsistens*, God is the prime cause of all creation, which also reflects God's causality as effect. So working back from creation as effect, by analogy, we may name the being of God, in all his perfections, as *ipsum esse subsistens*. This is a familiar pattern of argumentation from the Middle Ages, especially in its Neoplatonic form as the *exitus-reditus* of divine being and knowing.

Thus Cajetan grounds all metaphysics in the first principle of the existence of God. He writes: *omne quod est per aliud tale, proceditur ab eo quod est per se tale.*[275] That is, all creaturely beings have their reality only *per accident* because their being (existence) is distinct from their essence (substance). Their essence precedes existence, since to be really is *esse* and not *existentia*. Otherwise they would have existed before being. So also then, their existence (*esse*) is derived from a prior existence, which is "being itself or self-subsistent being."[276] God is being *per se* and not being *per aliud*. If there is no being that is being itself, then either there is nothing or the endless procession of being in general. Therefore "being itself" is a cause of all other being as *ex se ens* (being form itself) whose essence is "to be." Whereas the creature is *essentia* before *esse*, God is *esse* itself, and this constitutes his *essentia*. This creaturely distinction of *esse* and *existentia*, and the divine unity of *esse*, is the basis on which divine causality rests in Cajetan and in Aquinas.[277] As such Cajetan is restating and reaffirming Aquinas's position in the *ST*, book I, question 3, article 4, where Aquinas writes:

> God is not only his own essence . . . but also his own existence. This may be shown in several ways. First whatever a thing has besides its essence must be caused either by the constituent principles "of that essence . . . or by some exterior agent,—as heat is caused in water by fire." Therefore, if the existence of a thing differs from its essence, this existence must be caused either by some exterior agent or by its essential principles for nothing can be sufficient cause of its own existence, if existence is caused. Therefore that thing, whose existence differs from its essence, must have its existence caused by

---

[275]Cajetan, *D. Thoma De ente et essentia libellus*, in *S. Thomae Aquinatis doctoris angelici opusculum De ente et essentia*, ed. M. de Maria, S.J. (Rome, 1907), pp. 74-75. We will also use the English translation *Commentary on Being and Essence*, ed. L. H. Kendzierski and F. C. Wade (Milwaukee: Marquette University Press, 1964).

[276]Cajetan, *D. Thoma De ente et essentia libellus*, p. 75.

[277]See *ST* I, q. 13, art. 4c.

another. But this cannot be true of God, because we call God the first efficient cause. Therefore it is impossible that in God his existence should differ
from his essence.[278]

One can see from this citation how closely Cajetan interprets Aquinas from
his *De ente et essentia*. One can also see that Aquinas's basic conception of
existence remains consistent between his earlier and later works.

Indeed, these three propositions remain consistent with this text in the
ST, as Cajetan advises in chapter VI, question 15, of his commentary on that
same work. He affirms with Aquinas that God is unique in genus in respect
to the unity of essence and existence. Cajetan reasons that essences with a
genus are determined by the fact that it receives its being, thus God is distinguished from genus, because his essence is his existence.[279] Essences that
receive their *esse* are beings in that way, but God has no "way" of being as
such. He is being itself. Participated being is a being in a certain way, but
God's being is unparticipated. What does this mean for Cajetan? It means
that God's existence is *Existentia actualis ad nullum genus determinata, est
purum esse.*[280] That is to say, if God is undetermined by a specific difference,
a genus, like whiteness is not limited by some qualification, then he is "pure
being" or "being itself." While a genus is "predicamental" in its being, God's
being is not, or at any rate transcends all predicamentals.[281] Genus being is
limited and self-limiting. God's being is without limit. Genus being is finite;
God's being infinite.

This leads Cajetan to a further proof of the unity of being and essence in
God, namely, that in God *Esse est de conceptu quidditativo puri esse tantum.*
That is, only the quiddative (essential constitution) of the concept of God
will include *esse*, whereas the essential constitution of a genus being may
not include *esse* as constitutive of its existence, that is, as a power of its own
existence. They have being only in proportion to their essence. Cajetan
summarizes this first principle of his metaphysics as follows: "Existence
belongs to the concept of the quiddity of a thing because that thing is pure

---

[278]*ST* I, q. 4, art. 3.
[279]Ibid.; Cajetan, *D. Thoma De ente et essentia libellus*, p. 173.
[280]Actual existence without determinate genus is pure being.
[281]A *predicamental* is a secondary term that usually sits in relation to the categories and thus is not
capable of expressing a transcendental relation.

esse; furthermore that thing is pure *esse*, because it is not limited to any genus; also that thing is not limited to a genus, because it is identified with its existence."[282]

If God is not a predicamental nature, that is, because of his transcendent nature he is not ultimately subject to predication as such, how then can we name him from this first principle, being? The problem brings Cajetan to his second crucial affirmation, namely, that God as self-subsisting *esse* is the ground of all perfections. This concept of God as *esse subsistens* is the root of all his perfections and therefore the power and possibility of their denomination. That is, God as pure being is the root of all other divine perfections. Pure being is the most basic of all predications because it is nonpredicamental being itself. God is this, because he is it alone, uniquely. The problem of imperfection in God is eliminated if being is read a priori of God and a posteriori of the creature as a predicate. Divine being, according to this, is not a univocal concept, because it is not a genus being. Therefore, against the univocal position he posits the following. "Whoever possesses *esse* according to its fullness lacks no perfection of being. Whoever is *esse subsistens* possesses *esse* in its fullness. Therefore *esse purum subsistens* does not lack any perfection of being."[283] Thus, being, and all other perfections, have their actuality in "being itself." Therefore no man is called wise, good, just and so on unless he actually is so. There are, then, perfections that pertain to the being of the creature. But these are perfections guaranteed a priori by "being itself" as the source of all perfections a posteriori. As we have said, these perfections are possessed imperfectly because we have them individually. In God, however, all such perfections are eminent.[284] That is, in God all perfections are united in *esse simplicissima*.[285] Cajetan explains that divine *esse* is equivalent to all the perfections of all the genera, and it exceeds all these perfections taken singularly or together, since it is a thing of a superior and *inaccessible* order. For example, the sun is immanently light, but the moon only relatively so, yet the light reflected is really the light of the sun.[286]

---

[282]Cajetan, *D. Thoma De ente et essentia libellus*, p. 173.
[283]Ibid., pp. 174-75.
[284]Ibid., p. 175.
[285]Ibid.
[286]Ibid.

Cajetan clearly believes that God is essentially all his perfections and that everything participating, however imperfectly, reflects perfection nevertheless, "being" included. If a being is *ipsum esse subsistens,* it must be perfectly so. It is also, like the sun and its reflected light, "the cause of all other beings."[287] This third proposition is now the metaphysical basis of all possible denomination of divine perfections. He has proven God as the cause of all being already, by virtue of the participation of creation. He comments further on this in his commentary on the *ST* as follows. "Whatever is participated by a being is caused by the being, who essentially possesses what is participated. But *esse* is participated by all beings except God who is His *esse.* Therefore all beings are caused by God."[288]

In terms of his *esse subsistens,* God, as efficient cause, creates being *cum naturalissimum sit unicuique agere sibi simile.* That is, because God is the only perfect being, he is the cause of all other beings and their reflections of perfections.

> Since it is most natural for a thing to effect what is similar to it, and since it is impossible that one being, more perfect in the same line than another being which is such by its very essence, effect what is similar to it, it necessarily follows that the being which is essentially such be the first cause of other beings who are such only by participation, unless perhaps there should be another being who possesses in a more eminent way what is participated.[289]

But this is impossible since God is the highest of all such conceptions. Otherwise, there is an infinite regress of perfect being. This is essentially God's way of being as act. All potentiality is possible only as divine act. Thus the act of God is his existence, his being as such, and is to be summarized in that famous Thomistic dictum *actus purus.* This act of being extends itself to all other actual beings. "Every agent produces what is similar to itself: therefore to any active potency there corresponds as its proper object whatever is possible for that act which is the principle of acting."[290] In this way God's *esse* "contains within itself the total perfection of *esse.*" Furthermore, it excludes

---

[287]See also *ST* I, q. 14.
[288]See also *ST* I, q. 44, art. 1, art. 3; Cajetan, *Commentaria in Primam Partem Summa Theologiae* I, q. 44, art. 1.2.
[289]*ST* I, q. 14, art. 4.
[290]*ST* I, q. 25, art. 3, art. 4.

all generic *esse*. As such he is not a univocal cause. Cajetan concludes:

> There is a difference between a univocal cause and an equivocal cause. The univocal cause produces an effect on its own level; the equivocal does not. Moreover since *esse Dei* has two conditions; namely, that it transcends all genera and contains all perfections, and since no causable taken individually can be conceived to possess such conditions, it is necessary to consider the causable universally.[291]

So God's immediate and proper effect is *esse* because he is *ipsum esse subsistens*. He is being as being, the proper cause of living beings and thus the truth of being itself.[292]

So much for the all-too-brief descriptions of the metaphysics in Aquinas and Cajetan. What now may we say about the so-called analogy of being given this apparent accord between Aquinas and Cajetan, regardless of the variations of the treatment of analogy in Aquinas? Clearly analogy will call for some basic elements based on the preceeding description of metaphysics. Furthermore, it will not be surprising that such elements basically mirror Cajetan's analogy of proportionality.

Summary: Some difficulties with the intrinsic analogy. It would be helpful at this point to summarize what the "analogy of being" essentially looked like given the developments in the interpretation of Aquinas's metaphysics up to and after the fifteenth century, as illustrated in Cajetan, his followers and "correctors." If there was a "Catholic doctrine of analogy," it must have had the following elements, along with its attendant problems. It would appear, based on the preceding description of Thomistic metaphysics as it was commonly conceived in the late Middle Ages, that *being* was and still is considered to be an analogous term and essential as such to meta-

---

[291]*ST* I, q. 25, art. 4, art. 6.

[292]Compare also John F. Wippel, *The Metaphysical Thought of Thomas Aquinas: From Finite Being to Uncreated Being* (Washington, D.C.: The Catholic University of America Press, 2000), pp. 90-91, in the section "Parmenides and the Analogy of Being," where he concludes as follows with respect to the meaning of Aquinas's *De ente et essentia* for analogy: "Though Thomas does not spell this out for us in great detail, his reasoning seems to be this: because being (*ens*) itself is complex, including both quiddity and *esse*, and because *esse* is not realized univocally in two different members of the same species, neither is being so realized. It seems to follow, therefore, that for Aquinas, whether being is predicated of substances which differ specifically or of substances which belong to the same species and differ from one another only individually, it must be predicated of them analogically, not univocally" (*Metaphysical Thought of Thomas Aquinas*, p. 91).

physical description. Both Cajetan and Aquinas seem to affirm this—
Cajetan, in no uncertain terms, and Aquinas at least in terms of how he was
popularly understood and certainly in his *De ente et essentia*. If being is
analogous, then inferior beings express distinct modes of being. But being
cannot be univocal, since then every being would have the same mode of
being, God included. It cannot be equivocal, because then there is no point
of contact between the infinite being ascribed to God and finite being ascribed to the creature. This would be destructive of theological knowledge
altogether. Thus, the term *being*, as applied to finite and infinite being, and
so too substance and accident, is analogous by proper proportionality and/
or, depending on one's interpretation of Aquinas, intrinsic attribution of one
to another.[293]

In his *God as the Mystery of the World*, Jüngel has offered an interesting
interpretation of what happened to these forms of analogous predication, for
which he has been both hailed and criticized.[294] He suggests that Cajetan and
his followers conflated forms of analogy as understood in Aquinas. Based on
the foregoing analysis, it would appear that he was largely correct in his description of the conflation of these two forms of analogy, intrinsic attribution
and proportionality. This is necessarily so since the term *being* must be analogous rather than univocal or equivocal. Why so? And why did Cajetan finally come down to the analogy of proper proportionality? If we can agree
that the term *being* is analogous in a metaphysical way in Thomistic thought,
and not just in a logical or epistemological sense, a term that signifies a
quality or perfection, which is found to be intrinsic in all subjects about
which it is predicated but only according to a way that is proportionate, then
it makes sense to call this an analogy of proportionality. This is also underscored by the fact that, in Aquinas and Cajetan, *being* is a term that is found
properly and intrinsically in a prior way in infinite being, but also intrinsi-

---

[293]The problems with analogy as it relates to metaphysics have been pointed out by Catholic
scholars including Burrell, *Analogy and Philosophical Language*; Anderson, *Reflections on the
Analogy of Being*; and especially Henri Grenier, *Thomistic Philosophy*, 4 vols. (Charlottetown: St.
Dunstan's University Press, 1948); see esp. vol. 3, pp. 20-28.

[294]*GMW*, pp. 272-76. Perhaps the most thorough critique of Jüngel's position thus far is contained
in Rolnick's *Analogical Possibilities*, wherein he picks up on the critique of John Milbank, "Between Purgation and Illumination," in his *Word Made Strange*, pp. 171f; Gerard Rémy's "L'
Analogie selon E. Jüngel. Remarques critiques," *Revue d'Historie et de Philosophie Religiques* 66,
no. 2 (1986): 147-77.

cally in finite being, that is, in substance and accident, but again only proportionately. Thus it would seem that with reference to finite and infinite being,
substance and accident, *being* is analogous by proper proportionality. It is no
mere metaphor, making it simply a principle of logic or of hermeneutic/
epistemic consequence only, though the latter is certainly implied.[295]

Furthermore, as both Aquinas and Cajetan make clear in their respective
metaphysics, these subjects, infinite and finite being, substance and accident,
are all properly beings intrinsically, infinite being in a prior way, finite being
in terms of posteriority. They are so because they demonstrate a relation to
existence by their being—infinite being as being itself, finite being as created
being. In infinite being, essence and existence are identified, and so properly
substance without accident. Finite being exists by virtue of having received
existence, but infinite being, is substantially essence and so possesses existence in itself, is existence itself, whereas accident has existence only in a
finite subject. Now if this all were true only of the analogy of proportionality,
then contemporary scholars might have a case that Aquinas really teaches
the analogy of intrinsic attribution as *unius ad alterum*, or one to another,
but not the analogy of proportionality. But a case has been, and can still be
made, that one is a species of the other, or that they are virtually identical,
in that both constitute an *analogia entis*.[296]

For instance, in the analogy of intrinsic attribution, being is still analogous, by analogy of attribution, and properly so. If it were so by extrinsic
analogy of attribution only, as an effect and sign of infinite being, but not
intrinsically similar to infinite being, then, like the analogy of proper proportionality, intrinsic attribution presupposes an identity of essence and
existence in infinite being, and a real distinction per substance and accidents
in finite being. That is, both approaches share the same metaphysical basis,
the *analogia entis* of Cajetan and others since. Terms in the form of an intrinsic analogy of attribution, of one to another, signify a quality or perfection that is "essentially distinct" yet proportionately the same in each
analogate. These perfections, or qualities, are really objective qualities, yet

---

[295]See Aquinas, *De potentia*, q. 7, art. 7.

[296]See Reinhard Hütter's article, "Attention to the Wisdom of God—From Effect to Cause, from
Creation to God: A Relecture of the Analogy of Being According to Thomas Aquinas," in White,
Analogy of Being, pp. 209-45. See also my article "Causality and the Analogia entis: Reconsider-
ing Karl Barth's Rejection of the Annalogy of Being," *NV* 6, no. 2 (2008): 241-70.

analogically denominated. Thus in all cases of the predication of perfections, either by analogy of intrinsic attribution or by analogy of proportionality, we focus on one concept, which is perfect in infinite being, but only imperfectly known in its difference, in finite *analogatum*. That is, finite *analogatum* possess, intrinsically, the perfection of being, shall we say, in a *confused* manner, whereas it is inhered in infinite being perfectly and unconfused. This is the more express concept that determines the "proper proportion" by which finite analogates possess being. Thus the concept "being" is abstracted from imperfect finite being as perfect infinite being. That is, the prior quality of being in the infinite is the ground and basis of the perfection "being," because it is "being itself" as cause of all other being.[297]

The case now has been fairly well made, by means of the preceding, more metaphysically reflective account of analogy that Cajetan represents the mainstream of Catholic thought on analogy.[298] On that basis we could also make the case that some of the twentieth-century interpretations of the analogy of being, as the "Catholic doctrine," are in fact idiosyncratic despite making some real contributions to the discussion. It was in light of this possible interpretation of the *analogia entis* that Protestant theology evaluated late medieval theology. Because they saw the propensity for the principle to be interpreted toward a univocity of being, for the most part, it was rejected by Protestant theology as being *susceptible to* either an identity between God and creation, or a privileging of the human in relation to the divine. It was, furthermore, considered to be productive of a synergistic understanding of grace in late medieval sacerdotalism, which had supplanted the sovereign and gracious action of God in respect to salvation. Of course, we say "susceptible to" because there existed in the Catholic tradition other, less influential interpretations, based on the same Thomistic metaphysics, that avoided the extremes of agnosticism, sacerdotalism and synergism. But in the Reformation and modern period, up to Vatican II, these were hardly mainstream interpretations of the analogy of being. Protestantism was responding to this "susceptibility" or "tendency" and not always a real state of affairs in Thomism. There is no greater example of such criticism in Prot-

---

[297]See Cajetan, *Analogy of Names*, pp. 79-80.

[298]In essence this has been assumed by many Catholic commentators on analogy, including M. Pinedo, G. Phelan, Klubertanz, Lyttkens, E. Mascall and a host of others.

estant theology than Karl Barth, whom we shall invoke in our next chapter. Here we now want to briefly outline some of these tendencies with the analogy of being especially as they relate to the preceding metaphysical description of analogy. These are only a few of the problems that Protestant thought has discerned in the so-called Catholic doctrine of the *analogia entis*. There are other, lesser issues with it as a mode of theological predication as well.

For the sake of brevity here we shall now refer to both analogy of proportionality and intrinsic attribution of one to another as intrinsic analogy of one to another, since this is its conflated status in the late Middle Ages and Reformation/early modern era. The first two problems are directly related. The *first* problem to be encountered with intrinsic forms of analogy is the fact that terms such as *being, beauty, truth, goodness* and *One*, abstracted as they are from their imperfect representation in multiple *analogatum*, appear to be univocal by virtue of their relation to the one (*unum*), prime analogate. Thus we are already tempted to conclude that the categorical term *being* is univocal. This is so because the claim is that *being* in its infinite analogate is "perfect," but it is necessarily abstracted from a secondary, "imperfect" analogate. If we say, however, that perfection is only inferred and that it is abstracted only imperfectly, then it seems we have only a confused concept of being and not a perfect one, leaving us essentially bereft of the knowledge of being.

Second, if the term *being* must represent a perfection in God, however imperfectly abstracted, it remains somewhat univocal. The concept can only have "objective" meaning if the abstraction is perfect in each of the infinite and finite *analogatum*. If there is no difference in being, then it cannot express the differentiation by which the concept of being is abstracted. Again, it appears univocal, because an objective concept cannot at the same time be unobjective, or less objective. This is a contradiction in terms. If we say that they are only proportionally the same, then we cannot have access to objective infinite being, only subjective finite being.

This brings us to the *third* problem. If indeed we must have a perfect concept of being in order for it to be objectively knowable, then we are back to the same problem. If the term *being* expresses an objective concept that is the same in all the analogates of which it is said, then it must be a univocal concept. If, however, we say the perfect concept is represented in a confused act in finite being, we are left with an imperfect representation of the concept "being." Thus the term *being* cannot be represented as finite being in a confused act, because it is not an objective concept that can be known as perfect. Therefore the difficulty of univocity is not removed if real knowledge is the goal. How do we distinguish one being from another, in terms of degrees of perfection, if being represents its differentia in confused act? Either the concept "being" is a unified, or simple, conception applying to all particulars without degree, or there must be some distinction in finite being in confused act that allows for the abstraction of perfect being. The problem of univocity remains unresolved.

Fourth, being cannot represent its difference in a confused, finite being without including all existents in the similarity. This includes all celestial, animal and material beings. How then do we distinguish human being as a subject that has a special relation to existence, or is it the case that "being" is the designation of all things? If being is a formally perfect designation of God and the human, then it cannot serve as a general designation that returns knowledge of a perfect concept, "being." This problem extends, in my estimation, to the analogy of being in general and bespeaks its ambiguity on the side of agnosticism. Without some objective divine revelation to anchor the concept "being," it dissolves into either nature or God, and in neither case can it be an objective concept. This is why one can conclude that Aquinas is ultimately an existentialist. This is borne out both in his metaphysics and in his conception of analogy, just as it is in Cajetan.

When Jüngel writes the following, he is not, therefore, entirely misrepresenting the "Catholic doctrine of analogy." In fact, he is summarizing its most salient expression in our own time.

> Under the influence of Neoplatonic commentaries in Aristotle, the aspect of dependence was translated from the logical and hermeneutical context to the ontological during the period of Scholasticism, so that the hermeneutical dependence of any *analogatum* on the *analogans* (prime analogate) flowed over into the ontological dimension of dependence of being. The hermeneutical first thing appears as the ontological origin, which under certain circumstances can also be thought of as the ontic causer. The so-called analogy of [intrinsic] attribution now functions in such a way that the analogous pos-

sesses what is meant with the same word more originally than the other things named by the same word and thus appears as the cause in the causal nexus. . . . Analogy thus understood gained special significance in Thomas Aquinas for human talk about God and still determines Kant's usage of analogy in the context of the formation of concepts, which are appropriate to God.[299]

In this way the analogy of intrinsic attribution is conflated with the analogy of proportionality. The metaphysical principles of Cajetan and Aquinas support this conclusion, even if their various treatments of analogy do less so.[300]

Much of the debate about analogy and the modality by which theology may proceed in naming God has been dominated by a desire to reestablish a metaphysical approach, based on some idealized conception of the "Catholic doctrine of analogy." The issues involved extend beyond theological language to include the relationship between nature and grace, natural theology, divine-human agency, transcendence and immanence. We have chosen in this study to focus on analogy because it is a foundational way into expressing these important theological principles and their relation to one another. Though we cannot herein pursue any of these at length, the analysis of the concept of analogy, past and present, does serve us as an orientation to them in contemporary theology. In this respect the contemporary debate has been dominated by certain schools of thought in Protestant, Catholic and Orthodox Christianity. The discussion of the contemporary understanding began with Przywara in his early twentieth-century characterization of the *analogia entis,* which led to both an ecumenical dialogue and an ecumenical divide over the issue of analogy. The protagonists after Przywara include the likes of von Balthasar, among many others. The main antagonists on the Protestant side are Barth and Jüngel, again among others. We will focus on Barth and Jüngel in the second part of this book, since our interest resides in offering an alternative mode of analogy centered in Christology.

In sum, in these first two chapters we have sought to exposit the actual state of affairs in the theological development of the principle of analogy, and its final form in the concept of the "analogy of being," with a view to

---

[299]*GMW*, p. 272.
[300]*GMW*, p. 276.

establishing the fluidity of this principle, and yet the dominant influence of one form of it in the work of Cajetan's *The Analogy of Names*. The underlying motif has been to demonstrate the impossibility of contemporary readings as an attempt to offer an alternative reading of that history in an effort to establish a unitive "Catholic doctrine of analogy" that is basically Thomistic in character. Our overiding conclusion must be that no such unitive principle is operative in Aquinas, or in the history of the development of the idea of analogy as described by Przywara–von Balthasar. Even in the mature *Summae* nothing like a formal and final principle emerges as a settled doctrine. Even if in the principle of *the analogy of one to another* (*unius ad alterum*) we were able to secure this conception in Aquinas, his many statements elsewhere seem to militate against fixing it as the final form. Subsequent debate, from Henry of Ghent to Suárez, seems to have only indemnified this approach in terms of an *analogy of intrinsic attribution*, with considerable overtones and/or conflation in the direction of Cajetan's *analogy of proportionality*. At every step along the way we have had to take notice of the constant need to guard against the tendency toward univocity. Our brief analysis of the metaphysical foundations of analogy has confirmed this tendency and highlighted the problems attendant with such a reading of analogy.

While the contemporary interpretations of the Przywara–von Balthasar model insist that "the Catholic principle of analogy," as it should be understood, avoids such a philosophical problem as univocity imposes on language about God, one wonders if indeed it was not the influential criticism of Protestant thought that drives their desire to seek an "analogy of being within an analogy of faith." One fact is sure, that the characterization of analogy along these lines certainly is not entirely reflective of the tradition since Aquinas. Indeed, of all the recent attempts to explain the Protestant-Catholic divide on this issue, it seems best to investigate further the Protestant concept of the *analogia fidei*, as expressed in the two most significant attempts to establish that principle in Barth and Jüngel. Recent work by McCormack and Keith Johnson has opened up new avenues whereby we may understand the Protestant approach to analogy, especially its rejection of the analogy of being. But we also see in these recent approaches a possibility for reading the *analogia fidei* in its more positive direction and intent.

Chapter three of this work now requires us to account both for the Protestant critique of the analogy of being and its positive proposal for an analogy of faith in light of our survey of the development of the concept of analogy. Barth and Jüngel remain the most authoritative sources in Protestant theology, but recent work has made it possible to see their efforts in a new light, especially in terms of more fully fleshing out the christological orientation of the *analogia fidei*. It is to that task we must now turn.

3

ANALOGY IN KARL BARTH'S
CHURCH DOGMATICS

◆

UNDERSTANDING BARTH'S REJECTION OF THE *ANALOGIA ENTIS*

The preceeding analysis of the development of the concept of the analogy of being in classical and Latin thought has now put us in the best possible position to understand what was at the heart of Barth's "vehement" rejection of this principle as "the invention of the Antichrist" and how his proposal of an "analogy of faith" is substantially different and not just a slogan or a mere restatement of the same concept of the analogy of being, placed over against the Catholic view. The positive conception and use of analogy in Barth is qualitatively different from that expressed in Catholic thought, even in Hans Urs von Balthasar.

Those who criticize Barth's view as dismissive, reductionistic or a self-contradiction have often fallen victim to three dangers in reading Barth. The first is a general lack of close reading of Barth himself in favor of secondary readings, a fact we must note but cannot demonstrate in its fullness. The second danger is in reading Barth ahistorically in terms of his own development. Here the excellent work of Bruce L. McCormack's groundbreaking book *Karl Barth's Critically Realistic Dialectical Theology* has established that Barth cannot be understood apart from the historical context in which his theology developed. The third danger is the failure to read him all the way to the end of his dogmatic project. However, within a wholistic, genetic-historical understanding of Barth's rejection of the analogy of being that follows the Reformed-Scholastic criticism and rejection of it, one can see the emergence of a christological tone in Barth's theology that intensifies in his later work and becomes the central concept in his invocation of the analogy of faith in the *CD*. In fact, already in the early 1920s Barth was trying to find a place for analogical predication on an exclusively christological basis, though dialectic remains a central impulse throughout his works. This by no means indicates that we must see in Barth's rejection of the analogy of being a contradiction to his later invocation of the analogy of faith. It can also be demonstrated that the dialectical feature in Barth's theology is precisely the testing of all analogical predication by the christological criteria as the single root of God's self-revelation.

Barth's rejection of the analogy of being, taken together with his embrace of the analogy of faith, must be seen not just in the places where he takes the matter up directly but in the whole fabric of his concern for the singularity of revelation in all doctrinal expression.[1] Three specific places, besides the usual locations, within the *CD* can help us see further this concern for the singularity of revelation in Barth: his treatment and ultimate rejection of *vestigium trinitatis*, his caution against an appeal to any *analogia causalitatis*, and his final positivistic grounding of an *analogia fidei* in Jesus Christ as elected man and electing God.[2] We will use these themes in Barth's *CD* to underscore his concerns with Catholic theology, keeping in mind that they are by no means exhaustive of what Barth means in his rejection of the analogy of being. Rather, they are clear expressions of his central concern with "method," and they remain normative for him throughout. In the final analysis, these themes in the *CD* express his concern for responsible speech about God that corresponds to the substantial christological event of God's own self-giving. Thus theology can only point us to an analogy of faith. But it must be established that the analogy of faith is no empty concept in Barth's theology. In the final part of this chapter we will trace this concept out in terms of Barth's own Christology in his doctrine of reconciliation, where we find that the *analogia fidei* provides a powerful mode of expression in which theological predication can have its full bearing.[3]

---

[1] On the *analogia entis* see especially *CD* III/2, pp. 220, 244; on the *analogia fidei* and *relationis* see *CD* III/2, pp. 220-21, 323-24. On the general theme of the use of analogy see *CD* III/3, pp. 49-52, 421, 524-30; IV/1, pp. 108, 203, 634, 737, 768-70.

[2] On the *vestigium trinitatis* see *CD* I/1, §8.3, pp. 334-35. On causality and the *analogia entis* see *CD* III/3, §49.2, p. 91. On Jesus Christ as elected and electing God see *CD* II/2, §33.1-2, p. 99, and IV/I, p. 192.

[3] Here we shall focus on *CD* III/1, pp. 198-99, and Barth's understanding of the humility of the eternal Son, which is likely the crowning piece of his final version of the *analogia fidei*, *CD* IV/1, p. 192.

Nevertheless, the *analogia fidei* remains a concept that is not fully exhausted in Barth's theological corpus. Nowhere is it treated as a single theme at length. Rather, as with so many theological themes, it is worked out to the degree that his *CD* is one grand attempt at a christologically grounded *analogia fidei*. Barth's critics are often inattentive to this feature of his *CD*. One of the most incisive Barth scholars in this respect is Eberhard Jüngel. He is one of only a few scholars who have attempted to spell out Barth's appeal to the analogy of faith in terms of a consistent modality indicating how a christologically centered conception of analogy ought to be employed. Though the recent work of Bruce McCormack and Keith Johnson also sheds some light on this aspect of Barth's thought, Jüngel's remains the most penetrating and significant.[4] He calls this the "analogy of advent."[5] In his proposal, which will concern us in chapter four, he constructs an exposition of the *analogia fidei* with a view to a specifically social-linguistic understanding of language that he thinks offers a means for the christological delineation of the analogy of faith. Unpacking this in christological terms will be our final task. When taken together with Barth's treatment of analogy, the concept of correspondence (*Entsprechung*), based on the biblical witness to God's self-revelation in Jesus Christ, becomes a fruitful mode of theological predication. Our final chapter will combine our findings with respect to the analogy of faith in chapters three and four with some reflections on the threefold analogical modalities of participation, performance and parable, clearly recognizable in the prologue of John's Gospel, the high priestly prayer of Jesus (Jn 17) and the parabolic sayings of the Synoptic Gospels. Once we understand the dynamic movements of language, event and witness, we will finally be in a place to understand how theological predication might proceed. In this respect Bath's theological corpus will remain a significant resource for such a project. As von Balthasar well recognized in his magisterial treatment of Barth's theology, there is "much gun powder left unexploded" in the corpus

---

[4]See especially Bruce L. McCormack, "Karl Barth's Version of an 'Analogy of Being': A Dialectical No and Yes to Roman Catholicism," in Thomas Joseph White, O.P., *The Analogy of Being: Invention of the Antichrist or the Wisdom of God?* (Grand Rapids: Eerdmans, 2011), pp. 88-144, and McCormack's *Orthodox and Modern: Studies in the Theology of Karl Barth* (Grand Rapids: Baker Academic, 2008).

[5]The full scope of Eberhard Jüngel's proposal for an "analogy of advent" is worked out in his *GGW*, pp. 357-58; *GMW*, p. 281.

of Barth's work in respect to analogy and theological predication.[6]

Barth's rejection of the analogy of being. Since our immediate concern here is with Barth's attitude toward the *analogy of being* and the *analogy of faith*, we shall focus on those parts of the *CD* that demonstrate these concerns in clear and concise terms. It arises at the very beginning of the enterprise, where his positive concern for revelation in respect to the Trinity emerges, especially illustrated in terms of how he deals with vestiges of the Trinity. It reemerges again in his doctrine of creation and providence, where divine and human action has impotrant consequences for the direction of revelation, specifically in terms of an *analogia causalitatis*. Finally, it is also demonstrated in the positive description of an *analogia fidei*, in an *analogia relationis*, as an aspect of the chriostological determination of the divine-human correspondence in the elected and electing God-Man, Jesus Christ. Thus it is in the material development of his dogmatics that we may now proceed to uncover the final shape of Barth's *analogia fidei*. We shall do so first by means of understanding his rejection of the *analogia entis*, and then describing the precise nature of his *analogia fidei* in light of the whole corpus of the *CD*, with special reference to his conception of Jesus Christ as electing and elected God and Man. While we recognize that much of this material has already been covered in recent Barth scholarship, our intention here and in subsequent chapters is to establish a firm *anlogia fidei* in conjunction with the work of others who have taken their cue from Barth, and with a view in our final chapter to exposit this in more explicitly christological terms.

The question of the possibility of responsible speech about God is broached in the very first volume of the *CD*, especially in connection with the one doctrine Barth sees as the heart of the possibility of theology, namely, the doctrine of the Trinity. Barth's concern for the singularity of revelation remains the controlling principle of his description of the *analogia fidei* throughout the *CD*. This is one of the primary reasons why it constitutes a salutary option for the conduct of theological predication, for Protestant theology at least. But it is no less instructive for theology in other traditions. It arises right at the beginning of Barth's formal, material treatment of theology in volume one of the *CD*, under the title *vestigium trinitatis*, and as

---

[6]Hans Urs von Balthasar, *Karl Barth Darstellung und Deutung Seiner Theologie* (Koln: Kaiser Verlag, 1962), p. 65 (*The Theology of Karl Barth*, trans. E. T. Oakes [San Francisco: Ignatius, 1992], p. 69).

such predetermines much of what Barth will say subsequently about analogy. Therefore it is appropriate that we begin there, though few treatments of Barth take this into account where analogy is concerned.

Vestigium trinitatis *in Barth's CD I/1*. As always, for Barth, responsible speech about God remains the raison d'être of the theological discipline at all times. This is especially so at the place where theology must begin. Theology must be consciously aware, at all times and in all doctrinal locations, of its speech so that it allows God to speak for Godself as far as this is possible within linguistic boundaries. Jüngel suggests that, for Barth,

> the Christian faith proceeds from the prejudgment that God has definitively spoken in the Word of the cross as the gospel for mankind. Theology, therefore, orients itself to that speech which corresponds [*entspricht*] to the crucified Jesus Christ. Only in that fashion does it do justice to the claim that it is talk about God; that talk about God which regulates all other talk about God.[7]

This was the task with which Barth was preeminently concerned throughout the corpus of his *CD*. In *CD* II/1 Barth affirms:

> Our words are not our own property, but His. . . . We use our words improperly and pictorially—as we can now say, looking back from God's revelation—when we apply them within the confines of what is appropriate to us as creatures. When we apply them to God they are not alienated from their original object and therefore from their truth, but, on the contrary, they are restored to it. . . . Now it certainly does not lie in our power to return our words to their proper use. . . . In His revelation God controls His property.[8]

Such an improper use of "God's property" means that we will be limited in terms of how we may use language to express thought about God, on the basis of any kind of analogy.

For Barth the vestiges of the Trinity were a clear example of irresponsible speech about God.[9] Barth believes these attempts at an analogical description

---

[7]*GMW*, p. 227.
[8]*CD* II/1, pp. 229-30.
[9]On the question of the relationship between theological epistemology, revelation and the Augustinian conception of *vestigia trinitatis* as a form of learning through analogy, deeply influenced by Neoplatonic thought, see especially Luigi Gioia, *The Theological Epistemology of St Augustine's De Trinitate* (Oxford: Clarendon Press, 2008). This book constitutes a significant response to Lewis Ayres's *Augustine on the Trinity* (Cambridge: Cambridge University Press, 2004). His criticism of Augustine is shared by many contemporary scholars, including Olivier Du Roy,

of God's triune identity run the risk of a "theological abstraction" that tends to posit another root of revelation other than Scripture. So already at the beginning of the material description of dogmatics, the problem of theological language is a problem of the first order in Barth's *CD*. What he has to say about it is programmatic for the rest of his dogmatic enterprise under the concept of *analogia fidei*.

At this point we want to exposit this portion of the *CD* with a view to ascertaining the nature of Barth's initial solution to the problem of theological language and its implications for our present theological task, an understanding of the *analogia fidei*.[10] This passage clearly presages Barth's absolute rejection of the *analogia entis* in favor of an *analogia fidei*. In his rejection of *vestigium trinitatis* Barth is clearly breaking with all forms of natural theology, even though his later statements will allow for only one form of a qualified *vestigium trinitatis*, namely, Jesus Christ. He does so in such a way that there is no equation between an *analogia entis* and an *analogia fidei*. In fact the development of the idea of *vestigium trinitatis* was in the interest of an "essentially Trinitarian disposition supposedly immanent in some created realities quite apart from their possible conscription by God's revelation. Under the concept of *vestigium Trinitatis* the analogy of being would patently have to be considered a second root of revelation. It was a genuine *analogia entis*."[11] In essence, Barth's rejection of *vestigium trinitatis* is austensibly then also a rejection of *analogia entis*. Such an understanding is a beginning of a clarification that not only makes firm Barth's distinction between *analogia entis* and *analogia fidei*, but also underscores the content of that *analogia fidei*, though Barth does not flesh this out in the immediate context. Nevertheless, it

---

L'Intelligence de la foi en la Trinité selon saint Augustin (Paris: Études Augustiniennes, 1966); see especially John Milbank's "Sacred Triads: Augustine and the Indo-European Soul," in R. Dodaro and G. Laws, *Augustine and His Critics* (London: Routledge, 2000), pp. 77-102. See also Wayne J. Hankey, "Philosophical Religion and the Neoplatonic Turn to the Subject," in Wayne J. Hankey and Douglas Hedley, eds., *Deconstructing Radical Orthodoxy: Postmodern Theology, Rhetoric and Truth* (Burlington, VT: Ashgate, 2005), pp. 17-30.

[10]On Karl Barth's treatment of the *vestigium trinitatis*, see especially *GMW*, pp. 343-68, and Eberhard Jüngel, *God's Being Is in Becoming: The Trinitarian Being of God in the Theology of Karl Barth, a Paraphrase*, trans. John Webster (Grand Rapids: Eerdmans, 2001), pp. 17-27; see also Alan Torrance, *Persons in Communion* (Edinburgh: T & T Clark, 1996); Gioia, *Theological Epistemology of St Augustine's De Trinitate*, pp. 4-22.

[11]*CD* I/1, p. 335.

does form the background of his rather startling treatment of election in
CD II/2.

It was for the reason of responsible speech about God that Barth was
himself interested in a revised understanding of Trinity along economic
lines, and along the way he felt it necessary to pass judgment on this Augustinian and patristic conception of *vestigium trinitatis*. Barth's concern with
this doctrine has to do precisely with the relationship between revelation
and the triunity of God's being in terms of intradivine relations. Indeed, for
Barth, "the biblical doctrine of revelation is implicitly, and in some passages
explicitly, a pointer to the doctrine of the Trinity."[12] As such the biblical
witness to revelation has to do precisely with the Trinity as its "interpretation." In point of fact, the doctrine of the Trinity is "the exegesis of this
text," that is, of Scripture.

For Barth, only the biblical revelation of the "single Lordship of God
as Father, Son and Spirit" can be the root of the doctrine of the Trinity,
and there can be no other root from which this doctrine can stem. Barth
concludes:

> What we hear when with our human ears and concepts we listen to God's
> revelation, what we perceive (and can perceive as men) in Scripture, what
> proclamation of the Word of God actually is in our lives—is the thrice single
> voice of the Father, the Son, and the Spirit. This is how God is present for us
> in His revelation. This is how He Himself obviously creates a *vestigium* of
> Himself and His triunity. We are not adding anything but simply saying the
> same thing when we point out that God is present for us in the threefold
> form of His Word, in His revelation, in Holy Scripture, and in proclamation.
> This *vestigium* is plain and reliable. . . . In adhering to this, we shall not be
> accepting a second root alongside the first but just the one root of the doc-
> trine of the Trinity.[13]

Thus the doctrine of *vestigium trinitatis* poses a specific problem for the way
in which *we may speak* of the Trinity. It is a subversion of an *analogia fidei*
as such. In short, the doctrine of *vestigium trinitatis* implies, for Barth, a
genuine *analogia entis* according to which it is affirmed that the Creator,
God, has left traces of his being in the created order, which, through rational

---

[12]*CD* I/1, p. 333.
[13]*CD* I/1, p. 347.

reflection, we may know, apart from the scriptural principle of the incarnation. As Barth put it, "the concern here was with an essential Trinitarian disposition supposedly eminent in some created realities quite apart from their possible conscription by God's revelation."[14]

The importance of Barth's prohibition against *vestigium trinitatis* extends far beyond a mere critique of an inappropriate model for conceiving or establishing the truth of the doctrine of the Trinity in a natural theology. Barth himself recognized the problem as a fundamental one for and about theological language. He writes:

> The problem which is posed when the presence and knowability of these *vestigia trinitatis* are asserted is actually, then, of the greatest importance, not only for the question of the root of the doctrine of the Trinity, but also for that of revelation, of the grounding of theology in revelation alone, and finally even for that of the meaning and possibility of theology as distinct from mere cosmology or anthropology.[15]

What is of particular importance in his prohibition of the *vestigium trinitatis* is that Barth is both safeguarding and prescribing a fundamental rule for theological language, one that is already suggestive of the analogy of faith. This cannot be emphasized strongly enough in regard to Barth. Responsible speech about God is grounded in God's own self-revelation. There is no other source for theological talk than that of the revelation of God's triune being, as witnessed to in the Scriptures. As such, the doctrine of the Trinity is an *analogia fidei*, if by it we mean, as per Richard Muller, "the use of a general sense of the meaning of Scripture, constructed from the clear or unambiguous *loci*, as the basis for interpreting unclear or ambiguous texts." Muller correctly refers to this principle as "distinct from the more basic

---

[14]*CD* I/1, p. 335. "We might, of course, call this, and we can certainly call the form that God assumes in His unveiling as the Son or Word, the *vestigium trinitatis* (trace of the Trinity). But this is not what was meant in the development and use of the concept. The concern here was with an essential trinitarian disposition supposedly immanent in some created realities quite apart from their possible conscription by God's revelation. It was with a genuine *analogia entis* (analogy of being), with traces of the trinitarian Creator God in being as such, in its pure createdness. If it be acknowledged that there are *vestigia trinitatis* (traces of the Trinity), in this second sense then the question obviously arises—and this is why we must discuss the matter in the present context—whether we do not have to assume a second root of the doctrine of the Trinity alongside the one we have indicated in the previous sub-section."

[15]Ibid.

analogia Scripturae." Rather, "the *analogia fidei* presupposes a sense of the theological meaning of Scripture."[16]

The fundamental problem with *vestigium trinitatis* is that it seeks to talk of God with the language and concepts drawn from the natural realm, that is, solely within the world as such. This worldly language is inherently flawed and unsuitable for responsible speech about God because its verbal concepts and accompanying thought forms are fundamentally tied to humanity, and as such share in humanity's utter fallenness and alienation from God. Barth underscores this later point elsewhere in his *CD* when he describes human language as the most prominent example of the human situation of guilt, misery and separation from God. For Barth, the question that Christian theology must answer is how responsible speech about God is possible at all. Or even how the Scriptures, as human speech itself, can be the medium of God's revelation when human language in and of itself has no such capacity for responsible speech about God. Barth writes, "Theology and the Church, and even the Bible itself, speak no other language than that of this world which is shaped in form and content by the creaturely nature of the world and also conditioned by the limitations of humanity."[17] This capacity of language to convey revelation resides neither in human speech nor in the creaturely condition per se, but rather in the event of revelation, which is the sole object of authentic speech about God. In Barth's words, language is "seized" by revelation, and not vice versa.[18] Barth understands this possibility as "a venture which is, as it were, ascribed to language, and consequently to the world or man, from without, so that it is not really the possibility of the language, the world, or man, but the possibility of revelation."[19]

---

[16]Richard A. Muller, *Dictionary of Latin and Greek Theological Terms* (Grand Rapids: Baker Academic, 1985), p. 33.

[17]*CD* I/1, pp. 339-40. Barth writes: "The other impression we undeniably get from the whole material is that in varying degrees there must be 'something in' the connexion between the Trinity and all the 'trinities' to which reference is made here. Why should there not be something in it? The only question is what? Theology and the Church, and even the Bible itself, speak no other language than that of this world which is shaped in form and content by the creaturely nature of the world and also conditioned by the limitations of humanity: the language in which man as he is, as sinful and corrupt man, wrestles with the world as it encounters him and as he sees and tries to understand it."

[18]*CD* I/1, p. 348. Barth sees the doctrine of the Trinity as exclusively a "Church doctrine."

[19]*CD* I/1, p. 345.

Barth understood this to be the original intention behind the employment of *vestigium trinitatis*. It was a natural response of human individuals who were attempting to cast a "rational light," drawn from the world of experience, on the "unfathomable" mystery of God. Insofar as their attempts were serious and not an "idle game," we must ask the question as to whether there was "something in it" and if so, "what?"[20] Despite their best intentions, however, it was a process in which the fathers involved the church in dangerous theological language. What is at stake in such vestiges is the nature of the theological task itself and the threat of a μετάβασις εἰς ἄλλο γένος, through which the task and language of theology is fundamentally altered.[21] Barth labels this danger as the "transition from interpretation to illustration" and concludes, in regard to the employment of *vestigium trinitatis*, "We are plainly dealing with that non-obligatory, un-commissioned and dangerous possibility whenever theological language, as here, thinks it must not just be interpretation of revelation but also its illuminator. Interpretation means *saying the same thing* in other words. Illustration means saying the same thing *in other words*."[22] What is important is where we put the emphasis in our theological language. A precise line cannot be drawn, because traces of illustration can be found within interpretation just as interpretation is inevitably part of illustration. Yet Barth wishes to identify a direction denoted by each and employ this distinction as a criterion for theological language. The problem with illustration is that it posits a secondary root in terms of language about God. "We no longer trust revelation in respect of its self-evidential force. What we say about it must be buttressed and strengthened and confirmed by something other than itself."[23] In short, it represents a loss of confidence in the power of revelation to communicate clearly, thus necessitating a shift in confidence toward the inner capacity of human experience and language. In this respect, Barth says, "unbelief has already taken place," and therefore illustration already "stands under the interdict: Thou shalt not make unto thee any likeness."[24] Ultimately, the strident employment of *illustration* in

---

[20]Ibid.
[21]Ibid.
[22]Ibid.
[23]Ibid.
[24]Ibid.

theological language represents the abandonment of revelation as the sole source for speech about God.[25]

Interpretation, however, represents a process whereby the language of the theologian is centered on its object, which is constituted by the event of revelation. Interpretation is theological language that has allowed itself to be "seized" by revelation. Any appropriately formulated doctrine of the Trinity, and for that matter all Christian doctrine, will conform to this interpretive enterprise, which takes as its starting point the biblical witness to revelation.

> Theological language is not free to venture anything and everything. . . . To derive the Trinity consciously and intentionally from the scheme of man's consciousness or from some other creaturely order instead of Scripture is not the same thing as to derive it from Scripture and at the same time to grasp at a scheme which admittedly bears no small resemblance to that of man's self-consciousness and other creaturely orders.[26]

For Barth, the root of the doctrine must be found solely in the revelation to which Scripture bears witness. To root it anywhere else is to transform the Christian God into another "alien" god. "It is in the name of a pointer of this kind that we reject the doctrine of the *vestigia*," as an instance of *analogia entis*.[27] Such an *analogia entis* Barth detects to be at the very heart of what he declares would be the ultimate result of positing such *vestigia*, namely, German idealism. At the height of its development, the *vestigium trinitatis* could well issue in an absolutizing of subjectivity as in the idealist philosophy of Friedrich Wilhelm Joseph Schelling, with his "subject,

---

[25]See Jüngel, *God's Being Is in Becoming*, pp. 19-20. He was correct to identify Barth's concern as one with respect to the "capacity of language" for the "Trinitarian mystery of God," that is, as a hermeneutical problem. That it spoke of this revelation is a given; that it could really do so without itself being first grasped by revelation is precisely the problem with presupposing a *vestigium trinitatis*. It was as such an *analogia entis*.

[26]*CD* I/1, p. 335. "And if this question be admitted, then the further question can hardly be avoided: Which of the two roots of the doctrine of the Trinity that both call for consideration is the true and primary root, and which is a secondary 'runner'? But then we should also have to allow the question whether the derivation of the doctrine of the Trinity from the biblical revelation is not just the later confirmation of a knowledge of God which can be won from His revelation in creation quite apart from the biblical revelation. And then it is difficult to omit the final question whether these *vestigia* on which the doctrine of the Trinity is really based are in fact to be regarded as the *vestigia* of a Creator God transcending the world and not as determinations of the cosmos which must be viewed as strictly immanent and, because the cosmos is man's cosmos, as determinations of man's existence."

[27]Ibid.

object, subject-object" synthesis, or more likely George Wilhelm Friedrich Hegel with his "in-itself, for-itself, in-and-for-itself." Both dialectical models issue in an "absolute Spirit as synthesis." If these immanent absolutisms are not the product of *vestigium trinitatis*, they are no less unthinkable without the broader tendency to subjectivize trinitarian theology, if not directly as a development of Augustine's *vestigium trinitatis*. Should such a modality of analogy be considered as the hermeneutical key to the doctrine of the Trinity, it would equally have to involve a "logico-grammatical scheme" of signification under the subject, object and predicate function of language, as well. To that end we may certainly see such an immanent absolutization as a species of "the mediaeval construct of the religious consciousness," and therefore also "a variation on the general Augustinian argument from consciousness."[28]

Clearly the dispute for Barth is about the status of *analogia entis* to which *vestigium trinitatis* must refer. Such an *analogia entis* is not permissible, and Barth makes clear his reason for rejecting this theological method in *CD* II/1.

> Natural theology is the doctrine of a union of man with God existing outside of God's revelation in Jesus Christ. It works out the knowledge of God that is possible and real on the basis of this independent union with God. . . . Whatever we may think of its character as reality or illusion, this sphere arises and exists in the fact that man depends on himself over against God.[29]

However, as his treatment of *vestigium trinitatis* suggests, Barth's rejection of natural theology is rooted in his insistence on the singularity of the event of revelation witnessed to in the Scriptures as the sole source for theological speech. Therefore if revelation exists in nature, which Barth elsewhere affirms, it is not confirmed by any independent means apart from pointing to the revelation of God in the event of Jesus Christ. If there is a vestige of the Trinity in nature, it must be confirmed in that event, which Barth thinks is the case. Revelation comes to humanity exclusively as a product of God the Father's gracious, revelatory act in the incarnation of Christ and the subsequent procession of the Holy Spirit. There is not, and can never be, any human capacity for revelation outside this gracious event. Sin prohibits

---

[28]*CD* I/1, p. 338.
[29]*CD* II/1, p. 168.

any natural correspondence between God and humanity; therefore, Barth views attempts at natural theology as *hubris* when used as a basis for theological naming. It is a "cognitive-linguistic Pelagianism" that dispenses with grace.[30] It represents nothing less than the elevation of humanity to a place beside God, on an equal footing with him, outside grace. It is for this reason and this reason alone that Barth would brook no place in theology for any hint of *analogia entis* as he understood the phrase.[31] While the characterization of analogy will change over the course of the *CD*, nowhere does it amount to an embrace of the *analogia entis* or any of its derivitives and species.[32] All other attempts at analogy, by means of reference to human consciousness, soul, causality, intrinsic or extrinsic attribution of perfections, relationality, or being, do not return a capacity for language to express God in his revelation. They all fall under the same criticism as the principle of *vestigium trinitatis*.

In sum, Barth's rejection of the *vestigium trinitatis* amounts to a rejection of any other source for revelation and therefore any form of *analogia entis* as a basis for speaking about God. The doctrine of the Trinity, as the *interpretation* of revelation, represents the positive, christological alternative for authentic human speech about God as the one true *analogia fidei*. It is an alternative, however, that lies outside the realm of human experience and language as such. It must be given, and is given, in Jesus Christ. The doctrine of the Trinity, when correctly interpreted, grounds responsible speech about God in God's gracious commandeering of the language. It is *sola gratia*, and as such it has tremendous implications for the rest of Barth's dogmatic enterprise, especially, as we shall see, his doctrine of election. The material content of doctrine must be intimately linked with this *analogia fidei*, if it hopes to correspond to the witness to revelation in Scripture. This corre-

---

[30]*CD* II/1, p. 131.

[31]*CD* I/1, p. xiii.

[32]In 1962–1964, during discussions with students at Princeton University and the University of Tübingen, respectively, Barth responded very clearly to a question put by the students as to his "change of mind" on the *analogia entis*. He denied categorically that anything he had written since his rejection of it in the early *Dogmatics* can be read as a change of mind on the issue. Keith Johnson has made it clear that such a reading of Barth misses the inner connections that Barth establishes between God and the human in his mature *Dogmatics*. See Keith Johnson, *Karl Barth and the Analogia entis* (London: T & T Clark, 2010), pp. 226-27. For the often-misunderstood comment in Barth's later work, see his *The Humanity of God* (Philadelphia: John Knox, 1960), pp. 45-46.

spondence aims at an accurate account, as far as possible, of its author, God, who is its subject. Jesus Christ is as such the one true *vestigium trinitatis* and therefore also the one true *analogia fidei*. This understanding of the basic hermeneutical and ontological implications of analogy will follow Barth into the rest of the *CD*, as we shall now demonstrate by means of an extended exposition of his section in the *CD* on the doctrine of concursus and the divine accompanying (III/3). We will confirm this in the final section by means of an exposition of his alternative proposal for an *analogia fidei*, which will serve us as a basis for further exploration of this principle in chapters four and five.

Causality and Barth's rejection of the analogia entis. One of the most incisive and nuanced discussions of a similar concern to protect the singularity of revelation occurs in Barth's doctrine of creation, in *CD* III/3, especially in respect to the so-called *analogia causalitatis*. In fact this section goes to the heart of Barth's concern for and *analogia fidei* over against an *analogia entis*. It is a theme not traditionally focused on by scholars in relation to Barth's rejection of the *analogia entis*. This section of the *CD* illustrates both the complexity of the concept of analogy and the propensity for historical misunderstanding regarding the real intentions of Barth's appeal to the analogy of faith.[33] It is for these reasons that we must attend to it as another case in point of Barth's rejection of the *analogia entis*.

What is it about the concept of *causality* and causal argumentation that gives Barth pause for its consideration? Certainly the concept of CER has a central part to play in his rejection of any *analogia causalitatis*. In fact, Barth's rejection of the *analogia entis* can be better understood in the light of his rejection of the medieval understanding of causality that lies at the heart of the classical conception of analogy as CER. As we have seen, this is a feature of Catholic thought that has determined analogical predication from the beginning. It is in the light of this aspect of Barth's argument that

---

[33]The *locus classicus* is, of course, von Balthasar's well-known book *The Theology of Karl Barth: Exposition and Interpretation*, trans. Edward T. Oakes (San Francisco: Ignatius, 1992). See David Bentley Hart, *The Beauty of the Infinite: The Aesthetics of Christian Truth* (Grand Rapids: Eerdmans, 2003). J. Betz says something similar and somewhat in support of Hart in his "Beyond the Sublime: The Aesthetics of the Analogy of Being (Part One)," *ModT* 21, no. 3 (July 2005): 367-408. Betz accuses Barth of paying "little attention to detail" in his critique of Przywara. For part two, see *ModT* 22, no. 1 (January 2006): 1-50.

we can more fully understand one of the most important reasons why he remains concerned about it. This passage demonstrates that Barth is consistent in his rejection of this Thomistic conception of analogy in CD II/1, despite his opting for a form of analogical method and his apparent "misunderstanding" of "the Catholic principle" of analogy.

As we have seen, the appeal to causality in the Neoplatonic reading of Aristotle in the cosmology and theology of Pseudo-Dionysius (following the Neoplatonist, Proclus) is mediated through the philosophy and theology of Aquinas.[34] We have also demonstrated that this Dionysian/Proclan reading of causality, briefly stated in the medieval axiom that "effects resemble their cause," is employed throughout the Middle Ages as a fundamental epistemology for the knowledge of God and nature. That is, in Catholic thought it has sometimes functioned as a veritable metaphysics, a totalizing principle, a genus under which all else has its being and by which we may know being.[35] In this sense being is the only possible category by which we may know God, analogically. The argument must, of necessity, because of our finitude, be from human being to divine being, emphasizing dissimilarity but, again necessarily, affirming similarity, if knowledge is to be attained. Dissimilarity is only heavily emphasized where apophaticism is the ruling paradigm, but with a net negative return on the knowledge of God as such.

It has been suggested above that Aquinas, and medieval theology following him, appears to have derived an ontology of being from this quasi–Aristotelian-Neoplatonic conception of causality, which allowed for Immanuel Kant's demolition and reconfiguration of the argument from causality in his *Critique of Pure Reason* and *Critique of Judgment*, and in his subsequent description of divine providence in his *Lectures on the Philosophical Doctrine of Religion*. In this last work Kant attempts to secure the principle of the freedom of the human will over against the Scholastic, and Reformed-Scholastic, restriction of it on the basis of God's omni-

---

[34]W. J. Hankey, *God in Himself: Aquinas' Doctrine of God as Expounded in the Summa Theologiae* (Oxford: Oxford University Press, 1987).

[35]As we saw in chapter one, in Joseph Owens's groundbreaking study *The Doctrine of Being in the Aristotelian Metaphysics: A Study in the Greek Background of Mediaeval Thought* (Toronto: Pontifical Institute of Mediaeval Studies, 1951). Owens states with regard to the treatment of cause in the Aristotelian *Metaphysics* IV, "In this discussion Aristotle has linked 'universal' knowledge with knowledge 'through cause.'"

causality. In Reformed theology, up to and including Kant's time, this understanding of providence issued in the doctrine of *concursus*, which attempted to demonstrate at one and the same time the freedom of both the divine and human agents without the assimilation of one by the other. It is in light of this doctrine that Kant demolishes the CER as a secure source of the knowledge of God purely on the basis of empirical observation of natural causation.

In his treatment of "the divine accompanying" in the *CD* III/3, under the doctrine of providence, Barth is concerned to distinguish himself from any understanding of an *analogia causalitatis*, precisely by reformulating the Reformed doctrine of *concursus* over against the ontological approach to causality in Aquinas, the Jesuits (Przywara and Molina) and the Reformed-Scholastic approach where it follows Aquinas or Molina. Partly this is because of the Kantian critique, but more importantly it is because he considered the medieval form of the doctrine of "omnicausality" to be contrary to the doctrine of *creatio ex nihilo*, though he does hold to a form of causal argumentation that is christologically determined. A close reading of this section of Barth's *CD*, prefaced by a brief comment on his treatment of omnicausality and Molinism in *CD* II/1 (in order to set the context), will amply demonstrate that Barth is rejecting an ontology ingredient in what he calls "the *analogia entis*" more than he is rejecting any and all forms of analogy. This is so precisely because such an *analogia entis*, expressed also as an *analogia causalitatis*, is, as far as Barth is concerned, not to be found in the Bible. Furthermore, to the degree that it aids in establishing a knowledge of God apart from God's self-revelation as the Father of Jesus Christ, it represents a standpoint over against Christ, who is the sole *analogia fidei* to which theology can appeal for its theological speech.

As we have noted above, at the root of Barth's concern for the causal principle embedded in the concept of *analogia entis* is its tendency to fall under the Kantian critique. Kant's Copernican revolution is in essence his establishment of the principle of *causality* as a valid a priori judgment that enables us to make sense of our experience of objects in space and time.[36] This discovery came to him from his analysis of the physical sciences and

---

[36]Immanuel Kant, *Critique of Pure Reason*, trans. M. J. D. Meiklejohn (London: J. M. Dent and Sons, 1950), preface 4a.

mathematics, which were understood by Kant not merely to be about the apprehension of objects by means of sensible experience but as implying that the mind gives something to the determination of the object in space and time. The question that emerges for Kant is whether or not on this basis "we might be able to construct a real metaphysics as science."[37] The problem at the heart of this metaphysics is to rationally explain how we can admit to an a priori judgment, which does not turn out to be a fiction but expresses the real state of affairs. For Kant, the metaphysics of the scholastics (as embodied in Thomism) tended to ignore this a priori element within the mind in its determination of the knowledge of objects, which it assumed was knowable without in any sense being determined a priori by the mind.

This conclusion, in the *Critique of Judgment*, issues in a completely closed system of causality in which the knowledge of God is finally all but denied.[38]

> It is quite true that we cannot prove the existence of God as the moral author of the "World" simply from a consideration of nature as implying purpose. But it is the very character of reason that it cannot be satisfied with anything short of an absolute unity of principles, and therefore the knowledge of physical ends, when it is brought into relation with the knowledge of the moral end, is the means by which we are enabled to connect the practical reality of the idea of God with its theoretical reality as already existing for judgment.[39]

In sum, says Kant, *two* things must be kept in mind in regard to the moral proof of the existence of God in light of this closed system of ends. "In the first place, since we have no positive knowledge of the existence of a Supreme Being, on account of the necessary limitations of our knowledge to objects of sensible experience, we can only think or conceive the attributes

---

[37]Immanuel Kant, *Prolegomena to Any Future Metaphysics*, The Library of Liberal Arts (New York: Bobbs-Merrill, 1950). Kant writes: "My purpose is to persuade all those who think metaphysics worth studying that it is absolutely necessary to pause a moment and, regarding all that has been done as though undone, to propose first the preliminary question, 'Whether such a thing as metaphysics be even possible at all?'" (*Prolegomena to Any Future Metaphysics*, p. 3).

[38]Ibid., p. 432. Kant concludes that, "The conception, therefore, of an absolute end, i.e. of the possibility of the free realization of absolute moral laws by beings who are ends in themselves, presupposes the existence of a moral cause or author of the world; in other words, it presupposes the existence of God." But, says Kant, "we cannot assume that in the supreme cause of the world, which we must conceive of as an intelligence, there is the same contrast between reason as practical and reason as theoretical, and that a kind causality is required for the ultimate end which is different from that required for natural ends."

[39]Ibid.

of this Being by analogy."[40] It is not possible for us actually to know God, because there is nothing within our experience that reveals to us the nature of a being who transcends all experience. Secondly, it follows from this that, "though we are entitled to say that the Supreme Being must by His nature *correspond* to what we mean by intelligence and morality, this does not enable us to know Him as He is, nor can we predicate these attributes positively of Him."[41] Thus, according to Kant, the only manner in which we can realize for ourselves the nature of the Supreme Being is through the application of the idea of *final cause* or purpose, and that idea is only a regulative, not a constitutive, principle. Reason must take the form of the determinant judgment before we could absolutely determine the nature of God, and this is contrary to its fundamental character. The final result of Kant's whole enquiry was to place belief in God, freedom and immortality on a thoroughly rational basis, a result that at first sight seemed to be excluded by the necessary limitation of knowledge to the world of sense. This was his achievement for metaphysics. It was an achievement that he established due to the failure of scholastic metaphysics, and that as it was centered on the Thomistic/Aristotelian/Platonic epistemology of causality.[42]

Barth saw the danger in this emanationist argument from *causality* ingredient in analogical predication about God and its net negative return, and he warns of this problem throughout the *CD*.[43] My point here is simply to register this and not to render judgment as to the correctness of Barth's concern or to defend it per se. Barth's understanding of causality, especially in his treatment of primary and secondary causality, must be understood with special reference to his rejection of omnicausality and Molinism in his treatment of omnipotence in *CD* II/1, which is the proper dogmatic context for thinking here.[44]

There is no question that, in respect to his aversion to Neoplatonic em-

---

[40]See Immanuel Kant, *The Critique of Judgment*, trans. J. H. Bernard (Amherst, NY: Prometheus Books, 2000), pp. 348-49; *Lectures on the Philosophical Doctrine of Religion*, trans. and ed. Allen Wood and George Di Giovanni (Cambridge, Cambridge University Press, 1996), p. 422.

[41]Kant, *Critique of Judgment*, pp. 348-49.

[42]Kant, *Lectures on the Philosophical Doctrine of Religion*, p. 427.

[43]See John Betz's characterization of Barth's rejection of the *analogia entis* as an "unfair" and "abrupt" treatment of Przywara in "Beyond the Sublime: The Asthetics of the Analogy of Being (Part One)."

[44]*CD* II/1, pp. 529-30; III/3, pp. 89-154.

anationism, Barth also remains consistent throughout the *CD*. In respect to the predication of the perfections of God on the basis of any CER, Barth says:

> The fact that He (God) is one and the same does not mean that He is bound to be and to say and to do only one and the same thing, so that all the distinctions (perfections) of His being, speaking and acting are only a semblance, only the various refractions of a beam of light which are eternally the same. This was and is the way that every form of Platonism conceives of God. It is impossible to overemphasize the fact that here, too, God is described as basically without life, word or act. Biblical thinking about God would rather submit to the confusion of the grossest anthropomorphisms than to confusion with this, the primary denial of God.[45]

What is notable about this citation is the direct opposition Barth sees between the biblical descriptions of God's attributes and those of the Platonic tradition, which he sees as ultimately irreconcilable with the biblical witness. This is the primary attitude with which Barth begins his doctrine of God, and it expresses much about his approach toward those Platonizing principles that merely end in either the reduction of God to nonexistence, or to nothing but pure potential that is absolutely unknowable, unthinkable and unspeakable.[46] Barth sees the epitome of this reductionist approach to theology latent in the doctrine of *omnicausality*, expressed in terms of the classical doctrine of omnipotence, which he attributes to the Thomistic conception of *causality*. Says Barth:

> It is important to perceive the thrust of grace, mercy and patience in which God makes Himself our omnipotent God and applies His omnipotence beneficially to us as His omnicausality, although He does not need to do this or

---

[45]*CD* II/1, p. 496. Colin Gunton puts into perspective the importance of Barth's aversion to all forms of Platonic thinking, monist, dualist and emanationist, writing: "Thus, according to Barth revelation overthrows axiomatic monism of the kind that Hartshorne avows. . . . He wishes to preserve an understanding of God as one who really does things with, to, and for mankind, but who does them not because of necessitated metaphysical ties but because he freely and graciously chooses to do them. . . . The triumph of Barth's theology is a God who doesn't need man; therefore He can let man live" (*Becoming and Being: The Doctrine of God in Charles Hartshorne and Karl Barth* [Oxford: Oxford University Press, 1978], p. 154).

[46]Barth comments later in his treatment of the nature and provenance of the world that some Christian theologies lapse into "a monistic and or dualistic explanation" that is reductionist either on the side of the divine or the side of the world (*CD* II/1, p. 500).

> lose anything by doing it. . . . Absolutely everything depends on whether we distinguish His omnipotence from His omnicausality: not to the glory of an unknown omnipotent being who is beyond and behind His work; but to the glory of the omnipotent God who is present to us in His work and is known to us by His self-revelation; to the glory of His divinity, of the freedom of His love. Without which His love would not be divine love or recognizable as such.[47]

For Barth, this complete theological identification of God's omnipotence with his omnicausality leads to the perception that God is no longer the subject over his works and is "finally denied as such."[48] In exactly this way both the Protestant Reformed and the Catholic tradition demonstrate that it is not concerned with God, who is the subject of omnipotence and possesses it. Rather they are concerned with the bare concept of divine omnipotence, and with this "only as it denotes the *causal* basis of the natural system, i.e. the totality of finite causes and effects."[49] Barth is concerned to point out that a proper understanding of existence through divine *potentia* does not entail a metaphysics of necessity but allows for the freedom of God to decide what will and will not be. Causality must not be a principle that binds God to creation through a Neoplatonic doctrine of the "potency of participation."[50]

To drive home this tendency that Barth sees in the Thomistic and Reformed-Scholastic tradition, we can also note his treatment of Mo-

---

[47]*CD* II/1, p. 528. In regard to the absolute identification of power and causality in God, as per Aquinas, Barth writes, "If this is all there is to say, is not the conclusion irresistible that no potential can be ascribed to God intra se, as distinct from His operations ad extra, and therefore that impotentia must be ascribed to Him in Himself? Does God begin to be omnipotent only with the existence of a reality distinct from Himself, an extra in which His omnipotence can be omnicausality? Does it first exist as His relationship to this extra? But how is this in any sense possible if there is no corresponding being in God Himself? And how can God's relation *ad extra*, His omnicausality, be distinguished from all this outward activity?"

[48]*CD* II/1, p. 529. This is the problem, according to Barth, with Friedrich Schleiermacher's employment of causality as well. See Schleiermacher, *The Christian Faith* (Edinburgh: T & T Clark, 1992), §54-55.

[49]*CD* II/1, p. 530.

[50]Hankey, in "Radical Orthodoxy's Poiesis: Ideological Historiography and Anti-Modern Polemic," *American Catholic Philosophical Quarterly* 80, no. 1 (2006): 1-21, calls into serious question the radical orthodox appeal to participatory *poiesis* as the essence of Thomistic metaphysics, which places Aquinas's work squarely in the field of theology and not philosophy. But appeal to the Thomistic understanding of "participation" does not solve the problem of *esse* in Aquinas ("Radical Orthodoxy," p. 11). See also Hankey, *God in Himself*, p. 139.

linism that occurs in the same discussion of the attributes of God, but now with respect to omniscience. The basis of the critique that Barth levels at Molinism is the same as that raised against the absolute identification of omnipotence and omnicausality.[51] Barth recognizes that Thomism rejected the Molinist position, but ultimately came to an accommodation in relation to it (as did the Catholic Church in general). At the heart of this doctrine there is an inherent penchant for synergism expressed as an *analogia entis*, conveyed through a metaphysics of *causality*. Barth writes that

> an effective denial of Molinism is possible only when we cease to think in a God-creature system, in the framework of the *analogia entis*. It is possible only when theology dares to be theology and not ontology, and the question of a freedom of the creature which creates conditions for God can no longer arise. But this can happen only when theology is orientated on God's revelation and therefore [on] Christology.[52]

Here, in Molinism, Barth also sees the same operative monism in the treatment of God's foreknowledge that he saw in the treatment of God's omnipotence as omnicausality. Thomism could not ultimately deny Molinism for the same reasons. Barth writes, "The question remains whether this opposition [of Thomism to Molinism] springs from such an appreciation of the total distinction and relationship between God and the creature that it could really be carried through successfully, not merely offering an impressive resistance to the view adopted by the Jesuits, but basically excluding it. The answer is in the negative."[53] Why does Barth think this is so? He suggests that it is because

> the Thomist conception of the relation of God and the creature also offers the picture of a system, of the relationship of two quantities which in the last resort are comparable and can be grouped together under one concept (being). God's infinite superiority and the infinite subordination of the creature are

---

[51]In this follow-up discussion to omnicausality, Barth offers a severe critique of both Jesuitism and Thomism in the Catholic tradition in its dealing with the work of the Spanish Jesuit theologian Louis Molina (1535-1600) and his *Concordia Liberi Arbitrii cum Gratiae Donis*, "which can only be described as an illegitimate interest in an autonomy of the human will in its relation to the divine knowledge and to God generally" (*CD* II/1, pp. 569-70).

[52]*CD* II/1 p. 580.

[53]Ibid., p. 570.

beautifully set out and secured in this system. Yet in this remarkable relationship the two quantities are embraced in the common concept of being.[54]

So Barth concludes, "In this fundamental standpoint, which has priority
over all the others, Thomist and Molinist are unfortunately one."[55]

Furthermore, it is precisely the *causal* form of argumentation for this single
concept of being that lies at the root of Barth's problem with Molinism.[56] So
Barth raises a further question within this context that he deals with in a decisive manner elsewhere, under the providence of God in respect to the Scholastic doctrine of *concursus*, in *CD* III/3.[57] The question raised here, in the
context of his treatment of Molinism, regarding its doctrine of divine-human
cooperation, is: "If God and the creature are really both within a system of
being superior to both," so that "the occasional inversion of the concept A-B
to B-A" is permissible, then "can Molinism be rejected absolutely or *a limine*?"
The answer is again negative, and the same is true of the idea that it attempts
to establish, which is "namely of competition and co-operation on the part of
the creature in relation to God."[58] The treatment of the Catholic and Reformed-
Scholastic doctrine of *concursus* brings this critique of metaphysical causality
full circle in Barth's ongoing rejection of the *analogia entis*.

---

[54]CD II/1, p. 581. Barth places Przywara under the same kind of critique that he places Molina
through an oblique reference in this section to his treatment of the doctrine of Mary in *CD* I/2,
pp. 138-46, where, speaking about the comparison of Mary with *sophia* in Eccles 4, he writes,
"What is the meaning of this *sophia* proceeding from God, like God, yet immanent in the world?
E. Przywara purports to give us final clarity in the matter when he writes that there are contained
'in the Catholic doctrine of the *analogia entis* the possibilities of a true incarnational cosmos,
including body and soul, community and individual, because in their totality . . . they are "open"
to God. . . . In its final essence it is, as it were, already Mary's "Behold, the handmaid of the Lord.
Be it unto me according to thy word."'" Says Barth: "All this is what Mariology means, . . . which
involve a relative rivalry with Christ." Could this be a part of what Barth saw in Przywara's
doctrine of analogy as an "invention of the Antichrist"? (*CD* I/2, p. 145).
[55]CD II/1, p. 584.
[56]Ibid., p. 585. Barth's final word on Molinism clearly puts his problem with the Thomistic metaphysics of causality into perspective. "The most secure basis for this pattern is the work of
Thomas Aquinas himself, so that every step a Thomist takes, even if it seems to take him far
from the Jesuit counter-thesis, really serves implicitly to justify this counter-theory in advance.
Those who practice theology as ontology have not merely to admit the doctrine of the freedom
of the creature. Willynilly, they must themselves espouse it even if it means omitting some of
the radical conclusions of their protest. They affirm this doctrine when they undertake to practice theology as ontology. And it is not only Catholic theology in general which stands or falls
with this undertaking, but Thomism in particular."
[57]CD III/3, pp. 89-154.
[58]CD II/1, p. 581.

At the very beginning of his doctrine of providence, Barth is concerned to distinguish his position from the Catholic, Protestant Liberal and Reformed-Scholastic positions, which tended to reduce the preservation evident in the God-creature relation to a "logical necessity within which a given B is maintained by a given A, a given effect by a given cause."[59] The preservation of the creature is a work of divine favor and not expressive of a cooperative relationship in which God, of necessity, must act in a way consistent with a perceived form of CER. This resemblance is not to function, as with the Catholic form of the doctrine of divine simplicity, for instance, as a "self-imprisonment" of God. We must therefore avoid the Thomistic view of causality. But we can do so only "if we note the correlation between His [God's] work here and His work within the covenant of grace."[60] Only then can we be kept from the mistake of regarding either "the creature or its nexus as the sustaining principle of creation."[61] Barth elaborates as follows:

> As we consider His work within the covenant we shall be constantly aware of the fact that His indirect work here in the nexus of being is no less His free decision than is His direct work there in that other and spiritual nexus. And even here in the nexus of being ... we shall always distinguish sharply between the nexus of being which is the means and the One who uses this means.

Barth sees two problems with this reading of God and creation from the causal nexus, which he calls the "nexus of being." First,

> we understand the nexus of being of all created things (what Thomas described as the order by which one thing is dependent on another) quite one-sidedly and therefore falsely if we understand it only from the standpoint of the uniform interconnection of all being and events, for, as the (in this respect) far wiser older theology almost universally maintained, it has also the aspect of contingence in which all things must be considered according to their freedom.

Second, says Barth, "even if we do understand the creaturely nexus of being more comprehensively, its identification with the divine preservation involves a blind surrender of the concepts God and creation."[62]

---

[59]*CD* III/3, p. 59.
[60]Ibid.
[61]Ibid., p. 63.
[62]Ibid.

The only way to avoid this confusion of acting subjects is by a proper description of the God-human relationship that allows for the coexistence of both. This is Barth's aim in the redescription of the Thomistic and Reformed-Scholastic doctrine of *concursus*, which, in its Reformed expression, is grounded in a distinction between primary and secondary causality.[63] Barth wants to eliminate this dependence of the Reformed doctrine of *concursus* on the Thomistic distinction between primary and secondary causality, read as it was by Aquinas in the context of God's omnicausality.

Barth notes that it was in an attempt to "do justice to the problem of a co-existence and antithesis of the divine and creaturely action which should correspond with the testimony of Scripture" that Reformed Scholasticism developed the doctrine of primary and secondary causality in terms of the doctrine of the *concursus*.[64] Faced with this problem, Reformed Scholasticism formally borrowed from the philosophy of Aristotle and the theology of Aquinas.[65] This borrowing amounted to an "adoption and introduction of a specific terminology to describe the two partners whose activities are understood and represented in the doctrine of the *concursus*."[66] This was described in the quasi-synergistic terms of co-operation, in which the concept adopted and introduced was that of *cause*. For Barth, this Thomistic-Aristotelian—but ultimately Pseudo-Dionysian-Proclan—concept of cause becomes the controlling principle for the Reformed doctrine of *concursus* and its "kindred topics."[67] The term *cause* involves a question of "the relation between the divine and creaturely activity. But activity means *causare*. Activity is movement or action which has as its aim or object, a specific effect."[68] He further defines *cause* as

---

[63]It is hard to tell whether Barth thinks *concursus* is the Reformed-Scholastic doctrine that attempts to summarize and represent the Thomistic doctrine of primary and secondary causality, or whether the whole thing is Thomistic. Either way, whether he sees it as a Thomistic doctrine or a Reformed-Scholastic doctrine, they both end up in the same place, in a metaphysics of causality that loses both subjects in an eternal respect.

[64]*CD* III/3, p. 96.

[65]Ibid.

[66]Ibid.

[67]Ibid. Barth adds, "Now we cannot deny that even from the standpoint of the subject itself the concept *causa* could and necessarily did both advance and commend itself. It was indeed the whole problem of causa which had formed the topic for discussion even in the sixteenth century, and this not only in the doctrine of providence of Zwingli and Calvin but also in Luther's *De Servo Arbitrio.*"

[68]Ibid.

"something without which another and second thing either would not be at all, or would not be at this particular point or in this particular way."[69] He writes:

> A *causa* is something by which another thing is directly posited, or conditioned, or perhaps only partly conditioned, that is, by which it is to some extent and in some sense redirected and therefore altered. Now if we are speaking of the activity, and therefore the *causare*, of God and the creature, then wittingly and willingly or not, we are describing and thinking of both of them in terms of *causa*. And at once we have to begin our manipulation of the dialectic of the concept, and it was in this process that the older dogmaticians found inspiration and guidance in Aristotle and Thomas.[70]

This means that, for Barth, denoting God as *causa* "consists primarily and supremely in the fact that since He is the source of all *causae*, the basis and starting-point of the whole causal series, there is no *causa* which is either before or above him, but He is his own *causa: causa sui*."[71] Therefore, it also means that, since everything that exists apart from him was caused by him as an effect, all *causae* that exist outside him, with their own *causare*, "are not merely partly but absolutely conditioned by Him—indeed they are not merely conditioned but in the first instance posited by Him, seeing that they are created."[72] It was in this way that God was known and described according to the "older theology" as "*causa prima*, the *causa princeps*, the controlling cause which governs all other *causae* and their *causare*." Thus, Barth concludes, "this was the conceptual basis on which the older evangelical dogmatics understood the *concursus Dei* within the overruling of providence. As *causa prima*, or *princeps*, God cooperates with the operation of *causae secundae*, or *particulares*." The divine *causare* takes place in and with their *causare*.[73]

Barth does not fault the term *cause* directly for the tendency of this kind of argumentation to lead us astray vis-à-vis the biblical witness. In a very

---

[69] Ibid. He bases this on the "English" meaning of the word *cause*.
[70] Ibid.
[71] *CD* III/3, p. 98.
[72] *CD* III/3, p. 99. Furthermore, "all other *causae* can only affirm and attest Him as the one *causa*. All other *causare* can only affirm and attest His *causare causarum*."
[73] Ibid.

real sense "every terminology is a possible source of error."[74] There is no
doubt in Barth's mind, however, that the use of *causa* in describing primary
divine action and secondary human action did lead to a serious error in
Aquinas in regard to the biblical understanding of cooperation among the
acting subjects, God and the human. Indeed, the use to which it was put
obscured the biblical portrait of the God-human relationship, and precisely
on the basis of an Aristotelian-Neoplatonic conception of causality, which
was "completely apart from the message of the Bible."[75] Under the pressure
of this concept of cause "there emerged theological conceptions and assev-
erations which are foreign and even completely antithetical to that message."
Barth thinks that this has happened in the case of Thomism. This can also
be said about the Reformed tradition where it has followed Aquinas in this
matter.[76] Here Barth launches into a detailed discussion of Reformed Scholasticism, especially in its Lutheran expression, to demonstrate this fact. He
finds that while formally its use of the concept of cause is quite correct,
materially, its doctrine failed to be sensitive to the biblical witness. This was
the case to the degree that what Reformed Scholasticism hoped to preserve,
a biblical account of two acting subjects with eternal distinction, was lost.[77]

In short, the Thomistic-Reformed-Scholastic conception of *concursus*
leads one to a nonpersonal account of the divine-human encounter that
reduces the biblical portrait to a mere philosophical principle of the explanation of action. As a result, when the "older dogmaticians" spoke in terms
of the *causare* of the *causa prima* and the *causae secundae*, "neither in the
one case nor in the other had it any specifically Christian content."[78] To the
degree that it was an essentially unbiblical use of the term *cause*, Barth says,
it lacked any "definite safeguards" against the mischief that was inevitably
the result of an other-worldly reading of causality. "The enemies which it
was its business to repel, the enemy of synergism on the one hand and
monism on the other [which for Barth are internal to the Thomistic syn-

---

[74]Ibid. Here Barth wants to ensure his own right of access to a form of causal argumentation later
  and writes, "The term may well be useful in the developing and applying of the message of the
  Bible."
[75]Ibid.
[76]Ibid.
[77]*CD* III/3, p. 100.
[78]Ibid.

thesis], of the Papacy on the one hand and the Turk on the other, could also make use of exactly the same form."[79]

Barth only launches this critique of the use of causality in order to exposit the conditions under which a doctrine of *concursus*, based on cause, may be permitted. Here Barth is more explicit in his rejection of the analogy of being than anywhere else that can possibly be found in the *CD*, other than the statement so often referred to and so little understood, namely, the description of the *analogia entis* as "an invention of the Antichrist." His reasons for rejecting an *analogia causalitatis* further confirm our suspicion that this has to do with an ontology of the one and the many that always seems to lurk as a possible interpretation of Aquinas.

While this ontology may be denied, it cannot be done without taking into consideration Barth's concerns about this employment of causality, which he considers a form of metaphysics and as determinative of Catholic doctrine as a whole since Aquinas. On this basis, he writes, "We have to ask, therefore, on what conditions the concept can legitimately be applied to this Reformed doctrine of *concursus*."[80] Barth delineates five "preliminary conditions," the fulfillment of which is "dependent upon the fulfillment of one decisive condition," with which he deals in his conclusion to this section.[81] These conditions apply to any theological use of cause as an explanatory principle. The *first* condition, if the concept of causality is to be used effectively in theology, is that "the term *causa* must not be regarded as the equivalent of that of a cause, which is effective automatically"; as if "we had no choice but to think of *causa* as the term is employed in modern science," or for that matter in "natural philosophy." In that case "it is a concept which we could not apply either to God or to the creature of God," and so must be rejected.[82] This was a result of causal argumentation that Barth recognized to be at the heart of the Protestant Liberal (Ritschlian) criticism of causality in the light of the modern "scientific explanation of nature." Even though this is a mistaken interpretation of the Catholic/Reformed invocation of causality, the mechanistic understanding of causality appeared to liberal

---

[79]Ibid.
[80]*CD* III/3, p. 101.
[81]Ibid.
[82]Ibid.

Protestants as a threat to the Christian doctrine of God and so must be rejected. Here Barth recognizes that theology must use causal argumentation in a way that does not make it susceptible to the Humian-Kantian critique. But this is not his main concern in rejecting the Thomistic approach herein, and so we merely note it here as confirming what we said earlier.

His *second* condition comes closer to the mark when he writes, "If the term *causa* is to be applied legitimately, care must be taken lest the idea should creep in that in God and the creature we have to do with two 'things.' . . . But neither God nor the creature is a *causa* in this sense."[83] Barth is worried that the Catholic-Reformed doctrine of *concursus* has the tendency to reduce God and humanity to the status of things. In this event it is available to us as something we can access, realize and therefore "control." The causal concept, "like the concept of being, is certainly an invitation to error at this point."[84] But neither God nor the human can be conceived of as a cause in this way. Thus Barth rejects any and all attempts at objectivizing either God or humanity. More could be said about this, but we are still only approaching Barth's real concern, so we will move on.

Barth's *third* condition on the use of the word *cause* is one of the most revealing statements regarding Barth's overall concern in regard to Thomistic metaphysics for theology. He writes, "If the term *causa* is to be applied legitimately, it must be clearly understood that it is not a master-concept to which both God and the creature are subject, nor is it a common denominator to which they may both be reduced. . . . And if the concept is used, this invitation must be resisted at all costs."[85] *Causa*, says Barth, is not a "genus," according to which the "divine and creaturely *causa* can then be described as species." When theology speaks of the being of God and of the human, it is not "dealing with two species of the one genus being."[86] Furthermore, when Christian theology speaks christologically about the nature of God and the humanity of Christ, "we are not dealing with two species of the one genus nature."[87] Here Barth clearly rejects the CER principle, which he then

---

[83]Ibid.

[84]*CD* III/3, p. 102.

[85]Ibid.

[86]Ibid.

[87]*CD* III/3, p. 103. "To put it rather differently, it must be clearly understood that when the word *causa* is applied to God on the one side and the creature on the other, the concept does not

immediately applies to his understanding of analogy as follows:

> It is true, of course, that although there is no identity of the divine and crea-
> turely operation or *causare*, there is a similarity, a correspondence, a compa-
> rableness, an analogy. In theology we can and should speak about similarity
> and therefore analogy when we find likeness and unlikeness between two
> quantities: a certain likeness which is compromised by a great unlikeness; or
> a certain unlikeness which is always relativised and qualified by a certain
> existent likeness. The great unlikeness of the work of God in face of that of
> the creature consists in the fact that as the work of the Creator in the preser-
> vation and overruling of the creature the work of God takes the form of an
> absolute positing, a form which can never be proper to the work of the
> creature. But at the same time the divine work in relation to the creature also
> has the form of a conditioning, determining and altering of that which already
> exists. And inasmuch as the conditioning of another also belongs to creaturely
> activity, there is a certain similarity between the divine and the creaturely
> work. In view of this likeness and unlikeness, unlikeness and likeness, we can
> and should speak of a similarity, a comparableness, and therefore an analogy
> between the divine activity and the human. We have to speak of an *analogia
> operationis*, just as elsewhere we can speak of an *analogia relationis*.[88]

For many this passage is one of the locations where Barth offers a contradiction to his dismissal of what he calls the "doctrine of the *analogia entis*."
But surely Barth does not make this error. For that matter, those who have
pointed to this passage, and the extended discussion of *analogia relationis*,
have often failed to consider the wider context of Barth's theological development. Barth does not at all mean by *analogia operationis* what either
Aquinas or Przywara mean in their employment of analogy, notwithstanding
von Balthasar's critique (and those who follow it). In this very same context
Barth goes on to deny the analogy of being for the very same reason that he
has always rejected it, and in no uncertain terms. He writes,

> Indeed, it would be a mistake to try to compare them simply because they are
> both *causa*. . . . Therefore although the being of the Creator and that of the
> creature are unlike, in some respects they are like and therefore similar. There

---

describe the activity but the active subjects, and it does not signify subjects which are not merely
not alike, or not similar, but subjects which in their absolute antithesis cannot even be compared."

[88]*CD* III/3, p. 102.

is therefore an *analogia entis* between God and the creature. To that extent there is a master-concept, a common denominator, a genus (being), which comprises both God and the creature. And it would be a really serious mistake if we were to adopt this argument.[89]

Why does Barth think so? Because it is based on a mistaken Christology, which argues that Jesus Christ has a divine and a human nature, and that although the two natures are "unlike," they are also "alike and similar." There is therefore an attempt at a christological grounding of an *analogia naturae* between God and humanity that is not biblically warranted. "And to that extent we can speak of a master-concept, a common denominator, a genus (nature) which comprises both God and man. This is the type of mistake which we have to avoid at this point. This is the deduction which we have to recognize as false and therefore illegitimate."[90] Rather, Barth wants to lay clear emphasis on the fact of the differences between the two acting subjects. "The concept *causa* does not merely describe activities, but acting subjects. And between the two subjects as such there is neither likeness nor similarity; but utter unlikeness." In this sense the term *cause* may constitute a reduction to "one common denominator" in that they may be conceived as "belonging to the one genus. On the contrary, they cannot even be compared."[91] Rather, the *analogia relationis*, as a form of *analogia fidei*, has the capacity to correct this tendency and subsequently to provide a better basis for speaking about any cooperation between God and the human.

The *fourth* condition relates directly to the third, but "the third condition is the most important so far mentioned, and if it is fulfilled the fourth will also be fulfilled." So Barth deals with it very briefly. He writes, "When the causal concept is introduced, it should not be with either the intention or the consequence that theology should be turned into philosophy at this point, projecting a kind of total scheme of things."[92] In actuality this is for Barth an overriding concern in that he sees in the

---

[89]Ibid.

[90]*CD* III/3, p. 103.

[91]Ibid. Barth is unequivocal here. "They are unlike because their basis and constitution as subjects are quite different and therefore absolutely unlike, that is, there is not even the slightest similarity between them. The divine *causa*, as distinct from the creaturely, is self-grounded, self-positing, self-conditioning and self-causing."

[92]*CD* III/3, p. 104.

concept of causality the displacement of theology by philosophy. This, for Barth, destroys the specificity of theology as a science in its own right and represents its "defection" to philosophy.[93] But this concern, as expressed here, is really in preparation for his fifth and most crucial condition on the use of the term *cause*.[94] It at once summarizes and extends the other four conditions and is typical of Barth's whole theological enterprise. To miss it, and to misunderstand his intention in stating it, is to misunderstand Barth's approach to analogy altogether.

The *fifth* condition Barth sets on the use of the term *cause* is stated as follows: "If the causal concept is to be applied legitimately, its content and interpretation must be determined by the fact that what it describes is the operation of the Father of Jesus Christ in relation to that of the creature."[95] This, says Barth, is the only "positive condition" under which one may employ the causal concept in the doctrine of the *concursus*. It is, of course, the same condition that he places on *analogia relationis*.[96] Only in this respect can causal analogy be regarded as "theologically possible and incontestable." When it is interpreted in the light of Christology, the causal concept is certainly not exposed to the danger of becoming a means for interpreting the Christian faith as an ontology of the one and the many, of the *exitus* and *reditus* that marks the Neoplatonic and, to some degree, Thomistic systems of thought. Rather, the christological principle, regarding the use of *cause*, must be grounded in "the God who in the execution of His election of grace and the fulfillment of His covenant of grace willed and effected this inconceivable benefit, of the God who was already the Father of mercy and the God of all comfort (2 Cor. 1:3), of the God who thereby accomplished this eternal deliverance." It is in this sense that "He was already the Creator of the creature, and He is also its Sustainer, and the One who co-operates with it in its own work—always and everywhere."[97]

Thus, Barth concludes, and so may we, that only under these conditions

---

[93]*CD* III/3, pp. 105-6.

[94]See Barth's treatment of philosophy and theology in *CD* I/1, pp. 2-3; §6 and 7; II/2, pp. 148-55; III/1, p. 330. Barth does not dismiss philosophy, but its relation to theology cannot be determinative from the side of philosophy. Theology determines its own relation to philosophy.

[95]*CD* III/3, p. 106.

[96]Ibid.

[97]*CD* III/3, p. 105.

can one employ any conception of cause. But under these conditions *causa* has "a content in virtue of which it certainly embraces natural events and the uniformity of their processes, and yet cannot be identified with the narrow concept of a mechanical natural cause which effects and is effected automatically."[98] The concept *causa*, christologically grounded, also means that the subjects God and humanity cannot be identified on either side as a "thing."[99] This being the case, then, "we shall be delivered from the evil desire to find a master-concept, a common denominator, a genus, a synthesis, in which God and the creature can be brought together, and we shall be kept from the pleasure of finding analogies between the two subjects."[100] Finally, says Barth, the causal concept has

> no content in virtue of which it ceases to be part of the Christian confession and theological knowledge and becomes part of a philosophical scheme of things. For when the two subjects are so very different, but so closely inter-related, clearly it is only by revelation and in faith that the *causa princeps* and the *causa particularis* can be known both in and for themselves and in the *concursus* of their two-fold *causare*.[101]

Summary. We have seen how it is that, regardless of Barth's misunderstanding of the so-called Catholic conception of *analogia entis*, he has to be taken seriously on his own grounds and not on the grounds that his view is merely better stated in von Balthasar or Przywara. This mistake has led not a few interpreters of the tradition of analogy into an identification between the Przywarian–von Balthasarian view and the "Catholic" view that cannot be borne out in the details. Such a mistake not only sidesteps the serious concerns that Barth has leveled against post-Thomistic Catholicism in general, but it has also made it inattentive to that very same ontology of the one and the many through a reinterpretation of analogy of being in light of a doctrine of participation as process that is just as indebted to Neoplatonic

---

[98] Ibid.
[99] Ibid. Barth explains, "If the *causa prima* is the mercy of God, and the *causa secunda* is its object and recipient, then it follows that neither the one nor the other can ever be controlled by the one who meditates or speaks concerning them. For what is there here that we can 'realize'? We stand before the mystery of grace both on the one side and on the other. It is clear that the *causa prima* can be known only in prayer, and the *causa secunda* in gratitude, or else not at all."
[100] *CD* III/3, p. 106.
[101] *CD* III/3, p. 107.

philosophy.[102] This concern for the inadequacy of the *analogia entis*, and its entire subspecies, is now to be paired with Barth's equal concern for a positive *analogia fidei*, already pointed to in this section.

BARTH'S *ANALOGIA FIDEI*

The phrase *analogia fidei* really does encapsulate everything Barth wants to say, permit and commend theologically, as theology. "If the freedom of divine immanence is sought and supposedly found apart from Jesus Christ, it can signify in practice only our enslavement to a false God."[103] For this reason, says Barth, "Jesus Christ alone must be preached to the heathen as the immanent God, and the Church must be severely vigilant to see that it expects everything from Jesus Christ, and from Jesus Christ, everything; that He is unceasingly recognized as 'the way, the truth and the life' (Jn. 14:6)."[104] If Barth means many other things in his use of the phrase *analogia fidei*, especially over against the *analogia entis*, then they must also be related to this one core definition.

The problem is, however, that we may not anticipate all that Barth means by this within the confines of the first three main volumes of the *CD*. As we have suggested earlier, we cannot hope to extend, redefine or include this understanding within some broader conception of analogy apart from Barth's filling out of this christocentric understanding in volume IV of the *CD*.[105] This study has already extended this suggestion even further in affirming that the whole of the *CD* is, as such, an *analogia fidei*. It is a grand testimony to the fact that for Barth "Jesus Christ" was *everything* and everything he received was *Jesus Christ*. Theology is, in Barth's understanding, christological, and it is true to itself when its content is oriented entirely on the christological. The positing of an *analogia fidei* over against an *analogia entis* was, for Barth, a witness to the fact that sometimes theology became forgetful of its object, positing in its place another ("anti") Christ. This was a categorical mistake leading theology toward a "have not" status that "utterly lacked the fullness of God's presence."[106] That is, "if we separate our-

---

[102]Von Balthasar, *Theology of Karl Barth*, pp. 17-18.
[103]*CD* II/1, pp. 297-98.
[104]*CD* II/1, p. 298.
[105]*CD* IV/2, pp. 242-43, 605-11.
[106]*CD* IV/2, p. 242.

selves from Him, we are not even on the way to this richness, but are slipping back into an impoverishment in which the omnipresent God is not known."[107] If, therefore, theology is the demarcation of the immanence of God in his freedom, which is singularly exhibited in Jesus Christ, then

> Christology must always constitute the basis and criterion for the apprehension and interpretation of the freedom of God in His immanence. The legitimacy of every theory concerning the relationship of God and man or God and the world can be tested by considering whether it can be understood also as an interpretation of the relationship and fellowship created and sustained in Jesus Christ. Is it capable of adaptation to the fundamental insights of the church concerning the person and work of Jesus Christ—the *analogia fidei*?[108]

To put it another way, Barth is affirming that the person and work of Christ, which together constitute the true and complete *analogia fidei*, is the criterion by which all other methods of theology must be measured. Where there is incompatibility between that modality and any other "interpretation" of the relationship between God and the world, the adjustment must be made to this other interpretation so that it conforms to this principle.[109] If it is not "capable of adaptation" along this line, then it cannot stand as an authentic form of the witness to this relation. Such is the case with the Catholic view of analogy. In Barth's mind, the *analogia entis* adapted Christ to its modality of interpretation rather than vice versa.[110]

It is also of considerable interest here that Barth often uses the phrase *analogia fidei* as shorthand for "the gospel," expressed in the classic categories of the person and work of Christ, the mediator. In this respect Barth clearly stands in the Reformed-Scholastic tradition. In that tradition, as we saw, the phrase "analogy of faith" was often used in conjunction with the phrase "analogy of Scripture," but not synonymously. The overall harmony of Scripture, it was claimed, enabled interpretation through comparison of texts. But behind this principle of "Scripture interpreting Scripture" there stood the background theological principle of the "analogy of faith," "according to which the fundamental articles of faith enunciated in the basic

---

[107]Ibid.
[108]Ibid.
[109]Ibid.
[110]Ibid.

catechetical topics of Creed, Lord's Prayer and Decalogue, operate as interpretive safeguards upon the interpretation of particularly difficult texts."[111]
Thus in the mind of the Reformed exegete the "analogy of faith" represented
the conclusions "legitimately drawn from the larger body of New Testament
writings."[112] In the long run, according to the analogy of faith, Reformed
theology insisted that in all arguments for doctrine, whether they contain a
mixture of rational-speculative principles or texts of Scripture, "all portions
of the argument come either directly or indirectly from the text of Scripture
and the conclusion results from the collation of these texts."[113] The "analogy
of Scripture" compliments this method on the macro level, that is, by con-
formation of all doctrine with the "grammatical structures and figures" in
the text of the Bible as a whole. Muller concludes that the analogy of faith,
understood as described above, was the standard form of dogmatic exegesis
in the Reformed-Scholastic period.

> The prominence of faith as an element in the doctrine of Scripture and of the
> *analogia fidei* in the discussion of interpretation brought about a confessional
> and churchly model for exegesis and maintained the Spiritual and ecclesial
> reading of text necessary to the existence of dogmatic systems. Faith, both
> *fides qua* and *fides quae*, rather than reason, remained the norm for interpre-
> tation even granting the powerful and necessary role played by the rationality
> of the individual Protestant exegete.[114]

Certainly we may affirm that such a view of the *analogia fidei* must have
informed Barth's conception of it. It is also the case for Barth that Jesus
Christ, like the phrase *analogia fidei*, functions as shorthand for the gospel
of the *regula fidei* and the "general tenor" of Scripture. Such an attitude must
have been a large part of the motivation behind Barth's placing of the doctrine of the Trinity at the heart of his *CD*. But, of course, Barth has much
more in mind by *analogia fidei*, though this general Reformed-Scholastic
attitude remains its primary point of reference. The question must, on this
basis, be asked anew. What precisely does Barth mean by *analogia fidei*? The

---

[111]Richard Muller, *Post-Reformation Reformed Dogmatics: The Rise and Development of Reformed
    Orthodoxy, ca. 1520 to ca. 1725* (Grand Rapids: Baker Academic, 1998), 1:493f; see also p. 233.
[112]Ibid.
[113]Ibid.
[114]Ibid., p. 501.

answer must surely lead us to the conclusion that it is not, fundamentally, what he meant by *analogia entis*, and neither can it be said that the *analogia entis* is contained within Barth's *analogia fidei* as an *analogia relationis*. Rather, the key to the answer is its christological content.

The *analogia fidei*, as Barth conceived it, amounts to a "Copernican" revolution in the history of theology in general, and especially in Protestant theology. Barth has been hailed as charting nothing less than a new course for Christian theology.[115] The *analogia fidei* amounts to a new *theologia ratio*.[116] The question of how we might speak of God in human terms re-

---

[115]According to H. Hartwell, Barth represents an absolute revolution in theology. See his *The Theology of Karl Barth* (London: SPCK, 1964), p. 2; see also E. Busch, *Karl Barth: His Life from Letters and Autobiographical Texts* (Grand Rapids: Eerdmans, 1994), p. 2.

[116]For the most original location of Barth's formal definition of the analogy of faith, see his *Unterricht in der christlichen Religion*, vol. 1, *Prolegomena*, ed. Hannelotte Reiffen (Zurich: TVZ, 1985), pp. 39-40; Geoffrey W. Bromiley, trans., introduction to *The Gottingen Dogmatics*, vol. 1, *Instruction in the Christian Religion* (Grand Rapids: Eerdmans, 1990), pp. xxxii-xxxiii. There, commenting on the Helvetic Confession's affirmation of preaching the "Word of God," Barth writes, "As regards the prejudices, the most important is the question whether equation of preaching and God's Word is not itself an aberration from Protestantism, a catholicizing transmuting of the divine into something material, finite, and human. To this I reply: On the contrary, the Reformation orientation which took precisely this direction the most sharply, the church of Zwingli and Calvin, maintained this equation loudly and definitely from the very outset. The preaching of God's Word is God's Word; this is how the heading of the second section of the Second Helvetic Confession runs, and it then goes on to say that whenever God's Word is proclaimed in the churches by regularly called preachers, we believe that God's Word is proclaimed and is received by believers. No one, then, should either invent another Word of God or expect one from heaven. The parallel Lutheran statement is that of J. Gerhard, who says that it is one and the same Word of God whether it be presented to us in spoken or written form. From this confident assertion may we not at least ask whether there are not words which, although they are human words and mere words like any others, are also more than that on account of the knowledge or recognition to which they lead, on account of their impartation of truth from one person to another. The fact that they are human does not entail a humanizing of the divine. From the very first Protestantism has involved *a belief that the Logos takes human shape in spoken human words*. It has always reckoned with this possibility. That is beyond question. If some do not recognize the word that is spoken today as such, they are not following the Reformers but the Baptists, and they should ask themselves whether, with their rejection of God's Word in preaching, they are not secretly denying it in holy scripture and revelation as well" (pp. 32-33). McCormack notes that this is really where Barth first begins to work out this principle in earnest. See his "Barth's Version of an 'Analogy of Being,'" pp. 98-99. Some of the most critical works to consult (of the many available) on the actual exposition of Barth's doctrine of the analogy of faith include: Michael Beintker, *Die Dialektik in der "dialektischen Theologie" Karl Barths* (Munich: C. Kaiser, 1987). See also von Balthasar, *Theology of Karl Barth*, pp. 86-167; Kevin W. Hector, "God's Triunity and Self-Determination: A Conversation with Karl Barth, Bruce McCormack, and Paul Molnar," *IJST* 7, no. 3 (2005): 246-61; Johnson, *Karl Barth and the Analogia entis*; Eberhard Jüngel, *GMW*, pp. 232-373; *GGW*, pp. 307-512; Jüngel, *Barth-Studien* (Gütersloh: Benziger, 1982); Jüngel, *Unterwegs zur Sache*, Theologische Bemerkungen (Munich: Kaiser, 1972); Jüngel, *Zum Ursprung der Analogie bei Parmenides und Heraklit* (Berlin:

mained the great subterranean motive for his whole dogmatic enterprise. In short, the *analogia fidei* is really about how theological speech may responsibly correspond to the self-revealing God of the Bible in its witness to Jesus Christ.

As we have said, there is no systematic treatment of the *analogia fidei* as such in the *CD*. There are extended passages here and there that summarize his general attitude, but none can be taken on its own, or even as a collected whole, as his final word on the subject.[117] Later, as with the Reformed tradition, it is a general attitude that informs the development of the *CD* at every point. The point is always "what makes analogy, the *analogia fidei*," such that "it will be accurate to say of human words that they correspond to God."[118] In his book, *Anselm: Fides Quaerens Intellectum*, Barth defined the

---

de Gruyter, 1964); Amy Marga, "Partners in the Gospel: Karl Barth and Roman Catholicism, 1922–1932" (PhD diss., Princeton Theological Seminary, 2006); Bruce McCormack, *Karl Barth's Critically Realistic Dialectical Theology: Its Genesis and Development, 1909–1936* (Oxford: Clarendon Press, 1995); Battista Mondin, *The Principle of Analogy in Protestant and Catholic Thought* (The Hague: Martin Nijhoff, 1963); W. H. Neuser, "Karl Barth in Munster, 1924–1930," *Theologische Studien* 130 (1985): 37-40; Kenneth Oakes, "The Question of Nature and Grace in Karl Barth: Humanity as Creature and as Covenant-Partner," *ModT* 23 (2007): 595-616; Peter S. Oh, *Karl Barth's Trinitarian Theology: A Study in Karl Barth's Analogical Use of the Trinitarian Relations* (London: T & T Clark, 2006); Joseph Palakeel, *The Use of Analogy in Theological Discourse: An Investigation in Ecumenical Perspective* (Rome: Editrice Pontificia Universita Gregoriana, 1995), pp. 13-66; Wolfhart Pannenberg, *Analogie und Offenbarung. Eine kritische Untersuchung der Geschichte des Analogiebegrijfs in der Lehre von der Gotteserkenntnis* (Göttingen: Vandenhoeck & Ruprecht, 2007); Pannenberg, "Zur Bedeutung des Analogiegedankens bei Karl Barth. Eine Auseinandersetzung mit Urs von Balthasar," *Theologische Literaturzeitung* 78 (1953): 17-24; Erik Peterson, "Was ist Theologie?," in *Theologische Traktate* (Munich: Kösel, 1951), pp. 9-44; H. G. Pohlmann, *Analogia entis oder Analogia fidei? Die Frage der Analogie bei Karl Barth* (Göttingen, 1965), pp. 112-16; Erich Przywara, *Analogia entis*, Metaphysik (Munich: Kösel & Pustet, 1932); Eugene F. Rogers Jr., *Thomas Aquinas and Karl Barth: Sacred Doctrine and the Natural Knowledge of God* (Notre Dame, IN: University of Notre Dame Press, 1995); G. Söhngen, "Analogia fidei: Gottähnlichkeit allein aus Glauben?" and "Analogia fidei: Die Einheit in der Glaubenswissenschaft," *Catholica* 3 (1934): 113-36, 176-208; Söhngen, "Analogia entis oder analogia fidei?," *Wissenschaft und Weisheit* (1942): 91-100; Söhngen, "Bonaventura als Klassiker der Analogia fidei," *Wissenschaft und Weisheit* 2 (1935): 97-111; Archie J. Spencer, "Causality and the 'analogia entis': Karl Barth's Rejection of Analogy of Being Reconsidered," *NV* 6, no. 2 (2008): 329-76; Ingrid Spieckermann, *Gotteserkenntnis: Ein Beitrag zur Grundfrage der neuen Theologie Karl Barths* (Munich: C. Kaiser, 1985); Ferdinand Ulrich, *Logo-Tokos: Der Mensch und das Wort* (Einsiedeln: Johannes Verlag, 2003); Hans Wagner, *Existenz, Analogie und Dialektik, Religio pura sen transcendentalis* (Munich: Ernst Reinhard, 1953); Thomas Joseph White, O.P., "How Barth Got Aquinas Wrong: A Reply to Archie J. Spencer on Causality and Christocentrism," *NV* 7, no. 1 (2009): 241-70; White, *The Analogy of Being: Invention of the Antichrist or the Wisdom of God?* (Grand Rapids: Eerdmans, 2011).

[117]*CD* II/1, §27; III/2, pp. 220-23; III/3, pp. 49f; IV/1, pp. 768f; IV/2, pp. 242f.
[118]*GMW*, p. 281.

analogy of faith as a modality of theological speech that can only speak "with the certainty of faith":

> Theological statements as such are contested statements—challenged by the sheer incomparability of their object. It is just this very absoluteness of the revelation to which his statements apply that isolates the theologian in his meditation, as one who can think about himself. With only the relative power of the *ratio certitudinis* who often will be able to work only by experiment, who waits on the correction of others, who can never assume the ultimate certainty of even his best conceived statements, who will always understand his most profound *intelligere* as nothing more than *imbecillitas scientae meae*. There is one, and only one, apparent exception to this rule: The theologian speaks absolutely when his statements coincide with the text, or with the necessary inferences from the text of sacred Authority.[119]

Thus the analogy of faith is not to be conceived of as a tentativeness of theological statements. Neither is it merely the correction of one theology by another. It is rather, as with Reformed orthodoxy, the measure of correspondence between theological statements and "the texts of sacred authority."[120] Where there is coincidence, Barth would later say correspondences, between theological statements and the authoritative text, there and only there can a level of theological certitude be attained. The penetration through to the meaning of revelation is only on the basis of faith, because revelation is the knowledge of God given in and by God himself. Thus some sort of analogical basis exists between the actual revelation and its interpretation.[121] Therefore theology cannot, on this basis, arrive at a certainty unless and until it listens to the Bible, "the textual basis of the revealed object of faith."[122] Theology is not possible without such faith and obedience to it. "In the end, the fact that it reaches its goal is grace, both with regard to the perception of the goal and the human effort to reach it; and therefore in the last analysis it is a question of prayer and answer to prayer."[123] As such, the only analogy that can express God is an analogy of faith. This is the most appropriate place to begin an exposition of Barth's

---

[119]Karl Barth, *Anselm: Fides Quarens Intellectum* (London: SCM Press, 1960), pp. 30-31.
[120]Ibid.
[121]Ibid., pp. 39-40.
[122]Ibid.
[123]Ibid.

analogia fidei because it was here that the realization dawned on Barth that theology was a matter of faithful, prayerful obedience to the Word of the gospel in its total, biblical and therefore christological expression. But the analogy of faith is, as such, the act of theologizing itself, and not a metaphysically driven modality of philosophical method or language.

When Barth turns to the analogy of faith in the *CD*, he again wants to speak of it in terms of the veracity of our knowledge of revelation as it corresponds to the biblical witness.[124] Barth writes: "So far as I know, it was Anselm who first used the formula—paradoxical but very important and suitable for the whole problem [of theological language]—that the task of theology is *rationabiliter comprehendere (Deum) incomprehensible esse.*"[125] This idea is also picked up in the Fourth Lateran Council and repeated in Thomas Aquinas.[126] Such a position came to be associated with God, as a predicate of his being in Protestant thought. But it started out as an assertion of God's incomprehensibility apart from theology, making theological statements more articles of faith than rational propositions.

It was not considered so in the older *Dogmatics*, and in fact, though it was affirmed from even before Augustine, there was no clear reason for its affirmation.[127] Was it that they saw in it a "*doctrina ignorantia* in natural man," or was it a confession of the "hiddenness of God"? It seems to appear and disappear only as a problem and not as a doctrinal statement itself. Barth thinks it is likely related to the problems Platonic thought posed for theological speech. "The fact that this was not seen in the older theology seems to me to be explicable only on the grounds that in those times it was not finally clear whether they really wanted to understand the incomprehensibility of God from Plato and Plotinus or from Psalm 139 and from Paul, and therefore as an article of faith confirming the revelation of God as such."[128] At any rate it may be understood as a doctrine ultimately placing a limit on

---

[124]*CD* II/1, §27.2, pp. 204-54.

[125]*CD* II/1, p. 186; Anselm, *Monologion*, p. 64, translation: "to comprehend more rationally that God is incomprehensible," as cited in Karl Barth, *Anselm: Fides Quaerens Intellectum*, p. 44.

[126]*ST* I, q. 13, art. 7; *IV Lateran Council 1215*, in Henricus Denzinger, ed., *Enchiridion symbolorum et definitionum, quae de rebus fidei et morum a Conciliis oecumenicis et summis pontificibus emanarunt. In auditorum usum* (Los Angeles: University of California Library Press, 1856), p. 428.

[127]*CD* II/1, p. 181.

[128]Ibid.

what can and cannot be said theologically. "The assertion of God's hiddenness [which includes God's invisibility, incomprehensibility and ineffability] tells us that God does not belong to the objects which we can always subjugate to the process of our viewing, conceiving and expressing."[129] There is no naming (as per Augustine and Aquinas), as well as no description, a definition that does not finally "break apart" so that "it is actually not described and therefore not defined. . . . We lack the capacity both to establish His existence and to define His being."[130]

God, as such, apprehends and possesses us before any possibility of an apprehension of him. If it is the case that we resemble anything that we can then apprehend, it is only "the world and everything in it." *But there is no resemblance between the creature and the Creator.*[131] "The fact that we are created in the likeness of God means that God has determined us to bear witness to His existence in our existence. But it does not mean that we possess and discover an attribute within ourselves on the basis of which we are on a level with God."[132] On this basis alone, the *analogia fidei* is already radically different than the *analogia entis*. In fact, such a cosmology is the substance of the original sin, when the serpent whispered ever so softly, "You can be like God." So Barth affirms, "because we, therefore, do not find in ourselves anything which resembles God, we cannot apprehend Him by ourselves."[133]

In this respect Barth remains in the realm of irreconcilable dialectic, whether we put this difference in terms of the finite and the infinite, the absolute and the relative, being for itself and being in itself; all such oppositions remain dialectical and irreconcilable. Any reduction of one to the other is a reduction of God to the world.[134] Barth looks at this irreconcilable debate in multiple ways and comes to the same conclusion each time: "we cannot conceive of God, ourselves."[135] Furthermore, we cannot conceive of God on the basis of some preconceived sharing in humanity on the part of

---

[129]Ibid.
[130]*CD* II/1, p. 187; cf. Pseudo-Augustine, *De cognitione verae vitae* 7; *ST*, bk. I, q. 3, art. 5.
[131]*CD* II/1, p. 188. "We do not resemble God."
[132]Ibid.
[133]*CD* II/1, p. 189.
[134]Ibid.
[135]Ibid.

God in Christ Jesus. "We shall never say we resemble Him of ourselves."[136] If we share in this, it is only by the virtue of God's grace that makes it so, not some internal resemblance. In this sense theology, and the knowledge of God, is not a joint venture between us and God; it can only begin with God. There is, as such, no *analogia entis*.[137] This is the theological context against which we must view Barth's treatment of the analogy of faith in all volumes of the *CD*. Neither the section on *analogia fidei* in *CD* II/1, nor the section on *analogia relationis* in *CD* III/2 and/or the continuing discussion of the God-human correspondence in significant portions of *CD* IV/2 and IV/3 changes Barth's conviction that analogy must be rooted in a decision in God to reveal himself and not in some prior resemblance creation has to him. There is no theological ontology, epistemology or language without this prior, revelatory, and therefore christological orientation.

Thus christology is the "theological ontology" that drives Barth's *CD*. This is not an anthropological ontology, which one might perceive to be its basis if the section on *analogia relationis* in *CD* III/2 is the defining moment of Barth's *analogia entis*. Rather, we must begin with what Barth affirms of God, in his self-revelation, if we are going to understand how we are both unprepared and prepared for the reception of that revelation. We do not start, as with Aquinas for instance, with something innate to creation, but with a divine act. The whole of this act is contained in the trinitarian revelation of God to humanity in Jesus Christ as the decision to enter into partnership with humanity. Any other conception of theological ontology is considered to be a philosophical starting point, which Barth categorically rejects. Revelation is, as such, a circularity of the divine act. "A circular course is involved because God is known by God and only by God; because even as an action undertaken and performed by man, knowledge of God is objectively and subjectively both instituted by God, Himself and led to its end by Him; because God the Father and the Son, by the Holy Spirit is its primary and proper subject and object."[138] The "what" and "who" of God cannot be found anywhere else except "in God's act of revelation."[139]

---

[136]Ibid.
[137]Ibid.
[138]*CD* II/1, p. 204.
[139]*CD* II/1, p. 206.

In this sense God is who he is in his act and only as such is the one who reveals himself in his works. The works of God *ad extra* and *ad intra* are therefore indivisible. If a human theology succeeds in corresponding to this act of revelation, it is "in consequence of the fact that God does not wish to know Himself without Himself giving us a part in this event in the grace of His revelation."[140] Only on this basis may it have, as per Anselm, any certitude and/or confidence. But on this basis it does and can have a cognitive knowledge of God. "It is by God's revelation that we know God as the one who is absolutely perfect and self-sufficient, as the one whose being is absolutely self-determined and self-fulfilled and therefore self-enclosed, because in His being and for the felicity of His being He does not need another in the knowledge of whom He must first be confirmed and verified as the one He is."[141] In this sense God is in his act of revelation and always is to be known as who he is in this act. This is a dynamic actualism of the self-sustained and constantly faithful God, who guarantees what he includes in himself, even our being and action, and therefore our theology.

But Barth pauses here to comment on the status that philosophical description might have in relation to this *analogia fidei*.[142] "On the basis of His revelation we shall have to say this with quite another emphasis and weight than we could say it on the basis of a philosophical definition of the absolute. As such, God does not have to be [in his freedom] the object of our cognition. As such, He cannot be it at all."[143] Theological signification may have a relationship to philosophical description, but it is not to be displaced by it or misunderstood as equivalent to it. Certainly one may undertake a natural or philosophical description of God's revelation, and such endeavors do exist. But they are "false starts."[144] Any product of the creaturely realm will fall short in this respect. But human modalities to thought about God's self-revelation are nevertheless inevitable and therefore must be tested against the one *analogia fidei*. While philosophy can be conceived, controlled and

---

[140]*CD* II/1, p. 205.

[141]*CD* II/1, p. 206.

[142]See *CD* I/2, pp. 730-33. Barth is not totally dismissive of philosophy, but he frames its usefulness in terms of very tight constraints.

[143]*CD* II/1, p. 207.

[144]See Barth's Gifford lectures, *The Knowledge of the Service of God* (London: Hodder & Stoughton, 1960), pp. 4-5, 18.

conveyed within the respective rational powers of the human, revelation subjects itself to no such control. Revelation only comes to us as an act of the gracious God. "In what other way than in the gracious presence of God can we really have to do with God, Himself in a world-reality of this kind? It would not be God if His presence, objectively bestowed, did not become the necessary basis of our prayer and praise and thanksgiving. Only false gods can be presented to us in other ways."[145]

In this respect, philosophy and theology are two completely unrelated disciplines in that theology starts from faith, philosophy from reason. There is no continuity between them that is not uninitiated, authorized and overseen by the analogy of faith.[146] It is true that Barth affirms the validity of philosophy as a science in its own right.[147] He even goes so far as to affirm its necessary use by theologians who must "test" the coherence of the contemporary proclamation of the gospel.

The **analogia fidei** *in CD II/1, §27.* What then are we to make of Barth's initial description of the *analogia fidei* in light of the context he places it in, as described above? The whole of *CD* II/1, § 27 trades upon the limitations already imposed by a theology of incomprehensibility and the obscuration of any point of context in creation vis-à-vis a resemblance of God ingredient in nature, as with, for instance, creation in the *imago Dei*. Given these caveats, "the question how we come to know God by means of our thinking and language" means that the answer will exclude any human capacity to come to this "of ourselves."[148] It is also rather only by virtue of the grace of God, as it "comes to us and therefore to the means of our thinking and language," that it is possible at all. It is therefore a commandeering of thought and language as such, one in which God "adopts" us, our thought and speech. "We are permitted to make use, and a successful use at that, of the means given to us. We do not create this success. Nor do our means create it."[149] It is created in and through the revelatory action of God, in relation to which we can only stand in "awe."

---

[145]*CD* II/1, p. 207.
[146]*CD* II/1, pp. 225-26: neither correlation nor continuity but correspondence.
[147]Ibid.
[148]*CD* II/1, p. 224.
[149]Ibid.

"To know this is the awe in which our knowledge of God becomes true."[150]

Such language and thought has, therefore, a correspondence that is determined by the self-revealing God, precisely in a relationship in which there exists "a real fellowship between the knower and His knowing on the one hand, and the known on the other." To regard incomprehensibility as a negative is to deny God, his self-revelation, our knowledge of it and the grace, faith and truth in which it is given. Our knowledge of God takes place in "participation in the reality of the revelation of God," or else God is not revealed to us. "The way of human cognition of God has no goal at all, no *terminus ad quem*, which means that it probably has no beginning, no *terminus a quo*." This would amount to an illusion. But if indeed some participatory fellowship were to be affirmed, what would it be? In what would it consist? "Where do we find the veracity in which we apply to God, human words which, as such, are inadequate to describe Him, as we all do at every point when we speak directly or indirectly about God?"[151]

Furthermore, in light of this, what does it mean when we apply to God terms taken from the creaturely realm? Are we positing a relation of relative sameness or similarity, that is, some kind of "parity"?[152] We think we know what terms such as *wisdom, goodness, sovereignty* and the like mean in respect to the creaturely, but such an awareness is tentative. The same can be said for anthropomorphisms like *mouth, eye, ear* and so on. What happens to their meaning when we apply them to God? Can creaturely being, function and essence mean the same for God as it does for us? "Obviously we cannot affirm this, nor can the veracity of our knowledge be found in a likeness of this kind between our knowledge and Him as the known."[153] Such an assumption contradicts the confession of God's incomprehensibility, that is, his being revealed as hidden. The God who gives himself as hidden in his revelation, as the one revealed in his hiddenness, cannot be spoken of in such (univocal?) terms.[154] This kind of parity places God among the series of creatures and relatively identical with them.

We seem to be left with no alternative but to posit a complete "disparity"

---

[150]Ibid.
[151]Ibid.
[152]*CD* II/1, p. 225.
[153]Ibid.
[154]Ibid.

when creaturely terms are used to describe, name or designate God and his actions. Terms of quality, *being*, *goodness* and so on, or anthropomorphic terms such as *ear*, *eye* and so on appear to mean something quite different when applied to God.[155] This leads to an impossibility of the knowledge of God simply due to the fact that "if we know Him, we know Him by the means given to us."[156] Indeed, the fact that we have a knowledge of God must mean that "with our views, concepts and words, we do not describe and express something quite different from Himself, but in and by these means of ours—the only ones we have—we describe and express God Himself."[157] The very truth of our knowledge of God is otherwise in question, and theology is at an end. There is no relation, no revelation, no grace and thus no "fellowship with God." In fact, "the impossibility of the thesis of parity between our word and the being of God must not press us into the counter thesis of disparity between them."[158] Both alternatives are impossible for theology.

It was precisely in respect to this impossible situation that the "older theology" posited some aspect of analogy as a solution to the impasse. But the denial of both parity and disparity was not without recognition of the "elements of truth" in both alternatives. The term that analogy was meant to champion was *similarity*, which Barth refers to as "a partial correspondence and agreement and, therefore, one which limits both parity and disparity between two or more different entities."[159] But here we have a term "burdened by its use in natural theology" and thus in need of considerable qualification. While the term *similarity*, as the substantial meaning of analogy, is left to stand by Barth, it will have to be, at some point, subjected to an investigation as to the origin of this correspondence, especially in terms of its "partial" qualities. The veracity of revelation, as the truth about the self-revealing God, requires such a concept, however unsatisfactory. But if such a modality of naming is necessary, it is by virtue of divine ordination that it should be so and not as a humanly driven method. "Driven by the revelation of God we are pushed to the word 'analogy.'" But at the heart of *analogy* is a

---

[155]Ibid.
[156]Ibid.
[157]Ibid.
[158]Ibid.
[159]Ibid.; see also *CD* II/1, pp. 74-75.

relationship posited by the very act of revelation itself. Therefore, more than just establishing analogy, "we are inquiring into the relationship between what we may say about God with our words, which in themselves describe only the creaturely, and what God is and therefore what must be said of Him in words which are at our disposal."[160] The creatureliness of such words includes the creatureliness of words like *parity, disparity, likeness, unlikeness, similarity, dissimilarity* and *analogy. Analogy* is merely the best pick of a bad lot, because in all such words the "co-existence of comparable objects is obviously presupposed."[161] There is a real sense in which they are all inadequate because God is ultimately incomparable.[162]

What gives *analogy* its veracity, therefore, is not some secret power that it has (as for instance the supposition of a CER) but "on the strength of the 'nevertheless' of the true revelation of God, in which God posits Himself as a comparable object."[163] Here the christological determination of these terms now comes to the fore as the substance of their capacity to speak to the veracity of God's self-revelation. Such a christological determination of analogy is wholly absent from the Thomistic-Cajetanian definition of the term. In fact, the term has no special status as such apart from Christ, the content of revelation.

> In itself and as such it is no better than the words parity and disparity. Indeed in other contexts (as, for example, to describe the relationship between God and Christ) it would be quite out of place. It is not, therefore, correct in itself, even in this context. It becomes correct in this context because the relationship [posited in God's true revelation] which we have here to express in some sense attracts this word to itself, giving it in the sphere of our words, which are insufficient to be used in this way, the character of our designation for the divine reality of this relationship.[164]

The similarity posited in the term *analogy,* then, is a similarity given in revelation as what we know to be similar, namely, the humanity in which and by which God makes himself to be known. What gives the human and his

---

[160]*CD* II/1, p. 226.
[161]Ibid.
[162]Ibid. See Is 40; Job 28–38.
[163]*CD* II/1, p. 226.
[164]Ibid.

word the power of similarity is the similarity of being God posits for himself
in Jesus Christ, who is God and Man. Under this christological determination of the content of this similarity, "man with his human word 'similarity'
participates in the (as such) incomprehensible similarity which is posited in
God's true revelation, so that in it God participates in man and in his human
word."[165] Barth clearly distinguishes his understanding of analogy here from
those uses of analogy that might be "self-grounded upon a secret prejudice
in favour of an immanent capacity of this concept."[166] Such is probably the
case with its use in the "older theology," as he later points out. If it occurs
under the "compulsion of the object," it is the right modality. Jesus Christ is
such a compulsion. It is clear, however, that the compulsion referred to here
is the analogy God himself makes in the real relation that constitutes his
self-revelation in the God-Man, Jesus Christ. Here it must be underscored
that this is in no way understood as an analogy of being. It is, rather, the
essence of the analogy of faith. Here analogy must stand for the terminus ad
quem, the terminus a quo, and thus the alpha and omega of revelation, in
which we are made to participate in the revelation of the incomprehensible
God as "one who makes Himself comprehensible to us, without prejudice to
His hiddenness and therefore within the limits of our comprehension."[167]
This is why Barth's emphasis on the hiddenness, ineffability and incomprehensibility of God is qualatatively different from that of the "older theology"
and even Reformed orthodoxy.

But now Barth must ask about the origin of this analogy, this similarity
and therefore this correspondence. It does not arise as a power within the
language itself. It does not precede revelation, and it is not in and of itself a
participation essential to humanity itself. "It obviously subsists in God
Himself as the subject and Lord who in His revelation reveals Himself to us,
and as the Creator who in His revelation controls His own work."[168] Analogy
is not something we have control over. It is not, as mistakenly assured, an
aspect of our natural capacity to construct a theology from nature. "In His
revelation God controls His property, elevating our words to their proper

---

[165]*CD* II/1, p. 227.
[166]Ibid.
[167]Ibid.
[168]Ibid.

use, giving Himself to be their proper object, and therefore giving them truth. Analogy of truth between Him and us is present in His knowing, and this analogy of truth comes into being in virtue of the decision of His grace, which is to this extent the grace of His revelation."[169]

Therefore our words do not constitute theological truth by virtue of our anticipation of God's action, or of our capacity for kataphatic excess or our ability to "clarify" and so "press forward" to an understanding. Sin, finitude and the conditions of existence make such a provisional understanding impossible. As such, human thought and language can only follow insofar as God puts the truth of revelation at our disposal. "He has, therefore, to bestow the truth upon our knowing that is directed to 'creaturely objects'— the truth of similarity with Him."[170] The faith that we may have the truth of the creaturely analogy to the Creator can only be affirmed on that basis.

The problem with analogy as it is employed in the "older theology" is its objectification of the Creator through creaturely analogy, considered to be innate apart from divine giveness, that is, revelation. It can, according to this method, be counted on by virtue of its unchanging existence in created order itself. "It is not a dynamic quality of creaturely knowing, but an all too predictable and knowable copy of the divine in resemblance. It is not to be denied that a creaturely analogy is given. But it must be denied that it can be guaranteed in this or that creaturely resemblance."[171] Only where God has affirmed such an analogy can we make such an assumption about creaturely similarity. "It all depends upon our saying yes where—and only where—God has first said yes in His revelation." For Barth, only Jesus Christ constitutes the "deep secret" yes for analogy. Where we speak "what is given to us" to say, then we speak responsibly of God. We do theology in obedience and with the permission afforded it on the basis of God's revelation of himself as the known to be known. "All kinds of things might be analogous of God, if God had not made and did not make a very definite and delimited use of his omnipotence and revelation."[172] God in his freedom chooses the limit, scope and "definite possibilities" of such an analogy. It cannot therefore be an ar-

---

[169]*CD* II/1, p. 230.
[170]*CD* II/1, p. 231.
[171]Ibid.
[172]*CD* II/1, p. 233.

bitrary modality of analogy that is chosen. Such an arbitrary use of analogy precisely is sometimes employed in theology. In theology not everything that can be subjected to analogical predication should be. This is especially so with philosophical and world-cultural conceptions. "If it is going to be proclamation of God, it must rest on the choice made by God Himself."[173]

Here again we see the Reformed penchant for a necessary comparison with the substance of the gospel itself as the *analogia fidei* of all predication. All other forms of analogy risk becoming the "self-exposition of man" or the subjugation of revelation to such a criteria. What is the analogy of faith, then?

> It is the exposition of the revelation of God when it keeps to the human words which are placed at our disposal as we are confronted by God's revelation, and which are therefore designated as serviceable for this employment; when it follows the freedom in which God bestows His grace upon man generally and therefore upon his human views, concepts and words. It will then have something definite to say, and that with a good conscience, with the promise of relevance, i.e. of standing in a real relationship to the reality proclaimed by it, and with the justified claim and well grounded prospect of obtaining a hearing.[174]

Here Barth clearly underscores the need for responsible speech about God, which exists, obediently, within the confines laid out for it in the revelation of God himself. Only in this way can it be guaranteed relevance, truth and a hearing. Only as it stands in *correspondence* to the revelation of God in Christ Jesus can its terms, concepts and analogies be legitimate. Jesus Christ, as such, is the one and only *analogia fidei* in relation to which no other analogy is permitted, including the *analogia entis*. Even in this respect the similarity is only partial, and necessarily so given the disparity occasioned by the reality of the incomprehensibility of God, or rather, the hidden God who reveals himself as such. The correspondence is, in the final analysis, dialectical as much as it is analogical. "The insufficiency of the concept of analogy emerges in the fact that we have to introduce the word 'partial' when we define it more exactly. If we think that in the relationship between two creaturely entities, we have not to establish disparity or parity, but sim-

---

173Ibid.
174Ibid.

ilarity, we are left with a partial correspondence or agreement."[175]

The negative and positive stand in a direct correspondence to the revealedness of God in his hiddenness. In the positivity of the analogy there
is an *apophatic* element that is present, just as in the negativity there is something *kataphatic*. In Jesus Christ, the knowledge of God as the one who is
God and man carries within itself this dialectic of the givenness of God in
his hiddenness. The "Godness" of God and the "humanity" of man constitute the dialectical fulcrum on which the analogy of faith is worked out.
"Each step we take as we come from the hiddenness of God must, and will,
consist in a new reception of grace." It is the function of the priority of the
gospel, which always has the last word. Where analogy is forgetful of this
order of priority, as it was in the "older theology" and in "Reformed Scholasticism," especially in J. A. Quenstedt, it forgets also the dialectical nature
of God's self-giveness.[176] Here again the singularity of the root of revelation,
as per his discussion of vestigia, arises as the real motive for his advancement
of the *analogia fidei*.

Leaving aside the issue of justification, the question must be asked of
Barth: Did he remain true to this christological and dialectical determination of analogy, or does he ultimately succumb to a form of the analogy
of being in III/1 of the *CD*, under the concept of an *analogia relationis*? If so,
is theology still left with a fundamental *analogia entis* as the driving force of
theological speech? Przywara, von Balthasar and a number of scholars think
this about Barth. Were it not for the fact that such views of Barth stop at this
point in describing his view of analogy, there might be some grounds for
agreement, though by no means would it be conclusive. It is, rather, the fact
that Barth underwrites this christological determination of analogy both in
his doctrine of Jesus Christ as electing God and elected man, which follows
immediately after his description of the *analogia fidei*, and his later
grounding of the image of God in Jesus Christ, and the obedience of the Son,
in *CD* III/2 and IV/1. In light of these texts it becomes clear why von
Balthasar was wrong to attribute an *analogia entis* within Barth's *analogia
fidei* on the basis of *CD* III/1.[177] It is to these developments of Barth's thinking

---

[175]*CD* II/1, p. 234.
[176]*CD* II/1, p. 242.
[177]McCormack, "Barth's Version of an 'Analogy of Being,'" pp. 135-36.

that we must finally turn in our attempt to see the full dogmatic implications
and application of the *analogia fidei*.

The analogia relationis *as an* analogia fidei *in CD III/2, IV/1 and III/1.*
The context of Barth's employment of the *analogia relationis* (analogy of
relation) is in one of his main discussions of the anthropological principle
imago Dei. The key to the discussion is Barth's understanding of precisely
how, in the creation of humanity after the divine image, there is to be perceived "a genuine counterpart in God Himself leading to a unanimous decision" to create humanity. Is there "a secret prototype which is the basis of
an obvious copy, a secret image and an obvious reflection in the co-existence
of God and man, and also of the existence of man himself?"[178] The way in
which humanity comes to possess an image or "copy" of the divine, if at all,
is certainly not something attributable to humanity as a "divinizing" of its
being apart from God, but only as a correspondence willed for it by God.
"Man is not created to be the image of God but he is created in correspondence. That is, insofar as Jesus Christ is the prototype of the image of God
we have our being in Him as an image of God in correspondence, in that
His humanity is the prototype of all humanity and as such real man."[179] One
certainly could not arrive at an interpretation of the *imago Dei* as a copy of
the divine based on the Hebrew concept of דְּמוּת ("prototype") and צֶלֶם
("original"). In Genesis 1:26-27; 9:6 the indication is of a prototype that precedes the copy. But there can be no direct comparison between divinity and
humanity on this basis, since it would appear there is an imitation of the
divine copy. This copy is a decision, in God from all eternity, to create another, the copy being the prototype according to which the human was
created. Thus the image is constituted by virtue of a correspondence between the prototypical human and man himself. "Man is created by God in
correspondence with this relationship and differentiation in God Himself:
created as though he can be addressed by God but also as an I responsible
to God."[180] Thus the likeness is a likeness after a prototypical humanity and
not a likeness after the divinity, which can, by varying degrees or in total, be
lost in the fall or gained in redemption. "There is no basis for conception of

---

[178]Ibid. See also *CD* III/1, p. 1.
[179]*CD* III/1, pp. 132-33.
[180]*CD* III/1, p. 198.

the *Imago* in Gen. 1."[181] As such the *imago Dei* is an eschatological goal determined in the prototypical humanity of Jesus Christ from all eternity. This correspondence, then, is a correspondence in relation and an *analogia relationis* as such.

In this respect the New Testament use of the εἰκών is decisive in that the reference is always to the prototype itself, "to the form which is copied and essentially revealed in the image," i.e., Jesus Christ. Within this determination of the *imago Dei* there is no longer any need for images or likenesses after the divine, or any need to proscribe against them. Jesus Christ is the substantial meaning, real and imaged, of God and humanity. Neither is there any need of the Platonic conception of the creation as CER. In the face of these pagan conceptions, Paul's daring equation of the man Jesus, "who is the Messiah of Israel and the Son of God, directly with the divine image, is an unprecedented and radical innovation."[182] So we may conclude with McCormack that "the image of God finds its secure ground in a promise given in the covenant of grace—a promise that was realized fully and completely in the man Jesus, [and] is realized only provisionally and actualistically in believers."[183] The key, therefore, in understanding the substance of the image as it informs theological speech, is the way in which this correspondence takes place such that this is possible. This christological determination of the image of God is the conceptual key to Barth's understanding of the *analogia fidei*, but now under the rubric of the *analogia relationis*.

There is, says Barth, a severe limitation with respect to the *imago Dei* if what is in view is an *analogia relationis* misconstrued as an *analogia entis*. "We must not forget the limitation implicit in this term [*image*]. If the humanity of Jesus is the image of God, this means that it is only indirectly and not directly identical with God. It belongs intrinsically to the creaturely world, to the cosmos."[184] Hence, it does not belong to God's life *ad intra*, "the inner sphere of the essence" of God, but to his life *ad extra*. Therefore the humanity of Jesus Christ cannot present us with the knowledge of the inner life of God, which remains forever closed off to us. Rather he reveals to us

---

[181]*CD* III/1, p. 200.

[182]*CD* III/1, p. 203.

[183]Ibid.; McCormack, "Barth's Version of an 'Analogy of Being,'" p. 136.

[184]*CD* III/1, pp. 219-20.

God "in His relation to the reality distinct from Himself. In it we have to do with God and man, not God and God."[185] There precisely is where the real difference between humanity created in the image of God and God himself rests. "We cannot, therefore, expect more than a correspondence and similarity."[186] Theological speech, therefore, will avoid claims of identity. The eternal relations of the Trinity are a complete relation of unity of essence without the human. Thus the humanity of Jesus cannot function on this level. In respect to God in himself, there is a "complete disparity" between humanity and God.[187] God, in his freedom and grace, however, in the humanity of Jesus Christ, as a decision before all time, in eternity, provides a modality whereby God and humanity may be declared to us in Jesus Christ. On the level of his life *ad extra*, God accommodates himself to the human in Jesus Christ, who becomes the possibility and actuality of our blessedness, speech, thought and life. Thus, for all the dissimilarity of the human with respect to God's inner life, "there is a correspondence and similarity between the two relationships."

This is not a correspondence and similarity of being, "an *analogia entis*."[188] There is no possibility of such a correspondence on this level because it would be a correspondence to the life of God *ad intra*. The ground of this *analogia relationis* is not actually in creation, with humanity, as such, in a prior way. "It is a question of the relationship within the being of God and that of man on the other."[189] The correspondence exists in a relation of similarity determined in the inner life of God, but made real and explicit only in his life *ad extra*, but really in God as such. This is the *analogia relationis* in substance.[190]

The correspondence, and thus the possibility of thinking, speaking and knowing God, exists in the humanity of Jesus as "the direct correlative of His being for God" which reveals this "correspondence and similarity."[191] But, as the reflection of the being of God and humanity *ad extra*, it nevertheless

---

[185]Ibid.
[186]Ibid.
[187]*CD* III/1, p. 220.
[188]Ibid.
[189]Ibid.
[190]*CD* III/2, p. 221.
[191]Ibid.

follows the "essence of the being of God *ad intra*" and thus constitutes the form of the being of God *ad intra* as he expresses his life *ad extra*. "It is this inner being [of God] which takes this form *ad extra* in the humanity of Jesus Christ, and in this form, for all the disparity of the sphere and object, remains true to itself and therefore reflects itself."[192]

Hence the analogy is not inherent in creation or the creature apart from their determination in Jesus Christ, whose humanity is the only real possibility of an *analogia fidei*, precisely because of a divine decision in *analogia relationis*. Here we have a definition of analogy that seems quantitatively and qualitatively different from any other description we have encountered thus far.[193] Barth confirms this later in the same volume of the *CD* when he writes that the being of humanity is a being in correspondence as determined in the covenant partnership between God and the human. "If man is ordained to be God's partner in this covenant, and if his nature is a likeness corresponding to this ordination, necessarily it corresponds in this respect to the nature of God Himself. God has created him in this correspondence as a reflection of Himself."[194] But the analogy adheres to the relation, predetermined in the humanity of Jesus Christ, as a word *ad extra*, and not to the essential being of God *ad intra*.

In this respect the Catholic Mass fails to represent this *analogia relationis*, because it "repeats" as identifying the single event in God, which needs no repetition, only historical representation.

> The real presentation (representation) of the history of Jesus Christ is that which He Himself accomplishes in the work of His Holy Spirit where He makes Himself the object and origin of faith. Christian faith takes note of this, clings to it, and responds to it, without itself being the thing which accomplishes it [as with the Mass], without any identity between the redemptive act of God and faith as the free act of man.[195]

Barth faults such an identity of the human act and divine act as the root problem of the tendency toward a metaphysical *analogia entis*, and thus a christological paucity, in Roman Catholicism. This is a problem he hopes

---

[192]Ibid.
[193]Ibid. Barth clearly grounds this view in Scripture; see pp. 221-22.
[194]*CD* III/2, p. 323.
[195]*CD* IV/1, p. 767.

will be addressed by a movement within the Catholic tradition for a "christological renaissance" led by none other than von Balthasar. It is of course one that is more like his own attempt at a christological grounding in the *CD* than vice versa. In the final analysis it would appear that this view has never really left its Catholic propensity to identify human and divine act in its understanding of the Mass.[196] Indeed Barth bemoans the fact that the difference remains. "If only we were agreed . . . that the ultimate and the penultimate things, the redemptive act of God and that which passes for a response to it, are not the same thing. Everything is jeopardized if there is confusion in this respect."[197] In the act of redemption—thus in our justification and sanctification, and in our theological expression of it—there must be a correspondence to Jesus Christ himself who, as the substitution and representative of our humanity, is both the *analogans* and *analogatum*. He is "the parallel, the likeness—no more but no less—of His justifying being and activity."[198] Thus the essence of the *analogia fidei* is expressed in the cross of Christ. Similarity and dissimilarity between humanity and God is determined, not by the Christian, but by Christ, "not by a likeness established between us and Him from our side, but between He and us."[199]

Summary: Preliminary conclusions on the **analogia fidei**. The analogy of faith in Barth's *CD* has the following characteristics that distinguish it clearly from the *analogia entis*. *First*, analogy does not proceed from being but from action. It is a human correspondence to a divine revelation in act, the event of Jesus Christ, and therefore not theoretically accessible.[200] Being itself has the character of a category, whereas God is "Being in act." Only in this way does "the Word of God become a human thought, a human word."[201] *Second,* for Barth the analogy is exclusively determined from God, by God, in Jesus Christ. Only as and where God has acted may we determine a similarity in human act. *Third*, only God empowers human language insofar as it proceeds from, points toward and is grounded in this self-revelation of

---

[196]*CD* IV/1, p. 768.
[197]Ibid.
[198]Ibid.
[199]Ibid.; *CD* IV/2, p. 606.
[200]*CD* I/1, pp. 247-52.
[201]*CD* II/1, pp. 249-54.

God in Christ.[202] The incarnation of the Word is the very power of language to express God. That he has done so is a mystery and miracle as such.[203] In this event God "commandeers" language as his own property and commands us to make use of it.[204] Thus we may extend the use of this language to God because he, in the incarnate Word, applies it to himself.[205] The event of revelation sanctifies, makes real and realizable, the truth about his own being because he has sanctified us wholly in himself.[206] *Finally*, the *analogia fidei* stresses the hiddenness of revelation in that the words we use do not openly express God in his essence, but only in respect to his *Deus absconditus*.[207] That is to say, all knowledge of God is mediated knowledge grounded in the one mediator between God and the human, namely, Jesus Christ, who is both *Deus absconditus* and *Deus revelatus* at the same time.[208] There is an irremovable opacity between humanity and God that accrues to difference for difference's sake and thus will always require knowledge by mediation.[209]

The analogy of faith is precisely christological in three senses.

1. It is christological in terms of the analogy between the Father and the Son, in which God includes our humanity as a work *ad extra* and thus as an image of the Father in relation *ad intra*.[210]

2. It is christological in the sense of an analogy between Christ's humanity and his divinity. The divine and human coinhere in exactly the same analogous modality that God includes humanity in himself. There is an essential correspondence between the humanity in divinity of Jesus and the inclusion of humanity in the inner life of God, without eliminating the humanity or divinity of Jesus Christ.

3. In this way there can be an analogy between Christ's humanity and ours. The act of God, in taking up flesh, is the basis on which, exclusively, we may have any similarity to him.

---

[202]*CD* II/1, p. 231.
[203]Ibid.; *CD* I/1, pp. 125-86.
[204]*CD* II/1, p. 228.
[205]*CD* I/1, p. 153.
[206]*CD* I/1, pp. 153-54.
[207]*CD* I/1, p. 158.
[208]*CD* I/1, pp. 184, 276-77; II/1, p. 17.
[209]See especially Bouillard, *Karl Barth*, 2:210-11.
[210]*CD* III/2, p. 261.

But lest we conclude that there is an internal conflict in Barth's account of the *analogia fidei*, here a final word of qualification is needed.[211] Johnson's work on Barth and the *analogia entis* makes a point that is also relevant here. He takes pains to ground Barth's understanding of analogy in his doctrine of election, and he is correct to see this as a necessary qualification in understanding what Barth intends by *analogy*.

In fact, Barth's version of analogy cannot be understood apart from his doctrine of election.[212] The *analogia fidei* must be seen in light of the fact that for Barth, "Jesus Christ is the electing God and the elect human."[213] This election of God and humanity in the election of Jesus Christ includes Jesus Christ as electing God, as elected human, as electing human and as elected God.[214] "The concept of analogy emerges clearly from the foregoing considerations. The humility and obedience of the God-Man in time, in which true humanity is realized, finds its ontological ground in an eternal humility and obedience of the self-same Son, Jesus Christ."[215] We have already demonstrated this correspondence above, in our description of the christological grounding of analogy as a double action in the inner and outer life of God. "In other words, it is precisely by making this relation of correspondence to be realized actualistically and giving it a grounding in an eternal act of decision that Barth makes his concept of analogy (as correspondence) to be an analogy of being."[216] But of course, Barth does not mean at all what Przywara or von Balthasar had in mind. Jüngel, whom McCormack cites as an authority, makes it clear in his *God and the Mystery of the World* that this is not the case.[217]

The key, it seems, is not to read this understanding of analogy apart from the doctrine of election, as some Barth scholarship does. Indeed, it is only as we get to the later stages of the Barth's dogmatics, where he makes some critical adjustments to his doctrine of the electing God in Jesus Christ, that the final form of analogy emerges. In this respect von Balthasar was wrong

---

[211]McCormack, "Barth's Version of an 'Analogy of Being,'" pp. 88-143.
[212]Ibid., p. 122.
[213]Ibid., p. 120.
[214]Ibid., p. 122 n. 95.
[215]Ibid., p. 123.
[216]Ibid.
[217]Ibid., p. 123 n. 97.

to say that Barth's *analogia relationis* amounted to an analogy of being within an analogy of faith. That there is any relational ontology ingredient in an analogy of relationality is not attributable to some social ontology as its precondition. It is only in Jesus Christ and his enactment of the covenant that an *analogia relationis* is possible.[218] "The way of the Son of God into the far country is the way of obedience. This is (*in re*) the first and inner moment of the mystery of the deity of Christ." The second is that "for God it is just as natural to be lowly as it is to be high, to be near as it is to be far, to be little as it is to be great, to be abroad as it is to be home."[219] These two moments, the outer and inner, constitute the relational modality in which the Godhead exists. The humility that characterizes Jesus also accrues to the very being of God.

> If, then, God is in Christ, if what the man Jesus does is God's own work, this aspect of the self emptying and self humbling of Jesus Christ as an act of obedience cannot be alien to God. But in this case we have to see here the outer and inner side of the mystery of the divine nature of Christ and therefore the nature of the one true God—that He Himself, is also able and free to render obedience.[220]

This is the critical correspondence between Jesus Christ, the electing God of *CD* II/1 and the analogical relations by which we may know and describe him in *CD* III/2 and IV/2. It is grounded in his prior understanding of the inclusion of humanity in the triune life of God *ad extra* and is now taken up and made "the correspondence that has long lain at the heart of his concept of analogy." It resides in a "personal property" that is characteristic of the Son alone. This understanding of analogy in Barth is certainly far removed from what has often been made of it in Catholic circles. But in Barth it also differs somewhat from the classic Protestant understanding of the *analogia fidei*. In chapter five we shall have to discuss its implications for our own proposals. But in the meantime we need to explore further what this understanding means for another theologian who did more to advance a positive modality of the analogy of faith than anyone else in Protestant theology, namely, Jüngel. As such, our final form of the analogy of faith must be both

---

[218]*CD* IV/1, p. 192.
[219]Ibid.
[220]*CD* IV/1, p. 193. See also p. 177.

rooted in Barth and established in Jüngel's extension of it in terms of the
analogy of advent, to which we may now turn.

4

EBERHARD JÜNGEL:
APPROPRIATING THE ANALOGY OF
FAITH AS ANALOGY OF ADVENT

◆

John Webster is perhaps the foremost English-speaking expert on the work and theology of Eberhard Jüngel. He notes that the question of language is the "most striking" feature of Jüngel's multidimensional treatment of Christian theology.[1] Furthermore, of central importance to his work was the theology of his teacher and master, Karl Barth, who provided him with a "dogmatic framework of trinitarian and christological theory" and its understanding of the "centrality of the history of Jesus Christ as the root and ground of all Christian speech about the human and divine in their interrelation."[2] In this christological orientation of Barth, Jüngel finds sufficient grounds not only for his anthropology and ethics but also for the very possibility of theology as speech, thought and knowledge of God. "What Jüngel has taken from Barth, then, is not only dogmatic propositions but also a confidence about the enterprise of doing theology after the apparent erosion of many of its certainties."[3] Indeed, a careful reading of Jüngel will yield a rather well-designed conception of analogy that carries with it con-

---

[1]John Webster, "Introduction," in Eberhard Jüngel, *Theological Essays*, ed. and trans. John Webster (Edinburgh: T & T Clark, 1989), p. 3.

[2]Ibid. Webster is widely considered the most capable translator and careful interpreter of Jüngel's work in the English-speaking world. It is with respect that I recognize my indebtedness to his work in this chapter. Webster was especially attentive to the analogical direction of Jüngel's work and drew considerable conclusions from it for the theological task that we especially shall have to consider as we proceed.

[3]Ibid.

siderable possibilities, especially as an expansion of Barth's conception of the *analogia fidei*. But it is not without its problems, either.

This chapter is designed to offer Jüngel's approach as a critical part of the possible way forward for theology that will need further development under the category of parable in chapter five. One can see in Jüngel's approach to the problem of theological speech a very well-constructed example of what Barth's *analogia fidei*, christologically grounded, looks like in terms of a "social-linguistic" description. By the end of this chapter sufficient grounds for a revised understanding of the *analogia fidei*, as the christological content of theology, will be evident, as will its need to be filled out more fully in terms of the principle of correspondence (*Entsprechung*) inherent in Barth and Jüngel's approach. The second part of chapter five will attempt to do this by means of sketching out the shape of the christological determination of language as participation, performance and parable.

JÜNGEL: THE CONTEXT OF HIS THEOLOGICAL ENTERPRISE

Jüngel is by today's standards one of the most consequential Protestant theologians of our time. His contribution to Protestant theology is still being fully assessed and assimilated. "He is widely regarded as one of the most able, living interpreters of Barth. And his prowess as preacher and lecturer has won him acclaim from audiences wider than those of specialist theologians."[4] His introduction to English-speaking audiences, however, has largely been confined to specialists in theology, and European theology at that. Few studies to date have tried to position Jüngel's thought as a potentially significant contribution to the field especially in terms of evangelical Protestant faith.[5] One scholar of Jüngel's work, however,

---

[4] John Webster, *Eberhard Jüngel: An Introduction to His Theology* (Cambridge: Cambridge University Press, 1986), p. 1.

[5] Due to time constraints and language limitations, we are reliant on the works translated from the German, for the most part. We shall have recourse now and then to certain articles not yet translated. The works consulted include the following: Eberhard Jüngel, "God—as a Word of Our Language," in F. Herzog, ed., *Theology of the Liberating Word* (Nashville: Abingdon, 1971), pp. 24-45; *Death: The Riddle and the Mystery*, trans. Iain Nicol and Ute Nicol (Edinburgh: St. Andrews Press, 1974); "The Relationship Between 'Economic' and 'Immanent' Trinity," *Theology Digest* 24 (1976): 179-84; *God as the Mystery of the World: On the Foundation of the Theology of the Crucified One in the Dispute Between Theism and Atheism*, trans. Darrell L. Guder (Grand Rapids: Eerdmans, 1983); *Karl Barth: A Theological Legacy*, trans. Garrett E. Paul (Philadelphia: Westminster, 1986); *The Freedom of a Christian: Luther's Significance for Contemporary Theology*, trans. Roy A.

has gone a long way to redressing this situation. Webster's *Eberhard Jüngel:*

Harrisville (Minneapolis: Augsburg, 1988); *Theological Essays*, trans. J. B. Webster (Edinburgh: T & T Clark, 1989); "What Does It Mean to Say, 'God Is Love'?," in T. Hart and D. Thimell, eds., *Christ in Our Place: The Humanity of God in Christ for the Reconciliation of the World. Essays Presented to Prof. James Torrance* (Exeter, UK: Paternoster, 1989), pp. 294-312; "Life After Death? A Response to Theology's Silence About Eternal Life," *Word and World* 11 (1991): 5-8; "Toward the Heart of the Matter," *Christian Century* 108, no. 7 (1991): 228-33; *Christ, Justice and Peace: Toward a Theology of the State in Dialogue with the Barmen Declaration*, trans. D. B. Hamill and Alan J. Torrance (Edinburgh: T & T Clark, 1992); *Theological Essays II*, trans. J. B. Webster and A. Neufeldt-Fast (New York: T & T Clark, 1995); "On the Doctrine of Justification," *IJST* 1, no. 1 (1999): 24-52; "Theses on the Relation of the Existence, Essence and Attributes of God," *Toronto Journal of Theology* 17 (2001): 55-74; *God's Being Is in Becoming: The Trinitarian Being of God in the Theology of Karl Barth—A Paraphrase*, trans. J. B. Webster (Edinburgh: T & T Clark, 2001); *Justification: The Heart of the Christian Faith*, trans. Jeffrey F. Cayzer (Edinburgh: T & T Clark, 2001); "The Cross After Postmodernity," in Uwe Siemon-Netto, ed., *One Incarnate Truth: Christianity's Answer to Spiritual Chaos* (St. Louis: Concordia, 2002). Of the many essays, books and articles about Jüngel the following have been helpful: Ingolf Dalferth, ed., *Denkwürdiges Geheimnis: Beiträge zur Gotteslehre: Festschrift für Eberhard Jüngel zum 70* (Tübingen: Mohr Siebeck, 2004); Paul J. DeHart, *Beyond the Necessary God: Trinitarian Faith and Philosophy in the Thought of Eberhard Jüngel* (Oxford: Oxford University Press, 1999); Renate Enderlin, *Eberhard Jüngels Analogie des Advents* (Munich: GRIN Verlag, 2008); John Macken, "Autonomy and Ontology," in *The Autonomy Theme in the Church Dogmatics: Karl Barth and His Critics* (Cambridge: Cambridge University Press, 1990), pp. 143-54; Joseph Palakeel, "Eberhard Jüngel's Analogy of Advent," in *The Use of Analogy in Theological Discourse: An Investigation in Ecumenical Perspective* (Toronto: Editrice Pontificia Università Gregoriana, 1995), pp. 165-224; John B. Webster, ed., *Possibilities of Theology: Studies in the Theology of Eberhard Jüngel in his Sixtieth Year* (Edinburgh: T & T Clark, 1994); Webster, *Eberhard Jüngel*; Roland Zimany, *Vehicle for God: The Metaphorical Theology of Eberhard Jüngel* (Atlanta: Mercer University Press, 1994); Jonathan Case, "The Death of God and the Truth of the Triune God in Wolfhart Pannenberg and Eberhard Jüngel," *Journal for Christian Theological Research* 9 (2004): 1-13; Paul DeHart, "Eberhard Jüngel on the Structure of Theology," *Theological Studies* 57 (1996): 46-64; Matthias Haudel, "Zeitgenössische Neubegründung der Trinitätslehre: Eberhard Jüngel," in *Die Selbstschliessung des Dreieinigen Gottes: Grundlage eines ökumenischen Offenbarungs-, Gottes- und Kirchenverständnisses* (Göttingen: Vandenhoeck & Ruprecht, 2006), pp. 264-80; Christopher Holmes, "Jüngel on Aquinas," pp. 29-39, and "Divine Attributes According to Jüngel," pp. 99-144, in *Revisiting the Doctrine of the Divine Attributes: In Dialogue with Karl Barth, Eberhard Jüngel and Wolf Krötke* (New York: Peter Lang, 2006); Mark C. Mattes, "Eberhard Jüngel: Justification in the Theology of the Speech Event," in *The Role of Justification in Contemporary Theology* (Grand Rapids: Eerdmans, 2004), chap. 2; Bruce McCormack, "God Is His Decision: The Jüngel-Gollwitzer Debate Revisted," in B. McCormack and K. Bender, eds., *Theology as Conversation: The Significance of Dialogue in Historical and Contemporary Theology* (Grand Rapids: Eerdmans, 2009), pp. 46-66; Michael Murrmann-Kahl, "Eberhard Jüngels pantheistische Liebestrinität," in *"Mysterium Trinitatis"? Fallstudien zur Trinitätslehre in der evangelischen Dogmatik des 20. Jahrhunderts* (Tübingin: de Gruyter, 1997), pp. 108-34; Leo J. O'Donovan, "The Mystery of God as a History of Love: Eberhard Jüngel's Doctrine of God," *Theological Studies* 42 (1981): 251-71; G. Rémy, "L' analogie selon E. Jüngel. Remarques critiques. L' enjeu d' un debat," *Revue d'histoire et de philosophie religieuses* 66 (1986): 147-78; Philip Rolnick, *Analogical Possibilities* (Atlanta: American Academy of Religion Press, 1993); John Webster, "Justification, Analogy and Action: Barth and Luther in Jüngel's Anthropology," in *Barth's Moral Theology: Human Action in Barth's Thought* (Edinburgh: T & T Clark, 2004), pp. 179-214; S. D. Wigley, "Karl Barth on Anselm: The Influence of Anselm's 'Theological Scheme' on T. F. Torrance and Eberhard Jüngel," *SJT* 46 (1973): 79-97.

An Introduction to His Theology is still the best standard work about Jüngel available in English.[6] Of course, the reasons for Jüngel's lack of accessibility to English audiences are many and well documented. However, his critical insights on justification, anthropology, theological language and the doctrine of God, as well as his positive affirmation of the dogmatic enterprise as a whole, makes his work all the more important in an era when Protestant theology suffers from a lack of confidence, rigor and overall willingness. While his overconfidence about the possibility of theology might be a weakness, it may certainly also be viewed as a strength. His is a passionate, careful, critical and tenacious spirit. Jüngel everywhere proceeds with "intensity, rigor and the penetration of a powerful mind working within the structures of a passionate commitment."[7]

If one were to designate an overall theme of his dogmatic efforts, it would be his constant call for a responsible linguistic account of the God-human correspondence indicated at the heart of the gospel as a revelation of God in Jesus Christ. "Above all, he is anxious to avoid a reduction of the two-foldness of God and man to a single, self-consistent system."[8] In his most salient, dogmatic work, *God's Being Is in Becoming*, he writes,

> If revelation as event allows us to perceive "God in a mode of being . . . in which he can also exist for us" then it will be of the essence of revelation that this being for us also really reaches its final goal. Moreover, the fact that revelation is a concrete relation to concrete men must be grounded in the essence of the revelation itself, if "God's revelation has its reality and truth wholly and in every respect . . . within its self."[9]

The task of theology, in respect to this concrete "historical" event of the self-revelation of God and humanity, is to speak responsibly, such that God remains a Thou but the human really is and remains I, and as such a subject in humanity's own right. The very possibility of this dual relation of correspondence, without diminishment of either, rests in the divine act of revelation itself, that is, God's self-revelation as Father, Son and Holy Spirit:

---

[6]A further work in English that is also well worth considering is Rolnick's *Analogical Possibilities*, pp. 189-235.
[7]Webster, *Eberhard Jüngel*, pp. 3-4.
[8]Ibid.
[9]Jüngel, *God's Being Is in Becoming*, p. 32; *CD* I/1, pp. 314-15.

> Accordingly, the positive purpose of the doctrine of the Trinity, a purpose which it is the doctrine's task to defend "on the polemical front," is to make clear that, and in what way, the God who reveals himself can be . . . *(a)* "our God because in all His modes of being He is equal to Himself, one and the same Lord." And as this Lord he can be, *(b)* "our God . . . [in that] He can meet us and unite Himself to us, because He is God in His Three modes of being as Father, Son and Holy Spirit, because creation, reconciliation and redemption, the whole being, speech and action in which He wills to be our God, have their basis and prototype in His own essence, in His own being as God."[10]

Here Jüngel clearly wants to root the real distinction, yet the real revelation, in a christologically driven doctrine of the Trinity that remains faithful to Barth's impulse toward an *analogia fidei*. Though there are differences between Barth and Jüngel, by and large both theologians endeavor to "preserve the ontological distinction between God and the human even as they allow for participation in that history in which the being of God is realized. Thus, these ontologies held forth the promise of a real and genuine participation in the being of God."[11]

McCormack correctly notes that while Barth and Jüngel's theology of participation may be short on present realization, in the light of classical-metaphysical convictions, they nevertheless hold forth a greater eschato-logical promise than either Eastern or Western conceptions of theological ontology. The only reason such "Catholic" ontologies can make more promises in terms of the present realization of participation is that the subjects God and humanity are often confused in the broader philosophical grounding of the metaphysics of participation. As we shall see, Jüngel takes great pains to avoid such confusion. In fact, irresponsible speech about God is speech that fails to maintain the divine-human distinction in correspondence. To that extent, he supports Barth's reticence about the *analogia entis* and endeavors to clarify both Barth's and his own position in distinction from the Przywara–von Balthasar view. However, he rejects the *analogia entis* for precisely the opposite reason that Barth rejects it.

To that end we must clarify exactly what Jüngel finds problematic in the

---

[10]Jüngel, *God's Being Is in Becoming*, p. 32.
[11]Bruce McCormack, *Orthodox and Modern: Studies in the Theology of Karl Barth* (Grand Rapids: Baker Academic, 2008), p. 260.

classical approach to analogy, first by means of a general summary of his theological program. His argument that Aquinas's doctrine of analogy leads to the modern aporia with respect to the speakability of God has been variously criticized but not always completely understood in terms of its meaning for the analogy of faith. Thus we shall have to, once again, try to clarify the Aristotle-Aquinas-Kant continuum he so ably exposits. We shall then focus on his positive development of the analogy of advent, beginning with his appropriation of Barth's *analogia fidei*, its trinitarian grounding in the election of Jesus Christ and its attendant hermeneutical opacity with respect to *vestigium trinitatis*, which he takes up in his two most important works.[12] The narrowness of Jüngel's actual working out of the christological grounds for the analogy of advent will leave us in the position of having to return to Barth in chapter five to more fully flesh out this christological grounding of the analogy of advent and to draw a greater accord between Jüngel and Barth's conception of analogy as *analogia fidei*.

When Jüngel published *Gott als Geheimnis der Welt* (*God as the Mystery of the World*) in 1977, he was a relatively unknown Lutheran theologian teaching at Tübingen. Within the book Jüngel offered a revised understanding of the Reformed-Barthian conception of the "analogy of faith," but from the point of view of the Catholic and Protestant traditions as they related to the debates between dialectical theology, Catholic metaphysics and the so-called new hermeneutic. As a Lutheran theologian Jüngel was nevertheless steeped in the CD of his Reformed theology teacher, Barth. Yet he was equally supplied with the concepts of the new hermeneutics by his Lutheran New Testament teachers, Ernst Fuchs and Rudolf Bultmann.[13] Jüngel's interest is ultimately in combining these hermeneutical and theological concepts into a single method in which the insights of the new hermeneutics meet and are complemented by Barth's theology of the Word. As we have already indicated, central to his writings was the problem of the sheer possibility of thinking, speaking and knowing God in the midst of a culture that had become radically atheistic. For Jüngel the problem of atheism does not arise from an externally pagan and antitheistic culture but from within the Western Christian-metaphysical tradition itself. To

---

[12]See Jüngel, *God's Being Is in Becoming*, pp. 17-27; GMW, pp. 343-74.
[13]Webster, *Eberhard Jüngel*.

that end he traces the origin of the problem of possibility of theology as it arose in this theistic tradition, while at the same time attempting to go beyond the impasse between theism and atheism through a reconsideration of the ontological and theological grounds for the "thinkability," "speakability" and "knowability" of God.

Much to the surprise of those in the "new hermeneutic" school, Jüngel sides more with the dogmatic concerns of Barth in insisting that it is the principle of the relationship between the divinity and humanity of God that must supply the revelational grounds in advance for the possibility of thinking, speaking and knowing God. To think and speak of God, and therefore to know him, is to correspond precisely to the way in which God comes to us, since it is in the coming of God that the possibility of this correspondence exists. That this way might be analogical is precisely grounded in the one and only possibility of such an analogy, namely, the "Word of God," who comes to us as Jesus Christ of Nazareth. This being the case, the traditional modes of speaking and thinking about God by means of analogy required a new interpretation that does justice to the centrality of the event nature of the gospel of Jesus Christ, rather than an abstract conception of "being." The gospel conceives of the incarnation as an event that needs a witness and as such may be thought of as a "Word-event." The words used to signify this event must be, therefore, integral to the event itself, as a "language event." It is in this vein that Jüngel conceives of the phrase "analogy of advent" (*Analogie des Kommens* or *Analogie des Advent*). That is, it is a phrase that is wholly obedient to the Word of the gospel before any and all other claims to the linguistic signification of God. But this approach to the use of analogy in theology requires a radically revised theism, which entails the revision of many epistemological and ontological principles previously seen as essential to classical theism. With this conception of the "analogy of advent," Jüngel seeks to establish theology, and its possibility, on a theo-onto-linguistic basis that expresses its actual theological content. It is noteworthy that Jüngel's whole theological development begins with this interest in analogy.[14] That it issues in a complete revision of the concept of analogy, along the lines of an *analogia fidei*, should not be surprising. For him the

---

[14]Jüngel, *Zum Ursprung der Analogie bei Parmenides und Heraklit* (Berlin: de Gruyter, 1964).

question of analogy was synonymous with the possibility, or not, of theology.

Jüngel's training gave him a comprehensive grasp of the content of the Western philosophical and theological traditions. Philosophically, Jüngel is well acquainted with the works of Descartes, Kant, Fichte, Nietzsche, Spinoza, Leibniz, Hegel and Heidegger, among others.[15] His understanding of the traditions of German idealism, Cartesianism and existentialism are penetrating and have no small influence on his dogmatic decisions. So also is his grasp of the metaphysics of the classical theist tradition of medieval theology and philosophy, especially Anselm, Aquinas and Pseudo-Dionysius. The same can be said for his knowledge and understanding of the epistemological traditions of the Presocratics, Platonism and Aristotelianism.[16] All of these traditions are brought to bear on his revision of the epistemological grounds for God's thinkability, speakability and knowability. In terms of theology Jüngel represents a mixture of traditions, including patristic, medieval and modern schools.[17]

To a degree, therefore, Jüngel's theological enterprise attempts to reconcile the competing concerns of Barth and Bultmann. While he absorbed the principle of the centrality and singularity of revelation in dogmatics from Barth, he nevertheless appreciated, from Bultmann and his "new hermeneutics," the importance and primacy of the language we must employ in giving expression to that revelation.[18] Jungel saw the problems of hermeneutics and revelation to be closely related, especially as the division between dogmatics and exegesis was never so wide than during his education. Barth and Bultmann were, for him, equal opportunities to unite two formerly estranged disciplines in a new way, using complementary principles from both schools of thought. This has remained a central concern for Jüngel throughout his career.[19] Jüngel seeks to unite exegesis and dogmatics into a single theological method because he thinks it has important ramifications for one's capacity to think, speak

---

[15]On influences on Jüngel, see especially Webster, *Eberhard Jüngel*, pp. 25-29.

[16]In his Habilitationschrift, *Zum Ursprung der Analogie bei Parmenides und Heraklit*, Jüngel demonstrates considerable depth and prowess in the classics.

[17]Webster, "Introduction," in *Theological Essays*, pp. 3-5.

[18]This can be observed in his book *Paulus und Jesus: Untersuchung zur Prazisierung der Frage nach dem Ursprung der Christologie* (Tübingen, 1979).

[19]Webster, *Eberhard Jüngel*, pp. 25-33.

and know God.[20] Dogmatics poses the question: How may we we speak of God? Hermeneutics and exegesis pose the question: What is the meaning of God-talk? Jüngel could affirm simultaneously with Barth that "God is both the object and the subject of His self-revelation," and with Bultmann that God is nevertheless "a Word of our language."[21] But far from being in the constant thrall of Barth and Bultmann, Jüngel draws on his Reformed-Lutheran roots in order to give a theological expression to these seemingly competing concerns. This revised perspective is grounded in a conception of the theology of the cross, which he takes to be the place of the gospel wherein these concerns are synthesized in the historical event of Jesus Christ.[22] Jüngel shared with Barth and Bultmann the desire to divest theology of any anthropological/naturalistic presuppositions that might predispose it to some ground other than the gospel. To that degree, he affirms that he seeks a theology that runs "counter to Pannenberg and with Barth." Any conception of analogy would therefore have to be tempered and reinterpreted in light of such a concern. To that end he sees, with Barth, that the analogy of faith best expresses this avoidance of anthropocentrism. But where the early Barth took this in the direction of a radical differentiation between God and humanity, Jüngel wants to reinterpret the *analogia fidei* in the terms of a more linguistically and hermeneutically grounded modality of the speakability of God as an identity with humanity.[23]

Jüngel has made it clear that his theological quest is animated by two basic considerations: With Luther, he holds that humanity is radically and essentially distinct from God, who is its salvation; and with Barth he affirms that this distinction between God and humanity does not signify a contradiction between God and humankind but implies a correspondence or analogy. As the trinitarian God corresponds to God, humanity as humanity

---

[20]Ibid. Webster writes, "Jüngel's earliest explorations of this theme are informed by his conviction that the different theological disciplines all stand in relation to the 'Word of God': Theology is a science which is related in all its parts to the event of the Word of God and constituted as a science through that relation" (*Eberhard Jüngel*, p. 27).

[21]Ibid., p. 26.

[22]*GMW*, p. x.

[23]Jüngel, "Die Möglichkeit theologischer Anthropologie auf dem Grund der Analogie: Eine Untersuchung zum Analogieverständnis Karl Barths," *Evangelische Theologie* 22 (1962): 535-57; see also *Barth-Studien*, pp. 210-32.

must correspond to God. A correspondence (analogy) between God and humanity forms the foundation of all theology: "to think of the relation between God and man as a relationship of correspondence or as an analogical relation, means to think of it in the sense of an ever greater similarity, nearness and confidence between man and God even within the profound diversity, distance and strangeness."[24] Taking language, especially parable and metaphor, as the place of this ever-greater correspondence between God and humanity, Jüngel has succeeded in bringing a totally new dimension into the discussion of analogy. However, before we go to the analysis of his concept of analogy, we must briefly establish the theological foundation for it that he lays out in the early part of GMW.

Jüngel's theological enterprise as represented in GMW begins with a negative assessment of the status and problem of theology in the contemporary atheistic context in which he is doing theology. His goal, however, is to seek a positive ground where responsible speech about God may take place. Above all else, according to Jüngel, we must understand that the contemporary situation is rooted in a problematic mode in which theism formerly carried out its theological sentences. To that end Jüngel begins by expositing the roots of modern atheism as a product of an inherently problematic concept of God pursued within the metaphysical (classical theist) tradition of the Middle Ages and its accompanying "hermeneutics of signification." The fact that modern atheism finds its roots within, as opposed to outside, this tradition requires of the Christian faith that it renew its theology and epistemology in a direction that does not make it susceptible to atheistic thinking. Such a renewal is possible for Christian theology only from the point of view of revelation, that is, from a renewed understanding of the humanity of God as he is identified in the gospel of the crucified one, and as the event of language, of coming to speech in address and narrative. If God is to be thinkable and speakable, then it must be on the basis of the humanity of God (which is inimical to God's nature as primal decision). These three principles—the thinkability, speakability and humanity of God—constitute the sum and substance of what it is to know God in Jüngel's thought. God's thinkability and speakability are the elements essential

---

[24]R. Garaventa, "L'esito della teologia: Dio é altro dall'uomo (intervista a E. Jüngel)," Il Regno 2 (1987): 38-41.

to the knowledge (*ratio cognoscendi*) of God, while the humanity of God is the sum and substance of the being (*ratio essendi*) of God.[25] The principle that brings them together as responsible speech about God is correspondence (*Entsprechung*), which in Jüngel's thought substitutes for, or rather sums up, what is meant by the phrase "the analogy of faith" as it comes to expression especially in Barth's later theology. Our emphasis in this chapter will be decidedly on the "speakability," since its corollary is the "analogy of advent." But it must be understood here in the light of his overall concerns for thinking and revelation. Therefore we shall return to speakability more fully below but will touch on it here in light of his whole system of theology. At the end of the process it is the humanity of God that constitutes the revelatory and therefore the epistemological, linguistic and ontological basis for analogy.

The thinkability of God. Jüngel uses the Greek word *aporia* to describe the state of affairs with respect to classical theism and its difficulty in establishing the knowledge of God. In its cognate verbal form, ἀπορέω means "to be at a loss, confused or questioning in a perplexed manner." Nominally it can also mean "to be at a loss" or "in dismay" at a state of affairs.[26] The word has heuristic force and is not just descriptive of the development of classical theism. By using it Jüngel means to emphasize that the real aporia of modern thought about God in contemporary philosophy and theology has its corresponding initiating point in the aporia concerning thinking and speaking about God in the Middle Ages. The one is the direct product of the other. But the aporia, rather than being an end point beyond which theology cannot go, is rather an initiating point for a renewal of theology along the lines of a new *ratio*, namely, one informed by the humanity of God pointed out in the gospel. But how did this modern aporia come about? What is its connection to the aporia of theological language about God in the Middle Ages? The modern theological aporia originates in the epistemological presuppositions of the Cartesian reconfiguration of human self-understanding, together with its concomitant reconsideration of the world and God. It reaches its apogee in a form of Hegelianism that affirms the death of God in christological terms as an absolute identification of God with the world. As

---

[25]*GMW*, p. xii.
[26]G. W. H. Lamp, ed., *A Patristic Greek Lexicon* (Oxford: Clarendon Press, repr. 2007), p. 205.

such, the modern aporia is rooted in the emphasis on the necessity of God established in the metaphysical systems of theism of the Middle Ages.

In his analysis of the history of modern philosophy, especially its Cartesian beginnings, Jüngel discovers two critical and related contradictions of thought, as applied to the turn to the thinking self by means of systemic doubt.[27] *First* and foremost, there is in the Cartesian system an establishment of the self in God as a "methodological necessity" in order to secure an assurance of this thinking self for the human ego. This is rooted in a misreading of the ontological argument of Anselm, that God is the greatest of all possible thoughts and therefore must necessarily exist. This contradiction led naturally to the disintegration of the certainty of the knowledge of God insofar as God becomes a product of our capacity to think his existence. That is, he is relative to one's capacity to think his existence. Since, therefore, it can also be established that he is unthinkable, his nonexistence is equally plausible as a foundation for self-establishment.

A *second* contradiction followed the first in that this "necessary God" must exist without any imperfection and/or infirmity if he is to exist on a plane above the human self. But if such a necessary God is a product of human thought, he must nevertheless exist in and through humanity, since he can only be established to exist by means of human thought as above and yet within humanity. Such an intellectually conceived "necessary God" can only be the product of humanity and therefore subject to the dictates of humanity. This amounts to the banishment of a truly transcendent God and the institution of an exclusively immanent God "appropriate only to humanity."[28] The history of Cartesian subjectivity with respect to theology is the history of the coming to be of the "non-necessity" of God, in which "man is made the measure of all things," including his own humanity. God is "not necessary in any worldly sense," because "man can be human without God. . . . He can live without experiencing God."[29] God is banished from the world by means of the attempt to establish his existence, subjectively, through thought.

For Jüngel the point at which this modern aporia becomes manifest in an

[27]*GMW*, p. 122.
[28]*GMW*, p. 126.
[29]*GMW*, pp. 14-20.

atheism of cultural significance is in the so-called left-wing Hegelianism and its "hermeneutics of suspicion."[30] These hermeneuts of suspicion include Johann Gottlieb Fichte, Ludwig Feuerbach and Friedrich Nietzsche, though Fichte was hardly a Hegelian per se. He was rather a contemporary of Hegel who debated the same issues and came to conclusions in the opposite direction from him, namely, toward atheism. Fichte was not so much an atheist as he was a thoroughgoing rationalist who refused any idea of a rational justification for the existence of God. Contrary to Descartes, he saw rational doubt as the means to an establishment of pure reason without God.[31]

Feuerbach arrived at his negative assessment of the metaphysical necessity of God by means of an application to humanity of all the supposed "divine attributes." He discovered that the God of metaphysical necessity was really just a projection of our own human finitude and wish for transcendence on a being we call God. "The secret of theology is that it is, after all, only anthropology."[32] It was only a short step from there to Nietzsche's declaration of the death of God precisely by means of his metaphysical necessity. Once God becomes unthinkable, he becomes unspeakable and is thus supremely unknowable. That is, atheism is more plausible now than theism, or at least the theism of metaphysical necessity.[33]

This late modern atheism might best be expressed as the "displacement" of God by humanity. God's place in human self-understanding is "re-placed" by the human, but the replacement amounts to a "dis-placement" in that God no longer has any place. The "place-less-ness" of God is to be identified with the death of God in the modern world, where presence and absence are markers of existence and nonexistence. "God himself is negated along with his absence."[34] In this sense the Cartesian *cogito* is the sign under which we may signify the death of God. If the Middle Ages was an exercise in the unknowability of God, modernity follows it with an affirmation of his

---

[30]*GMW*, pp. 63-69, deals with Hegel's significance for modern atheism at length and with important ramifications for Jüngel's theology of the cross.

[31]See especially Johann Gottlieb Fichte, *Grundlage der gesamten Wissenschaftslehre* (1794/95; 2nd ed. 1802), Foundations of the Entire Science of Knowledge, trans. Peter Heath, in *Fichte: Science of Knowledge (Wissenschaftslehre)*, ed. Peter Heath and John Lachs (Cambridge: Cambridge University Press, 1982), pp. 35-36.

[32]Ludwig Feuerbach, *The Essence of Christianity* (New York: Harper & Row, 1985), pp. 221-22.

[33]*GMW*, pp. 128-50.

[34]*GMW*, pp. 52-55.

unthinkability, and atheism/agnosticism, or the unknowability of God, becomes the only alternative.[35]

The shocking thing about this state of affairs is that it is precisely a development internal to the Western Christian tradition. Modern atheism as it comes to expression in the hermeneutics of suspicion, and as it is embedded in the modern philosophical notion of the necessity of God, is the result of a prior condition within theism and is therefore the cause of atheism. The emphasis on the simplicity, perfection and transcendence of God, in terms of radical otherness as the God who is "fundamentally and exclusively over us," lent itself to a form of radical doubt that ultimately led to God's displacement and banishment.[36] The God of medieval metaphysics was not amenable to a God who may share in the suffering, death and perishability that was the predominant expression of the modern human condition. Furthermore, speaking ontologically, the perfect God of metaphysical signification was established more on a philosophical than a biblical basis. He was a product of the classical tendency to identify existence and essence as the real but at the same time expressible only as the "distinction between essence and existence" due to the epistemological lack within the realm of finite human knowing (the *ratio cognoscendi* could never really know God's unity as a *datum*, only as an a priori proposition). When modern philosophy, following Descartes, posited God as a being necessary to our own thought and existence, it no longer saw him as a unity but precisely as a rational distinction between essence and existence. Such a rational conception of God had the effect of introducing a split between God, as he is in himself, and our rational perception of God. The net result is to establish a God beyond God, making the intellectual apprehension of God itself a threat to the God beyond the rationally perceptible God. In the Middle Ages the capacity to think was synonymous with knowledge. If, with late modern philosophy, we see God as beyond our capacity to think him (as per Fichte and Feuerbach), we must also conclude with the tradition of classical theism that he is unspeakable and therefore unknowable as well.[37] If the presence of God is synonymous with the denial of the majestic aspects of his being, such

---

[35]*GMW*, pp. 150-51.
[36]*GMW*, p. 48.
[37]*GMW*, pp. 101-4.

as his omnipotence, then it must also extend to his omnipresence. In this way the attempt to establish God as a product of our capacity to think him leads to impossibility of thinking God as God, as per classical theism. Modernity thus becomes the nursery that brings forth atheism from theism. Or as Jüngel puts it, "Proof of the necessity of God is the midwife of modern atheism."[38] In this sense atheism is the flip side of theism.

The problem that this state of affairs poses for doing theology in the late modern period is obvious. If theology is going to overcome the latent agnosticism and atheism of its own systems of thought, it must first overcome this way of doing the doctrine of God. Jüngel thinks that "atheism can be rejected only if one overcomes theism, which is the presupposition of modern metaphysics and its disputation."[39] Theology may do so in two ways: *First*, it must strive to think "God" as he is, that is, as he gives himself to be known in Scripture and the gospel and not after the classical philosophical modality of a distinction in the being of God between essence and existence. This will deny to thought the capacity to insert its own presence between the essence and the existence of God.[40] *Second*, in short, it will return to a biblical concept of the unity of God wherein existence and essence are consistently thought of as a unity. By means of the gospel, theology can offer the world, and its nonnecessity of God, a God who is "more than necessary." According to Jüngel, we need look no further than our own experience of the world to establish this possibility.[41] The human "experiences his existence and the being of his world as a being which has been plucked from nothingness. . . . God is experienced as the Being who disposes over being and nonbeing. Such a Being . . . cannot be conceived of as dependent on some other being. . . . God has no ground. . . . As a groundless being, God is not necessary and yet more than necessary."[42] That God is "more than necessary" means that he is beyond the confines of our capacity to think him as necessary and contingent. This means that "God is interesting for his own sake," but also "that man and the world are interesting for their own sake"

---

[38]*GMW*, p. 19.
[39]*GMW*, p. 43.
[40]*GMW*, pp. 153-55.
[41]*GMW*, p. 31-32.
[42]*GMW*, p. 24.

particularly because God makes humanity "interesting in a new way."[43] The very same God who, from above, determines the distinction between being and nothingness is precisely the God who, from below, is in the midst of this contradiction and is vulnerable to it, in his humanity, in the very same way.[44] In this sense the perfect God of splendid isolation, who is a prisoner of his own glory, is supplanted by the God of the gospel who identifies himself not just with but as the crucified. The death of God, far from signifying his absence, confirms his identity as a "totally new from above" who is present in the crucified one.[45] In this sense only can God become "thinkable" again.

Jüngel draws on a number of late and contemporary sources in theology to confirm this new identity of God with the crucified, including Luther, Dietrich Bonhoeffer and, to a degree, Hegel. In concert with Bonhoeffer he sees the modern atheistic impasse as a turning point in theology. It is a possible renewal of theology along the lines of Luther's *theologia crucis*.[46] This is a fundamentally christological move that enables late modern humanity to think God in close connection with his perishability, as a unity, and thus as his concretization in human states of affairs.[47] The gospel points us to the God who dies in our place rather than an absolute and perfect being of metaphysical signification.[48] "Talk about the death of God implies, then, in its true theological meaning, that God is the one who involves himself in nothingness."[49] In God's identification with the death of the man Jesus Christ of Nazareth, nonbeing is undone and rendered powerless. The dialectic of being and nonbeing, of life and death, is resolved in God, who is love. Thus God's identification with the crucified is the revelation of God as mystery, the mystery of the world.[50] God is only above us insofar as he is with us, and he is with us only insofar as he is above us. He is the event of the mystery of God's condescension and identity in and with Jesus Christ the crucified one—that is, as the *Word* of the gospel.

---

[43]*GMW*, p. 34.
[44]*GMW*, pp. 34-35.
[45]*GMW*, pp. 44-48.
[46]*GMW*, p. 92.
[47]*GMW*, pp. 182-205.
[48]*GMW*, p. 199.
[49]*GMW*, p. 219.
[50]*GMW*, p. 220.

Thus the thinkability of God can only be grounded in the *Word* as its hermeneutical possibility. In Scripture God comes to the world as a capacity for human thought via the revelation of his Word. The very thought of God constitutes a divine address in which the human is borne by God. The thought of God is the event of divine encounter as such.[51] It is the address of humanity by God in such a way that "reason can . . . only think God in that it follows after faith." Faith is the divinely enabled venturing of the self, as ego, in the direction pointed out by God himself. The self-grounding of thought (*Selbständigkeit*) is the correspondence of faith in terms of a "thinking after," a self-positing act of "being taken along" and "a correspondence of thinking and being, thanks to the addressing feature of language."[52] Human self-positing happens when "thought so affected by God affirms the Word as the place where God is thinkable."[53] There is no possibility of the renewal or redemption of language without the integral connection between thought and speech. God is speakable because he is thinkable, but he is only thinkable because he has spoken in his Word. The Word of his address constitutes the only possibility of thought and speech about God.

The speakability of God. So much for the problem of God's thinkability as the epistemic grounds for analogy in Western thought. What are its implications for God's speakability as the linguistic ground for theology? To be precise, the core of Jüngel's concern is, as we have said, responsible speech about God as a distinct possibility. Thus speakability is the heart of the matter. But how to establish the speakability of God "in an age of the verbal place-less-ness of God" is not immediately self-evident.[54] To begin with we must affirm against the classical theist tradition that thinking about God is not the source of the speakability of God. Rather the opposite is true, but only in terms of God's own Word of address, that is, *his* spoken Word. God becomes thinkable and speakable only on this basis. It is a hermeneutical matter from the outset in that speakability as a divine given entails a relationship initiated from the divine side respecting God's spoken Word and human language. To avoid ending in theology's silence, one has to conceive

---

[51]*GMW*, pp. 160-67.
[52]*GMW*, pp. 166-70.
[53]*GMW*, p. 166.
[54]*GMW*, pp. 55-56.

of the possibility of theological speech as invested with a theology of language from the very beginning. Such a view must avoid "the ontological priority of thought over speech."[55] Thinking God presupposes "talk about God."[56] The priority of speech follows from the fact that thinking is "thinking after." Thought follows faith, which follows a Word of address, which is heard and followed by language.[57] This is so for theology because "God has spoken to us definitively" in his Word, Jesus Christ, and so "we must conceive of God himself as the one who speaks . . . not only in order to communicate something, but to communicate himself."[58] But it is not to be determined by thinking; rather, "what is to be thought is preceded by what is spoken."[59] It is the material of the spoken Word that gives birth to thought. "It is not reason which leads to speaking, but rather speaking leads to reason and to thought. . . . God must first of all speak, if he is to let himself be thought." The question of the thinkability of God is then resolved by whether "God is speakable on the basis of such a Word of God."[60] This is the central concern to be exposited in the relation between revelation and language. To do so is to do theology.

For Jüngel correspondence means that revelation and language exist in a proper tension that establishes the priority of revelation together with the necessity and legitimacy of language. This is a theme that first emerges in his early writings, especially his work *Paulus und Jesus*, which consisted of a blending of exegetical and dogmatic themes. It is given further expression in his very well-written paraphrase of Barth's doctrine of the Trinity, *God's Being Is in Becoming.*[61] Both of these works highlight the dialectical nature of the relationship between revelation and language. In a later essay, "Metaphorical Truth," Jüngel attempts a synthesis between these dialectical poles by means of a metaphorical understanding of the relationship between revelatory truth and language.[62] This synthesis is further developed in his essay

---

[55]*GMW*, p. 252.
[56]*GMW*, p. 230.
[57]*GMW*, p. 253.
[58]*GMW*, pp. 12-13.
[59]*GMW*, pp. 253-54.
[60]*GMW*, p. 254.
[61]See especially Webster, *Eberhard Jüngel*, pp. 40-42.
[62]Besides *GMW*, see "Metaphorical Truth," in *Theological Essays*, pp. 16-71, and "The World as Possibility and Actuality," in *Theological Essays*, pp. 95-123.

"The World as Possibility and Actuality," in which he establishes the ontological priority of the possibility over actuality, in that the truth does not correspond to the actual, as per classical theism, but to the possible as more than actual. Truth is the disclosure of being as the event of the investing of language with being. To the degree that language is invested with being, truth and language correspond to the event of divine speech. Metaphor brings to language the possibility of this correspondence. Thus correspondence is to be correlated with and corrected by means of metaphor, which has the capacity to reveal the new being of God's speech-act. In this sense possibility must precede actuality, but to the degree that actuality is given its true being by means of metaphor. It does so precisely by comparing realities that are otherwise worlds apart, thus giving actuality the capacity to give place to the new without destroying the integrity of the language or stretching it beyond its normal capacities. The familiar is used to signify the unfamiliar, thus granting to language a capacity for disclosing the content of the divine speaking in ordinary language. But it does so precisely in that it points beyond the familiar and ordinary to the dialectic inherent in the speech-act of God himself, as revelation.

Here we come to the central axiom of Jüngel's argument for the speakability of God. The classical conception of language, as signs that signify, tends to present God as ultimately the incomprehensible (unthinkable) and therefore unspeakable.[63] The most important theological question is "whether that to which the word refers must itself exist beyond the word, outside of the language context in which it is found?"[64] Here Jüngel employs the doctrine of the sacraments together with the poetic function of language and concludes, "Language has still other functions than that of signifying. One of its functions is that of address."[65] Jüngel affirms, "It is the address character which first makes it human," since "the word of address affects not only the consciousness of the person addressed but his whole being."[66] Insofar as the human is addressed, he is a subject. Address constitutes an event that "takes place," as it happens "in the very event of the Word"; "words allow

---

[63]*GMW*, p. 8.
[64]*GMW*, pp. 9-11.
[65]Jüngel, "Metaphorical Truth," p. 57; "Anthropomorphism: A Fundamental Problem in Modern Hermeneutics," in *Theological Essays*, pp. 72-94, 92-93.
[66]*GMW*, p. 11.

something to happen which is present in the words or with them or through them."[67] This is for Jüngel "a language event" in which humanity hears language as addressing speech, which involves the speaker (God) and the hearer (humanity) by bringing "God and the addressed person together lingually" (really and actually and therefore ontically as a function of language). It is in this sense that Jüngel affirms that "God becomes thinkable on the basis of his speakability."[68] Thus the basis of God's speakability and thinkability is not relegated to the capacity of language to signify but to its metaphorical capacity to be invested with the speech event of God. That is, God is thinkable and speakable in his self-revelation as the Word of the Gospel. God alone, in his speech, can say and determine the content of the word "God." Revelation is thus necessarily obedient of this Word of address.

This revelation comes to speech as "Word event" and thus amounts to a commandeering of language for revelation, a gain to speech. The capacity of language to speak "God" is not abolished but established by this divine commandeering. God himself renders human language capable of speaking himself, by means of his identification on the human side with the crucified one.[69] The speakability of God is first a hearing of divine speech and only then as a "coming to speech." The Word of revelation, understood as God's speech-act, is a testimony to humanity as participants in "linguistic being (*Sprach-Wesen*)," the unity of which is "his being in the world (in time and space)," which is "maintained by the linguistic nature (*Sprachlichkeit*) of his existence."[70] This is the divine solution to the aporia of God's "incomprehensibility." Thus the aporia of the ineffability of God and the problem of anthropomorphism is overcome by the humanity of God (the Word become flesh), which is the material ground for thinkability and speakability. If God is both thinkable and speakable on this basis, then he is also knowable.

It is in this way that the humanity of God constitutes the basis of the thinkability and speakability of God: "to think God's being as love means then to think God's thinkability on the basis of his speakability, and his speakability on the basis of the correspondence he has established between

---

[67] *GMW*, p. 10; "Gott als Geheimnis," pp. 83-98.
[68] *GMW*, pp. 11-12.
[69] Ibid.
[70] Eberhard Jüngel, "Grenzen des Menschseins," in *Entsprechungen: Gott—Wahrheit—Mensch*, Theologische Erörterungen II (Munich: Kaiser, 1980), pp. 357-59.

God and man."[71] But this is a movement of God in history that has its beginning in the the incarnation of the Son. It proceeds from there to the revelation of God as love and his identification with humanity in the self-exposition of God as economic and immanent Trinity. Insofar as a correspondence of relation exists eternally in the Trinity, and this relation has been displayed in the sending of the Son and Spirit in the economy of salvation, so also there exists a relational correspondence between God and the human. This is the humanity of God disclosed in his divine speech. That is, "divinity's own humanity" is the "material insight" that "the humanity of God taught us to think of God as the subject of himself who is free in the event of love, and that led to the formal insight that God can be known and thought only on the basis of his own being."[72]

Being is not, therefore, self-realization or self-assertion through thought and signification. It is rather God's self-identification with perishability. Precisely the death of God constitutes the ground of his speakability, not his nonexistence. Jüngel concludes: "The positive meaning of the talk about the death of God would then imply that God is in the midst of the struggle between nothingness and possibility."[73] The identity of the existence and the essence of God with perishability is the possibility and actuality of the existence of God as "being and nothingness" and as the "struggle between life and death," which become concrete in the historical fact of the death and resurrection of Jesus: "suffering annihilation in himself, God shows himself to be the victor over nothingness."[74] The dialectic between being and non-being as love is the ontological ground of the thinkability, speakability and knowability of God.

The humanity of God is revealed precisely in the christological destiny toward perishability. The incarnation, God's Word of address, is the identification of God's humanity with ours as the speakability of a God who loves in freedom. The crucified Lord Jesus Christ is the revelation of God as love. On the cross God is defined as love. The predicative statement "God is love" (1 Jn 4:8) means that "God lives as love."[75] Here, in the demonstration of

---

[71]*GMW*, p. 300.
[72]*GMW*, p. 299.
[73]*GMW*, p. 217.
[74]*GMW*, p. 218.
[75]*GMW*, pp. 220-22.

love, act and being constitute a single revelation of the divine-human correspondence that witnesses to the onto-theological being, existence and express-ability of God.[76] It is the unique form of encounter that constitutes "the event of a still greater selflessness within a great, and justifiably very great self-relatedness. Love is mutual surrender."[77] It is "a radical distancing" that "takes place in favour of a new nearness to oneself and the beloved."[78] We have love not by means of our own self-awareness, but by means of a divine-human correspondence that "transforms itself in the promises of a new being."[79] Furthermore, "love carries death within itself," as the possibility of being in its struggle with nonbeing. It is the possibility of life over death.[80] If the essence of being itself is love, God's being and essence is love because God is the "unity of life and death in favour of life."[81] The answer to the question that arises with God's self-identification with humanity in Jesus Christ, especially with respect to perishability, is contained for Jüngel in the doctrine of the Trinity, to which he appeals at this juncture. However, his clearest expression of this is in his little book *God's Being Is in Becoming*.

In *God's Being Is in Becoming*, Jüngel explains the possibility of God's self-identification with perishability in human terms as follows. Proper speech about God's being-as-object "cannot be located in the human mind, making God an object of subjective knowing, but comes from God's giving of himself to the subject as an object which can be known." It consists in the fact that "God has become expressible."[82] God is available as an object for subjective apprehension, but only as he has made himself to be such. This is not to say that God is once again removed from us, as object over against subject, but rather God's objectivity must be understood in terms of its determination within human existence. The anthropological significance of God's being-as-object resides in the fact that in God's being-as-object, God has brought human existence into a definite relationship with himself.[83] The subjective reality of the human individual is not thereby excluded but

---

[76]*GMW*, pp. 314-15.
[77]*GMW*, p. 317.
[78]*GMW*, pp. 318-19 and 390-91.
[79]*GMW*, p. 321.
[80]*GMW*, p. 324.
[81]*GMW*, p. 325.
[82]Jüngel, *God's Being Is in Becoming*, pp. 45-47.
[83]Ibid., p. 46.

contained in God's being-as-object in relation to the human. The polarization of God's existence over against his subjectivity is based on an illegitimate understanding of objectivity, which fails to consider the primary and secondary objectivity of God. Along with Barth, Jüngel wants to establish human existence and God's speakability without reducing God to a label for human states of affairs. God's being-as-object is not the antithesis of human subjectivity but is its inner possibility and actuality, just as God's being-as-object is God's own actuality and possibility.

To speak of God's being-as-object as the possibility of God's self-expression to humanity is to speak of his *being-in-coming*. Furthermore, to speak of God in this way is not to make God's ontological existence into a mere instance of flux, but to speak of the way in which God chooses to be in his self-interpretation. As such, God's being is "self-relating-being," in that each eternal mode of God's being "becomes what it is only together with the two other modes of being." This is expressed, according to Barth, in the doctrines of *perichoresis* and *attribution* as applied to the three eternal modes of God's being. As an attribute particularly ascribed to God, *becoming* is a function of his being. It indicates the manner in which God's being is, as "ontological place." It is "the becoming which is proper to God's being." It has a christological rather than a metaphysical ground. Jüngel, with Barth, is concerned to identify God's divine nature with the nature manifested in Jesus Christ in that "the God whose being is in [be]coming can die as a human being."[84]

This ontological place of God's being is one that he has chosen from eternity, for himself. It is the place of God's eternal election of himself in that he is "his own double." God's being, as a being in becoming in Jesus Christ, "is the place of His choice." God's freedom and aseity are therein not circumscribed but fully realized. Jesus Christ is substantially the predicate of God's own being by God's *primal decision* to be in history before history. In the primal decision God has subjected himself to the threat of nonbeing in the death of Jesus on the cross. But this risk is precisely the undoing of nonbeing in that God triumphs over it, because in the moment of self-denial God becomes God's self, since this suffering and death are willed by God himself.

---

[84]Ibid.

God's being is a being-in-becoming in that God has chosen to identify with humanity in Jesus Christ. Such an entry into history is God's subjection of himself to historicity and possibility as his own aim. This does not entail a contradiction in God's "being," but is God's "being-in-act."[85]

In sum, in the intratrinitarian life of God, God has freely chosen obedience to suffering and death. In his *God as the Mystery of the World* Jüngel put a finer point on this, stating: "God is God even in the death of the Son."[86] This necessarily presupposes a second eternal mode of being in the Godhead as the relation and differentiation of Father and Son. The third eternal mode necessarily follows, in that "next to the Father and the Son, the Holy Spirit is a third relationship, namely, the relationship between the relationships of the Father and the Son, . . . and thus an eternally new relationship of God to God," in which God remains eternally Father and Son in the Spirit as advent, "the event [coming] of God."[87] The trinitarian grounding of God's being is an eternally new relationship in that God comes from God: "the Father, who loves of himself; the Son, who has always been loved; and the constantly new event of love between the Father and the Son which is the Spirit."[88] It is in this sense that the economic Trinity constitutes the ground of the expressability of the immanent Trinity, and only in this way may the two concepts be spoken of as identical. The trinitarian nature of God is known only from the story of Jesus, and not from the inner life of God per se. As such, and following the analysis of Barth, the crucified Jesus is the only vestige of the Trinity.[89]

God's speakability is as the triune God, who is in the crucified Jesus, the "mystery of the world."[90] Furthermore, he is the mystery as the newly added plus of humanity and as the one who truly comes to the world as its own. "God came to the world as man." Therefore in his identity with Jesus Christ, "God is the actual mystery of the world."[91] In that God comes from God, he is the event of his eternal coming. What is more, "God in his becoming is

---

[85]Ibid., p. 66.
[86]*GMW*, pp. 391-92.
[87]*GMW*, p. 82.
[88]*GMW*, p. 83.
[89]*GMW*, p. 85.
[90]*GMW*, pp. 376-96.
[91]*GMW*, p. 379.

aiming at the becoming of creation." Temporal being is enfolded in the eternal election of God in Jesus. It has a beginning and an end that is ontologically given and knowable in the eternal generation of the Son. As such, Jesus Christ is the primal "image" of humanity that constitutes the divine image breathed into humanity at creation.[92] "The Son of God coming eternally from God aims at the man who temporally comes from God."[93]

Summary: The problem of analogous talk of God. What Jüngel has been describing in the first part of his magnum opus, *God as the Mystery of the World*, and in his *God's Being Is in Becoming*, are the theological grounds for the use of analogy. The grounds for analogy will be therefore relagated to a christological *analogia fidei*. Three principles have emerged with respect to those grounds. *First*, God's thinkability, speakability and knowability must be revised and understood in light of the humanity of God. God is thinkable only as "being in coming." "God's being is in coming."[94] "The statement 'God's being is in coming' implies first of all that God's being is the event of his coming to himself. . . . God is eternally coming to himself." God "always comes as God from God to God."[95] The economic expression of this coming is as the mystery of the triune God to whom Jesus points us, and in which "God comes from God the Father, to God the Son, as God the Holy Spirit."[96]

Second, God comes to the world in the same mode of address as his own Son. In the historical personage of Jesus Christ of Nazareth, God identifies himself with humanity, as it is narrated in the gospel of Jesus Christ. This is a story that must be told. The legitimacy of the storytelling in linguistic terms is underwritten by the event itself as divine address in the Word. God comes to language as language, speech, address, parable and metaphor.[97] *Third*, God's coming as a Word of address constitutes revelation as a language-event. God's coming to the world is compared to this Word of address as the

---

[92]Jüngel, "Der Gott entsprechende Mensch: Bemerkungen zur Gottesebenbildlichkeit des Menschen als Grundfigur theologischer Anthropologic," in *Entsprechungen*, p. 314.

[93]*GMW*, p. 384.

[94]*GMW*, p. 275. See also Jüngel, "Das Verhältnis von ökonomischer und immanenter Trinität. Erwägungen über eine biblische Begründung der Trinitätslehre—im Anschluß an und in Auseinandersetzung mit Karl Rahners Lehre vom dreifaltigen Gott als transzendentem Urgrund der Heilsgeschichte," in *Entsprechungen*, pp. 265-75, p. 271; "Das Verhaltnis von 'okonomischer' und 'immanenter Trinitat,'" (1975): 275-91.

[95]*GMW*, p. 380.

[96]*GMW*, p. 381.

[97]Ibid.

exclusive grounds and possibility for analogy, and nowhere else.

God is speakable only on the basis of the distinction between God's being as being in himself and his being as Father, Son and Holy Spirit. *Correspondence* is the careful theological delineation of this distinction. In God's coming to the world there is implied "a fundamental distinction between God and world."[98] This distinction is arrived at from the side of God first as "a distinction of the world based on God."[99] It is grounded in God's own being as his own capacity to be intrinsically the one who comes to himself and has his existence in himself without creation. "God became man in Jesus Christ in order to distinguish definitely between God and man forever." The uniqueness of Jesus "effects a concrete distinction between God and world."[100] According to Jüngel, "The difference between God and man, which is constitutive of the essence of Christian faith, is thus not the difference of a still greater dissimilarity, but rather, conversely, the difference of a still greater similarity between God and man in the midst of a great dissimilarity."[101] Thus God's coming to the world as his eternal Word, in the eternal mode of his Son, is God's primal act of election, differentiation and thus correspondence. Such an election, differentiation and correspondence is expressible only by an analogy of faith in the event of the incarnation.[102]

What, then, is the concept of correspondence in its essence? The knowability of God is precisely the humanity of God. It is not in the first instance the capacity to think God. It is possible only as the encounter between God and the world as the humanity, self-identification and vulnerability of God. Only on this basis may language "correspond" to God. But on this basis a true correspondence is possible and actual. It is not guaranteed by thought or ontology but only by the self-identification of God with perishability in the crucified Lord Jesus Christ, the *theologia crucis* or Word of the cross. This is a Word of address that interrupts rather than confirms human autonomy and metaphysics; "the essence of the addressing Word is approached through interruption." This interruption is a threefold correspondence: "of thought to faith, of being to love, of speech to metaphor." This is the

---

[98]*GMW*, pp. 368-76.

[99]*GMW*, p. 380.

[100]*GMW*, pp. 94-95.

[101]*GMW*, p. 288.

[102]Jüngel, "The Invocation of God," in *Theological Essays*, pp. 159-60.

movement that Jüngel traces out in the rest of *GMW*. The hermeneutical and ontological key is analogy, or properly speaking, the analogy of coming, of advent, to which we can now turn to complete the picture and indicate our way forward.[103]

JÜNGEL'S PROPOSAL FOR AN ANALOGY OF ADVENT

As we have seen, very early in Jüngel's theological endeavors he sought to clarify the relationship between God and humanity, and their autonomy, in Barth's theology. He does this by paying careful attention to the problems of analogy and ontology in Barth, from a Reformed perspective.[104] Jüngel is critical of von Balthasar, Gottlieb Söhngen, Przywara and Wolfhart Pannenberg's interpretations here because all have failed to understand Barth's distinction between *analogia fidei* and *analogia entis*, and his rejection of the latter. Jüngel takes great pains to explain what Barth was about in his use of *analogia fidei*. Analogy is not just a question of a certain linguistic method for speaking about God, but it is a substantive proposal on Barth's part that entails "the being of the man Jesus" as the "ontological and epistemological basis for all analogy."[105] As Jüngel suggested in a later article: "In theology, analogy is pertinent; as the ontological structure of the relationship between God and his creation; as a hermeneutical model for formulating theological concepts, that is to say, as the condition of the possibility of appropriate human discourse about God; and as the starting point for an ethical theory of the Christian faith."[106] Jüngel is concerned to show that, understood correctly, Barth's appeal to the analogy of faith helps resolve the problem of whether a christologically determined anthropology can affirm the reality of the human person positively.

This issue can be illustrated in Pannenberg's rejection of Barth's doctrine

---

[103]*GMW*, pp. 165-66.

[104]Jüngel, "Die Möglichkeit theologischer Anthropologie auf dem Grunde der Analogie," *Barth Studien* (1982): 210-32. Cf. E. Przywara, "Metaphysik, Religion, Analogie," in *Analogia entis: Schriften* (Einsiedeln: Johannes Verlag, 1962), 3:334; G. Söhngen, "Die Weisheit der Theologie durch den Weg der Wissenschaft," in *Mysterium Salutis: Grundriss Heilsgeschichtlicher Dogmatik* (Einsiedeln: Benziger, 1965); W. Pannenberg, "Person als Subjekt," in J. Feiner and J. Löhrer, eds., *Grundfragen Systematischer Theologie*, Gesammelte Aufsätze II (Göttingen: Vandenhoeck, 1967), pp. 80-95. See *GGW*, pp. 307-8.

[105]Jüngel, "Die Möglichkeit, p. 212.

[106]Jüngel, "La Signification de l'analogie pour la théologie," in P. Gisel and P. Secretan, eds., *Analogie et Dialectique*, Essais de Théologie Fondamentale (Geneva: Labor et Fides, 1982), pp. 247-58.

of *analogia fidei*. Pannenberg thought that it tended to put the emphasis in the analogy on the universal element of analogy, resulting in an emphasis on epistemology, which Barth never intended. Such a concern is an "abstraction," which once again posits the human as the subject of knowing. This is also the case with the Catholic doctrine of *analogia entis*, which is precisely why Barth rejected it. Analogy is not concerned with the human subject as knowing agent. In agreement with Barth, Jüngel affirms that *analogia entis* ultimately did away with the distinction between God and humanity, but *analogia fidei* makes the distinction greater without denying one or the other because it is grounded in Jesus Christ. Such a characterization of analogy can only be understood in light of Barth's treatment of the image of God in humanity. "The category of the *imago dei* . . . is identical only with the historical name of Jesus Christ. The person called by that name is the man who expresses God."[107] The image of God is made personal, particular and definable in Jesus Christ. As such, Christ functions as a definition of humanity. This is so not only because the christological grounding of the human is its natural constitution, but also because this humanity is borne by Jesus Christ, and, as such, he becomes the defining act of this humanity. Humanity is human "on the basis of the reality of this one man who expresses God."[108] As a result, humanity, grounded in Jesus Christ, "expresses God." Correspondence (*Entsprechung*) is not to be understood initially in imperative terms as a command requiring response. This would attribute to humanity a certain autonomy, which would again lead to the modern insistence on a certain possession of *humanum* apart from God, which would once again compromise the christological grounding and put humanity back in as the subject. The Word constitutes humanity by addressing it. The humanity of the human is the veritable result of God's "speech act" in Jesus Christ. That is, the mood is first in the indicative rather than imperative. Therefore, the analogy between God and the human in which *Gott spricht* and *der Mensch entspricht* is "an ontological repetition" in which humanity is contingent for its very being on Jesus Christ, the Word of God.[109]

---

[107]Jüngel, "Die Möglichkeit," p. 226; *GMW*, pp. 389-96. Cf. Webster, *Eberhard Jüngel.*
[108]*GGW*, p. 389.
[109]Webster, *Eberhard Jüngel*, p. 104.

For Jüngel, as with Barth, the determination of humanity cannot rest on the Western metaphysical tradition whose theism amounts to a mere human projection of its own self-understanding. It must come from God's self-revelation as the truly human person in Jesus Christ. The reality of revelation alone is Jüngel's guide in his attempt to show that Barth's use of the analogy of relation (*analogia relationis*), in the later parts of the *CD*, must be understood exclusively in the sense of the *analogia fidei*.[110] This is quite different than the understanding of analogy which Gottlieb Söhngen and von Balthasar propose can be found in Barth. If revelation alone provides the sole basis for analogy, then such analogies must be found in Jesus Christ. In God's self-revelation in Christ is the correspondence of God's being to God's self. It is, in Barth's words, the "primal act" in which correspondence can be found and the one on which all other analogies are based. Grace is primary in both an ontological and and a noetic sense.

In Jüngel's treatment of Barth's conception of *analogia fidei*, one must note that, following Jüngel's careful and largely affirmative treatment of Barth's understanding of *analogia relationis*, he clearly underlines how Barth was able to remain faithful to his early emphasis on anthropology as established by the divine Word of address. There is no knowledge of God or human beings by means of this negative mode. Only in God's self-revelation in Jesus Christ as the truly human individual can there be a ground for analogy. Such an analogy is an *analogia relationis* because in Christ humanity corresponds to God, insofar as the inner being of God corresponds to the being of Christ and thus to humanity. As such, theological analogy can only be established christologically. This correspondence is supremely action, because of God's prior action. Human freedom and action are a reality only in this prior act wherein God posits God's self and, in this self-positing, posits the other. The determination of the human is thus restricted to this determination in God. There is no real humanity outside this humanity. Freedom and genuine action are not the products of natural law or conscience, and neither are they given in any idealist or metaphysical concept of being-in-and-for-itself.

A question remains here whether Jüngel has not "also brought in an el-

---

[110]John Macken, *The Autonomy Theme in the Church Dogmatics* (Cambridge: Cambridge University Press, 1990), pp. 144-49.

ement that does not interpret, but rather is foreign to, Barth's understanding"
of analogy. As Webster points out, in Jüngel's suggestion of a partial *humanum* outside Christ, there is an "anthropological reductionism" in that
Jüngel tries to hold together a christological grounding of the human with
the suggestion that humanity can be human, in part, without God. That is,
a certain *humanum* is attributable to humanity in terms of its capacity for
language, independent of its status in Christ. However, for Jüngel, to be
"truly human" means that we can become more human in Christ. Christ
amounts to a "freely added plus," a superadded reality in which humanity
"becomes ever more human."[111] In this way God makes humanity, which is
"interesting for its own sake, more interesting."[112] The problem is that this
introduces a contradiction to his statement that "to be human is to express
God." Here Jüngel goes beyond Barth and to a degree annuls the positive
influence Barth has had on his anthropology and doctrine of analogy.[113] This
being said, however, we can attribute to Jüngel a more fruitful way forward
in theological analogy based on Barth's later "theoanthropology."[114]

Jüngel's description of the problem of analogy. At the core of his delib-
erations regarding the speakability of God in *GGW* is his analysis of the
problem of *analogical speech* in theology.[115] This is a pivotal concern for
Jüngel because it provides both a locus of the problem and, rightly understood, its solution in respect to God's speakability.

Jüngel begins his formal discussion of analogy in *GMW* under the rubric
"The Problem of Analogous Talk About God." His aim therein is to lay bare

---

[111]Jüngel, *Was ist ein Sakrament? Vorstösse zur Verständigung* (Freiburg: Herder, 1971), p. 53; "Extra
Christum Nulla salus—als Grundsatz natürlicher Theologie? Evangelische Erwägungen zur
'Anonymität' des Christenmenschen," *Zeitschrift für Theologie und Kirche* 72 (1975): 337-52.

[112]*GGW*, p. 43; *GMW*, p. 34.

[113]See particularly Jüngel's article, "On Becoming Truly Human: The Significance of the Reformation Distinction Between Person and Works for the Self-Understanding of Modern Humanity,"
in *Theological Essays II*, trans. John Webster and A. Neufeldt-Fast (New York: T & T Clark,
1995), pp. 216-40. There he writes, "The human person should have or possess something, but
not possess him or her self" (p. 234). Cf. Webster, *Eberhard Jüngel*, pp. 90-91.

[114]Webster, "Justification, Analogy and Action: Passivity and Activity in Jüngel's Anthropology,"
in Webster, ed., *Possibilities of Theology*, pp. 106-41.

[115]*GGW* (English trans., *GMW*). This work represents one of Jüngel's greatest achievements and
is the best possible entry point to his mature thought on analogy. See also his *Gottes Sein ist im
Werden* [*God's Being Is in Becoming*] (Munich: de Grutyer, 1976). See also his two essays "Die
Möglichkeit theologischer anthropologie auf dem Grunde der Analogie: Eine Untersuchung
zum Analogieverständnis Karl Barths," and "Metaphorical Truth," in *Theological Essays*.

the aporia generated by the apophatic-Thomistic tradition of philosophy and theology, which, by way of the metaphysics of negation and causal necessity, established analogy as the primary means of theological discourse. Jüngel takes the apophatic tradition to task for its careless employment of *analogia nominum* and the closely related principle of *analogia entis*. God as mystery and as love cannot ultimately be conceived of by this method. Jüngel writes,

> The love of God articulated in this way will never be able to overcome the chasm between God and man (the world), which is characterized by infinite superiority. That God spoken of as love in this way remains "above us" (*supra nos*) in the dimension of causes. And that is, all the way through, the actual theological weakness of the classical form of the doctrine of analogy. Analogy understood in this way puts God, as the unknown initiator of this world, firmly above the world and exclusively beyond it.[116]

Yet Jüngel recognizes the necessity of analogy in speaking about God. He states that "there can be no responsible talk about God without analogy. Every spoken announcement which corresponds to God is made within the context of what analogy makes possible."[117] Thus the task that Jüngel sets for himself in *GMW* does not amount to a wholesale rejection of the method of analogy but rather intends "to expose what is problematic in previous applications of analogy."[118] As Rolnick observes, "Much is at stake in this analysis; for if he is right about the failure of the tradition . . . then his own constructive claim for analogical predication would have imperial ramifications for theology."[119]

In describing the problem, Jüngel turns first to Kant's analysis of analogical method in order to point back to Aquinas, whose own method, according to Jüngel, bore the seeds of the Kantian approach. It would appear that Jüngel sees Kant as the epitome of the problem because "Kant stood within a classical theological tradition, even though he very likely was unaware of it."[120] As such he represents the culmination of the aporia latent

---

[116]*GMW*, p. 279.

[117]*GMW*, p. 281.

[118]Rolnick, *Analogical Possibilities*, p. 200.

[119]Ibid., p. 200.

[120]*GMW*, p. 263. One wonders whether Kant was so unaware of his proximity to the apophatic tradition as Jüngel suggests. In his *Lectures on the Philosophical Doctrine of Religion*, trans. and

within the classical doctrine of analogy, especially as it was understood and employed by Aquinas. Kant attempts to solve the aporia of God's speakability by appealing to the method of analogy in his *Lectures on the Philosophical Doctrine of Religion*. However, in his more programmatic *Critique of Pure Reason* Kant was led to conclude that, on the one hand, judgments based on perceptual experience must be made within the limits of this experience if they are to be responsible judgments.[121] On the other hand, given a finite world, God is beyond perceptual experience and thus incapable of linguistic description. Yet, God is of singular importance to Kant's "moral imperative" because "the ultimate proportion of virtue and happiness cannot be determined within the limits of this world alone."[122] Nevertheless, for Kant, God remains basically meaningless. A being whose representation is based on nothing but the pure concepts of our subjective understanding is

---

ed. Allen Wood and George Di Giovanni (Cambridge, Cambridge University Press, 1996), Kant refers to the Scholastic theologians who believe that "every attribute of God is in fact God himself." This of course was a fundamental axiom of Thomistic and apophatic theology, and it leads Kant to the conclusion that such a view makes God "a necessary idea of our understanding, because he is the substratum of the possibility of all things." However, because we represent these attributes "under the limitations of our being," we can only ascribe these attributes to God in an "impure way" because we have no experience of these except via the negative. Thus, in the case of infinity for instance, "I cannot come a single step further in my cognition of God by applying the mathematical concept of infinity to him." This is so because what God possesses by way of the "highest perfection" (infinity) I only possess imperfectly (finitely) in experience. Thus we can never know what infinity means as ascribed to God. Therefore God is unknowable as such. "The only thing I can know is that he is greater than any number I can think" (Immanuel Kant, *Religion and Rational Theology*, ed. and trans. A. W. Wood and G. D. Giovanni [Cambridge: Cambridge University Press, 1996], pp. 335-552). Cf. *GMW*, pp. 362-65.

[121]Immanuel Kant, *Critique of Pure Reason*. In the concluding chapter of that great work, Kant comments on the implications of judgments based on experience for "belief in God" as follows: "Now we must admit that the doctrine of the existence of God belongs to doctrinal belief. For, although in respect to the theoretical cognition of the universe I do not require to form any theory which necessarily involves this idea, as the condition of my explanation of the phenomena which the universe presents, but, on the contrary, am rather bound so to use my reason as if everything were mere nature. . . . But the word belief refers only to the guidance which an idea gives me, and to its subjective influence on the conduct of my reason, which forces me to hold it fast, though I may not be in a position to give a speculative account of it" (p. 468).

[122]Rolnick, *Analogical Possibilities*, p. 201, citing Kant's *Prolegomena to Any Future Metaphysics*, ed. L. W. Back (Indianapolis: Bobbs-Merrill, 1950), p. 103, where Kant writes, "If we represent to ourselves a being of the understanding by nothing but pure concepts of the understanding, we then indeed represent nothing definite to ourselves, and consequently our concept has no significance." Here Rolnick admits that, like Aquinas and David Burrell, "Kant's setting of the problem is similar . . . how to preserve the transcendence of God and yet relate God to the world." This problem follows Kant right into *The Critique of Practical Reason*, trans. L. W. Beck (New York: The Liberal Arts Press, 1956), p. 134.

ultimately indefinite to ourselves and thus of no consequence or significance. This being must be brought into the sensible world in order to be concrete.[123] The only way to achieve this is by some sort of analogy based on practical reason. Kant writes: "But if we think of it by properties borrowed from the sensuous world, it is no longer a being of understanding, but is conceived phenomenally and belongs to the sensible world."[124] Kant forms a conception of God, albeit unknowable, by means of analogy to sensible conceptions, which may be known by experience.

It is here that Jüngel sees the reflection of the classical doctrine of analogy. Kant limits the judgments based on analogy to the "relations" that the sensible world has to a being whose conception lies beyond the sensible world. In so doing we avoid the attribution of properties of representative objects of experience to a Supreme Being and thus avoid "dogmatic anthropomorphism."[125] But we attribute them to "the relation of this being to the world and allow ourselves a symbolical anthropomorphism, which in fact concerns language only and not the object itself."[126] This allows Kant to "speak of a highest essence," as if "the world were the work of a supreme artificer."[127] It is here that Jüngel takes exception to Kant's reductions of anthropomorphic language to a mere symbolism. Jüngel writes:

---

[123]The clearest treatment of this idea is found in Kant's *Prolegomena to Any Future Metaphysics*, pp. 103-4; *GMW*, pp. 263-64.

[124]Kant, *Prolegomena to Any Future Metaphysics*, p. 103.

[125]See Kant's *Lectures on the Philosophical Doctrine of Religion*, pp. 384-85, wherein he defines "symbolical anthropomorphisms" as follows: "Anthropomorphism is usually divided into the vulgar kind, when God is thought of in human shape, and the subtle kind, where human perfections are ascribed to God but without separating the limitations from them. The latter kind of anthropomorphism is a particularly dangerous enemy of our pure cognition of God." While the former are immediately recognized as errors, the latter *anthropomorphismus subtilis* often "creep into our concept of God and corrupt it." Kant seems to suggest that certain forms of analogy have created this problem in the past and therefore calls for a "transcendental theology" that "puts us in a position to remove from our cognition of God everything sensible inhering in our concepts, or at least by its means we become conscious that if we predicate something of God which cannot be thought apart from the conditions of sensibility, then we must give a proper definition to these predicates, even if we are not always in a position to represent them in a manner wholly free from faults." This can be done only if "our reason voluntarily relinquished its claim to have cognition of the nature of God and his attributes, as to how they themselves are constituted internally, and, if mindful of its weakness, it never tried to exceed its bounds but were content to cognize only so much about him . . . as it has need of." The theological interests of humanity can only be served best through symbolic anthropomorphisms, *per viam analogiam*.

[126]Kant, *Prolegomena to Any Future Metaphysics*, p. 106.

[127]*GMW*, p. 264.

Kant ascribes to language a hermeneutically decisive function for the definition of the relation of God and the world, and thus for the problem of the thinkability of God. . . . The "symbolic anthropomorphism" is the corresponding achievement of language. Through such "symbolic anthropomorphisms," which are limited to mere statements about relations, God is not actually known.[128]

As we have seen, the problem for Jüngel is that in the Western metaphysical tradition God cannot actually be known and is, furthermore, incapable of being thought as knowable. The result is that "the infinite difference between God Himself and human (anthropomorphic) talk about God, is not silenced, concealed, or circumvented, but rather is directly expressed."[129] Kant's understanding of analogy does not emphasize the imperfect similarity of two conceptions but "a perfect similarity of relations between two quite dissimilar things."[130] For Jüngel, Kant's proposal is identical with the *analogy of being* because this type of analogy employs the resemblance between cause and effect, which implies a definite relation between them. Jüngel concludes that Kant has actually combined two different types of analogical method known in the classical tradition as *analogy of proportionality* and *analogy of intrinsic attribution*. Both of these are related in the tradition to the *analogia nominum*, or analogy of names.[131]

Jüngel proceeds to clarify this point, and prepare for his analysis of Aquinas, by noting the development of these two models of analogy in Aristotle. For Jüngel, Aristotle becomes the shared ground between Kant and Aquinas in their understanding of *analogia nominum*. This being the case, the concealed aporia in this model of analogy applies across the board to Kant, Aquinas and Aristotle and calls for a renewed understanding and approach to the use of analogical method. To properly understand this shared ground, Jüngel launches into a brief discussion of the development of the analogical method in its two forms in Aristotle. In Jüngel's opinion, Aristotle gave precision to the Platonic tradition of analogy initially in his analysis of metaphor.

---

[128]Ibid.
[129]*GMW*, p. 265.
[130]Kant, *Prolegomena to Any Future Metaphysics*, p. 106.
[131]*GMW*, p. 266.

Summarizing his analysis, Jüngel notes that the point of agreement between the two analogical models is that each model names on the basis of relations.

> The first model of analogy understands analogy to be a proportion which, on the basis of similar (identical) relations between dissimilar things, allows comparison with each other within the relation of relations. Thus one speaks of an analogy of proportionality (*analogia proportionalitatis*). The second model of analogy understands analogy, on the basis of the noncomparable relations of different things to the one thing they have in common, as a simple analogy of relation (*analogia proportionis*) or also the analogy of attribution.[132]

Thus in an analogy of proportionality a:b::c:d, whereas in the analogy of intrinsic attribution, b, c and d all relate to "a" from which they receive their common name, that is, a:(a)b::(a)c:(a)d. At this point Jüngel turns to an in-depth analysis of the analogy of attribution with a view of pointing out a peculiarity in its structure. Whereas the analogy of proportionality employs merely the correspondence between compared entities, the analogy of attribution implies the *dependence* of "many things" on the "one common thing." The "many things" are ordered by and dependent on the "one common thing," which is the "hermeneutical first principle." According to Jüngel this is precisely what Aquinas calls the "analogy of order," whereby the description "hermeneutical order" primarily means that this analogy is constituted by an *analogans* (the one thing that makes the analogy) on which the thing named after it depends as the *analogatum* (that which is analogized).[133]

According to Jüngel's analysis, an important development of this analogy of order took place through the scholastic (Thomistic) appropriation of Aristotle's models of analogy. His conclusion bears repeating: "The hermeneutical first thing appears as the ontological origin which under certain circumstances can also be thought of as the ontic cause."[134] Here we are reminded of one of the primary reasons for Barth's rejection of the *analogia entis*, with respect to causality, and it would appear that Jüngel shares this concern.

---

[132]*GMW*, p. 271; see also Aristotle, *Nicomedian Ethics*, p. 1096b, lines 25-31.
[133]*GMW*, p. 271. Jüngel refers to Aquinas's *ST* I, q. 13, art. 5.
[134]*GMW*, p. 272.

Thus the *analogans*, through the influence of mystical theologians such as Psuedo-Dionysius the Areopagite (*Divine Names* and *Mystical Theology*), possesses the original meaning of the word, compared those entities named by the same word, and is designated as the cause in a "causal nexus."[135] "Analogy thus understood gained special significance in Thomas Aquinas for human talk about God and still determines Kant's use of analogy in the context of the formation of concepts which are appropriate for God."[136] While both models of analogy play a significant role in Scholastic theology and the Western metaphysical tradition, it is important to recognize with Jüngel that both these traditions represent a conflation of these analogical methods and contributed to the aporia concerning God's speakability in a profound way. Before bringing this argument to a close, Jüngel brings the full weight of the critique to bear on Aquinas's analogical method.

Aquinas employed the method of analogy of attribution understood as the mediating point between univocity and equivocity with the purpose of solving the problem of how common affirmative predicates, taken from created order, can speak of God.[137] In a similar fashion to Kant and Aristotle, Jüngel finds both forms of analogy used in Aquinas, with a particular emphasis on the analogy of attribution, though conflation of the two models are present in Aquinas. Jüngel affirms, on the basis of the works of G. Scheltens, that Aquinas discontinued the strict usage of the analogy of proportionality that he stressed in his *De veritate*.[138] However, Aquinas would eventually connect these two methods in such a fashion that analogy of attribution would come to represent *both* a hermeneutic and an ontic priority. Aquinas's reworking of analogy called for the rejection of "names" (*nominum*) which univocally may be ascribed both to God and the creatures because "then God would not be adequately distinguished as the highest cause, from everything which had been caused."[139] Aquinas writes, "Univocal predication is impossible between God and creatures. The reason for this is that every effect which is not a proportional result of the power of the

---

[135]Ibid.
[136]Ibid.
[137]Ibid.
[138]*GMW*, p. 271; see also Rolnick, *Analogical Possibilities*, p. 204.
[139]*GMW*, p. 272.

efficient cause receives the similitude of the agent not in its full degree, but in a measure that falls short."[140]

Conversely, we do know God *from his creatures*, a fact that prohibits the equivocal naming of God and creatures. Thus predication about God and creatures can only be expressed analogically: "that is, according to an order or relation to some *one thing*."[141] Leaving aside predication about God, Jüngel notes a hermeneutical distinction here in Aquinas's development of analogy. Aquinas distinguishes two subtypes of the analogy of attribution based on the analogy of many things to the one identical thing. He writes: "Since it is always presupposed that at least two different things have two different relations to the one common thing, in the second instance the one thing (*unum*) might relate to itself as that one common thing to which the other one relates itself in another fashion."[142] To illustrate this shift in Aquinas, Jüngel recalls the famous health example to which Aquinas refers. Here Jüngel demonstrates a distinction between the hermeneutic and ontic "first thing." The Aristotelian example shows that the human body, medicine and urine can all be called "healthy." "The one thing to which all three things are related is, for Thomas, health *per se*, but it is thought of as subsisting in a definite existing thing."[143] In other words, the *unum* exists in a concrete being because health is predicated about medicine and urine "in relation and in proportion to health of the body, of which the former is a *cause* and the latter a sign."[144] This prior thing in relation to which the other things are ordered is a prior thing in a hermeneutic, not an ontic sense. It is an order of *knowing*. Significantly, here Jüngel reminds us of Aquinas's epistemological principle of the priority of knowing over language.

Epistemologically, then, the health of the body comes before the analogy of things. Ontological primacy must be given to medicine as the hermeneutical first thing because "it is to be regarded as the cause" of the health of the body. The result is that the ontic priority of the "one thing," on the basis of which the other things are named, does not play any role in the *modus sig-*

---

[140]*ST* I, q. 13, art. 5, as quoted in *GMW*, p. 272.
[141]*SCG*, bk. I, cap. 34, as quoted in *GMW*, p. 272 (emphasis added).
[142]Ibid., p. 273. As cited above.
[143]Ibid.
[144]*ST* I, q. 13, art. 5, as per *GMW*, p. 273.

nificandi. The analogy of being (*analogia entis*) is presupposed as the basis of the spoken analogy within the order of participation and causality. It receives no independent emphasis. This brings out the Thomistic view that talk about God must not employ the analogy of attribution whereby the "many things" are related to the one "because this would either place God in the same series as the other *analogata,* or would relate God to a third and higher principle."[145] Thus the first form of the analogy of attribution must be rejected (i.e., a dominant relation of the many to the one). It appears the only analogical method of predication about God that Thomas permits is that method whereby the "one thing" that is the common element in the many things has hermeneutical primacy in the analogy of naming if it "first subsists in God himself and *therefore* in the creatures caused by God."[146] With the concept of goodness, for example, God would possess goodness by virtue of the possession of his own being. Correspondingly, God distributes this goodness to creatures of his agency. Herein lies the problem for Jüngel. For comprehension, this analogy requires a "conceptual reversal": "For the goodness which God possesses first by his being, is first known and named by its possession in the creature."[147] In Jüngel's words, "They have it in their particular way of being as those who have been *caused,* and thus based on that, we can know and name what has its original being in God himself."[148] This has the effect of translating a hermeneutical principle into one of metaphysical necessity. Without the ontological basis of a CER there would be no hermeneutical function for analogy.

The result of this analysis is that Aquinas's method of analogy has combined the analogy of attribution, analogous naming "according to which the one thing is proportioned to another," with the first model of analogy based on the Aristotelian category of metaphor, that is, the analogy of proportionality.[149] Thus being is derived from the fact that this *unum* possesses the common element in such a way that it is identical with it. Therefore the other things relate themselves to the common element by possessing the common element, albeit in a derivative fashion. "The so-called 'analogy of attribution'

---

[145]Rolnick, *Analogical Possibilities,* p. 205.
[146]*GMW,* p. 275.
[147]Rolnick, *Analogical Possibilities,* p. 205.
[148]*GMW,* p. 275.
[149]*GMW,* p. 276.

has drawn into itself the so-called 'analogy of proportionality' when the issue is analogous talk about God."[150]

Jüngel is now in a position to draw the lines of continuity between Kant and Aquinas in their use of analogical method. Jüngel claims that this connection is valid because this conceptual reversal of the analogy of attribution is employed by Kant, who placed emphasis on the analogy of proportionality (in the Thomistic understanding) as the "causal nexus" of the analogy of intrinsic attribution. Behind this stands the unexpressed presupposition that "God has given perfection to God's being as the creature has the same perfection to the creature's being."[151] This essentially expresses an analogy of proportionality a:b::c:b. Jüngel's conclusion states the point succinctly: "Whereas in the 'mode of signification' the language of the world functions as the hermeneutical *analogans*, and talk about God as the hermeneutical *analogatum*, the content expressed by this analogous talk about God is expressed in the hermeneutical *analogatum* as ontic *analogans* (*causa*), the world on the other hand as ontic analogatum (*causatum*)."[152]

The aporia now comes into focus. On the basis of this thorough critique of the use of analogical method in speech about God, Jüngel is now in a position to reveal the aporia, which he considers to be concealed in this method. On the basis of his analysis Jüngel concludes that both Kant and Aquinas are dependent on the same analogical method, which is traceable to Aristotle's model. This means that, in terms of the theological tradition, the critique of Kant's understanding of analogy by Jüngel applies equally to that of Aquinas. That is, this method of analogy allows for predication about God only as an unknown entity. The logic of this method keeps God out of the world and emphasizes the infinite qualitative distinction between God and the world to the point of his unthinkability, unknowability and unspeakability. This Thomistic-Kantian model was designed to protect God's aseity from "dogmatic anthropomorphism."

This leaves Jüngel with the all-important question of the viability and validity of God's speakability in terms of any Thomistic conception of analogy. "The question to be decided is whether God is speakable only as

---

[150]Ibid.
[151]Rolnick, *Analogical Possibilities*, p. 206.
[152]*GMW*, p. 277.

the one who actually is unspeakable, and can be made known only as the one who is actually unknown."[153] On the basis of this understanding of analogy, the problem becomes one of speaking about God without "humanizing" his divine essence "since language in all its forms of expression is bound to the form of being of speaking man."[154] Jüngel explains, "By using the pure analogy of relation (analogy of proportionality) which preserves the absolute differentness of the things being related to each other, it appeared that a possibility which maintained the difference between God and man was given for appropriate talk about God."[155] This desire to protect the aseity of God is, for Jüngel, a shallow victory, because in doing so the apophatic tradition has made him unknowable and more importantly unspeakable. If God is speakable only by "symbolic anthropomorphism" and not as God *in se*, then God cannot in essence be known. Therefore the apophatic tradition has given us an "unbearably sinister riddle." The final result is that "the analogy of attribution defines so precisely the unknowness of God that it vastly increases that unknowness into God's total inaccessibility."[156] In its attempt to solve the problem of God's speakability, it has created the larger problem of the relevance of God's speakability at all.

This is a crucial link in Jüngel's critique of the Western metaphysical tradition, which has led to the modern problem of God's relevance, thinkability, knowability and speakability, which contemporary atheistic philosophies have, rightly so, put forth. To make the connection firmer, Jüngel illustrates the final result of this tradition by focusing on the skepticism of Spinoza, whose concept of divinity excluded any attribution of human characteristics. While Kant tries to avoid this extreme position, he nevertheless falls into it on the basis of his shared conviction that God and human beings remain "infinitely distinct" from each other. Jüngel rejects this "suspicion of absurdity" as contrary to Christian belief and proposes a way whereby the distinction between God and humanity can be maintained as thinkable, knowable and speakable, but via different means than the logic of the metaphysical tradition. He notes that there is a "God-enabled, a God-inspired, even a God-

---

[153]Ibid.
[154]Ibid.
[155]Ibid.
[156]*GMW*, p. 278.

demanded anthropomorphism which moves far beyond the naiveté of 'dogmatic anthropomorphism.'"[157] The question raised is whether one can employ analogy in such a way that it corresponds to faith in the incarnate God. Jüngel proposes a rediscovery of christological anthropomorphism in opposition to the metaphysical tradition's avoidance of it. Perhaps God's speakability can be grounded in such a christologically centered endeavor.

The analogy of advent: The gospel as analogy, christologically grounded. Thus far we have seen that throughout *GMW*, Jüngel has been pointing out that "the metaphysical 'God of signification' is inherently prone to the metaphysical death of the Descartes-Fichte-Feuerbach-Nietzsche syndrome."[158] God's necessity and imperishability become the cause of his metaphysical death. If God becomes thinkable only on the basis of his speakability, then a new understanding of analogy is needed.[159] Of particular importance here is Barth's critique contained in his *CD* I/1. Barth saw this as an attempt to establish God's existence by means of natural theology and anthropology. Jüngel considers it a partial misunderstanding of what *analogia entis* attempts to do and responded to Barth in an important article that won the praise of Barth.[160] For Jüngel, theology involves the cognitive moments of understanding, thought and speech about faith. In this sense, Western theological and philosophical metaphysics has yielded both an unsatisfactory theism and atheism. The value of atheism lies in its unveiling of the concealed aporia in the apophatic tradition of theism. Jüngel affirms that we must think and speak of God in a new way, based on the certainty of faith, which encounters and confronts unbelief. Yet, "in this sense, the certainty of faith is not comparable to the certainty of understanding."[161] Faith and understanding (including thought and speech) are distinct but perform related tasks in speaking about God. In opposition to the Cartesian grounding of the self by methodological doubt, Jüngel posits a self-understanding that begins with faith that is "a movement out from the self toward another. . . . If faith (theology) does not lead thought (philosophy), then

---

[157]*GMW*, p. 280.
[158]Rolnick, *Analogical Possibilities*, p. 210.
[159]*GMW*, p. 281.
[160]Jüngel, "Die Möglichkeit."
[161]Rolnick, *Analogical Possibilities*, p. 209.

thought inevitably turns back upon itself in the self-reflectivity of the *cogito*."[162] Faith prevents this reflexive self-contemplation by going out to the other. "By relating the self to the other, faith functions to guarantee the distinctiveness of each one" between humanity and God or humanity and humanity.[163]

This other-directedness of thought is typologically characterized as *address* and represents an alternative to self-directed thought. For Jüngel, this *address* character of faith is grounded in the historical death of God in Jesus Christ as the confrontation of being with nonbeing. It is this "Word of address" that forms the basis of his proposal for an analogical method, which can allow for speech about God.[164] By this method Jüngel attempts to close the "metaphysical gap" introduced by the Thomistic-Kantian theory of analogy so that "God becomes thinkable on the basis of his speakability."[165] As such, the analogy of advent involves the *addressed, address* and *addressee* simultaneously. Because God is *in* the Word, the Word of address affects the addressed in the totality of their being.[166] The language event is God's self-relation in the Word, and in coming to humanity in the Word Jesus Christ, God comes into relation to humanity. In distinction from the "linguistic displacement of God" as God *supra nos*, Jüngel locates God in the Word, as he is interpreted in the Word, so that God in being occurs in the Word. As such, God is subject to the temporality of this world in the death of Jesus Christ on the cross. This being the case, the metaphysical distanciation of God is avoided, and the way is open for participation in God through the addressing Word of God. Jüngel concludes,

> For the certainty of faith is the certainty that it is dealing with God himself. Faith is participation in God himself. Certainly faith does not force itself into a position between God and God. It is the essence of faith to let God be God. . . . Then God's being must be thought as a being which allows that it be participated in, that is, a being which turns outward what it is inwardly.[167]

---

[162]Ibid., p. 210.
[163]Ibid.
[164]Ibid., p. 211.
[165]Ibid.
[166]*GMW*, pp. 11-12.
[167]Ibid.

This happens in the Word and only in the Word of God.[168]

In the earlier work cited above, *God's Being Is in Becoming*, Jüngel clearly aligns himself with Barth's conception of God's being as "being in becoming."[169] This being of God is grounded in the creative act whereby God relates himself to himself and proceeds from himself in movement toward nonbeing. For the being of God, this means the "threat of negation." Jüngel explains,

> For in Jesus Christ the No expressed in the justification of the sinner together with the Yes to man strikes from the first, and therefore once for all, God himself. If from this there results for man the consoling statement that the "rejection cannot again become the portion or affair of man," then there results for God at the same time the dangerous statement: "in God's eternal purpose it is God himself who is rejected in his Son."[170]

Consequently, since God in Jesus Christ has entered into a covenant with lost humanity, God has already accounted for the serious "threat of negation" to his eternal being. "In precisely this way God maintains to the end his Yes to himself and his Yes to man. And precisely in this maintenance, God's being remains in *becoming*."[171]

Though the seeds for Jüngel's approach to analogy are reflected here in his book on the Trinity, his doctrinal development shifts in *GMW* to the thesis of "God's being as *coming*." The change represents only a slight shift in his understanding of God's being in relation to creation, since Jüngel still insists throughout his writings that in the creative act God goes out from God's self into nonbeing. The location of this negation and its confirmation is the cross, because in the death of Jesus Christ, God's Son, is nothing less than the death of God and the revelation of God's self-giving being. "The cross of Christ discloses the divine self going out to the nothingness of death and perishability, just as the *creatio ex nihilo* of the world began in God's self and went forth creatively into the nothingness."[172] The God of apophatic-metaphysical signification is impassable and separate from this world, and therefore unthinkable, unknowable and unspeakable. But if in the Word,

---

[168]*GMW*, p. 176. This can happen because participation in being is essential to the word of address in the sense that the being of the speaker is expressed in the word.

[169]Jüngel, *Doctrine of the Trinity*; *God's Being Is in Becoming*.

[170]Jüngel, *God's Being Is in Becoming*, p. 78. Here Jüngel is quoting from Barth's *CD* II/2, p. 167.

[171]Ibid., p. 8. Emphasis original.

[172]Rolnick, *Analogical Possibilities*, p. 214.

Jesus Christ, God comes to God's self and at the same time to humanity, then God's speakability and therefore thinkability must be predicated on the basis of the crucified God in the Word, Jesus Christ. It is in the Word that theology must be grounded because God's being in relation to himself and humanity is reflected there. Theology, as speech about God, proceeds from a risk of faith in going out from the self, just as the divine being risked the encounter with nonbeing. Theology can speak of God and humanity when it looks to the self-disclosure of God as man on the cross. In Jesus Christ, God and humanity are in correspondence (*Entsprechung*) to each other. Theology gains its speech in faithfulness to this correspondence. Understood in this way, the gospel of Jesus Christ can be seen as "the human Word which corresponds to the divine mystery" revealed in the cross and can be established as a doctrine of analogy, which makes God speakable.[173] In this way Jüngel has given theology the task of true correspondence, as responsible speech about God, based on the prior address of God's Word in Jesus Christ. To accomplish this correspondence, a proper model of analogy that is rooted in the analogy of faith as witnessed to in Scripture is required.

As a preface to his discussion of the gospel as analogy in section 18 of *GMW*, Jüngel explores Barth's distinction between the *analogia fidei* and the *analogia entis*. Besides his brief discussion in the first paragraph of section 18, Jüngel has also raised the issue in his article "*Die Möglichkeit.*"[174] Therein he writes that "what we must decide now is what makes analogy the '*analogy of faith*' in the sense that we can say of human words that they truly 'correspond to God.'"[175] He understands analogy as the ontological movement whereby God comes to speech and has done so in the gospel. For Jüngel, analogy is the portrayal of God's essence in the human words of the gospel. This calls for a renewed investigation into the value of anthropomorphic speech. Anthropomorphic language provided the apophatic tradition with part of its desire to distinguish God from the world as "totally other." On the basis of his analysis of analogy and subsequent call for an *analogia fidei*, Jüngel now embraces anthropomorphic language in the gospel as an absolutely necessary and appropriate way of speaking about God. Such language

---

[173]*GMW*, p. 261.
[174]Rolnick, *Analogical Possibilities*, pp. 217-18.
[175]*GMW*, p. 281.

speaks of God as mystery, which is the bond between the divine and human nature in the Word of the gospel. Both the mystery and the anthropomorphic language that expresses it are christologically grounded and motivated. We need to arrive at an understanding of human speech about God that goes beyond mere toleration for anthropomorphism as an inadequate way of speaking about God to a positive appreciation of the fact that reorganizes "from the outset the anthropomorphic structure of human speech."[176] Analogy functions on the basis of the doctrine of God. Contrary to the *via negativa*, whereby God's inexpressibility is emphasized, Jüngel develops a view of the analogy between God and humanity that accounts for this basic characteristic of human speech.

Because of this new possibility of speech about God, Kant's view of symbolic/dogmatic anthropomorphism must be discarded in favor of christologically grounded anthropomorphic language. We must move beyond the "naiveté of dogmatic anthropomorphism and the skepticism of symbolic anthropomorphism" in order to ascertain a theological use of analogy "which corresponds to faith in the incarnation of God."[177] In the gospel, says Jüngel, God has revealed his humanity by the execution of his divinity. The execution of his divinity is an "event of correspondence" about which the gospel, and only the gospel, speaks. "God is thinkable as one who speaks because and to the extent that he is human-in-and-of-himself."[178]

Returning to his previous discussion of the aporia, Jüngel now recounts the results of the Kant-Aquinas link. Jüngel reaffirms here that the theological aporia, which resulted from the Thomistic appropriation and modification of Aristotelian–Pseudo-Dionysian analogical method, "became visible in Kant's philosophy as the actual accomplishment of this doctrine of analogy."[179] The idea of God that emerges from this method remains essentially empty, because the unknown x, which is to be known via analogy, remains unknowable. Jüngel concludes, "What remains unthinkable is that God himself relates in this relationship, relates to himself and at the same time to the world. And thus that talk about God made possible by 'knowledge

---

[176]*GMW*, p. 260.
[177]*GMW*, p. 280.
[178]*GMW*, pp. 286, 289.
[179]*GMW*, p. 283.

after analogy' is basically only a linguistic ingredient which is indispensable only to the point that the objects must let themselves be defined by thoughts."[180] In other words, God's unknowability is the only fruit of statements about God. "Analogy serves, therefore, to make expressible in speech the unknowable God in his unknowability."[181] The final result of the Kantian analogy is the formula x:a::b:c. According to this analogy, "God is inaccessible and remains beyond the boundaries of all grasping, and any concept that could define him." Speech about God is resolved into a mystery about mystery. The world relation is a perfect similarity of relations surpassed by a greater dissimilarity of the relation x:a. The relation x is unknown and unknowable. *Analogia entis*, thus understood, "has doubtless the advantage of being the most thoroughgoing hindrance to a closed system which forces together God, man and the world."[182]

Jüngel understands God in the Barthian sense as being in coming. When this understanding of God is written over the Kantian analogy of proportionality (x:a::b:c), a new correspondence between God and the world relation is possible. Jüngel writes: "One must understand analogy as an event which allows one (x) to come to the other (a) with the help of the relationship of a further other (b) to even one more other (c). The issue is an analogy of advent, which expresses God's arrival among men as a definitive event."[183] According to this model, the world relation (b:c), despite its inability on its own to speak about God, now does so. It is possible because a new light illumines it, that is, that God comes to the world "and makes use of the obvious in this world in such a way that he proves himself to be that which is even more obvious against it."[184] This obviousness appears in the form of parables about the kingdom of God. Like the hidden treasure, one will give everything to find that which is of greater value (i.e., God). This is only possible where God overcomes the "worldly obviousness" (b:c) and comes to it by means of correspondence whereby God ceases to be the unknown (x). In the analogy of advent God (x), in coming to the world (a), ceases to be an unknown x. God arrives as revelation, as a being in our

---

[180]Ibid.
[181]Ibid.
[182]*GMW*, p. 284.
[183]*GMW*, p. 285.
[184]Ibid.

language. It is a linguistic arrival, expressed in terms of a relation as x→a::b:c. "Briefly put: the Gospel is to be understood as the event of correspondence."[185]

If the gospel is understood as the analogy of advent, then the criterion for this correspondence can only be *the event about which the gospel speaks*. Only this event as the formal structure of analogy can be a "hermeneutical enabling and ontological release" for God's speakability.[186] This event, as the subject of the gospel, is also contained "in the Pauline phrase *logos tou staurou*" (1 Cor 1:18). The Word of the cross draws in talk about God as an event, in being as discourse. Both event and speech share in the power by which it comes. The content of this Word "shares itself in such a way that a distinction between it and talk about it can be made only through an abstraction. What is expressed in the Word of the cross is thus itself the full relation of language."[187] Jüngel is proposing that, in the address function of language, "mystery is in the expression of being which occurs as the Gospel is spoken."[188] Divine being as such is a lingual participation. This Word as event represents not a yes and/or no, but a definitive yes. "The name of Jesus Christ as the crucified one is responsible for this definitiveness. For in him all God's promises are 'yes' so that, in prayer, and thus through him, human speech must become 'amen' whereby God in the Word is honored."[189]

The availability of God in language, as event, is properly speaking what the Bible means by "revelation." Herein the *analogia fidei* takes place "in which human words do not come close to God but rather God as the Word comes close to man, in human words."[190] By this means God carries out his own "divine humanity" in order to make clear the distinction between his humanity and humanity's humanity in terms of dependence and derivation of one from the other. "The Christian faith confesses that God's becoming man, the incarnation of the Word of God in Jesus Christ, is the unique, unsurpassable instance of a still greater similarity between God and man taking place within a great dissimilarity."[191] In the midst of this similarity and

---

[185]*GMW*, p. 286.
[186]Ibid.
[187]*GMW*, p. 287.
[188]Rolnick, *Analogical Possibilities*, p. 236.
[189]*GMW*, p. 287.
[190]*GMW*, p. 288.
[191]Ibid.

in the midst of such great dissimilarity, it must be affirmed that Jesus is the parable (*Gleichnis*) of God. This Easter faith is the fundamental proposition of a hermeneutics of God's speakability. "As such, it is the approach to a doctrine of analogy which expresses the gospel as correspondence."[192]

This correspondence is not inherent in language but comes to language from God in Jesus Christ as a "personal parable from the Father." Parables, like metaphors, are address forms of speech. They depart from the customary uses of language and represent a "lingual renewal," which constitutes the address function of parable and metaphor. This is how analogy functions so that "what grips us is that correspondence which mediates between the unknown and the already known, the foreign and the customary. . . . Analogy grips us. It causes the character of address found in metaphor and parable."[193] Metaphors and parables are socializing phenomena and are distinct from other forms of addressing speech. They move language beyond what was actually there before. They are creative in that their use involves an event wherein the subject, the discourse and the hearer, "are represented in a differentiated unity."[194] The parables do emphasize the great dissimilarity between the kingdom of God and the world, but only to the degree that "the great dissimilarity in a still greater similarity is emphasized."[195] This is why the kingdom of God is expressed in parables, understood as analogy—in order that its absolute distinction from the world is ultimately surpassed by a greater similarity so that "the kingdom of God comes into language in the parable as a parable, and thus comes to the hearer."[196] This amounts to the surpassing nearness of the kingdom of God. "Thus the parable, although it speaks the language of the world, speaks at the same time in truth and speaks genuinely of God."[197] We shall say more about this in chapter five.

The value of parable over the Kantian analysis of dogmatic-symbolic anthropomorphism is that parable as analogy preserves the distinction between God and humanity, while at the same time combining God and humanity "in one and the same event," that is, in Jesus Christ as parable. Christian theology

---

[192]*GMW*, p. 289.
[193]*GMW*, p. 290.
[194]*GMW*, p. 292.
[195]*GMW*, p. 294.
[196]*GMW*, p. 295.
[197]Ibid.

opposes speech about God that describes him in terms of likeness to humanity but affirms speech about God "as this particular man," Jesus Christ. It must avoid symbolic or dogmatic anthropomorphism, which are designed to protect God's impassability. Jüngel concludes: "God and perishability are thought together in the Christian faith when the faith speaks of God as a man and in the process says 'God' and does not require that one always speak of man instead of God. Rather, what must be done is to speak of God as a man in such a way that this man, whose name is Jesus, can be named, confessed, and called on as God."[198] Both Jesus and his parables are the representation of the nearness of God to humanity, nearer than humanity's own proximity to itself. Analogy is "the still greater similarity within such a great dissimilarity between God and man" and is, as the linguistic-logical expression of God's being, the hermeneutical ground for evangelical speech about God. By means of analogy as lingual event, the being of God realizes himself "*in the midst of such great self-relatedness as still greater selflessness, and is as such love.*"[199]

Jüngel on vestigium trinitatis *and the hermeneutical problem posed by* analogy. Having begun our description of the Protestant concern for an *analogia fidei* over an *analogia entis* with Barth's treatment of the *vestigium trinitatis*, we may now come full circle in order to see how for Jüngel, christologically grounded, the vestiges express a positive mode of the analogy of faith. In his treatment of this principle, in both *God's Being Is in Becoming* and *GMW*, Jüngel has correctly noted the basic link between the interpretive hermeneutic, which Barth prescribes in his rejection of the doctrine of *vestigium trinitatis*, and his working concept of revelation as God's own self-interpretation.[200] Commenting on Barth's rejection of *vestigium trinitatis*, Jüngel writes, "Revelation cannot be brought to speech 'by a possibility of logical construction.'" In agreement with Barth, he thinks that would be just an *analogia entis*. But the language in which the revelation shall be able to come to speech must, as it were, be "commandeered" by revelation. "Where such commandeering of the language by revelation, for revelation becomes event, then there is a gain to language. It consists in fact that God as God comes to speech."[201]

---

[198]*GMW*, p. 298.
[199]Ibid., emphasis original.
[200]Jüngel, *God's Being Is in Becoming*, p. 17; *GMW*, pp. 348-49.
[201]Jüngel, *God's Being Is in Becoming*, p. 11.

As Jüngel also notes, it is axiomatic for Barth that God's revelation is revelation of God's self. In the threefold repetition of revelation, God reveals
himself as revealer, revelation and revealedness. Both Barth and Jüngel regularly express this relation in the strongest terms of the identity between the
event of revelation and the eternal God.[202] The event of revelation is the event
of God's self-interpretation to humanity.[203] In other words, the veracity and
finality of revelation is already guaranteed by the fact that the God who reveals
himself as himself is this self-revealing God eternally.[204] Jüngel identifies this
vorgebildet as the principle of correspondence (*Entsprechung*), in that God in
his self-revelation corresponds to himself as he is eternally. As Jüngel puts it,
"God's being *ad extra* corresponds essentially to his being *ad intra* in which it
has its basis and prototype." In simpler terms, God's self-interpretation (revelation) "is interpretation as correspondence."[205] Here we have the fundamental possibility for theological language, but only as it orients itself to the
event of revelation, to some secondary point of reference, and not, as with the
older interpretation of *vestigium trinitatis*, understood as *analogia entis*.

Expressed in trinitarian terms the thesis is that "the economic Trinity
corresponds to the immanent Trinity."[206] Jüngel suggests that for Barth this
thesis functions as a hermeneutic rule, the effect of which is to ground all
theological language in its own object, the eternal reality of God. The only
verification for this thesis is in the bare statement of God's self-revelation. It
is not a doctrine in the classic sense of that word but represents a kind of
summary of the way in which Barth employs the doctrine of the Trinity as
a critical criterion for responsible talk about God. Any statements about
God *ad intra* must find their counterpart and interpretation in statements
about God *ad extra*, that is, in his self-revelation as witnessed to in Scripture.
The language of the economic Trinity finds its basis and authentication in
the immanent Trinity, to which it corresponds. Jüngel summarizes this hermeneutic principle admirably: "The revelation of God thus 'commandeers'

---

[202]*CD* I/1, p. 522; *KD* I/1, p. 503.

[203]Jüngel, *God's Being Is in Becoming*, p. 21.

[204]*CD* I/1, pp. 307-8; *KD* I/1, pp. 403-4.

[205]Jüngel, *God's Being Is in Becoming*, p. 23.

[206]Ibid. Jüngel comments, "Gott entspricht sich," *Gottes Sein ist im Werden*, p. 35. This is the full
weight of Jüngel's statement "Gottes entspricht Sich," and while the statement "the economic
Trinity corresponds to the immanent Trinity" is not found in the *CD* as such, certainly this is
Barth's understanding of God's self-revelation.

language not as a dumb aggressor but enters into language as a movement of speech. Thus the revelation of God itself is the enabling of interpretation of revelation ... 'because revelation is the self-interpretation of this God.'"[207] But revelation as the self-interpretation of God is the root of the doctrine of the Trinity. The doctrine of the Trinity is then consequently the interpretation of revelation and therewith the interpretation of the being of God made possible by revelation as the self-interpretation of God.

Thus, as for Barth, so also with Jüngel, there can be no possibility of *analogia entis* in any form in theology by means of appeal to natural vestiges.[208] But if the *vestigia* are christologically determined, at the place of God's own self-interpretation, there also we may affirm a *vestigium trinitatis*. It is in this historical event that "worldly speech" may be included in the self-revelation of God. This is an aspect of vestiges as the interpretation of revelation, the full meaning of which Barth failed to see.[209] *Vestigium trinitatis* means that the world "must be conceived as within the concept of revelation." Thus human history, conceived of as within revelation itself, is marked off as a "special human history" not in itself but in the power of its coming in Jesus Christ of Nazareth. "Then it is necessary to say of that history that it is the trace of the triune God, the vestige of the Trinity."[210] Preeminently this must be seen in that most human and worldly event, the crucifixion. "The man Jesus and his death on the cross would basically not affect faith in God if God himself had not come to the world in this human life and death."[211] The essence of the speakability of God consists in this "coming and going away of God," under the conditions of human sin and frailty. Therein we may speak of the loving Father, "who identifies with Jesus in his death," making it possible to speak of and believe in the Son. "To believe with Jesus in God the Father means, with all the necessity of Easter, to believe in Jesus as God the Son. But this faith is not derived from man; it is possible only in the power of the Spirit, who comes to man. To believe in God with Jesus and to believe in Jesus as God means

---

[207]Jüngel, *God's Being Is in Becoming*, p. 15.

[208]In Torrance's article he seems to agree with Jüngel here, as does Paul D. Molnar in his *Divine Freedom and the Doctrine of the Immanent Trinity: In Dialogue with Karl Barth and Contemporary Theology* (New York: T & T Clark, 2002), pp. 259-60.

[209]*GMW*, p. 348.

[210]*GMW*, p. 349.

[211]Ibid.

thus to believe in the Holy Spirit."[212] This is the only possible source for faith in a triune God in history, and thus it is the one exclusive vestige of the Trinity and possibility for speech. Barth comes close to affirming this in *CD* I/1 but does not give it the significance for speech about God that Jüngel attributes to it. As such Jüngel extends Barth's conception of the *analogia fidei* in terms of real, worldly states of affairs for theological language. To that degree, his analogy of advent marks a real advance on Barth's position. But it may be extended further still, as we will see in our final chapter.

Summary. The gospel of Jesus Christ is the essence of Jüngel's counterproposal to an *analogia entis*. It is what he really means by the analogy of advent. Speech about God cannot be grounded in its predetermination as the thinkability of God. This is a metaphysical "dead end" for theology. The speakability of God must be grounded in a divinely determined correspondence in which God comes to speech as the historical inclusion of theological language in the real vestige of this coming—that is, as the self-interpretation of God as Father, Son and Holy Spirit. It is exclusively located in Jesus Christ of Nazareth, the God-Man, born among humanity, as man, crucified, dead and buried, but coming forth from the grave as the very power of human signification.

The question of the viability of this analogy of advent remains to a large degree unanswered. There have been some limited reactions and appraisals of Jüngel's treatment of analogy, but a full response, or working out of its implications, is still forthcoming. As it is, we can gain some insights as to its viability by evaluating and analyzing the response to Jüngel to date. This has been done to a limited degree in Webster's work on Jüngel, but the full impact remains to be drawn out. If we combine Jüngel's extension of the analogy of faith, in the analogy of advent, with Barth's christological grounding of the *analogia fidei* in his doctrine of Jesus Christ as electing and elected God and man, sufficient ground would exist to expand the analogy of advent from its constriction to parable to include the coming of God in his Word as participation and performance. This would result in a more robust christological grounding of the *analogia fidei*. Let us now demonstrate this as a way of drawing our analysis of the possibility of theology to a close.

---

[212]*GMW*, p. 368.

5

THE CHRISTOLOGICAL
CONTENT OF THEOLOGY
AS *ANALOGIA FIDEI*

◆

Karl Barth's theology displays a Chalcedonian Christology that is fully affirmative of "one person in two natures." He regards Christ as "complete in humanity" and "complete in Deity." Furthermore, Barth affirms that "when these two natures met in Christ, they did so 'without separation or division' and yet also 'without confusion or change.'"[1] Granted, Barth never takes over or interprets the tradition without criticism, alteration and/or correction. But he was and remained essentially Chalcedonian. Despite his difference of approach from the mainstream of Barth interpretation, Bruce McCormack also seems to suggest Barth's faithfulness to Chalcedon. But whereas the so-called Yale School interpretation of Barth sees no possibility of an affirmation of any kind of analogy of being, McCormack sees an "analogy of being," of sorts, though by no means in terms of Przywara and/or von Balthasar.[2] In McCormack's analysis their detection of an analogy of being rests on wrong questions and a one-sided emphasis in Barth's

---

[1]George Hunsinger, "Karl Barth's Christology: Its Basic Chalcedonian Character," in *Disruptive Grace: Studies in the Theology of Karl Barth* (Grand Rapids: Eerdmans, 2000), pp. 131-47. See also Thomas F. Torrance, *Karl Barth: Biblical and Evangelical Theologian* (Edinburgh: T & T Clark, 1990), pp. 169, 201; Bruce L. McCormack, "The Ontological Presuppositions of Barth's Doctrine of the Atonement," in Frank A. James III and Charles E. Hill, eds., *The Glory of the Atonement: Biblical, Historical and Practical Perspectives* (Downers Grove, IL: InterVarsity Press, 2004), pp. 346-66.

[2]McCormack, "Barth's Version of an 'Analogy of Being,'" in Thomas Joseph White, O.P., *The Analogy of Being: Invention of the Antichrist or the Wisdom of God?* (Grand Rapids: Eerdmans, 2011), pp. 123-35.

corpus. Is it possible to find a mediating position between Protestant and Catholic theology that will enable us to affirm a Chalcedonian Christology, yielding an analogy of faith? The answer to this question would have implications, epistemically and ontologically, such that a ground for God's speakability could be established in a way that would bring greater agreement on analogy and its usefulness. In the hopes of at least initiating this discussion, this chapter will build on the positive description of the christological ground of analogy in order to demonstrate this possibility.

Our analysis thus far must lead us to the conclusion that if theological language is possible at all, it is only on a basis rooted in the one event of revelation, Jesus Christ of Nazareth. All attempts at an *analogia entis* fail, precisely because they are insufficiently oriented to this revelatory event. We will establish this possibility first by means of an expanded exploration of the fundamental christological orientation of Barth's *CD*. At the end of the day, what matters most to Barth is the grounding of all theological speech in the one reality that determines the divine-human correspondence, the similarity in ever-greater dissimilarity, at every turn. It is grounded in Jesus Christ as electing and elected God and man, which is the essence of the self-revelation of God. We have suggested already that it is in this sense that the whole of the *CD* is an *analogia fidei*, in that every loci has its defining moment in Jesus Christ. But insofar as it does this, it delivers us a real, knowable image of God and the human, or a *bona fidei* analogy. To demonstrate this we will need to revisit the doctrine of election under the rubric of Jesus Christ as the elected and electing God, and follow this up with an exposition of Barth's conception of Jesus Christ as the elected and electing human. The dialectic of this double election renders "God for man and man for God" as the correspondence ingredient in this revelation, and therefore as a real ontological possibility for theological speech. Speech about God that is not oriented on this christological dialectic cannot be counted as truly theological speech.

The result of our analysis of Barth's Christology will leave us with the possibility of describing the divine-human correspondence in terms of an analogy of faith that has three dimensions. These three dimensions will act as summary features of the multifaceted nature of the coming of God to speech, as an extension of both Barth's designation of an *analogia relationis/*

fidei and Jüngel's suggestion of an analogy of advent. Thus in part two of this chapter we will offer the possibility of theological speech first as analogy of *participatory* Word, grounded in and limited by the christological confines of revelation, and not to be understood as a general metaphysics of being available in nature. We will then combine it with an analysis of the possibility of theological speech as an analogy of *performative* Word, precisely because of the "event" nature of revelation. This means also, finally, we may affirm an analogy of *parabolic* Word, in a further conjunction with Jüngel as an instance where participation and performance are given real shape and scope in the teachings of Jesus. These three dimensions mark off God's revelation in Jesus Christ the *Word* as a gain to language with respect to speaking God. Problems and limitations will remain, of course, especially in terms of how a new dialogue about analogy might emerge and whether it is possible to have a theological ontology without the metaphysics of being. In the end, we may find a way to partially ameliorate the impasse on both the Catholic and Protestant side by offering a Chalcedonian view of theology that will be at least a good starting point.

Jesus Christ as Electing and Elected God and Man

Jesus Christ as electing God. In his primary work Barth sets out to establish a dogmatics that is entirely grounded, expressible and knowable in Jesus Christ of Nazareth. In his attempt to accomplish this, there is no loci, no methodological principle and/or interrogation of the tradition left untouched. This is a grand *analogia fidei*, the essence of which may be located either in the doctrine of the Trinity as a whole (I/1), and/or in God the Creator (III/1), and/or in God the Reconciler (IV/1), and no doubt, had he written it, in God the Redeemer as well (the projected volume V that was never written).[3] This christologically defined *analogia fidei* dominates the whole of the *CD* and all of its parts.[4] But if one were to ask for a christological center from which the God-human correspondence resonates to all

---

[3]Barth's ethics of redemption in the *Ethik* is often pointed to as an indication of how vol. V might have been shaped. Karl Barth, *Ethics*, ed. G. W. Bromiley, trans. D. Braun (Edinburgh: T & T Clark, 1981), pp. 461-516. The German text can be found in Barth, *Gesamtausgabe II. Akademische Werke: Band I & II* (Zürich: Theologischer Verlag, 1973, 1978).

[4]For a clear demonstration of this, see especially Eberhard Busch, *The Great Passion: An Introduction to the Theology of Karl Barth* (Grand Rapids: Eerdmans, 2009), pp. 184-85.

its parts, it would have to be located in Barth's doctrine of God proper, precisely in his description of Jesus Christ as elected and electing God and man. As we have noted, within Protestant interpretation a number of Barth scholars, especially Jüngel and McCormack, have affirmed this as Barth's absolute christological center, from which one may ultimately define the *analogia fidei* and the *analogia relationis* as a theological ontology that drives language in terms of its capacity to correspond (*Entsprechung, Entspricht*) to God's Word of address (*Spricht*).[5]

The degree to which a theology remains centered on Jesus Christ is the degree to which it remains theology. The *analogia fidei*, the Word and the gospel are, historically, synonyms that bespeak and confirm this faithfulness, the degree to which Barth remained faithful, and therefore the degree to which his theology may be a Word of the gospel, an *analogia fidei* and a witness to the revelation of God in Jesus Christ. It is a decision not left in his hands or ours but, by Barth's own admission, in God's.[6] His doctrine of Jesus Christ as elected and electing God epitomizes this intention and is offered here both as an example that we may, with some reservations, follow, and as a demonstration par excellence of what it means to attempt to consistently ground theology in Christology. We shall, of course, have to qualify this, but first we must hear what Barth is attempting to say.

In reference to a "true *analogia fidei*" that is rooted in a doctrine of election, in the preface to II/2 of the *CD*, Barth frets about the fact that in this respect he had to leave the framework of his Reformed tradition "to a far greater extent than in the first part of the doctrine of God."[7] He wishes he could have followed John Calvin's doctrine of predestination "much more closely" than in taking the radical turn he actually does. It was, he says, his meditation on Scripture in this respect that invariably led him to reconstruct the doctrine of election. It is to Barth's credit that his efforts at reconstruction once again raised the profile of the doctrine, though hardly diminishing its place under the doctrine of soteriology in the Reformed tradition. In Barth's understanding, the foundations of the doctrine of predestination are not to

---

[5]Bruce McCormack, *Karl Barth's Critically Realistic Dialectical Theology: Its Genesis and Development, 1909-1936* (Oxford: Clarendon Press, 1995), pp. 14-15.
[6]See his lecture "Evangelical Theology," in Barth, *An Introduction to Evangelical Theology* (Grand Rapids: Eerdmans, 1984), p. 8.
[7]*CD* II/2, p. x.

be located anywhere other than the doctrine of God's self-revelation in the event of Jesus Christ. The answer to the question will lead to a different "form" of the doctrine and therefore "with it, our whole dogmatic system, and the church's proclamation informed by that system."[8] Here, says Barth, "we must recall the basic rule of all Church dogmatics: that no single item of Christian doctrine is legitimately grounded, or rightly developed or expounded, unless it can of itself be understood and explained as part of the responsibility laid upon the hearing and teaching church towards the self-revelation of God attested in Holy Scripture."[9]

For this reason the theologically accurate rendition of the doctrine of election will not be beholden to a tradition, even if it is Reformed.[10] Neither will it be subject to some pedagogical imperative or priority in the interest of the "care of souls."[11] Nor can experience dictate to us the place, scope and shape of the doctrine of election, as though failure to hear the gospel should mitigate or qualify the application of the doctrine.[12] It most certainly cannot be determined by some abstract principle of the "omnipotent will" of God, hidden in a mysterious *decretum absolutum* as yet to be revealed. "On such a view predestination is only one moment within the world-order established and executed by the principle of freedom and necessity, proclaimed under the name of God. The doctrine of predestination is only one moment in a deterministic scheme."[13] When we oppose this view, we must be aware of coming down on the side of determinacy. God defines himself as self-determined in his Word, that is, as he exists in Jesus Christ. "If in this way we ask further concerning the one point upon which, according to Scripture, our attention and thoughts should and must be concentrated, then from first to last the Bible directs us to the name of Jesus Christ."[14] In this name alone do we discern the divine decision of God to move toward us as "the Lord and Shepherd of His people."[15]

The Reformed doctrine of predestination was often predetermined on

---

[8]Barth appears to mean the Reformed system of dogmatics (*CD* II/2, p. 34).
[9]*CD* II/2, pp. 35-36.
[10]*CD* II/2, p. 36.
[11]*CD* II/2, p. 37; see John Calvin, *Institutes of the Christian Religion* III.21.1.
[12]*CD* II/2, p. 39; Calvin, *Institutes* III.24.12-15.
[13]*CD* II/2, p. 45; *ST* I, q. 12, ad. 2; Calvin, *Institutes* III.21-24.
[14]*CD* II/2, p. 55.
[15]Ibid.

the basis of a concept of God, in general, and not always on the basis of
the biblical witness. Therefore a corrective is required in terms of directing
us to Jesus Christ as the name, content and agent of God's election, both
of himself and the human. The Scriptures point us to this fact in no uncertain terms. It extends all the way back to the covenant of God with
Noah in Genesis 9:9, which includes "every living creature of all flesh that
is upon the earth" (Gen 9:10). It is confirmed and affirmed in God's covenant with Abraham (Gen 12:1-3; Is 55:3; Jer 32:40) and in his covenant
with Israel at Sinai (Ex 32:13; Is 45:23; 54:9; 62:8). In the New Testament
election is only meaningful and expressed in direct relation to Jesus Christ
(Rom 9–11; Eph 1:3-5, 9-11; 2 Tim 1:9). "In these texts it is not of any importance whether the mention of God's will and purpose preceding the history,
or more specifically the expression (ἐκλεκτός), [are] meant to refer to the
eternity of God in itself, or 'only' to the beginning of creation, and therefore
of the universe and time."[16] This leads Barth to a crucial decision, which
he frames as follows:

> In its simplest and most comprehensive form the dogma of predestination
> consists, then, in the assertion that the divine predestination is the election of
> Jesus Christ. But the concept of election has a double reference—to the elector
> and to the elected. And so, too, the name Jesus Christ has within itself the
> double reference: the one called by this name is both very God and very man.
> Thus, the simplest form of the dogma may be divided at once into the two as-
> sertions that Jesus Christ is the electing God, and that he is also elected man.[17]

In essence, though, the double relationality of election is fourfold: Jesus
Christ is electing God and elected God, he is elected man and electing man.
The revelation of God in Christ is precisely constituted by this double
election and is grounded in the triune life of God from all eternity, "because
he is the Son of the Father," and therefore has no need of election, but nevertheless "we must add at once that He is the Son of God elected in oneness
with man, and in the fulfillment of God's covenant with man."[18] How well
does this compare to the idea of election as a secret *decretum absolutum*?
Not well at all, as a matter of fact. It is "crowded out" by virtue of the fact

---

[16]*CD* II/2, p. 103.
[17]*CD* II/2, pp. 103-4.
[18]*CD* II/2, p. 103.

that what was once secret and marked off as inscrutable has now become a *datum* of revelation.[19] In the light of this, "how can the doctrine of predestination be anything but 'dark' and obscure if in its very first tenet, the tenet which determines all the rest, it can speak only of a decretum absolutum?"[20]

Rather, we can now say, on the basis of John 1:1-2, that the revelation of the Word is the revelation of Jesus Christ as the electing and elected God and humanity, and as such a correspondence. Where such an election is hidden, there can be no assurance of faith. But this is precisely where the tradition that stems from Augustine through Aquinas to Calvin in fact leaves us. "And all the earnest statements concerning the majesty and mystery of God, all the well-meaning protestations of His fatherly loving-kindness, cannot in any way alter the fact that we necessarily ought to let ourselves be appeased. How can we have assurance of our own election except by the Word of God?"[21]

Such assurance can only come if Jesus Christ, as the Word of God, is electing and elected God.[22] At first glance one would suspect Barth of wanting to secure a place for confidence on the part of humanity in its election of God, but precisely the opposite is true, in both forms of the doctrine. The doctrine of election as a *decretum absolutum* is a temptation to root assurance in our own faith, while on the other hand the doctrine as revealed in the electing God, Jesus Christ, finds its proper basis as a divine decision, and exclusively so. "In no depth of the God-head shall we encounter any other but Him. There is no such thing as God-head in itself."[23] Barth does not want a doctrine of *decretum absolutum,* because it appears to posit a God beyond God in his self-revelation, in eternal splendid isolation. "There is no such thing as a will of God apart from the will of Jesus Christ."[24] This is no mere "mirror of our own election" but the real election that can be known and "contemplated by us."[25] Precisely, Jesus Christ reveals the will of God in election, rather than maintaining its hiddenness.

---

[19]*CD* II/2, p. 104.
[20]Ibid.
[21]*CD* II/2, p. 110.
[22]Ibid. Barth sees this as the chief problem with Calvin.
[23]*CD* II/2, p. 115.
[24]Ibid.
[25]Ibid.

He tells us that he is the one who elects us because he elects himself. "In the very foreground of our existence in history we can and should cleave wholly and with full assurance to Him because in the background of history, in the beginning with God, the only decree which was passed, the only word which was spoken and which prevails, was the decision which was executed by Him."[26] We can thus say with assurance, and full knowledge, that we are the elect of God. Because Jesus Christ is not only electing God, he is, in congruence with the fullness of his divinity and humanity, elected God as electing human. Now our faith is, in Jesus Christ, the cause, or concurrent cause, of our election.[27]

To be fair to Calvin, he does attempt to ground his doctrine of election christologically, so as to "assure" the faithful of their salvation.[28] However, the dilemma with respect to assurance remained because of the *decretum absolutum*. In response, Calvin attempted to ground such assurance in an "individual's testimony of works."[29] But Barth saw this as highly problematic because it took the "good works of grace" to confirm their election. This was ultimately a "happy inconsistency" that led Calvin to believe he could unify "the Christological beginning and the anthropological conclusion of his thinking" with the possibility that there might be a "relapse into a primitive doctrine of self-justification."[30] This amounted to a "smuggling of Pelagianism through the back door of a '*syllogismus practicus*,'" or system of practices.[31]

The question that must be raised in respect to analogy, in light of Barth's doctrine of Jesus Christ as electing God, is precisely its implications for the doctrine of the Trinity. It would appear that the *Deus absconditus* of the immanent Trinity is now fully the *Deus revelatus* of Jesus Christ as electing God. Is there a contradiction here between the hiddenness of the inner life of God and the full disclosure of his most primal act in the concept of Jesus Christ as electing God? The whole point of Barth's doctrine of the Trinity is

---

[26]*CD* II/2, p. 116.
[27]See also *CD* III/3, the divine accompaniment.
[28]Calvin, *Institutes* III.21.2-3.
[29]Ibid., III.21.3-4.
[30]Ibid.
[31]On this see R. T. Kendall, *Calvin and English Calvinism to 1649* (Oxford: Oxford University Press, 1979); John E. Colwell, *Actuality and Provisionality* (Edinburgh: Rutherford House, 1989), p. 231.

to demonstrate the fact that God is known and constituted in his self-revelation as Father, Son and Holy Spirit, precisely as Jesus Christ, the *Word* of God. In the place of the *decretum absolutum* is now Jesus Christ, electing God, as Father, Son and Holy Spirit. In essence, then, the incarnation is the most salient aspect of the triune life of God, *ad extra*. This is the way in which God chooses to be God, and thus to be electing God and elected man. Barth later confirms this in reference to reconciliation, suggesting that the event of the atonement, accomplished by Christ in time, "is not simply one history among others and not simply the reaction of God against human sin. It stands at the heart of the Christian message and the Christian faith because here God maintains and fulfills His Word as it is spoken at the very first."[32] The question as to whether the incarnation or the Trinity is God's first thought here is beside the point. The whole of the divine drama is caught up with God's eternal covenant of grace, which he makes the goal of creation in general. Jesus Christ is, as such, the "content and form" of the primal Word of God and so "the beginning of all things," of creation, reconciliation, redemption and all humanity.[33] God's covenant with humanity, enacted in the electing God, Jesus Christ, precedes, is the purpose, the "command" and the "pledge," "by which He pledges and binds man to Himself" and himself to man. "At the beginning of all things in God there is the Gospel and the Law, the gracious address of God and the gracious claim of God, both directed to man, both the Word of the *Deus pro nobis* who is one God and beside whom there is no other."[34]

Thus the fact that the incarnation is more than just a solution to human sin, and is rather the original, primal determination of God and humanity in himself, is itself a theological ontology that theology and its language are required to work within. That this is the case in Barth's theology has been pointed out most succinctly in Jüngel's *God's Being Is in Becoming*, wherein he writes, "If I have understood correctly this decisive locus of Barth's doctrine of election, then the being of the man Jesus with God is to be understood in the sense of the enhypostasis and anhypostasis of the human nature

---

[32]*CD* IV/1, p. 46. Colin Gunton sees this as the divine logic of love, "making present in its earthly actuality its eternal reality." Colin Gunton, *Yesterday and Today: A Study of Continuities in Christology* (London: SCM Press, 1983), pp. 132-33.

[33]*CD* III/1, p. 42.

[34]*CD* IV/1, p. 53.

of Jesus Christ."[35] How might this help us understand Barth's option for Jesus Christ as electing and elected God? Jüngel explains, "If the being of the man Jesus in the beginning with God is not to be understood in the sense of a projection of temporal existence into eternity, then we must speak of this temporal existence of Jesus in the sense of the anhypostasis."[36] That is, "Jesus' existence would not be what it is if it were not already in the 'eternal decision of God by which time is founded and governed."[37] But Barth must also affirm that this is precisely so in that "this existence really is temporal existence," which Jüngel calls enhypostatic, then adds, "He who 'by nature is God,' the man Jesus, is in the beginning with God. In this way he corresponds as elected man to the God who elects, and in unity with the Son of God is 'in concerto and not in abstracto' Jesus Christ."[38] If indeed this is the case, theologically, and if we may agree with Barth and Jüngel here, then obviously this has the character of an ontological determination of the creature and creation in the person and work of Jesus Christ, the one true analogy of faith. As Jüngel notes in the footnote to this section, here Jesus Christ stands in place of the *theologia naturalis* that Barth radically rejected, simply because it was, and always will be, the wrong starting point. As such Barth now affirms nature as in the beginning with God but as determined christologically. That which could not be affirmed when dogmatics had to begin with God's revelation of himself as Father, Son and Holy Spirit, and therefore as God's being without creation, can now be seen as, christologically, God's being in the beginning with creation, but only as the being of the elect man Jesus.

This seems to be the best way to understand Barth's position with respect to natural theology as it relates to the possibility of theology. This is a "Christological surpassing" of all natural theology, and, as Jüngel affirms, absolves Barth of the charge that "Barth's rejection of any natural theology withheld from humanity the theological significance which is its due."[39] But here also

---

[35]Eberhard Jüngel, *God's Being Is in Becoming: The Trinitarian Being of God in the Theology of Karl Barth—A Paraphrase*, trans. J. B. Webster (Edinburgh: T & T Clark, 2001), p. 46.
[36]Ibid.
[37]Ibid., p. 96; *CD* II/2, p. 99.
[38]Jüngel, *God's Being Is in Becoming*, p. 97. It is on this basis that Jüngel will place the possibility of a real, linguistic correspondence as both elected man and, "in concreto and not in abstracto," the electing Son of God, Jesus Christ. *CD* II/2, pp. 96-97.
[39]Jüngel, *God's Being Is in Becoming*, p. 96.

we may locate a real principle of human participation in God that remains untrammeled by the emanationist misconceptions of the *exitus* and *reditus* of divine being. In Reformed theology participation cannot be understood in this manner. But this does not mean that Reformed theology is thereby incapable of a true participation in the being of God. The key is indeed to be thoroughly christological.[40] Elsewhere in the *CD*, Barth offers a formal christological and trinitarian description and ground of such participation, but in the context of a warning that "it will not do to merely offer a divinization of the human essence of Christ."[41]

> If we shall shake the spell [that compels us to think of the need to divinize humanity in the humanity of Christ], and try to think of the God-head of God in biblical rather than pagan terms, we shall have to reckon, not with the mutability of God, but with the kind of immutability which does not prevent him from humbling himself and therefore doing what he willed to do and actually did do in Jesus Christ, i.e. electing and determining in Jesus Christ to exist in divine and human essence in the Son of God and son of man and therefore to address His divine essence to His human, to direct it to it. . . . What is, then, the divine essence? It is the free Love, the omnipotent mercy, the holy patience of the Father, Son and Holy Spirit.[42]

Perhaps, then, the thought of election and the thought of Trinity are one and the same thought, or two sides of the same theological coin. Perhaps

---

[40]Ibid., pp. 96-97; see also pp. 97-98. Here we see more clearly the Reformed basis for such a conception of christologically grounded participation. Jüngel writes, "Equally, Barth's doctrine of the being of the man Jesus in the beginning with God may also be understood as a Reformed counterpart to Lutheran teaching about the participation of the human nature of Jesus Christ in the omnipresence of the *logos incarnatus* [incarnate Word]. Cf. *CD* IV/2, p. 81, where Barth describes it as inadequate to speak of 'a divinization of human essence in Jesus Christ,' and instead brings the doctrine of the *communicatio gratiarum* (communication of graces), which includes the proper concern of the *communicatio idiomatum* (communication of properties), to its rightful place as an indication of the 'fullness of the concretion' which, in the 'movement which is made to human essence,' is God's 'event.' . . . If the christological aphorism is grounded in the Lutheran doctrine of justification, the Reformed aphorism emerges from the doctrine of predestination. In both cases we are dealing with aphorisms. We need to discover what is lost if we blunt the sharpness of either statement" (Jüngel, *God's Being Is in Becoming*, p. 97 n. 91). In this respect Todd Billings's recent exposition of participation in Calvin misses the mark for a proper doctrine of participation in Reformed theology and as such represents an imposition of a more Catholic doctrine on Calvin and the Reformed tradition. See Todd Billings, *Calvin, Participation and the Gift* (Oxford: Oxford University Press, 2007), pp. 105-41; see also *CD* IV/2, p. 81.
[41]*CD* IV/2, p. 85.
[42]*CD* IV/2, pp. 85-86.

indeed this is the full definition of the phrase "God is." He is, as he is, in himself as Father, Son and Holy Spirit, whose being and existence is made known as the electing and elected God and man, Jesus Christ, the God who loves in freedom. This is the God who has and "maintains the initiative" in this event, without which human participation, indeed the participation of creation, cannot be conceived. "The Father, He Himself, gives Himself up. This offering is therefore, elected and determined by His own majesty—the majesty of the divine Subject."[43] This is the theological ground of all possible correspondence in being, speech and action, as seen from the side of Jesus Christ as electing God. But the story can only be completed from the point of view of Jesus Christ as elected man, to which we must now turn, as the second essential element in the divine-human correspondence. We may merely note, in passing over to this, that there hardly seems to be any real grounds for Barth to alter the order of his dogmatics when the triune God already prefigures Jesus Christ as electing and elected. Its basic Chalcedonian character remains intact. In his recent study, *Reconciled Humanity: Karl Barth in Dialogue*, Hans Mikkelsen has referred to this principle of double election "in line with the Councils of Nicea and Chalcedon" in that the "act of atonement presupposes that Jesus, the Son, has the same being (οὐσία) as God the Father" and that as such it fits well with the *an-en hypostatic* tradition of Chalcedon.[44] Jüngel's approach is also very much in line with this.[45]

   Jesus Christ as elected man. If we were to end our grounding of corre-

---

[43]Ibid.

[44]Hans Mikkelsen, *Reconciled Humanity: Karl Barth in Dialogue* (Grand Rapids: Eerdmans, 2010), p. 149.

[45]Ibid., pp. 151-54. On the hermeneutical significance of this principle, see Eberhard Jüngel, "Jesus Wort und Jesus als Wort Gottes. Ein hermeneutischer Beitrag zum christologischen Problem," in Eberhard Jüngel, *Unterwegs zur Sache* (Munich: Chr. Kaiser Verlag, 1972), pp. 126-44. Jüngel comments: "We have to distinguish between and correlate en- and anhypostasis as two different relations at the same time which differ in an ontic way while they are ontologically identical. This is due to the pre-easterly Jesus historically existing and thus revealing the anhypostasis of his being (which he can do ontologically because of the power of the enhypostasis of his being in the form of *logos*). On the other hand the enhypostasis which enables and characterizes his whole being is being revealed in the form of the resurrected as the existence of Jesus Christ" ("Jesus Wort und Jesus als Wort Gottes," p. 137, as per Mikkelsen, p. 152). See also Hunsinger, *Disruptive Grace*, pp. 263-67; Bruce L. McCormack, "Grace and Being: The Role of God's Gracious Election in Karl Barth's Theological Ontology," in John Webster, ed., *The Cambridge Companion to Karl Barth* (Cambridge: Cambridge University Press, 2000), pp. 92-110.

spondence merely in the one-sidedness of Jesus Christ the elector, we would run the risk of invalidating the temporal in light of the eternal, and be no better off than we were with Calvin's *decretum absolutum*. The question that determines the truth of the matter of God's correspondence to the human in Jesus Christ, the electing God, is its actualization as an *event* in history, in time, and therefore as a temporal/eternal achievement of God precisely in election. The ontology ingredient in the election of God and man in Jesus Christ must accrue to history as much as to eternity. Without the temporal action, the eternal decision is an illusion.[46] But Barth goes on to great lengths to ensure that the eternal correspondence, decided from the beginning, in which Jesus Christ is electing and elected God and man, is real history and not just "eternal history." "Jesus Christ is the eternal decree of God before all time. Jesus Christ is the history in Palestine which reveals this decree."[47] Barth refuses to identify a priority of order, insisting on a dialectical relation between the two, the eternal and temporal Jesus Christ. As such, time stands in an analogical relation of correspondence to eternity. It is constituted by an eternal, triune relation made real and possible in the economy of salvation, and as such is irreducible to time or eternity, from a human perspective. In III/2 of the *CD* the human is described christologically as being in God's time, but with particular reference to human or "given time," but, again, grounded in Jesus Christ, in a dialectical fashion, as God for man and man for God. Just as the temporality of humanity is confirmed in the electing God, so the temporality of God is affirmed in Jesus Christ the elected man.[48]

Furthermore, Jesus Christ as elected man is the realization, revelation and accomplishment of the eternal decree, the covenant. In the temporal history of Jesus Christ, God's faithfulness, his constancy, his affirmation of his covenant with humanity, is the "consequence of a presupposition already

---

[46]See J. Thompson, "The Humanity of God in the Theology of Karl Barth," *SJT* 29 (1976): 249-69. See also his *Christ in Perspective: Christological Perspectives in the Theology of Karl Barth* (Grand Rapids: Eerdmans, 1974), pp. 20-35; R. H. Roberts, "Eternity and Time in the Theology of Karl Barth: An Essay in Dogmatic and Philosophical Theology" (PhD diss., University of Edinburgh, 1975); R. W. Jenson, *Alpha and Omega: A Study in the Theology of Karl Barth* (New York: Wipf and Stock, 2002); and Jenson, *God After God: The God of the Past and the God of the Future as Seen in the Works of Karl Barth* (New York: Sheed and Ward, 1969).
[47]Jenson, *God After God*, pp. 150-55.
[48]*CD* III/2, p. 134; see also pp. 437-38; *CD* II/1, pp. 608-10.

laid down by Him, as the fulfillment of a decision which underlies and therefore precedes that actualized, 'earlier' divine decision, as the successful continuation of an act which God had already begun."[49] But, again, this is a consequence of who God is. It is an irreconcilable dialectic about which we must use words like *presupposition*, or *beginning*, or *already*, but we really mean the one being of God in his action. It is his will as Creator, reconciler and redeemer to overcome the transgression of humanity from his own side in his real identification with humanity in Jesus Christ. Perhaps the term that might best represent the coinherence of the eternity-time dialectic as it relates to the decree of God, to be and act as he is and does in Jesus Christ as electing and elected, is *mediator*. This action, the divine decision to proceed, as Father, Son and Holy Spirit in the electing and elected God-Man, is "a work of faithfulness" in respect of his covenant. It is an "affirmation and confirmation of the institution of the covenant between Himself and man which took place in and with creation."[50] This he accomplishes in the face of a rebellion, despite it and as the "one who overcomes it as the mediator between God and man."[51] In this sense *the mediator* is the representation and realization of the fulfillment of "the original and basic will of God."[52] He is, as such, the sum and substance of the divine correspondence, the actual and actualized Word who, as parabolic mystery, performs the divine-human correspondence in history.

So, just as God is the electing God in Jesus Christ, he is also elected man. As such, he is both the subject and object of his election. If the eternal nature of God's being is his being in act, does this not mean that his being in act is a "being-in-becoming" in the temporal history of the man Jesus of Nazareth? Jüngel sees this as a necessary corollary of the double election of God and humanity.[53] "The temporal history of Jesus Christ is the fulfillment in time of God's eternal resolve. The fulfillment in time of God's eternal resolve is God's existence as man in Jesus Christ."[54] But Jüngel goes further. "God's existence as man is not only God's existence as creature, but equally God's

---

[49]*CD* IV/1, p. 36.
[50]Ibid.
[51]*CD* IV/1, pp. 36-37.
[52]Ibid.
[53]Jüngel, *God's Being Is in Becoming*, p. 98.
[54]Ibid.

handing of himself over to the opposition to God, which characterizes human existence. The consequence of God's self-surrender is his suffering of opposition to God which afflicts human existence in opposition to God—even to death on the cross."[55] This election of humanity is thus specific and not confined to some general anthropology. It is in keeping with "the Christological assertion of tradition" (Chalcedon) with which Barth believes himself to be in unity. "But the Christological assertion of tradition tells us no more than that in His humanity Jesus Christ was one of the elect."[56] More precision is needed if we are to understand this in relation to the first assertion (electing God) and God's primal will, (triune) revelation.

In fact, God was more than becoming in his election of the man Jesus Christ. The election of humanity in Jesus Christ tells us that "before all being and becoming in time, before time itself, in the pre-temporal eternity of God, the eternal divine decision as such has as its object and content, the existence of this one created being, the man Jesus of Nazareth, and the work of this man in His life and death, His humiliation and exaltation, His obedience and merit."[57] In short, the resolve or decision of God "has the mediatorial role of the man Jesus Christ of Nazareth, in view from the beginning."[58] Because the divine decision of a covenant of grace is in view, "Jesus Christ is not merely elect, He is the elect of God."[59] When Ephesians 1:4 speaks of our election "in Him," it speaks exclusively of the only possible election, the election of us in Jesus Christ. To be sure, this is no overcoming of the divine nature by humanity, or vice versa. Rather, the election of Jesus Christ the man is the election of "real man."[60] This is not, therefore, the election of humanity under the conditions of sin, but the election of humanity as determined in the covenant of grace wherein Jesus Christ is "God for man and man for God"—that is, the prototype of humanity that constitutes its creation in divine image. Theological anthropology proceeds on the basis of a theological determination of humanity in the primal decision of

---

[55]Ibid.
[56]*CD* II/2, pp. 116-17.
[57]Ibid.
[58]Ibid.
[59]Ibid.
[60]*CD* III/2, p. 71; see my *Clearing a Space for Human Action: Ethical Ontology in the Theology of Karl Barth* (New York: Peter Lang, 2003), p. 270.

God to elect man in Jesus Christ. It is conceived wholly as image of the prototype and not as fallen. It is a relation to God established, confirmed and enacted in the *Word* of God.[61] The act is *performed* from the side of God, it is *participated* in from the side of our humanity, guaranteed in the *performance*, and it is witnessed to, *parabolically*, linguistically and actually, in our designation from the side of God as witness to the *Word*. As such, Jesus Christ is the exclusive source of our correspondence with God. "It is clear that there can be no question of a direct equation of human nature as we know it ourselves with the human nature of Jesus, and therefore of a simple deduction of anthropology from Christology."[62]

Our knowledge of humanity and the truth of humanity in Jesus Christ are two different yet similar realities, on the level of our apprehension of it. It will only ever be possible to indicate a general (parabolic-analogical) correspondence of similarity because "human nature, as it is in ourselves, is always a debatable quantity; the human situation as we know and experience it is dialectical. We exist in antithesis, we cannot escape or see beyond."[63] Our life is without the unity that marks the being of humanity in and with God, in Jesus Christ. We are a contradiction to ourselves, in this respect, and therefore always in a self-deception in which we refuse to recognize the truth about ourselves. But what exists as unsynthesized antithesis in us is posited as a complete unity in the humanity of Jesus Christ.[64] Thus it is only as we look to Jesus Christ, the one true *analogia fidei* of God and humanity, that we have knowledge of ourselves.

It is all grounded in the concept of the humanity of Jesus Christ as relational-prototypical image. With the word *image*, Barth reminds us, "we must not forget the limitations implicit in this term. If the humanity of Jesus is the image of God, this means that it is only indirectly and not directly identical with God. It belongs intrinsically to the creaturely world, to the cosmos. Hence it does not belong to the inner sphere of the essence, but to the outer sphere of the work of God."[65] Were it otherwise, neither the knowledge of God nor humanity would be possible. The very function of

---

[61]*CD* III/2, pp. 19-41.
[62]Ibid.
[63]*CD* III/2, p. 47.
[64]Ibid.
[65]*CD* III/2, p. 219.

the mediatorial role of Jesus Christ as electing God and elected human requires this distinction. The revelation of God in the God-Man, Jesus Christ,
"does not present God in Himself [*De Deo*], and in His relation to Himself,
but in His relation to the reality distinct from Himself."[66] This is why it is a
product of his life *ad extra* and not directly *ad intra*. In Jesus Christ we have
the revelation of God and man, not "God and god" or the "Human and
humanity." "Between God and God, the Father and the Son, and the Son and
the Father, there is unity of essence, the perfect satisfaction of self-grounded
reality, and a blessedness eternally self-oriented and self-renewed. But there
can be no question of this between God and man, and it cannot therefore
find expression in the humanity of Jesus, in His fellow-humanity as the
image of God."[67]

Clearly this places the accent on correspondence and similarity, but just
as clearly it sets a severe limit on the employment of the concept of image
as a modality of access. The "disparity" is real and complete, grounded in
the very concept of image itself. In the "older theology" disparity is more
often than not grounded in the human as incapacity conjoined with sin.
Here it accrues to the humanity of Jesus and is much more of an ontological
condition of our creation in the image. "It is in the humanity, the saving
work of Jesus Christ that the connection between God and man is brought
before us."[68] It is in this christologically grounded relation, above, that the
possibility of our salvation, our reality and our action consists. There is a
"great disparity" between the Father-Son relationship and our relationship
with God. It is an ontological gap that can only be bridged from the side of
God, and according to his electing grace. But in this event is not only the
revelation of very God of very God, but also very man of very man, or as
Barth so often shortens it, "God for man and man for God."[69]

Jesus Christ as electing and elected God as correspondence in speech.
Having already suggested, on the basis of McCormack's treatment of election
in Barth, that the *analogia relationis* can only be understood in the light of
Jesus Christ as electing and elected, we are now able to precisely define how

---

[66]Ibid.
[67]Ibid.
[68]Ibid.
[69]Jüngel, *God's Being Is in Becoming*, pp. 96-98.

this Christology works with respect to theological language. The whole discussion leads Barth to that point in *CD* III/2, because "for all the disparity— and this is the positive sense of the term image—there is a correspondence and similarity between the two relationships."[70] Once again Barth makes it clear that this is not an *analogia entis*. "The being of God cannot be compared with that of man." The analogy does not rest on a comparison of being but a comparison of relation, which, as we saw in Barth, à la McCormack and Jüngel, is a relation that has ontological grounding in the very election of God from all eternity. Thus it is a relation "within the being of God," but also "between the being of God and man."[71] Therefore "it is not a question of this two-fold being," but it is a question of "the two relationships [in both their eternal and temporal reality] as such." In this sense the relation between God and humanity is an image of the relation between Father and Son. "Between these two relationships as such—and it is in this sense that the second is an image of the first—there is correspondence and similarity, there is an *analogia relationis*."[72]

But this relation, as a divine decision in the electing God, Jesus Christ, is a relation in Trinity. It "consists in the fact that" as God posits himself as Father, Son and Holy Spirit, he does so in the freedom of his will to proceed "into a far country" to engage the creature as his creature.[73] To put it another way, and here Barth returns to the trinitarian grounding of God's revelation and therefore the revelation of his being in act, he is the one who loves in freedom. The similarity and correspondence consists in the fact that as Father, Son and Holy Spirit, he is the one who loves in freedom. Once again, the question of the order appears in a dialectical tension; the being and action of God are indivisible, and to that degree so are act and being. As John Colwell puts it, "That God is related *ad extra* as well as *ad intra*, that He loves man in Jesus Christ as a reiteration of His self-relatedness, is an outcome of the *a posteriori* necessity of His grace, not any *a priori* necessity constrained in the external object of His love."[74] The correspondence follows the "essence of the inner being of God" and not some accidental relation in creation. But since the being of God *ad intra* and the works of

---

[70]Ibid., p. 107.
[71]*CD* III/2, p. 220.
[72]Ibid.
[73]Ibid.
[74]Colwell, *Actuality and Provisionality*, p. 250.

God *ad extra* are indivisible (*sunt indivisa*), God in his works remains true to his inner life so that, despite the dissimilarity, a similarity exists. "Hence the factuality, the material necessity of the being of the man Jesus Christ for His fellows, does not really rest in the mystery of an accident or caprice but on the mystery of the purpose and meaning of God, who can maintain and demonstrate His essence even in His work, and in His relation to this work."[75] As with the declaration of the glory of God, in his inner being, and in his triune relation in the economic Trinity, so also in the relation of himself with humanity, in the Son as Word, his glory is declared (Jn 1:14-18; 17:1-18).

Therefore language about God orders itself according to this correspondence. It speaks, carefully and responsibly, *only* about the sum and substance of this relation in correspondence. In this sense, and this alone (*sola*), it may and can speak of a correspondence and similarity "within the creaturely world and its history."[76] This is the history of a covenant, of a relation, of a real divine-human correspondence in Jesus Christ. The question remains as to how, precisely, this responsible speech is now to proceed. What are the limitations and possibilities of theological language carried out on this basis? Unfortunately, due to the scope of this project, we can only sketch out the approach here. We cannot begin to work out a dogmatics either in part or whole, even by way of example with a single loci. That task will have to come under a different cover. Hopefully, however, enough of a start can be achieved here to indicate what the full shape and scope of such a dogmatics will entail. In the final sections of this chapter it remains for us to sketch the possibility of theology as an analogy of participated Word, performative Word and parabolic Word. Thus one may also posit them as the substance of an *analogia fidei* with the full capacity to bring God to speech, as a gain to language. Its Chalcedonian character will continue to show itself, making the approach at once Christological, analogical and ecumenical.

THE POSSIBILITY OF *ANALOGIA FIDEI* AS CHRISTOLOGICAL CORRESPONDENCE

Is it impossible to speak meaningfully of God? In order to fully grasp our claim to the possibility of theological speech, let us once again remind our-

---

[75]*CD* III/2, p. 221.
[76]Ibid.

selves of the problem of analogy, this time in its recent modern criticism. From the start this study has been about the very real existential struggle to understand how language may serve as a referent to God in such a way that it can be said "this or that statement is theologically true," or better, "this or that statement is theologically meaningful." The question of analogy, as we have shown, is at the epicenter, as suggesting both the necessary possibility and the inevitable impossibility of the capacity of language to convey the being of divinity. More than being proffered as a logical or epistemological/ hermeneutical solution to the impasse, it appeared as a natural, ontologically driven recourse, a "metaphysics of being." Was this a mere accident of reason, or is there something ontologically innate about this recourse to the analogy of being?

In doing the research for this study, one does not have to go far to find modern critics who note the impossibility of analogy to convey any meaningful speech about God that may pass for knowledge. Jüngel and Barth's engagement of the issue was precisely in response to this state of affairs. As a matter of fact, it seems that theological agnosticism, even atheism, is the motivator for all such analogical approaches. Even within the Christian faith scholars have pointed to analogy, especially as classically conceived in the medieval period, as part of the problem rather than the solution. Étienne Gilson once wrote,

> if then we take the divine attributes one by one and ask whether each of them is to be found in God [by virtue of having been first identified in us], we must reply that they are not there, at least as such and as a distinct reality, and since we can in no way conceive an essence which is nothing but an act of existing, we cannot in any way conceive what God is, even with the help of such attributes.[77]

In the same tradition, E. L. Mascall locates the problem in causal argumentation, stating, "the world requires as its cause a being totally transcending

---

[77]Étienne Gilson, *The Christian Philosophy of St Thomas Aquinas*, trans. L. K. Shook, History of Christian Philosophy in the Middle Ages (New York: Random House, 1955), pp. 105-7; E. L. Mascall, *Existence and Analogy* (New York: Anchor Books, 1967); Frederick Ferré, "Analogy in Theology," in *The Encyclopedia of Philosophy* (New York: McMillan Press, 1967), 1:41-44; see also Kai Nielsen, "Analogical Talk About God: A Negative Critique," *The Thomist* 40 (1976): 32-60. For a response to these arguments against the possibility of analogy, see, for example, W. N. Clarke, *Explorations in Metaphysics: Being—God—Person* (Notre Dame, IN: University of Notre Dame Press, 1995), pp. 123-49.

it in every respect; but how can we even affirm the existence of such a being, if an experience of the world gives us no words by which to define Him?"[78]

In his influential article on analogy in *The Encyclopedia of Philosophy*, titled "Analogy in Theology," Frederick Ferré asks the same question, in his evaluation, as to whether analogy may convey meaningful truth about God. He offers six substantial reasons why it is, in his opinion, virtually impossible, the fifth of which is a devastating critique of the analogies of emanation we have discussed in the late medieval period. "Even if it could be demonstrated," he writes,

> through some "chain of being" conception of ontology, that causes universally "resemble" their effects in some important way, one must still refrain from attributing the properties of a "cause" to God in any univocal sense. . . . If God is to be spoken of as "first cause" of the world, that attribution must be proposed in some nonunivocal sense. Thus, even if an analogy of attribution can be shown to hold informally among objects in the world, it appears to founder helplessly in an infinite regress of equivocations on its key word, "cause" when applied in hopes of gaining knowledge of God.[79]

The same is true, he affirms, of analogies built on intrinsic similarities. In view of the modern critique of language and logic, the claims of analogy appear difficult to defend.

In fact, two studies since have gone a long way toward denying the concept of analogy as a route to divine predication as knowledge. Both studies, not surprisingly, have focused on the problem and possibility of analogy as conceived by Thomas Aquinas. Kai Nielsen, in his influential article, "Analogical Talk of God: A Negative Critique," boldly asserts that "the classical doctrine of analogy has been used to try to show how terms involved in God-talk have an appropriate meaning even if the key statements involving God-talk are not verifiable in principle."[80] In Nielsen's mind, the conclusions often drawn from analogical speech are caught up in a process of mutual verification, but without the necessary verification of experience, such as the principle of falsification put forward by Antony Flew, for instance. All analogical language cannot be rooted in experience, where

---

[78]Nielsen, "Analogical Talk About God," pp. 32-33.
[79]Ferré, "Analogy in Theology."
[80]Nielsen, "Analogical Talk About God," p. 33.

the ideas about God are conceived.[81] He too criticizes the position of analogy argued from causality and sees it as the central problem. In this modality of analogy, "there must be some univocal predication possible concerning God if there is to be analogical predication at all, but the crucial point of all Thomist and Neo-Thomist predication is that it is precisely non-univocal." But cause can only accrue to God and creation univocally, as it relates to experience or verifiability. "In short even if such a theory of analogy can be worked out for terms like 'caused' and 'knows,' it does not work for God-talk."[82]

In an even more penetrating critique of the Thomistic conception of analogy, John S. Morreall has effectively denied it any sense of surety of knowledge if the criterion is the rule of noncontradiction with respect to empirical experience, and especially if the argument is from causality. The problem with such an approach to analogy, and thus speech about God, is that it cannot account for anything in our experience, and so we must extrapolate beyond ourselves. "A real problem arises when we try to consider alternatives to talking about God in language designed to talk about ourselves, for the only possible alternative seems to be agnosticism."[83] If we cannot accurately represent "him" as somehow similar to ourselves, then knowledge of God seems impossible. As Carnades suggested, it seems that our notion of deity must be either anthropomorphic or meaningless; or, in Feuerbach's words, "a being without qualities is one which cannot become an object to the mind, and such a being is virtually non-existent."[84]

Morreall then proceeds to apply this critique, respectively to negative theology and the Thomistic concept of analogy, which he thinks came out of this negative theology and the causal argument that sits at the core of this Thomistic version of analogy. In that respect he sees negative theology as problematic because "any position which tried to hold that God could only be described by denying that God is material, changing and so on, with any property one could think of, is reducible to the position that God cannot be described at all."[85] The *via negativa* is therefore insufficient, so Aquinas is

---

[81]Ibid., pp. 50-51.
[82]Ibid., p. 55 n. 52.
[83]John S. Morreall, *Analogy and Talk About God* (Atlanta: Scholars Press, 1984), p. 2.
[84]Ibid.
[85]Ibid., p. 7.

forced to "make some true *affirmative* statements about God."[86] This was, according to Morreall, the motive behind Aquinas's appeal to analogy. After a brief analysis of Aquinas's theory and its historical development, Morreall comes to the conclusion that the Thomistic transformation of the classical mode of analogy absolves him from having to make "actual analogies," as one is forced to do in mathematics. Similarities can be actual or implied, but are always assumed, yet not always present. "It is fine to leave the actual similarity unstated, of course, but only as long as it can be presupposed. In theology the similarity is often both not stated and not presupposed. But it is nonsense to say that one knows of a similarity between creatures and God, but that he does not know what it is."[87] Thus such "unspecified similarities" cannot be the basis of any theological knowledge as such. Analogy only works if "extended meanings are specifiable extrapolations from ordinary meanings."[88] When this criterion is applied to the principle of causal resemblance, which Morreall does in the rest of his critique of Aquinas, the results for analogical speech are dubious at best. "The fact that some artists are self-expressive or self-revelatory in their work, that is, does not justify effect-to-cause inferences in just any case of artistic production. It is important to see here, as in the case of final causality, that our inferences are only as good as our familiarity with the effect and the cause and the connection between them."[89] Of course, the problem with CER in theology is that we only have familiarity with the effect, as such. Even at that we claim only an indirect knowledge of the cause. Analogy thus seems tentative, almost agnostic.

We have adduced these critiques here simply to point out the difficulty embedded in analogical ways of speaking about God. Much more could be said in terms of depth, breadth and scope of the critique. The impression one gets is that there are many more arguments against theological language than for, and this is to be expected given the modern and late modern criticism of theology since Kant. One of the reasons, as we have said, that Jüngel and Barth take up the issue is that there were modalities of theological

---

[86]Ibid.
[87]Ibid., pp. 9-10.
[88]Ibid.
[89]Ibid., p. 27.

speech in the tradition that left Christian discourse open to these criticisms. Now that we have arrived at their proposals, what can we say for the possibility of analogy, in the light of Jüngel and Barth's proposal for an *analogy of faith*? Are the criticisms of theological predication established by modernity final, such that we must rule out our possibility of theological knowledge or meaning, as such? Indeed there is hope for just such a possibility, even among the philosophers today, as Anthony Kenney, in his *The God of the Philosophers*, suggests:

> I suppose that few people claim to know that there is a God; most believe it as a matter of faith. But traditionally faith was faith in God as Saviour, not as Creator; it was faith in, not the existence of God, but in the promises of a God whose existence was taken as so obvious that only ill will could account for the failure to recognize it. Faith was demanded in God's promises to his chosen people, or in his revelation in Jesus, not in there being a God who could promise or reveal. Even against such a background it is no easy matter to show that such faith is reasonable; without such background its rationality is even more difficult to establish. The absolute commitment demanded by religious traditions is a deliberate giving of assent beyond what the evidence demands. The justification of this is the most important task for the theist philosophy of Religion.[90]

While this may be true about the philosophy of religion and theism in general as a philosophical task, in theology the task is intraecclesial, and indeed in Barth and Jüngel, among others, the task has precisely concerned a move away from philosophical theism toward the God of the Bible. If we take Barth's analogy of faith—and Jüngel's expression of it in terms of the analogy of advent—seriously, then we may note three ways in which God, in the Bible, corresponds to us, and we to him, in Jesus Christ, about which we may speak in faith. That is, as participatory Word, performative Word and parabolic Word. Our *analogy of faith* confines itself to these modalities of biblical attestation in respect to the knowledge and speakability of God. It does not attempt a rational justification in the name of philosophical theism. Together these principles provide a modality of analogy wherein the real extension of real similarities become possible.

---

[90]Anthony Kenny, *The God of the Philosophers* (Oxford: Oxford University Press, 1987), p. 127.

Participation, performance and parable: Toward a christo-onto-theological paradigm. The reader should know that the alliteration here is quite accidental and not intended as a literary device. All three of these categories have contemporary currency and can be demonstrated to have direct theo-ontological connections to the principle of incarnational revelation that forms the core of the gospel.[91] Taken together, they intend to extend the normal descriptions of linguistic reflection in theology, precisely by each being grounded in the christological mode of God's self-revelation, as opposed to some metaphysics or sociolinguistic theory of language in the first instance.[92] Very often these modes of linguistic description of the function of theology are taken up without reference to one another, as it relates to gospel revelation. Here we combine these three common ciphers in order to both fill out the capacity of language, thus avoiding a narrowness of linguistic function, and to open theology up to the full range of the theological/christological content of the gospel. Furthermore, because of their direct christological content, these may well qualify as modes of the *analogia fidei,* as classically understood. As well, it is their social-linguistic similarity that constitutes their capacity to function as principles inherent in the epistemic grounds for theology. Let us first offer a basic definition of what we mean by these three forms of the analogy of faith. We shall then unpack each in turn as we see them witnessed in certain key portions of Scripture.

In respect to the analogy of participatory Word, this principle seems self-evident in that it is perhaps the most immediate and natural christological feature of a theo-ontological basis for the analogy of faith.[93] It is, so to

---

[91]On the relationship between analogy, participation and the sociolinguistic conception of theology, see especially Hans Boersma, *Heavenly Participation: The Weaving of a Sacramental Tapestry* (Grand Rapids: Eerdmans, 2011); P. A Rolnick, *Analogical Possibilities: How Words Refer to God* (Atlanta: Scholars Press, 1993), p. 41; see also David Burrell, *Analogy and Philosophical Language* (Oxford: Oxford University Press, 1996) and his *Knowing the Unknowable God: Ibn-Sina, Maimonides, Aquinas* (Notre Dame, IN: University of Notre Dame Press, 1986), pp. 1-2. On performance, see especially Hans Urs von Balthasar, *Theo-Drama* (San Francisco: Ignatius, 1997); Kevin J. Vanhoozer, *The Drama of Doctrine* (Louisville: John Knox, 2005). On parable and analogy, see Eberhard Jüngel, *Paulus und Jesus* (Tübingen: J. C. B. Mohr, 1962), pp. 87-88; *GMW*, pp. 281-82.

[92]Participation can be seen as a product of a metaphysical system whose counterpart is an analogical method of predication. On this see W. N. Clarke, *The Philosophical Approach to God: A Contemporary Neo-Thomist Perspective* (Winston-Salem, NC: Wake Forest University Press, 1979), p. 55.

[93]Classical Christian conceptions of participation seem almost devoid of any christological

speak, the heart of the matter in that Christianity espouses, preeminently, God's participation in and with humanity precisely as a Word of address. In this Word, sign and the signified are one, and thus the "very Word" of God. That it should supply the natural ground for an *analogia fidei* as well as the theo-ontological ground for our own witness to this express Word seems axiomatic. However, in this context, what precisely do we mean by *participation*? Are we referring back to a sacramental principle in order to ground the analogy it represents? Is this a participation grounded in the historical event of the incarnation? Or is it primarily a reference to an idealized conception of "heavenly participation" wherein "Christology" appears as a phantom of history, realized in a "kind of Platonist-Christian synthesis"?[94]

Rather, by *participation* we mean, as per Romans 6:8, our participation in the death and resurrection of Christ in terms of a συνήσομεν. That is, to participate in and with Christ is to live, move and have our being in him. It is as much the participation in this life as it is in a "future glory." Both are key elements moving us toward this participation. Our participation means our fellowship with Jesus Christ of Nazareth in the full range of human experiences that his life represents for us. In theological terms it is the *duplex gratia* of our justification and sanctification that constitutes the ground of our capacity to know, invoke and act in the Christian life. It is our *unio cum Christo* (union with Christ), achieved in this double grace, that Protestant faith refers to when we speak of participation. That it takes on an analogical scope is again axiomatic given its prefiguring in the life, death and resurrection of the God-Man, whose reality can never be conceived of as identical with any creaturely state of affairs, in terms of sameness. Rather, it can be so only in terms of similarity and only at the behest of the self-revealing God, who alone, as our Father and the Father of the Son, enacts this analogy of participatory Word, as an *analogia fidei*.

So also we must regard any analogy of performative Word as grounded in the single act of God the Father in the history of his Son, Jesus Christ of Nazareth. In defining this particular function of language as a possible *ana-*

---

ground, though the idea is used as a mode of description for the Christian life, theology and liturgy in general. But this is an instrumental understanding of participation. See especially Clarke, *Philosophical Approach to God*, pp. 55-56. See also *ST* I, q. 2, art. 3.

[94]See Boersma, *Heavenly Participation*, p. 162.

logia fidei, christologically rooted, we are asking about the relative effects of the incarnation of the Word as an act of God. That is, the gospel presents itself, in its literary form, as a "theo-drama" under the direction of God, who is the primary producer, director and actor. As such, it is in the literary record of this act that we can come into touch with the drama of salvation as a "theo-drama" of Word and deed.[95] *Drama* here is not just narrowly referring to a literary-performative designation for the gospel story. Far from being merely a pointer to something that transcends the dramatic activity, the act is itself in the drama as Word, event and record. Scripture itself may then be the realization of God's act in history. It is God's direct "communicative action" in and through the Word of address (Jn 1:1-18). The total realization of this drama in theology includes a full account of the gospel as divinely spoken and performed Word together with human witness and action, by way of *correspondence*. This correspondence involves us in a divine-human encounter in which we enact, and reenact, the truthful statements of the gospel as doctrine (teachings) in such a way that they establish a true correspondence with this initial witness in terms of experience, act and thought about the comprehensive revelation of God in Jesus Christ. God's *acts*, his creation, rejection, election, reconciliation and redemption of his people, by means of the drama of the life, death, resurrection and ascension of Jesus Christ, establish the comprehensive ground of the witness. It is the play, creation is the stage, and the drama unfolds in correspondence with the eternal, divine drama of the inner life of God the Father, Son and Holy Spirit. It is this double capacity (or should we say triple?) for performative action, between God and humanity, that is grounded and guaranteed in the person and work of the Word. He is, as such, the possibility of the divine-human encounter and correspondence. In this sense, as with participation, it can serve as a mode of the christologically determined *analogia fidei*. It not only brings God to speech, but it is the enactment of God as speech.

Participation and performance have the character of a double correspondence as both divinely ordered action and human correspondence. Christology, the affirmation of the capacity in God for this divine-human par-

---

[95]Here we are conflating the definitions offered in Vanhoozer and von Balthasar, whose works are cited below.

ticipation and performance, finds further grounding in the gospel as parabolic witness, that is, as an analogy of parabolic Word. Again, the key is Christology. As with participation and performance, in Jesus Christ of Nazareth revelation is brought to expression and expressibility by means of indirect reference. Taking our cue from Jüngel, we define the *analogia fidei* here in terms of parable as a "hermeneutical enabling" of human talk about God, on the analogical level, due to its capacity, metaphorically, to narrate, name and bring to speech the faith represented in the gospel. The language of faith is, in part, constituted by parable because the parabolic device expresses the capacity of language to bring God to speech. It renders the gospel communicable because "it signifies a new way of dealing with the world and each other." As such, "a theological theory of language has to accord metaphorical speech a dogmatically fundamental and therefore hermeneutically decisive function . . . because linguistic expressions often have to assume new meaning in order to signify theological states of affairs."[96]

That Jesus Christ of Nazareth leads the way in this mode of speech, precisely as the embodiment of the meaning and capacity for parable, certainly places parable on the order of a hermeneutical key where theology is concerned. In the very same way that God addresses us in the parabolic Word, so the Word addresses us. Indeed, in the address of parable itself is the capacity of language to be freighted with a divine-human correspondence that marks it out as a particular form of the *analogia fidei*. Parable is "a language event of creative freedom" and as such possesses the "original lingual unity of freedom and forcefulness" that is "the essence of analogy." Parable, then, as an *analogia fidei*, is "the addressing event of freedom" in that it is "an enhancement of language" precisely focused on the event of the incarnation.[97]

Therefore, taken together with participation and performance, parable is an equally forceful and hermeneutically necessary element in a more robust christological *analogia fidei*. Unlike Jüngel, however, it cannot perform this hermeneutical function in the absence of the larger christological paradigm afforded in participation and performance. All three modes of the analogy

---

[96]Eberhard Jüngel, "Metaphorical Truth: Reflections on Theological Metaphor as a Contribution to a Hermeneutics of Narrative Theology," in *Theological Essays*, ed. and trans. John Webster (Edinburgh: T & T Clark, 1989), pp. 49-50.
[97]Ibid.

of faith constitute the single *analogia fidei* and must be held together. In the rest of this chapter we will expand on these definitions by comparing the respective elements with their christological expressions in the New Testament Gospels. In respect to participation and performance we will confine our exposition and expansion to John's Gospel (chapters 1 and 17 and a few related texts), though examples and texts may well be drawn from other areas of the New Testament. In regard to parable we will confine ourselves to indirect references to a very few examples from the Synoptics, especially the parables of the kingdom. Our goal here is to establish these as principles that drive a christologically defined *analogia fidei*. We cannot in any way hope to be exhaustive in our exposition of them. They are merely suggestive at this stage.

The possibility of theology as the analogy of participatory word. The theme of participation has been a subterranean motif in this study, but its criticality has never been too far out of sight. From the very beginning Christian theology has traded, either implicitly or explicitly, on the assumption that there is some sense of a divine participation in creation and that creation has a capacity for or is at least caused to participate in God. This principle sits at the heart of all attempts to define analogy. The point is precisely how it is to be understood, such that the divine-human correspondence is not obliterated on either side. The principle has become all the more critical since it has been deployed as a key element in recent Catholic and Protestant attempts at a "new metaphysics," or at least a new "sacramental theology."[98]

In Protestant theology, the so-called radical orthodox group has been leading the charge in this respect. Its chief architect and exponent, John Milbank, has called for a new "theological" metaphysics that fearlessly established theological discourse in its own right, without respect for the modern criticism of theology. What emerges in the process is a heavily sacramental ontology that trades on Neoplatonic and Christian resources, which have been reinterpreted, historically reordered and augmented in ways that defy traditional interpretations. The essential position of the radical orthodoxy group suggests that in Augustine and Aquinas, at least, one can observe a theological ontology that avoids the traps of philosophical

---

[98]See, for instance, Boersma, *Heavenly Participation*, pp. 162-64.

determinism and that may be revived in the postmodern situation in the interest of a resurgent theology. This whole approach traded on an account of the modern rejection of metaphysics described in Milbank's *Theology and Social Theory: Beyond Secular Reason*.[99]

In this seminal book Milbank argues that theology must no longer allow itself to be seen as a discourse that exists outside philosophical and secular discourses. Theology, far from being a humble science, now needs to assert itself in the face of a modern, secular reason, which finds itself "at an end" and precisely so because it was itself "a metaphysics" of a "religious" nature.[100] The so-called postmodern critique has absolved Christian theology from the requirement of being measured by secular reason for its truth claims. Along with other members of the "Cambridge school," radical orthodoxy attempts to "resurrect" Christian orthodoxy in the face of this "modern religion." In the process, particularly through what they call a "theological turn" in the French School of Phenomenology and the *Nouvelle Theologie*, they have attempted to repristinate the "orthodox" principle of participation as a key element in the new theological ontology. But to do so they felt it absolutely necessary to retrieve a Neoplatonic understanding of the "One," which they claim was a driving principle of theological orthodoxy in the early to late medieval period.[101] In essence, Milbank defines such participation (according to his reading of Aquinas) as the capacity of created being to participate in "uncreated intelligible light" in that

> the *intellectus* or "higher reason" enjoys a certain very remote approximation
> to the divine intuition or immediate intellectual vision, which operates
> without recourse to divisive unfolding. Hence it enjoys some vision of the
> pure divine form without matter, only known to our *modus cognoscendi* as
> the diverse transcendental of Being, unity, truth, goodness and beauty.[102]

---

[99]See also John Milbank, "'Between Purgation and Illumination': A Critique of the Theology of Right," in *Christ, Ethics and Tragedy: Essays in Honour of Donald Mackinnon*, ed. Kenneth Surin (Cambridge: Cambridge University Press, 1989), pp. 161-96.

[100]John Milbank, *Theology and Social Theory* (Oxford: Blackwell, 1990), pp. 1, 260. See also his *The Suspended Middle: Henri De Lubac and the Debate Concerning the Supernatural* (Grand Rapids: Eerdmans, 2005); and "Only Theology Overcomes Metaphysics," *New Blackfriars* 76 (1995): 325-42.

[101]Milbank elsewhere refers to this capacity for participation as reciprocity in terms of gift giving and forgiveness. See especially his "The Soul of Reciprocity," *ModT* 17, no. 3 (July 2001): 335-91; see especially pp. 344-45, where he asks and answers the question: Is reciprocity onto-theological? See also his *Being Reconciled: Ontology and Pardon* (London: Routledge, 2003), p. 8.

[102]See John Milbank and Catherine Pickstock, *Truth in Aquinas* (London: Routledge, 2001), p. 113

John Marenbon has already answered the question as to whether Milbank has correctly interpreted Aquinas, so we shall leave this issue aside.[103] Here we merely want to note that something like this is representative of the concept of participation at play in this school of thought. It is a view of participation that is very much dependent on a Neoplatonic conception, and not really representative of even a Thomistic sacramental view. Anthony Kenney has reminded us that in the view of radical orthodoxy, participation has been virtually severed from its sacramental context in Aquinas thought. Their view ignores the fact that in Aquinas, "what the Christian sees and tastes in the Eucharist are the accidents of the bread and wine, whereas what Christ takes the place of in this miracle, is their substance."[104] Clearly theology cannot appeal to such a view of participation and expect to be free of the kind of metaphysics Milbank himself eschews.

In another recent offering of a participatory metaphysics, this time from the Eastern Orthodox perspective, David Bentley Hart takes a similar approach to radical orthodoxy. In his book *The Beauty of the Infinite: The Aesthetics of Christian Truth*, he calls for an *analogia entis* that is grounded in a participatory taxonomy of *perichoresis*. He calls his an *analogia verbi*, and it does come closer to what we intend to suggest by an analogy of participatory word. Hart states that "the analogy between God and creation, so the book of wisdom seems to suggest, is not one between the here below and the far above, between lesser and greater powers, human and divine forces within the order of being."[105] Rather, he suggests, "all of creation is the sign of God's power in its very want of divinity, in the failure of even its greatest beauty and splendor to attain to the Majesty of God. . . . The proportions of created things, their orders of magnitude, quantity, and beauty, tell of an infinite proportion—an infinite interval—if ever yet greater magnitude, 'quantity' and beauty."[106] On this understanding analogy is the principle of

---

n. 24; For a severe criticism of this approach, see John Marenbon, "Aquinas, Radical Orthodoxy and the Importance of Truth," in Wayne J. Hankey and Douglas Hedley, eds., *Deconstructing Radical Orthodoxy: Postmodern Theology, Rhetoric and Truth* (Burlington, VT: Ashgate, 2005), p. 53.

[103]Marenbon, "Aquinas, Radical Orthodoxy," pp. 49-63.

[104]Kenny, *God of the Philosophers*, p. 41.

[105]See David Bentley Hart, *The Beauty of the Infinite: The Aesthetics of Christian Truth* (Grand Rapids: Eerdmans, 2003), p. 300.

[106]Ibid.

the embeddedness of the infinite as "infinite interval" or "whole infinity" in which God dynamically moves thought toward himself. "Its essential impetus is a desire that wills the downfall of all mere concepts when they encounter the persistent interval within analogy, because the interval is analogy's power."[107]

There is a sort of *epektasis* at work in this form of analogy in that "language, drawn on by the beauty of the Word who is the distance containing all the words of creation, traverses the analogical interval between God and creation."[108] This is an action of God between creations, "proportions" and God's "proportions of peace" that issues in an endless, kataphatic progress of language limited only by the "measure of charity revealed in Christ," which, of course, like God, because he is the revelation of God, is infinite in proportions.[109] Hart claims that this is no epistemological or metaphysical grounding of theological language. It is grounded in one event. "I want to consider principally how analogy (as a linguistic event) constitutes, for Christian thought, a true (and so peaceful) rhetorical style."[110] One is immediately struck by this rather startling claim to be locating analogy in event rather than in epistemologically driven metaphysics of being, and so he might well be an ally for our own attempt to disabuse theological language of its oftentimes metaphysical casting. But this is premature in Hart's respect. There is no doubt that Hart's position on analogy is driven here by the influence of von Balthasar and especially Przywara. To the degree that there is congruence between their views and the views of Jüngel and Barth, we certainly have grounds for considering this conception of an *analogia verbi*. But a closer look at the grounding of his view of analogy in a participatory understanding of trinitarian perichoresis reveals an internal contradiction in his disavowal of analogy as metaphysical epistemology.

We cannot pursue this here at length, but only note the contradiction. Further on in his *Beauty of the Infinite*, in the course of his treatment of the Trinity, we note with puzzlement the following, clearly metaphysical grounding of trinitarian participation. He starts by commenting on the eco-

---

[107]Ibid., p. 301.
[108]Ibid.
[109]Ibid.
[110]Ibid.

nomic Trinity as being full, in its economic mode, of the "accommodations of a supreme ontic principle with inferior reality, but are rather all equally present in every divine action, each wholly God even as they differ."[111] Yet they constitute together, as the *missio Dei*, the one action of God *ad intra* and *ad extra*. In the process of this trinitarian differentiation in unity, Christian theology struggled to account for "what the Areopagite calls (τὸ τῆς οὐσίας διάφορον)."[112] That is, how could theology, with its limited capacity for reference, account for the differentiation of substance under the concept of being, especially of a "highest being"? In the process theology, with no small aid from Pseudo-Dionysius, replaced the *exitus-reditus* procession of the one with "God's perichoresis as unity and difference, and the tragicomic ambiguity of emanated finitude was displaced by the joy of God's immanent diverse fullness and of finitudes gratuity."[113] In Hart's mind, this replacement of substance ontology with the perichoretic unity in difference, which also constitutes an "analogical interval between the Trinitarian infinity and the gift of created glory," is a substitution of a philosophical on-

---

[111]Hart, *Beauty of the Infinite*, p. 182.

[112]Ibid. On "the repetition of essence" see Pseudo-Dionysius, *De ecclesiastica hierarchia*, chap. 4, sect. 3.1. The passage to which Hart refers is precisely summarized by a metaphysics of *exitus-reditus* that he says he disavows. It reads as follows. "The holy consecration, then, which we are now extolling, is, as I said, of the perfecting rank and capacity of the Hierarchical functions. Wherefore our Divine Leaders arranged the same, as being of the same rank and effect as the holy perfecting of the Synaxis, with the same figures, for the most part, and with mystical regulations and lections. And you may see in like manner the Hierarch bearing forward the sweet perfume from the more holy place into the sacred precincts beyond, *and teaching, by the return to the same,* that the participation in things Divine *comes to all holy persons, according to fitness,* and is undiminished and altogether unmoved and stands unchangeably in its identity, as beseems Divine fixity." Clearly this follows the definition Pseudo-Dionysius offers at the head of chap. 3, where he writes, "In my opinion a hierarchy is a sacred order, a state of understanding and an activity approximating as closely as possible to the divine. And it is uplifted to the imitation of God in proportion to the enlightenments divinely given to it" (*De ecclesiastica hierarchia*, chap. 3, sect. 1.1). Further on, in the opening paragraphs of chapter 4 Pseudo-Dionysius explains the participatory foundation of all such hierarchies as summed up in oneness as follows. "One truth must be affirmed above all else. It is that the transcendent Deity has out of goodness established the existence of everything and brought it into being. It is characteristic of the universal Cause, of this goodness beyond all, to summon everything to communion with him to the extent that this is possible. Hence everything in some way partakes of the providence flowing out of this transcendent Deity which is the originator of all that is. Indeed nothing could exist without some share in the being and source of everything. Even the things which have no life participate in this, for it is the transcendent Deity which is the existence of every being" (chap. 4, sect. 1.1). Here it is the absolute oneness of all that pervades the thought of Pseudo-Dionysius.

[113]Hart, *Beauty of the Infinite*, p. 183.

tology for a "theological ontology" that constitutes our knowledge of God as freely transcendent. But could such a theological ontology even deliver the knowledge of God sought after in the "transcendence imaginable within classical metaphysics"?[114]

With these words Hart's free theology of kataphatic excess returns to its rootedness in a Proclan–Pseudo-Dionysian ontology that led Aquinas down a very narrow road of conceivable and knowable predicates. It was to the credit of Barth and Jüngel that they could see through this attempted trinitarian grounding of metaphysics in the Neoplatonic-driven *analogia* of Pseudo-Dionysius and his followers. Clearly what Hart means by *analogia verbi* and what the tradition knows as *analogia entis* exhibit no real "difference in substance." Everything, in terms of the power of signification, is rested in the gift, the glory of God in creation, and insofar as analogy returns this gift it participates in the *analogia verbi* that underwrites it.[115] To go with Hart here would really be a step back rather than a step forward in determining the nature of an analogy of participatory Word. But before we continue further on in our delineation of participation, we should note the recent efforts of an emerging and influential evangelical-Catholic-Reformed theologian, Hans Boersma.

Like those of the radical orthodox group and the Eastern Orthodox faith, Hans Boersma sees the need for a mode of theological discourse that recaptures the sacramental nature of the task. His recent book, *Heavenly Participation*, is the latest of a number of other publications toward this end.[116] It is nothing short of a call to evangelical Christianity to return to a rootedness

---

[114]Ibid.

[115]Ibid.

[116]See also Boersma, "Accommodation to What? Univocity of Being, Pure Nature, and the Anthropology of St. Irenaeus," *IJST* 8 (2006): 266-93; "Analogy of Truth: The Sacramental Epistemology of the Nouvelle Theologie," in Gabriel Flynn and Paul D. Murray, eds., *Ressourcement: A Movement for Renewal in Twentieth-Century Catholic Theology* (Oxford: Oxford University Press, 2013); "Being Reconciled: Atonement as the Ecclesio-Christological Practice of Forgiveness in John Milbank," in James K. A. Smith and James H. Olthuis, *Radical Orthodoxy and the Reformed Tradition: Creation, Covenant, and Participation* (Grand Rapids: Baker Academic, 2005); *The Nouvelle Theologie and Sacramental Ontology: A Return to Mystery* (Oxford: Oxford University Press, 2009); "On the Rejection of Boundaries: Radical Orthodoxy's Appropriation of St. Augustine," *Pro Ecclesia* 15 (2006): 418-47; "Redemptive Hospitality in Irenaeus: A Model for Ecumenicity in a Violent World," *Pro Ecclesia* 11 (2002): 207-26; "Sacramental Ontology: Nature and the Supernatural in the Ecclesiology of Henri de Lubac," *New Blackfriars* 88 (2007): 242-73.

in "truth as a sacramental reality." This is a reality, he claims, "that lies anchored in the truth of the eternal Word of God."[117] His inspiration for this call comes initially from his reading of Milbank and company, but he soon moves beyond them to the *Nouvelle Theologie*, itself the initial influence on Milbank. Indeed, he even sounds like Milbank in terms of positing the theological task as needing to be taken up in the face of the failure of modernity. "The certainty of Cartesian and Baconian methods may long have held sway in Western culture. More and more, however, evangelicals are realizing that the univocal view of truth implied in these methods is deeply problematic—and most certainly unfitting for theological discourse that aims at the mystery of God."[118]

Whatever one might say about this characterization of modernity, and there are as many problems as there are truisms therein, one cannot fault the positive proposal Boersma puts forward in terms of an analogically driven conception of participation. Following one of the later *Nouvelle Theologie*, Henri Bouillard, Boersma calls for an *analogia veritatis*, or an "analogy of truth" that, like Hart's *analogia verbi*, is rooted in a participatory ontology. Equally, like the radical orthodox and the Orthodox position, his, so he claims, is a "theological" ontology rather than an epistemologically driven metaphysical ontology. The term itself is one he takes over directly from the *Nouvelle Theologie*, but the content is very much shaped by his own theological outlook. To begin with, Boersma is much more sensitive to the problematic nature of the *analogia entis* in its historical development, a history that Hart seems wholly oblivious to. In his earlier discussion of this theme (chap. 4) Boersma notes that the concept of analogy that Aquinas adopts and amends places Aquinas

> within the longstanding Platonist-Christian tradition. . . . Following the Great Tradition, he tries to walk the same fine line. On the one hand, because there is a participatory link between our existence and God's, it is possible for us to talk about God in human language. On the other hand, Thomas is also convinced that when we talk about God, we always have to remember the infinite difference that remains.[119]

---

[117]Boersma, *Heavenly Participation*, pp. 6-7.
[118]Ibid., p. 169.
[119]Ibid., p. 73.

By insisting that ultimately, in thought and in word, God is incomprehensible, Aquinas shows himself to be part of the great tradition, and faithful to it. Thus our participation and our analogical speech are "merely" so. Here Boersma attempts to shield Aquinas from the charge that his doctrine of participation actually protects theology from undo Neoplatonic influence. Others remain skeptical of this mitigation of Neoplatonism in Aquinas.[120]

Unlike Hart, however, Boersma rightly draws attention to the tendency toward univocity in late medieval thought, instantiated in Scotus and, as he correctly notes, indemnified in the tendencies of later medieval theology, especially Suárez. But what precisely does Boersma mean by an *analogia veritatis*? Is it equivalent to Aquinas's understanding of analogy, or is it more like that of Suárez? Was there a sacramental conception of analogy, understood as an *analogia veritatis*, that became a dominant mode of doing theology in some period before (perhaps Augustine) or after Aquinas?[121] Perhaps he is following Przywara and von Balthasar, but then neither in his major work on the *Nouvelle Theologie* nor in this smaller missive are we given any indication of his thinking. That aside, what is this form of analogy? Boersma answers:

> This notion is a sacramental principle that seems to underscore two things: on the one hand, it means that, just like a sacrament, human discourse participates in divine truth, so that God's truth is really present in the dogmatic statements of the Church; on the other hand, it also means that, just as with a sacrament, the mystery of the divine truth infinitely transcends the human words themselves.[122]

According to Boersma, this was an approach that the *Nouvelle Theologie*

---

[120]See chap. 3 above and my article "Causality and the '*analogia entis*': Karl Barth's Rejection of Analogy of Being Reconsidered," *NV* 6, no. 2 (2008): 329-76.

[121]His understanding of analogy is very akin to Lewis Ayres's description of Augustine's conception of "discursive analogy," wherein "Augustine models the mind's exercising of itself through showing us his own process of reflecting on different conditions of intelligible and sensible reality. In this process Augustine does not move consistently from corporeal likenesses that are easier to grasp but less revealing to likenesses more difficult to grasp but that better reveal relationships or modes of existence possible within the intelligible realm. Instead Augustine performs for us a discursive interplay between these levels as he tries to draw the mind into recognizing both its abilities to reason about the intelligible and the constant threat that it will be seduced into importing inappropriate material conditions" (Lewis Ayres, *Augustine and the Trinity* [Oxford: Oxford University Press, 2010], pp. 288-89).

[122]Boersma, *Heavenly Participation*, p. 164.

borrowed from Gregory of Nyssa in that "the notion implies real heavenly participation, while at the same time it retains infinite transcendence."[123] But, when Boersma brings this into comparison with the classical concept of *analogia entis*, the same ontology that has been appealed to since Suárez applies. Just as the *analogia entis* was a "sacramental principle" protecting against the Neoplatonic tendency to identify God and creation, so "the analogy of truth" maintains that one can speak not only of "an analogous sacramental relationship between the being of God and that of the creature," but even more so it can also speak of "an analogous or sacramental relationship between the truth of God and the creature."[124]

But, again, one fails to see the real distinction here between truth and being. In Aquinas truth is "being itself," and "being itself" is truth, and the truth of truth is that it is a predicate applied perfectly to God, as is "being itself," and only imperfectly of the creature, as existential being, in a relation of priority and posteriority. The same can be said of the other transcendental categories he mentions, such as goodness and beauty. These are all analogically ordered and may stand in the place of being, or truth, but only in respect to an analogy of one to another where the priority rests on the determination of the quality in God. Once again this is more like an *analogia participationis* than an *analogia veritatis*. The one difference between Boersma's approach to analogy and those of his contemporaries is that he more consciously grounds analogy in the real sense of the Word as *the* sacrament. Here his appropriation of Bouillard's thought, that transubstantiation might actually obscure rather than make plain the divine act, has potential for a true analogy grounded in a sacramental word. In this modality truth itself exists in the nexus of a correspondence between God's decision to be truth in the Word of address in such a way that includes the human capacity for such correspondence.

Here precisely the work of Barth and Jüngel could be brought to bear in an expanded definition of an analogy of participatory Word. In fact, the apprehension one has with respect to all three approaches described thus far is the insufficient christological grounding of participation and Word. All three views resort to an ontology that is ultimately to be found in Neo-

---

[123]Ibid.
[124]Ibid.

platonism before it is found in Jesus Christ the Word. This is not to gainsay the possible accord between Christianity and certain aspects of Neoplatonism, but, as this study has demonstrated, this sort of ontology was more concerned with being and God in himself (*De Deo*), as *ipsum esse subsistens*, than it was with the eternal subsistence (by virtue of a primal divine election) of God and humanity in Christ.[125] From the beginning the principle of participation, grounded as it is in a Neoplatonic-Aristotelian ontology of CER, would direct theology away from its object rather than toward it, so that the kataphatic excess would turn out to be more of an anthropology than theology. In that respect Feuerbach was right.

What then should an analogy of participatory Word look like? Clearly, as per John 1:1-18 and chapter 17, the God-human correspondence must be grounded thoroughly in the participatory nature of the triune relation and procession, but from the perspective of Jesus Christ the *Word* as electing God. In these passages there is a basis for a theology of participation that is defined from the point of God's action in Jesus Christ, exclusively, so that nothing in creation, either as gift or reflection of his glory, predisposes this participation.

In John's Gospel, especially in the prologue and the farewell discourses of John 13–17, there appears to be, in the relationship of Jesus with his disciples, an analogy to the participatory relationship he has with the Father. According to John's Gospel, this relationship of the Father and the Son is often cast in terms of a relationship determined from before time in the primal will of God. "I glorified You on the earth, having accomplished the work which You have given Me to do. Now, Father, glorify Me together with Yourself, with the glory which I had with You before the world was" (Jn 17:4-5). The glory of God in this passage, and this is the sense of the word *glory* throughout John's Gospel, accrues to Jesus Christ as a condition of the Father-Son relation before the cosmos could ever declare such glory. It is completely outside the creaturely world. This is the clear sense of the parallel references to glory to the Father "on earth" (ἐπὶ τῆς γῆς) and "the glory which I had with You before the world was" (as in, started to exist; καὶ νῦν δόξασόν με σύ, πάτερ, παρὰ σεαυτῷ τῇ δόξῃ ᾗ εἶχον πρὸ τοῦ τόν κόσμον

---

[125]See Jüngel's, *God's Being Is in Becoming*, pp. 20-21, 93-98.

εἶναι παρὰ σοί). The unity of the glory that Christ *had* with God, from the beginning, is constitutive of the glory he declares, in the present tense, on earth. The connection between them is clearly the work of God *ad extra* in the phrase "the work which You have given Me to do" (τὸ ἔργον ἐτελείωσα ὃ δέδωκάς μοι ἵνα ποιήσω). Clearly the present work of salvation in the action of the Son is the work elected for him before the world began. But the unity of the Father and the Son consists in a mutual participation, from before all time, in this work, such that the *glory* of God is revealed entirely, and exclusively, in this work.[126]

Creation, the cosmos, is the stage on which this eternal relation is exhibited in the decision of God to submit himself to the temporal expression of this glory. The glory of creation is constituted in and by this divine participation of the Father and Son. The very tenses of the verbs, "I had" (εἶχον, imperfect) and "having finished" (τελειώσας, aorist active participle), indicate a perfection in time of a decision enacted in eternity. It is therefore the work (τὸ ἔργον) of John 17:4 that constitutes the sum of the participatory relation of the Father and Son. What is more, it is having "accomplished" this work. The glory of God is completely constituted in the work of God, that is, in the incarnation of the Word of God. This is the meaning of the prologue as well, when John states in the same past tense, "we saw His glory, glory as of the only begotten from the Father, full of grace and truth."[127] The glory of the Father and of the Son are constituted by the work of God, but

---

[126]The author gratefully acknowledges the fact that there has been much scholarly work completed on the origins, textual development, theology and history of interpretation of the Gospel of John to date. We shall have occasion to draw selectively from these sources and, where necessary, to temper our conclusions with respect to our own interpretation so that we are not taking liberties with the text. However, we retain the rights respective to the fields of historical and systematic theology to have primary regard here for the history of the interpretation of John within the broad framework of orthodox Christianity, especially in recognition of the important role that this Gospel plays in dogmatics. It is to this end that we will, for the next several pages, be primarily concerned with an interpretation of John 17 and the prologue of John's Gospel. An exhaustive exegetical treatment of the whole of John 17, the prologue and other texts is simply beyond the scope of our present endeavor. See also Boersma, *Heavenly Participation*, pp. 40, 188. Boersma calls John 1:1-5 "the key that unlocks the entire Christian message," p. 40. The key is incomplete without verses 14 and 18, however. Hart, *Beauty of the Infinite*, includes in his work a centrally placed exegesis of the English text of the several key Johannine texts including John 1:1; 10:30; 15:26; 17:11. See pp. 178-79.

[127]John 1:14: καὶ ἐθεασάμεθα τὴν δόξαν αὐτοῦ, δόξαν ὡς μονογενοῦς παρὰ πατρός, πλήρης χάριτος καὶ ἀληθείας. Translation: "And we beheld His glory, glory as of the only unique one from the Father, full of grace and truth."

include the capacity of creation both to be the context for the display of this glory and the comprehension of this glory, while not innately in possession of this glory.

Furthermore, this work of participatory glory in John's Gospel is a work of obedience. The full sense of how glory accrues to God the Father in the obedience of the Son is contained in the phrase τὸ ἔργον ἐτελείωσα ὃ δέδωκάς μοι ἵνα ποιήσω, which may also be translated "the work which you gave to me, so that [in order that] I should do." The final verb is in the aorist active subjunctive, clearly emphasizing the character of the work as both a command and an already predetermined accomplishment, again guaranteeing the temporal in the eternal as the substance of the divine revelation in the elected Word. The principle "the works of God *ad extra* and *ad intra* are indivisible" expresses perfectly the procession of God as an eternal decision to declare his glory in and through the obedience of the Son, the mediator, who makes real, knowable and expressible the participation of the Father and the Son in the procession. Twice more in this passage the Gospel writer declares this glory to be "out of this world" in no uncertain terms (Jn 17:14, 16). Jesus Christ is not of this world in respect to his being, the revelation of God: "I have given them Your word; . . . [t]hey are not of the world . . ." καθὼς ἐγὼ οὐκ εἰμὶ ἐκ τοῦ κόσμου, "even as I am not of the world."

When John 15:9; 17:23, 26 refer to the fact that the Father loved the Son, it demonstrates a participation in relation that transcends the expression of the glory of God in the incarnation and includes us by virtue of the aorist tense of ἠγάπησα (Jn 15:9, aorist active indicative). This is a reference to "what is as it was," in terms of what continues as it began in that pretemporal beginning. "Hence Jesus is in the Father (10:38; 14:10, 20; 17:21), the Father is in Him (10:38; 14:10; 17:21, 23), and He and the Father ('we') are one (10:30; 17:11, 22), and so He is sent by the Father into the world (17:3, 8, 18 etc.)."[128] The full extent of the participatory Word is contained in this divine history of salvation. Therefore also, and as such, the full scope of our inclusion in it is guaranteed in the incarnation of the Word, in which our humanity is both defined and determined in the obedience of God, to be our glory. "This is the original, the relationship within the divine being, the inner divine co-

---

[128]*CD* III/2, pp. 220-21.

existence, co-inherence and reciprocity."[129] If the questions arise, How do I participate? What is the constitution of my being in participation? the answer cannot come from "some generally concerned *humanum,*" some perceived cosmological causal resemblance, or some *ratio essende,* apart from Jesus Christ. The resemblance and *ratio* are in him alone. He is true humanity in the correspondence of his obedience to the Father as the guarantor of the possibility and actuality of our being, in his role as electing God and elected man. Participation, as such, cannot be the basis of a similarity or relation or resemblance grounded in a generally intuitable state of affairs. It is truly a revelation. It is truly a revelation as event, in the Word incarnate.

Thus, insofar as we look to the *Word,* λόγος, we see an analogy of participatory Word. "And in full correspondence and similarity there is the relationship between God and man represented within the creaturely world, as a history played out in the cosmos, in the man Jesus, in His fellow humanity, in His relationship to His disciples."[130] This is the possibility and actuality of our participation in God. In that the humanity of Jesus Christ belongs to the Father, in the eternal decision of his will to be for us in Jesus Christ, so also do his disciples. Just as the Son is, therefore, loved, so also, in the same transtemporal tense, are the disciples established in the love of God. The disciples are thus, by analogy of participation, given to the Son by the Father in a double sense. Just as the Son received them from all eternity, they are given to Jesus so that, as the Son is glorified in the Father from all eternity, in the inner life of God, so the glory of the Son is repeated in the history of Jesus Christ. "I have glorified Him [in eternity past] and will glorify Him again [in the temporal realization of eternity future]."[131] The temporal interval is the full display of this glory as the economy of salvation. The double tension of being "in the world" and yet "not of the world" here refers not to the task of the disciple in respect to each domain but rather illustrates the dialectical nature of our twofold participation in the being of God *ad intra* and *ad extra.*

Again, note the parallelism between John 17:5 and John 17:10. The glory

---

[129]*CD* III/2, p. 221.

[130]Ibid.

[131]On the question of the parallel designation of "glory" to both the Son and the Father, see G. B. Caird, "The Glory of God in the Fourth Gospel: An Exercise in Biblical Semantics," *NTS* 15 (1969): 265-77.

that was Christ's in the primal election of God, from all eternity, as δόξασόν, is now applied to Jesus, in exactly the same respect as δεδόξασμαι. The *analogia participationis* continues throughout John 17 and elsewhere in the Gospel. It occurs in respect to the Son not being of the world, so therefore we are not of the world (Jn 17:14, 16). In the same respect that he is in the Father, so we are in him (Jn 14:20). In the same way that the Father is in him, so, analogously, he is in us (Jn 17:23). To the degree that the glory of the Father and the Son is demonstrated in their unity, so also, by analogy, our participation in one another in unity demonstrates that same glory.[132] To the very same degree and in the very same respect that the Son is sent into the world, so also does he send his disciples. Here we would add that the end of Matthew's Gospel envisions the same analogy of participation with respect to mission. We are to go, just as God has gone; we are to proclaim, just as he proclaimed; and our baptism in the name is an inclusion of us in the very being of God in the Word, so that the promise "I am with you always" is an ontological reality of the disciples' existence (Mt 28:19-20).[133]

Under these conditions, certainly with biblical qualifications and expansions from Paul and elsewhere, we may say there is a participation that yields a possibility to speech as a capacity for correspondence. But there is nothing in Scripture to support a direction of participation from humanity upward. We are caused to participate in the Word.

> And if we now read: "Neither pray I for these alone, but for them also which shall believe on me through the Word: they all may be one: as thou, Father, art in me, and I in thee, that they also may be one in us: that the world may believe thou has sent me" (17:20-21), we are obviously reminded, even in this context of the bursting of the inner circle of the community outwards in favor of all men, of the whole world. He who is already glorified by the Father in His relationship to Him is again glorified in them, in His relationship to man. Thus the divine original creates for itself a copy in the creaturely world. The Father and the Son are reflected in the man Jesus. There could be no plainer reference to the *analogia relationis* and therefore the *imago dei* in the most central, i.e. the Christological sense of the term.[134]

---

[132]Ibid., p. 273.
[133]Ibid.
[134]*CD* III/2, p. 222. Elsewhere in the same volume Barth describes the full panorama of the parallelism between the Son and the Father in respect to glory as follows: "There is no 'own,' no 'of

This seems as robust a concept of participation as one might find in the less christologically oriented conception of participation in the Catholic tradition. More importantly, it lies within the boundaries set for it in the biblical witness to our participation in Christ. But has it fully exhausted the biblical concept of participation in God at precisely this point? The answer is, of course, not entirely. It is to the detriment of Barth's theology that he never gets to any real sense of the full procession of God, in the Holy Spirit. This absence of the determination of the God-human relation pneumatologically remains a serious lacuna in Barth's corpus. Its absence is salutary in that it is a reminder to us all that no correspondence between God and the human can be conceived outside the third article of the Creed. It is not that Barth intended to do this, but questions remain as to why he finished the cycle of *CD* before he got to it. Some chalk it up to his health, others to his reticence with respect to the Holy Spirit, already demonstrable from his doctrine of the Trinity. Still others, like Phillip Rosato, see it as a product of his "reduction" of the Holy Spirit to the noetic. Whatever the reason, there were as many resources available in John 13–16 for a robust conception of participation in the Holy Spirit as there were for the Father-Son relation in John 17.

Despite this assessment, however, others are more inclined to see a positive role of the Spirit in Barth precisely in respect to his understanding of the Holy Spirit and participation. John E. Colwell has gone a good distance in confirming this interest on Barth's part. The possibility of both the place of the Son and the Holy Spirit is guaranteed in Barth by the principle of Jesus Christ as electing and elected. "The primal decision of God is prior, not simply in a chronological sense as that which has always been from the very beginning, but in an ontological sense as the basis of the actualization of man's election in Jesus Christ."[135] As such, then, "the actualization of God's

---

Himself, no neutral sphere, from which things might be sought or said or done as from the seat of a will distinct from that of His Father. But what then does He seek, say and do? He does His works by the command and authority and in the name of His Father (10:25). . . . And on this ground Jesus did not hesitate to adopt the absolute ἐγώ εἰμι—spoken without predicate—of the Old Testament God ([Jn] 8:24, 58, 13:19). In the sense of Deut. 32:39, and also in the sense of these Johannine texts, the implication is: 'I am He who alone can heal' He thus described and claimed as His own the δόξα only for God (2:11, 9, 16, 11:40), as is affirmed by the Prologue: 'We beheld his glory' (1:14)" (pp. 63-64).

[135]John E. Colwell, *Actuality and Provisionality: Eternity and Election in the Theology of Karl Barth* (Eugene, OR: Wipf and Stock, 2011), p. 280 n. 54.

eternal degree in the event of Jesus Christ ontologically comprehends the real event of man's participation in Jesus Christ" in that the eternal decision of God includes, from the beginning, "the history in which it is made visible and becomes operative as the Word of God, proclaimed and received."[136] This event happens "in the pure simultaneity of God's time" and "man's actual participation in the election of Jesus Christ."[137] As such our participation is a dependent participation. Just as the election of Jesus Christ is God's eternal will, so also is our participation in this election. The ultimate ground of this participation is the perfection of God. "It is something isolated and complete."[138] Thus it is "the foreordination which precedes all creaturely life." It cannot be assailed on any grounds within the creature or creation. "It has the character not only of an unparalleled 'perfect' but also of an unparalleled 'present' and future."[139] It is before, with and after time in the sense that it is determined in the one eternity of God. It is a happening that has "happened" and "is the principle of all happening everywhere." As an act of the divine will, therefore, it is also a performative word. As such we may also say that there is an analogy of performative Word.

But how do we know that history, the temporality of the man Jesus Christ of Nazareth, is not some mere Platonic form, over against which the real is placed in transcendental perfection? Because, and this marks as a crucial difference between biblical and classical definitions of participation, "the relationship between Jesus Christ and other men is not just ontological, it is also authentically dynamic, though the dynamic is never independent of the ontological."[140] That is to say, participation is trinitarian. It is an event of the threefold self-repetition of God as a primal decision of the Father, the performative act of the Son, and the realization of the Holy Spirit.[141] As Colwell correctly points out, for Barth, "the work of the Holy Spirit is no more an addendum to the completed work of the Son than the work of the Son is an addendum to the eternal decision of the Father, rather the Holy Spirit makes this completed work subjectively known and real (because objectively

---

[136]Ibid., p. 281.
[137]Ibid.
[138]Ibid.; CD II/2, p. 183.
[139]CD II/2, p. 183.
[140]Ibid.
[141]CD IV/1, p. 158.

known and real) in the life of the individual."[142] God is reconciling God, and humanity is reconciled humanity, not only because God is, himself, this God and this man, and this reconciler and reconciled, this lost and this found, but also because "it is in His Holy Spirit that it is present and an event for us."[143] He, the Holy Spirit, is "the fixed point from which there can be these later developments." In this sense, also, "the Spirit constitutes the subjective condition which is necessary for the apprehension and recognition of the self-manifestation of God in Christ; for the Spirit is God knowing Himself, and to receive the Spirit is to participate in that knowledge."[144] The analogy of participation requires this subjective reception of the Holy Spirit as its only real temporal possibility. "Because the participation of individual man in the election of Jesus Christ is an event of the Holy Spirit, it is an event of God's freedom, an event in which He remains free Lord in respect of the actual realization of His ontological definition of man in the existence of individual men."[145] In the Holy Spirit our participation is assured as a divine, free act. The whole of Barth's treatment of the Christian life and reconciliation trades on this participatory possibility made real in the calling and gift of the Holy Spirit. It is the definition, goal and content of our lives as the elect of God. It is a participation in community because it is a participation determined in the triunity of God.[146]

Of course, a caution is in order here before we pass over into a full description of the preformative aspect that the analogy of participatory Word envisions. There is a sense in which, in our time, the issues of analogy, participation, performance and parable, along with other circumstantial theological conceptualities, are displacing the main thrust of the material content. As Webster correctly notes, the ultimate concerns of dogmatics are decided in respect to its *materia*, wherein circumstantial issues must be subordinated. This is true not only of the issue of analogy in general, but of this and other treatments of the themes related to it. Ultimately we must be about the "illumination of the Gospel, of which it is a conceptual celebration," and as

---

[142]Colwell, *Actuality and Provisionality*, p. 284.
[143]Ibid.
[144]*CD* IV/1, p. 158.
[145]Colwell, *Actuality and Provisionality*, p. 284.
[146]*CD* II/2, p. 449; *CD* II/2, pp. 345-49; *CD* IV/1, p. 6.

such we "ought not to distort theology's relation to its proper object."[147] Precisely this can become the case with the concept of participation. Webster is correct to note that one should remain "uneasy" with some of the uses to which participation has been put of late.[148] He sees it as having "slender exegetical foundations," but he also worries about "its often drastically schematic history of Christian thought, and its apparent lack of concern with the hypertrophy or atrophy of some tracts of Christian teaching."[149] One such neglected tract, in his mind, is the doctrine of the perfection of God, which he identifies as the larger material concern that shapes any conception of participation and/or analogy. We have already seen the importance of this in Barth's approach. In this respect Webster thinks the Reformed tradition has much to offer, especially "its most sublime modern exposition in the work of Karl Barth." Much more than a mere "transcription of modernity's defects," Barth's own treatment of divine perfection makes such criticism of his work hard to sustain.[150]

> In its most measured and intelligent expositions, when [Reformed theology] has been determined to keep its eye on scripture and eager to learn from catholic Christianity, that tradition has been able to shake itself free from a dialectical metaphysics without recourse to the opposite, and to commend a theology of God's perfection, which is the eternal depth of His creative triune goodness as the one who loves, elects, accompanies, reconciles, and glorifies creatures, so making resplendent His own glory.[151]

Our own approach here would do well to remember these admonitions, and indeed to place our understanding of analogy as participatory word, performative word and parabolic word under this larger material concern.

For instance, we would do well to remind ourselves that God's perfection is "the limitless abundance of his life, the sheer plenitude that he is in himself

---

[147]John Webster, "Perfection and Participation," in White, *Analogy of Being*, p. 381.

[148]See Todd Billings, *Participation in Calvin* (Oxford: Oxford University Press, 2005). Billings mistakes Calvin's basis for an appeal to participation as existing in a form of perfection understood as Neoplatonic *methexis*. But Calvin's understanding of participation is strictly limited to participation in Jesus Christ as determined in the history of Jesus Christ with humanity and not in a general creational understanding of participation, of which Calvin is not a little suspicious.

[149]Webster, "Perfection and Participation," p. 380.

[150]Ibid.

[151]Ibid.

as Father, Son and Spirit." His perfection is "the infinite ocean from which flows the tide of God's long act toward creatures."[152] In all of its parts, therefore, dogmatics will be concerned to explicate this perfection. It can only be this material concern that dictates dogmatics in all its parts. Insofar as it does this, it is explication and repetition of the divine name "I am He" (Is 41:4). Christian theology cannot, therefore, be, or go along with, the accounts of the philosophies of religion as such. The God of the Bible is not even able to gain ascendency over their respective "deities." Such a being only emerges "out of the need for a perfect being as causal explanation of features of the contingent world."[153] Such philosophical accounts remain forgetful, in both their modern and premodern modalities, of the triunity of God. "The doctrine of the Trinity plays little role, the weight of the edifice being borne by deity, its logical structure and cosmological function."[154]

The perfection of God observable in Scripture is that of Father, Son and Holy Spirit, the perfection of whose inner life is the source of all creaturely life. Philosophical concepts of God subsume this notion "beneath the project of determining the necessary attributes of a supreme causal power from which all things can be explained." The result is a God who is built more on the image of creation, leading in consequence to "an insufficiently determinate concept of divine perfection."[155] However, if theology keeps its eye on Scripture and is attuned to the best aspect of the tradition, it is able to point to God's "singular, noncomparative, nonderivitive identity."[156] When first we say that God is God, that he comes from himself and goes to himself, then we are able to determine, dogmatically, the "sheer originality and singularity of the one who displays and magnifies his inherent perfection in the history of the covenant and supremely in the missions of the Word and the Spirit."[157]

Taken in the context of these material concerns, what then may we say about an analogy of participatory Word, and the *analogia entis* in particular? Certainly those who promote an *analogia entis* must not just dismiss the

---

[152]Ibid., p. 381.
[153]Ibid.
[154]Ibid.
[155]Ibid., p. 382.
[156]Ibid.
[157]Ibid.

broad lines of Barth's rejection but must also attend to where it makes a dogmatic difference in his system of thought, as, for instance, his doctrines of election and providence, both of which we have covered herein. But Reformed dogmatics may also learn from its interlocutors, in correcting the distinctions of its own theology. "There is nothing self-evidently pantheistic about theologies of participation, no obvious compromise of the distinction between the agenetic and the genetic orders of reality."[158] But neither will a Reformed dogmatics rush to judgments about its own conceptions and proclamation based on the hearsay of its interlocutors. We cannot expect to increase the "catholicity" of the faith by a rush to judgment either way. Neither can we add a lick to the perfection of dogmatics in doing so. Instead, a truly Reformed dogmatics will be guided by some basic rules of thumb in respect to catholic dialogue. "The first is that any account of the relation of God's perfect life in himself to created reality will be adequate to the degree to which it is shaped and formed by the biblical canon."[159] That is, it must be "warranted" by Scripture and/or "required" by Scripture. This is also true of any conceptions of participation as well. In the imagery Barth used in his *Evangelical Theology*, we do not stand over the shoulders of the prophets and apostles to correct their "theological exercise books"; rather, they stand over us, correcting our theological "exercise books."[160]

Second, we need an "anatomy of the economy" of biblical revelation as a set of concepts that are secondary to the biblical description of God in his relation to creation. That is, certain material concerns will assert mastery over the merely occasional concerns. Thus, for instance, issues like election, reconciliation, providence and covenant will exercise a determinative influence on the narrative, since they are constitutive of what God is doing in the story of redemption. Finally, dogmatics will not be required to wait for the findings of metaphysics to arrive. Certainly dogmatics must not displace exegesis in favor of metaphysics, either, for reasons of tediousness or unwillingness to be corrected thereby. Exegetical correction is the essence of the dogmatic enterprise, and it fails to be true to itself when it refuses to submit

---

[158]Ibid., p. 387.
[159]Ibid., p. 388.
[160]Ibid., p. 387. See Karl Barth, *Evangelical Theology: An Introduction* (Grand Rapids: Eerdmans, 1985).

to this. With these caveats in mind, however, it is possible for theology to find a modality of analogy in which language may serve theology. Webster's conclusion is thus salutary.

> If this, or something like it, is what is meant by the *analogia entis*, then the polemical situation looks rather different; if this is what Barth failed or refused to see, then he deserves to be taken to task. But Ephesians ought at least to register the question whether God's goodness is such that he is beyond ontological difference. It is without doubt easy to slide into a mythological account of the divine economy, in which God is simply a magnified voluntary agent, contracted to certain relations and acts: however infinite the magnification, it always misses God's true infinity.[161]

It is hard to tell whether indeed Webster thinks that, on balance, the *analogia entis* has been susceptible to this, but the warning comes out of his reading of the history of dogmatics and is greatly informed by Barth's critique of the tradition, so we may take from him, and Barth still, these cautions in respect to analogy and its hybrids, including participation. These cautions will now follow us into the second possibility for analogy, the analogy as performative word.

The possibility of theology as the analogy of performative word. To say the least, the redemptive action of God is presented in dramatic fashion in the Bible as a whole. As such, God is a dramatic God. If the cosmos is the stage on which this drama unfolds, then God is the performative force of the play. But if the human creature has been included, from the eternal decision in Jesus Christ to be for the creature, then, as covenant partner, we too have an act to perform, one given to us in the electing and elected God-Man, Jesus Christ. In this way the human act is performed in analogy to the divine act, but the divine act is the basis of the possibility of this similarity in performance. Language, as such, is performative and so may be called on, again in analogical fashion, to reflect the drama of the divine in the order of salvation. Indeed the Scriptures begin with such a "performative function of language," ascribed solely to God.

> By the word of the LORD the humans were made,
> And by the breath of His mouth all their host. . . .

---

[161]Webster, "Perfection and Participation," p. 394.

For He spoke, and it was done;
He commanded, and it stood fast. (Ps 33:6, 9)

In sum, God acts in and through his performative Word of address, and the content of the script is his covenant with humanity, in which script humanity is given and created for a definitive performance of their own. "But our primary emphasis must not be upon the fact of this accompaniment of history of the covenant of grace by that of creaturely being, this coordination, integration and co-operation of the later," but that it "is the work of God."[162]

God's address to the human, in his performative Word of creation, is not only the causal power of creation but also designates a role to creation in that it is given a particular place in the drama. From the beginning we are called not only to be addressed but to address, as responsible agents who are the "stewards of creation" and as such are given "dominion." This is all the language of performance, act and corresponding address, and the Scriptures everywhere employ this language. Performative language is, as such, "self-involving" but it is also necessarily narrative, prose, history, poetry and report. Between actors, scripts and the drama that unfolds, the performative analogy between God's Word of address and our obedient response becomes the basis of our capacity for such performance.

Contemporary theology, in some sectors, has seen somewhat of a revival in such performative approaches to grounding the theological task. We shall look, briefly, at two such attempts, that of von Balthasar's *Theo-Drama* and an evangelical attempt influenced by his approach by Kevin J. Vanhoozer in *The Drama of Doctrine: A Canonical Linguistic Approach to Christian Theology*. The latter has much to commend in respect to drawing out an *analogia dramatis in verbi*. But before we go there we should offer a brief summary of some of the theoretical background with respect to the performative aspect of language, with the goal to simply point out that all language has a performative aspect, though it is also more than this. Issues of genre, grammar, sociality and indication also play key roles in the way language functions, so we must caution ourselves against making too much of the performative aspect. That said, however, it is clear that verbal performance is a key aspect of the dynamic of revelation in Scripture, so we should mine

---

[162]CD III/3, p. 41.

it for its linguistic potential to speak of divine revelation.

Why would we choose the word *performance* here and not *drama*? In recent times the performative aspect of language has been theoretically laid out in the works of linguists such as Donald Evans, John L. Austin and John R. Searle.[163] The performative function of language is an underlying motif in much of the existentialist works of the nineteenth and twentieth centuries, especially in Kierkegaard, Bultmann, Fuchs and Heidegger.[164] "Existentialist models of hermeneutics have sought to capture the dimension of self-involvement and audience-related address which such texts pre-suppose. But the era of existentialism, associated especially with Heidegger and Bultmann, has largely passed."[165] Nevertheless, this movement did provide some insights as to how language functions, namely, by means of the principle of "self-involvement." For us, performance must be expanded from the concept of self-involvement to include the larger sphere of divine-human correspondence. It is theologically axiomatic that in revelation God is "self-involved" from all eternity. But few have thought to apply this principle to language itself, and therefore speech as the self-involvement of God, particularly as λόγος, as event, as performative Word (Jn 1:1-18). Austin uses this aspect of existentialist hermeneutics to explore "the logical connections" between texts that focus on origins, or "creation texts," and the actual coming-to-be of the physical universe. In the creation texts of the Bible, the Word of God is seen as a "causal power" in the sense of the actual speaking bringing about the actual "states of affairs." This is due to the "executive force" of the divine *fiat*, and thus one may call such language "performative."[166] In such events it is not just a matter of the linguistic observation of an aggregate coming-to-be from nothing, through force, but of a performative role assigned to the entity that comes to be. These "states" of affairs that mark this coming to be, in their linguistic expression, call the readers first to a certain status, in this case creatures, and then to an address, in the case of the Bible a revelation of God's Word, and finally to a responsible role as actors. But in biblical literature every one of these linguistic positions has its analogy in the prior action of God.

---

[163]See Anthony C. Thistleton, *New Horizons in Hermeneutics* (Grand Rapids: Zondervan, 1992), pp. 271-72 nn. 1-54.
[164]Ibid., p. 273.
[165]Thistleton, *New Horizons*, p. 274.
[166]Ibid.

The performative Word of God, which, as we have seen, is eternally electing God and elected human, includes the call of our humanity in Christ to correspond to this performative Word. To the degree that God is Creator, we participate in creation; to the degree that he is actor, we have our corresponding act; to the degree that he addresses us, in him through Jesus Christ as man for God and God for man, we address him. Or as Jüngel puts it so succinctly, *Gottes spict der Mensch entspricit; Der Mensch sprict Gottes entsprict.*[167] The christological determination of the human is the ground of all such performative correspondence. But in Scripture this correspondence in act does not rest only on an existential hermeneutic of encounter as such, since, as Austin correctly notes, "for a certain performative utterance to effectively involve people and perform acts, certain statements have to be true."[168] That is, there is a "correspondence to facts" that mark such speech acts as authentic correspondence. Donald Evans, in his *Logic of Self-Evident Involvement*, employs Austin's approach to cause-effect language not to the self-evident sensory intuition of the universe, but to states of affairs in which self-involvement is the key to understanding the cosmos. Thus the linguistic description of the origins of creation in the Bible cannot be confined to mere narrative or the logic of responding to states of affairs. The language of self-involvement is the key to the linguistic capacity to describe these states of affairs. In other words, language does not function apart from human knowing, truth telling and revelatory proclamation. It is itself caught up in the enterprise. To the degree that this is true of language, theology is free to explore the depths to which performative language may appropriate, analogically, this mutual divine-human correspondence that sits at its heart.

Indeed there have been a few very sophisticated attempts at doing so, with some significant results that are worth exploiting as a contribution to an analogy of performative word. One such approach comes from the second movement of von Balthasar's massive Theological Trilogy, namely, his five-volume Theo-Drama, the first volume of which is titled *Theo-Drama: Theological Dramatic Theory: Prolegomena.* The Theo-Drama is really the heart of his trilogy, following on his first movement, *Theological Aesthetics*, and in its final movement, *Theo-Logic.* These correspond to the disciplines

---

[167]See *GMW*, p. 296.
[168]See Thistleton, *New Horizions*, p. 275 nn. 7-8.

of aesthetics, which is theophany or revelation, and dramatic theory, which is theopraxy and logic, but as theologic. "These three parts cannot be separated from one another."[169] Von Balthasar's "dramatic" dogmatics demonstrates no small influence from the Protestant schools of hermeneutics and dogmatics, despite his intention, as a Catholic theologian, to sacramentalize these influences in order to demonstrate the "heart" of Catholic theology. As a pattern of the full implications of an *analogia dramatis*, we may certainly learn the scope of a possible analogy of performative Word. But we must also note its limits. It is to Vanhoozer's credit that he has been able to employ von Balthasar's approach while avoiding its pitfalls.

We cannot offer anything like a comprehensive treatment of von Balthasar's proposal for a theo-drama here. This would require a whole study of its own, since it takes him five hefty volumes to explicate it.[170] Rather, here we are interested in the implications his theo-drama has for analogy, especially in its performative-linguistic aspect. Vanhoozer correctly identifies the term *theo-drama* as a reference to the action of God as Creator, reconciler and redeemer, as described in the Scriptures.[171] It is a drama in which, for von Balthasar, the church itself is "caught up."[172] In fact Vanhoozer sees von Balthasar's whole approach as caught up in the navigation of the difficult relationship between divine and human action. Taking his cue from speech-act theory, as does Vanhoozer to some degree, von Balthasar is interested in drama as a way of avoiding the predetermination of the relationship in metaphysical terms, using metaphysical categories. The recapture of the narrative, performative and self-involved nature of language offers a new possibility for describing the God-human correspondence. The key component is, however, action. "The Gospel is something said about something done."[173] It is, for von Balthasar, epitomized in the Eucharist. "Here, basically, theater is the self-actualizing analogy between creation and redemption: the analogy is discovered and beheld in the full seriousness of truth made manifest but

---

[169]Von Balthasar, *Theo-Drama* 1:15-17.

[170]For the ecumenical significance of von Balthasar's trilogy, see R. A. Howsar, *Hans Urs von Balthasar and Protestantism: The Ecumenical Implications of His Theological Style* (Edinburgh: T & T Clark, 2005).

[171]Vanhoozer, *Drama of Doctrine*, p. 17.

[172]Ibid.

[173]Ibid., p. 46.

keeps an awareness of the fluidity of meanings, an awareness that recognizes creation in its functionality (and to that extent its reality), sees through it and allows it its limited validity."[174] Here, divine act, speech and symbol are brought together in one performative analogy in which the being of God and the being of creation are dialectically related in the symbol of the bread and wine.

The correspondence inheres in each as act: the act of God, the act of the Word, as it comes to us, and the act of remembrance in which the human finds its corresponding act. God's act of creation is spoken (Gen 1:1) and is enacted in a single Word (Jn 1:1-18). Vanhoozer writes, "This is a point of far-reaching significance: speaking is one of the things that God does: speaking is one of God's mighty acts."[175] One could go further and affirm that God is as he speaks because his being and action are one. Insofar as the λόγος is the one speech-act of God, the λόγος is itself God's being in act. This is the act determined in Jesus Christ, from all eternity, in that he is electing God, and as such determines to be spoken as this λόγος ἄσαρκος in the eternal decision, in his temporal identity with Jesus Christ of Nazareth, but as eternal dimension to be so identified. The self-preserving of this eternally spoken λόγος is not limited to an act of repeated symbols from the human side but is eternally enacted in the procession of God from the Father and the Son, in the Holy Spirit (Jn 16:13-15). Unfortunately, though von Balthasar sees this connection between human and divine action well, his limitation of it to the Catholic Church alone is regrettable, as is his insistence that it can only be properly mediated in the Catholic conception of the Mass.[176]

However, the act of God in language has been recognized as a modality of correspondence since Origen, who often spoke of a triple incarnation of Word (λόγος) in theophanies, in the incarnation of the Word in Jesus Christ and in the incarnation of the Word in Scripture, the very words themselves being the enfleshment of the λόγος.[177] Again Vanhoozer hints at this in his

---

[174]Von Balthasar, *Theo-Drama* 1:117.

[175]Vanhoozer, *Drama of Doctrine*, pp. 46-47.

[176]Von Balthasar, *Theo-Drama* 1:117.

[177]See K. J. Torjesen, *Hermeneutical Method and Exegetical Procedure in Origen of Alexandria* (Tübingen: de Grutyer, 1989). See also my "Influences on Origen's Doctrine of the Incarnation" (ThM thesis, Regent College, 1994), p. 150.

reference to Hebrews 1:1-2 but misses the history of this concept in Alexandrian thought. Von Balthasar is quick to attribute this form of the conception of revelation as speech-act in Origen, especially in its connection with divine-human correspondence. "In the suffering of the God-Man a role has been left for the believer, and evidently it is not a superfluous or dispensable one (Col. 1:24); the action and passion of Christ can rightly be termed 'symbolic' (Origen) in view of the interpretation of this 'symbol' by the body of Christ, which is the church."[178] Of course, von Balthasar fails to see, in this appeal to Origen, that there is an eclipse of the body of Christ and the literal Word, such that real correspondence in Origen is only given lip service, while all action is absorbed into the single, eternal divine act. In this respect the church itself would not represent a true correspondence in God but merely its "symbolic" realization. It is precisely the freedom of the Holy Spirit, as the realization of all true correspondence in act, that prevents such a reduction. Vanhoozer is sensitive to this possibility in von Balthasar's approach when he criticizes it in respect to Barth's conception of "speech-act." "The germ of the idea is present in the Fourth Gospel itself. Balthasar admires Goethe's translation of John 1:1 *'Am Anfange awar die Tat'* (In the beginning was the deed). By placing Goethe's translation in tension with John, Balthasar produces the notion of *Tatwort* (deed-word)."

Where Barth mentions speech-acts (*Rede-tat*), von Balthasar thinks of deed-words as being qualitatively different, though on closer investigation the difference appears to be only semantic.[179] The two emphases can be combined under the broader rubrics of divine discourse and communicative action. "God's words do 'many and various' things: God asks question (Gen. 4:9), makes promises (Gen. 12:2) and issues commands (Gen. 22:2)."[180] Vanhoozer is quite correct to see that the concept of deed-word cannot display the full correspondence of the divine-human act. "God speaks in and through human words, not only to reveal but to promise, exhort, command, warn," etc. Scripture is thus a "vital ingredient in the economy of divine communicative action." Indeed, in respect to the Word as *witness*,

---

[178]Spencer, "Influences on Origen's Doctrine of the Incarnation," p. 151.
[179]See especially Barth's exposition of the prologue of John's Gospel in his *Witness to the Word* (Grand Rapids: Eerdmans, 1987), p. 14.
[180]Vanhoozer, *Drama of Doctrine*, pp. 47-48.

Scripture is *the* vital ingredient.[181] What is the place of the Word in the economy of the whole complex of God, the world, humanity, the witnesses and believers? What role does it play? What is its path from him who speaks it to those who hear it? That is, what takes place, and where is it spoken and heard? Finally, at the climax, who is the Word? But this brings us to the point where the concept has served its turn, where the reality of Jesus Christ that is concealed in the proclamation of the Evangelist takes its place with power, where the equation is solved: "Καὶ αὕτη ἐστὶν ἡ μαρτυρία τοῦ Ἰωάννου, ὅτε ἀπέστειλαν, Jn. 1:19."[182] The *Word* is the one, single speech-act of God. "The Word is where God is. Hence it must belong to God and be of the same nature as God. No more and no less than God Himself was and is needed if the Word is there, and is and *will be* spoken. He *had* to speak it. But He *has* spoken it. And He speaks it *again*. To this Word, the human word of the Evangelist bears witness."[183] Scripture, as witness, is the very meeting point of the divine-human correspondence, the divine-human performance in analogical terms. Theology as a human word thus may correspond to the divine Word, if only analogically.

It is interesting that in the history of theology we have always required an analogical understanding of the correspondence between divine and human being, but not its speech as act. Yet it would appear that this *analogia dramatis in verbi*, as described by von Balthasar, precedes any *analogia entis* in every way. Thus the need for a nonmetaphysical theology of drama, or better a dramatic theology, seems called for. More could be said, of course, about von Balthasar's proposal and indeed has been said.[184] But

---

181See Barth, *Witness to the Word*, p. 27.

182Ibid.

183Ibid.

184Much has been written in respect to the aesthetic-dramatic aspect of von Balthasar's theology. The most important works include P. Casarella, "The Expression and Form of the Word: Trinitarian Hermeneutics and the Sacramentality of Language in Hans Urs von Balthasar's Theology," *Renascence* 48 (Winter 1996): 111-35; Louis Dupre, "The Glory of the Lord: Hans Urs von Balthasar's Theological Aesthetic," in David L. Schindler, ed., *Hans Urs von Balthasar: His Life and Work* (San Francisco: Ignatius, 1991), pp. 183-20; Jeffrey Ames Kay, "Balthasar: A Post-Critical Theologian?," in Gregory Baum and Marcus LeFebure, eds., *Neoconservatism: Social and Religious Phenomenon* (Edinburgh: T & T Clark, 1981), pp. 84-89; Kay, *Theological Aesthetics: The Role of Aesthetics in the Theological Method of Hans Urs von Balthasar* (Bern: Herbert Lang, 1975); John R. Kevern, "Form in Tragedy: Balthasar as Correlational Theologian," *Communio* 21 (Summer 1994): 311-30; Manfred Lochbrunner, *Analogia caritatis: Darstellung und Deutung der Theologie Hans Urs von Balthasars* (Freiburg: Herder, 1981); John J. O'Donnell, *Hans Urs von*

we have established enough here to point us in a direction that exceeds the narrow confines of von Balthasar's ecclesially driven *Theo-Drama*. Vanhoozer's proposal for an *analogia dramatis* comes much closer to what we intend and thus deserves our attention before we offer our own analogy of performative Word.

Vanhoozer is currently a leading American evangelical theologian whose interest in the problems associated with Scripture, tradition and theological hermeneutics led him to the establishment of a new modality of theology in the evangelical Protestant vein. The tenor of his publications prior to *The Drama of Doctrine* gave every indication of what this new proposal was to become. It is ecumenical in scope, Reformed-evangelical in orientation and superbly scriptural/canonical in substance. While taking his cue for the theme of drama from von Balthasar and the linguistics of performative act, he has very effectively adapted it to the evangelical concerns for revelatory authority based on the Protestant principle of *sola Scriptura*. But one would do a great disservice to Vanhoozer by narrowing its scope to a specifically evangelical set of issues, or even by limiting it to an exercise in theological method in the service of such a narrow concern. This is a work of dogmatics in and of itself. Its subtitle, *A Canonical Linguistic Approach to Christian Doctrine*, places it within the scope of the current, broad ecumenical discussion. At the same time, Vanhoozer is influenced by George Lindbeck's *Nature of Doctrine*, von Balthasar's *Theo-Drama* and Barth's revelatory theology of the Word as dynamic divine act.[185] It is, in short, a rare example of North American evangelical engagement of critical sources, modalities and influences on contemporary theology that does not surrender its evangelical outlook. It does, however, deeply enrich that outlook by virtue of this ecumenical engagement. His purpose is clearly and very positively stated in the preface. Vanhoozer writes, "This present book sets forth a post-conservative, canonical-linguistic theology, and a directive

---

Balthasar (London: Geoffrey Chapman, 1992); Edward Oakes, *Pattern of Redemption: The Theology of Hans Urs von Balthasar* (New York: Continuum, 1994); Angelo Scola, *Hans Urs von Balthasar: A Theological Style* (Grand Rapids: Eerdmans, 1995); David Stuart Yeago, "The Drama of Nature and Grace: A Study in the Theology of Hans Urs von Balthasar" (PhD diss., Yale University, 1992).

[185]See George Lindbeck, *The Nature of Doctrine: Theology in a Postliberal Age* (New Haven, CT: Yale University Press, 1987).

theory of doctrine that roots theology more firmly in Scripture while preserving Lindbeck's emphasis on practice."[186]

Leaving aside his references to "postconservative theology," the meaning of which is dubious, what is of interest is the connection between drama (practice, action), canon and linguistics. For him, this approach involves accounting for human "saying" and "doing" and their relationship to divine "saying" and "doing." The two are not to be separated in a privileging of theory over praxis or vice versa. The Bible renders one concept that combines these in a perfect performance that is divine in its source and orientation, namely, "the Word" (λόγος), which is nothing less than the revelation of the God of the gospel. "The task of theology is to enable hearers and doers of the Gospel to respond and to correspond to the prior Word and act of God, and to be thus drawn into this action."[187] The location of this "performative Word" is Scripture as a whole. The performative "voice" of God is its core unitive reality. God's voice is his act, and his act is his voice, from the performative act of creation, "In the beginning . . . God said, 'Let there be light'" (Gen 1:3), to the covenantal drama that God undertakes to act on behalf of humanity in Noah, Abraham, Israel, David and Jesus Christ, the latter being the "very Word" to such a degree that we may identify God in and with this performative "Word."[188] While the locus classicus is John 1:1-18, we may also witness to this performative Word as the substance of all God's acts recorded in Scripture.[189]

> The Word of God can be parsed in several different ways: (1) a divine communication via human language (Mark 1:11); (2) the person of Jesus Christ (John 1:14-18); (3) the preaching of the Gospel, especially by the apostles (Acts 4:31); (4) the Words of Scripture (2 Tim. 3:16). At times the discussion of how these senses interrelate has been distorted by the tendency to make divine revelation the overarching category. God's speech does more, however, than make God known.[190]

That is, when we limit God's revelation to mere saying without doing, or

---

[186]Vanhoozer, *Drama of Doctrine*, p. xiii.
[187]Ibid., pp. 44-45.
[188]Ibid.
[189]Ibid.
[190]Ibid., p. 45.

mere doing without saying, we undercut revelation itself, which is always and at all times both at once.[191] The tendency to downplay the act in favor of the "written Word" or the "written Word" in favor of the act alone is to obviate the substance of revelation on one side for the other.[192] The key to avoiding this dialectic is to approach the speech act of God from the perspective of canon. "An adequate doctrine of Scripture must locate the canon in the broader economy of the Gospel."[193] It seems that Vanhoozer wants to locate God's performative act in such a way that it is more clearly discernible, nameable and therefore speakable. For this reason Scripture, as canon (as a moment in the history of God's redemptive act that is clearly marked off and can be pointed to), must be elevated above all other claims to such revelatory knowledge. "The Bible is the means by which the apostolic memory of what God was doing in Christ is given specificity and substance."[194] If indeed we are to "locate" the moment of "light" implied in the creative act (Gen 1:3) that is clearly visible on the scene of history, as a coming of God in Word and deed, then we must agree with Vanhoozer, Barth and the whole of Reformation thought that Jesus Christ is this exclusive Word. Thus "the Bible— not only the Gospels but all of Scripture—is the (divinely) authorized version of the Gospel, the necessary framework for understanding what God was doing in Jesus Christ. Scripture is the voice of God that articulates the Word of God: Jesus Christ."[195]

This position has enormous consequences for the capacity of language to convey such a revelatory performance. Language is not, nor was it ever, a mere "tool for information processing." It has within its very structure ontological consequences. Language as "communicative action" is the very witness of God's capacity and freedom to include within himself, as essential to his being, this communicative act. The Scriptures are replete with the witness to this essential nature of the acting God. From creation to exodus, from settlement to exile, in promise and in deed, Jesus Christ is the summation of all such performance, canonically speaking. When Christian theology forms its predicates, names its divinity, describes its

---

[191]Ibid.
[192]Ibid.
[193]Ibid., p. 45 n. 38.
[194]Ibid., p. 46.
[195]Ibid.

place in this salvation history, it participates, by the very language it uses, and thus by analogy, in this performative Word. "The task of theology is to ensure that we fit into the action so that we are following rather than opposing Jesus Christ."[196]

Vanhoozer has a designation for such theological work. He calls it *analogia dramatis* in contradistinction to von Balthasar's *Theo-Drama*. Whereas von Balthasar seems more concerned to base theology on some "ideal" or "experience," an *analogia dramatis*, rather, is concerned with "understanding how God brings covenantal blessings out of a situation of covenantal unfaithfulness."[197] Language is properly engaged in analogy when it does not substitute a metaphysics of idea, or the infinite, for the prima facie act of redemption.[198] Further along in the same chapter he clarifies this concept in connection with what he calls an analogy of communicative action. This is precisely the linguistic function of "passing on" (*paradosis*), via translation, interpretation and "patterns of communicative action," the substance of the divine act as far as analogy will allow. Thus theology is a task in and for the church. It is its "mission." But theology must be careful in respect to such an analogical communication.

> As we shall see, the analogy is not guaranteed simply by repeating as if by rote the same form of words. No, the analogy between divine communicative action and the church's communicative action is the analogy of word-deeds and deed-words. Only when the church's speech and action are analogous to the divine communicative action [as an *analogia dramatis*] does it *participate* in the divine mission to the world. Theology's special task is to preserve the integrity of the church's communicative action.[199]

In all its preaching, liturgy, "sacraments" and ministerial action, it performs, by analogy, the communicative act whereby God shows himself to be for us in Jesus Christ. As such, this analogy of communicative action is not confined to literary action, but also inheres in symbol, liturgical performance, response and indeed the whole of the Christian life. We are, in this way, the *verba visibilia*. It is canonical first and therefore also, in a secondary sense,

---

[196]Ibid., p. 57.
[197]Ibid., p. 50.
[198]Ibid.
[199]Ibid., p. 74.

creedal, catholic, pastoral and ecumenical. As such, the *analogia dramatis* "remains theologically fruitful." Furthermore, it is "both adequate to the subject matter of Christian theology and conducive to resolving certain longstanding dichotomies . . . that have led the church to undervalue, or even to neglect [some would even say reject] its rich doctrinal heritage."[200]

Much more could be said by way of expanding on and illustrating Vanhoozer's proposals. We have had to content ourselves with a broad description. In terms of what we are proposing here, this treatment of an *analogia dramatis* goes a long way toward our own conception of an analogy of performative Word. The problem with drama, of course, is that it is play and suggests a lack of seriousness in respect to acting. The Latin word for performance is *effectus*, and when referring to the divine act we must remain in the realm of reality, not theater. Theater does help convey the idea that our act of faith can only indirectly imitate the divine act. But the realization of redemption is no mere drama. The act of God is his essence, and his essence is his act. Theology as performance approximates reality more than drama, so we must deepen the task of theology and insist that theological language endeavor to describe real "states of affairs." When we look for guidance to how theology may be constituted as an analogy of performative Word, we are inevitably drawn to the prologue of John's Gospel. It is the one place in Scripture where language, and its writer, is pushed to the limits, in order to witness to this performative act. The words *become, flesh, dwelling, glory, was, was with* and, of course, *Word* strain to perform the event in the fullness of its reality. The passage requires a closer look to bear this out. An extended exegesis of parts of this passage would serve us well as an initial definition of the analogy of performative Word. But as with participation so also here we can hardly be exhaustive, and must be merely descriptive. We shall use the United Bible Society Greek text (1983) and the NIV (1984) of the Bible, which read as follows, respectively:

Ἐν ἀρχῇ ἦν ὁ λόγος, καὶ ὁ λόγος ἦν πρὸς τὸν θεόν, καὶ θεὸς ἦν ὁ λόγος. 2. οὗτος ἦν ἐν ἀρχῇ πρὸς τὸν θεόν. 3. πάντα δι᾽ αὐτοῦ ἐγένετο, καὶ χωρὶς αὐτοῦ ἐγένετο οὐδὲ ἓν ὃ γέγονεν. 4. ἐν αὐτῷ ζωὴ ἦν, καὶ ἡ ζωὴ ἦν τὸ φῶς τῶν ἀνθρώπων. 5. καὶ τὸ φῶς ἐν τῇ σκοτίᾳ φαίνει, καὶ ἡ σκοτία αὐτὸ οὐ κατέλαβεν.

---

[200]Ibid., p. 402.

6. Ἐγένετο ἄνθρωπος ἀπεσταλμένος παρὰ θεοῦ, ὄνομα αὐτῷ Ἰωάννης·
7. οὗτος ἦλθεν εἰς μαρτυρίαν, ἵνα μαρτυρήσῃ περὶ τοῦ φωτός, ἵνα πάντες
πιστεύσωσι δι᾽ αὐτοῦ. 8. οὐκ ἦν ἐκεῖνος τὸ φῶς, ἀλλ᾽ ἵνα μαρτυρήσῃ περὶ τοῦ
φωτός. 9. Ἦν τὸ φῶς τὸ ἀληθινόν, ὃ φωτίζει πάντα ἄνθρωπον ἐρχόμενον εἰς
τὸν κόσμον. 10. ἐν τῷ κόσμῳ ἦν, καὶ ὁ κόσμος δι᾽ αὐτοῦ ἐγένετο, καὶ ὁ κόσμος
αὐτὸν οὐκ ἔγνω. 11. εἰς τὰ ἴδια ἦλθε, καὶ οἱ ἴδιοι αὐτὸν οὐ παρέλαβον. 12. ὅσοι
δὲ ἔλαβον αὐτόν, ἔδωκεν αὐτοῖς ἐξουσίαν τέκνα θεοῦ γενέσθαι, τοῖς
πιστεύουσιν εἰς τὸ ὄνομα αὐτοῦ, 13. οἳ οὐκ ἐξ αἱμάτων, οὐδὲ ἐκ θελήματος
σαρκός, οὐδὲ ἐκ θελήματος ἀνδρός, ἀλλ᾽ ἐκ θεοῦ ἐγεννήθησαν.

14. Καὶ ὁ λογός σὰρξ ἐγένετο καὶ ἐσκήνωσεν ἐν ἡμῖν, καὶ ἐθεασάμεθα τὴν
δόξαν αὐτοῦ, δόξαν ὡς μονογενοῦς παρὰ πατρός, πλήρης χάριτος καὶ
ἀληθείας.

15. Ἰωάννης μαρτυρεῖ περὶ αὐτοῦ καὶ κέκραγε λέγων· Οὗτος ἦν ὃν εἶπον, Ὁ
ὀπίσω μου ἐρχόμενος ἔμπροσθέν μου γέγονεν, ὅτι πρῶτός μου ἦν. 16. Καὶ ἐκ
τοῦ πληρώματος αὐτοῦ ἡμεῖς πάντες ἐλάβομεν, καὶ χάριν ἀντὶ χάριτος· 17. ὅτι
ὁ νόμος διὰ Μωϋσέως ἐδόθη, ἡ χάρις καὶ ἡ ἀλήθεια διὰ Ἰησοῦ Χριστοῦ
ἐγένετο.

18. θεὸν οὐδεὶς ἑώρακε πώποτε· ὁ μονογενὴς υἱὸς ὁ ὢν εἰς τὸν κόλπον τοῦ
πατρός, ἐκεῖνος ἐξηγήσατο.

1. In the beginning was the Word, and the Word was with God, and the Word
was God. 2. He was with God in the beginning. 3. Through him all things were
made; without him nothing was made that has been made. 4. In him was life,
and that life was the light of men. 5. The light shines in the darkness, but the
darkness has not understood it.

6. There came a man who was sent from God; his name was John. 7. He
came as a witness to testify concerning that light, so that through him all men
might believe. 8. He himself was not the light; he came only as a witness to the
light. 9. The true light that gives light to every man was coming into the world.

10. He was in the world, and though the world was made through him, the
world did not recognize him. 11. He came to that which was his own, but his
own did not receive him. 12. Yet to all who received him, to those who be-
lieved in his name, he gave the right to become children of God—13. children
born not of natural descent, nor of human decision or a husband's will, but
born of God.

14. The Word became flesh and made his dwelling among us. We have seen
his glory, the glory of the One and Only, who came from the Father, full of
grace and truth.

15. John testifies concerning him. He cries out, saying, "This was he of whom I said, 'He who comes after me has surpassed me because he was before me.'" 16. From the fullness of his grace we have all received one blessing after another. 17. For the law was given through Moses; grace and truth came through Jesus Christ.

18. No one has ever seen God, but God the One and Only, who is at the Father's side, has made him known.

In this critical and central description of revelation as performative Word, there are three primary acts around which this conception of analogy revolves, in its most critical places: Act one is contained in John 1:1-5, the primal divine act of being from all eternity, in the speaking of the Word (λόγος). Act two is contained in John 1:6-8, the act of *witness* that comes into being and therefore is a response of faith to the primal act. Act three is contained in John 1:14, 18, where there is the realization of the primal act in the act of the incarnation of the spoken Word of God, "who has made Him [God] known," (ἐκεῖνος ἐξηγήσατο). On the basis of this central text, let us explore how we may understand the nature of the divine-human correspondence in this threefold reciprocal act, the one true analogy of performative Word.

Act one: John 1:1-5. The performative nature of God's self-revelation is announced in the very opening of the prologue with its indirect but no less clear reference to Genesis 1:1, "In the beginning," contained in the Ἐν ἀρχῇ of verse 1. In the LXX the pattern is the same, Ἐν ἀρχῇ. In Genesis 1:1, however, the context is the beginning of creation, whereas John 1:1 has a point beyond and before time in mind with its ἀρχῇ. Before creation, before any word that was spoken to bring creation into existence, the λόγος was (ἦν). The λόγος was eternally spoken before creation. He arrives on the scene of history in action, as Creator.[201] The Word did not "come into being" or arise with creation but "was." Furthermore, the Word "was with God" (πρὸς τὸν θεόν) and with God "in the beginning" (ἐν ἀρχῇ πρὸς τὸν θεόν). Additionally, the λόγος, in the beginning with God, partook of the divine nature in terms of equality (καὶ θεὸς ἦν ὁ λόγος). Thus the λόγος was the agent enacting the beginning of all being. He was, as per the Vulgate, *in initio*.[202] As such, he

---

[201]J. H. Bernard, *A Critical Commentary on the Gospel According to John* (New York: Scribners, 1924).

[202]Barth, *Witness to the Word,* p. 17.

was above or beyond creation and therefore all ἐγένετο (becoming). "His being is not temporal; it is eternal being, that in principle precedes all time and encloses all time. The Athanasians were right when they based on this passage their thesis that there was no time in which *Logos* was not. In fact, John means that the Logos was, in principle, before all time."[203]

One could put the question thus: Who else but God could be in the beginning, before time, with God? The answer Barth gives suggests that to be with God in the beginning is to "belong to God." One commentator confirms this, stating: "The preposition [πρός] 'with' in the phrase 'the Word was with God' indicates both equality and distinction of identity, along with association. The phrase can be rendered 'face to face' with." As such, the proposition implies "personality, co-existence, with the creator, and yet an expression of His creative being."[204] Indeed, "expressive," but not in terms of typical representation in abstraction, rather as God "expressed" in that God's Word is pronounced from himself.

John 1:2 serves to summarize and emphasize the threefold act of God announced in John 1:1, the eternal speaking of the Word, the eternal being with the Word, and the eternal belonging of the Word, only with added emphasis on its eternal nature, in that "He was with God in the beginning." Calvin cuts to the chase, translating the opening line as "In the beginning was the Speech," and commenting,

> As to the evangelist calling the Son of God, *the speech*, the simple reason appears to me to be, first, because he is the eternal wisdom and will of God; and secondly, because He is the lively image of His purpose; for as speech is said to be among men the image of the mind, so it is not inappropriate to apply this to God, and to say that He reveals Himself to us by His speech.[205]

That John uses this designation, ὁ λόγος, is expressive of his desire to proclaim that the wisdom (σοφία) of the Hermetic Greeks, or the Word (דָּבָר;מֵאמָר) of the Hebrews, or indeed the reason (λόγος) of the Hellenistic Greeks, is now spoken and given shape and meaning as the act of God in

---

[203]Ibid., p. 20.
[204]M. C. Tenney, *The Expositors Bible Commentary*, vol. 5, *John* (Grand Rapids: Zondervan, 1988), p. 28.
[205]John Calvin, *Commentary on the Gospel According to John*, vol. 1 (Grand Rapids: Eerdmans, 1980), p. 25.

His eternal *speech* (λόγος). Barth goes even further, suggesting

> the thought reached with the third sentence in verse 1 is that the Logos can
> belong to God and can be in the beginning with God, not because he is the
> person who has the required nature, essence, or operation in the first instance,
> or, as we should say in the language of dogmatics, is in the mode of the eternal
> Father, but because he is the second person, who, as we should say, in the
> mode of the eternal Son shares the same nature with the *person* of the Father
> in the same dignity and perfection.[206]

Thus before creation there is in God a "two-fold relation," as Calvin puts it,
concealed in eternity but now revealed as concealed in creation as the deed,
the act of revelation, and the Word, the sum, substance, witness and content
of the act.[207] This is the first act, but it is an act coterminous with eternity,
without beginning, without end and without equal.

We have yet to speak about the leading role directly, the λόγος, in these
first two verses. The term λόγος has a long and complex history, as is well
attested to in Gerhard Kittel's *Theological Dictionary of the New Testament*.[208]
"At the very head of the train of thought sketched by the term λόγος there
stands, not a concept, but the event which has taken place, and in which
God declares Himself, causing His Word to be enacted."[209] This declaration
is not just a mediation of the Word in the words of Jesus but "is the fact of
Christ as such."[210] Others have considered the λόγος to be a borrowing
from Philo, Hermes, the Hebrew concept of wisdom (σοφία) or even the
Aramaic and Hebrew tendency to personify Word in the terms of God's
creative act.[211] All such conceptions were no doubt known to the Evangelist,

---

[206]Barth, *Witness to the Word*, p. 22.

[207]Calvin, *Commentary on the Gospel According to John*, p. 26.

[208]H. Kleinknecht, "λόγος," *TDNT* 4:91-136.

[209]Ibid., 4:125.

[210]Ibid.

[211]Articles consulted on the background, purpose and meaning of the prologue of John's Gospel
include: K. Aland, "Eine Untersuchung zu Joh 1, 3-4," *ZNW* 59 (1968): 174-209; P. Borgen,
"Observations on the Targumic Character of the Prologue of John," *NTS* 16 (1969-1970): 288-
95; Borgen, "The Logos Was the True Light; Contributions to the Interpretation of the Prologue
of John," *NovT* 14 (1972): 115-30; T. Boman, *Hebrew Thought Compared with Greek*, trans. Jules
L. Moreau (Philadelphia: Westminster Press, 1960), pp. 58-69; A. Culpepper, "The Pivot of
John's Prologue," *NTS* 27 (1980-1981): 1-31; C. Demke, "Der sogenannte Logos Hymnus in
Johanneische Prolog," *ZNW* 58 (1967): 45-68; C. H. Dodd, *The Interpretation of the Fourth
Gospel* (Cambridge: Cambridge University Press, 1953), pp. 263-85, 294-96; F. L. Cross, ed.,
Studies in the Fourth Gospel (London: Mowbray, 1957), pp. 9-22; M. D. Hooker, "John the Bap-

and one may well surmise that these may have acted as external forces causing the Evangelist to point to Jesus Christ as the one true λόγος. Certainly, the call to "believe in" Jesus Christ as the λόγος is good reason to suppose that he is attempting to be evangelistic from the outset. Some commentators think "belief" is really the unifying theme of John's Gospel, given his strategic use of πίστις.[212] Certainly, all the Gospels are told from the perspective of a call to faith in a way that takes account of their various communal situations.[213] But there are deeper motives here at work than mere cultural reflection or evangelism.

It is clear that employing the term λόγος as a locum tenens in John 1:1-3 amounts to "simply the designation of a place which something or someone else will later fill."[214] Indeed, judged on the basis of how often the term λόγος occurs in lieu of "Jesus Christ," or as a designation, one seems puzzled at the lack of reference beyond the prologue (Jn 1:1-5, 14) and Revelation 19:13, which are the only direct occurrences. In each situation the λόγος stands in for Christ. "His is the place which at one and the same time is occupied, reserved, and delimited by the predicates which are ascribed to the Logos by the history which is narrated about him."[215] The question as to why John makes this substitution is intriguing, and scholars are still attempting to uncover the external motives driving the Evangelist's choice (to say nothing of those who deny the status of the prologue as belonging to the Gospel at all). None of the reasons posited for the Evangelist's choice could adequately explain his intentions. The Bultmanian supposition is that the λόγος is for the Evangelist "the revealer."[216] Bultmann correctly places the emphasis on

---

tist and the Johannine Prologue," NTS 16 (1969–1970): 354-58; J. Jeremias, The Revealing Word: The Central Message of the New Testament (London: SCM Press, 1965), pp. 71-90; E. Käsemann, "The Structure and Purpose of the Prologue to John's Gospel," in New Testament Questions of Today (London: SCM Press, 1969), pp. 138-67; J. T. Sanders, The New Testament Christological Hymns (Cambridge: Cambridge University Press, 1971), pp. 2-57. Many other commentaries were also consulted, the best of which, for our purposes, included those partial or complete commentaries by J. H. Bernard, Karl Barth, G. R. Beasley-Murray, C. K. Barrett, R. E. Brown, R. Bultmann, G. B. Caird, John Calvin, E. Heachen, C. Keener, B. Lindars, L. Morris, M. C. Tenney and B. F. Westcott.

[212]Merrill C. Tenney, John: Gospel of Belief (Grand Rapids: Eerdmans, 1975), pp. 11-12.

[213]On the Johannine community see R. E. Brown, The Community of the Beloved Disciple (New York: Paulist, 1979).

[214]Barth, Witness to the Word, p. 23.

[215]Ibid.

[216]Rudolf Bultmann, Commentary on John, Hermeneia (Philadelphia: Fortress, 1982), pp. 13-14.

address, in the "broadest sense" implied by the term.[217] However, while the words spoken by Jesus Christ are included in this address, they do not limit the scope and weight of the address as divine "speech-act." That is, "Word" is the Creator-Word, the act in Word and the Word in act, though care must be exercised that we do not read more into the λόγος than is there.[218] There is an "inner necessity" in John's substitution of λόγος for Jesus Christ. John is driving us toward the witness to the Word that now unfolds before us, in John the Baptist first (as Jn 1:5-6, 19 clearly indicate), but in the rest of the Gospel preeminently.

Where the Word of God is, there is the gospel; where the gospel, the Word of God. "Hence it must belong to God and be of the same nature as God. No more and no less than God Himself was and is needed if the Word is there, and is and will be spoken. He had to speak it. But He has spoken it. And He speaks it again."[219] This is God's act as threefold repetition, from eternity to eternity, known now in Jesus Christ the God-Man as Father, Son and Holy Spirit. But, and here is the substance of the analogy, "To this Word the human word of the Evangelist bears witness."[220] That is, our corresponding witness is the inhabitation of the word of the witness by the Word of God. The fact of witness, of human correspondence, of human speech, is always, and at every moment, underwritten, or not, in the freedom of God but as this eternal speech-act, act-speech. All our witness is grounded, in terms of its capacity and content, in this one, single, divine, eternal, historically real and realized act of God who comes in the flesh. All our witness is derived from this act, in terms of its power, correctness and possibility, just as all our witness goes responsibly, powerfully and actually to that act in an interplay of similarity and dissimilarity that both permits and immediately limits theology. To this single speech-act, act-speech, theology must remain responsible in its witnessing.

Why must theology be so singularly obedient to this analogy of performative Word? Because πάντα δι' αὐτοῦ ἐγένετο, καὶ χωρὶς αὐτοῦ ἐγένετο οὐδὲ ἓν ὃ γέγονεν: "Through him all things were made; without him nothing

---

[217]See also Barth, *Witness to the Word*, p. 26.
[218]Ibid.
[219]Ibid., p. 27.
[220]Ibid.

was made that has been made." That is, "all things" that come into being and are contingent come into being by virtue of the "essential being" or Word of God.[221] Harking back, as John does, to Genesis 1–3, we affirm with Genesis that the phrase "And God said" is followed by the coming into existence of all that was spoken.[222] But the Word spoken is no "mere passive instrument," as it was with Philo and intertestamental Jewish thought. No, the reference to καὶ χωρὶς αὐτοῦ ἐγένετο οὐδὲ ἓν ὃ γέγονεν makes such passivity impossible. Before the Word there was no other mediating agency, whether inert (matter) or animated (angels); there was only the active agency of the Word. There is still only the active agency of the Word, and there will only ever be the active agency of the Word.[223] Such an agency enfolds all other agents, in terms of conceiving them, positing them and corresponding to them as Word. Again Calvin's comment is salient. "Having affirmed that the speech is God, and having asserted his eternal essence, he now proves his Divinity from his works. And this is the practical knowledge, to which we ought to be chiefly accustomed."[224] That is to say, herein the Word sets the limits and possibility of the knowledge of God via his works, namely, his work as speech-act, act-speech. Calvin summarizes this possibility for a "practical knowledge" of God as follows:

> Accordingly, the ordinary mode of expression is here employed, that the Father made all things through the Son.... Now the design of the Evangelist is, as I have already said, to show that no sooner was the world created than the Speech of God came forth into external operation; for having formerly been incomprehensible in his essence, he then became publically known by the effect of his power.[225]

Calvin recognizes, of course, that the philosophers of the past had already identified "God as the Master builder," but from there had flown off into all kinds of "frivolous speculations," where clearly, based on this passage, all we need to know about the CER is to be read off from "this inspired declaration, well knowing that it conveys far more than our mind is able to comprehend."[226]

---

[221]Bernard, *A Critical Commentary*, p. 3.
[222]Ibid.; see Ps 33:6; 147:15; Is 55:11. Compare 2 Esdras 6:38, *Wisdom of Solomon* 9:1.
[223]Bernard, *A Critical Commentary*, p. 3.
[224]Calvin, *Commentary on the Gospel According to John*, p. 30.
[225]Ibid., p. 30.
[226]Ibid.

Again, M. C. Tenney confirms this intuition when he writes that "the priority of Christ over creation is taught here and it also is mentioned in Colossians 1:16 and Hebrews 1:2."[227] Clearly the limits of practical theological naming are to be determined in the revelation of the Word. Barth observes,

> The *dia* in all these passages [Col 1:16; Heb 1:2; Jn 1:3] denotes the role of the
> means, or, rather, of the mediator whose existence and function, in the mind
> of the author and of that insightful age, explain the unheard of fact that the
> dark, lower world is possible and actual alongside the pure and lofty God.
> Through him and only through him, through the Revealer, is this possible.[228]

In short, there is no natural theology, no metaphysics, no word of humankind that can rise to the task of revelation. "So great is God that it is only the Revealer who can originally bind Him and the world together."[229] Whatever might be said for other forms of mediation between "a God" and the world, the New Testament is concerned with only one mediator between God and the world, and the one who gives us both, namely, Jesus Christ. But the New Testament is also concerned with mediation in act as speech, to which the literary word must bear witness. He himself relativizes all pretentions and pretenders to revelation. Our witness is something, or not, "only as it is related to the Word. Its existence is conceivable only in the light of the Word. Its own function is lent it by the Word, by the Word that was [and is] *theos.*"[230] The Scriptures are totalizing in this respect. "For by Him all things were created: things in heaven and on earth, visible and invisible, whether thrones or powers or rulers or authorities; all things were created by Him and for Him."[231] As witness, theology is not revelation, but as revelation the Word witnesses to the Father. Barth is, at this point, correct to conclude: "The witness is not the Revealer, nor is he a witness to himself but to the Revealer. To be sure, this is not yet said in verse 3, but within the total context the way is undoubtedly prepared for it. And in this preparatory purpose I discern the special Johannine emphasis with which the contem-

---

227Tenney, *John: Gospel of Belief,* p. 29.
228Barth, *Witness to the Word,* p. 31.
229Ibid.
230Ibid., p. 34.
231Ibid. The parallel is unmistakable: πάντα δι' αὐτοῦ ἐγένετο, καὶ χωρὶς αὐτοῦ ἐγένετο οὐδὲ ἓν ὃ γέγονεν.

porary idea of the mediating role of the *Logos* is adopted."[232]

In sum, the mediator is the one act of God's speech, and the one Word of God's act to which all our theological witness is to be oriented, as an analogy of performative Word, in light of which there can be no other pretenders. But now we must turn to the content of this analogy in act two: the witness to the Word in John 1:6-8, 15. We shall see in act 3 (Jn 1:14, 18) that witness and Word are combined in a "double correspondence" summarized in the mediation of revelation in the Word.

Act two: John 1:6-8. Ἐγένετο ἄνθρωπος ἀπεσταλμένος παρὰ θεοῦ, ὄνομα αὐτῷ Ἰωάννης: "There was a man sent from God whose name was John." Whence this interruption? What is this perturbation of the divine act in the role of an "amateur" actor? The text leaves off the leading role in John 1:5 with no indication of a transition or "particle" connecting it with what had hitherto been said.[233] It almost feels like a moment of discord, the clearing of a throat in the audience while the prime actor is in the midst of his oration. In the words of J. H. Bernard, "It is a sentence quite distinct form the verse of the Logos Hymn which goes before."[234] The transition is certainly in keeping with the discord often felt on the human side in respect to "speech" about the divine. Barth is correct, on one level at least, to consider the introduction of the witness of John the Baptist as the "crux" of the passage. He writes: "vv. 6-8 and v. 15 constitute an interruption which we should like to expunge in the interest of smoother reading."[235] But they are indeed there and cannot, by any means, be overlooked because of their awkwardness.

> Those who have studied John's Gospel know what is the exegetical crux of the prologue. It is concrete and palpable in verses 6-8 and verse 15. . . . They tell us that the author wants to show us at once what is the relationship of this John to the Word, to the light about which verses 1-5 and verses 9-13 speak, to the incarnate Word that is seen by us, to Jesus Christ, as will at last be openly stated in verse 17. He, this John, is not himself this Word; He is a man sent by God. He is not himself the light; he is a witness to it. He bears witness that the one who comes after him surpasses him, as he is before him in principle.[236]

---

[232]Ibid., p. 35.
[233]Bernard, *A Critical Commentary*, p. 7.
[234]Ibid.
[235]Barth, *Witness to the Word*, p. 13.
[236]Ibid.

The goal of his coming is that, through his witness, all might believe in the light. Here the witness is determined in and by the Word. The Word is present in and with the witness. But how must we characterize this presence of the Word in the act of the witness? The Word is present, according to John 1:1-5, "antecedently." "His presence precedes our self-presence, and fashions into a counterpart to itself."[237] John's presence or arrival on the scene is not somehow a presencing of Christ as an "extension or modification of our presence to ourselves." He is not ours to possess as if by rights. Webster puts this point in John's Gospel in sharp relief when he writes, "The presence of Christ is divine self-presence, and as such becomes a human present autonomously, in spontaneous fulfillment of its own determination, by virtue of the action of the Holy Spirit, and not by human acts of projection or reconstruction."[238] John's record of the Baptist should be read here in similar terms. He is no self-positing witness, but is posited as witness, in witness, to the self-positing Word.

> Accordingly, our presence to ourselves is not a stable and settled disposition of ourselves by which all other presences are measured, and before which Jesus Christ may be summoned to appear as a further object of our attention. It is "eschatological." Our human self-presence is a function of the fact that Jesus Christ presents Himself to us in the Spirit's power, he creates a human present as the auxiliary of His presence, overcoming our pretended self-sufficiency, and making us into new creatures of God who confess that he is before them. The paradigm of His antecedent presence as the risen one is thus the effortless, unfettered and wholly effective coming of Jesus Christ: "Jesus came and stood among them" (Jn. 20:26).[239]

Clearly this is the sense of the witness here. John is posited by God as the object of his act and not self-posited and in possession of the object of its witness. John has his own faith, his own baptism, and as such is a witness to his own light, to be sure, but the Word is not that faith, that light, that witness. Nevertheless, the Baptist is posited as an active, effective witness to the light. He is, as such, "partnered" to the act of the divine revelation of the light as performative Word. In this respect, God and the daybreak of (his)

---

[237]John Webster, *Confessing God: Essays in Christian Dogmatics II* (London: T & T Clark, 2005), p. 132.
[238]Ibid.
[239]Ibid.

reality belong together.[240] In the wake of Ἐν ἀρχῇ ἦν ὁ λόγος, there "arose a man" (Ἐγένετο ἄνθρωπος). The verb ἐγένετο is here in the aorist tense. The present tense (γίνομαι) means to "come to be," whereas the Word always was.[241] But, as one commentator correctly points out, in John the Baptist, "the human agent for introducing the Word to men is presented." It is his "function" that accrues to his being and vice versa. As such, he is ἀπεσταλμένος, or "sent," almost in apostolic terms. It is a word of "authority" and "commission" and thus defines his primary role with respect to the divine λογός.[242] It was a title that both the Baptist and Paul would claim to have received from heaven.[243] In John 3:28 he reminds us that, while he was "sent" (ἀπεσταλμένος) before the Word, the light, he was not the light.

What is the function here of being the "sent one"? This is the primary role of a secondary actor, who, nevertheless, proclaims, per analogy of performative Word, the Word in a reflective manner. Here John the Evangelist is speaking about the possibility of confusing one with the other. Thus it is critical to differentiate the witness from the Word.[244] Barth comments, "This is precisely what should not happen in the relationship of revealer, witness and hearers" that the Baptist typifies.[245] But, and here is "the content of the possibility that the speech of the witness" may correspond to the speech of God: "If ἐγένετο and ἄνθρωπος definitely distinguish him from the Logos, the predicate, ἀπεσταλμένος παρὰ θεοῦ, brings him close, and even in a sense puts him in the same sphere and gives him the same function, for the same verb describes Jesus also as 'sent by God' in John 5:36, 38; 7:29; 20:21."[246] There is nothing here that accrues to the Baptist by virtue of his nature that is not given by God. "Sent by God" here means, as per Calvin, that the Evangelist intends us to see him as sent "by the command of God," and that, as such, "God is the author of his ministry." As a matter of fact, "what is as-

---

[240]Wolf Krötke, as per my *Clearing a Space*, p. 307.

[241]In the words of Leon Morris, "John came into existence but Jesus was in the beginning" (*The Gospel According to John*, New International Commentary on the New Testament [Grand Rapids: Eerdmans, 1971], p. 88).

[242]See Tenney, *Gospel of John*, p. 23; Morris, *Gospel According to John*, p. 89; Bernard, *A Critical Commentary*, p. 130.

[243]See John 3:28; 1 Corinthians 4:7.

[244]See also John 5:35, where he is referred to as ἀγαλλιαθῆναι πρὸς ὥραν ἐν τῷ φωτί. Barth, *Witness to the Word*, p. 17.

[245]Ibid., pp. 18-19.

[246]Ibid.

serted by John is required in all the teachers of the church, that they be called by God; that the authority of teaching may not be founded on any other than on God above."[247] Indeed, as Calvin confirms, and so also the majority of commentators on John since him, this is precisely the calling and anointing of the disciples as witnesses attested to in John 20:21-22. In this passage the disciples stand in a series of divine acts, from the sending of the Son, and with the Son the Father's sending of the Spirit, to now the sending of the "witnesses" in and with the authority of the analogy of performative Word.

When, in John 20:21, Jesus says καθὼς ἀπέσταλκέν με ὁ πατήρ, κἀγὼ πέμπω ὑμᾶς, it would appear, as Calvin suggests, that "His words amount to a declaration, that hitherto He has discharged the office of a teacher, and that, having finished his course, he now confers on them the same office."[248] Furthermore, what comes with this appointment to the apostolic office of teaching is the same authority to possess, proclaim and witness to the Word as the "Word" himself. They possess the same authority as he by virtue of their being "sent" in the same economic order as himself and the Holy Spirit. "It is not without reason, therefore, that Christ communicates to His apostles the authority which he received from the Father, that thus He may declare that the preaching of the Gospel was committed to Him, not by human hands, but by the command of God."[249] In confirmation of this calling, Jesus ἐνεφύσησεν (breathed on them), saying, Λάβετε πνεῦμα ἅγιον (receive the Holy Spirit). In Calvin's understanding, there is no possible witness to the Word without divine enablement, "for no man can speak a word concerning Christ unless the Spirit guide his tongue (I Cor. 12:3) so far is it from being true that there is any man competent to discharge faithfully and honestly all the duties of so excellent an office."[250] As we have said, Calvin is followed here by a host of commentators since.[251]

In his commentary on John, the Catholic scholar Raymond Brown notes that what we have here (in Jn 1:6; 20:21-22) is an "*analogia verbi* in which human words have the exact force of the Word Himself," in that the witness

---

[247]Calvin, *Commentary on the Gospel According to John*, p. 36.
[248]Ibid., p. 266.
[249]Ibid.
[250]Ibid., p. 267.
[251]See, for instance, B. F. Westcott, J. H. Bernard, G. R. Beasley-Murray, C. K. Barrett, Raymond Brown.

"can affirm a partial truth in finite human words, since these words are analogous participations in His external Word."[252] While it would appear that Brown seems to claim a metaphorical identity between our words and the Word here, to the degree that we cannot go so far ourselves, his comment does attest to the nature of the double act of sending in the sent Word and the sent witness. C. K. Barrett puts it in much more balanced terms when he comments on John 20:21-22 as follows:[253]

> The two verbs [πέμπω and ἀπέσταλκέν] seem to be used synonymously in this gospel. . . . (note especially the use of the word [πέμπειν] in the phrase ὁ πέμψας με (πατήρ), and that it is used of the sending of the Paraclete, 14:26; 15:26; 16:7). In each [passage] the same pattern of sending is noted. The Father sends the Son, and the Son sends the "apostles." . . . In view of the generally synonymous use of the words ἀποστέλλειν and πέμπειν, and the construction of this sentence (καθώς . . . καί . . .) it does not seem possible to distinguish between two kinds of sending. . . . Parallelism, not contrast, between two missions is emphasized here. . . . It follows that in the apostolic mission of the church . . . the world is veritably confronted not merely by a human institution but by Jesus the Son of God (13:20; 17:18).[254]

Therefore it also follows that, insofar as Jesus' obedience is reflected in his relationship to the Father who seals and sanctifies his work, and the Holy Spirit, who empowers him, in its life, ministry and theology the church stands in the same obedient lineage, with the same authority, but only insofar as it is vested in the Word of God and vice versa.[255] As such, the Baptist, in John 1:6-8, 15-17, 19, and following in the rest of John, is not just a historical personage but, like the λόγος, is for Jesus Christ. He is a substitution for us all, as his witness. He is a "revealer" in the sense that, like the λόγος, he is "sent from God." John the Baptist and John the Evangelist are shedding "light" on the redemption that has come into the world. In doing so, their witness is analogically parallel, and effective as parallel, with the same authority as the sending mission of God. It is, in the drama of revelation, the

---

[252]See Raymond Brown, "*The Sensus Plenior* in the Last Ten Years," *Catholic Biblical Quarterly* 25 (1965): 262-85; M. M. Waldstein, "Analogia Verbi: The Truth of Scripture in Rudolph Bultmann and Raymond Brown," *Letter and Spirit* 6 (2010): 115.

[253]On "sent" and "sending" see John 1:6-8, 19; 3:17, 34; 5:36, 38; 6:29, 57; 7:29; 10:36; 17:3-25.

[254]C. K. Barrett, *The Gospel According to John*, 2nd ed. (London: SPCK, 1978), p. 342; see verse 19.

[255]Ibid., p. 569.

secondary role, but no less critical to the play. To be sure neither he, nor the Evangelists, nor any of the apostles, are the "light," but the "light" of the Word is, nevertheless, the power of their witness. We are not φῶς, but we are μαρτυρήσῃ περὶ τοῦ φωτός. As Barth comments,

> At all times and in all circumstances the bearer of the Christian message, having his own light, is the Word that is incarnate in the fullness of time. But the witnesses of the remotest past and most distant future have in principle a similar share in revelation, or render a similar service to it. There applies to all of them the caveat that in themselves, if they do not misunderstand themselves they are only witnesses.[256]

Thus we are only always, but of necessity, the reflection of this role. But we are still in the anticlimax of the play. The crux, the third act, is about to arrive, and in its arrival Word and witness are combined in an analogical relation that is reflexive and participatory. This occurs in John 1:14-18, but with particular reference to 14 and 18. In this third act the analogy of performative Word is finally and unequivocally christologically founded and established.

In sum, in John 1:14 the possibility and foundation of theological speech (as witness) is laid. It is directly proportional to, and in relation to, the full realization of the incarnation of the λόγος. All similarity and dissimilarity, as well as all correspondence in being, act and Word are herein delimited and defined. Outside this final act there is no other possibility of correspondence, of similarity or, for that matter, dissimilarity. Analogy is herein, finally and fully, christologically determined. Thus a closer look is required if we are to determine the limits and nature of the analogy of performative Word. It would not be an exaggeration to say that John 1:14 also is one of the most commented-on passages of Scripture in Christian history; so, again, we will have to be selective in terms of our interpretation of it, especially in the light of verse 18.

Act three: John 1:14, 18. Revelation is, in its essence, a divinely ordered correspondence of a human-divine unity in difference as speech-act, or as per Vanhoozer, word-deed, deed-word. John 1:14, 18 reads as follows: Καὶ ὁ λόγος σὰρξ ἐγένετο καὶ ἐσκήνωσεν ἐν ἡμῖν, καὶ ἐθεασάμεθα τὴν δόξαν

---

[256]Barth, *Witness to the Word*, p. 59; see also *CD* IV/3.3 §72.

αὐτοῦ, δόξαν ὡς μονογενοῦς παρὰ πατρός, πλήρης χάριτος καὶ ἀληθείας.
... θεὸν οὐδεὶς ἑώρακεν πώποτε: ὁ μονογενὴς υἱὸς ὁ ὢν εἰς τὸν κόλπον τοῦ
πατρὸς ἐκεῖνος ἐξηγήσατο: "The word became flesh and made his dwelling
among us. We have seen his glory, the glory of the One and Only, who came
from the Father, full of grace and truth. . . . No one has ever seen God, but
God the One and Only, who is at the Father's side, has made him known." In
sum, we have here in the incarnation of the Word the closest possible proximity and correspondence of the Word and its witness, divinity and humanity, in analogical relation, determined in the one act of God as the possibility and power of revelation and its spoken witness. It is the prime
analogate (trusted *analogans*) in the series of analogates (*analogatum*) that
bring into comparison divine action as speech and human action as witness
to the speech. Divine speech is to God as it comes to human witness. Everything that has gone before this in John 1 brings us to this conclusion. We
know that the Word of God is spoken eternally in God and is with God and
is God in nature, autonomy, personhood and action. He is the light that has
shone in creation, which is the product of his hand, and he, not creation or
the creature, is that light. The Baptist is "not that light" but really does testify
to it in terms that are substantially the same as its origin, in the order of its
sending. "Thus the revelation of the Word, and in the revelation, the Word
itself, comes into the world. Not known by the world, not accepted by those
to whom it originally applies, it is still mighty and victorious, it still creates
its own hearers and recipients, because it is the Word, God's Word. Of this
subject it is now said: 'σὰρξ ἐγένετο.'"[257]

In light of this, the substance of the analogy is this Word "become flesh."
That which the *analogia entis* sought after but failed to achieve, because it
could only premise it on the basis of a physically intuited CER, is here, in
Jesus Christ the Word, removed from sensory intuition apart from incarnation and placed entirely within the drama of God, to which all forms of
intuition, analytic and synthetic, must now mark their orientation. This is
a cosmic event. It is one in which not we but God makes the analogy, precisely in the form of speech. What exegetical grounds can we adduce for
such a conclusion?

---

[257]Barth, *Witness to the Word*, p. 61.

Clearly the key word between verses 14 and 18 is ἐγένετο. As B. F. Westcott succinctly notes: "The announcement of the mystery of the incarnation, embracing and completing all the mysteries of revelation, corresponds . . . to the declaration of the absolute being of the Word in verse 1."[258] That is, "He who was beyond time" is now "revealed for a space to the observation of men." The term used to introduce this divine act is ἐγένετο. It immediately points out the difficulty of human language to speak to this divine speech. "Owing to the inherent imperfection of human language as applied to the mystery of the Incarnation," ἐγένετο cannot adequately express the divine act.[259] However, this becoming is not to be seen as a change of essential nature. "The Word remains the Word" in his becoming.[260] Bernard explains further: "The Logos did not just become 'a man' but He became 'man' in the fullest sense; the divine person assuming human nature in its completeness. To explain the exact significance of ἐγένετο in this sentence is beyond the powers of any interpreter."[261] In the words of Paul, the "mystery" of the gospel is great (Eph 3:1-10). Whether or not Docetism played a part in John's choice of words, σάρξ and ἐγένετο, here is beside the point when considered in relation to the theological principle of revelation he is aiming at.[262] All we know for sure is that the aorist tense of the verb ἐγένετο indicates an action in time.[263]

The term is certainly stronger than Paul's affirmation in 1 Timothy 3:16 that Jesus was God "manifested" (ἐφανερώθη) in the flesh (σάρκος). G. Richter comes closest to the meaning of ἐγένετο when he writes, "The verb γίνομαι in connection with the predicative noun [σάρξ] expresses that a person or a thing changes its property or enters into a new condition, becomes something that it was not before."[264] While the term elsewhere can mean to be "born," as in John 18:37, its meaning far surpasses that basic defi-

---

[258]B. F. Westcott, *The Gospel According to St. John* (Grand Rapids: Eerdmans, 1950), p. 10.

[259]Ibid.

[260]Barrett, *Gospel According to John*, p. 165; see also Paul's understanding of the Son of God becoming flesh (Rom 1:3; 8:3; 1 Tim 3:16).

[261]Bernard, *A Critical Commentary*, p. 20.

[262]On the docetic background of John, see Bultmann, Barrett, Morris, etc.

[263]Morris, *Gospel According to John*, p. 102.

[264]See G. R. Beasley-Murray, *Gospel According to John*, Word Biblical Commentary (Waco: Word, 1987), pp. 13-14.

nition here.[265] Calvin understands this to be a begetting of the Word from "before all ages," the Word who now dwells in the form of humanity in a unity of divinity and humanity that "does not hinder the two natures from remaining distinct, so that his divinity retains all that is peculiar to itself and his humanity holds separately whatever belongs to it."[266] Either way, the commentators seem to be clear on one fact, that this becoming is an extraordinary one, out of character with all other becoming, yet at the same time the basis and source of all other becoming.

But how can the speech of God become, without surrendering something essential to his nature in his becoming, that is, his eternally begotten nature as attested to in John 1:1-5? How indeed can any form of speech convey the dialectic contained in an unbegotten God becoming human? We know that creation has its begetting in consequence of the action of the divine Word, the deed-word or speech-act. How then can we understand that ἐγένετο can apply also to his "becoming" in the flesh? The contrast indeed has already been provided. The witness, in John 1:6-8, is a becoming that is determined by the ἐξουσία of the Word (Jn 1:12-13). Precisely, as it happens, the Word becomes flesh in an identity with the "becoming" of the witness. "His action is that He, so to speak, loses Himself among those who can still be only objects of His action."[267] His existence, though it is the eternal ground of all existence, is now an existence after the same manner of the witness. He is in the "flesh"—"just as anything else or as anyone else exists."[268] Here, finally, the eternal reality of the divine thinking of God and humanity together is realized in historical correspondence. This is no combination of divinity and humanity in some higher synthesis. "It can mean only to think both the λόγος and the ἐγένετο with the strict similarity with which they are given us in Scripture."[269]

Thus the "becoming" here is a divine assumption of flesh (σάρξ) that bespeaks the internal ground of all witness and speaking. It is a miraculous act in which the whole of human action and reaction is enfolded as its ground, its going forth and its return. "As the Word of God becomes flesh

---

[265]See C. Keener, *The Gospel of John: A Commentary* (Peabody, MA: Hendrickson, 2003), 1:407 n. 413.
[266]Calvin, *Commentary on the Gospel According to John*, p. 46.
[267]*CD* I/2, pp. 133-55; *CD* IV/3.2, pp. 159-60; see also *CD* IV/3.2, p. 610.
[268]*CD* I/2, p. 160.
[269]*CD* I/2, p. 161.

He assumes or adopts or incorporates human being into writing with His divine being, so that this human being, as it comes into being, becomes as a human being the being of the Word of God."[270] This is the ground of all analogy because it is the internal and external possibility of such analogy. This is the one *analogia fidei*, in that it is the source of all possible begetting, speech, correspondence and action. But, precisely as such it is the possibility of all human becoming, speech correspondence and action. There is no *tertium quid* between these two becomings, combined in the single begetting of the Word. This is the force of the word *flesh* here. It is no mere appearance, no mere idea, no mere trace in creation or mind. It is an event, an act, in space and time. God is this one who acts in his Word. "His manhood is only the predicate of His Godhead, or better, and more concretely, it is only the predicate, assumed in inconceivable condescension, of the Word acting upon us, the Word who is the Lord."[271]

This is the *Deus dixit*. It is the resolution of the problem of speaking and knowing the Word of revelation and our participation in that revelation. In the words of Calvin, "as long as Christ remains outside of us, and we are separated from him, all that he has suffered and done for the salvation of the human race remains useless and of no value for us. Therefore, to share with us what he had received from the Father, he had to become ours and to dwell within us."[272] This is no human doing, however, in that there is nothing in us that is given and/or achieved by us. It is a work of the Paraclete, the Holy Spirit, as teacher and illuminator. Just as the Word comes to flesh, so there corresponds a second sending of the Holy Spirit to its human witness. "So the miracle of faith cannot be seen psychologically but only through the Son who as He Himself assumes human nature gives us a share in His fellowship with the Father."[273] This is the "self-enclosed circle of the *Deus dixit*" that we cannot and must not leave in the name of some "clear conceptuality." This self-enclosed circle is the place of the possibility of speech that corresponds to the divine speaking. "Our only option is to

---

[270]*CD* I/2, p. 160.

[271]*CD* I/2, p. 163.

[272]John Calvin, *Institutes of the Christian Religion*, ed. J. T. McNeill, trans. Ford Lewis Battles, Library of Christian Classics (Philadelphia: Westminster Press, 1960), III.1.1.

[273]Barth, *The Göttingen Dogmatics: Instruction in the Christian Religion* (Grand Rapids: Eerdmans, 1996), pp. 192f.

describe the point where God's Word is not only *God's* speech, God's address to us, but also God's address to us that is *heard* by us."[274] In this way,
"God meets us as man without ceasing to be God," but humanity is also able
to meet God without ceasing to be humanity. As such, "the event of eternity
and of eternity's union with time is an event which can now be narrated."[275]
What Barth is affirming in his appeal to John 1:14 is that theology is not only
concerned with Jesus Christ, but it is also determined by him. In short,
"church dogmatics must, of course, be christologically determined as a
whole and in all its parts."[276]

The key to this christological orientation is indeed John 1:14, but it cannot
be fully understood as such without the affirmation of John 1:18, especially
the reference to not seeing and to making known: θεὸν οὐδεὶς ἑώρακεν
πώποτε: ὁ μονογενὴς υἱὸς ὁ ὢν εἰς τὸν κόλπον τοῦ πατρός, ἐκεῖνος
ἐξηγήσατο. Here the background is more clearly that of Exodus 33 and
especially Exodus 34, wherein Moses is in some sense authorized to speak
on God's behalf but within strict boundaries that close off the revelation of
the "glory of God." Herein, what was once considered impossible (hubris,
even), that a human could not only witness but witness *to* the fullness of
grace and truth (πλήρης χάριτος καὶ ἀληθείας), now receives its full possibility in the very vision of the one who quite literally "exegetes" God. Where
Yahweh and Moses stand over against each other as the incompatible, incomparable and incomprehensible God in respect to his witness, now the
witness (the Evangelist and John the Baptist) stands in Jesus Christ the Word
as, albeit secondary, witnesses to the grace and truth of God that constitutes
the exegesis of his glory; but nevertheless, in comparison to the Word they
still stand "very much in the shadow" of God's self-revelatory Word.[277] What
Moses could only reflect in his face and reiterate on tablets of stone is now
fully embodied in Jesus Christ the λόγος. Jesus at once embodies and transcends the Torah so that, by proxy, the witnesses have a revelation "of greater
authority than that of Moses."[278] Indeed, the rejection of Jesus is disobe-

---

[274]Ibid., p. 192. Emphasis original.
[275]Christopher Hasper, *Eschatalogical Presence in Karl Barth's Göttingen Dogmatics* (Oxford: Oxford
    University Press, 2010), p. 6.
[276]*CD* I/2, pp. 123-63.
[277]Barth, *Witness to the Word*, p. 126.
[278]Keener, *Gospel of John*, 1:360.

dience in respect to the *Torah* as such.[279] "The contrast does not simply mean that God has broken his prophetic silence and spoken again; it means that all that God had already spoken was contained in Jesus, the ultimate embodiment of all God's Word," indeed its essence as the act of revelation.[280] The substance of this revelation is now reaffirmed as ὁ μονογενὴς υἱὸς ὁ ὢν εἰς τὸν κόλπον τοῦ πατρός. That is, "one of whom it can be predicated that He is unique in His being, and God, is none other than the 'only begotten Son' (ὁ μονογενὴς υἱός)."[281] The designation "the One and Only, who is at the Father's side" may then be taken as equivalent to κύριος, υἱὸς τοῦ θεοῦ and λόγος. It may also be taken to mean that the revelation consists in the full declaration of the glory of God as grace and truth.

Furthermore, that he is the ἐξηγήσατο of God means that he is the substance of our witness in terms of capacity and content. Indeed, our "seeing" of Jesus Christ is a seeing of the Father, and the sending of Jesus Christ, as the revelation of God, constitutes the sending of the witness (Jn 14:9; 16:30; 20:21). It is the one act of God in which the content, form, power and actuality of God's self-revelation are met in a dual correspondence of witness. Bernard correctly identifies ἐκεῖνος ἐξηγήσατο as the climax of the prologue in that it is he, the λόγος of John 1:1-5, 14, who reveals and interprets the Father. It is now this primary and secondary witness who will be "exhibited to the world" in the rest of the Gospel.[282] This exegesis transcends the ordinary modalities of witness, knowing and sensory intuition. Only the incarnation of the Word can suffice as the ground of such a witness.[283] Indeed, the Word incarnate is the very power and possibility of its being "recounted" or "narrated," as Barrett prefers to interpret ἐξηγήσατο.[284] While our capacity to exegete the Father is a secondary one, hidden with Christ in God, the Word's is a primary one.

> The final word of the prologue is that he [Christ the λόγος] is the exegete, the communicator, the one with whom we have to do, he who is μονογενής, whose information about himself is original, primary and authentic reve-

---

[279]Ibid.
[280]Ibid., 1:361 n. 42.
[281]Westcott, *Gospel According to John*, p. 15.
[282]Bernard, *A Critical Commentary*, p. 33.
[283]Tenney, *Gospel of John*, p. 34.
[284]Barrett, *Gospel According to John*, p. 170.

lation. . . . He, this ἐκεῖνος, definitely establishes the validity of the οὗτος ἦν of vs. 1 and 2, the validity of the witness of John, both the Baptist and the Evangelist.[285]

In sum, only in these terms may we speak of an *analogia fidei* as an analogy of performative Word. He is its original power in the act of God from all eternity. He is its sum and substance in its secondary act, and as such the very possibility of our having a role in the *analogia dramatis*. The role of the secondary witness is determined in the threefold act of God in deciding to send the λόγος as his primary witness. Our secondary witness consists only in the power granted to it in the sending of the Spirit, which is its ground and power. In this sense theology must receive *"everything from Jesus Christ and from Jesus Christ everything."*[286] Theology is entirely ordered on this incarnate Word. As such, then, it is Christ himself, and not just Christology, that is its center, power and possibility. While theology strives, in its creeds, confessions and sentences, toward clarity, the point of speaking about God is not a final systematic act of well-ordered statements, but a process whereby the living Word of God is made known and witnessed to in every instance. In this threefold act we have the possibility of theology as an analogy of participatory Word, an analogy of performative Word and therefore also as an analogy of parabolic Word, or the possibility of language itself to witness. This third modality is our final step in establishing the *analogia fidei* on a more substantial christological basis. Notice that the three acts establish the content of the revelation, its witness and its coming to speech as hermeneutical enablement of that speech. The possibility of theology resides in the power that Jesus Christ himself affirms in his own parabolic mode of discourse and being.[287]

The possibility of theology as the analogy of parabolic Word. In his monumental book, *God as the Mystery of the World*, Jüngel refers to "the man Jesus" as the "parable of God" based on the insight that "the translation of the

---

[285]Barth, *Witness to the Word*, pp. 131-32.

[286]*CD* II/1, p. 320. Emphasis original.

[287]*Analogia participationis in verbi* refers to a sharing or partnership, a working together with the word. In the phrase *analogia effectus verbi* we mean actual doing, execution, performance, including its effects and results with the word. By *analogia parabola verbi* we mean the enigmatic nature of the threefold form of theological discourse as analogy given in and by the Word, Jesus Christ.

model of human talk to God is based on the certainty of a God who is human in his divinity" so that "God is thinkable as one who speaks because and to the extent that he is human in and of himself."[288] The task of this final section is simply to determine how this basic insight can be conceived as a critical part of a christologically grounded *analogia fidei*, but not the most exclusive or definitive aspect. We are not intending here to resolve the other modes of analogy into this one linguistic reference. Theology will always be more than the capacity of language to express God. The analogy of parabolic Word follows quite naturally on the strength of God's speech-act, or word-deed, in the incarnation of the Word, but now concerns itself with the problem of how human "word-deeds" may reflect, in real terms, this coming to speech on the part of God. Whereas Aristotle, Aquinas and Kant, as Jüngel regularly points out, limit the capacity of language in their various analogical proposals, producing only "symbolic anthropomorphism," we seek, through the categories of participation, performance and parables, to "tremendously escalate the possibilities of language" in terms of thinking and speaking about God.[289] For us, based on our analysis of the Gospel of John, the gospel is fundamentally analogous as the "speech" of God. It begins with the affirmation that divinity fundamentally possesses its own humanity, and that the incarnation is the historical instantiation of this reality as revealed knowledge. As we saw in chapter four, Jüngel refers to this as the analogy of advent, which is in contradistinction to an *analogia nominum* and an *analogia entis*, these latter two being too restrictive of language.[290]

Parable is the essential element in any analogy of advent. Whereas, for Jüngel, the *analogia entis* is ultimately based on a "still greater dissimilarity between God and the world," parable as analogy enables the "difference . . . of a still greater similarity" between God and the world in the midst of "a great dissimilarity."[291] This is the "hermeneutical thesis" posed by the *ana-*

---

[288]*GMW*, pp. 289-95.

[289]See Rolnick, *Analogical Possibilities*, p. 255; John Macken, *The Autonomy Theme in the Church Dogmatics* (Cambridge: Cambridge University Press, 1990), p. 143; John B. Webster, *Eberhard Jüngel: An Introduction to His Theology* (Cambridge: Cambridge University Press, 1991), pp. 110-19.

[290]See Joseph Palakeel, *The Use of Analogy in Theological Discourse: An Investigation in Ecumenical Perspective* (Toronto: Editrice Pontificia Università Gregoriana, 1995), p. 208.

[291]*GMW*, p. 288; *GGW*, p. 393.

logia fidei, understood now as "event," "word-deed" or "speech-act."[292] Specifically, "the Christian faith confesses that God's becoming man, the incarnation of the Word of God in Jesus Christ, is the unique, unsurpassable instance of a still greater similarity between God and man taking place within a great dissimilarity."[293] The key to understanding this hermeneutical dialectic is the relationship established in the divine encounter. In this coming of God to humanity, the identification of God with humanity preserves the difference between God and humanity while establishing the "nearness," or better, the "presence" of God with humanity.[294] Only the incarnation, as opposed to some natural identification of God with nature, can demonstrate this relation of identity in a difference. There is to be no displacement of difference into identity here, since a relation of nearness would be destroyed. Identity dismisses the nearness, while absolute difference "establishes an absolute distance."[295] All such absolutizing ends in either distance or identity without relation. "By contrast, the mystery of the God who identifies with the man Jesus is the increase of similarity and nearness between God and man which is more than mere identity and which reveals the *concrete difference* between God and man in its surpassing mere identical being."[296] Here precisely Jesus Christ has the total character of a parable, not in the sense that he is analogous to a parable, but in the sense that in his being he embodies the fundamental relations in similarity and dissimilarity that make parabolic language possible and meaningful. As such, Jesus is the "parable of God," and this christological statement is "the fundamental proposition of a hermeneutic of the speakability of God." The analogy of faith, as an analogy of advent, must be understood as essentially a parable that "corresponds" to God.[297]

It is on the basis of this incarnate parable, wherein God's speaking corresponds, as we have seen, to human speech and witness, that theological speech is exclusively possible. It is the natural outflow of the principle that God is, primordially, human in his divine decision. Parable is the "herme-

---

[292]Ibid.
[293]*GMW*, p. 288; *GGW*, p. 392.
[294]Ibid.
[295]*GMW*, p. 288; *GGW*, p. 394.
[296]Ibid.
[297]*GMW*, pp. 288-89; *GGW*, p. 394.

neutical" enablement of language to speak of God in this decision. This possibility is based on Jüngel's assertion that "God is not an object outside language to which language distinctly refers; God comes into human language."[298] The event of the coming of the Word of God leaves no excess, so that God is really revealed in the Word.[299] Accordingly, "all valid analogy is founded on and to be known in the being of the man Jesus Christ."[300] In short, we may agree with Webster's assessment of Jüngel here when he writes that what is being propounded in Jüngel's understanding of parable is "the conviction that the language of the New Testament 'brings to speech' revelation, that it is the place where God's Word is encountered and so is both authoritative and determinative of the mind's response to it. The 'extentionality' of the texts forestalls any autonomous 'intentionality.'"[301] Parables are examples par excellence of this revelatory function of language.

But why parables? we might ask. For Jüngel the concepts of parable, metaphor and analogy have at the core a capacity to bring together "the intellectual and temporal involvement in narrative" in ways better than almost all other forms of linguistic discourse.[302] Parables, analogies and metaphors are "nonconceptualizing language-events." The relationship between God and his Word and humanity and its word constitutes an ontological relation that is grounded in God's speech but, for that reason, extends to language. "The analogy is also here in its relation as a matter of language."[303] That is, "the analogy itself is in an eminent sense a language event" because in the speaking of God there is a relation between God and the world such that God becomes a possibility of speech, but only insofar as God comes to speech and corresponds not as a capacity of language itself. "To correspond to God is a possibility that comes to language from God, and certainly not as a matter of chance."[304]

In his Paulus und Jesus, Jüngel undertakes an extensive study of the

---

[298]Rolnick, Analogical Possibilities, p. 255.
[299]Ibid.
[300]Macken, Autonomy Theme, p. 145.
[301]Webster, Eberhard Jüngel, p. 48.
[302]See R. Zimany, Vehicle for God: The Metaphorical Theology of Eberhard Jüngel (New York: Mercer University Press, 1994), pp. 26-27.
[303]Ibid.; GMW, p. 289; GW, p. 394.
[304]GMW, p. 289; GW, p. 395.

parables of the kingdom in Matthew, Mark and Luke, the essential results of which he summarizes in *GMW*.[305] The essential point there, as here, remains that, on the basis of God's inclusion of humanity in himself, we may speak of Jesus as the parable of God. The crux of the analysis, however, is to establish how the disciples were enabled to move from being mere hearers of the parables of Jesus "to faith in Jesus as the parable of God." To understand this is to understand the analogical function of parables as such. Before he gets to this analysis directly, however, he sets the movement in the context of a hermeneutical discussion since, in his opinion, this is the movement that theology has to explicate. Here he works to distinguish parable as analogy from the predominant Aristotelian view. Though we cannot follow Jüngel exhaustively here, the following critical points emerge in respect to the hermeneutical distinction that must be made between the biblical view of metaphor as parable and analogy and the commonly accepted Aristotelian definition of metaphor.[306]

Parable, metaphor and analogy exist in close relationship as linguistic forms due to their ability to narrate. While parable may be regarded as "an extended metaphor" and metaphor may be deemed an "abbreviated parable," narrative is immanent in both forms of discourse, as it is in analogy as well.[307] What distinguishes metaphor from parable is the fact that metaphor "implies narrative" through naming, whereas parable "always presupposes language's process of naming and is directed to portraying a process, an event through the movement of language."[308] That is, both parable and metaphor "address" the hearer through a form of discourse that "departs from customary language use," so that there is a "lingual renewal" of language in relation to its existential context. "This new usage makes what exists communicable in a qualitatively new way."[309] Analogy functions similarly, so that we may affirm that parable is a type of analogy in that it also enables language toward "a new way of dealing with what exists" so also that language is renewed, and precisely in the "new" there is address. Parable and analogy may be said to be "the language of faith" in that something is "signified" in

---

[305]Jüngel, *Paulus und Jesus*, p. 135.
[306]Ibid.
[307]Jüngel, "Metaphorical Truth"; Palakeel, *Use of Analogy*, p. 205.
[308]*GMW*, p. 290; *GGW*, p. 396.
[309]Ibid.

the new usage made of language by parable and/or analogy. Jüngel summarizes the effect this has on analogy as follows:

> Analogy as a process of speech is an eminently socializing phenomena in that it binds together in a fellowship not only the address of the hearers but also the speaker engaged by the analogy with his hearers. . . . As analogous talk about God, they (with the help of the speaker who is communicatively competent) create situations in which the subject of the talk becomes generally understandable, because those addressed become discoverers to all of whom the something discloses itself.[310]

That is to say, parable, metaphor and analogy possess a special force not possible in other forms of address, such as a command or request, for instance. They express "more in language than was real until now," and they do so by "involving the person who is addressed in the being of what is being talked about, or they *mediate* the topic of talk to the being of man. . . . They 'signify' a new way of understanding 'the world and each other' such that 'the new' and the accustomed 'are brought' into a relation that is already known," establishing "a correspondence which mediates between the unknown and the already known" so that what was divided, remote and unrelated are now brought into a relation of nearness, in difference, but with greater similarity.[311] Parable as analogy breaks the modality of direct discourse and identity. "If a parable were an equation, then it would be a thesis, and then its 'content' would in fact be a theme which could be abstracted from the 'form' of the parable. But a parable is not a thesis and has no theme at all. Rather, it is an event which then makes something else happen."[312] In this "happening" there is a coalescence of the subject of the parable with the persons addressed. Something happens in the parable, and it happens in such a way that then something also happens through the parable.[313] "This is a unique function of language that brings something new and different" by means of concepts both familiar and similar, yet completely different in meaning. "In a parable, language is so focused that the subject of the discourse becomes concrete in language itself and thus defines anew the people addressed in

---

[310]*GMW*, p. 291; *GGW*, p. 397.
[311]*GMW*, p. 290. Jüngel prefers the word *correspondence* (*Entsprechung*) to *similarity*.
[312]*GMW*, pp. 293-94; *GGW*, p. 401; Jüngel, *Paulus und Jesus*, p. 107.
[313]*GMW*, pp. 292-93; *GGW*, p. 399.

their own existence."[314] What parable, and therefore also analogy, brings is
an event that surpasses direct speech with a greater capacity to concretize
transcending principles or ideas. As such, they are "language events of creative freedom" that constitute "the essence of analogy," which is "the addressing event of gripping freedom. As such it is both an enhancement of
language and its precise focusing."[315]

Parables, as such, "ignite" understanding through indirect reference.
Jesus does this supremely in his parables of the kingdom, wherein "the
kingdom becomes understandable not by means of a mere definition (this
is the kingdom) kept as a kerygma or preached concept (the kingdom of
God is *like* . . .)."[316] "In that sense parables serve as the language of faith
generally. Of all the parables representative of the language of faith . . . Jesus'
parables of the kingdom of God are especially instructional because, although they are not the adequate ground, they are the hermeneutical preparation for kerygmatic talk about Jesus as the Son of God."[317] Parables, as
such, have an analogical power to express "God's future" in such a way as to
bring an eschatological "foretaste" of that future. As uttered by Jesus, they
are a "sacramental relation" in that the sign and the things signified become
"efficacious." Parables are "divine acts" in which "the new time of God's reign
is already present," as proclaimed by Christ.[318] "The parables of Jesus do not
speak of God as a man. But they speak of God in such a way that they tell
about the world of men. They don't do this by putting the world in God's
place, so that some kind of general wisdom would emerge as the point of
the parables." Rather, "their concern is the kingdom of God and that means
that they are dealing with the intertwined work of God's relationship to Jesus'
hearers and their relationship to God."[319] In parabolic discourse, there is no
basis here for a direct comparison between God and the world. There is no
such internal comparison assumed to be present in parable. To assume this
would be to "leave the world itself" so that no real relation between God and

---

[314]*GMW*, pp. 292-93; *GGW*, p. 400 n. 22.
[315]*GMW*, p. 292.
[316]Ibid., pp. 87, 110.
[317]*GMW*, p. 293; *GGW*, pp. 400-401.
[318]Jüngel, *Paulus und Jesus*, p. 101.
[319]*GMW*, p. 293.

the world would be possible.[320] "These parables do presuppose the dissimilarity of the kingdom of God and the world in the sense of a fundamental difference, but they only emphasize this difference so that the great dissimilarity in a still greater similarity is emphasized."[321]

Thus the kingdom of God comes to speech primarily in the form of an analogy in terms of its "strangeness" and "abstract difference" but in a way that ultimately "surpasses" this strangeness with a "greater familiarity" in the sense of a concrete differentness from the world, which benefits the world.[322] It is the "activity of the kingdom" of God in Jesus' telling of the parables that makes possible this relation between God and the world. This is how the kingdom of God "is," but only in terms that "the following relationship corresponds to it." The kingdom of God (x), unknown in the world and not even knowable within the world's terms, relates itself to the world (a) in a relationship which in the world corresponds to the way things happen, as, for instance, in the story of the treasure in the field (Mt 13:44). This yields the following linguistic model: $x{\rightarrow}a{::}b{:}c$.[323] Insofar as the kingdom of God came into language in this way (as parable), it has the capacity to address the hearer. It is brought into language by the storyteller, immanently exemplified in Jesus but also as a capacity given to all such storytellers. The worldly side of the parable, b:c, is certainly "received according to the mode of the receiver but only by virtue of the fact that a prior 'x' comes to 'a'" such that it is the speech of God. "God comes into language." He "enters into words," and only to this extent may we say that, in parable, God comes to language such that a relation is established. So Jüngel concludes, "Bringing God to expression in language thus follows after the relation of the kingdom of God to the world and consequently has its criteria in the fact that at the very great distance away of the eschatological kingdom of God is surpassed by a still greater nearness."[324] In this way parables, and therefore metaphors and analogies, though they be worldly modalities of speech, still may speak truthfully of God and the world at the same time. Indeed such a word, despite the incomprehensibility of God, is still a knowledge of God "sufficient

---

[320]Ibid.
[321]*GMW*, p. 294.
[322]*GMW*, p. 295.
[323]Ibid.
[324]Ibid.

unto salvation."[325] Any one of the parables of the kingdom can adequately demonstrate "the still greater nearness of the far distant kingdom of God."[326]

Summary. So much for the hermeneutical possibility of an analogy of parabolic Word, admittedly only sketched herein. What is its significance with respect to the question of theological speech in light of the analogy of being and our own proposal for an *analogia fidei* along the lines of participation, performance and parable? The question that brings them all together and what is the significance of our own *analogia fidei* is precisely how God comes to us as participation, performance and parable in time. For language to have the capacity to be freighted with the being of God, there must exist a divine relation to time that does not so completely exclude God from time, so that such a relation is impossible, but to relate God to time so that such a greater distinction is obviated. Here we return to the central principle that grounds the whole enterprise of an *analogia fidei*, namely, Jesus as God for man and man for God. If we take God's relation to time to mean absolute difference, we reduce language to mere "symbolic anthropomorphism." If, however, we take God's relation to time in terms of an absolute identity, we are driven to "dogmatic anthropomorphism." Neither approach is an option for a Christian modality of theological speech. Both are the result of an *analogia entis* toward a univocity of being or an *analogia entis* toward an incomprehensibility of being.[327] Dogmatic anthropomorphism leads us to speak of God as though he were the highest man, with a consequent loss of his distinction from humanity and vice versa. When theology loses both subjects, it loses its raison d'être. "The fatal thing then about naive 'dogmatic' anthropomorphism is ultimately that it cannot withstand theological enlightenment but rather, when once theologically enlightened, asserts that God is in the final analysis not speakable at all."[328] Is this not, after all, the deep secret negation contained in the inevitable grounding of our knowledge of God in a testable experience of the world, known in principle as CER? Is it not the case that at the end of the day the *via negativa*, the *via eminentia* and the

---

[325]*GMW*, p. 295 n. 25.
[326]Ibid.
[327]*GMW*, pp. 296-97.
[328]*GMW*, p. 297.

via analogia (understood as an *analogia entis*) are precisely "philosophical insights" that lead to the unspeakability of God? In respect to this history, one is inclined to agree with Jüngel: "Since one is no longer allowed to think of God as a divine *ego* according to the analogy of a human *ego*, a divine *ego* which is addressable as a Thou, he becomes unspeakable as his own subject, that is, as God."[329]

Some theologians of participation tend this way. God's "co-humanity" must not be permitted to become a cipher for his de-divinization or humanity's re-divinization.[330] In this respect we only achieve the concomitant loss of our own humanity wherein we separate ourselves from ourselves and from others "in order to seek after the place of the distant God, man himself now being an essence of the distant."[331] When Jüngel wrote this in the 1970s, he had in mind both the death-of-God theologies and the theologies of radical alterity. In our own time it has come back on the scene in terms of a resurgent theological metaphysics of radical orthodoxy and the renaissance of Eastern Orthodoxy. "In opposition to 'dogmatic' anthropomorphism and the fatal consequences which may be ascribed to it, it may be said of parable as analogous talk about God that it preserves the concrete distinctiveness of God and man (world). It preserves the distinctiveness, however, in that it combines God . . . and man in one and the same event, in the parable itself." But this is also true of the participation of God in and with the world in his spoken word. It is verified in the performative act of his speaking, to which our analogy of performative Word may correspond.[332]

But this is precisely the ground necessary to avoid the pitfalls to theological speech on the side of mere Kantian "symbolic anthropomorphism." "The parable, as concrete spoken implementation of the analogy between God and man, does not recede into merely symbolic anthropomorphism, which would articulate, in spite of such a great similarity between God and man, a still greater dissimilarity."[333] The language of total difference and/or total identity can, at either end, be pushed in the direction of agnosticism at

---

[329]Ibid.
[330]Ibid. See esp. p. 297 n. 27.
[331]Ibid.
[332]Ibid.
[333]Ibid.

best, or atheism at worst, despite Kant's desire to "create a space for faith."[334] Just as it is impossible to identify God and humanity, it is also impossible to speak of God without humanity, but only because of the divine decision. We cannot hope to speak of God "like" a man if we cannot affirm the sense in which he came "as a man." Christian theology preserves the dialectic precisely in its doctrine that Jesus Christ the Son of God became a man. On the one hand, parable, as a linguistic category, contains within it the capacity, as analogous talk about God, to hold in balance an *analogia participationis* that might descend into dogmatic anthropomorphism when participation is seen as an exclusive privilege of creation itself. On the other hand, as a linguistic cipher, parable is a form of analogy that tempers the tendency to read an absolute difference between God's speech-act and the corresponding human witness. In parable, participation between divinity and humanity is assumed, while performance is the very act of God coming to the speech of the storyteller. "Christian talk about God stands and falls with its being able to speak of God as a man. . . . God and perishability are thought together in the Christian faith when the faith speaks of God as a man and in the process says 'God' and does not require that one always speak of man instead of God."[335] It does this when it says this man, Jesus Christ, is God for man and man for God, because he is electing God and elected man. In this sense truly God has come closer to humanity than humanity has, or can, come to itself. In this regard Jüngel is entirely correct to call Jesus Christ of Nazareth the parable of God. If there is a theological ontology, surely this must be its shape and scope. This is the Christian God of the Bible: the one who, despite his great dissimilarity, his greater distance and his utter difference is still more concerned with a greater nearness, and a "still more intensive relationship."[336] Love is constituted by the fact that, in his great love, God speaks a Word that included the possibility of our own speech, action and correspondence. Theology knows no other metaphysics and needs no other ontology than the incarnate Word, witnessed to in the Scripture as Jesus Christ of Nazareth. He is the one true analogy, the *analogia fidei*.

---

[334]See Immanuel Kant, *Religion Within the Limits of Reason Alone* (New York: Harper & Row, 1983), p. 13.

[335]*GMW*, p. 297.

[336]*GMW*, p. 298.

Furthermore, as theology moves forward, we will need to give some attention to the question about the power of language, which Jüngel's proposal for an "analogy of advent," through parable, raises. Analogy is a function of language and as such comes under the general criticism about the power of language as a means for religious discourse. One of Jüngel's particularly keen observations of Kant is that language receives a reduction in its capacity for speech about God in Kant's notion of analogy. Its power to express knowledge is limited to "symbolic anthropomorphism," which has for its subject an object that remains beyond the sphere of the sensible world. The best knowledge that can be achieved is that the object of religious knowledge is unknowable.

Jüngel wants to introduce new possibilities for religious discourse in his reshaping of analogy into an analogy of advent. God is not outside language but comes to the world in human speech. This coming is the advent of the gospel that addresses us as the Word of God. God is in the Word. In his treatment of the analogy of advent, Jüngel "takes us to the heart of his concern to explore the character of the relationship between God and man. For he views analogical language, like metaphor, as a form of predication which corresponds to the proper distinction between God and the world."[337] This is Jüngel's real "dogmatic" concern in his treatment of analogy. Truth is expressed in analogical language as a fundamental interpretation of human life relations. Webster summarizes this function of analogy in Jüngel very well:

> The analogy of advent is thus the linguistic equivalent of the proper relation of God and the world. The divine and the human are not confused, either by envisaging divine immanence within the human or by resolving the human into a sign whose value is exhausted in pointing to God. Divine and human are substantial in themselves; but by coming to the world God allows the human and worldly to speak of him, and so grants it new and further significance.[338]

Jüngel is not concerned with the "absolution" of reality but with introducing new "possibilities" within reality itself. Analogical language is not a literal description of reality, but it is not less than what is actually real, either. It is "referential to more than actuality, precisely because it is metaphorical lan-

---

[337]John Webster, "Eberhard Jüngel on the Language of Faith," *ModT* 1, no. 4 (July 1985): 261.
[338]Webster, *Eberhard Jüngel*, p. 48.

guage. The suspension of literal reference allows the linguistic identification of states of affairs beyond the actual."[339] In the coming of God as parable, the interruption of the human horizon has created a space for God's speakability.

Webster offers an important caveat, however, to Jüngel's investment of power in language. The danger is that he "tends to elevate metaphor, parable and analogy to the position where they become the only appropriate modes of Christian speech." He does this by compressing "the multi-level, pluriform nature of Christian religious language, and so fails to be alert to the range of its possibilities."[340] Religious language certainly needs liberation from the "hegemony" of literal speech, but not to the degree that its freedom of form is further curtailed by one mode of speech, namely, parable. In the long run it is Jüngel's "dogmatic quest" for a proper account of the distinction between God and humanity, and its responsible explication in theology, that reduces his efforts to a prescription for religious discourse rather than a description of its way forward. There are also realities in Christian expression that lie beyond linguistic description and cannot be reduced to language. Not only language "but patterns of thought and strategies of action both ritual and ethical" must aid in "bringing God to speech." The Christian faith is not reducible to words but incorporates the transformation of humanity, of which language is only one of its cultural mandates. Speech about God involves, in the true "Barthian" sense, human response in "decision and deed."[341]

---

[339]Ibid., p. 261.
[340]Webster, *Eberhard Jüngel*, p. 50.
[341]Ibid., p. 51.

CONCLUSIONS

◆

This study was undertaken with a view to establishing the possibility of theology along the lines of a deepened understanding of the christological content of the analogy of faith. In the process it insisted on maintaining the distinction between the *analogy of being* and the *analogy of faith* and therefore recognizes the ecumenical differences that remain between Catholic ways of doing theology and the Protestant modality. Is it the case, therefore, that we have closed off any opening for dialogue? Certainly not! The one principle that unites the desire for a theology that speaks effectively about God is the christological element. It is my opinion that a close reading of some contemporary offers for a revised version of theological speech along the lines of analogy of being fails the test in this respect.

With Barth we affirm the possibility of a deeper christological grounding of analogy in the work of Erich Przywara and especially Hans Urs von Balthasar. But a recognition of this insight on their part does not have to entail, on the part of Protestantism, an abandonment of their suspicion with respect to the analogy of being, or the synergistic tendencies latent, and sometimes operative, in Catholic theology. There is every reason to believe that the singular contribution of Protestant thought to the issue of analogy is in the supplying of a positive christological *analogia fidei*. A few conclusions may now be ventured on this basis.

First, in the so-called postmodern era (or better, late modern era), when it would appear that the "epistemological collapse" of the modern project now opens the way for a revised "theological ontology" with its own metaphysics of an *analogia entis* of sorts, we need be no less critical of any metaphysics that threatens the theological primacy of the revelatory Word. Far from wanting to institute either a theopanism on the one side, or pantheism on the other, Eberhard Jüngel strove to maintain the ontological difference between God and the human, precisely in correspondence. This was the fundamental principle he learned from his theological master, Karl Barth. On the large scale of twentieth- and twenty-first-century theology, even in respect to Przywara and von Balthasar, Barth continues to be a veritable "cornucopia" of theological insight, especially where theological predication is concerned. Despite our best efforts herein, the full scope of the dominance of his christological *analogia fidei* remains to be completely exposited. It is clear that any future work in theological method related to analogy must strive to take as full an account of this christological ground for the *analogia fidei* as did Barth, and, following his intuition, von Balthasar.

Furthermore, despite the attempts on the part of some scholars from all of the major Christian traditions to undermine the Protestant concern as a misunderstanding, clearly Protestantism, from within its own theological concerns, had and still has a right to be concerned about the *analogia entis*. Just as the case for the differences between Barth, Przywara and von Balthasar may have been based on overblown misunderstanding, so it is also a mistake to dismiss the differences as a problem Protestantism has with the proper foundations of theological predication. This is an oversimplification in the opposite direction. The differences between Protestant and Catholic theology on this issue were and still are real, and they remained so for both Barth and Przywara.

Last, Christian theology has to accept the fact that very early on in its development it adopted a principle, which we designated herein as CER, that had latent within it a Platonic cosmology that predisposed theological epistemology toward a totalizing metaphysics, often with the capacity for both pantheism and/or theopanism. We have purposely avoided herein a direct answer as to whether this Platonic principle accords with Scripture's epistemic point of view, or if indeed Christian theology ought to trade on it. But it has become clear by now that metaphysically oriented theological epistemologies that did trade on this became susceptible to dogmatic anthropomorphism on the one hand and symbolic anthropomorphism on the other. The CER principle also tended to trade a general theopanism for a concrete form of divine incarnation. Either way, for theology, the only corrective must be an insistence on a real, substantial christological content for any use of analogy. It must be a christological *analogia fidei*.

BIBLIOGRAPHY

Adams, Marilyn McCord. "Final Causality and Explanation of Scotus's 'De Primo Principio.'" In *Nature in Medieval Thought: Some Approaches East and West*, edited by Chūmaru Koyama, pp. 153-84. Studien und Texte zur Geistesgeschichte des Mittelalters 73. Leiden: Brill, 2000.

Aertsen, Jan. *Medieval Philosophy and the Transcendentals: The Case of Thomas Aquinas*. 3 vols. Studien und Texte zur Geistesgeschichte des Mittelalters 52. Leiden: Brill, 1996.

Aiken, Wyatt D. "Essence and Existence, Transcendentalism and Phenomenalism: Aristotle's Answers to the Questions of Ontology." *Review of Metaphysics* 45 (1991): 29-55.

Aland, K. "Eine Untersuchung zu Joh 1, 3-4." *ZNW* 59 (1968): 174-209.

Alston, William P. *Divine Nature and Human Language: Essays in Philosophical Theology*. Ithaca, NY: Cornell University Press, 1989.

Ambühl, Hans. "Metaphysik und Ontologie bei Aristoteles." *Freibürger Zeitschrift für Philosophie und Theologie* 41 (1994): 223-28.

Ameriks, K. "The Critique of Metaphysics: Kant and Traditional Ontology." In *Cambridge Companion to Kant*, edited by Paul Guyer, pp. 269-302. Cambridge: Cambridge University Press, 1992.

Ammonius, Hermiae. *On Aristotle's Categories*. Translated by S. Marc Cohen and Gareth B. Matthews. Ithaca, NY: Cornell University Press, 1991.

Anawati, Georges C., O.P. "Saint Thomas d'Aquin et la Mitaphysique d'Avicenne." In *St Thomas Aquinas, 1274-1974*, edited by É. Gilson, 2:449-66. Commemorative Studies. Toronto: Pontifical Institute for Mediaeval Studies Press, 1974.

Anderson, James F. *The Bond of Being: An Essay on Analogy and Existence*. St. Louis: B. Herder, 1949.

———. *The Cause of Being: The Philosophy of Creation in St. Thomas*. New York: B. Herder, 1952.

————. *An Introduction to the Metaphysics of St. Thomas Aquinas.* Chicago: Henry Regnery, 1953.

————. *Reflections on the Analogy of Being.* The Hague: Martin Nijhof, 1967.

Anderson, T. C. "Aristotle and Aquinas on the Freedom of the Mathematician." *The Thomist* 36 (1972): 231-55.

Anzinger, Herbert. *Glaube und kommunikative Praxis: eine Studie zur vordialektischen Theologie Karl Barths.* Munchen: Chr. Kaiser Verlag, 1991.

Aquinas, Thomas. *Commentary on the Book of Causes* [*Super librum De causis expositio*]. Translated and annotated by Vincent A. Guagliardo, Charles R. Hess and Richard C. Taylor. Vol. 1 of *Thomas Aquinas in Translation.* Washington, D.C.: The Catholic University of America Press, 1996.

————. *Compendium of Theology.* Translated by R. J. Regan. Oxford: Oxford University Press, 2009.

————. *Corpus Thomisticum, Editio aureo numismate donata Summo Pontiiice Leone XIII.* Romae: Ex Typographia Forzani Et S., 1979.

————. *De ente et essentia.*

————. *De Principiis Naturae.*

————. *Lectura Romana in Primum Sententiarum Petri Lombardi.* Edited by Leonard E. Boyle and John F. Boyle. Toronto: Pontifical Institute of Mediaeval Studies, 2006.

————. *In librum Dionysii De divinis nominibus expositio.* Available at www.corpusthomisticum.org/cdn00.html.

————. *In Metaphysicorum.*

————. *On Being and Essence.* Translated by Armand Maurer. Toronto: Pontifical Institute of Mediaeval Studies, 1949.

————. *Peri hermeneias.*

————. *Quaestiones disputatae de potentia Dei.* Edited by Raymund Spiazzi. Taurini: Domus Editorialis Marietti, 1953.

————. *Quaestiones quodlibetales.*

————. *Sententia libri Ethicorum.*

————. *Sententia libri Metaphysicae.*

————. *Summa Contra Gentiles.* Dominican Fathers Edition of the Leonine Text. London: Burns and Oates, 1924.

————. *Summa Theologiae.* Dominican Fathers Edition of the Leonine Text. London: Burns and Oates, 1924.

————. *Super Boethium De Trinitate.*

———. *Super Isaiam.*

Aristotle. *De anima.*

———. *Metaphysics.*

———. *Nicomachian Ethics.*

———. *Nicomedian Ethics.*

———. *Physics.*

———. *Poetica.*

Armstrong, A. H., ed. *The Cambridge History of Later Greek and Early Medieval Philosophy.* London: Cambridge University Press, 1967.

Ashworth, E. Jennifer. "Can I Speak More Clearly Than I Understand? A Problem of Religious Language in Henry of Ghent, Duns Scotus and Ockham." *Historiographia Linguistica* 7 (1980): 29-38.

Aubenque, Pierre. "Aristoteles und das Problem der Metaphysik." *Zeitschrift für philosophische Forschung* 15 (1961): 321-33.

———. "Les origins neoplatoniciennes de la doctrine de l'analogie de l'etre." In *Neoplatonisme: mélanges offerts a Jean Trouillard*, pp. 19-22. Les Cahiers de Fontenay. Fontenay-aux-Roses, 1981.

———. "Sur l'inauthenticité du livre K de la Métaphysique." In *Zweifelhaftes im Corpus Aristotelicum: Studien zum einigen Dubia, Akten des 9*, edited by Moraux Paul and Wiesner Jürgen, pp. 318-44. Symposium Aristotelicum, Berlin, September 1981. Berlin: Walter de Gruyter, 1983.

Augustine. *Confessions.* Translated by Maria Boulding. Works of Saint Augustine I/1. Hyde Park, NY: New City Press, 2002.

———. *Confessionum.* PL vol. 32.

———. *Contra Academicos.* PL vol. 32.

———. *Contra Academicos.* Edited by Johannes Quasten. Translated by John J. Omera. Ancient Christian Writings 12. Westminster, MD: The Newman Press, 1950.

———. *Contra Iulianum haeresis Pelagianae defensorem libri sex.* PL vol. 44.

———. *De civitate Dei.* PL vol. 41.

———. *De diversis quaestionibus LXXXIII liber unus.* PL vol. 40.

———. *De doctrina christiana.* PL vol. 40.

———. *De Genesi ad litteram.* PL vol. 34.

———. *De Genesi ad litteram imperfectus liber.* PL vol. 34.

———. *De Genesi contra Manicheos.* PL vol. 42.

———. *De immortalitate animae.* PL vol. 40.

———. *De liber arbitrio.* PL vol. 32.

———. *De quantitate animae liber unus.* PL vol. 32.

———. *De Trinitate.* Books XIV-XVI. PL vol. 42.

———. *De vera religione liber unus.* PL vol. 34.

———. *De vita beata.* PL vol. 47.

———. *Enarrationes in Psalmos.*

———. *Epistolae.* PL vol. 35.

———. *In Evangelium Johannis tractatus.* PL vol. 35.

———. *On Christian Belief.* Edited by Boniface Ramsey. Translated by Edmund
Hill, Ray Kearney, Michael Campbell, Bruce Halbert and Michael Fiedrowicz.
New York: New City Press, 2005.

———. *On Christian Teaching* [*De doctrina christiana*]. Translated by R. P. H.
Green. Oxford World's Classics. New York: Oxford University Press, 1997.

———. *Retractationum.* PL vol. 47.

———. *The Trinity.* Translated by Edmund Hill. New York: New City Press, 1991.
PL vol. 42.

Ayres, Lewis. *Augustine and the Trinity.* Cambridge: Cambridge University Press,
2004.

Bäck, Allan. "What Is Being Qua Being?" In *Idealization XI: Historical Studies
on Abstraction and Idealization,* edited by Coniglione Francesco, Poli Ro-
berto and Rollinger Robin, pp. 37-58. Amsterdam: Rodopi, 2004.

Barrett, C. K. *The Gospel According to John.* 2nd ed. London: SPCK, 1978.

Barth, Karl. *Anselm: Fides Quaerens Intellectum: Anselm's Proof of the Existence
of God in the Context of His Theological Scheme.* Translated by Ian W. Rob-
ertson. London: Pickwick, 1985.

———. *Church Dogmatics, Vol. I-IV.* Translated and edited by T. F. Torrance and
G. W. Bromiley. Edinburgh: T & T Clark, 1965, 2004.

———. *Die Kirchliche Dogmatik, Band I-IV.* Zürich: Evangelischer Verlag-
Zollikon A. G., 1932.

———. *Ethics.* Edited by G. W. Bromiley. Translated by D. Braun. Edinburgh:
T & T Clark, 1981.

———. "Fate and Idea in Theology." In *The Way of Theology in Karl Barth: Essays
and Comments.* Edited by M. Rumscheidt. Allison Park, PA: Pickwick, 1986.

———. *Gesamtausgabe II. Akademische Werke: Band I & II.* Zurich: Theologischer
Verlag, 1973, 1978.

———. *God Here and Now.* Translated by Paul M. van Buren. New York: Routledge, 2003.

———. *How I Changed My Mind.* Edinburgh: St. Andrews Press, 1969.

———. *The Humanity of God*. Philadelphia: John Knox, 1960.

———. *Instruction in the Christian Religion*. Vol. 1 of *The Göttingen Dogmatics*. Translated by Geoffrey W. Bromiley. Grand Rapids: Eerdmans, 1990.

———. *An Introduction to Evangelical Theology*. Grand Rapids: Eerdmans, 1984.

———. "Kirche und Theologie." *Zwischen den Zeiten* 4 (1926). Reprinted in *The Beginnings of Dialectical Theology*, edited by J. M. Robinson, 1:21-58. Richmond, VA: John Knox, 1968.

———. *The Knowledge of God and the Service of God*. London: Hodder & Stoughton, 1960.

———. *Prolegomena, 1924*. Vol. 1 of *Unterricht in der christlichen Religion*. Edited by Hannelotte Reiffen. Zurich: TVZ, 1985.

———. *Protestant Theology in the 19th Century: Its Background and History*. Grand Rapids: Eerdmans, 2002.

———. *Witness to the Word*. Grand Rapids: Eerdmans, 1986.

Barth, Timotheus. *Studies in Philosophy and the History of Philosophy*. Vol. 3. Washington, D.C.: Catholic University of America Press, 1965.

Bastit, Michel. *Naissance de la loi moderne: La pensée de la loi de saint Thomas à Suarez*. Paris: Presses Universitaires de France, 1990.

Bates, Todd C. *Duns Scotus and the Problem of Universals*. New York: Continuum, 2010.

Baurschmidt, F. C., and J. Fodor. "John Duns Scotus and Modern Theology." *ModT* 21, no. 4 (October 2005): 539-42.

Beach, J. D. "Separate Entity as the Subject of Aristotle's Metaphysics." *The Thomist* 20 (1957): 75-95.

Beasley-Murray, G. R. *Gospel According to John*. Word Biblical Commentary. Waco: Word, 1987.

Beintker, Michael. *Die Dialektik in der "dialektischen Theologie" Karl Barths*. Munich: C. Kaiser, 1987.

Pope Benedict XVI. "Faith, Reason and the University: Memories and Reflections." *Libreria Editrice Vaticana* (2006): 10.

Berchman, Robert. *From Philo to Origen: Middle Platonism in Transition*. Chicago: Scholars Press, 1984.

Berkouwer, G. C. *The Providence of God*. Translated by Lewis B. Smedes. Grand Rapids: Eerdmans, 1952.

Bermon, Pascale. *Lumières médiévales: saint Bernard, Averroès, saint Thomas d'Aquin, Duns Scot*. Conférences de la Faculté Notre-Dame, 2008–2009. Saint-Maur: Parole et silence, 2010.

Bernard, J. H. *A Critical Commentary on the Gospel According to John.* New York: Scribners, 1924.

Betz, John R. *After Enlightenment: The Post-Secular Vision of J. G. Hamann.* Oxford: Blackwell, 2008.

———. "Beyond the Sublime: The Aesthetics of the Analogy of Being (Part One)." *ModT* 21 (July 2005): 367-411.

———. "Beyond the Sublime: The Aesthetics of the Analogy of Being (Part Two)." *ModT* 22 (January 2006): 1-50.

Beumer, B. "*Gratia supponit naturam.* Zur Geschichte eines theologischen Prinzips." *Gregorianum* 20 (1930): 381-406, 535-52.

Bieler, Martin. "Karl Barths Auseinandersetzung mit der analogia entis und der Anfang der Theologie." *Catholica* 40 (1986): 241-45.

Billings, Todd. *Calvin, Participation and the Gift.* Oxford: Oxford University Press, 2007.

———. *Participation in Calvin.* Oxford: Oxford University Press, 2005.

Blondel, Maurice. *L'action.* Paris: Presses Universitaires de France, 1995. Reprint of 1983 ed.

Blumenthal, H. J., ed. *Neoplatonism and Early Christian Thought: Essays in Honour of A. H. Armstrong.* London: Variorum Publications, 1981.

Bobik, Joseph. *Aquinas on Matter and Form and the Elements.* Notre Dame, IN: University of Notre Dame Press, 1998.

Boersma, Hans. "Accommodation to What? Univocity of Being, Pure Nature and the Anthropology of St. Irenaeus." *IJST* 8 (2006): 266-93.

———. "Analogy of Truth: The Sacramental Epistemology of the Nouvelle Theologie." In *Ressourcement: A Movement for Renewal in Twentieth-Century Catholic Theology,* ed. Gabriel Flynn and Paul D. Murray, pp. 81-105. Oxford: Oxford University Press, 2013.

———. "Being Reconciled: Atonement as the Ecclesio-Christological Practice of Forgiveness in John Milbank." In *Radical Orthodoxy and the Reformed Tradition: Creation, Covenant, and Participation,* ed. James K. A. Smith and James H. Olthuis, pp. 157-71. Grand Rapids: Baker Academic, 2005.

———. *Heavenly Participation: The Weaving of a Sacramental Tapestry.* Grand Rapids: Eerdmans, 2011.

———. *The Nouvelle Theologie and Sacramental Ontology: A Return to Mystery.* Oxford: Oxford University Press, 2009.

———. "On the Rejection of Boundaries: Radical Orthodoxy's Appropriation of St. Augustine." *Pro Ecclesia* 15 (2006): 418-47.

———. "Redemptive Hospitality in Irenaeus: A Model for Ecumenicity in a Violent World." *Pro Ecclesia* 11 (2002): 207-26.

———. "Sacramental Ontology: Nature and the Supernatural in the Ecclesiology of Henri de Lubac." *New Blackfriars* 88 (2007): 242-73.

Boethius, Manlii Severini Boetii. *Opera Omnia*. PL vols. 63 and 64.

Boland, Vivian. *Ideas in God According to St. Thomas Aquinas: Sources and Synthesis*. New York: Brill, 1996.

Boman, T. *Hebrew Thought Compared with Greek*. Translated by Jules L. Moreau. Philadelphia: Westminster Press, 1960.

Bonaventure, Saint Cardinal. *Commentaria in Sententiis P. Lombardi*.

Bonner, Gerald. *St. Augustine: Life and Controversies*. 3rd ed. New York: Morehouse, 2002.

Borgen, P. "The Logos Was the True Light; Contributions to the Interpretation of the Prologue of John." *NovT* 14 (1972): 115-30.

———. "Observations on the Targumic Character of the Prologue of John." *NTS* 16 (1969–1970): 288-95.

Bos, Egbert Peter. "A Scotistic Discussion of 'Deus est' as a *propositio per se nota*. Edition with an Introduction." *Vivarium* 33 (1995): 197-234.

Bosley, Richard N., and Martin M. Tweedale, eds. *Basic Issues in Medieval Philosophy: Selected Readings Presenting the Interactive Discourses Among the Major Figures*. 2nd ed. Orchard Park, NY: Broadview, 1997.

Bouillard, Henri. *Karl Barth: Genese et evolution de la theologie dialectique*. 3 vols. Paris: Aubier, 1957.

———. *The Knowledge of God*. Translated by Samuel D. Femiano. New York: Herder & Herder, 1968.

Boulnois, Olivier. "Analogie et univocité selon Duns Scot: La double destruction." *Les études philosophiques* 3, no. 4 (1989): 347-69.

———. *Être et représentation: Une généalogie de la métaphysique moderne à l'époque de Duns Scot (XIIIe–XIVe siècle)*. Épiméthée, Paris: Presses Universitaires de France, 1999.

———. "Puissance neutre et puissance obédientielle: de l'homme à Dieu selon Duns Scot et Cajétan." In *Rationalisme analogique et humanisme théologique: la culture de Thomas de Vio "Il Gaetano": actes du Colloque de Naples, 1-3 novembre 1990*, ed. Bruno Pinchard and Saverio Ricci, pp. 31-69. Napoli: Vivarium, 1993.

———. "Reading Duns Scotus: From History to Philosophy." *ModT* 21 (2005): 603-8.

Boyle, Leonard. *The Setting of the Summa Theologiae of St. Thomas.* Toronto: Pontifical Institute of Mediaeval Studies, 1992.

Brague, Rémi. *Aristote et la question du monde. Essai sur le contexte cosmologique et anthropologique de l'ontologie.* Paris: Presses Universitaires de France, 2001.

Breil, Reinhold. *Der kosmologische Gottesbeweis und die Einheit der Natur: Thomas von Aquin—Duns Scotus—Leibniz—Wolff—Kant.* Veröffentlichungen der Johannes-Duns-Skotus-Akademie für Franziskanische Geistesgeschichte und Spiritualität Mönchengladbach 11. Kevelaer: Butzon und Bercker, 2000.

Brentano, Franz. *On the Several Senses of Being in Aristotle.* Berkeley: University of California Press, 1975.

Brisson, L. "The Reception of the Parmenides Before Proclus." *Zeitschrift für antikes Christentum* 12 (2008): 99-113.

Brito, Emilio. *La christologie de Hegel: Verbum Crucis.* Paris: Beauchesne, 1983.

———. *Dieu et l'etre d'apres Thomas d'Aquin et Hegel.* Paris: Paris University Press, 1991.

———. "Dieu en movement? Thomas d'Aquin et Hegel." *Revue des sciences religieuses* 62 (1988): 111-36.

Brock, Stephen L. *Action and Conduct: Thomas Aquinas and the Theory of Action.* Edinburgh: T & T Clark, 1998.

Brown, Jerome V. "Avicenna and the Unity of the Concept of Being: The Interpretations of Henry of Ghent, Duns Scotus, Gerard of Bologna and Peter Aureoli." *Franciscan Studies* 25 (1965): 117-50.

———. "Duns Scotus on the Possibility of Knowing Genuine Truth: The Reply to Henry of Ghent in the 'Lectura prima' and the 'Ordinatio.'" *Recherches de théologie ancienne et medieval* 51 (1984): 136-82.

———. "John Duns Scotus on Henry of Ghent's Theory of Knowledge." *The Modern Schoolman* 56 (1978/79): 1-29.

Brown, Peter. *Augustine of Hippo: A Biography.* Rev. ed. Berkeley: University of California Press, 2000.

Brown, R. E. *The Community of the Beloved Disciple.* New York: Paulist, 1979.

———. "*The Sensus Plenior* in the Last Ten Years." *Catholic Biblical Quarterly* 25 (1965): 262-85.

Brunner, Emil. *The Christian Doctrine of Creation and Redemption: Dogmatics Volume II.* Philadelphia: Westminster Press, 1952.

———. *Natural Theology.* Translated by Peter Fraenkel. London: Geoffrey Bles/ The Centenary Press, 1946.

Buchanan, Emerson. *Aristotle's Theory of Being*. Cambridge: Cambridge University Press, 1962.

Buckley, James J., ed. *Knowing the Triune God: The Work of the Spirit in the Practices of the Church*. Grand Rapids: Eerdmans, 2001.

Buckley, J., and W. McFague Wilson. "A Dialogue with Barth and Farrer on Theological Method." *Heythrop Journal* 26 (1985): 274-93.

Bukowski, T. P. "Beyond Aristotle . . . and Beyond Newton: Thomas Aquinas on an Infinite Creation." *The Thomist* 68, no. 2 (2004): 287-314.

Bultmann, Rudolf. *Commentary on John*. Hermeneia. Philadelphia: Fortress, 1982.

Burnaby, J. *Amor Dei: A Study of Religion in St Augustine*. London: Hodder & Stougthon, 1938.

Burnet, John. *Greek Philosophy: Thales to Plato*. London: MacMillan, 1961.

Burrell, David. *Analogy and Philosophical Language*. New Haven, CT: Yale University Press, 1973.

———. *Aquinas: God and Action*. Notre Dame, IN: University of Notre Dame Press, 1979.

———. "Aquinas on Naming God." *Theological Studies* 24 (1963): 183-212.

———. "Beyond a Theory of Analogy." *Proceedings of the American Catholic Philosophical Association* 46 (1972): 114-22.

———. *Faith and Freedom: An Interfaith Perspective*. Malden, MA: Blackwell, 2004.

———, ed. *God and Creation: An Ecumenical Symposium*. Notre Dame, IN: University of Notre Dame Press, 1990.

———. "John Duns Scotus: The Univocity of Analogous Terms." *The Monist* 49 (1965): 639-58.

———. *Knowing the Unknowable God: Ibn-Sina, Maimonides, Aquinas*. Notre Dame, IN: University of Notre Dame Press, 1986.

Busch, Eberhard. "God Is God: The Meaning of a Controversial Formula and the Fundamental Problem of Speaking About God." *Princeton Seminary Bulletin*, no. 7 (1986): 101-13.

———. *The Great Passion: An Introduction to the Theology of Karl Barth*. Grand Rapids: Eerdmans, 2009.

———. *Karl Barth, His Life from Letters and Autobiographical Texts*. Grand Rapids: Eerdmans, 1994.

Caird, G. B. "The Glory of God in the Fourth Gospel: An Exercise in Biblical Semantics." *NTS* 15 (1969): 265-77.

Calvin, John. *Commentary on the Gospel According to John.* Vol. 1. Reprint, Grand Rapids: Eerdmans, 1980.

———. *Institutes of the Christian Religion.* Edited by J. T. McNeill. Translated by Ford Lewis Battles. Library of Christian Classics. Philadelphia: Westminster Press, 1960.

Caputo, John D. *Heidegger and Aquinas: An Essay on Overcoming Metaphysics.* New York: Fordham University Press, 1982.

Carabine, Deirdre. *The Unknown God: Negative Theology in the Platonic Tradition, Plato to Eriugena.* Louvain: Peeters, 1995.

Casarella, P. "The Expression and Form of the Word: Trinitarian Hermeneutics and the Sacramentality of Language in Hans Urs von Balthasar's Theology." *Renascence* 48 (Winter 1996): 111-35.

Case, Jonathan. "The Death of God and the Truth of the Triune God in Wolfhart Pannenberg and Eberhard Jüngel." *Journal for Christian Theological Research* 9 (2004): 1-13.

Cessario, Romanus. *A Short History of Thomism.* Washington, D.C.: The Catholic University of America Press, 2003.

Chabada, Michal. *Cognitio intuitiva et abstractiva: Die ontologischen Implikationen der Erkenntnislehre des Johannes Duns Skotus mit Gegenüberstellung zu Aristoteles und I. Kant.* Veröffentlichungen der Johannes-Duns-Skotus-Akademie für franziskanische Geistesgeschichte und Spiritualität 19. Mönchengladbach: Kühlen Verlag, 2005.

Chadwick, Henry. *Augustine: A Very Short Introduction.* New York: Oxford University Press, 2001.

———. *Augustine of Hippo: A Life.* New York: Oxford University Press, 2009.

Chavannes, H. *L'analogie entre Dieu et le monde selon saint Thomas d'Aquin et selon Karl Barth.* Paris, 1969.

Chenu, M. D., O.P. "Creation et Histoire." In *St Thomas Aquinas, 1274-1974,* edited by É. Gilson, 2:391-401. Commemorative Studies. Toronto: Pontifical Institute for Mediaeval Studies Press, 1974.

———. *Toward Understanding Saint Thomas.* Translated by A.-M. Landry, O.P., and D. Hughes, O.P. Chicago: Henry Regnery, 1963.

———. *Toward Understanding St. Thomas.* Edited by Marcia L. Colish and Peter Lombard. 2 vols. New York: E. J. Brill, 1994.

Cherniss, Harold. *Aristotle's Criticism of Plato and the Academy.* New York: Russell and Russell, 1962.

Clark, Mary T. *Augustine.* Washington, D.C.: Georgetown University Press, 1994.

————. *Augustine.* Outstanding Christian Thinkers. Edinburgh: T & T Clark, 2005.

Clarke, W. Norris. *Explorations in Metaphysics: Being—God—Person.* Notre Dame, IN: University of Notre Dame Press, 1994.

————. *The One and the Many: A Contemporary Thomistic Metaphysics.* Notre Dame, IN: University of Notre Dame Press, 2001.

————. *The Philosophical Approach to God: A Contemporary Neo-Thomist Perspective.* Winston-Salem, NC: Wake Forest University Press, 1979.

Code, Alan. "Aristotle's Metaphysics as a Science of Principles." *Revue Internationale de Philosophie* 51 (1997): 357-78.

————. "Owen on the Development of Aristotle's Metaphysics." In *Aristotle's Philosophical Development: Problems and Prospects,* edited by Wians William, pp. 303-25. London: Rowman & Littlefield, 1996.

Colish, M. L. *Avicenna's Theory of Efficient Causation and Its Influence on St. Thomas Aquinas.* Atti del Congresso Internazionale Tommaso d'Aquino nel suo settimo centenario. Rome-Naples: Vatican Press, 1975.

Collins, James. "Przywara's 'Analogia Entis.'" *Thought* 65 (1990): 265-77.

Colwell, John E. *Actuality and Provisionality: Eternity and Election in the Theology of Karl Barth.* Eugene, OR: Wipf and Stock, 2011.

Compier, H., J. Rieger and K. Pui-Lan. *Empire: The Christian Tradition.* New Readings of Classical Theologians. Minneapolis: Fortress, 2007.

Copleston, Frederick. *Augustine.* Vol. 2 of *History of Philosophy.* Suffolk, UK: Chaucer Press, 1972.

Cornford, F. M. *From Religion to Philosophy: A Study in the Origins of Western Speculation.* Princeton, NJ: Princeton University Press, 1912. Rev. ed., 1991.

————. *Plato's Cosmology.* Oxford: Oxford University Press, 1937.

Coulter, James A. *The Literary Microcosm: Theories of Interpretation of Late Neoplatonists.* Leiden: E. J. Brill, 1976.

Courtine, Jean F. *Inventio analogiae. Metaphysique et ontotheologie.* Paris: J. Vrin, 2005.

Crombie, I. M. *An Examination of Plato's Doctrines.* 1963. Reprint, London: Taylor Francis Press, 2012.

Cross, F. L., ed. *Studies in the Fourth Gospel.* London: Mowbray, 1957.

Cross, Richard. *Duns Scotus.* Great Medieval Thinkers. New York: Oxford University Press, 1999.

————. "Duns Scotus and Suarez at the Origins of Modernity." In Hankey and Hedley, eds., *Deconstructing Radical Orthodoxy,* pp. 65-78.

————. *Duns Scotus on God.* Aldershot, UK: Ashgate, 2004.

————. *The Metaphysics of the Incarnation: Thomas Aquinas to Duns Scotus.* Oxford: Clarendon Press, 2002.

————. "Where Angels Fear to Tread: Duns Scotus and Radical Orthodoxy." *Antonianum* 76 (2001): 7-41.

Crouzel, Henri. *Origen.* New York: Harper & Row, 1989.

Culpepper, A. "The Pivot of John's Prologue." *NTS* 27 (1980–1981): 1-31.

Currey, Cecil B. *Reason and Revelation: John Duns Scotus on Natural Theology.* Chicago: Franciscan Herald Press, 1977.

Dalferth, Ingolf U., ed. *Denkwürdiges Geheimnis: Beiträge zur Gotteslehre: Festschrift für Eberhard Jüngel zum 70.* Geburtstag: Mohr Siebeck, 2006.

————. *Theology and Philosophy.* Eugene, OR: Wipf and Stock, 1988.

Dauphinais, M., and M. Levering. *Aquinas the Augustinian.* Washington, D.C.: Catholic University of America Press, 2007.

Davies, Brian. *The Thought of Thomas Aquinas.* Oxford: Oxford University Press, 1992.

Davis, C., and P. A. Riches. "Metanoia: A Theological Praxis of Revolution." In *Theology and the Political: The New Debate,* ed. Creston Davis, John Milbank and Slavoj Žižek, pp. 22-51. Durham, NC: Duke University Press, 2005.

De Ferrari, Roy J. *A Lexicon of St. Thomas Aquinas Based on the Summa Theologica and Passages of His Other Works.* Baltimore: Catholic University of America Press, 1948.

De Libera, A. *L'Art des généralités. Théories de l'abstraction.* Paris: Aubier, 1999.

De Molina, Luis. *On Divine Foreknowledge.* Translated by Alfred J. Freddoso. Cornell Classics in Philosophy. Reprint, Ithaca, NY: Cornell University Press, 2004.

De Muralt, André, Valentín Fernández Polanco and Francisco León. *La estructura de la filosofía política moderna: sus orígenes medievales en Escoto, Ockham y Suárez.* Tres Cantos: Ediciones Istmo, 2002.

De Rijk, L. M. "On Boethius' Notion of Being. A Chapter of Boethian Semantics." In *Meaning and Inference in Medieval Philosophy,* ed. N. Kretzmann, pp. 1-29. Synthese Historical Library 32. Boston: Kluwer, 1988.

De Vio, Thomas, Cardinal Cajetan. *The Analogy of Names and The Concept of Being.* Translated by Edward A. Bushinski. Pittsburgh, PA: Duquesne University Press, 1953.

————. *Commentary on Being and Essence.* Edited and translated by L. H. Kendzierski and F. C. Wade. Milwaukee: Marquette University Press, 1964.

————. *D. Thoma De ente et essentia libellus.* In *S. Thomae Aquinatis doctoris angelici opusculum De ente et essentia*, edited by M. de Maria, S.J. Rome, 1907.

———. *De Nominum Analogia, De Conceptu Entis*. Edited by P. N. Zammit, O.P. Rome: Angelicum, 1934.

———. *In De Anima Aristotelis Commentaria*. Edited by J. Coquelle, O.P. Rome: Angelicum, 1938.

———. *In De Ente et Essentia De Thomae Aquinatis Commentaria*. Edited by M.-H. Laurent, O.P. Turin: Marietti, 1934.

———. *In Porphyrii Isagogen Commentaria*. Edited by I. M. Marega, O.P. Rome: Angelicum, 1934.

———. *In Praedicamenta Aristotelis Commentaria*. Edited by M.-H. Laurent, O.P. Rome: Angelicum, 1939.

———. *In Summa Theologiae St. Thomae Aquinatis Commentaria*. Leonine ed. Rome, 1882.

———. *Opuscula Omnia*. Venice, 1956.

De Vogel, Cornelia J. *Rethinking Plato and Platonism*. Leiden: E. J. Brill, 1986.

DeHart, Paul J. *Beyond the Necessary God: Trinitarian Faith and Philosophy in the Thought of Eberhard Jüngel*. Oxford: Oxford University Press, 1999.

———. "Eberhard Jüngel on the Structure of Theology." *Theological Studies* 57 (1996): 46-64.

Demke, C. "Der sogenannte Logos Hymnus in Johanneische Prolog." *ZNW* 58 (1967): 45-68.

Denzinger, Henricus, ed. *Enchiridion symbolorum et definitionum, quae de rebus fidei et morum a Conciliis oecumenicis et summis pontificibus emanarunt. In auditorum usum*. Latin ed. Los Angeles: University of California Library Press, 1856.

Descoqs, P. *Institutiones Metaphysicae Generalis*. Paris, 1925.

Dillon, John. "Image, Symbol and Analogy: Three Basic Concepts of Neoplatonic 'Allegorical Exegesis.'" In *The Significance of Neoplatonism*, ed. R. Blaine Harris, pp. 247-62. Albany: State University of New York Press, 1976.

———. *The Middle Platonists*. London: Duckworth, 1977.

———. *The Middle Platonists, 80 B.C. to A.D. 220*. Rev. ed. Ithaca, NY: Cornell University Press, 1996.

Dillon, John, and Sarah Klitenic Wear. *Dionysius the Areopagite and the Neoplatonist Tradition: Despoiling the Hellenes*. Ashgate Studies in Philosophy and Theology in Late Antiquity. Aldershot, UK: Ashgate, 2007.

Dobson, R. B., and A. Vauchez, eds. *Encyclopedia of Middle Ages*. Cambridge: James Clark, 2000.

Dodaro, R., and G. Lawless. *Augustine and His Critics: Essays in Honour of Gerald Bonner*. London: Routledge, 2000.

Dodd, C. H. *The Interpretation of the Fourth Gospel*. Cambridge: Cambridge University Press, 1953.

Doolan, Gregory T. *Aquinas on the Divine Ideas and Exemplar Causes*. Washington, D.C.: Catholic University of America Press, 2008.

Du Roy, Olivier. *L'Intelligence de la foi en la Trinité selon saint Augustin*. Paris: Études Augustiniennes, 1966.

Dupre, Louis. "The Glory of the Lord: Hans Urs von Balthasar's Theological Aesthetic." In *Hans Urs von Balthasar: His Life and Work*, ed. David L. Schindler, pp. 183-20. San Francisco: Ignatius, 1991.

Dutari, Julia Cesar. *Christentum und Metaphysik Das Verhaltnis beider nach der Analogielehre Erich Przywaras (1889-1973)*. Munich: Berchmanskolleg Verlag, 1973.

Dutari, Julio. "Die Geschichte des Terminus'Analogia entis'und das Werk Erich Przywara." *Philosophisches Jahrbuch* 77 (1970): 164-92.

Effler, Roy. *John Duns Scotus and the Principle Omne quod movetur ab alio movetur*. Franciscan Institute Publications Philosophy Series 15. St. Bonaventure, NY: Franciscan Institute, 1962.

Emery, Gilles. *Trinity in Aquinas*. Ypsilanti, MI: Sapientia Press of Ave Maria College, 2003.

Enderlin, Renate. *Eberhard Jüngels Analogie des Advents*. Munich: GRIN Verlag, 2008.

Enders, Markus. "Das metaphysische Ordo-Denken in, Spätantike und frühem Mittelalter: Bei Augustinus, Boethius und Anselm von Canterbury." *Philosophisches Jahrbuch* 104 (1997): 335-61.

England, F. E. *Kant's Conception of God: A Critical Exposition of Its Metaphysical Development Together with a Translation of the Nova Dilucidatio*. London: Unwin Brothers, 1928.

Fabro, C. "The Intensive Hermeneutics of Thomistic Philosophy: The Notion of Participation." *Review of Metaphysics* 27 (1974): 449-91.

———. "The Overcoming of the Neoplatonic Triad of Being, Life, and Intellect by Saint Thomas Aquinas." In *Neoplatonism and Christian Thought*, edited by Dominic J. O'Meara, part 2, chap. 10. London: Variorum Press, 1982.

———. *Participation et causalite selon s. Thomas d'Aquin*, Chaire card., *Mercier* 2. Louvain/Paris: University of Paris Press, 1961.

———. "Platonism, Neo-Platonism and Thomism: Convergencies and Divergencies." *Neo Scholastic* 44 (1970): 69-100.

Farthing, John L. "The Problem of Divine Exemplarity in St Thomas." *The Thomist* 49 (1985): 183-222.

Ferejohn, Michael T. "Aristotle on Focal Meaning and the Unity of Science." *Phronesis: A Journal for Ancient Philosophy* 25 (1980): 117-28.

Ferré, Frederick. "Analogy in Theology." In *The Enclyclopedia of Philosophy*, 1:41-44. New York: Macmillan, 1972.

Feuerbach, Ludwig. *The Essence of Christianity.* New York: Harper & Row, 1985.

Fichte, Johann Gottlieb. *Grundlage der gesamten Wissenschaftslehre.* 1794/95. 2nd ed. 1802. Translated by Peter Heath. In *Fichte: Science of Knowledge (Wissenschaftslehre)*, edited by Peter Heath and John Lachs. Cambridge: Cambridge University Press, 1982.

Fitzgerald, Allan, ed. *Augustine Through the Ages: An Encyclopedia.* Grand Rapids: Eerdmans, 1999.

Flint, Thomas P. *Divine Providence: The Molinist Account.* Cornell Studies in the Philosophy of Religion. Ithaca, NY: Cornell University Press, 2006.

Follon, Jacques. "Le concept de philosophie première dans la 'Metaphysique' d'Aristote." *Revue Philosophique de Louvain* 90 (1992): 387-421.

Fraser, Kyle A. "Aristoteles ex Aristotele: A Response to the Analytic Reconstruction of Aristotelian Ontology." *Dyonisius* 20 (2002): 51-69.

Frei, Hans. "The Doctrine of Revelation in the Thought of Karl Barth." PhD dissertation, Yale University, 1956.

Freudenberg, Matthias. *Karl Barth und die reformierte Theologie: Die Ausseinandersetzung mit Calvin, Zwingli und den reformierten Bekenntnisschriften während seiner Göttinger Lehrtätigkeit.* Neukirchen-Vluyn: Neukirchener Verlag, 1997.

Garaventa, R. "L'esito della teologia: Dio e altro dairuomo (intervista a E. Jüngel)." *Il Regno* 2 (1987): 38-41.

Gawronski, Raymond. *Word and Silence: Hans Urs von Balthasar and the Spiritual Encounter Between East and West.* Grand Rapids: Eerdmans, 1995.

Geiger, Louis Bertrand. "Dissimilitude, Transcendence et Perfection du Principe Divin. Aperies et Solutions." *Dialogue* (1962): 17-35.

———. *La Participation dans la philosophie de S. Thomas d'Aquin.* 2nd ed. Bibliothèque thomiste 23. Paris: Vrin, 1995.

Gersh, Stephen. *From Iamblichus to Eriugena: An Investigation of the Prehistory and Evolution of the Pseudo-Dionysian Tradition.* Studien zur Problemgeschichte der antiken und mittelalterlichen Philosophie 8. Leiden: Brill, 1978.

———. *Middle Platonism and Neoplatonism: The Latin Tradition.* 2 vols. Notre Dame, IN: Notre Dame Press, 1986.

———. *Neoplatonism After Derrida: Parallelograms.* Leiden: Brill, 2006.

———. *A Study of Spiritual Motion in the Philosophy of Proclus.* Leiden: Brill, 1973.

Gersh, Stephen, and Maarten J. F. M. Hoenen, eds. *The Platonic Tradition in the Middle Ages: A Doxographic Approach.* New York: Walter de Gruyter, 2002.

Gerson, L. P. *Aristotle and Other Platonists.* Ithaca, NY: Cornell University Press, 2005.

Gertz, Bernhard. *Glaubenswelt als Analogie: Die Theologische Analogielehre Erich Przywaras und ihr Ort in der Auseinandersetzung um die Analogie Fidei.* Düsseldorf: Patmos-Verlag, 1969.

Gilson, Étienne. *Being and Some Philosophers.* Toronto: Pontifical Institute of Mediaeval Studies, 1952.

———. "Cajetan et l'existence." *Tijdschrift voor Philosophie* (June 1953): 267-86.

———. *The Christian Philosophy of St. Augustine.* Translated by L. Lynch. New York: Random House, 1960.

———. *The Christian Philosophy of St Thomas Aquinas.* Translated by L. K. Shook. New York: Random House, 1955.

———. *History of Christian Philosophy in the Middle Ages.* New York: Random House, 1955.

———. *Jean Duns Scot: Introduction à ses positions fondamentales.* Études de philosophie médiévale 42. Paris: Vrin, 1952.

———. *The Spirit of Mediaeval Philosophy.* Notre Dame, IN: University of Notre Dame Press, 1991.

———, ed. *St Thomas Aquinas, 1274-1974.* Commemorative Studies. Toronto: Pontifical Institute for Mediaeval Studies Press, 1974.

Gioia, Luigi. *The Theological Epistemology of St Augustine's De Trinitate.* Oxford: Clarendon Press, 2008.

Goergen, A. *Kardinal Cajetans Lehre von der Analogie; ihr Verhältnis zu Thomas von Aquin.* Speyer: Pilger-Verlag, 1938.

Goodman, Lenn E., ed. *Neoplatonism and Jewish Thought.* Albany: State University of New York Press, 1992.

Gregory, John. *The Neoplatonists: A Reader.* 2nd ed. New York: Routledge, 1999.

Gruber, J. *Kommentar zu Boethius De Consolatione Philosophiae.* 2nd ed. New York: de Gruyter, 2006.

Gunton, Colin E. *Act and Being: Towards a Theology of the Divine Attributes.* Grand Rapids: Eerdmans, 2003.

———. *Becoming and Being: The Doctrine of God in Charles Hartshorne and Karl Barth.* Oxford: Oxford University Press, 1978.

———. *Intellect and Action: Elucidations on Christian Theology and the Life of Faith*. Edinburgh: T & T Clark, 2000.

———. *Yesterday and Today: A Study of Continuities in Christology*. London: SCM Press, 1983.

Gutas, Dimitri. *Avicenna and the Aristotelian Tradition: Introduction to Reading Avicenna's Philosophical Works*. Leiden: E. J. Brill, 1988.

Guyer, P. *Kant and the Claims of Knowledge*. Cambridge: Cambridge University Press, 1987.

Hackforth, R. "Plato's Cosmogony." *Classical Quarterly* 9 (1959): 17-25.

Hadot, Pierre. "L'image de la Trinite." *Studia Patristica* 6 (1962): 404-32.

———. *Philosophy as a Way of Life*. Edited and translated by Arnold I. Davidson and Michael Chase. Oxford: Basil Blackwell, 1995.

———. *Plotinus: The Simplicity of Vision*. Translated by M. Chase. Chicago: University of Chicago Press, 1993.

Hahn, Robert. "Aristotle as Ontologist or Theologian? Or, Aristotelian Form in the Context of the Conflicting Doctrines of Being in the Metaphysics." *Southwestern Journal of Philosophy* 10 (1979): 79-88.

Hall, Alexander W. *Thomas Aquinas and John Duns Scotus: Natural Theology in the High Middle Ages*. New York: Continuum, 2007.

Hall, Douglas C. *The Trinity*. Leiden: Brill, 2008.

Halper, Edward C. "Being Qua Being in Metaphysics Gamma." *Elenchos* (1987): 43-62.

———. *One and Many in Aristotle's Metaphysics. Book alpha—delta*. Las Vegas: Parmenides Publishing, 2009.

Hankey, W. J. "Aquinas and the Platonists." In *The Platonic Tradition in the Middle Ages: A Doxographic Approach*. Edited by Stephen Gersh and Martin Hoenen. New York: de Gruyter, 2002.

———. "Aquinas' Doctrine of God Between Ontology and Henology." In *Colloque La philosophie et la question de Dieu. Histoire, développement, perspectives Université Laval les 10, 11 et 12 avril 2003* (dans le cadre des grands colloques organisés par Yves-Charles Zarka, du CNRS, Paris).

———. "Aquinas, Pseudo-Denys, Proclus and Isaiah VI.6." *Archives d'histoire doctrinale et littéraire du Moyen Âge* 64 (1997): 87-90.

———. *God in Himself: Aquinas' Doctrine of God as Expounded in the Summa Theologiae*. New York: Oxford University Press, 1987.

———. "Mind." In *Augustine Through the Ages*, edited by A. D. Fitzgerald, pp. 563-67. Grand Rapids: Eerdmans, 1999.

———. "Participatio divini luminis, Aquinas' Doctrine of the Agent Intellect: Our Capacity for Contemplation." *Dionysius* 22 (2004): 149-78.

———. "Philosophical Religion and the Neoplatonic Turn to the Subject." In *Deconstructing Radical Orthodoxy: Postmodern Theology, Rhetoric and Truth*, edited by Wayne Hankey and Douglas Hedley, pp. 17-30. Aldershot, UK: Ashgate, 2005.

———. "Pope Leo's Purposes and St. Thomas' Platonism." In *Atti dell' VIII Congresso Thomistico Internazional*, VIII:39-52. Vatican City: Vatican Press, 1982.

———. "Radical Orthodoxy's Poiesis: Ideological Historiography and Anti-Modern Polemic." *American Catholic Philosophical Quarterly* 80, no. 1 (2006): 1-21.

———. "Reading Augustine Through Dionysius: Aquinas's Correction of One Platonism by Another." In *Aquinas the Augustinian*, edited by M. Dauphinais, B. David and M. Levering, pp. 243-57. Washington, D.C.: Catholic University of America Press, 2007.

———. "Self and Cosmos in Becoming Deiform: Neoplatonic Paradigms for Reform by Self-Knowledge from Augustine to Aquinas." In *Reforming the Church Before Modernity: Patterns, Problems and Approaches*, edited by C. M. Bellitto and L. I. Hamilton, pp. 39-60. Aldershot, UK: Ashgate, 2005.

———. "Theoria Versus Poesis: Neoplatonism and Trinitarian Difference in Aquinas." *ModT* 15 (2003): 387-415.

———. "Thomas' Neoplatonic Histories: His Following of Simplicius." *Dionysius* 20 (2003): 153-78.

———. "Why Philosophy Abides for Aquinas." *The Heythrop Journal* 42, no. 3 (2001): 329-48.

Hankey, Wayne, and Douglas Hedley, eds. *Deconstructing Radical Orthodoxy: Postmodern Theology, Rhetoric and Truth*. Aldershot, UK: Ashgate, 2005.

Harmless, William, ed. *Augustine in His Own Words*. Washington, D.C.: Catholic University of America Press, 2010.

Harrington, Larry Michael. "A Thirteenth-Century Textbook of Mystical Theology at the University of Paris: The Mystical Theology of Dionysius the Areopagite in Eurigena's Translation with the Scholia Translated by Anastasius the Librarian and Excerpts from Eurigena's Periphyseon Edition, Translation, and Introduction." In *Dallas Medieval Texts and Translations* 4. Paris/Leuven/Dudley: Peeters, 2004.

Harris, C. R. S. *Duns Scotus*. 2nd ed. New York: The Humanities Press, 1959.

Harris, R. Bain. *The Significance of Neoplatonism*. New York: State University of New York Press, 1976.

Harrison, Carol. "Augustine." In *The Early Christian World*, edited by Philip Esler, pp. 1205-27. New York: Routledge, 2001.

Hart, David Bentley. *Beauty of the Infinite: The Asthetics of Christian Truth*. Grand Rapids: Eerdmans, 2003.

———. "The Mirror of the Infinite: Gregory of Nyssa on the Vestigia Trinitatis." *ModT* 18, no. 4 (2002): 541-61.

Hart, Trevor A. "Anselm of Canterbury and John McLeod Campbell: Where Opposites Meet?" *Evangelical Quarterly* 62 (October 1990): 311-33.

Hartwell, H. *The Theology of Karl Barth*. London: SPCK, 1964.

Hasper, Christopher. *Eschatalogical Presence in Karl Barth's Göttingen Dogmatics*. Oxford: Oxford University Press, 2010.

Haudel, Matthias. "Zeitgenössische Neubegründung der Trinitätslehre: Eberhard Jüngel." In *Die Selbsterschliessung des Dreieinigen Gottes: Grundlage eines ökumenischen Offenbarungs-, Gottes- und Kirchenverständnisses*, pp. 264-80. Göttingen: Vandenhoeck & Ruprecht, 2006.

Hector, Kevin W. "God's Triunity and Self-Determination: A Conversation with Karl Barth, Bruce McCormack, and Paul Molnar." *IJST* 7, no. 3 (2005): 246-61.

Hegel, G. W. F. *Lectures on the History of Philosophy*. Translated by E. S. Haldane and F. H. Simpson. New Jersey: Humanist Press, 1983.

Heidegger, Martin. *Aristotle's Metaphysics Θ 1-3*. Indianapolis: Indiana University Press, 1995.

———. *Being and Time*. Translated by John Macquarrie and Edward Robinson. New York: Harper & Row, 1962.

———. *Die Kategorien- und Bedeutungslehre des Duns Scotus*. Tübingen: J. C. B. Mohr, 1916.

———. *Gesamtausgabe*, I. Abteilung, Band 1. Frankfurt am Main: Vittorio Klostermann, 1978.

———. *Hegel's Phenomenology of Spirit*. Translated by Parvas Emad and Kenneth Maly. Bloomington: Indiana University Press, 1988.

———. *An Introduction to Metaphysics*. New York: Doubleday, 1961.

———. *Kant and the Problem of Metaphysics*. Translated by James S. Churchill. Bloomington: Indiana University Press, 1962.

———. *The Phenomenology of Religious Life*. Translated by Matthias Fritsch and Jennifer Anna Gosetti-Ferencei. Bloomington: Indiana University Press, 2004.

———. *What Is Called Thinking*. Translated by J. Glenn Gray. New York: Harper & Row, 1968.

Heidl, György. *Origen's Influence on the Young Augustine: A Chapter of the History of Origenism.* Notre Dame, IN: Notre Dame University Press, 2003.

Heimsoeth, H. *Transzendentale Dialektik. Ein Commentar su Kants Kritik d. reinen Vernunft.* Berlin: de Gruyter, 1967.

Henle, Robert John. *Saint Thomas and Platonism. A Study of the Plato and Platonici Texts in the Writings of Saint Thomas.* The Hague: Martinus Nijhoff, 1956.

Henrich, D. *Der Ontologische Gottesbeweis. Sein Problem und seine Geschichte In der Neuzeit.* Tübingen: Mohr Siebeck, 1960.

Henry of Ghent. *Summae Questionum Ordinarium.* 1520 ed. St. Bonaventure, NY: Franciscan Publications, 1953.

Henry, Paul. "Augustine and Plotinus." *Journal of Theological Studies* 38 (1937): 20-38.

Heppe, Heinrich. *Reformed Dogmatics.* Grand Rapids: Eerdmans, 1978.

Higton, Mike, and Stephen R. Holmes. "Meeting Scotus: On Scholasticism and Its Ghosts." *IJST* 4 (2002): 67-81.

Hochschild, Joshua P. "Cajetan on Scotus on Univocity." *Proceedings of the Society for Medieval Logic and Metaphysics* 7 (2007): 32-42.

———. *The Semantics of Analogy: Rereading Cajetan's De Nominum Analogia.* Notre Dame, IN: University of Notre Dame Press, 2011.

Holmes, Christopher. "Jüngel on Aquinas," pp. 29-39, and "Divine Attributes According to Jüngel," pp. 99-144. In *Revisiting the Doctrine of the Divine Attributes: In Dialogue with Karl Barth, Eberhard Jüngel and Wolf Krötke.* New York: Peter Lang, 2006.

Hombert, Pierre-Marie. *Nouvelles recherches de chronologie augustinienne.* Collections des Études Augustiniennes. Série antiquité 163. Paris: Institut d'Études Augustiniennes, 2000.

Hooker, M. D. "John the Baptist and the Johannine Prologue." *NTS* 16 (1969–1970): 354-58.

Howsar, R. A. *Hans Urs von Balthasar and Protestantism: The Ecumenical Implications of His Theological Style.* Edinburgh: T & T Clark, 2005.

Hughes, Christopher. *On a Complex Theory of a Simple God.* Ithaca, NY: Cornell University Press, 1989.

Hume, David. *Dialogues Concerning Natural Religion.* In *Writings on Religion,* ed. Anthony Flew. La Salle, IL: Open Court, 1993.

Hunsinger, George. "Karl Barth's Christology: Its Basic Chalcedonian Character." In *Disruptive Grace: Studies in the Theology of Karl Barth,* pp. 131-47. Grand Rapids: Eerdmans, 2000.

Husain, Martha. "The Multiplicity in Unity of Being 'qua' Being in Aristotle's 'pros hen' Equivocity." *New Scholasticism* 55 (1981): 208-18.

Hütter, R. "Attention to the Wisdom of God—From Effect to Cause, from Creation to God: A Relecture of the Analogy of Being According to Thomas Aquinas." In White, *Analogy of Being*, pp. 209-45.

———. "Karl Barth's Dialectical Catholicity; Sic et Non." *ModT* 16, no. 2 (April 2000): 137-57.

Ignatius, Brady, O.F.M. "John Pecham and the Background of Aquinas's De Aeternitate Mundi." In Gilson, ed., *St Thomas Aquinas*, 2:141-79.

Ingham, Mary Beth, and Mechthild Dreyer. *The Philosophical Vision of John Duns Scotus*. Washington, D.C.: Catholic University of America Press, 2004.

Jaeger, Werner. *Aristoteles: Grundlegung einer Geschichte seiner Entwicklung [Aristotle: Fundamentals of the History of His Development]*. Translated by Richard Robinson. Oxford: Clarendon, 1948.

———. *Theology of the Early Greek Philosophers: The Gifford Lectures, 1936*. Oxford: Oxford University Press, 1947, 1952.

Janz, Paul D. *God, The Mind's Desire*. Cambridge: Cambridge University Press, 2004.

———. "Radical Orthodoxy and the New Culture of Obscurantism." *ModT* 20, no. 3 (2004): 363-407.

Jenson, Robert W. *Alpha and Omega: A Study in the Theology of Karl Barth*. New York: Wipf and Stock, 2002.

———. *God After God: The God of the Past and the God of the Future as Seen in the Works of Karl Barth*. New York: Sheed and Ward, 1969.

———. *The Knowledge of Things Hoped For: The Sense of Theological Discourse*. New York: Oxford University Press, 1969.

Jeremias, J. *The Revealing Word: The Central Message of the New Testament*. London: SCM Press, 1965.

Johnson, Keith L. "*Analogia entis*: A Reconsideration of the Debate Between Karl Barth and Roman Catholicism, 1914-1964." PhD dissertation, Princeton Theological Seminary, 2008.

———. *Karl Barth and the Analogia Entis*. Edinburgh: T & T Clark, 2010.

———. "Reconsidering Barth." *ModT* 26, no. 4 (2010): 633-50.

Johnson, Mark F. "Aquinas' Changing Evaluation of Plato on Creation." *American Catholic Philosophical Quarterly* 66, no. 1 (1992): 81-88.

Jones, Paul Dafydd. *The Humanity of Christ: Christology in Karl Barth's Church Dogmatics*. London: T & T Clark, 2008.

Jordan, Mark D. *The Alleged Aristotelianism of Thomas Aquinas.* The Étienne Gilson Series 15. Toronto: Pontifical Institute of Mediaeval Studies, 1992.

————. "The Grammar of *Esse*." *The Thomist* 44 (1980): 1-26.

Jüngel, Eberhard. "Anthropolomorphismus als Grundproblem der neuzeitlicher Hermeneutik." In *Verifikationen: Festschrift für Gerhard Ebeling zum 70. Geburtstag*, edited by E. Jüngel et al., pp. 499-521. Tübingen: Mohr Siebeck, 1982.

————. *Barth-Studien.* Gütersloh: Benziger, 1982.

————. *Christ, Justice and Peace: Toward a Theology of the State in Dialogue with the Barmen Declaration.* Translated by D. B. Hamill and Alan J. Torrance. Edinburgh: T & T Clark, 1992.

————. "The Christian Understanding of Suffering." *Journal of Theology for Southern Africa* 65 (1988): 3-13.

————. "The Cross After Postmodernity." In *One Incarnate Truth: Christianity's Answer to Spiritual Chaos*, ed. Uwe Siemon-Netto, pp. 98-108. St. Louis: Concordia, 2002.

————. "Das Sakrament-was ist das? Versuch einer Antwort." In *Was ist ein Sakrament? Verstösse zur Verständigung*, E. Jüngel and K. Rahner, pp. 11-40. Friburg: Herder, 1971.

————. "Das Verhaltnis von 'okonomischer' und 'immanenter Trinitat.'" *Erwägungen über eine biblische Begründung der Trinitätslehre—im Anschluß an und in Auseinandersetzung mit Karl Rahners Lehre vom dreifaltigen Gott als transzendentem Urgrund der Heilsgeschichte* (ZThK 72, 1975): 265-75.

————. *Death: The Riddle and the Mystery.* Translated by Iain Nicol and Ute Nicol. Edinburgh: St. Andrews Press, 1974.

————. "Der Gott entsprechende Mensch. Bemerkungen zur Gottesebenbildlichkeit des Menschen als Grundfigur theologischer Anthropologie." In *Neue Anthropologie*, Bd. 6: *Philosophischer Anthropologie*, edited by H. G. Gadamer and Paul V. Vogeler, pp. 342-72. Munich: Deutscher Taschenbuch Verlag, 1980.

————. "Die Moglichkeit theologischer Anthropologic auf dem Grunde der Analogie." In *Eine Untersuchung Zum Analogieverständnis Karl Barths*, pp. 210-32. Gütersloh: Mohn, 1982.

————. *The Doctrine of the Trinity.* Translated by H. Harris. Edinburgh: Scottish Academic Press, 1976.

————. "Extra Christum Nulla salus—als Grundsatz natürlicher Theologie? Evangelische Erwägungen zur 'Anonymität' des Christenmenschen," *Zeitschrift für Theologie und Kirche* 72 (1975): 337-52.

————. *The Freedom of a Christian: Luther's Significance for Contemporary The-*

ology. Translated by Roy A. Harrisville. Minneapolis: Augsburg, 1988.

————. "God—as a Word of Our Language." In *Theology of the Liberating Word*, edited by F. Herzog, pp. 24-45. Nashville: Abingdon, 1971.

————. *God as the Mystery of the World: On the Foundation of the Theology of the Crucified One in the Dispute Between Theism and Atheism.* Translated by D. Guder. Grand Rapids: Eerdmans, 1983.

————. *God's Being Is in Becoming: The Trinitarian Being of God in the Theology of Karl Barth.* Translated by John Webster. Grand Rapids: Eerdmans, 2001.

————. "The Gospel and the Protestant Churches of Europe: Christian Responsibility for Europe from a Protestant Perspective." *Religion, State and Society* 21, no. 2 (1993): 137-49.

————. *Gott als Geheimnis der Welt. Zur Begründung der Theologie des Gekreuzigten im Streit zwischen Theismus und Atheismus.* 7th ed. Tübingen: Mohr Siebeck, 2010.

————. *Gottes Sein ist im Werden.* Tübingen: Mohr Siebeck, 1986.

————. "Grenzen des Menschseins." In *Entsprechungen: Gott—Wahrheit—Mensch,* pp. 355-61. Theologische Erörterungen II. Munich: Kaiser, 1980.

————. "The Invocation of God as the Ethical Ground of Christian Action." In *Theological Essays,* edited and translated by J. B. Webster, pp. 154-72. Edinburgh: T & T Clark, 1989.

————. *Justification: The Heart of the Christian Faith.* Translated by Jeffrey F. Cayzer. Edinburgh: T & T Clark, 2001.

————. *Karl Barth: A Theological Legacy.* Translated by Garrett E. Paul. Philadelphia: Westminster, 1986.

————. "'Keine Menschenlosigkeit Gottes.' Zur Theologie Karl Barths zwischen Theismus und Atheismus." In *Barth-Studien,* pp. 332-47. Gütersloh: Mohn, 1982.

————. "La Signification de l'analogie pour la théologie." In *Analogie et Dialectique. Essais de Théologie Fundamentale,* edited by J. L. Marion, pp. 247-58. Geneva: Labor et Fides, 1982.

————. "Metaphorical Truth." In *Theological Essays,* translated by J. B. Webster, pp. 16-71. Edinburgh: T & T Clark, 1989.

————. "On Becoming Truly Human: The Significance of the Reformation Distinction Between Person and Works for the Self-Understanding of Modern Humanity." In *Theological Essays II,* translated by J. B. Webster and A. Neufeldt-Fast, pp. 216-40. New York: T & T Clark, 1995.

————. "On the Doctrine of Justification." *IJST* 1, no. 1 (1999): 24-52.

————. *Paulus und Jesus: Eine Untersuchung zur Präzisierung der Frage nach dem*

Ursprung der Christologie. Tübingen: J. C. B. Mohr, 1962.

———. "The Relationship Between 'Economic' and 'Immanent' Trinity." *Theology Digest* 24 (1976): 179-84.

———. *Theological Essays*. Edited and translated by John Webster. Edinburgh: T & T Clark, 1989.

———. "Theses on the Relation of the Existence, Essence and Attributes of God." *Toronto Journal of Theology* 17 (2001): 55-74.

———. *Unterwegs zur Sache*. Theologische Bemerkungen. Munich: C. Kaiser, 1972.

———. "Von der Dialektik zur Analogie; Die Schule Kierkegaards und der Einspruch Petersons." In *Barth-Studien*, pp. 127-79. Gütersloh: Mohn, 1982.

———. "What Does It Mean to Say, 'God Is Love'?" In *Christ in Our Place: The Humanity of God in Christ for the Reconciliation of the World. Essays Presented to Prof. James Torrance*, ed. T. Hart and D. Thimell, pp. 294-312. Exeter, UK: Paternoster, 1989.

———. *Zum Ursprung der Analogie bei Parmenides und Heraklit*. Berlin: de Gruyter, 1964.

———. "Zur Kritik des sakramentalen Verständnisses der Taufe." In *Karl Barth's Lehre von der Taufe*, edited by E. Viering, pp. 161-64. Gütersloh: Mohn, 1971.

Kant, Immanuel. *The Cambridge Edition of the Works of Immanuel Kant: Lectures on Metaphysics*. Translated and edited by Kanrl Ameriks and Steve Naragan. Cambridge: Cambridge University Press, 1997.

———. *The Cambridge Edition of the Works of Immanuel Kant: The Critique of Pure Reason*. Translated and edited by Paul Guyer and Allen Wood. Cambridge: Cambridge University Press, 1998.

———. *The Critique of Judgment*. Translated by J. H. Bernard. Amherst, NY: Prometheus Books, 2000.

———. *Critique of Practical Reason*. Translated by Lewis White Beck. The Library of Liberal Arts. New York: The Liberal Arts Press, 1956.

———. *Critique of Pure Reason*. Translated by N. Kemp Smith. New York: Palgrave Macmillan, 2005.

———. *Lectures on the Philosophical Doctrine of Religion*. Translated and edited by Allen Wood and George Di Giovanni. Cambridge, Cambridge University Press, 1996.

———. *Lectures on Philosophical Theology*. Translated by Allen Wood and Gertrude M. Clark. Ithaca, NY: Cornell University Press, 1978.

———. *Prolegomena to Any Future Metaphysics*. The Library of Liberal Arts. New York: Bobbs-Merrill, 1950.

————. *Religion and Rational Theology.* Translated and edited by A. W. Wood and G. D. Giovanni. Cambridge: Cambridge University Press, 1996.

————. *Religion Within the Limits of Reason Alone.* New York: Harper & Row, 1983.

Karamanolis, George E. *Plato and Aristotle in Agreement? Platonists on Aristotle from Antiochus to Porphyry.* Oxford: Clarendon Press, 2006.

Käsemann, E. "The Structure and Purpose of the Prologue to John's Gospel." In *New Testament Questions of Today*, pp. 138-67. London: SCM Press, 1969.

Kaufmen, Gordon. *The Theological Imagination: Constructing the Concept of God.* Philadelphia: Westminster Press, 1981.

Kay, Jeffrey Ames. "Balthasar: A Post-Critical Theologian?" In *Neoconservatism: Social and Religious Phenomenon*, ed. Gregory Baum and Marcus LeFebure, pp. 84-89. Edinburgh: T & T Clark, 1981.

————. *Theological Aesthetics: The Role of Aesthetics in the Theological Method of Hans Urs von Balthasar.* Bern: Herbert Lang, 1975.

Keener, C. *The Gospel of John: A Commentary.* 2 vols. Peabody, MA: Hendrickson, 2003.

Kelly, Bernard. *The Metaphysical Background of Analogy.* London: Blackfriars, 1958.

Kendall, R. T. *Calvin and English Calvinism to 1649.* Oxford: Oxford University Press, 1979.

Kenny, Anthony. *The Five Ways.* London: Routledge, 1969.

————. *The God of the Philosophers.* Oxford: Oxford University Press, 1987.

Ketchum, Richard. "Being and Existence in Greek Ontology." *Archiv für Geschichte der Philosophie* 80, no. 3 (1998): 321-32.

Kevern, John R. "Form in Tragedy: Balthasar as Correlational Theologian." *Communio* 21 (Summer 1994): 311-30.

Kierkegaard, Søren. *Kierkegaard's Concluding Unscientific Postscript.* Translated by David F. Swenson. Princeton, NJ: Princeton University Press, 1968.

————. *Philosophical Fragments: Johannes Climacus.* Translated and edited by Howard V. Hong and Edna H. Hong. Princeton, NJ: Princeton University Press, 1985.

Kiernan, Thomas P., ed. *Aristotle Dictionary.* New York: Philosophical Library, 1962.

King, P. "Augustine's Encounter with Neoplatonism." *The Modern Schoolman* 82 (2011): 213-26.

————. "Introduction." In *Augustine: Against the Academicians and The Teacher.* Ancient Christian Writers 12. Chicago: Paulist Press, 2012.

Kirk, S., and J. E. Raven, eds. *The Presocratic Philosophers*. Cambridge: Cambridge University Press, 1960.

Klagge, J., and N. Smith. *Methods of Interpreting Plato and His Dialogues*. OSAP Supplement. Oxford: Oxford University Press, 1992.

Kleinknecht, H. "λόγος." *TDNT* 4:73-136.

Klibansky, Raymond. *The Continuity of the Platonic Tradition During the Middle Ages*. London: Warburg, 1951, 1981.

Klubertanz, George P. *Introduction to The Philosophy of Being*. New York: Meredith, 1963.

———. *St. Thomas Aquinas on Analogy: A Textual Analysis and Systematic Synthesis*. Chicago: Loyala University Press, 1960.

Kremer, Klaus. *Die neuplatonische Seinsphilosophie und ihre Wirkung auf Thomas vonAquin*. Studien zur Problemgeschichte der antiken and mittelalterlichen Philosophie I. Leiden: Brill, 1966.

Kretzman, Norman, ed. "Boethius and the Truth About Tomorrow's Sea Battle." In *Ammonius on Aristotle on Interpretation 9 with Boethius on Aristotle on Interpretation 9*. Translated by D. Blank and N. Kretzmann. Ithaca, NY: Cornell University Press, 1998.

———. *The Cambridge History of Later Medieval Philosophy: From the Rediscovery of Aristotle to the Disintegration of Scholasticism, 1100-1600*. Cambridge: Cambridge University Press, 1988.

Lafont, G. "Raconter Dieu sans analogie. 'Eberhard Jüngel: Dieu mystere du monde.'" *Dieu, le temps et le etre* (1986): 282-95.

Lakebrink, Bernhard. "Analektik und Dialektik: Zur Methode des Thomistischen und Hegelschen Denkens." In *St Thomas Aquinas, 1274-1974, Commemorative Studies*, ed. É. Gilson, 2:459-88. Toronto: Pontifical Institute for Mediaeval Studies Press, 1974.

Lamp, G. W. H., ed. *A Patristic Greek Lexicon*. Reprint, Oxford: Clarendon Press, 2007.

Lancel, Serge. *Saint Augustine*. London: SCM Press, 2002.

Langston, Douglas C. "Scotus' Epistemological Doctrine of Univocity." PhD dissertation, Princeton University, 1978.

Lash, Nicholas. "Where Does Holy Teaching Leave Philosophy? Questions on Milbank's Aquinas." *ModT* 15, no. 4 (1999): 435-44.

Lee, Jung Young. "Karl Barth's Use of Analogy in His Church Dogmatics." *SJT* 22 (1969): 129-51.

Leftow, B. *Time and Eternity*. Ithaca, NY: Cornell University Press, 1991.

Leo XIII. *Aterni Patris: Opera Omnia* of Thomas Aquinas. Rome, 1882.

Lewry, O. P. "Two Continuators of Aquinas: Robertus de Vulgarbia and Thomas Sutton on the 'Perihermeneias' of Aristotle." *Mediaeval Studies* 63 (1981): 58-130.

Libera, Alain de. *La querelle des universaux: De Platon à la fin du Moyen Age.* Paris: Des travaux, 1996.

Lindbeck, George. *The Nature of Doctrine: Theology in a Postliberal Age.* New Haven, CT: Yale University Press, 1987.

Llano Cifuentes, A. "The Different Meanings of 'Being' According to Aristotle and Aquinas." *Acta Philosophica* 10 (2001): 29-44.

Lloyd, G. E. R. *Polarity and Analogy: Two Types of Argument in Early Greek Thought.* Cambridge: Cambridge University Press, 1966.

Lochbrunner, Manfred. *Analogia caritatis: Darstellung und Deutung der Theologie Hans Urs von Balthasars.* Freiburg: Herder, 1981.

Lombard, Peter. *The Sentences of Peter the Lombard.* Translated by Giulio Silano. Toronto: Pontifical Institute of Mediaeval Studies, 2007.

———. *The Sentences, Book I: The Mystery of the Trinity.* Translated by Giulio Silano. Toronto: Pontifical Institute of Mediaeval Studies, 2007.

Lonergan, Bernard J. *Verbum: Word and Idea in Aquinas.* Edited by David B. Burrell. London: Darton, Longman & Todd, 1968.

Long, S. D. *Saving Karl Barth: Hans Urs von Balthasar's Preoccupation.* Philadelphia: Fortress, 2014.

———. *Speaking of God: Theology, Language and Truth.* Grand Rapids: Eerdmans, 2009.

Long, Stephen A. *Analogia Entis: On the Analogy of Being, Metaphysics, and the Act of Faith.* Notre Dame, IN: University of Notre Dame Press, 2011.

———. "Obediential Potency, Human Knowledge, and the Natural Desire for God." *International Philosophical Quarterly* 37, no. 1 (1997): 45-63.

Louth, Andrew. *St John Damascene.* New York: Oxford University Press, 2002.

Ludwig, Walter D. "Aristotle's Conception of the Science of Being." *New Scholasticism* 63 (1989): 379-404.

Lyttkens, Hampus. *The Analogy Between God and the World: An Investigation of Its Background and Interpretation of Its Use by Thomas of Aquino.* Uppsala: Almquist and Wiksell, 1952.

MacDonald, S. "Boethius's Claim That All Substances Are Good." *Archiv für Geschichte der Philosophie* 70 (1988): 245-79.

MacIntyre, Alasdair. *First Principles, Final Ends and Contemporary Philosophical Issues.* Milwaukee: Marquette University Press, 1990.

Macken, John. *The Autonomy Theme in the Church Dogmatics*. Cambridge: Cambridge University Press, 1990.

Madec, Goulven. *Introduction aux 'Revisions' et à la lecture des oeuvres de saint Augustin*. Collection des Études Augustiniennes. Séries Antiquité 150. Paris: Institut d'Études Augustiniennes, 1996.

Madigan, Patrick. *Christian Revelation and the Completion of The Aristotelian Revolution*. New York: University Press of America, 1988.

Marenbon, J. "Aquinas, Radical Orthodoxy and the Importance of Truth." In *Deconstructing Radical Orthodoxy*, ed. W. Hankey, pp. 49-64. Leuven: Catholic University Press, 2008.

——. *Boethius*. New York: Oxford University Press, 2002.

Marga, Amy. "Partners in the Gospel: Karl Barth and Roman Catholicism, 1922– 1932." PhD dissertation, Princeton Theological Seminary, 2006.

Marrone, Steven P. "The Notion of Univocity in Duns Scotus's Early Works." *Franciscan Studies* 43 (1983): 347-95.

Mascall, E. L. *Existence and Analogy*. New York: Anchor Books, 1967.

Mattes, Mark C. *The Role of Justification in Contemporary Theology*. Grand Rapids: Eerdmans, 2004.

McCormack, Bruce. "The Being of Holy Scripture Is in Becoming: Karl Barth in Conversation with American Evangelical Criticism." In *Evangelicals & Scripture: Tradition, Authority and Hermeneutics*, edited by Vincent Bacote et al., pp. 55-75. Downers Grove, IL: InterVarsity Press, 2004.

——. "God Is His Decision: The Jüngel-Gollwitzer Debate Revisted." In *Theology as Conversation: The Significance of Dialogue in Historical and Contemporary Theology*, edited by B. McCormack and K. Bender, pp. 46-66. Grand Rapids: Eerdmans, 2009.

——. "Grace and Being: The Role of God's Gracious Election in Karl Barth's Theological Ontology." In *The Cambridge Companion to Karl Barth*, edited by John Webster, pp. 92-110. Cambridge: Cambridge University Press, 2000.

——. *Karl Barth's Critically Realistic Dialectical Theology: Its Genesis and Development, 1909-1936*. Oxford: Oxford University Press, 1997.

——. "Karl Barth's Version of an 'Analogy of Being': A Dialectical No and Yes to Roman Catholicism." In *The Analogy of Being: Invention of the Antichrist or the Wisdom of God?*, edited by Joseph White, pp. 88-144. Grand Rapids: Eerdmans, 2011.

——. "The Ontological Presuppositions of Barth's Doctrine of the Atonement." In *The Glory of the Atonement: Biblical, Historical and Practical Perspectives*, ed. Frank A. James III and Charles E. Hill, pp. 346-66. Downers Grove, IL: InterVarsity Press, 2004.

——. *Orthodox and Modern: Studies in the Theology of Karl Barth*. Grand Rapids: Baker Academic, 2008.

McInerny, Ralph. *Aquinas and Analogy*. Washington, D.C.: Catholic University of America Press, 1996.

——. *The Logic of Analogy*. The Hague: Martin Nijhoff, 1971.

——. *Preambula Fidei: Thomism and the God of the Philosophers*. Washington, D.C.: Catholic University of America Press, 2006.

——. *Rhyme and Reason: St. Thomas and Modes of Discourse*. Milwaukee: Marquette University Press, 1981.

McTighe, T. P. "Contingentia and Alteritas in Cusa's Metaphysics." *American Catholic Philosophical Quarterly* 64 (1985): 55-71.

Mechels, Eberhard. *Analogie bei Erich Przywara und Karl Earth: Das Verhaltnis von Offenbarungstheologie und Metaphysic*. Neukirchen-Vluyn: Neukirchener Verlag, 1979.

Meng, J. Chua Soo. "Reginald Garrigou-Lagrange OP on Aristotle, Thomas Aquinas, and the Doctrine of Limitation of Act by Potency." *The Modern Schoolman* 78, no. 1 (2000): 71-87.

Merlan, Philip. *From Platonism to Neoplatonism*. 3rd ed. The Hague: Martinus Nijhoff, 1968.

Mikkelsen, Hans. *Reconciled Humanity: Karl Barth in Dialogue*. Grand Rapids: Eerdmans, 2010.

Milbank, John. *Being Reconciled: Ontology and Pardon*. New York: Routledge, 2003.

——. "'Between Purgation and Illumination': A Critique of the Theology of Right." In *Christ, Ethics and Tragedy: Essays in Honour of Donald Mackinnon*, ed. Kenneth Surin, pp. 161-96. Cambridge: Cambridge University Press, 1989.

——. "Only Theology Overcomes Metaphysics." *New Blackfriars* 76 (1995): 325-42.

——, ed. *Radical Orthodoxy: A New Theology*. London: Routledge, 1999.

——. "Sacred Triads: Augustine and the Indo-European Soul." In *Augustine and His Critics*, ed. R. Dodaro and G. Laws, pp. 77-102. London: Routledge, 2000.

——. "The Soul of Reciprocity." Part 1. *ModT* 17, no. 3 (2001): 335-91.

——. "The Soul of Reciprocity." Part 2. *ModT* 17, no. 4 (2001): 485-507.

——. *The Suspended Middle: Henri de Lubac and the Debate About the Supernatural*. Grand Rapids: Eerdmans, 2005.

————. *Theology and Social Theory*. Cambridge: Blackwell, 1998. 2nd ed., 2006.

————. *The Word Made Strange: Theology, Language, Culture*. Malden, MA: Blackwell, 1997.

Milbank, John, and Catherine Pickstock. *Truth in Aquinas*. London: Routledge, 2001.

Miller, Mitchell H. *Plato's Parmenides: The Conversion of the Soul*. Pittsburgh: Pennsylvania State University Press, 1991.

Minio-Paluello, L. *Opuscula: The Latin Aristotle*. Amsterdam: Hakkert, 1972.

Molnar, Paul D. *Divine Freedom and the Doctrine of the Immanent Trinity: In Dialogue with Karl Barth and Contemporary Theology*. New York: T & T Clark, 2002.

Mondin, Battista. *The Principle of Analogy in Protestant and Catholic Theology*. The Hague: Martinus Nijhoff, 1968.

Montagnes, Bernard. *The Doctrine of the Analogy of Being*. Translated by E. M. Macierowski. Milwaukee: Marquette University Press, 2004.

Moreau, Joseph. "The Platonic Idea and Its Threefold Function: A Synthesis." *Irish Philosophical Quarterly* 9 (1969): 477-517.

Morewedge, Parviz, ed. *Neoplatonism and Islamic Thought*. Albany: State University of New York Press, 1992.

Morreall, John S. *Analogy and Talking About God: A Critique of the Thomistic Approach*. Washington, D.C.: University Press of America, 1979.

————. *Analogy in Aquinas*. Claremont, CA: American Academy of Religion Press, 1984.

Morris, Leon. *The Gospel According to John*. New International Commentary on the New Testament. Grand Rapids: Eerdmans, 1971.

Mortensen, J. R. *Understanding St. Thomas on Analogy*. Rome: The Aquinas Institute for the Study of Sacred Doctrine, 2006.

Muller, Richard A. *Dictionary of Latin and Greek Theological Terms*. Grand Rapids: Baker Academic, 1985.

Muller, Richard. *Post-Reformation Reformed Dogmatics: The Rise and Development of Reformed Orthodoxy, ca. 1520 to ca. 1725*. Vol. 1, *Prolegomena to Theology*. Grand Rapids: Baker Academic, 1998.

————. *Post-Reformation Reformed Dogmatics: The Rise and Development of Reformed Orthodoxy, ca. 1520 to ca. 1725*. Vol. 4, *The Triunity of God*. Grand Rapids: Baker Academic, 2003.

Narbonne, Jean-Marc. *Hénologie, ontologie et Ereignis (Plotin-Proclus-Heidegger)*. Paris: Les Belles Lettres, 2001.

———. "Ontologie et hénologie; divergence ou convergence?" *Laval Théologique et Philosophique* 51 (1995): 541-49.

Nash, R. "Divine Illumination." In *Augustine Through the Ages, Encyclopedia*, edited by Allen D. Fitzgerald, pp. 438-41. Grand Rapids: Eerdmans, 1999.

Natorp, Paul. "Thema und Disposition der aristotelischen Metaphysik." *Philosophische Monatschefte* 24 (1887): 37-65, 540-74.

———. "Über Aristotele's Metaphysik K 1-8." *Archiv für Geschichte der Philosophie* 1 (1888): 178-93.

Neder, Adam. *Participation in Christ: An Entry into Karl Barth's Church Dogmatics*. Louisville, KY: Westminster John Knox, 2009.

Neilsen, Niles C. *The Analogia Entis of Erich Przywara*. PhD dissertation, Yale University, 1951.

———. "Analogy and the Knowledge of God: An Ecumenical Appraisal (Roman Catholic and Protestant Interpretations in Relation to the Debate About the Analogy of Being Between Erich Przywara, S. J., and K. Barth)." *Rice University Studies* 60 (1974): 21-102.

Nemetz, A. A. "Logic and the Division of the Sciences in Aristotle and St. Thomas Aquinas." *The Modern Schoolman* 33 (1956): 91-109.

Neuser, W. H. "Karl Barth in Munster, 1924-1930." *Theologische Studien* 130 (1985): 37-40.

Nielsen, Kai. "Analogical Talk About God: A Negative Critique." *The Thomist* 40 (1976): 32-60.

Oakes, Edward. *Pattern of Redemption: The Theology of Hans Urs von Balthasar*. New York: Continuum, 1994.

Oakes, Kenneth. "The Question of Nature and Grace in Karl Barth: Humanity as Creature and as Covenant-Partner." *ModT* 23 (2007): 143-67.

O'Connell, Robert J. "The De Genesi contra Manichaeos and the Origin of the Soul." *Recherches Augustiniennes* 39 (1993): 129-41.

———. "Faith, Reason, and Ascent to Vision in St. Augustine." *Augustine Studies* 21 (1990): 83-126.

———. *The Origin of the Soul in St. Augustine's Later Works*. New York: Fordham University Press, 1987.

———. "Pre-Existence in the Early Augustine." *Revue des etudes Augustiniennes* 26 (1980): 176-88.

———. *St. Augustine's Confessions: The Odyssey of Soul*. Cambridge, MA: The Belknap Press of Harvard University Press, 1969.

——. *St. Augustine's Early Theory of Man*. Cambridge, MA: Harvard University Press, 1968.

——. "Where the Difference Still Lies." *Augustine Studies* 21 (1990): 139-52.

O'Daly, Brian. "Augustine on the Origins of the Soul." In *Platonismus et Christentum: Festschrift für Heinrich Dörrie*, edited by H. D. Blume and F. Mann, pp. 245-57. Jahrbuch für Antike und Christentum Supplement 10. Münster in Westfalen: Aschendorff, 1983.

O'Donnell, James J. *Augustine: A New Biography*. New York: HarperCollins, 2005.

O'Donnell, John J. *Hans Urs von Balthasar*. London: Geoffrey Chapman, 1992.

O'Donovan, Leo J. "The Mystery of God as a History of Love: Eberhard Jüngel's Doctrine of God." *Theological Studies* 42 (1981): 251-71.

O'Farrell, Frank. "Aristotle's Categories of Being." *Gregorianum* (1982): 87-131.

Oh, Peter. *Karl Barth's Trinitarian Theology: A Study in Karl Barth's Analogical Use of the Trinitarian Relation*. Edinburgh: T & T Clark, 2006.

O'Meara, Dominic J., ed. *Neoplatonism and Christian Thought*. Albany: State University of New York Press, 1981.

O'Meara, Thomas Franklin. *Erich Przywara, S.J.: His Theology and His World*. Notre Dame, IN: Notre Dame University Press, 2002.

——. *Thomas Aquinas Theologian*. Notre Dame, IN: University of Notre Dame Press, 1997.

O'Rourke, Fran. *Pseudo-Dionysius and the Metaphysics of Aquinas*. Studien und Texte zur Geistesgeschichte des Mittelalters 32. Leiden: Brill, 1992.

Owen, Gwilym Ellis Lane. "Aristotle on the Snares of Ontology." In *New Essays on Plato and Aristotle*, edited by Bambrough Renford, pp. 69-176. New York: Humanities Press, 1965.

Owens, Joseph. "Aquinas as Aristotelian Commentator." In *St Thomas Aquinas, 1274-1974, Commemorative Studies*, ed. É. Gilson, 1:213-38. Toronto: Pontifical Institute for Mediaeval Studies Press, 1974.

——. "Aristotle and Aquinas." In *The Cambridge Companion to Aquinas*, ed. N. Kretzmann and E. S. Stump, pp. 38-59. Cambridge: Cambridge University Press, 1993.

——. "Aristotle and Aquinas on Cognition." *Canadian Journal of Philosophy*, Supplement 17 (1991): 103-23.

——. *Aristotle's Gradations of Being in Metaphysics E-Z*. Edited by Lloyd P. Gerson and Patzig Günther. South Bend, IN: St. Augustine's Press, 2007.

——. *The Doctrine of Being in the Aristotelian Metaphysics: A Study in the Greek*

Background of Medieval Thought. Toronto: Pontifical Institute of Mediaeval Studies, 1951.

———. "Is There Any Ontology in Aristotle?" *Dialogue* 25 (1986): 697-707.

———. "Theologie und Ontologie in der 'Metaphysik' des Aristoteles." *Kant-Studien* 52 (1960/61): 185-205.

———. "Theology and Ontology in Aristotle's *Metaphysics*." In *Articles on Aristotle, Vol. 3—Metaphysics*. London, Duckworth, 1979.

Paasch, J. T. *Divine Production in Late Medieval Trinitarian Theology: Henry of Ghent, Duns Scotus, and William Ockham*. Oxford Theological Monographs. New York: Oxford University Press, 2012.

Palakeel, Joseph. *The Use of Analogy in Theological Discourse: An Investigation in Ecumenical Perspective*. Rome: Pontificia Universita Gregoriana, 1995.

Palmer, Humphrey. *Analogy: A Study of Qualification and Argument in Theology*. London: Macmillan, 1973.

Pannenberg, Wolfhart. *Analogie und Offenbarung: Eine kritische Untersuchung zur Geschichte des Analogiebegriffs in der Lehre von der Gotteserkenntnis*. Göttingen: Vandenhoeck & Ruprecht, 2007.

———. *Metaphysics and the Idea of God*. Translated by Philip Clayton. Grand Rapids: Eerdmans, 1990.

———. *Systematic Theology I*. Grand Rapids: Eerdmans, 1991.

———. "Zur Bedeutung des Analogiegedankens bei Karl Barth. Eine Auseinandersetzung mit Urs von Balthasar." *Theologische Literaturzeitung* 78 (1953): 17-24.

Pasnau, Robert. *Metaphysical Themes 1274–1671*. Oxford: Clarendon Press, 2011.

Paulus, J. *Henri de Gand: Essai sur les tendances de sa Mitaphysique*. Paris, 1938.

Pelikan, Jaroslav. *The Mystery of Continuity: Time and History, Memory and Eternity in the Thought of Saint Augustine*. Charlottesville: University Press of Virginia, 1986.

Peterson, Erik. *Theologisch Traktate*. Munich: Kaiser Verlag, 1928.

Phelan, Gerald B. *Saint Thomas and Analogy*. Milwaukee: Marquette University Press, 1941.

Philoponus. *Against Proclus On the Eternity of the World 6-8*. Translated by M. Share. The Ancient Commentators on Aristotle. London: Duckworth, 2005.

Pickstock, Catherine. "Duns Scotus: His Historical and Contemporary Significance." *ModT* 21, no. 4 (2005): 543-74.

———. "Modernity and Scholasticism: A Critique of Recent Invocations of Univocity." *Antonianum* 78 (2003): 3-46.

Pitschke, Carsten. "Maius quam cogitari possit. Der Gottesbeweis des Anselm von Canterbury und seine Kritik durch Kant und Hegel." *Theologie und Glaube* 94 (2004): 416-34.

Plato. *Cratylus.*

———. *Laws.*

———. *Gorgias.*

———. *Meno.*

———. *Parmenides.*

———. *Philebus.*

———. *Republic.*

———. *Statesman.*

———. *Timaeus.*

Plotinus. *Ennead, Volume I: Porphyry on the Life of Plotinus.* Translated by A. H. Armstrong. LCL 440. Cambridge, MA: Harvard University Press, 1969.

Pohlmann, H. G. *Analogia entis oder Analogia fidei? Die Frage der Analogic bei Karl Barth.* Gottingen: Vandenhoeck & Ruprecht, 1965.

———. "Mistakes of Fact and Agent Voluntariness: Aristotle, Aquinas, and Conformity to Will." *The Modern Schoolman* 80, no. 2 (2003): 99-113.

Proclus. *Commentary on Plato's Parmenides.*

———. *Commentary on Plato's Timaeus.*

———. *The Elements of Theology.* Translated by E. R. Dodds. Oxford: Clarendon Press, 1963, 2004.

Prouvost, Géry. *Thomas d'Aquin et les thomismes.* Paris: Le Cerf, 1996.

Przywara, E. *Analogia entis.* Schriften III. München: J. Kosel und F. Pastef, 1932.

———. *Analogia entis: Metaphysics, Original Structure and Rhythm of All.* Edited and translated by David B. Hart. Grand Rapids: Eerdmans, 2014.

———. *Analogia entis. Metaphysik.* Munich: Kosel & Pustet, 1932.

———. "Die Reichweite der Analogie als katholischer Grundform." *Scholastik* XV (1940): 339-63, 508-32.

———. "Metaphysik, Religion, Analogie." In *Analogia entis: Schriften.* Einsiedeln: Johannes Verlag, 1962.

———. "Neu Philosophie." In *Ringen der Gegenwart I.* Augsberg: Fischer, 1925.

———. *Ringen de Gegenwart: Gesammelte Aufsatze, 1922-1927.* Vol. 2. Augsburg: Benno Filser Verlag, 1929.

———. *Schriften* I, *Fruhe religose; Schriften* II, *Religionsphilosophische; Schriften* III, *Analogia entis, Metaphysik: Ur-St'ruktur und All-Rhythmus.* Einsiedeln: Johannes Verlag, 1962.

Pseudo-Dionysius the Areopagite. *The Complete Works*. Edited and translated by P. Rorem and C. Luibheid. Classics of Western Spirituality. New York: Paulist Press, 1987.

Quenstedt, Johann Andreas. *Theologica Didactio Polemica sive Systema Theologicum*. Lipsiae: Thomam Fritsch, 1715.

Rachid, A. "Dieu et 'etre selon Al-Farabi: le chapitre de 'l'etre' dans le Livre des Lettres." In *Dieu et l'etre: 'exegeses d'Exode 3, 14 et de Coran 20, 11-24*, pp. 179-90. Centre d'etudes des religions du livre, CNRS. Etudes augustiniennes. Paris, 1978.

Rahner, Karl. *The Trinity*. Translated by Joseph Donceel. New York: Herder & Herder, 1970.

Reale, Giovanni. *The Concept of Philosophy and the Unity of Metaphysics of Aristotle*. Translated by John R. Catan. Albany: State University of New York Press, 1980.

———. *Il concetto di "filosofia prima" e l'unità della metafisica di Aristotele. Con due saggi sui concetti di potenza-atto e di essere*. 6th ed. Milano: Vita e Pensiero, 1994.

Reilly, J. P. *Cajetan's Notion of Existence*. The Hague: Moulten, 1971.

Reiner, Hans. "Die Entstehung und usprüngliche Bedeutung des Names Metaphysik." *Zeitschrift für philosophische Forschung* 8 (1954): 210-37. Translated as "The Emergence and Original Meaning of the Name 'Metaphysics,'" by P. Adler and D. Paskin, *Graduate Faculty Philosophy Journal* 13, no. 2 (1990): 23-53.

Rémy, Gerard. "L' Analogie selon E. Jüngel. Remarques critiques." *Revue d'Historie et de Philosophie Religiques* 66, no. 2 (1986): 147-77.

Reyna, R. "On the Soul: A Philosophical Exploration of the Active Intellect in Averroes, Aristotle, and Aquinas." *The Thomist* 36 (1972): 131-49.

Richard, Jean. "Theologie Evangelique et Theologie Philosophique a Propos, d'Eberhard Jüngel." *Science et Esprit* 38, no. 1 (1986): 5-30.

Richards, Jay Wesley. "Barth on the Divine 'Conscription' of Language." *Heythrop Journal* 38, no. 3 (1997): 247-66.

Riches, John. "The Biblical Basis of Glory." In *The Beauty of Christ: An Introduction to the Theology of Hans Urs von Balthasar*, ed. Bede McGregor, O.P., and Thomas Norris, pp. 65-78. Edinburgh: T & T Clark, 1994.

Rist, J. M. *Augustine: Ancient Thought Baptized*. Cambridge: Cambridge University Press, 1994.

———. *Plotinus: The Road to Reality*. Cambridge: Cambridge University Press, 1967.

Robb, James H. *Man as Infinite Spirit*. Milwaukee: Marquette University Publications, 1974.

Robinson, Richard, trans. *Aristotelis Metaphysica: Bk Gamma*. Oxford: Oxford University Press, 1957.

———. *Plato's Earlier Dialectic*. Ithaca, NY: Cornell University Press, 1941.

Rocca, Gregory P. *Speaking the Incomprehensible God: Thomas Aquinas on the Interplay of Positive and Negative Theology*. Washington, D.C.: Catholic University of America Press, 2004.

Rodgers, Mary. *The Neoplatonic Metaphysics and Epistemology of Anselm of Canterbury*. Lampeter, UK: Mellon, 1997.

Rogers, Eugene F. "Schleiermacher as an Anselmian Theologian: Aesthetics, Dogmatics, Apologetics and Proof." *SJT* 51 (1998): 342-79.

———. *Thomas Aquinas and Karl Barth: Sacred Doctrine and the Natural Knowledge of God*. Notre Dame, IN: University of Notre Dame Press, 1995.

Rogers, Katherine A. "The Traditional Doctrine of Divine Simplicity." *Religious Studies* 32 (June 1996): 165-86.

Rolnick, Philip A. *Analogical Possibilities: How Words Refer to God*. American Academy of Religion Academy Series 81. Atlanta: Scholars Press, 1993.

Rorem, Paul. *Eriugena's Commentary on the Dionysian Celestial Hierarchy*. Toronto: Pontifical Institute of Mediaeval Studies, 2005.

Rosenberg, Jean Randall. *The Principle of Individuation: A Comparative Study of St. Thomas, Scotus and Suarez*. Philosophical Studies 121. Washington, D.C.: Catholic University of America Press, 1950.

Rotelle, J. E., and B. Ramsey. *The Works of Saint Augustine: A Translation for the 21st Century*. New York: New City Press, 1990.

Routila, Lauri. *Die aristotelische Idee der ersten Philosophie. Untersuchungen zur onto-theologischen Verfassung der Metaphysik des Aristoteles*. Amsterdam: North-Holland Press, 1969.

Ruello, F. J. "La mystique de l'Exode,' Dieu et l'etre." In *Dieu et l'etre: 'exegeses d'Exode 3, 14 et de Coran 20, 11-24*, ed. Centre d'etudes des religions du livre, CNRS, pp. 213-43. Etudes augustiniennes. Paris, 1978.

Runia, D. T., and M. Share, trans. *Proclus' Commentary on Plato's Timaeus. Vol 2, Book II: Proclus on the Causes of the Cosmos and its Creation*. Cambridge: Cambridge University Press, 2008.

Rutten, Christian. "La stylometrie et la question de 'Métaphysique' K." *Revue Philosophique de Louvain* 90 (1992): 486-96.

————. "Science de l'être et théologie dans la *Métaphysique* d'Aristote. Essay d'analyse génétique." *Kernos* 11 (2001): 227-35.

Saffrey, H. D. "New Objective Links Between the Pseudo-Dionysius and Proclus." In *Neoplatonism and Christian Thought*, edited by Dominic J. O'Meara, pp. 55-63. Studies in Neoplatonism: Ancient and Modem III. Albany: State University of New York Press, 1982.

————. "Nouveaux liens objectifs entre le Pseudo-Denys et Proclus." *Revues scientifiques philosophiques et theologiques* 63 (1979): 3-16.

————. *Sancti Thomae de Aquino Super Librum de Causis Expositio*. Fribourg: Societe Philosophique, 1954.

Sanders, J. T. *The New Testament Christological Hymns*. Cambridge: Cambridge University Press, 1971.

Sauter, Gerhard. *Protestant Theology at the Crossroads*. Grand Rapids: Eerdmans, 2007.

Scheeben, M. J. *Nature and Grace*. Translated by C. Vollert. London: Herder, 1954.

Schomakers, B. "The Nature of the Distance: Neoplatonic and Dionysian Versions of Negative Theology." *American Catholic Philosophical Quarterly* 82 (2008): 593-618.

Schulz, Michael. *Sein und Trinität: Systematische Erörterungen zur Religionsphilosophie G. W. F. Hegels im ontologiegeschichtlichen Rückblick auf J. Duns Scotus und I. Kant und die Hegel-Rezeption in der Seinsauslegung und Trinitätstheologie bei W. Pannenberg, E. Jüngel, K. Rahner und H. U. v. Balthasar*. Münchener theologische Studien 2, 53. St. Ottilien: EOS-Verlag, 1997.

Schumacher, Lydia. *Divine Illumination: The History and Future of Augustine's Theory of Knowledge*. Challenges in Contemporary Theology. Oxford: Wiley-Blackwell, 2011.

Scola, Angelo. *Hans Urs von Balthasar: A Theological Style*. Grand Rapids: Eerdmans, 1995.

Scotus, John Duns. "Commentary on the Sentences." In *A Scholastic Miscellany: Anselm to Ockham*, edited by Eugene R. Fairwather, pp. 428-436. Philadelphia: Westminster, 1956.

————. *God and Creatures: The Quodlibetal Questions*. Translated by Felix Alluntis and Allan B. Wolter. Washington, D.C.: Catholic University of America Press, 1975.

————. *Ordinatio, Opera Omnia*. Edited by Scotistic Commission. 11 vols. Vatican City: Typis Polyglottis Vaticanis, 1950.

————. "The Oxford Commentary on the Four Books of the Sentences." In *Philosophy in the Middle Ages*, edited by Arthur Hyman and James J. Walsh, pp. 555-604. Indianapolis: Hackett, 1973.

————. *Philosophical Writings: A Selection*. Translated by Allan Wolter. Indianapolis: Hackett, 1987.

————. *A Treatise on God as First Principle*. Edited by Allan B. Wolter. 2nd rev. ed. Chicago: Franciscan Herald Press, 1983.

Seddon, Frederick A., Jr. "The Principle of Contradiction in *Metaphysics, Gamma*." *New Scholasticism* 55 (1981): 191-207.

Sellers, W. "Metaphysics and the Concept of a Person." In *The Logical Way of Doing Things*, edited by K. Lambert, pp. 219-252. New Haven, CT: Yale University Press, 1969.

Shiel, J. "Boethius' Commentaries on Aristotle." In *Aristotle Transformed*, edited by Richard Sorabji, pp. 349-372. London: Duckworth, 1990.

Skousgaard, Stephen. "Wisdom and Being in Aristotle's First Philosophy." *The Thomist* 40 (1976): 444-74.

Söhngen, Gottlieb. "Analogia entis in analogia fidei." In *Antwort: Karl Barth zum Seibzeigsten Geburtstag*. Zurich: Evangelischer Verlag AG, 1956.

————. "Analogia entis oder analogia fidei?" *Wissenschaft und Weisheit: Zeitschrift für augustinisch-franziskanische Theologie und Philosophic in der Gegenwart* 9 (1942): 91-100.

————. "Analogia fidei: Die Einheit in der Glaubenswissenschft." *Catholica* 3, no. 4 (1934): 176-208.

————. "Analogia fidei: Gottähnlichkeit allein aus Glauben?" *Catholica* 3, no. 3 (1934): 113-36.

————. *Analogie und Metaphor; Kleine Philosophie und Theologie der Sprache*. Freiburg/München: K. Alber, 1962.

————. "Bonaventura als Klassiker der Analogia fidei." *Wissenschaft und Weisheit* 2 (1935): 97-111.

————. "Die Weisheit der Theologie durch den Weg der Wissenschaft." In *Mysterium Salutis: Grundriss Heilsgeschichtlicher Dogmatik*. Einsiedeln: Benziger, 1965.

Sorabji, Richard, ed. *Aristotle Transformed: The Ancient Commentators and Their Influence*. London: Duckworth, 1990.

Spencer, Archie J. "Causality and the '*analogia entis*': Karl Barth's Rejection of Analogy of Being Reconsidered." *NV* 6, no. 2 (2008): 329-76.

————. *Clearing a Space for Human Action: Ethical Ontology in the Theology of Karl Barth*. New York: Peter Lang, 2003.

————. "Influences on Origen's Doctrine of the Incarnation." ThM thesis, Regent College, 1994.

Spieckermann, Ingrid. *Gotteserkenntnis. Ein Beitrag zur Grundfrage der neuen Theologie Karl Barths.* Munich: C. Kaiser, 1985.

Staley, K. M. "Aristotle, Augustine, and Aquinas on the Good and the Human Good: A Note on 'Summa Theologiae' I-II, qq. 1-3." *The Modern Schoolman* 72, no. 4 (1995): 311-22.

Starr, B. E. "Adolf Von Harnack." In *Augustine Through the Ages*, edited by A. D. Fitzgerald, pp. 414-416. Grand Rapids: Eerdmans, 1999.

Steel, C. "Proclus on the Mirror as a Metaphor of Participation." In *Mirroir et savoir. La transmission d'un theme platonicien, des Alexandrins à la philosophie arabo-musulmane. Actes du colloque international tenu à Leuven et Louvain-la-Neuve, les 17 et 18 novembre 2005*, edited by D. De Smet, M. Sebti and G. De Callatay, pp. 79-96. Leuven: Leuven University Press, 2008.

Stevens, Annick. *L'ontologie d'Aristote au carrefour du logique et du reel.* Paris: Vrin, 2000.

Stevenson, J. G. "Being 'qua' Being." *Apeiron* 9 (1875): 42-50.

Suárez, Francisco. *Metaphysicarum Disputationum, in quibus et universa naturalis theologia ordinate traditur, ad quaestiones ad omnes duodecim Aristotelis libros pertinentes, accurate disputantur: cum indicibus necessarius.* 1st ed., Rome. Salamanca ed., 1597. Moguntiae ed., 1600.

Sullivan, J. B. *An Examination of First Principles in Thought and Being in the Light of Aristotle and Aquinas.* Washington, D.C.: Catholic University of America Press, 1939.

Surin, K. *Ethics and Tragedy; Essays in Honor of Donald Mackinnon.* Cambridge: Cambridge University Press, 1989.

Sweeney, Eileen C. "Three Notions of *resolutio* and the Structure of Reasoning in Aquinas." *The Thomist* 58, no. 2 (1994): 197-243.

Swinburne, Richard. *Revelation: From Metaphor to Analogy.* New York: Oxford University Press, 1992.

Talanga, J. "On the Immortality of the Mind in Aristotle and Thomas Aquinas." *Filozofska Istrazivanja* 13, no. 1 (1992): 31-43.

te Velde, Rudi A. *Aquinas on God.* London: Ashgate, 2008.

————. *Participation and Substantiality in Thomas Aquinas. Studien und Texte zur Geistesgeschichte des Mittelalters, xlvi.* Leiden: Brill, 2009.

Tenney, M. C. *Expositors Bible Commentary.* Vol. 5, *John.* Grand Rapids: Zondervan, 1980.

———. *John: Gospel of Belief.* Grand Rapids: Eerdmans, 1975.

TeSelle, Eugene. *Augustine the Theologian.* Eugene, OR: Wipf and Stock, 2002.

Teske, Roland. "The Image and Likeness of God in St Augustine's *De Genesi ad litteram liber imperfectus.*" *Augustinianum* 30, no. 2 (1990): 441-51.

———. "Origen and St. Augustine's First Commentaries on Genesis." In *Origeniana quinta.* Louvain: The Catholic University Press, 1992.

———, trans. "Saint Augustine on Genesis." The Fathers of the Church 84. Washington, D.C.: Catholic University of America Press, 1991.

———. "Soul." In *Augustine Through the Ages,* edited by A. D. Fitzgerald, pp. 807-12. Grand Rapids: Eerdmans, 1999.

———. "St Augustine's View of the Original Human Condition in *De Genesi contra Mamchaeos.*" *Augustinian Studies* 22 (1991): 141-55.

Thistleton, A. *New Horizons in Hermeneutics.* Grand Rapids: Zondervan, 1992.

Thompson, J. *Christ in Perspective: Christological Perspectives in the Theology of Karl Barth.* Grand Rapids: Eerdmans, 1974.

———. "The Humanity of God in the Theology of Karl Barth." *SJT* 29 (1976): 249-69.

Tillich, Paul. *Systematic Theology.* Vol. 2. Chicago: University of Chicago Press, 1969.

Torjesen, K. J. *Hermeneutical Method and Exegetical Procedure in Origen of Alexandria.* Tübingen: de Grutyer, 1989.

Torrance, Alan J. *Persons in Communion: An Essay on Trinitarian Description and Human Participation.* Edinburgh: T & T Clark, 1996.

Torrance, T. F. *Karl Barth: Biblical and Evangelical Theologian.* Edinburgh: T & T Clark, 1990.

———. "The Theology of Karl Barth." *The Scotsman* 14 (April 1952): 4-25.

Tracy, Thomas F. *God, Action, and Embodiment.* Grand Rapids: Eerdmans, 1984.

Ulrich, Ferdinard. *Logo-Tokos.* Der Mensch und das Wort. Einsiedeln: Johannes Verlag, 2003.

Upton, Thomas. "Aristotle on Existence: Escaping the Snares of Ontology?" *New Scholasticism* 62 (1988): 373-99.

Ury, William. *Trinitarian Personhood: Investigating the Implications of a Relational Definition.* Eugene, OR: Wipf and Stock, 2002.

van den Berg, R. M. *Proclus' Commentary on the Cratylus in Context.* Ancient Theories of Language and Naming, Philosophia Antiqua 112. Boston: Brill, 2008.

Vanhoozer, Kevin J. *The Drama of Doctrine.* Louisville: John Knox, 2005.

Vaught, Carl G. *Metaphor, Analogy, and the Place of Places: Where Religion and*

Philosophy Meet. Waco, TX: Baylor University Press, 2004.

Verbeke, Gérard. "Aristotle's Metaphysics Viewed by the Ancient Greek Commentators." In *Studies in Aristotle,* edited by Dominic O'Meara, pp. 107-28. Washington, D.C.: The Catholic University of America Press, 1981.

———. "L'objet de la métaphysique d'Aristote selon des études récentes." *Revue de Philosophie Ancienne* 1 (1983): 5-30.

———. "La doctrine de l'être dans la *Métaphysique* d'Aristote." *Revue Philosophique de Louvain* (1952): 471-78.

von Balthasar, Hans Urs. "Analogic und Dialektik: Zur Erklarung der theologischen Prinzipienlehre Karl Barths." *Die Religionis* 22 (1944): 171-216.

———. "Analogie und Natur: Zur Erklarung der theologischen Prinzipienlehre Karl Barths." *Theologisch Zeitschrift* 23 (1945): 3-56.

———. *Convergences: To the Sources of Christian Mystery.* Translated by E. A. Nelson. San Francisco: Ignatius, 1983.

———. "Creation and Trinity." *Communio* 15 (1988): 285-93.

———. *Explorations in Theology.* 5 vols. San Francisco: Ignatius Press, 1988–1991.

———. *Glory of the Lord: A Theological Aesthetics.* 7 vols. Edited and translated by J. Fessio and J. Riches. San Francisco: Ignatius Press, 1982–1991. German ed., *Herrlichkeit: Eine theologische Asthetik I–III.* Einsiedeln: Johannes Verlag, 1961–1969.

———. *Skizzen zur Theologie.* Einsiedeln: Johannes Verlag, 1960–1986.

———. *Theo-drama. Theological Dramatic Theory.* 5 vols. San Francisco: Ignatius Press, 1988. German ed., *Theodramatik I–IV.* Einsiedeln: Johannes Verlag, 1973–1983.

———. *Theologik.* 3 vols. Einsiedeln: Johannes Verlag, 1985–1987.

———. *The Theology of Karl Barth.* Translated by E. T. Oakes. San Francisco: Ignatius, 1992. German ed., *Karl Barth Darstellung und Deutung seiner Theologie.* Koln: Kaiser Verlag, 1951.

———. *The Word Made Flesh.* 2 vols. Translated by A. V. Littledale and A. Dru. New York: Ignatius, 1964–1965.

Wagner, Hans H. *Existenz, Analogie, Dialektik. Religio pura sen transcendentalis.* Munich: Ernst Reinhard, 1953.

Waldstein, M. M. "Analogia Verbi: The Truth of Scripture in Rudolph Bultmann and Raymond Brown." *Letter and Spirit* 6 (2010): 115.

Wallis, R. T. *Neoplatonism.* 2nd ed. London: Duckworth, 1995.

Ward, Graham. *Barth, Derrida and the Language of Theology.* Cambridge: Cambridge University Press, 1995.

Webster, John B. *Confessing God: Essays in Christian Dogmatics II*. London: T & T Clark, 2005.

———. *Eberhard Jüngel: An Introduction to His Theology*. Cambridge: Cambridge University Press, 1986.

———. "Eberhard Jüngel on the Language of Faith." *ModT* 1, no. 4 (July 1985): 235-76.

———. "Justification, Analogy and Action: Passivity and Activity in Jüngel's Anthropology." In *Possibilities of Theology*, edited by John Webster, pp. 106-42. Edinburgh: T & T Clark, 1994.

———. "Perfection and Participation." In *The Analogy of Being: Invention of the Antichrist or the Wisdom of God?*, ed. Thomas Joseph White, O.P., pp. 379-94. Grand Rapids: Eerdmans, 2011.

———, ed. *The Possibilities of Theology: Studies in the Theology of Eberhard Jüngel in His Sixtieth Year*. Edinburgh: T & T Clark, 1994.

Wedin, Michael. "The Science and Axioms of Being." In *A Companion to Aristotle*, edited by Anagnostopoulos Georgios, pp. 125-143. Malden, MA: Wiley-Blackwell, 2009.

Weinandy, Thomas G. *The Father's Spirit of Sonship: Re-conceiving the Trinity*. Edinburgh: T & T Clark, 1995.

Westcott, B. F. *The Gospel According to St. John*. Grand Rapids: Eerdmans, 1950.

White, R. M. *Talking About God: The Concept of Analogy and the Problem of Religious Language*. London: Ashgate, 2010.

White, Thomas Joseph, O.P. *The Analogy of Being: Invention of the Antichrist or the Wisdom of God?* Grand Rapids: Eerdmans, 2011.

———. "How Barth Got Aquinas Wrong: A Reply to Archie J. Spencer on Causality and Christocentrism." *NV* 7, no. 1 (2009): 241-70.

White, Victor. *Holy Teaching: The Idea of Theology According to St. Thomas Aquinas*. London: Blackfriars, 1958.

Wigley, D. "Karl Barth on Anselm: The Influence of Anselm's 'Theological Scheme' on T. F. Torrance and Eberhard Jüngel." *SJT* 46 (1973): 79-97.

William of Ockham. *Dialogus*. Translated by John Scott. London: The British Academy, 1999.

Williams, Rowan. "Creation." In *Augustine Through the Ages*, edited by Allen D. Fitzgerald, pp. 251-54. Grand Rapids: Eerdmans, 2005.

Williams, T., ed. *The Cambridge Companion to Duns Scotus*. Cambridge: Cambridge University Press, 2003.

———. "The Doctrine of Univocity Is True and Salutary." *ModT* 21 (2005): 575-85.

Wippel, John F. *Metaphysical Themes in Thomas Aquinas I*. 2 vols. Washington,

D.C.: Catholic University of America Press, 1984.

———. *The Metaphysical Thought of Thomas Aquinas: From Finite Being to Uncreated Being*. Washington, D.C.: Catholic University of America Press, 2000.

Wolter, Allan B. *Scotus and Ockham: Selected Essays*. St. Bonaventure, NY: Franciscan Institute, 2003.

Worthen, J. F. "Augustine's *De trinitate* and Anselm's *Proslogion*: 'Exercere Lectorem.'" In *Augustine: Presbyter Factus Sum* [Collectanea Augustiniana], edited by Joseph T. Lienhard et al., pp. 517-29. New York: Peter Lang, 1993.

Woznicki, Andrew N. *Being and Order: The Metaphysics of Thomas Aquinas in Historical Perspective*. New York: Peter Lang, 1990.

Yeago, David Stuart. "The Drama of Nature and Grace: A Study in the Theology of Hans Urs von Balthasar." PhD dissertation, Yale University, 1992.

Yu, Jiyuan. *The Structure of Being in Aristotle's Metaphysics*. Dordrecht: Kluwer, 2003.

Zagzebski, L. T. *The Dilemma of Freedom and Foreknowledge*. New York: Oxford University Press, 1991.

Zechmeister, Martha. *Gottes-Nacht: Erich Przywara Weg Negativer Theologie*. Munster: Lit Verlag, 1997.

Zeitz, James V. "Erich Przywara: A Visionary Theologian." *Thought* 58 (1983): 145-57.

———. "Erich Przywara on Ultimate Reality and Meaning: '*Deus Semper Major*.'" *Ultimate Reality and Meaning* 12 (1989): 192-201.

———. "Spirituality and the *Analogia entis* According to Erich Przywara." Washington, D.C.: University Press of America, 1982.

Zimany, R. *Vehicle for God: The Metaphorical Theology of Eberhard Jüngel*. Atlanta: Mercer University Press, 1994.

Zimny, Leo. *Erich Przywara: Sein Schriftum, 1912–1962*. Eisiendeln: Johannes-Verlag, 1963.

NAME INDEX

SUBJECT INDEX

281, 285, 288-89, 293-97, 303,
305, 307-8, 314-18, 330-31,
322, 338, 340-41, 343, 345,
348-49, 353, 355-56, 359-61,
364-67, 369, 370-72, 375
  in Barth, 21, 100, 181,
    183-95, 211, 217-18,
    221-22, 224-29, 234-35
  as historical event, 21,
    27-28, 233, 242, 247, 259,
    263, 280, 287, 289, 302,
    316, 331
  in Jesus Christ, 13, 16, 191,
    220-28, 234, 242, 247-48,
    254, 258-59, 294, 307
  in Jüngel, 242-43, 257-60,
    263, 281, 284-85, 287-89,
  by Scripture, 13, 255-56
  transcendent, 13, 18
  See also Christology
sacerdotalism, 174
sacrament, 324-27, 350
sacramental ontology, 319
sanctification, 234, 316
Scholasticism, 176, 194,
  199-200, 273-74
Scripture, 13-14, 16-17, 21,
  27-28, 79-80, 97, 104, 109,
  124-25, 185-88, 190-92, 203,
  213-15, 233, 253, 255, 282, 288,
  294-96, 315, 317, 332, 336-51,
  359, 364-65, 368, 382, 386
self-revelation of God, 26-27,
  29, 99, 181-82, 187, 195, 199,
  220, 223, 225-26, 235, 242,
  247, 258, 267, 288-89, 292,
  295, 315, 353, 371
signification, 16, 90, 111,
  127-28, 133, 221, 245, 248, 254,
  259, 277, 279, 281, 290, 324
similarity/dissimilarity, 21, 35,
  49, 53-54, 56, 60-61, 76, 113,
  292, 306-9, 313-16, 331, 339,
  357, 365, 368, 373-74, 377, 379,
  381-82
  in Aquinas, 104, 109, 119,
    123, 132, 135-37, 139-40,
    159-60, 165-66, 176
  Augustinian, 76-77, 81, 86,
    103
  in Barth, 194, 208-9,

223-28, 232-34, 236
  in Jüngel, 248, 264, 272,
    284-87
skepticism, counterargument
  to, 68-69
soteriology, 294
soul, 22, 74-86, 295, 320
  in Aquinas and Cajetan,
    94, 159, 161, 163
  Augustinian theology of,
    67, 88
  in Barth, 192, 201
  Classical view, 32, 44, 58,
    62, 68
speakability/unspeakability of
  God, 15, 17, 27, 119, 144, 198,
  244-49, 255-65, 268, 274,
  277-90, 309-14, 374, 381, 384
speech-acts, 345-46, 349, 357,
  365, 374
substance, 116-17, 164
Summa Contra Gentiles
  (SCG), 23, 41-42, 92, 100-123,
  126-28, 131-32, 153
Summa Theologiae (ST), 23,
  94-100, 123-36, 153, 170, 194
suprasensibility, 40, 54
symbol (σύμβολον), 59-62,
  271-72
synergism, 142, 174, 200, 205
synonymity, 127
Synoptic Gospels, 182, 319
temporality of God, 280, 303,
  334
theo-drama, 317, 340, 342-43,
  347, 350
theopantheism, 386-87
thinkability/unthinkability of
  God, 27, 191, 198, 245-46,
  248-59, 263, 272, 277-83, 290,
  373
Thomism, 41, 100, 152, 174, 196
  Barth on, 199-205
Thomistic analogy, 312
  misunderstanding of, 100
Trinity, 299, 301, 308-9, 322-23,
  334
  Augustinian doctrine of,
    22, 76
  in Barth, 183, 186-87,
    190-92, 232, 256, 298

  in Jüngel, 239, 243-44, 256,
    259-63, 281, 288-90
triunity, human, 82-84
truth and being, 327
unity of God, 96-99, 253-54
univocity, 23, 24, 49, 103, 113,
  120-23, 126, 128-30, 135, 141,
  169, 171-72, 175-76, 223, 274,
  312, 325-26
  in Aquinas, 165-65
  of Duns Scotus, 23, 105,
    143-51, 162, 164, 165
  See also predication
vestigium trinitatis, 22, 26,
  65-66, 74, 76
  Augustinian doctrine of,
    77-85, 88
  Barth's rejection of, 181,
    183-93
  in Jüngel, 244, 287-90
via analogia, 381
via causalitatis, 99
via eminentia, 99, 380
via negativa, 99, 133, 380. See
  also apophatic theology
wisdom, 38, 116, 216, 245, 260,
  321, 354-55, 378
  in Aquinas, 111-12, 114,
    116-17, 120, 122-23, 127
  Aristotelian, 42, 45-51
  Augustinian, 71-73, 84, 86
  in Barth, 223
  See also knowledge
witness, 21, 213, 219, 306,
  316-17, 345, 348-49, 355, 357,
  359-66, 369-72, 374, 382
  Scripture as, 13, 17, 27, 182,
    186-87, 190-92, 198, 205,
    218, 282, 288, 296, 315,
    318, 333, 346, 351-53, 357,
    368, 382
Word (λόγος), 13, 27, 70-73,
  184, 233-35, 244-45, 247,
  254-56, 258-59, 263-69,
  280-82, 285, 290, 293-95,
  297-301, 304, 306, 309,
  314-18, 328-36, 339, 342, 344,
  346, 348-82
  triple incarnation of, 344

SCRIPTURE INDEX

STRATEGIC INITIATIVES IN EVANGELICAL THEOLOGY

IVP Academic presents a series of seminal works of scholarship with significant relevance for both evangelical scholarship and the church. Strategic Initiatives in Evangelical Theology (SIET) aims to foster interaction within the broader evangelical community and advance discussion in the wider academy around emerging, current, groundbreaking or controversial topics. The series provides a unique publishing venue for both more senior and younger promising scholars.

While SIET volumes demonstrate a depth of appreciation for evangelical theology and the current challenges and issues facing it, the series will welcome books that engage the full range of academic disciplines from theology and biblical studies, to history, literature, philosophy, the natural and social sciences, and the arts.

Editorial Advisory Board

Published Volumes

Finding the Textbook You Need

The IVP Academic Textbook Selector
is an online tool for instantly finding the IVP books
suitable for over 250 courses across 24 disciplines.

www.ivpress.com/academic/